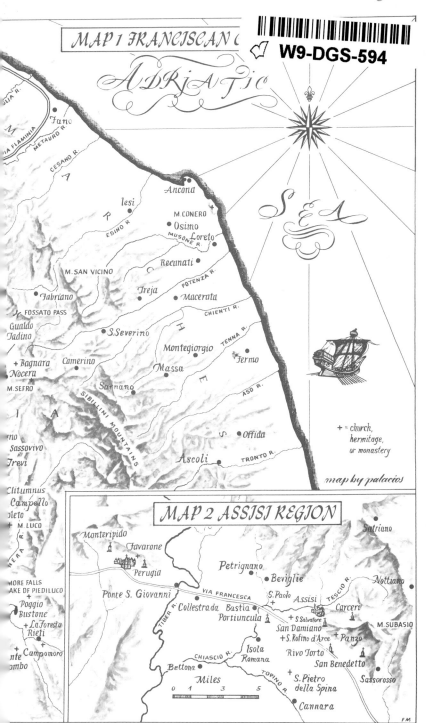

o-cat

W9-DGS-594

MAP 1 FRANCISCAN

ADRIATIC

SEA

+ = church,
hermitage,
or monastery

map by palacios

MAP 2 ASSISI REGION

SAINT FRANCIS OF ASSISI

OTHER FRANCISCAN BOOKS IN ENGLISH

BY OMER ENGLEBERT

Adventurer Saints [Junipero Serra, Giles of Assisi]
The Last of the Conquistadors, Junipero Serra, 1713-1784

BY IGNATIUS BRADY, O.F.M.

Legend and Writings of St. Clare (with Sr. M. Frances, SMIC)

TRANSLATIONS:

The Marrow of the Gospel by Cajetan Esser, O.F.M et al.
The Order of St. Francis and *Love's Reply* by Cajetan Esser, O.F.M.
St. Anthony, Doctor of the Gospel by Sophronius Clasen, O.F.M.

BY RAPHAEL BROWN

Our Lady and St. Francis (St. Francis Texts 1)
Fifty Animal Stories of St. Francis (St. Francis Texts 2)
The Wounded Heart: St. Charles of Sezze, Franciscan Brother
Franciscan Mystic, The Life of Blessed Brother Giles of Assisi

TRANSLATIONS:
The Little Flowers of St. Francis
The Perfect Joy of St. Francis by Felix Timmermans
The Revelations of St. Margaret of Cortona by Ange Marie Hiral, O.F.M.
An Apostle of Two Worlds, Good Father Frederick Janssoone, O.F.M. by Romain Légaré, O.F.M.

SAINT FRANCIS OF ASSISI

A biography

by Omer Englebert

A new translation

by Eve Marie Cooper

Second English Edition
revised and augmented
by
Ignatius Brady O.F.M. and *Raphael Brown*
with introduction, appendices, and comprehensive
bibliography covering modern research

Franciscan Herald Press
Publishers of Franciscan Literature
Chicago, Illinois 60609

X 14521489

BX
4700
. F6
E 612
1965

SAINT FRANCIS OF ASSISI: A biography by Omer Englebert.
New translation by Eve-Marie Cooper from second French edition, *Albin Michel*, Paris, France. Second English edition, texts
and notes revised by Ignatius Brady O.F.M. and Raphael Brown.
New introduction, appendices, and comprehensive bibliography of
modern research on St. Francis by Raphael Brown. Library of
Congress Catalog Card Number: 64-14252, copyright 1965 by
Franciscan Herald Press, 1434 West 51st Street, Chicago, Illinois
60609. Designed by Publication Associates and made in the United States of America.

IMPRIMI POTEST:
    Dominic Limacher O.F.M.
    Minister Provincial

NIHIL OBSTAT:
    Mark Hegener O.F.M.
    Censor Deputatus

IMPRIMATUR:
    Most Rev. Cletus F. O'Donnell, D.D.
    Vicar General, Archdiocese of Chicago

April 16, 1965

"The Nihil Obstat and the Imprimatur are official
declarations that a book or pamphlet is free
of doctrinal or moral error. No implication is
contained therein that those who have granted the
Nihil Obstat and Imprimatur agree with the contents,
opinions, or statements expressed."

THE EDITORS OF THIS BOOK GRATEFULLY DEDICATE IT TO

THOMAS OF CELANO
BROTHERS LEO, RUFINO, & ANGELO
ANGELO CLARENO
THE COMPILERS OF THE SPECULUM PERFECTIONIS
AND THE LEGENDA ANTIQUA OF PERUGIA
ARNAUD DE SARRANT
GIACOMO ODDI
MARIANO DA FIRENZE
CONSTANTIN SUYSKENS
NICCOLO PAPINI
FRANCOIS VAN ORTROY
JOHANNES JOERGENSEN
UMBERTO COSMO
MAURICE BEAUFRETON
ANDREW G. LITTLE
F. C. BURKITT
WALTER W. SETON
EDOUARD D'ALENCON
HILARIN FELDER
ANDRE CALLEBAUT
LIVARIUS OLIGER
MICHAEL BIHL
AGOSTINO GEMELLI
DOMENICO SPARACIO
LEONE BRACALONI
BENVENUTO BUGHETTI
LAURENTIUS CASUTT
EZIO FRANCESCHINI
GIUSEPPE ABATE
NESTA DE ROBECK
FAUSTA CASOLINI
MALCOLM D. LAMBERT
ALEXANDRE MASSERON
OMER ENGLEBERT
FRANCIS DE BEER
ARNALDO FORTINI
AUGUSTO VICINELLI
ENGELBERT GRAU
OKTAVIAN VON RIEDEN
KAJETAN ESSER
LUCIANO CANONICI

HENRI D'AVRANCHES
ST. BONAVENTURE
UGOLINO DI MONTE S. MARIA

BARTHOLOMEW OF PISA
MARCOS DE LISBOA
LUKE WADDING
CANDIDE CHALIPPE
PAUL SABATIER
MICHELE FALOCI PULIGNANI
MONTGOMERY CARMICHAEL
ALFONS FIERENS
GRATIEN DE PARIS
HAROLD E. GOAD
PASCAL ROBINSON
CUTHBERT OF BRIGHTON
FREDEGAND D'ANVERS
LUIS DE SARASOLA
FERDINAND M. DELORME
LEONARD LEMMENS
VITTORINO FACCHINETTI
PIERO BARGELLINI
NICOLA CAVANNA
GIROLAMO GOLUBOVICH
ZEFFERINO LAZZERI
DOMENICO CRESI
RAPHAEL HUBER
FRANCESCO ATTAL
ROSALIND BROOKE
JOHN R. H. MOORMAN
STEPHEN J. P. VAN DIJK
EDOUARD SCHNEIDER
JACQUES CAMBELL
DOMINIQUE BONIN
ARDUINO TERZI
FIDENTIUS VAN DEN BORNE
LOTHAR HARDICK
SOPHRONIUS CLASEN
ALBERTO GHINATO
GIACINTO PAGNANI

HOLY SPIRIT LIBRARY
89 0585
CABRINI COLLEGE, RADNOR, PA.

Foreword

Of the making of books about St. Francis of Assisi, there is no end — so much so that the constitutions of the French Canadian Province of the Order of Friars Minor stipulate that each friar must read one such book every year. While one can only rejoice over the spiritual good which each and any of these books may effect in its readers, it is legitimate to question whether that good may not diminish insofar as the books become repetitive.

Hence the need for new materials and for new treatment of old materials. And this need applies equally to the two aspects of every saint or officially acknowledged master and model of the Christian life: his deeds and his spirituality. The first are the primary concern of the biographer; the second, though of basic importance in biography, is usually treated more extensively in works on the Saint's doctrine or message or significance.

In this book, we are dealing almost entirely with biographical data. Consequently, our fundamental obligation to the reader is to see that the events of the Saint's life are presented as faithfully as possible in the light of objective historical truth, *to the extent to which that factual truth has been established by the latest findings of modern, critical scholarship.* In other words, we must try to "get the facts straight" as they are known today.

So much important research has been performed in Europe in the past twenty-five years as to render the standard biographies of St. Francis of Assisi seriously out of date, despite the enduring merits of many of their pages. Those by Father Cuthbert and

Johannes Joergensen are based on the state of knowledge prevailing forty years ago or earlier. In 1947 the Abbé Omer Englebert began to make use of some of the source materials published in the 1920's, notably the *Legenda Antiqua* of Perugia (1922) and the *Liber exemplorum* (1927). But most of the important new studies and discussions, such as those concerning the site of the Saint's home and of the composition of the Canticle of Brother Sun, appeared in the 1950's and early 1960's, and Fortini's great work appeared in 1959. Consequently, Englebert's revised second French edition of 1956 is also out of date; actually, its only noteworthy changes consisted of numerous minor corrections of facts and references supplied in the helpful critical review by Père Dominique Bonin, O.F.M.

Edward Hutton's 1950 English translation of Englebert's first edition was shown to be gravely faulty by Ignatius Brady, O.F.M., in *Franciscan Studies* in 1953. It was clear that a thorough revision was needed. The Franciscan Herald Press therefore acquired the English-language rights and an authorization to publish an entirely new English second edition, in a second translation by Miss Eve Marie Cooper of Montreal, to be brought up to date by Father Ignatius and myself.

Once the new translation was available, our first task was to make a careful revision of the text and especially of the numerous quotations from the sources. On finding that many were paraphrases rather than quotations, we either omitted the quotation marks or supplied our own translations. Both of us thoroughly checked and occasionally corrected the Notes, and I added many new Notes, which are enclosed in brackets. The English version of the Testament and several Prayers of the Saint is by Brady, and that of the Canticle of Brother Sun is mine.

Because studies of the life of St. Francis have been crippled throughout these productive decades by the lack of a comprehensive subject bibliography, it was decided that this new English edition should be equipped with a Research Bibliography covering all important materials since 1939, with a selection of outstanding older publications. In this connection, the point to be stressed is that the best documented works, both old and recent, themselves contain ample bibliographical references to previous publications which have been omitted in our compilation. An asterisk precedes the reference number of such works in the Research Bibliography, and two asterisks denote items which are especially rich bibliographically.

In addition, to serve as an introduction to the most important contributions, I have provided a Guide to Research on St. Francis of Assisi 1939-1963, which surveys in succession the subject fields of the Bibliography: Documentation, Life, Spirituality, Orders, and Places. A detailed Table of Contents of the Bibliography precedes its two Lists of Abbreviations. For reasons of economy, the latter have been used extensively; similarly, throughout the Guide, Notes, and Appendices, the reader is constantly referred to the 1575-item Bibliography for complete data. There too he will often find references to reviews and abstracts of important books and articles in the principal Franciscan and some general historical journals, which can be of time-saving aid to the researcher by providing evaluations, corrections, or condensations of the publications in question.

It is an interesting fact that much of the extensive research and discussion of the last quarter century has concentrated on subjects that are peripheral to the life of St. Francis, such as his home and family. So too most of the colorful wealth of material provided by the monumental new four-volume biography by Arnaldo Fortini in 1959 tends to fill in the background of life in Assisi early in the 13th century, rather than to supply new data concerning the actual deeds and events of the Saint's career. As a result, we have inserted (in brackets) fourteen major factual emendations into Englebert's 21 chapters (see pages 58, 59, 63, 107, 125, 135, 174, 180, 182, 221, 251, 287, 308, 328).

The essence of the new materials will be found, therefore, in the Guide, the Notes, and above all in these seven Appendices; II Chronology; III Family; IV Birth, Baptism, and Name; V Homes; VI Wars; VII Companions; VIII The Canticle of Brother Sun. Appendix I on the Sources is mostly by Englebert, with a few pages which I have added (paragraphs enclosed in brackets).

The perhaps surprising list of eighty names on the dedication page represents the major medieval and modern scholars whose writings and research have been used in preparing this edition, as all must do who undertake the study of the life of St. Francis. However, beyond our debt to them, I wish to acknowledge here my warm gratitude to the following friends for their valued advice or kind assistance in consulting, borrowing, or obtaining, often though generous gifts, valuable materials and publications: Ignatius Brady, OFM; Irenaeus Herscher, OFM; Jacques Cambell, OFM; Dominique Bonin, OFM; Arduino Terzi, OFM; Goffredo Ligori, OFM; Giacinto Pagnani, OFM; Luciano Canonici, OFM; Kajetan Esser, OFM; James Van der Veldt, OFM; Marion A.

Habig, OFM; Denis McGuckin, OFM; Henry Demko, OFM;
Dominic Unger, OFM Cap; Oktavian von Rieden, OFM Cap;
Giuseppe Abate, OFM Conv; Arnaldo Fortini; Angelo Sacchetti
Sassetti; Nello Vian; Eugene Willging; John Alden; Bernard Pee-
bles; Peter Petcoff; and Nesta de Robeck. May St. Francis reward
them!

In 1228 Friar Thomas of Celano was the first to record (in *I
Celano*, 37) the epochal fact that through St. Francis of Assisi
"*Christi renovatur Ecclesia*," the Church of Christ is being renewed.
Today, when the Holy Spirit, working through the Second Vatican
Council, is again renewing the Church, has the Little Poor Man
of Assisi a vital part to play, through his followers, or has he, as
someone has had the termerity to say, "been downgraded in recent
years"?

On October 4, 1963, at a general congregation of the Council
in St. Peter's Basilica, one (non-Franciscan) bishop after another
rose to insist on the urgency and timeliness of the Poverello's
spirituality of voluntary Christian poverty and love of the poor,
echoing these not-to-be-forgotten words uttered the previous November 11 by the beloved Pope John XXIII: "The Church, which
is the Church of all, wishes in a special way to be the Church of
the Poor." Those who have followed closely the powerful under-
currents of thought and aspiration among the Council Fathers
testify that a growing number are convinced that the Holy Spirit
will bring about the renewal of the Church in the spirit of poverty and in the service of the poor.

The part which St. Francis of Assisi will play in this post-Council
renovation of the Church will of course depend entirely on the
extent to which his friends and followers, in and out of his three
Orders, succeed in living and radiating his spirit. May this book
add its mite to that noble process of renovation by brushing a
few bits of dust away from his image, so that some of those thousands who still look to him for guidance and self-renewal may
perceive more vividly and accurately the supreme timeliness of his
message as indelibly etched in the incarnate drama of his daily
life and actions.

Father of the Poor, pray for us, and renew The Church of Christ
in our Times as you did in yours!

Raphael Brown

Washington. D.C.
July 23, 1964

Contents

Guide to Research on
St. Francis of Assisi 1939-1963

According to Dom David Knowles, "the number of English scholars who are fully aware of the amount of first-class critical work that has been accomplished by continental scholars on this period of religious history [1209-1330] could probably be counted on the fingers of one hand." It is perhaps futile to deplore a similar ignorance among English and American historians and students of the enormous mass of writings by continental scholars on the life of St. Francis during the last quarter of a century.

However, it may be a constructive criticism to point out that there is no medium through which those historians can conveniently follow the development of that research, apart from the invaluable yet highly specialized Capuchin journal *Collectanea Franciscana*, with its thorough coverage of current production and particularly with its indispensable cumulative *Bibliographia Franciscana*. But as that splendid journal is primarily a tool for the advanced scholar specializing in Franciscan history, there remains a serious lacuna for the would-be well-informed historian and student, in that no Franciscan periodical in the English language undertakes to abstract or review current literature in this field. In vain one looks for such coverage in *Franciscan Studies* or *Catholic Historical Review*; while the latter's responsibility is obviously far smaller, actually it prints more than the former (since 1953).

1

It is axiomatic today that bibliographical control of a subject is an absolute prerequisite to its mastery. Yet with utter disregard of that axiom, the study of the life of St. Francis of Assisi has groped and stumbled along for nearly four productive decades without a comprehensive bibliography, i.e. since that of Facchinetti in 1928 (A7). The wealth of monographic studies appearing in various journals has consequently remained largely unknown and unused. It is high time that this inefficient situation come to an end. The Research Bibliography in this book will, we hope, for some time eliminate any excuse for such lack of proficiency. It is the aim of this Guide to serve as a necessarily limited introduction to the major contributions of European scholars to our knowledge of St. Francis of Assisi in recent decades. The Guide will survey their work in the same topical order as the Bibliography: Documentation, Background, Life, Spirituality, Orders, Places. Subtopics will be printed for the first time in italics.

(A) Documentation

A few notes on the major Franciscan historical journals besides the indispensable *Collectanea Franciscana*; almost equally useful to the student for their articles and reviews or abstracts are the following: *Archivum Franciscanum Historicum, Etudes Franciscaines, Franziskanische Studien, Miscellanea Francescana, Studi Francescani,* and *Wissenschaft und Weisheit,* with *Frate Francesco* and *Italia Francescana* also helpful, though edited more for the general reader.

Piana's survey of basic Franciscana since 1880 (A17) is especially useful. Of course the new Ooms & Frascardore *Bibliografia delle bibliografie francescane* (A15) will be invaluable.

As to the *bibliography* of St. Francis himself, one can only regret that Fortini's (A8) 1000 items, all arranged in a single author alphabet, are far from being as comprehensive as one would wish; while rich in materials on Italian history, they do not include many important articles in the Franciscan periodicals.

For other major recent bibliographies, see that word in the Subject Index of the Bibliography.

Of the *writings of St. Francis,* the new English editions (A30, A33) are accurate and readable, but lack the helpful annotations, introductions, and indexes to be found in the French editions (A36, A37, A39), the Italian editions of Vicinelli (A43) and Cambell (A42), and especially in the third edition of the new German version by Esser and Hardick (A41). Cambell's fundamental study of the authenticity and textual problems is probably definitive (though not mentioned by A33). Esser has supplied critical editions and basic studies of the Saint's Testament (A62) and Rule for Hermitages (A61).

Regarding the *sources*, it should go without saying that the critical Quaracchi edition of the 13th-century texts in *Analecta Franciscana* X (A64) supersedes all earlier editions. We can only hope and strongly urge that Volume XI, to include the 14th-century texts, be edited and published in the near future.

Meanwhile excellent translations and studies of the *Vitae* by Friar Thomas of Celano have appeared in recent years in several languages (A88-A92), with the German edition as usual the most scientific in apparatus (A90). Of three dissertations dealing with his lives of St. Francis (A97, A99, A101), the first by Francis de Beer, OFM, on the Saint's conversion, succeeds in being the most abstruse and subtle. Treating only *I Celano*, 1-36, and *II Celano*, 3-18, the author tries to demonstrate that in the First Life the Saint's conversion is described from the point of view of the psychology and spirituality of the individual, whereas in the Second Life it is viewed through the prism of the Order. The study by Fidentius van den Borne, OFM (A102), though unfortunately hidden in a Dutch journal, is no doubt one of the best ever written.

The outstanding new edition and study of St. Bonaventure's Legends are those of Sophronius Clasen, OFM (A105, A108).

Among the minor sources, we must welcome the critical edition being prepared by Alberto Ghinato, OFM, of the *Anonymus Perusinus* (A126), and the recent critical edition of Jacques de Vitry's Letters (A128), with McDonnell's valuable though not exhaustive pages on him (A129). The early Franciscan Chronicles of Jordan of Giano, Thomas of Eccleston, and (in part) Salimbene of Parma have had useful new translations and commentaries (A130-A132, A135, A140-A142).

For an outline and evaluation of the fundamental 1939 study of the famous so-called Legend of the Three Companions by the Conventual scholar Giuseppe Abate, which is still not known and appreciated as it should be, see the last part of Appendix I on the Sources.

Though not yet ready, Mrs. Rosalind Brooke's edition and study of The Writings of Brother Leo in Nelson's Medieval Texts will probably be a major contribution toward the final solution of what is called in Italy *la questione francescana*, i. e. the identification of those writings in the several late compilations. Bishop Moorman's significant suggestions in his important *Sources* . . . (A268) are also considered in Appendix I. Another important milestone toward that goal is the 1963 edition and study of the mid-14th century Barcelona Codex by Jacques Cambell, OFM (A210), which contains several hitherto unknown anecdotes about Brother Giles.

Thanks to the useful tables of parallel texts in five major sources published by Andrew G. Little in 1926 (A265), scholars analyzing incidents in the life of St. Francis have increasingly used the comparative method which is absolutely necessary in order to ascertain *all* relevant details supplied by *all* extant texts of the same anecdote. However, owing perhaps to the lack of a set of complete tables, insufficient use has been made of the secondary 14th-century compilations or codices published, with helpful references to parallel versions, by Bihl (A205), Bughetti (A207, A208), Delorme (A211, A212, A213), and Oliger (A220, A221). The only writer who has duly exploited them is Moorman, in his little-known but rich *New Fioretti* (A84).

The extended controversy over the place of origin of The Canticle of Brother Sun, which is summarized in Appendix VIII, Part 2, has resulted in new studies of the reliability of our two principal sources for that incident, the *Speculum Perfectionis* of Sabatier (A151, A152) and the *Legenda Antiqua* of Perugia (A148), by Abate (C160:344-355), Fortini (FNV II,479-486), and Bigaroni (C163:39-49). But a definitive analysis of their historicity, and especially of the important unique details in the *Legenda*, must await the publication of the Sarnano manuscript of the latter, which Abate promised a quarter of a century ago.

The *Actus-Fioretti* has been the subject of illuminating new studies and excellent new editions, as noted at the end of Appendix I. The extensive bibliography in A166 must be consulted for works before 1958 that are not included in items A158-A186 in the Research Bibliography in this book.

The only major biography of St. Francis that has appeared since 1939 is the monumental new *Nova Vita di San Francesco* (A296) by the former mayor and outstanding historian of Assisi, Prof. Arnaldo Fortini. Privately published by the author in 1959 (but now distributed by Vallecchi in Florence), this 2265-page work in four volumes (bound in five) consists of the following parts: Volume I (bound in two) is a narrative biography in 17 chapters totaling 819 pages; Volume II presents in 549 pages eleven documented studies on sources, the home of the Saint, his youth, the war against Perugia, his first years after conversion, his companions, the family and home of St. Clare, the Sisters and history of San Damiano, lay friends of the Poverello, and the problem of the origin of the Canticle of Brother Sun; Volume III (658 p.) begins with a section describing the city and district of Assisi in the 13th century, with its municipal organization and customs, followed by a catalog of its archival collections and concluding with over 100 pages of texts of 62 significant documents between 1140 and 1298; Volume IV contains a 1000-item bibliography in one alphabet by author; a 200-page index; and a map of Assisi and another of its district.

Obviously from this outline of its contents, Fortini's work by its very nature and amplitude forms an epochal contribution to research on the background of the life of St. Francis which no one writing on that subject can fail to mine and exploit with rich fruit. It must be noted with regret, however, that this encyclopedic study cannot be considered a definitive biography. Its strongest points for the historian are to be found in its author's mastery of the documentary materials dealing with the history of Assisi in the 12th and 13th centuries which appear in Volumes II and III. The biography itself is written in an often eloquent and always readable neo-d'Annunzian style which strives to bring history to life by a more or less generous injection of imaginative coloring, somewhat in the manner of André Maurois and Emil Ludwig. The resulting cinerama tends at times to be almost too colorful or more dramatic than objective reality itself. In a fair number of instances, e.g. its system of chronology (see Appendix II) and its confusing of the two Count Conrads (see Appendix VI, Part 1), the author's research should have been more exacting; in others, such as his relative neglect of events outside of Umbria and especially in the Valley of Rieti, his treatment should have been more impartial. As Oktavian von Rieden has remarked, the long chapter on Egypt represents a mixture of fact and fiction. Nevertheless, all future writers on St. Francis will be glad to acknowledge their gratitude to Arnaldo Fortini for the wealth of materials and insights which he has generously contributed to our knowledge of the life and times of St. Francis of Assisi.

While the Dutch Pater Fidentius van den Borne, OFM, has not yet published a biography of the Poverello, his numerous substantial studies of the sources and problems and other biographies (A102, A275-A277, A318-A320, E167, E235, E235a; cf A321) lead one to hope that he will soon give us one of the best of all. Père Dominique Bonin, OFM, of Montreal, may soon complete a two-volume biography which will also mark a milestone in this field.

(B) Background

Limitations of space and the subject's indirect connection with the life of St. Francis preclude more than a brief mention of just a few outstanding items in this section of the Research Bibliography.

In the field of *art*, the reader must remember that the world of the Poverello was Romanesque through and through. The new Gothic style was born in France during his lifetime and reached central Italy only after he died. For a vivid panorama of the churches, paintings, and sculptures which he actually saw there, consult B15-B18, B20-B24, B27, B27a.

As to the revolutionary countercurrent of medieval *heresies*, Borst has made a basic study of the Cathari (B29), and Esser has explored the contrasts between their spirituality and that of Francis (B32). For these movements as a whole, Grundmann's amply documented surveys (D199a, B34) are unsurpassed.

Fortini's comprehensive *La lauda in Assisi e le origini del teatro italiano* (B52) is rich in unpublished materials on the *laudesi* and their popular religious poetry, inspired by the Franciscan spirit, which played a significant role in the evolution of Italian literature and drama. Cellucci (B50) has made an excellent study of the literary qualities of the early Franciscan *legendae*.

The relationship between traditional Benedictine *monasticism* and St. Francis, against the background of the numerous great monasteries in Central Italy which he visited, has not yet been scientifically studied; for available materials, see B57-B87. The potential influence of that master of eremiticism, St. Peter Damian, on his eremitical spirituality might provide a fruitful field to explore; for outstanding recent works on St. Peter Damian, see B67, B69-B72, B74, B80.

(C) Life

The complex problems of the *chronology* of the life of St. Francis have been inadequately treated by Cresi (C1), Fortini (C3), and Terzi (C9); for the various elements involved, see Appendix II, and for my conclusions, see the Table in its Part 15.

The major controversy over the location of the *home* in Assisi of the Saint's father, covering over 1000 pages (C11-C28), is outlined in Appendix V. While rejecting Fortini's new third site, I incline to believe that the evidence is strong both for San Francesco il Piccolo (without the Stalletta-birth fable) and for the Chiesa Nuova site, as having been homes of Pietro di Bernardone respectively in the infancy and the youth of Francis.

New materials supplied by Abate (C33) and Fortini (C36) concerning the *family, birth, and childhood* of the Saint, with data on his baptism and name, are described in Appendixes III and IV. The debated question as to how gay was his *youth* is treated in Note 42 of Chapter 1. Felder's book on Francis and *chivalry* is still fundamental, though Fortini (C48) has added some new local data.

Again Fortini's detailed account of the prolonged hostilities between Perugia and Assisi, culminating in the *Assisi-Perugia War* in 1202 (C63), forms one of the most valuable parts of his work. So too Prof. Van Cleve (C68) has thoroughly documented the *War in Apulia*.

The *conversion* of St. Francis, as described in both *Vitae* by Thomas of Celano, has been perhaps too minutely analyzed by Francis de Beer (A97). Esser (C72) defends the authenticity of the short prayer recited before the beautiful 12th-century Crucifix of San Damiano, which has been described by Bracaloni and Vavalà (C69).

Among the Saint's *missions*, the background of the siege of Damietta in 1219 is now better known thanks to the important chapter by Prof. Van Cleve on "The Fifth Crusade" in the new University of Pennsylvania *History of the Crusades* (C89), and thanks also to Donovan's and Mansilla's studies on Cardinal Pelagius (C81, C84) and to Gottschalk's biography of Sultan Al-Malik al Kamil (C83). Among the recent Franciscan literature on the Saint in Egypt and the Holy Land, the works of Roncaglia (C97, C98, C121, C122), Ghinato (C112), and Oktavian von Rieden (C120) are outstanding and indispensable. Important studies of the early Franciscan missions in the Near East have also been published (C92, C93, C95, C101).

On both *The Christmas Crib* and *The Stigmata*, the remarkable Capuchin scholar Oktavian von Rieden has contributed richly documented and thoroughly rewarding monographs (C134, C135, C143). His work on the Stigmata is so comprehensive in treatment and bibliography that no other item need be listed on that subject. When completed, it will of course require abstracting for the general reader.

The two aspects of the famous Canticle of Brother Sun which have been the subject of extensive controversies in recent years — the meaning of its often repeated *per* and the place of its composition — are considered, with relevant literature (C144-C186), in Appendix VIII. My conclusions are: (1) *per* can be taken as meaning either "for" or "by," depending on which early source one follows; (2) the Canticle was not composed in the Valley of Rieti or in the Bishop's Palace in Assisi, as lately claimed, but in the chaplain's house at San Damiano, as stated in the sources.

A scientific monograph has still to be written on the *illnesses and doctors* of St. Francis, using the materials listed under C186a-C194. Likewise on his *death* (C195-C200; cf Notes 18 & 21 of Chapter 21) and on his *relics* (C201-C216), which are as scattered as the articles, mostly before 1939, dealing with them.

Bihl's 1928 article on the *canonization* (C218) remains the best work on the subject, though Lazzeri has just made an interesting contribution (C219a). Regarding the Saint's *cult in liturgy*, a minor controversy over the authorship of his Preface (C223, C225, C226, C227) seems not to have come to a conclusion. Cambell (C222) has published a usefully annotated collection of 13th-century liturgical texts. The *papal visit* of John XXIII to Assisi in 1962 has been duly described (C229, C232; cf C230.)

In *iconography*, Kaftal (C240a), Villain (C253), and Réau (C249) have written general surveys, while others have studied the Saint in the paintings of Titian (C233), El Greco (C238a), Benozzo Gozzoli (C247), and Rubens (C250). Finally, five early 20th-century artists — Jose Benliurre y Gil, Maurice Boutet de Monvel, Eugène Burnand, Jose Segrelles, and Dom Pedro Subercaseaux Errazuriz, OSB — have created sets of splendid illustrations of scenes in the life of St. Francis which deserve to be remembered, though published before 1939 (C254-C258).

(D) *Spirituality*

It is probably in the field of the spirituality of St. Francis that the most fruitful and significant work has been done in the last quarter of a century, mostly by prolific kerygmatic German writers.

A scientific study has not yet been made of the Saint's spiritual roots in the *humus* of the *Bible*; cf D1-D5.

Probably the forthcoming article in the *Dictionnaire de spiritualité ascétique et mystique* (under *Frères mineurs*) will provide a hitherto lacking thorough and up-to-date survey of the Poverello's spirit and practice of *contemplation, mysticism, and prayer*. Meanwhile, as we have seen, Esser has edited and commented on his Rule for Hermitages (A61), and Clasen has written a few excellent pages on the life lived therein by the Saint and his companions (D10). Dacian Bluma, OFM, has devoted a well documented dissertation (D6) to a constitutional history of Franciscan houses of recollection (cf D18). The place of Christ in the prayer life of the Saint has been carefully explored by Oktavian von Rieden (D21) in his masterpiece, *Die Leiden . . .* (D139), noticed below under Theology.

We also still lack a critical appreciation of the Poverello's almost unique attitude toward *creatures* (cf D24-D4). For an undocumented collection of practically all extant anecdotes dealing with animals, see D28 and D29.

His fervent cult of the *Eucharist* has been well studied by Esser (D49), Franceschini (D50), and Bertrand Cornet, OFM (D48). The latter especially delineates in some detail the contemporary background which induced Francis to promote a clearcut reform in this realm, inspired by the Fourth Lateran Council and supported by Honorius III.

In the complex realm of 13th-century *liturgy*, we are fortunate to have the thoroughly documented masterpieces of Van Dijk and Walker (D60, D62), which throw new light on that period in which, owing largely to the new spirit and practical requirements of the friars, the principal liturgical books were reformed, abbreviated, and reorganized in a way that inevitably reminds one of the liturgical "revolution" taking place in the Church in our times. The authors' incisive treatment of the several questions pertaining to St. Francis and the divine office (D60:179-212) is especially enlightening. However, the Poverello's insistence on the supreme spiritual value of a single conventual Mass daily is not explained (D60:52) as satisfactorily — "the reason given is not clear . . . seems to have been for fear of gain" — as it was in 1937 by Octave d'Angers, Cap (D68:482-3): the supernatural communitarian or social value of all members of a religious family uniting in offering the sacrifice was spiritually more fruitful. Nussbaum's work (D56) supplies the historical background of the evolution of the private Mass, which also summarized in D60:45-57.

The humble and simple yet profound *mariology* of St. Francis has been duly studied by Esser (D73), Feliciano de Ventosa (D74) and Brown (D70-D72).

The basic principles of the Poverello's masterful doctrine on voluntary Christian *poverty* have been carefully re-examined by several writers (see Bibliography Subject Index), notably by Esser (D82), Hardick (D84), and Lambert (D87; cf D91a).

The only important new study of the Saint's concept of the *priesthood* is that of Clasen (D98).

For recent studies on various aspects of the *theology* of St. Francis, the reader will find a helpful list of topics under that word in the Subject Index of the Bibliography. Of outstanding value are the contributions of Kajetan Esser, OFM (D114-D126), especially his paper on Francis' ecclesiology (D125), and the definitive masterpiece of Oktavian von Rieden, Cap (D139), on the sufferings of Christ in the spirituality of the Poverello.

Among general *miscellaneous studies* (D150-D186), those of Laurentius Casutt, (D151), Clasen (D151), Lekeux (D168), and Lortz (D169) are noteworthy for their stimulating re-evaluation of the psychology and ideals of the Saint. Interesting autobiographical tributes by modern writers appear in Rossetti's *San Francesco vivo* (D177). Fernando de Maldonado, Cap (D188), has written a well-documented monograph on the Saint's pedagogical method. Several important studies of his relations to medieval spirituality are listed in D197-D204.

(E) Orders

Comprehensive coverage of recent research on the founders of religious Orders — whether it be Francis, Dominic, or Benedict — must necessarily include important new works on the early history of their Orders, and with our Saint they are three in number; hence this section of the Bibliography (E1-E247), with an addendum on his friend, St. Dominic (E248-E255).

The most useful new works on early *Franciscan history* are those by Brooke (E3), Esser (E16), Huber (E27), Lazaro de Aspurz (E32), and Sevesi (E42); Bishop Moorman's comprehensive history of the Order to 1517 has not yet appeared.

On the *Franciscan Spirituals and Joachimism,* Bloomfield's critical survey of Joachim of Flora (E48) is indispensable, and the 1963 dissertation by Thaddeus of New Durham (E56a) on the Spirituals no doubt covers the latest and best studies, though I have not yet seen it. Alberto Ghinato has contributed a welcome new edition of Angelo Clareno's *Chronicon* (E57), and the works by Doucet (E60) and Lydia von Auw (E64-E66) have extended our knowledge of that controversial figure.

The *rules* of the First Order have been the subject of some disagreement and discussion, with Quaglia (E86-E88) contending there really was none before 1221 — a thesis effectively refuted in Bihl's 1946 review. However, as Cambell stressed in 1960, Quaglia has demonstrated the basic originality of the Franciscan Rules in contrast to others then in use. Casutt's analysis (E78) is also important. But the most constructive clarification appears in the German *Werkbuch,* also available in English and French (E91).

The still unclear *clericus-laicus* problem (E92-E99) is sketched in Appendix VII, Part 4. But we must note with gratitude a basic new study of the Franciscan lay brotherhood (E92).

In the important field of early *Franciscan biography,* much remains to be done, as shown in Appendix VII, owing to recent controveries about several of the companions of St. Francis. The new Italian *Martirologio* (E101, E102) and *Aureola serafica* (E108), with Habig's excellent *Franciscan Book of Saints* (E106), serve as useful handbooks.

Regarding important friars who were companions or contemporaries of the Poverello, Grau's article (E112) unfortunately does not cover the new data and arguments of Fortini (E111) and Terzi (E115). *Blessed Brother Giles* has been studied by Hardick (E120), Brown (E121), and Gamboso (E123). *St. Anthony of Padua* has found an excellent biographer in Clasen (E136-E140), as well as several important studies by others (E141, E143, E144, E147, E150, E151, E153). On the recent re-evaluation of the enigmatic *Brother Elias* (E154-E167), see Appendix VII, Part 3, under his name, and Note 16 of Chapter 14.

St. Clare and her *second order* account for about 60 items in the Bibliography (E168-E222a), as the 700th Anniversary of her death brought forth a number of useful works, notably those by Grau (E191-E194, adapted in English by Brady, E170), by Fortini (E181-E185), Franceschini (E186-E189), and the authors of the Assisi symposium (E206). The minor controversy between Abate and Fortini (E214-E218) over the site of her home is also important for the history of the Duomo of San Rufino (see Note 2 of Chapter 8).

No outstanding new research has been done in recent years on the still obscure origins of the *Third Order*. However, we now have a valuable handbook of Tertiary biographies, *These Made Peace* (E230), as well as useful lives of St. Elizabeth of Hungary (E238) and Blessed Luchesio (E246-E247).

A thorough study still has to be made of the friendship and meetings and mutual influences of Saints Francis and Dominic, which Vicaire's definitive biography of the latter (E255; cf E252) and Hinnebusch's article (E251) treat only in passing.

(F) *Places*

Though he was in fact one of the greatest hermits in the history of the Church, St. Francis traveled so often from one of his twenty-odd hermitages to another, always preaching in the towns in between, that today there is in Italy an organized movement to have him appointed Patron Saint of Tourists. While much research must still be done on the topographical and chronological problems connected with his travels — particularly on the dates of his long tours in Northern and Southern Italy — a good deal of useful literature is now available on the places he visited and the friaries or hermitages he founded in *central Italy*. For reasons of convenience, his relations with Rome and the papacy have been included in this section of the Guide and Bibliography.

The maps and works on *medieval roads and topography* (F1-F13) will be found useful in general and especially for the background of Appendix II, Parts 8 and 14, dealing with major highways and pilgrims routes through Umbria; see also the maps in this book.

By far the most detailed and helpful guidebooks are the provincial ones published by the Touring Club Italiano (F55, F136, F149, F181). Of the more recent travel books on *Franciscan Central Italy* as a whole, the only one worthy to rank with the best older works is that by Secret (F47); of course von Matt's illustrations (F43), as always, are superlative.

The outstanding research on the Poverello in the Valley of Rieti in *Lazio* performed by the retired Bishop Arduino Terzi, OFM, in his monumental *Memorie* and other writings (F59, F60, C181-C186), has been noted in Appendix VIII, Part 2. His important archaeological discoveries and restorations at Greccio, Poggio Bustone, and La Foresta will remain an enduring monument to his remarkable contributions to our knowledge of the life of the Poverello long after historians will have disproved his thesis for the composition of the Canticle of Brother Sun at La Foresta (see Appendix VIII, Part 2).

Turning to *Rome and The Papacy*, with *The College of Cardinals*, again Msgr. Terzi has given us a finely illustrated though not ideally critical book on *San Francesco d'Assisi a Roma* (F122). But the only new study of the important episode of the Fourth Lateran Council in the Saint's life is unfortunately written in Dutch (F113). Similarly, we can only regret that Kartusch's important dissertation (F100) on the Cardinals of his times has not been published, as also that Paschini's basic monograph on Cardinal John of St. Paul (F104), though printed in 1940, is still almost unknown (see Chapter 5, Note 23).

Another minor controversy has centered in recent years on the date of the Saint's visit to the Hermitage of St. Benedict at *Subiaco* (F123-F128). If and when established, its conclusions may be helpful in solving some chronological problems.

As noted at the end of Appendix I, and in Appendix II, Part 12, Giacinto Pagnani, OFM, has written some valuable studies on the *Fioretti* (A177-A179) and on the beautiful garden which produced it, *The Marches* (F132, F142).

In *Tuscany*, we now have excellent monographs on Francis and Arezzo (F150), Siena (F157), and San Quirico d'Orcia (F161), with a useful discussion of the first friary in Florence (F155, F156).

On *Umbria*, besides several outstanding new descriptive works (F163, F167, F175, & F177), the Università degli Studi in Perugia has contributed a fundamental symposium (F195) and stimulated further research into the medieval history of the province, in recent years under the direction of Prof. Arnaldo Fortini.

For the latter's invaluable books and brochures on the history of *Assisi*, see F233-F239; cf F212, F213, F240. Cristofani's still useful 1866 history of the town was reprinted in 1959 (F232). The *Bolletino* of the Deputazione di storia patria per l'Umbria has published significant studies on the legend and cult of the early bishop San Rufino (F231) and on Umbrian folklore (F203), as well as a helpful cumulative index of its articles (F185).

On Assisi's *Churches and Monasteries*, the early history of the Portiuncula has at last been clarified by Canonici (F248); see also Note 3 of Chapter 4. The ruined San Benedetto has been treated (F258, F261), as has San Damiano (F264). Of course the Basilica of San Francesco and the Sacro Convento continue to attract students (F266-F272, F277-F279).

Helpful monographs have appeared on St. Francis in Gubbio (F294) and Trevi (313). Two recent studies of early Franciscan history in Perugia (F304, F306) concentrate on the second half of the 13th century.

For *Northern Italy*, Alessandria (F316, F317) and Novara (F319) have been well covered. In *Southern Italy*, early Franciscanism in the mountainous Abruzzi is the subject of still another bitter dispute (F324-F329).

Of the Poverello's twenty *Hermitages*, the following have received noteworthy new treatment; apart of course from those of the Valley of Rieti: Bellegra (F346, F348) — thanks to Pope John's visit; Le Celle di Cortona (F362); Monte Casale (F363); L'Alberino in Siena (F370); La Verna (F376, F379, F382); the Carceri (F385, F389); Monte Luco (F393, F394); La Romita (F396); Lo Speco di Sant' Urbano (F399); Trasimene Island (F400); and — thanks to the late English novelist Phyllis Bottome — San Francesco del Deserto near Venice (F402). However, it should be noted that many of the hermitages are also described in works on Franciscan Central Italy and Umbria. I am devoting my next book to them and to the contemplative and eremitical spirituality of their Founder (F344).

Fiction was naturally not included in the Research Bibliography. Nevertheless it may not be out of place to mention here two outstanding fictional biographies based on careful research — Felix Timmermans' *De Harp van Sint Franciscus* (Antwerp & Amsterdam, 1931), with English translations by Molly Bird, *The Harp of Saint Francis* (Ranchi, 1949), and by Raphael Brown, *The Perfect Joy of St. Francis* (NY, 1952) — also translated into German, French, and Japanese; and *The Bright Thread; A Novel of St. Clare of Assisi*, by J. Steffan (NY, 1962).

Lastly, a footnote on a lately popular apocryphal item: the so-called Peace Prayer of St. Francis. There is no text in all the Franciscan literature of the first several centuries which contains any passage like it. James Meyer, OFM (A31:333) quotes a text in Brother Giles' *Sayings*, Ch. 1, which very indirectly, not "strongly recalls" it; but there is no connection between the two. Irenaeus Herscher, OFM, has traced it back only to 1938 in Italy; see *The Letters of George Santayana*, ed. by Daniel Cory (NY 1955) 323.

Introduction

There is no Saint about whom so much has been written as St. Francis of Assisi. But the publications dealing with him overflow the narrow bounds of devotional literature. For not only are Catholics to be found in the long procession of his admirers, but Protestants, pantheists, rationalists, and persons indifferent to religion.

What is the reason for the Poverello's universal popularity? The biography which you are about to read will doubtless furnish some indication. Like those masterpieces in which each generation discovers new riches, his life contains ever timely lessons and is an inexhaustible source of inspiration.

Francis is one of those men of whom humanity will always be proud. His qualities compel sympathy. His faults — if any — are charming. His sanctity has in it nothing esoteric, effeminate, or intimidating. His natural gifts arouse general admiration. His teaching breathes forth such freshness, poetry, and serenity that even the most blasé may find in it reasons for loving life and for believing in God's goodness.

He is pleasing to all by his nobility, his disinterestedness, and his goodness. This knightly man walks nobly forward to-

17

ward the high goal which he has set for himself. He knows nothing of mediocre thinking, pious falsehood, or petty intrigue. If he feels reverence toward those in high place, if he gladly obeys not only his superiors but likewise his equals and his inferiors, he has about him none of the toadying proper to flatterers and slaves.

The truth is that he was born a prince; and why should he flatter any man, when he himself despises all temporal goods? He leaves the honors to others, stands apart from the wranglings of men, takes no thought for the morrow, and abandons his woodland shelter to an ass obstinately bent on occupying it. So long as he has any money, he gives it to anyone who wants it; and when his money is all gone, he runs after beggars to give them his clothes.

Now if intelligence consists in the bandying about of abstractions or in a bent for organization, philosophers and public servants may flatter themselves that they possess more of it than he. But if intelligence consists in common sense and in the discernment of men's hearts, Francis is assuredly inferior to none. But where he is truly without a peer is in his faculty for loving.

All his brethren benefit from his affection. The first place is given to persons afflicted with leprosy. Next come highwaymen and those other sinners for whom his heart overflows with tender love and forgiveness. For he judges no man, reserving for his own sins the total weight of his scorn. He honors the least of his kind, treats every man with respect, and speaks graciously and courteously to all.

Can it be that he is unaware of the baseness of the human heart? He sees it as clearly as does the most pessimistic of psychologists; but he prefers to look at the noble aspects of the soul, leaving to the evil-doer the self-esteem necessary for his redemption. Neither does the evil which seems to triumph in this world escape him; but rather than dwell on those riddles which Christ Himself refuses to clarify, he devotes his time to promoting the kingdom of righteousness and to urging men to earn their salvation. We are grateful to him for such optimism.

We feel no less gratitude for the joy that he radiates. Since riches, pleasure, and ambition mean nothing to him, since he has renounced all that engenders dissatisfaction, resentment, and remorse, what cause would he have to be sad? He is gay, requires cheerfulness of all who approach him, and does not insist on all men following his own peculiar pattern of virtue. His self-imposed austerities cause none to suffer. His faith is neither intolerant nor aggressive. His own continence does not lead him to condemn lawful human affection. Far from desiring to enslave men's wills, he permits each one to follow the Holy Spirit's inspirations. And in those times of inquisitions and fierce conflicts, he neither debates nor argues, limiting himself to recommending peace.

The sources of poetry which he discovered will never fail thirsty souls. Ever the inspired poet, he grasps the hidden relations of things, creates new formulas, improvises moral fables in perfect taste, and enacts delightful personifications. He dramatizes, stages, mimics like a *jongleur*, and when words fail him, calls music to his aid. He composes sublime canticles reminiscent of the most beautiful Psalms in the Bible.

A man can be a saint without being an artist. Great mystics have written volumes without being able to express themselves. But for Francis the means of expression are always equal to the themes that he invents or renews. For he has discovered many new themes which have since entered into mankind's heritage. And as for those traditional themes that he takes up, he enriches them with an orchestration so natural, so exquisite, and so new that his endowments as an epic poet shine through even Thomas of Celano's rhetoric and the threadbare prose of Brother Leo.

One of his merits is that of having restored speech to the

long dumb fraternal voice of creation. He awakens slumbering creatures. His eyes perceive the unity of God's plan. Contemplating nature with that fresh gaze with which the first man looked upon it on the world's first morning, he rediscovers in it the traces of divine love and beauty. He loves plants and animals, and urges the elements to join him in praise of their common Benefactor. And wonder of wonders, nature, recognizing itself in this ingenious interpreter, shakes off for him its hostility and reserve. His brother fire refrains from burning him, his brother wolf tenders its paw, while his sister swallows come hastening to his sermons.

These anecdotes and many others which we shall retell prove St. Francis' eternal timelessness. For it will not do to see in him only the founder of an Order, a saint on the calendar of saints, or an historic figure to be studied by the learned.

Francis is a sincere man with whom every honest man is delighted to converse, a former sinner who has found happiness and passes on its recipe to his brethren. Here is a being inebriated with love, illumined with divine light, preserved from error by his humility and common sense, expressing sincerely and without harshness those few concepts essential to the life of the soul. He is a master of inner freedom and a universal intercessor.

His personality is not dependent on time, place, or school. He calls himself a man of no booklearning and declares that he has no other master than the Almighty. And indeed, aside from a few popular songs, liturgical texts, the catechism and the Gospel, he knows nothing at all. He is marked by no system and makes no attempt to create a new one. Thus nothing that he has said is dated; no alteration is to be found in the heritage he has left us. East and West, youth and greybeard, plain men and connoisseurs may all help themselves to his riches and ask of him the secret of peace of soul.

*   *   *

This is not the place to show how Francis, whom all men loved in life, was likewise beloved after his death.

To reasoners and logicians, to be sure, who count on logic and compulsion to resolve all problems, he remains a stranger. Nor is he appreciated by authoritarian politicians who aspire to load down the human soul with those chains from which the Sermon on the Mount had delivered it.

But he has always fascinated those who are sensible to mystery and beauty. How many souls have learned sanctity in his school! How many poets have celebrated him! What famous artist has not dedicated some masterpiece to him! Even in our own time, how many skeptics, wearied with philosophy and sophism, have been brought back by him to the truth of the Gospels.

Artists and the learned of every age have been interested in this "man without learning." It is true (as we shall see later on) that their attitudes toward him have sometimes varied.

It is the lover of Christ crucified, the man with the stigmata, the most perfect imitator of Christ that the literature and art of the Middle Ages celebrate in him.

It is thus that he appears to St. Bonaventure, to Jacopone da Todi, to Giotto, and to a multitude of painters and authors of "legends" in the thirteenth and fourteenth centuries. It is thus that he is sung by Dante, who places him, because of his resemblance to our Lord, above all the doctors and founders of orders. It is thus that he is praised by the *Imitation of Christ*, which, as we know, names no other saint. As for the *Fioretti*, whose vogue was so great in the fourteenth and fifteenth centuries, the following phrase which serves as a prologue becomes the recurring theme of the whole volume: "Be it noted first of all that our blessed Father St. Francis was conformed to Christ in all his acts."

This theme, become stereotyped, was taken up again by Bartholomew of Pisa in his book *Of the Conformities*, which developed St. Francis' forty resemblances to our Lord. Innumerable copies of this work, approved by the General Chapter of 1399, were circulated. Many extracts of it were made; it was translated and reprinted; for one hundred and fifty years it held popular sway.

The learned and the story-tellers of the Renaissance, among them the ex-Franciscan Rabelais, poked much fun at scholasticism, canon law, legends of the saints, religious in general and Franciscan friars in particular, but not one of them touched St. Francis.

It was quite different with the Protestants. The attack started from Brandenburg, where in 1542 Erasmus Alber declared that he had found in the *Conformities* proof of the power exercised by Satan over monks. According to him, if it was not the devil who imprinted the stigmata, it was he who persuaded the Franciscans to believe in them, to neglect the Bible, and to become stubborn about their *Conformities*, like the Turks with their Koran.

Alcoranum franciscanorum — such was the title of the massive volume wherein Alber exploited as a pamphleteer the work of Friar Bartholomew. Luther wrote a preface for it. He who admired St. Francis and qualified him as *"vir admirabilis et spiritu ferventissimus,"* ("an admirable man, exceedingly fervent in spirit"), declared that he "carefully preserved the *Book of Conformities* against the day when the Papists should say that they had never troubled the water. Then I shall know," he added, "what a stink to set under their noses."[1]

The *Alcoran* enjoyed an immense vogue. In less than fifteen years, two editions appeared in Latin, three in German, one in English, and one in French. The latter, which was published in Geneva in 1556 by Conrad Badius, was entitled, *"The Koran of the Cordeliers* [Greyfriars] — a collection of the most notorious stupidities and blasphemies . . . of those who have dared to compare St. Francis to Jesus Christ, taken from the great *Book of the Conformities*, formerly composed by Friar Bartholomew of Pisa, who in his lifetime was a Cordelier."

In an introduction which he joined to that of Luther, Conrad Badius dubbed Bartholomew a fanatic and foolish monk, and declared that all the devils put together could not have spewed out as many lies and blasphemies about God as are contained in the cursed and execrable book of the *Conformities*. His sources of information moreover permitted him to assert in verse that Francis was in Hell and that his disciples would rejoin him there:

> Tipsy Greyfriars, idolatrous vermin,
> Masked monsters, source of error most unclean,
> Your Francis who, by teaching heresy,
> Has led astray a great part of the world,
> For his virtues lies in Hell's deepest pit,
> With an iron chain most handsomely adorned,
> Reigning and flourishing with Lucifer.
> And you, likewise, who follow in his train,
> Shall not you too have your own place in Hell?
> To such offspring, such heritage is meet.

And for two hundred years, Osiander, Pierre Dumoulin, Duplessis-Mornay, Jurieu, and all the polemists and theologians of the Reformation in Germany and the Netherlands, as well as in Switzerland and France, took their text from the *Conformities* to rail against Francis and attempt to embarrass the Church of Rome.

But was this book of Bartholomew de Pisa really so wicked? "I do not hesitate to see in it the most important work written on the life of St. Francis," wrote the Protestant pastor, Paul Sabatier. "One may boldly place [its author] in the first rank of compilers. Nowhere does he make St. Francis the equal of Christ, and he even forestalls criticism on this point."[2] We must then give due credit to Friar Bartholomew for having reported all that had been published up to his time on the Little

Poor Man. It is true, say the Fathers of Quaracchi, that he did wrong to collect all sorts of miracles and visions which would be considered today as unlikely and ridiculous.[3]

Except for Bayle and the ecclesiastical authors, most of the savants of the seventeenth century ignored St. Francis. We also know that cultivated minds of the period despised the Middle Ages and Gothic art and that the poetic side of Christian hagiography escaped them. Only St. Augustine interested these reasoners. The Jansenists, who translated the Lives of the Desert Fathers, would have been scandalized by the *Fioretti*. Apparently this work was unknown to them, as it was to La Fontaine, who would have loved it, or to Pascal, who made a pact with holy poverty a few months before his death. And no one even dreamed of disturbing the folios of Wadding and of Bartholomew of Pisa, which gathered dust in libraries.

Bayle likewise refrained from consulting them. He read the *Koran of the Cordeliers*, adding a few sly insinuations and obscenities, and so drew up the article in his *Dictionnaire*, in which eighteenth century writers found their material.

Nothing disposed these indigent souls for an appreciation of the Little Poor Man. "All those who say that people can be happy and free in poverty are liars, fools, and madmen," wrote the Marquise du Deffant, who was very unhappy herself amid her riches.[4]

The editors of the *Encyclopédie* regretted that Francis had obligated his friars to continence. "How many arms lost to agriculture and the arts!" groaned De Félice. "How many celibates [living] at the expense of those who obey the laws of nature!"[5]

The spectacle of Friars Minor begging for alms saddened Voltaire, who had, as we know, a private income of 140,000 pounds a year:

> I am not over-pleased with that man Francis,
> Who thought a real Christian should go begging in the street,

And wanted his sons, those robust lazybones,
To take an oath to live at our expense![6]

There existed at that time relaxed Franciscans; and ever since the "Grey Eminence" [i.e. Fr. Joseph, Capuchin, adviser to Richelieu], certain among them mingled too freely in politics not to have made many enemies. It was not just the friars, though, but Francis himself whom Voltaire detested. With his customary inexactitude,[7] he assures the readers of his *Essai sur les moeurs* that the *Conformities* "were written in the time of St. Francis," adding that the "aberrations of the human mind have never gone further."[8]

What poet today would not give fifty thousand verses of the rhymer of the *Henriade* for the ten strophes of the *Canticle of the Sun?* Voltaire, moreover, understood nothing of this masterpiece. The author, in his eyes, is nothing but "a raving fanatic, who goes about stark naked, talks to animals, catechizes a wolf, and makes himself a snow-wife."[9]

Alone among the philosophers and their successors, Lalande and Stendhal appreciated the Poverello. Lalande also deplored the snow-wife and the sermon to the birds; but he did concede to the Founder of the Franciscans "genius of a high order, exemplary virtue, persuasive eloquence, indefatigable zeal, and rare constancy."[10] As for Stendhal, while traveling in Umbria in about 1815, he wrote: "Personally, I consider St. Francis of Assisi to be a very great man," a declaration well worthy of the perceptive mind of its author, but which was not noticed by anyone when it appeared.[11]

So for four centuries the Little Poor Man was either ignored or ridiculed by those whom we would style today the intellectuals. Even to the poets of the time, he was unknown. At this period he was familiar only to the world of art. Painters, especially, remained true to him.

Clearly, we are not speaking here of religious writers, historians, or preachers, who, either because of their state of life or their piety, continued to be preoccupied with him.

In 1728, the *Histoire de saint François d'Assise* by Father
Candide Chalippe was published, and it was reprinted for one
hundred and fifty years. The author's source was Wadding.

A more considerable event from the standpoint of historical
science was the publication in 1768 by the Bollandists of the
Legend of the Three Companions and the *Vita prima* by
Thomas of Celano, which up to that time had not been published. No less important was the discovery in 1806 of the *Vita
secunda* by the same author.

As for the orators, a panegyric of St. Francis was always
preached twice a year, on the occasion of the Portiuncula and
on his feast day (October 4th), by the Cordeliers and the
Capuchins with whom France teemed at that period. Their sermons dealt with the saint's virtues and power as a wonder-
worker: "Our Father St. Francis could work a miracle as easily
as I can swallow a glass of wine," exclaims the famous Olivier
Maillard (died, 1502). Often it is the theme of the *Conformities* which reappears: "The sufferings of St. Francis are, in a certain sense, greater than those of Christ; and the wounds which
he received are in some ways holier, longer lasting, and cruel-
er," declared Father Senault when preaching on the stigmata.
We may be sure that he bolstered up this paradox with as
much subtility as orthodoxy. The sermons of Abbé Boileau
and of Father Lejeune developed similar considerations.[12]

Bossuet alone brings up the subject again and with lyric
audacity exalts the sublime extravagance of the stigmatized
Saint of Alverna. Already, at Metz about 1652, celebrating in
St. Francis "the most ardent, the most enthusiastic, perhaps
the most desperate lover of poverty ever to be found in the
Church," Bossuet said that he wished no other ornament for
his speech than "this illustrious, this generous, this wise and
triumphant folly of the Christian religion."[13]

Twenty years later, he took up this theme at Saint-Germain,

when in a sort of diptych, he compared the folly of the Cross with that of the Poverello. "The Infinite goes forward only by gigantic steps. He leaps over hill and dale, from Heaven to the Crib, from the Crib by leaps to the Cross, from the Cross to the tomb and the depths of Hell, and from there to highest Heaven. All this is done without order and without measure." To this generous effusion of love which brought about our salvation, one man responded in kind: "By the same steps whereby the Infinite united with the finite, the finite must rise to the Infinite. He must free and liberate himself from every rule of prudence that restrains him, so as to lose himself in the Infinite. And this losing himself in the Infinite, because it transcends all rules, appears as an aberration. Such is the folly of Francis."[14]

When Napoleon reopened the churches of France and rationalism went out of style in literature, one might have expected that Chateaubriand would have made room for St. Francis of Assisi in his *Génie du christianisme*. But he waited until 1833 to pay him homage. In his *Mémoires d'outre-tombe*, he speaks as a poet "of the brotherly love which the Poverello extended even to animals," and insists on the social import of his Order:

"My Patron Saint," he writes, "inaugurated a considerable step forward in the Gospel, which has not been sufficiently remarked. He completed the introduction of the people into religion. By clothing the poor man with a monk's habit, he obligated the world to charity; he raised the beggar in the eyes of the rich; and a proletarian Christian militia, he set up the model of the brotherhood of man which Christ had preached, a brotherhood which will be the fulfillment of this as yet undeveloped segment of Christianity, and without which there will never be complete liberty and justice on earth."[15] These lines appeared only in 1850.

Apparently, it is to the Germans Goerres and Hase, and to

the Frenchmen Michelet, Renan, and Sabatier that credit is due for having attracted to St. Francis the unparalleled sympathy which he enjoys in our time among men of letters.

Johann Joseph Goerres, a former member of the *Tugendbund*, had already been converted to Catholicism when a chance reading of the *Canticle of the Sun* revealed to him the poetic genius of the Poverello. His opuscule, *Der Heilige Franciscus von Assisi, ein Troubadour* (Strasbourg, 1826), shared his discovery with the public and crossed the frontiers of his country. In it, he likewise celebrated the Middle Ages and chivalry, and built up a thesis on the relations of poetry and mysticism that delighted German Romanticists and found its defenders in France.

Twenty years later, on reaching the two great Orders of the thirteenth century, Jules Michelet, in his *Histoire de France*, was ready to dismiss them both in a few lines; "Born under the sanguinary inspiration of Citeaux, amid the crusade of Languedoc, the Order of St. Dominic was the chief auxiliary of the Pope before the founding of the Jesuits. [Its members] were charged with regulation and repression; they conducted the Inquisition and the teaching of theology, while the Franciscans overran the earth in all the turbulence of inspiration, falling and rising from obedience to freedom and from heresy to orthodoxy, embracing the whole world and animating it with ecstasies of mystical love."[16]

Then Michelet leafed through Thomas of Celano and St. Bonaventure. These old texts enchanted him. He was fascinated; and this visionary historian wrote an essay on St. Francis which ranks among his finest pages.[16]

In 1849 Antoine Frédéric Ozanam brought out *Les Poètes franciscains. . . . avec un choix des petites fleurs de saint François* (*The Franciscan Poets, with Selections from 'The Little Flowers of St. Francis'*). Except for the part dedicated to Jacopone da Todi, this beautiful volume dealt almost entirely with him whom the author called "the Orpheus of the Middle Ages."[17]

A few months previously, Abbé Riche had published a complete translation of the *Fioretti*.[18] French readers could thus enjoy a masterpiece which people had been reading in Italy ever since the invention of printing, and which subsequently was translated a dozen times more in French.

It was in 1856 that the *Franz von Assisi* of the Protestant Karl Hase appeared in Leipzig, of which the French adaptation by Charles Berthoud furnished the occasion for a celebrated study by Ernest Renan.

"Francis of Assisi possesses an extraordinary interest for religious criticism," wrote Renan. "He is, after Christ, the man who had the most limpid conscience, the most absolute naïveté, the most vivid sentiment of himself as a son of the Heavenly Father. God was in a very real sense his beginning and his end. His life is a poetic madness, a perpetual intoxication with divine love. For a whole week he delighted in the song of a cicada. His eyes, clear and deep like those of a child, penetrated to the inmost secrets, those things which God conceals from the wise and reveals to the humble.

"The thing that distinguishes him in his age and in every age is his complete originality . . . . His kind of piety comes solely from himself . . . . He despises nothing; he is indifferent to nothing; he loves everything. For everything he has a smile and a tear. A flower throws him into an ecstasy — in nature he sees only brothers and sisters . . . . All things for him possess meaning and beauty. We know that admirable hymn which he himself calls the *Canticle of the Creatures*,[19] the most beautiful piece of religious poetry since the Gospels and the most complete expression of modern religious feeling . . . . In it there is nothing strained as in the mode of Port-Royal and the mystics of the French school of the seventeenth century, nothing exaggerated or frenzied as in the Spanish mystics.

"One might say that Francis of Assisi was the only perfect Christian since Christ. His great originality lies in his having undertaken — with boundless faith and love — to carry out the program of Galilee. . . . The thesis of the *Book of the Conformities* is true. Francis really *was* a second Christ, or, rather, he was a faithful mirror of Christ.[20] The fundamental theme of the Gospel is the vanity of earthly things, which turn man aside from the Kingdom of God. This is likewise the main theme of Francis of Assisi. The bird appears to him, as to Jesus, to lead a perfect life. For a bird has no barn; it sings without ceasing; it lives by God's grace, and it wants for nothing.

"After Christianity itself," continued Renan, "the Franciscan movement is the greatest popular achievement known to history. One feels in it the simplicity of men who know only nature and what they have seen or heard in church, and who combine the whole in the freest fashion. We are a thousand miles away from Scholasticism. Francis of Assisi is virtually the only man in the Middle Ages . . . whose mind was never infected by the subtleties of the Schools."[21]

In 1864, during a journey in Italy, Hippolyte Taine in turn discovered St. Francis. Together with Dante and Giotto, whom he inspired, it is the Poverello, according to Taine, who marks the peak of the civilization of the Middle Ages. "This period is unique," he writes. "The thirteenth century is the flower and culmination of living Christianity . . . . After it there remains only Scholasticism, decadence, and fruitless gropings . . . . At that time love burst forth with extraordinary force, and St. Francis was its herald . . . . [In him], the natural boundaries separating the different realms of thought are obliterated and vanish . . . . Ponderous tangible matter and the framework of dull formulas melt and evaporate on the heights of mystical contemplation, until nothing remains but a melody, a perfume, a luminous ray, or a symbol, that débris of earthly images having no intrinsic value or serving no other purpose than prefiguring the imponderable and ineffable hereafter."[22]

The examples of Michelet, Taine, and Renan were later followed by numerous essayists, such as Emile Gebhart, Arvède Barine, Marcel Hébert, Georges Lafenestre, Teodor de Wyzewa, Louis Gillet, Andre Pérate, Edouard Schneider, Nicolas Ségur, Camille Mauclair, and Abel Bonnard, who dedicated sometimes truly remarkable writings to the Poverello.

Meanwhile, the Germans, K. Müller, H. Thode, Voigt, and Cardinal Ehrle pursued their learned researches, and the chronicles of Jordan of Giano, Thomas of Eccleston, Fra Salimbene, and Angelo Clareno were published in Germany, England, and Italy.

However, it cannot be affirmed that before 1894, Franciscan origins were studied any more than any other important chapter in church history.

* * *

It was Paul Sabatier who aroused interest in the subject and caused it to take on a hitherto unheard-of amplitude. He himself tells us the origin of his Franciscan vocation.

"One December morning in 1884, at the end of a class in Hebrew at the Collège de France, Ernest Renan was talking to a little group of students who had gathered around him before leaving the classroom. They were hoping that with his customary informality he would add some reflection of a general nature to the technical lesson, in which would be felt not the erudite and scholar, but the philosopher, the father, the old man at life's sunset, more preoccupied with the things of eternity than he was pleased to appear to be.

"This day, repeating a verse from the Gospel that was often on his lips, he said to them: 'Yes, Mary has chosen the better part. The most permanent thing in the backdrop of history is the religious effort. *There* is the soul; *there* is life.' Then looking down at the ground as though he had just been gazing at his own open grave, he added, 'When I began to work, I dreamed of devoting my life to the study of three periods — blessed be the illusions of youth! Three periods: the origins of Christianity together with the history of Israel, the French Revolution, and the wonderful religious renewal brought about by St. Francis of Assisi. I have been able to complete only the first third of my program. But you, Monsieur Leblond,' he said to a young man who appeared sound and healthy (but who died shortly afterward from overwork), 'must become the creator of the religious history of the Revolution.'

" 'And you,' he continued, addressing [Paul Sabatier] and placing his hand on his shoulder to keep him from slipping away, 'shall be the historian of the Seraphic Father. I envy you. St. Francis has always smiled on his historians. He saved the Church in the thirteenth century, and ever since then his spirit has remained strangely alive. We need him. If we really want him, he will come back . . . .'

"Someone came to tell Renan that his carriage was waiting. He entered it painfully; and from the carriage door which he held half open, he called out to them in a voice — gay, but at the same time filled with emotion — 'Farewell, children!' "[23]

The *Life of St. Francis* that Paul Sabatier published in 1894 has been read and translated in all the world. It pleased scholars by its solid documentation, men of letters by its literary quality, and everyone by the delicate touch with which this psychologist and poet analyzed the soul of his hero. Rome, however, placed the book on the Index, because of the too Protestant opinions of its author. Sabatier had less confidence in Thomas of Celano, the official biographer, and St. Bonaventure, the Minister General, than in Brother Leo, the confessor and confidential friend of the Saint. For forty-five years he continued his researches, often believing he had discovered, and sometimes actually discovering, documents emanating from or inspired by that intransigent memorialist, Brother Leo.

Sabatier's publications had widespread repercussions. Professional historians became interested, some of them favoring his thesis and others resolutely or moderately hostile to it. Each of these sought out new sources to bolster up his viewpoint. These they found and are finding still. Some have helped to clear up the question, others to obscure it — nearly all have provoked discussions which are far from closed. In short, aside from the history of the origins of Christianity, perhaps no problem of scholarship in the past sixty years has put so many scholars to work or involved so much effort.

*   *   *

Among the innumerable "lives" of St. Francis which have been published, the greater part furnish more proof of devotion than of information. Others are "essays," necessarily partaking of the disadvantages of this type of literature. As for the biographies properly so called, the best are incontestably those of Sabatier, written in French; of Joergensen, written in Danish; and of Father Cuthbert, written in English.

To these works of permanent value which continue to be read, is it desirable to add a new book? Our excuse has been to believe that if we cannot do better than our predecessors, we can at least do differently, and that, coming a half century after the most recent of them, we are able to make use of texts and studies not available to them. For, in truth, few figures out of the past are better known today than the Poverello.

How many new documents have appeared since the year 1865, when Renan in pleased surprise observed that "his marvelous legend may be studied at close range and confirmed in its broad outline by historical criticism!" The discussions they have provoked would fill a library. To list and analyze them would alone require an extensive monograph. In order not to lengthen the present Introduction out of all proportion, we have assigned such a study to the end of the volume.

Let us briefly summarize it so that the reader may know the historical basis for the biography he is about to read, and be able to identify the references accompanying our text.

Every life of St. Francis ought to make use of the Saint's own testimony and that left by persons who knew him.

His own testimony is to be found in his writings, comprising the two Rules which he composed, the Testament which he dictated before his death, a few letters and exhortations, and some prayers.

The testimony left by those who knew him is to be found in the Legends of Thomas of Celano and of St. Bonaventure, in those writings inspired or written by Brother Leo and the first Franciscans, and in the chronicles of certain contemporaries. Unrivaled among the latter, we place those of Jacques de Vitry and Jordan of Giano, which confirm admirable pages in Thomas of Celano and the *Fioretti*, in which we had not dared until then to place too much credence.

For six centuries, the most celebrated Legend of the Poverello was that of St. Bonaventure, written between 1260 and 1263. It was at one and the same time very precise, very politic, and very incomplete. It was precise in that it said nothing that was not true. It was politic, in that it aimed at appeasing the dissensions in which the Order was embroiled. And it was incomplete in that it maintained silence on whatever would have shown that the Franciscan institute had turned aside from certain intentions of its Founder. Every stop was pulled to accredit it. Not only did the Chapter of 1263 approve it; but three years later the Chapter of Paris ordered that it should be the sole one to be read thenceforth, and that the other Legends were to be destroyed.

It was the writings of Thomas of Celano and Brother Leo that this decree had particularly in view. Certain Spirituals, however, put forth little zeal to carry out the decree, and a few of the copies earmarked for destruction escaped. A number have been found, and these constitute the basis of every serious biography of St. Francis.

The three most important works of Brother Thomas are: the *Vita prima*, which he wrote by order of Gregory IX immediately following the Saint's death; the *Vita secunda*, which he composed by order of the Minister General Crescentius between 1244 and 1247; and the *Tractatus de miraculis*, which first saw the light between 1250 and 1253.

The presumed author of the *Dies irae*, Thomas of Celano is not only a talented writer, but an able and conscientious historian. Although received in the Order by Francis himself, he lived with him hardly at all. But he did write under the control and sometimes at the dictation of witnesses of his life.

Brother Leo, the confessor and best friend of the Saint, was scarcely ever separated from his master. Brother Angelo and Brother Rufino, the two other members of the literary team of the Three Companions (*Tres Socii*), were likewise his constant associates. Now in 1244, at the request of Minister Crescentius, they pooled their memories and made of them a long Memorial which Friar Thomas drew from abundantly. [The so-called *Legend of the Three Companions* does not contain the text of that Memorial, and was probably written several decades later.] Crescentius' appeal was general, addressed to all those especially associated with St. Francis. Thus it is probable that other friars responded to it, and that they, too, told what they knew.

Which of the Three Companions held the pen? It is generally believed to have been Brother Leo, but the question itself is of small moment. Much more important would be to know the fate of the famous Memorial after it was utilized by the author of the *Vita secunda,* and also to know what became of the other works of St. Francis' confessor.

For the decree of 1266 was much more deadly to their writings than to those of Thomas of Celano. After seven centuries, we have almost succeeded in reconstructing the entire work of the latter. But we are still far from having collected all the writings of Brother Leo.

According to recent criticism, the *Legenda antiqua* of Perugia may reproduce the major part of them, the so-called *Legend of the Three Companions* a few passages, and the *Phillipps Manuscript* some ten chapters. As for the *Speculum Perfectionis,* this is not, as was first believed, an authentic work by Brother Leo, but a late compilation strongly inspired by him. Finally, in the *Chronicle of the Twenty-four Generals,* and in the *Actus-Fioretti,* we have composite collections giving still more place to legend, yet containing ample testimony to the Leonine tradition and that of the first Franciscans.

*   *   *

For the historian, having all this material assembled before him is not enough. Unless he would limit himself to publishing a few volumes of text and argument, he must — once he has completed his research and examined the opinions of the critics — make a choice.

The biographers of the Poverello have invariably done so. And that is why, depending on the source they choose, the "St. Francis" that they present is so different.

Now which is the most authentic? All are agreed that it is not St. Bonaventure's. The work of the Seraphic Doctor can serve only to give us information on the spiritual life of the Little Poor Man. But between Thomas of Celano and Brother Leo, whom are we to choose? Some prefer to trust only the first, and others swear by Leo and his friends. But neither of the two deserves to be blindly followed.

For it so happens that Celano sins by omission, for example when he does not dare insist on certain of the most characteristic traits in the physiognomy of St. Francis. These, among others, are his predilection for manual labor and the care of victims of leprosy, or the prohibition placed on his friars against ever receiving any favors or privileges from the Roman curia.

The testimony of Brother Leo also requires close examination. Bitterness over the evolution taking place in the Order on the part of one who had been beaten on orders from Brother Elias for his intransigent fidelity to the traditions of his Father is understandable. The words and writings of his old age must have shown its effects, and still more the works of the Spirituals who received his confidences and persisted in invoking his testimony. Passion does not favor impartiality. Hence, if it be wise to complete Thomas of Celano by Brother Leo, it is sometimes no less wise to correct Brother Leo and his continuators by Friar Thomas. And it is always well to compare all of them with the writings of Francis himself. That is the method we have followed.

This would be more easily handled if we possessed all the authentic texts of Brother Leo. But we have seen that we are still in the preliminary stages on this point, i.e. of attempting to identify them in later compilations, and of disengaging the verbal tradition going back to Brother Leo from the alterations introduced by the Spirituals.

Such difficulties are no drawback for certain critics, who resolve them as they present themselves and go on their merry way. Others, less dogmatically-minded, are more circumspect. To take an example from Scholasticism, we know that the Thomistic School is absolutely convinced of the real difference between essence and existence, of the analogy of being, and a number of other theses about which the Scotist School adopts a diametrically opposite view. Is it necessary to add that both these rivals have arguments at their disposal which have permitted them for centuries to win brilliant victories over each other?

Among the problems offered to historians of Franciscan origins, many are scarcely more advanced than those separating Thomists and Scotists. In these problems, the sequence of the story has sometimes compelled us to appear to take sides. Let the reader not deem himself bound, however, to embrace our opinion. For it is to clarify facts and enable him to form an intelligent judgment that we constantly send him back to the sources.[24]

In addition to the texts attributed to Brother Leo, the miraculous tales in the primitive documents likewise offer him an opportunity to exercise his own judgment. For what are we to think of the visions, apparitions, and other divine interventions reported in them? Christians who come across their equivalents in the Gospel will doubtless be able to admit them without great difficulty. But what of others?

Faithful to the method which consists in believing or denying a fact according to one's concept of its possibility or impossibility, a rationalist will say: "In view of the studies I have made on the existence and nature of God, and the light I have acquired on angels and demons; in view, in fine, of the impossibility I and my friends have always experienced in seeing any visions or performing any miracles, I conclude that Francis was never the object of the supernatural favors attributed to him."

A man who reasons in this way does so as a philosopher rather than as a historian. This we have taken care not to do. Besides, we are not sufficiently convinced that the first Franciscan biographers were less intelligent and honest than we are, to dare to dispute with them on so delicate a subject. We have therefore preferred to record their statements accurately and respectfully.

Not (be it said in passing) that we have translated them word for word. To do so would have been to give our book at times the appearance of a collection of Latin translations. It would seem better either to give a faithful résumé of the original or else render it in good French [or English].[25] This procedure offers no inconvenience, since the notes always permit recourse to the original Latin and even very frequently to the literal translations which have been made from it.

*   *   *

In short, the aim of this book would be to inspire confidence and at the same time not weary the reader. To this end the author has applied himself to follow the rules of good criticism, while attempting to bring order into a mass of details.

Hagiographers — in order to embellish their subject — often yield to the temptation to comment and to mix in all sorts of instructive and edifying reflections. We have endeavoured not to imitate them in this respect. First, because there already exist a number of books of analysis or of synthesis on St. Francis in which this work has already been done. Next, because such considerations, necessarily subjective, run the risk of slighting the historic truth, which it is so difficult to come by. Every eyewitness account is already an interpretation. The most impartial witness can report what he has seen and heard only through the medium of his own personality. A fresh attempt of this sort would thus serve merely to increase the possibility of distorting facts.

Rather than expatiate on St. Francis ourself, we have — insofar as possible — let those speak who knew him, believing that once in possession of authentic evidence, the reader will be able to draw his own conclusions.

Let him gather then as he will the elements of poetry or of moral beauty that will be given him here. Let him draw for himself that portrait of the Poverello which seems to him most faithful. Let him delight in, let him meditate and dream about, and if possible, be edified by his meeting with the most evangelical and most charming of the saints. For there is no saint more capable of preparing a pathway to God in his heart.

OMER ENGLEBERT

Paris
July, 1956

- 1 -

Origins and Life in the World

In St. Francis' day, the world known to the west was limited to Europe, North Africa, and the Near East, where the Crusaders had fought and traded for a century.

The political and social configuration of the European states was no by means that of today. France was only half as big; Spain was partly in the hands of the Moors; and England continued to exercise her suzerainty over Normandy, Brittany, and the Aquitaine. The Holy Roman Empire embraced not only Germany, Austria, Switzerland, and Bohemia; but spilled over into the Walloons, Lorraine, Burgundy, and Provence. To this, Italy — except for the Pontifical States — also belonged.

In the Italian Peninsula, however, frequent revolts flared, which Frederick Barbarossa (1152-1190), Henry VI (1190-1197), Otto IV (1197-1214), and Frederick II (1214-1250), had the utmost difficulty in quelling. To maintain his domination, the Emperor relied on the nobility, whose members held their fiefs from him and exercised the functions of podestàs, judges, and consuls in his name.

Born of the necessity of keeping in check the anarchy following upon the barbarian invasions, the feudal regime com-

41

prised, as we know, two classes of men — the *majores* or *boni homines* (the great or the nobility) and the *minores* (the common people).

The *majores* were the nobles, the knights, the lords, who constituted in those times of general brigandage a permanent police force. Everyone was born into his hereditary rank (duke, marquis, count), with his local position and landed property, with the certainty of never being abandoned by his liege lord, and also with the obligation, should need arise, of dying for him. Thanks to these warriors, the *minores* were protected. They could work in peace and eat their fill — no longer in fear of being liquidated or led away at the point of the lance as captives with their families. But they paid dear for this protection, sometimes in quitrents and service, and sometimes even with the loss of freedom.

The *minores* were of two sorts: villeins and serfs. The latter, attached to the lord's land, belonged to their master like so much livestock and enjoyed no independence whatever. The others, farm laborers in the country, craftsmen, or merchants in the towns, were free men, with the right to own property and move about freely. The serf, then, was really a slave; the villein was free in body, but subject to taxation and forced labor. The noble, who shared with the churches and monasteries nearly all the wealth of the period, was not taxed, owing only a vassal's homage to his lord.

The Crusades, which were in part commercial expeditions, transformed the feudal system. Up to then, craftsmen and laborers worked for the local market, with no other outlets than the castle or monastery. After the discovery and pillage of the treasures of the Byzantine Empire, hitherto unsuspected routes opened up to trade and industry. Innumerable ships dotted the Mediterranean; the Roman highways, destroyed by the barbarian invasions, were rebuilt; and from one end to the other of Europe raw materials and manufactured products were exchanged. Many artisans became rich, and some merchants reaped immense fortunes.

These newly rich remained nonetheless villeins or *minores*, crushed beneath the burden of quitrents and services, deprived of any voice in the government of the towns. Their fortunes, however, soon permitted their voices to be heard. They compelled the temporal and spiritual lords to grant them economic privileges and to admit them to their councils, thus becoming themselves *majores*.

From concession to concession, the lord, who up to then had made all appointments to public employment, was also constrained to grant to other citizens consuls of their own choosing, charged with lawmaking, administrating, and handing down justice. From then on, the commune was born, a sort of new suzerainty, bound like any vassal domain to its lord, and like it, obliged by the feudal oath, to place troops at his service.

The serfs did not benefit from the social transformation. For to become a freeman and lay claim to the title of "citizen," one must own a house and enjoy a certain revenue. Consequently, only a small number of privileged villeins could belong to the commune. The serfs on the glebe and of the crafts thus remained just as poor and enslaved as before. Indeed, their plight was often worse than before, so greedy and cruel did their new masters prove to be. Having no protection, the greater part among them began to form a wretched proletariat in the outkirts of the city, whose freemen were concerned only with sending them off to fight.

*　*　*

Now the Italian citizens of the time declared war, and fierce war, at will. These associated merchants constituting the commune were insatiable — forever having some quarrel to pick with their neighbors. When these neighbors blocked off the roads with taxes and tolls, they attacked them, if they felt themselves strong enough. If they were too weak, they allied themselves with other merchants, with some powerful lord, even with the emperor, so as to snatch the coveted river, bridge, forest, or strip of land from the rival commune.

And woe to the vanquished! Their city was razed, entire villages were destroyed, and crops burned. Prisoners — those who escaped from the massacre — were mutilated or tortured with a refinement of cruelty. At Forlì, for instance, men were shod like mules. And, lest any should forget, annual festivals were celebrated in which pigs, rams, asses, and other grotesque animals appeared on the scene, charged with making the hereditary enemy seem despicable.[1]

Thus to the old seignoral rivalries were now joined undying hatreds and feuds between the communes, while within their walls they were often torn apart by partisan or family struggles, to the loss of their inner peace. "We learn," wrote Innocent III, "that you continue to lay waste cities, destroy castles, burn villages, oppress the poor, persecute churches, and reduce men to serfdom. Murder, violence, and rapine are rife, with quarreling and wars."[2]

At the time of St. Francis' youth, at any rate, these reproaches of the Pope were deserved as much by Assisi as by the communes of the Marches to which they were addressed. "Not only had war, with its orgies and disorders, become a necessity and a habit, but it had become the preferred occupation, the ruling passion, and the whole life of this city, in which the word 'peace,' no longer had any meaning."[3]

It is a mistake, then, to see in the end of the twelfth century and in the beginnings of the thirteenth a sort of golden age wherein peace and the practice of the Gospel flourished. It is true that in this period men built hospitals for the sick and abbeys whose walls resounded to the chanting of the divine praises, the land was adorned with a white flowering of churches, prayers and pilgrimages multiplied, Crusades were preached, knights professed to defend the widow and the orphan, and troubadours went all over Europe singing their courtly refrains. But if we stop to think that these hospitals, these cathedrals and monasteries were often the "remorse in stone" by means of which great sinners attempted to atone for their crimes and violence, and if we observe in addition that heresy and immorality corrupted Christian people, and that never before had the "little man" been the victim of so much social injustice, we may well conclude that the times of St. Francis yielded to none in calamities and scandals.

* * *

Umbria, where St. Francis' life was spent, is situated in Central Italy, between the March of Ancona and Tuscany. This region, full of contrasts and beauty, affords to man's spirit a variety of scenery which is truly captivating: solitary peaks and charming valleys, streams lazily meandering along the plain, torrents cascading down ravines, fields of wheat and unproductive volcanic soils, forests of ilex and fir, silver-leaved olive trees, engarlanded vines running along the mulberry trees, and clumps of black cypress mounting guard at way-side chapels. The winter is rugged, the summer scorching, autumn and springtime marvelously mild. The people are handsome, somewhat rude of manners, kindly, and thoughtful.

The artistic riches of the country are scarcely inferior to its natural beauties. Rarely does one see so many masterpieces accumulated in so small a space. For without mentioning the churches and palaces, who does not know Perugia with its Signorellis, its Lorenzos, and its Peruginos; Assisi with its Giottos and its Cimabues; Spoleto and its Filippo Lippis; Spello and its Pinturicchios; Montefalco with its Benozzo Gozzolis; and finally, Trevi, Cortona, and Foligno? "Florence and Pisa seem almost Boeotian to me, after seeing Perugia and Assisi," wrote Renan.[4]

Perched almost all of them on hilltops, these little towns appear ethereal in the diaphanous light that bathes them. The crenelated battlements of their ancient walls speak eloquently of the struggles which blood-reddened them for centuries — but these are memories that the gentle Franciscan legend has now obliterated. For Umbria, "the Galilee of Italy," has long been the country of the Poverello, the kingdom of peace in which poets and mystics alike have been spiritually naturalized.[5]

*   *   *

Assisi, where Francis was born toward the close of 1181 or the beginning of 1182,[6] then belonged to the Empire.

The city's founders, so it is said, were those Umbrians who, overcome by the Etruscans, joined with their conquerors and were subsequently beaten with them by the Roman legions in the third century before Christ. It became a Roman municipality, and later gave birth to the poet Propertius, if we are to believe the inscription on the temple of Minerva still standing in the Piazza. The sight of that edifice threw Goethe into an extraordinary state of exaltation. "It was," he exclaims, "the first monument of antiquity that it was given me to see; and I could not see enough of it."

It is claimed that the city was evangelized about the year A.D. 50 by St. Crispoldo, a disciple of St. Peter; but it is St. Rufino who is reputed by the Assisians to have really converted them two centuries later. Condemned to death and drowned in the Chiascio, he was first buried in a temple to Diana, near this river; then in 412 his body was solemnly brought into the city.

The latter had, in the thirteenth century, the same boundary lines as in the time of St. Rufino. It has changed little since, with its sloping streets and its old houses of rose-colored stone; and its population is still below 10,000.[7] Terraced on a spur of Mount Subasio, whose summit soars some 4000 feet, Assisi beholds at its feet the vast plain extending from Perugia to Spello, Foligno, and Spoleto. Here silence, solitude, and peace reign supreme. In the evening one may hear — so still is it — the murmur of the water in the fountains.

We must climb to the ruins of the Rocca, the ancient feudal castle, to have a sweeping view of the entrancing landscape.

On our right, our gaze extends over the immense Valley of Spoleto; on our left, there is the wild desolation of the mountains; behind, an arid ravine; ahead, the city with its somber towers, its crenelated gates, its houses that seem to stand on tiptoe to see better; and finally, its Franciscan monuments which form its immortal glory: the grandiose Basilica, with its two superimposed churches, guarding the tomb of St. Francis; the Chiesa Nuova, over the site of the family residence; the Cathedral of San Rufino where he was baptized; the Basilica of St. Clare, replacing the Church of San Giorgio, where he learned to read; the bishop's palace where he stripped off his garments to give them to his father; the home of Bernard of Quintavalle, his first disciple; the Church of San Nicolò, where the two consulted the Gospels to learn their vocation; the Church of San Damiano which the Poverello restored with his own hands; and finally, down in the plain, St. Mary of the Angels, the Portiuncula, where he died.[8]

* * *

Some traces still remain of the house where Francis passed the first twenty-five years of his life. If it resembled its neighbors which are still standing, the house had five or six rooms. Peter Bernardone, father of the future saint, was one of the richest cloth merchants in the city. Pica, his mother, gave birth to at least [two] children;[9] of whom one, Angelo, had two sons, Piccardo and Giovanni.[10]

In the sixteenth and seventeenth centuries, when men too readily "discovered" noble lineages for the Saints, writers boasted of Bernardone's noble origin and gave him the Moriconi of Lucca for ancestors. But such a genealogy was a pure fabrication. Besides, Francis often affirmed that he was born a commoner.[11] All that can actually be said is that at this time when the cloth trade led so often to wealth, and wealth to nobility, Bernardone could hope to see his son become a knight, and therefore a gentleman.

If he himself was not born to the purple, did Francis' father at least marry a noblewoman? To prove that he did, French historians have had her born in Provence, alleging the authority of a seventeenth-century French author, Claude Frassen. "Pica," he writes, "comes from the illustrious house of Bourlemont, as appears in an ancient manuscript preserved in the archives of that house." But it is difficult to attach any importance to this unverifiable testimony.[12]

*   *   *

Peter Bernardone was on one of his frequent trips to France when his son was born.[13]

Thanks to the peace maintained by Barbarossa in the Empire, Central Italy enjoyed great prosperity, and the cloth trade especially flourished. As Italian wools, however, were good only for the manufacture of coarse stuffs, to find better materials, merchants of the peninsula were obliged to frequent the fairs of Provence and Champagne, where Europe, Asia, and Africa exchanged their products.

Without waiting for the father's return, Dame Pica had the newborn baby carried to the baptismal font of San Rufino

Church, where he was christened John.[14] Was this name afterward changed into another, not found in the martyrology? Celano, who mentions the fact, gives no reason. He observes, though, that the Poverello always celebrated the feast of his heavenly patron, St. John the Baptist, with especial devotion.[15]

"It was the father," say the *Three Companions*, "who, in his joy, had him named Francis on his return from his far journey."[16] Was it a compliment on his part to the country where he traveled so much and did so much business?

But those who do not take everything in the *Legend of the Three Companions* for Gospel truth rather surmise that John was dubbed "Francesco" when later on people saw that he enjoyed speaking French so much and singing the songs and lays of the French troubadours.[17] His father knew French, and no doubt, taught it to his son, for French at that time served as a business medium everywhere in the West.[18]

* * *

Francis' biographers have noted that he was "a man without learning." That is, he studied neither theology nor canon law, and was unversed in any of the ecclesiastical or profane sciences of the time. Is this one of the reasons why everything about him arouses so warm a response in men of every clime and culture? Men taught him the catechism and the alphabet. God and his own native genius taught him the rest.

A few steps away from the family home stood a school that was an annex of San Giorgio Church. There it was that Francis learned to read and write.[19] This elementary schooling included Latin, often used still in sermons and public deliberations. As for writing, it would seem that Francis never became very proficient in it, as in the rare autographs we have of him the handwriting is quite ordinary. Besides, he wrote little. Ordinarily, he dictated to Brother Leo, and for signature drew a T-shaped cross.[20]

The school from which the young man derived the most benefit was that of the songs of chivalry and of the *gai savoir* which was then all the rage.[21]

For years, the most famous troubadours of France wandered through Italy, visiting the castles, enlivening gatherings and tournaments, bringing the Courts of Love into style, endlessly rhyming the legendary history of Charlemagne, of the knights of the Round Table, and of the doughty warriors who emulated them. They also sang of woman; for as Don Quixote says, "There can no more be a knight without a lady than a tree without leaves or a sky without stars."[22] But the love they celebrated was the love that is purified by sacrifice and loyalty, and the heroes whose exploits they extolled, were always "knights without fear and without reproach."

The troubadours had for pupils and interpreters the *jongleurs*, with whom the land teemed. They expressed themselves in a "Franco-Italian" jargon, spoken nowhere and yet understood by all. They were to be met on pilgrim routes and in cities, parroting over and over in their peculiar style the consecrated themes, before their enthusiastic — or resigned — hearers. The use of rhyme became so trite that professionals complained: "We shall have to give up singing, for there isn't a drunkard now who doesn't set his hand to writing a song."[23]

At every step in the life of St. Francis, we shall be reminded of the songs of chivalry, of the troubadours, and even of the *jongleurs*. Like Ronald of Montauban, the cousin of the brave Roland, we shall see him building churches to atone for past sins. Like King Arthur, he will assemble his knights of the Round Table at the Chapter of Pentecost. He will compose music and verse, and will praise the Lord in song while pretending to accompany himself on the viol. We shall hear him make use of phrases from the poetry of chivalry to express his inmost being and to draw men after him.

* * *

If we are to believe Thomas of Celano, the upbringing of the little Bernardone boy was dreadful. "In our day, and even from the cradle," he writes, "Christian parents are wont to bring up their boys in softness and luxury. These innocents are barely able to lisp when they are taught shameful and abominable things. They are scarce weaned before they are forced to utter obscene words and commit indecent acts. Should they attempt to resist, the fear of ill-treatment would get the upper hand over their resistance. The more perverted they become, the more pleased are their parents; and when they grow up, they rush of their own accord into more and more criminal practices." And the diatribe continues with a profusion of redundant and balanced phrases.[24]

But we should remind ourselves here that Friar Thomas is one of those authors who sometimes let themselves be carried away with words — stopping only when they run out of them.

Writing more calmly, St. Bonaventure states that in his youth Francis "was nurtured in vanity among the vain sons of men"; which adds up to saying that he was not sanctified from the cradle and that his character training may have been sketchy.[25]

His father, however, does not seem to have been a bad man. A domineering and vain burgher, he was fond of his gold, liked to be in the public eye, and was desirous of rising in the social scale. He was an ordinary Christian, in no rush to get to Heaven and putting off all active concern for his salvation. Meanwhile, happy and prosperous in this life, he was intent on seeing that his son did not run through his property and that he should be an honor to him.

Italian or Provençal, noblewoman or commoner, Dame Pica was in any case his superior. Ordinarily she was a meek creature, submissive and retiring, but one who, on occasion, dared brave her husband's wrath. "A friend of everything good," wrote Thomas of Celano, correcting in his second Legend[26]

the exaggerations of the first, she practiced every virtue in a
rare degree, and reminds one of St. Elizabeth by the name she
had prophetically given to her child. 'You shall see,' said she
to those scandalized by his youthful errors, 'that he will become a son of God.' "[27]

* * *

Peter Bernardone lost no time in introducing his son into
his business.

It was the custom then to advertise one's wealth by one's
clothing, and luxury was, for the most part, confined to dress.
Men vied with one another in wearing the richest and most
showy textures.[28] Even some priests sought to distinguish
themselves in this respect, since a decree of 1213 had to forbid them to ape the sartorial luxury of the ladies.[29]

So Francis waited on customers in a well-patronized shop.
He went on horseback to the fairs of Spoleto, Foligno, and
other places. He may have accompanied his father to Champagne and to Provence. Later on, he declared that he loved
France in a special manner and desired to end his days there,
because (he said) there, more than anywhere else, men showed
reverence for holy things and particularly for the Blessed Sacrament. Was this an observation that he had already made in
the course of his youthful journeys?[30]

At any rate, never did anyone see a more affable and charming merchant. In addition he was, says Thomas of Celano,
"most prudent in business."[31] But it soon became evident that
if Francis excelled in making money, he was still better at
spending it.

Naturally liberal, he gave abundant alms. "Love for the poor
was born in him," writes St. Bonaventure; and he had made
a special resolution never to refuse anyone who solicited alms
in God's name. Only once, detained by a customer, did he

brusquely turn away a beggar, but he regretted it at once. "What!" he said to himself, "if this man had come to borrow money for one of your noble friends, you would have been proud to give it to him; and you dare to show him the door when it is the King of kings who sends him to you?" And dashing out after the beggar, he made amends.[32]

It was not just in charity, however, that Francis spent his money.

By his way of looking at things, observes one of his biographers, he was the exact opposite of his father. "Much more whimsical and less thrifty, he lived above his station, rushing pell-mell into pleasure and throwing away everything he earned on feasts and sumptuous clothing." He even rigged himself up like a *jongleur* "by sewing pieces of sacking onto his best clothes. Prompt to leave the dinner table or his father's counter at the first signal from his friends, he was always ready, day or night, to run singing with them through the town."

At that time there were youth groups in Assisi, in which boys from middle class homes, mingled with a few nobles, had good times together. And the year round, there were well-wined banquets, noisy gatherings, farandoles danced through the streets of the little city, and nocturnal serenades beneath the balconies of local beauties. There was feasting and laughter, poetry and music, eccentricities and follies, and also (alas!) real disorders. For debauchery was rife in Assisi, and the excesses of these night prowlers often compelled the authorities of the commune to intervene.[33]

"Certain it is that from time to time Francis' parents reproached him for his conduct: 'You are no prince's son,' they would say to him, 'to throw money away like water, and feed so many parasites at your expense.' But rich and indulgent, they overlooked his vagaries and avoided crossing him."[34]

After all, this prodigal youth was a charming and affectionate son, who would eventually "straighten out"; and meanwhile, Peter Bernardone must have been flattered to see him getting in with the nobility.

*   *   *

One naturally wonders just how far the young man's waywardness actually went during this period of his life, of which, later on, he was so bitterly to reproach himself with having "lived in sin."[35] In what sense are we to take this rather vague expression? In order not to say — on this delicate subject — more than we know, let us limit ourselves to citing the evidence.

First of all, we have Thomas of Celano putting the final brush strokes to the sombre picture whose first lines we have quoted:

"What do you think becomes of them" (these children whose fearsome training he has depicted), "once they pass through the portals of youth? Free at last to pursue their inclinations and swept up in the maelstrom of pleasure, these voluntary slaves of sin, whose members serve only iniquity, eagerly rush into every vice. There is no longer anything Christian about them but the name, and they become boastful sinners who would deem it a disgrace to preserve a semblance of decency. Such was the miserable apprenticeship which made up the youthful existence of the man whom we now venerate as a saint. He wasted his life up to his twenty-fifth year, surpassing his comrades in foolishness, and drawing them with him into vanity and evil. He was fond of jests and songs and jokes, liked to dress in fine and flowing garments, and was lavish with his money, thereby attracting to his retinue many youths who made a career of wickedness and crime.

"Thus he went on, the proud and magnificent leader of this perverse army, through the streets of Babylon. And so it went, until that day when — to keep him from utter loss of his soul — the hand of the Lord fell upon him and transformed him.

Then was Francis converted; so that sinners, following his example, might thenceforth trust in God's mercy."[36]

This language is clear. True, quite a bit of rhetoric is mixed in; but not enough, it would seem, to take all the meaning out of the words. And it must be agreed that Friar Thomas, had he so willed, might have employed his rhetoric to say something else. For instance, it would have been easy for him to show the flighty youth remaining pure in spite of his bad company; and certainly, nothing prevented him from retracting on this point in his second *Legenda*, as he did for several others. Yet he changed nothing.

All the accounts written in the next thirty years give us the same theme. Seven or eight years later, Julian of Speyer, using Thomas of Celano's very words, cited St. Francis' example to sinners, to inspire them likewise to trust in God's readiness to forgive.[37]

In 1238, Pope Gregory IX, the intimate friend of the Poverello, praised St. Francis for "having embraced chastity, after having given himself over to the seductions of the world."[38]

Finally, preaching to a General Chapter of the Order, Cardinal Eudes of Chateauroux did not hesitate to declare that "in the beginning, Francis was a great sinner; but, sated with carnal pleasures, he took the road leading to holiness, so that no sinner need thenceforth despair of his salvation."[39]

His Franciscan audience could not have been offended at this portrait of the culpable youth of their founder since they themselves when chanting Matins alluded to it in the following antiphon:

> *Hic vir in vanitatibus*
> *Nutritus indecenter*
> PLUS SUIS NUTRITORIBUS
> SE GESSIT INSOLENTER.

"As a child, he received a very bad upbringing, and later

he did not scruple to go beyond his masters in immorality."[40]

The first Friars Minor believed then that their Father had been a sinner. But those of the following generation found this to be an inadmissable stain in so sublime a life. It pained them to admit that the flesh marked by the sacred stigmata had ever been defiled, and that the purity of the seraphic Francis had been less than that of St. Dominic, of which the Friars Preachers were so proud.

Then it was that the Chapter of 1260 recast the last two verses of the compromising strophe, making it read that, fortunately, divine grace had preserved the seraphic Father from every error:

> Hic vir in vanitatibus
> Nutritus indecenter
> DIVINIS CHARISMATIBUS
> PREVENTUS EST CLEMENTER.[41]

At almost the same time, St. Bonaventure definitely settled the question by writing that "despite the young debauchés he had associated with, Francis had never yielded to the seductions of the flesh";[42] and as henceforth his *Legend* had the sole right to exist, this became the prevailing opinion.

*   *   *

But sinner or not, it would be an error to think of the youthful Francis as a rake. One cannot imagine him as either corrupt or corrupting; and if there were some weaknesses in his life, assuredly baseness was not among them. No one (thank God) has revealed to us the name of the little lady who may have momentarily captivated his heart. But if Francis loved, it was nobly and in the manner of the knights of chivalry whose ideals he shared. He was a prey to temptations of the flesh (since we shall see him later on rolling in the brambles and in the snow to get rid of them);[43] but his deportment and his speech were always perfectly proper. "Never did an offensive or coarse word come from his mouth; and if anyone spoke improperly to him, he resolved not to reply."[44]

His nobility of soul extended to everything. He was, we are told, dignity and graciousness itself. "Avoiding wounding anyone, and being most courteous to all, he made himself universally loved. To see the refinement of his manners, one would have taken him for the son of some great nobleman." In short, he was born a prince, and everyone gladly forgave him "for wanting to be in the forefront of things. Thus he soon came to be known beyond his immediate circle, and many began to predict for him a glorious destiny."[45]

Among them was "that simple man, somewhat of a prophet," writes St. Bonaventure, "who never met him without taking off his cloak and spreading it under his feet, replying to the mockers that, in honoring Peter Bernardone's son in this way, he was but anticipating the universal homage of posterity."[46]

It may well be imagined that Francis' ambitions were not confined to measuring out cloth in his father's house and to feasting in company with the fops whom he fed at his expense. He had faith in his star, and he dreamed of becoming famous.

*   *   *

At that time, fame was to be acquired in war, and those who liked fighting found opportunities galore.

Francis himself had grown up in an atmosphere of civil war. For almost thirty years, his native city had been demanding its freedom. In 1174, the merchants of Assisi had tried to shake off the imperial yoke; but they had run up against something stronger than themselves; and in 1177, Frederick Barbarossa, going up to La Rocca, had installed his lieutenant, Duke Conrad of [Urslingen], charged to hold them in check.[47] From that time onward, the great feudatory lords regained the upper hand; and the middle class, stripped of all political rights and burdened with taxes, meditated projects of vengeance.

Peter Bernardone's son was about fifteen, when in 1197 the succession of Henry VI, owing to the rivalries to which it gave rise, had momentarily placed the affairs of Germany in an evil pass. This was the signal in Italy for a general uprising against German supremacy. The communes sized the goods of the Empire, drove out its representatives, and occupied its fortresses. Innocent III profited by the interregnum to support the revolted cities and to attempt to bring several of them under his authority. Specifically, he ordered Duke Conrad to turn Assisi over to him. Betraying the cause of the Empire, the Duke left La Rocca and hastened to Narni to do homage for his fief to the papal legates. No sooner had he set off than the Assisians rushed to attack the German garrison defending the fortress. It was in vain that the papal legates called on the besiegers to surrender the keep. With no great desire to give themselves a new master, the latter braved the papal excommunication, took the citadel by storm, and totally demolished it. They thereupon formed a communal government, whose first concern was to provide the city with a stout enclosure, so as to forestall any renewed offensive by the enemy. These ramparts — parts of which still stand — were finished with incredible speed, and stones from the dismantled fortress were used in their construction. Can we doubt that Francis took part in this work, learning as he did so the building trade in which we shall see him excel?

One would prefer to believe, however, that he took no part in the massacres which followed.

Not content with having driven out the Germans, the next

thought of Assisi's burghers was to rid themselves of the feudal aristocracy, which, by its toll charges and vexations of every sort, hampered the city's trade. Then began dreadful reprisals. The castles dominating the heights were burned and many of their owners executed. The lords found in the city were put to death and their palaces demolished. The goods of all those nobles in whom the German hegemony found its support were confiscated.

Delivered from its oppressors, was Assisi at last to enjoy its newly won liberty in peace? Not so, for Perugia, the eternal rival, aroused by the nobles of Assisi who took refuge in it and who burned to recover their lost status, now entered upon the scene. In 1201 Perugia declared war on her neighbor, and a fierce duel between the two communes ensued which lasted for at least a decade.

It was during this murderous period that in November, 1202, the battle of Ponte San Giovanni was waged by the Tiber below Perugia. Francis fought in it bravely, was taken prisoner, and carried away as a hostage to Perugia. His captivity probably lasted until the month of November 1203,[48] [. . . though] the war continued — interrupted by truces and new massacres — up to 1210, when Francis [perhaps] contributed to restoring peace to his fellow-townsmen.

Meanwhile, the long months he passed in the Perugian prison dampened neither his military ambitions, his knightly courage, nor his gaiety.

"As he lived in the manner of the nobles, it was with the knights that he was imprisoned. Now, while the latter were bewailing their fate, he laughed at his chains, and always appeared cheerful.

" 'Are you crazy?' asked one of his companions, 'to crack jokes in the fix we're in?'

" 'How can you expect me to be sad,' he replied, 'when I

think of the future that awaits me, and of how I shall one day be the idol of the whole world?' "

Among the captives, there was an unbearable young noble, shunned by all. Francis alone did not turn his back on him. In fact, he did so well that he ended up by taming him and reconciling him with his companions.[49] For already, no one could resist his charm and goodness.

- 2 -

Conversion

Several painters of the thirteenth century have preserved for us the features of the Little Poor Man. We admire, "as if he were living in our time, this slight Italian figure, slender and pale, with his beautiful large eyes, his fine and regular features, his smiling, almost merry, countenance, and extreme expressiveness."[1]

Of all these paintings, that of Cimabue in the Lower Church of the Saint's Basilica in Assisi is perhaps the most faithful.[2] It dates from around 1265 and corresponds quite well with Thomas of Celano's description.

"Francis," says the latter, "was a man of almost medium height, rather slight in build, joyous and kindly of countenance. He had a round head, a low forehead, kind, black eyes, straight brows, a straight well-shaped nose; small, and as it were, uptilted, ears. His speech was penetrating and ardent; his voice, strong and musical. His teeth were well-spaced, even, and white; his mouth small, and his beard scanty. He had a slender neck, short arms, tapering fingers and nails. He was lean, with slender legs, and small feet.[2]

"He had a good intellect and an excellent memory. His great

eloquence melted men's hearts. Ever courteous and mild, he was open-handed, seldom angry, quick to forgive, knew how to keep a secret, and adapted himself to the most diverse temperaments. Though one of the greatest of the saints . . ."[3]

But let us not anticipate. We are only in 1203; and that year, the aspirant to knighthood who leaves the Perugian prison has not yet dreamed of sainthood.

*   *   *

On the contrary, he resumed his life of business and pleasure, and then fell gravely ill. "In fact, Francis never had any health," affirm those who knew him. "From his youth, he could live only surrounded by constant care."[4]

Had his long imprisonment weakened him? Or, once liberated, anxious to make up for lost time, had he overtaxed his strength? At any rate, he now spent long weeks in bed; during which time his thoughts began to take a different tack.

"When he was out of danger," writes Thomas of Celano, "he arose, and, leaning on a cane, began to take a few steps in his room. Shortly after, he was able to venture outdoors for the first time; and wanted to go and enjoy the country, which had always been enough to make him happy. But this time, neither the beauty of the fields and the smiling vineyards, nor anything pleasant to the sight was able to charm him. Astonished at the change, he reflected that it is foolish to become attached to those things that lose their appeal from one day to the next; and, profoundly disillusioned, he sadly returned home.

"These, however," Thomas adds, "were but surface impressions. Vice is second nature; and those bad habits which have taken root in the soul are not eradicated all at once. So, as soon as he felt really well again, Francis began to prepare for new exploits."[5]

He continued to dream of military glory and of chivalry.

Chivalry was the nobility of the times. It was not, moreover, reserved to the sons of aristocrats. Those of the upper middle class could also aspire to it, if they were able to furnish their equipment and were deemed worthy to be dubbed a knight. Being knighted involved the double ritual of the conferring of knighthood and the accolade.

The first consisted in the conferring of the armor. The accolade was the symbolic blow with the fist which the new knight received from his sponsor. The candidate passed the night before the altar on which his armor reposed. In the morning, he heard Mass, and on his knees, took the oath to use his sword in the service of God and the oppressed. His sponsor then gave him the accolade on the back of his neck and embraced him, saying: "In the name of God, of St. Michael, and of St. George, I dub you knight. Be brave, courageous, and loyal."

* * *

Francis had just learned that a count of Assisi, [perhaps] named Gentile, was preparing to leave for Apulia, where the eternal struggle between Church and State had flared up anew.[6]

By his marriage with Constance, heiress of the Norman princes, the Emperor Henry VI had added to his crown the title of "King of the Two Sicilies." After his death, his widow had decided to confide the tutelage of their son, the young Frederick II, to Pope Innocent III. But the German princes were too fearful lest the patrimony of St. Peter should aggrandize itself at their expense, to brook that so able a pope should be the protector of their future emperor. So they arrayed themselves on the side of Markwald, the former lieutenant of Henry VI, who, on the strength of an alleged will made by the dead king, claimed the precious guardianship for himself. Now the interests of both sides were too involved to permit them to come to an understanding, so it was necessary to have recourse to arms.

Thus had the struggle continued since 1198. At first, the pontifical armies had been defeated. But the situation changed when in 1202 Gautier de Brienne entered the service of Innocent III. The Norman captain scored victory over victory; and those interpreters of the populace who did not like the Germans — the Provençal and Italian troubadours — sang his exploits far and wide. From the entire peninsula, soldiers rushed to range themselves under the banner of the glorious knight.

Francis likewise decided to join the papal armies. "He was certainly less opulent and less wellborn than the lord of Assisi, his companion," we are told; "but he set off moved by noble sentiments. The other thought especially of the spoils, while Francis thought only of glory" and of being knighted on the field of battle.[7]

Feverishly, he made ready.

The equipment of a knight cost a small fortune; and that is why so many young lords, unable to defray the cost, were finally eliminated from the ranks of the nobility. It consisted of the hauberk or coat of mail, and the cuisse covering the thighs to the knees, the greaves or jambeaux and sollerets, protecting the shins and feet, the helmet covering the head, the sword whose hilt was a reliquary, the lance with its pennant, the buckler with its coat of arms, and the surcoat or flowing robe which covered the whole person. In addition, there was the horse and its armor, consisting of chain mail protecting the flanks and the chamfron protecting the head; and finally, the squire, likewise armed and mounted, by whom the knight was attended as he set out for war.

One may well imagine that Francis, who had no intention of being outdone by anyone, did things in the grand manner.

Meanwhile, "he met a knight so ill-clad that he was almost naked." Did the seedy warrior implore his charity? Or was

Francis spontaneously touched by his dilapidated appearance? Be that as it may, the fact is that "he gave to him generously, for the love of Christ, the sumptuously embroidered garments he was wearing."[8]

He had acted like St. Martin, Thomas of Celano writes, and like St. Martin, he received his reward from God in a symbolic vision that he had the following night:

He saw in a dream his father's house changed into a marvelous palace filled with arms. The bales of cloth had disappeared, and were replaced by magnificent saddles, shields, lances, and all kinds of knightly harness. Moreover, in one room of the palace a beautiful and charming bride was waiting for her bridegroom. Francis, thunderstruck, was wondering what all this could mean when a voice revealed to him that the soldiers and this beautiful lady were reserved for him. He awoke with happiness, since this vision, as he thought, could only be symbolic of the success he was to achieve.

Such was not, however, the true interpretation of this strange dream, and doubtless, the ambitious youth became aware of this, when his joy was followed by a deep gloom and he found he had to make a real effort to get started on his way.[9]

*　　*　　*

But off he went. One morning, his kinsfolk saw him galloping off on horseback, followed by his squire, on the road which winds along the flanks of Mount Subasio. From Foligno, he headed toward Spoleto, whence he could reach Rome, then southern Italy. But it was written that he should nevermore serve under an earthly standard, and should thenceforth have no other master but God.

At Spoleto, where he stopped for the night, the mysterious voice spoke to him again in his sleep. "Francis," it said to him, "where are you going like this?"

"I am going to fight in Apulia," replied the young man.

"Tell me," the voice continued. "From whom can you expect most, the master or the servant?"

"From the master, of course!"

"Then why follow the servant, instead of the master on whom he depends?"

"Lord, what would You have me do?"

"Return to your own country. There it shall be revealed to you what you are to do, and you will come to understand the meaning of this vision."

Francis awoke, and unable to go back to sleep, spent the rest of the night in reflection. Abandoning his project, he took the road back to Assisi the next day. He was then about twenty-five years old.

All were amazed that he appeared in no wise humiliated at his setback, and that, on the contrary, he appeared gayer than ever, saying: "You will see that some day I am going to be a great prince just the same!"[10]

"But he was a changed man," observes Friar Thomas, "as his friends soon found out." The chronicler gives us a most realistic account of his last party:

"His friends had come to propose him as 'king of youth,' and had given him the scepter of his new dignity, which (if truth be told) merely signified their desire to fill their bellies at the expense of the so-called 'king.' Too polite to refuse, Francis offered them once more one of those banquets which permitted them to surfeit themselves with food. Then these gluttons spilled out over the sleeping city, singing their drunken refrains. Francis came behind them, his fool's scepter in his hand. But far from joining in with their songs, which disgusted him, he began to pray.

"Then it was that divine grace came upon him, enlightening him as to the nothingness of earth's vanities and revealing to him the invisible realities. Suddenly, he was inundated with such a torrent of love, submerged in such sweetness, that he stood there motionless, neither seeing nor hearing anything. They might have cut him in pieces, he said later, and he would not have moved.[11]

"His companions, however, missing him, turned back to look for him. But they scarce recognized him, so changed was his countenance. 'What's wrong with you,' they asked, 'that you're not following us any more? Are you planning to get married? And has your sweetheart turned your head?'

" 'You're right!' replied Francis. 'I *am* thinking of marrying! And the girl to whom I intend to plight my troth is so noble, so rich, and so good, that none of you ever saw her like!' "[12]

Who was the lady of his thoughts? Francis himself did not know yet. It was only later that he was to find her. While waiting, he sought her, created her little by little (if I may dare so to speak), up to the day when the Gospel disclosed the features and name of his future bride.

Certain it is that this feast was Francis' last, and that he thereafter remained faithful to the mysterious bride his heart had chosen. "He tried hard," says Thomas of Celano, "to conceal from everyone the change that had been wrought in him; but he nonetheless lost all taste for business, and gradually he was seen to withdraw from the world."[13]

* * *

Here, as elsewhere, we shall make no attempt to explain the workings of grace in the soul of St. Francis. Who would presume to indicate the why and wherefores of similar phenomena? Neither St. Luke, writing of Mary Magdelene, nor St. Paul and St. Augustine, writing of themselves, ever attempted to show how faith succeeds doubt, nor the way whereby the soul suddenly passes from indifference or hate to fervor and mystical love. Has the Almighty, who can do more than we can ever comprehend, ever revealed those laws on which His miracles depend?

All that anyone can say is that Francis is now a man who has found love and who claims to be enlightened from on high. And he will act as such, consenting to pass for a religious visionary in the eyes of the blind who walk in darkness, and accomplishing acts described as "madness" by those who have never loved.

One might add that all that was best of his youthful ideals and ambitions was to survive in him. Like an artist who, changing his inspiration, does not thereby change his technique, he will shed nothing of his nobleness or his originality. A knight was what he had dreamed of becoming; a knight he will remain till his death.

His biographers often call him *miles Christi*.[14] But the expression should not be taken as St. Paul understood it when speaking of Christians,[15] or St. Augustine, Jerome, and Benedict when speaking of monks.[16] To them, *miles* evoked the Roman legionary, the brave foot soldier who endured war's fatigues and won the victory.

The word took on a nobler meaning in the Middle Ages. It no longer designated the soldier who goes on foot, but the mounted warrior, the lord, the knight.[17] *Miles Christi*, as pictured by historians of the Crusades, is the brother in arms, the champion, the "vassal of Christ."[18] And so it is that Francis is to look on his service of the suzerain chosen by him in the night of Spoleto.

He is to proclaim himself the "herald of the Great King," and the "standard bearer of Christ," and he will call his followers his "companions of the Round Table." He is to wear a sack in the form of a cross, to recall together his Master's death and the colors of his Lady Poverty. We shall see him a knight in his joyous enthusiasm, his courtesy, his liberality, his uprightness, his horror of minutiae. He is to be chivalrous in thought, deed, and troth. For these things were, as we know, fundamental points in the code of chivalry.

The liege man (*homo legalis*) was obliged to respond to the call of his suzerain, to fight, and if need be, to die for him. To withdraw from this engagement out of cowardice or through some legal loophole would be a breach of faith, a dishonor, and for the felon it meant the death penalty on earth, while waiting "to go and burn in hell-fire with the devils."[19]

Honor and undying fidelity were to characterize the holiness of the Poverello. Once he has paid homage to the Master, who said: "Whoever does not follow me is not worthy of me," Francis, filled with valor, will think only of imitating Him in His life of poverty and suffering; constantly conceiving new exploits, endeavoring to vie with Him in love and goodness, burning to become a martyr, and finally dying marked with the stigmata of his passion.

* * *

At this point in our story, however, young Francis, who has just broken with his past, and who seeks another goal for his life, is still ignorant of the road to follow to the happiness promised him. But he relies on God to show him the way; and that he may hear the Lord's voice again, he meditates and prays.

He also seeks to unbosom himself to a friend. He makes a confident of a young man of his own age who shared his tastes and consented to accompany him on his walks. Both went by preference to a grotto near town; and as they walked, they talked of the precious treasure for which they aspired.[20]

Arriving at the grotto, Francis would go in alone, and remain alone with God. And there, in a long and anguished prayer — for his soul, torn by a thousand conflicting thoughts, could not find peace — he would implore God to show him the way. He would bewail his past sins, which he now held in horror, trembling lest he fall into them again. And all this made him suffer so intensely that his face would be drawn when he rejoined his companion.

One day, however, he came forth in peace, for God had delivered him from uncertainty and had enlightened him. He was so brimming over with joy that no one could help noticing it. As he could neither explain his joy nor contain it, he would put people off by saying that if he had come back from Apulia before he got there, it was that he might accomplish his exploits in his own country. Or else he would start talking again about the peerless princess whom he hoped to wed.[21]

This princess was Lady Poverty.

* * *

Loving poverty does not mean limiting yourself to loving the poor, while taking care that you yourself lack nothing. It means becoming poor with them. It means refusing to enjoy yourself while they are suffering; and it means to embrace, as our Lord did, their state and their neediness. Such is the form of heroism that the sanctity of St. Francis was to take.

People remarked that his love for the outcasts had increased. He gave them, we are told, more and more alms. If he had no money, he would give them his cap, his belt, some portion of his clothing — sometimes even his shirt. He also bought sacred vessels for needy priests. And when his father was absent, he would place much more food than was necessary on the family table, thinking of the beggars who would come after the meal for the leavings. This little stratagem, of course, did not escape his mother; but she said nothing against it, for she loved and admired him more than her other children. In short, Francis reached the point where he was concerned solely with the poor and was happy only in their company.[22]

"The truth was," writes Thomas of Celano, "that he had become one of them, thinking only of sharing their life of privations." He loved Poverty itself.

In the course of a pilgrimage made to Rome, an opportunity was afforded him to wear the colors and livery of his austere princess. It may have been his confessor who imposed the journey on him as a penance; or perhaps the idea came to him of its own accord, since he had — like all Christians of his time — a great devotion to the Apostles.

Arriving at St. Peter's tomb, he was scandalized to see the pilgrims so niggardly with their money and making such mean offerings. "Really!" he thought. "This is no way to honor the prince of the Apostles!" And taking his purse filled with gold, he flung it toward the altar. The gold pieces rolling on the pavement caught the attention of the crowd, who marveled at such munificence. The gesture was chivalrous and right in St. Francis' style, for he was never one to stop and look at the sordid side of things; and so it was a matter of indifference to him, should his gold go to prelates, already, perhaps too rich.

When Francis had finished his devotions, he went out, encountering in front of St. Peter's the beggars with whom this place teems at all times. There it was that he proposed to one of them that they change clothes — an offer which, as one may well imagine, was not turned down. Putting on the wretched fellow's rags, and mingling with the troop of beggars, he begged along with them, shared their sordid meal, and found so much happiness in his taste of this kind of life that he would have asked nothing better than to keep on with it. Indeed he would have become a beggar there and then, had it not been for his desire to spare his family the shame of seeing him in this state.[23]

After his return to Assisi, he became more solitary than ever and gave himself over more and more to prayer. Sometimes he was tempted to quit, and for some time he was troubled by a strange obsession.

There was a woman in the city, some devout old crone, perhaps, who had so ugly a hump on her back, that the poor old creature appeared a monster. For a long time, Francis was obsessed with the fear that this same hump would grow on his back if he kept on in his way of life. It was the Devil, (a fallen angel, and therefore grotesque) who suggested this ridiculous thought to discourage him. But God came to his assistance. Francis, said the well-known voice, if you would find Me, despise earthly things; deny yourself, and prefer bitterness to sweetness. For this is the price you must pay to understand all these things.[24]

The young man "promised to obey," and God soon sent him a final trial.

* * *

The Saint himself has related in his Testament how he became "converted."

"During my life of sin," he writes, "nothing disgusted me like seeing victims of leprosy. It was the Lord Himself who urged me to go to them. I did so, and ever since, everything was so changed for me that what had seemed at first painful and impossible to overcome became easy and pleasant. Shortly after, I definitely forsook the world."

If we are to believe the chronicler, Matthew of Paris, there were no fewer than twenty thousand lazarets in Europe at that time. Everywhere, one would run across these unfortunates, whose putrefying flesh, oozing ulcers, and pestilential odor brought disgust. The young dandy had such a horror of them that if he saw one two miles away, he would turn his horse's head and gallop off, holding his nose. And he sent someone else to take alms to him.

But one day, at a bend in the road, he suddenly found himself facing a man afflicted with leprosy. His first reaction was to turn back. But he immediately changed his mind; and dismounting, he embraced the wretch, gently putting some coins in his hand. He thereupon felt a great happiness pervade his whole being. It was God keeping His promise and changing bitterness to sweetness for him who had preferred bitterness to sweetness.

But the young man was not content with this first victory. He sprang to the saddle and rode to a neighboring lazaret, apparently, San Lazaro d'Arce, about two miles from Assisi. Francis entered this "last refuge of all human misery." He assembled its unfortunate inmates and begged their pardon for having so often despised them; he lingered some time in their company; and while waiting to come and live near them, "he distributed money to them and left only after kissing them all on the mouth."[25]

- 3 -

The Restorer of Churches

About three-quarters of a mile below Assisi stands the little convent of San Damiano. Built on a hillside, on an elevation from which the whole plain may be viewed through a curtain of cypresses, it has become the residence of the Friars Minor after having been that of the Poor Ladies.

But in the spring of 1206, all that was there among the wheat fields sparsely set with olive trees was a ruinous chapel. Within, suspended over the altar, hung a mild and serene Byzantine crucifix. Although the church was no longer frequented, an in-indigent priest was still attached to it, living, no doubt, on alms and the suffrages of the faithful.[1]

"Now one day as Francis was passing, he entered the chapel. Kneeling before the wooden crucifix, he began to pray, when suddenly the figure of Christ, parting its painted lips, called him by name and said, 'Francis, go repair My house, which is falling in ruins.'

"It would be impossible," the biographer continues, "to describe the miraculous effect that these words produced on the hearer, since the latter declared himself incapable of expressing it. But one may reverently conjecture that Christ then impressed on his heart the sacred wounds with which he was later to mark his stigmatized body. For how many times in the future was not the blessed man to be met along the road, shedding compassionate tears over the Savior's Passion?"[2]

It was not a rare thing for knights to become builders of churches, in expiation of the faults committed in their adventure-filled lives. Had not one of the four sons of Aymon, men said, abandoned his military career to help build the Cathedral of Cologne?

Francis may have believed himself called on to imitate him; for, taking literally an order evidently applying to the Church of Christ itself, he at first thought that he was to restore the chapel of San Damiano. He at once offered the priest money for oil and a lamp, so that a suitable light might burn before the image of Christ crucified.[3] But where was he to find the necessary resources for rebuilding the chapel?

That need not be an obstacle! Francis thought of his horse and the bales of cloth at home. He returned home, made up a bundle of the most precious stuffs, then fortifying himself with the sign of the cross, leaped to the saddle and set off at a gallop for Foligno. There (as he usually did) he met customers who bought his merchandise. He also sold them his horse, so that he had to make the ten miles back to Assisi on foot.[4]

When he returned, the priest of San Damiano was in the chapel. Francis kissed his hands, detailed his plans to him, and attempted to give him the receipts from his sale. But the priest took this at first for a practical joke. Was not this risky money, which might embroil him with Francis' family? And then, how was a man to believe in the sudden conversion of this young fop, who even yesterday was scandalizing the whole town by his follies? So Francis did not succeed in having his gift accepted. But he did win the priest's confidence and got his permission to stay with him. As for the purse that was burning his fingers, he tossed it like a dead weight into the corner of a window and thought no more about it.[5]

Meanwhile, Peter Bernardone was in a towering rage and

deeply distressed at learning what his son had done. Assembling his friends and neighbors, he rushed to San Damiano "to seize the fugitive and bring him home."

Fortunately, the new hermit had taken care to secure a place of refuge — a sort of dug-out under a house that no one, except a friend, knew about. As the conspirators drew near, he ran and hid in it, and let them shout it out. He hid for a whole month, eating in his cave the little food that was brought him, and beseeching God to help him carry out his plans. And in this dark retreat, the Lord sent him such consolation and delight as he had never known.[6]

The time came, however, when, blushing at his fears, he left the hiding place; and resolved to face the music, he headed for town. He was exhausted by his austerities. People seeing him gaunt and wan — he who a short time before had been so full of life — thought that he had lost his mind, and began to yell, "Lunatic! Madman!" Urchins slung stones and mud at him; but he went on, without appearing to notice their taunts.

Hearing the hullabaloo, Peter Bernardone came out of the house and saw that it was his son they were harrying. He became furious. Hurling himself on Francis like a fierce wolf on an innocent lamb, he dragged him into the house, where he chained him and shoved him into a dungeon. He spared neither arguments nor blows to wear down the rebel, but the latter refused to be shaken.[7]

Personal business, however, obliged the father to leave; and Francis' mother profited by this to try her hand at swaying her son. Seeing that he remained inflexible, one day when she was alone in the house, she broke his chains and set him free. The father's fury knew no bounds, when, on his return, he learned of the prisoner's escape. He launched into reproaches against his wife;[8] then attempted a final move at San Damiano, where Francis had again settled.

But trial had steeled his courage. He came forth now with assurance, with peaceful heart and joyous mien. He calmly walked up to his father, declaring that he no longer feared either irons or blows and that he was ready to endure all things for the love of Christ.[9] Feeling that all hope was lost for the time being, Peter Bernardone concerned himself only with recovering the Foligno sales money and sending the young rebel into exile. This respectable citizen hoped in this way to get the son who shamed him out of the way, and perhaps by cutting off his living, to bring him back home some day.[10]

Shouting angrily on the way, he rushed to the palace of the commune, and swore out a warrant before the consuls. The magistrates charged a town crier to summon Francis to appear before them. But the young man, who was bothered neither about exile nor about giving back the money, refused to obey; and claiming that having gone into God's service, he was no longer under civil jurisdiction, he declined to appear. The consuls declared themselves incompetent and rejected the plaintiff's claim, leaving him with no recourse but to appeal to the jurisdiction of the Church.[11]

* * *

The Bishop of Assisi at that time was Lord Guido, who occupied his diocese until after the saint's death. He formally bade the accused to appear before his tribunal. "I will go before the bishop," replied Francis, "for he is the father and master of souls."

The judgment was most probably rendered in public, in the piazza of Santa Maria Maggiore, in front of the bishop's palace.

"Put your trust in God," said the bishop to the accused, "and show yourself courageous. However, if you would serve the Church, you have no right, under color of good works, to keep money obtained in this way. So give back such wrongly acquired goods to your father, to appease him."

"Gladly, my Lord," replied Francis, "and I will do still more."

He went within the palace and disrobed; then, with his clothing in his hands, he reappeared, almost entirely nude, before the crowd. "Listen to me, everybody!" he cried. "Up to now, I have called Peter Bernardone my father! But now that I purpose to serve God, I give him back not only this money that he wants so much, but all the clothes I have from him!" With this, Francis threw everything on the ground. "From now on," he added, "I can advance naked before the Lord, saying in truth no longer: my father, Peter Bernardone, but: our Father who art in Heaven!"

At this dramatic climax the bishop drew Francis within his arms, enveloping him in the folds of his mantle. The spectators, catching sight of the hair shirt that the young man wore on his skin, were dumbfounded, and many of them wept. As for Peter Bernardone, unhappy and angry, he hurriedly withdrew, taking with him the clothing and purse.[12]

And that was the way Francis took leave of his family.

One would like to think that he saw his mother again, and from time to time showed some mark of tenderness toward this woman who admired him and had had an intuition of his sublime destiny. But the biographers make no further mention of her.

* * *

For some time after that, Francis did no more about San Damiano. The funds on which he had counted had vanished, and he had not yet learned that poverty sufficeth for all things.

He had first to go in search of suitable clothing, since all that he had to cover him was a little coat full of holes that the bishop's gardener had given him after the scene of the day before. He drew a cross on it with chalk by way of a coat of arms; then he set out through the woods singing the Lord's praises in French at the top of his lungs.[13]

His heart was overflowing with joy. There was to be no more now of circumspection and feeling his way. A pathway of light opened straight before him. He was consecrated to the Master's service; he had just been made Christ's knight and had solemnly espoused Lady Poverty. God was rewarding him by making him happy.

He was making the woods ring with his songs when some robbers, scenting a prey, rushed up. This man with his threadbare cloak was a disappointment to them. "Who are you?" they asked.

"I am the herald of the Great King!" replied Francis with assurance.

As he did not yet have the gift of taming wild beasts, the robbers beat him up and threw him into the snow at the foot of a ravine. "There you are, oaf!" they shouted as they made off. "Stay there, God's herald!"

Francis climbed out of the slush-filled hole only with great effort, and when the ruffians were out of sight and hearing, he went on his way, singing louder than ever.[14] He then directed his footsteps to a monastery, where he thought the monks would consent to clothe him in exchange for work.

The monks took him on as a kitchen helper but gave him nary a stitch to cover him. For food, they let him skim off a little of the greasy water they fed the pigs. It is true that afterwards, when Francis' reputation for sanctity began to be established, the prior was ashamed at the way he had treated him and came to beg his forgiveness. And he obtained it easily, for the saint said that he had very pleasant memories of the few days spent in his kitchen.[15]

It was at Gubbio that an old friend gave him something to

wear. So afterward men saw him wearing a hermit's garb —
a tunic secured at the waist by a leather belt, sandals on his
feet, and a staff in his hand.[16] He next stayed a while with the
lepers, living in their midst, bathing their sores, sponging off
the pus from their ulcers, and giving them loving care for the
love of God.[17]

Then he went back to San Damiano.[18]

*   *   *

There, the chaplain still recalled recent events, and Francis
had to reassure him by telling him of the bishop's encouragement and approval. After this, the restoration of the chapel
could begin.

As Francis had no money with which to buy materials, he
was obliged to beg for them. He went through the city crying, "Whoever gives me a stone will receive a reward from
the Lord! Whoever gives me two will have two rewards! Whoever gives me three will receive three rewards!" Sometimes,
like a *jongleur* who sings in order to earn his salary and repay
his benefactors, the collector would interrupt his rounds to
sing to the glory of the Most High.

And whether he addressed himself to men or to God, whether he begged for hewn stone or celebrated the divine attributes, the Little Poor Man (his biographers observe) "always
spoke in a familiar style, without having recourse to the
learned and bombastic words of human wisdom."[19] Is this an
allusion to the jargon and to the false science that flourished
in the schools? One thing certain is that here you have defined the man and the style, which go together in St. Francis.

Simple he was in his person, having but one aim and one
object, honestly and openly sought. Simple he was in speech,
knowing what he said, and saying only what he knew; avoiding lengthy, pompous, and obscure discourse, speaking — like

Jesus in the Gospels — to make himself understood and to be useful to others. Picturesque and sublime, his talks, coming from the heart, reached men's hearts, delivering them from their sadness and their sins, and revealing to them the happiness that comes from belonging to God.

Moreover, if many still held the new hermit to be a madman and persisted in insulting him, many already were beginning to understand him; and, moved to the depths of their being, they wept as they listened to his words. They saw him carrying stones on his back and striving to interest everyone in his project. Standing on his scaffolding, he would joyously hail the passers-by. "Come here a while, too," he would shout, "and help me rebuild San Damiano!"

It may be that crews of masons responded to his appeals, and working under his direction, helped him in his tasks. It was then, accounts tell us, that he predicted that virgins consecrated to God would soon come and take shelter in the shadow of the rebuilt chapel.[20]

One can imagine how he drove himself — he who had always been petted and pampered by his parents. Taking pity on him, his priest-companion began — poor as he was — to prepare better food for him than that with which he himself was satisfied.

Francis, at first, raised no objections; but seeing that he was being mollycoddled, he said to himself: "Francis, are you expecting to find a priest everywhere who will baby you? This is not the life of poverty that you have embraced! No! You are going to do as the beggars do! Out of love for Him who willed to be born poor and to live in poverty, who was bound naked to the Cross, and who did not even own the tomb men laid Him in, you are going to take a bowl and go begging your bread from door to door!"[24]

So Francis went begging through the town, a large bowl in his hands, putting everything that people gave him into it.

When it came to eating this mess, he felt nauseated. He managed, however, to get it down, and found it better than the fine food he used to eat at home. He thereupon thanked God for being able — frail and exhausted as he was — to adjust himself to such a diet; and from then on, he would not let the priest prepare anything special for him.[22]

Let no one imagine, however, that he was not sometimes subject to false shame. For instance, one day when oil was needed for the chapel lamp, he went up to a house where a party was in progress, with merrymakers overflowing into the street. Recognizing some old friends and blushing to appear before them as a beggar, he started back. But he soon retraced his steps and accused himself of his cowardice before them all. Then, making his request in French, he set off again with his oil.

Thomas of Celano observes here that "it was always in French that St. Francis expressed himself when he was filled with the Holy Ghost; as if he had foreseen the special cult with which France was to honor him one day," and wanted to show himself grateful in advance.[23]

*   *   *

No one, though, ever loved his homeland more than he did, or was more beloved by its people. But the veneration of his fellow-citizens did not come in a day. A considerable number of them began by mocking him at will, including his brother Angelo, eager to show himself for once witty at Francis' expense.

This happened very likely in a church, where Francis was praying one wintry morning, shivering with cold beneath his flimsy rags. Passing near him with a friend, the brother remarked to his companion, "Look! There's Francis! Ask him if he won't sell you a penny's worth of his sweat!"

Francis could not help smiling. "It's not for sale," he replied gently. "I prefer to keep it for God, who will give me a much better price for it than you."[24]

The barbed shafts no longer struck home. Only one thing continued to distress him, and that was his father's attitude toward him. For every time that Peter Bernardone met his son, he became infuriated and cursed him.

A son like Francis could not remain under the spell of a father's curses. So to an old beggar named Albert, he made the following offer: "Adopt me as your son, and I will share the alms I receive with you. Only whenever we meet my father and he curses me, you make the sign of the cross over me and give me your blessing."

The arrangement was to Albert's advantage, and we may be sure that he had no scruples about giving as many blessings as there were curses to ward off. So, addressing the wrathful merchant, Francis would say to him, "You see that God has found a way to offset your curses, for he has sent me a new father to bless me."[25]

Evidently Peter Bernardone was sensitive to ridicule and ended by taking things more calmly, for we hear no more of him in the biographies. No doubt, he lived long enough to behold the rising star of the Little Poor Man. And who knows if, on seeing his son honored by important personages, he did not put as much zeal into acknowledging him as he had into denying him?

- 4 -

"Discovery" of the Gospel
and First Recruits

We do not know how many churches Francis repaired during the two or three years he gave himself up to this occupation, while continuing to care for lepers. Biographers mention three, all of them in the neighborhood of Assisi: San Damiano, which we know already; [probably San Pietro della Spina on the plain west of San Damiano;] and finally, the Portiuncula, lost at that time in deep woods, and today enclosed within the walls of the basilica of St. Mary of the Angels.[1]

The Portiuncula belonged to the Benedictine Abbey of Mount Subasio; but the monks had long since abandoned it and cared less and less about it. "The chapel was, then, completely deserted, and no one ever set foot in it," writes Thomas of Celano, "when, pained at this state of things, Francis, the devoted client of the Virgin Mary,[2] resolved to settle there and restore it."

The Portiuncula, which was to become the cradle of the Franciscan epic, "was the place that Francis loved most in the whole world," wrote St. Bonaventure. Everything conspired to endear it to him: its name, linking the concept of poverty to

84

the name of the Mother of God; its isolation in the midst of the great silent forest; without counting the proximity of the Santa Maddalena and San Salvatore leprosaria situated about three miles from there, and both of them near Assisi.[3]

It was while hearing Mass in the restored chapel that Francis received the revelation of his true vocation. This event [probably] took place on the 24th of February, 120[8], the feast of St. Matthias,[4] while the priest was reading the Gospel passage in which Jesus maps out a rule of conduct for his apostles. "Go," said the Savior, "and preach the message, 'the Kingdom of Heaven is at hand!'. . . . Freely you have received, freely give . . . . Do not keep gold, or silver, or money in your girdles, no wallet for your journey, nor two tunics, nor sandals, nor staff; for the laborer deserves his living.

"And whatever town or village you enter, inquire who in it is worthy; and stay there until you leave. As you enter the house, salute it, saying, 'Peace to this house.' "[5]

Francis had made great spiritual progress and received much light since beginning his life of penance and charity; but this time, he felt that God had taken away the last veil and finally illumined his path.

The better to understand these sacred lines, he asked the priest to explain them and comment on them. The priest, perhaps a Benedictine from Mount Subasio, explained the Gospel passage — that Christ's disciples had been commanded to preach repentance everywhere, to take nothing with them, and to trust in God alone to supply all their needs.

Francis thrilled with happiness at this revelation and exclaimed enthusiastically: "That is what I want! That is what I seek! I long to do that with all my heart!" On the instant, he threw away his staff, took off his shoes, and laid aside his cloak, keeping only a tunic; replaced his leather belt with a cord, and made himself a rough garment, so poor and so badly cut out that it could inspire envy in no man.[6]

That, as Francis recalled in his Testament, was a day of decision, a day to be remembered, in which "the Most High personally revealed to me that I ought to live according to the Holy Gospel"; and in which he himself, in his childlike candor and knightly loyalty, adopted forever this literal way of interpreting the Savior's words. For (Thomas of Celano observes here), "it was not as a deaf man that he heard the Lord's words" — as a deaf man who opens or closes his ears according to circumstances and his own convenience. As for him, "not only did he learn by heart all our Lord said, but he never lost sight of it, and constantly endeavored to observe it to the letter."[7]

* * *

Francis knew now that it was not to build chapels that God was calling him, but to co-operate in the restoration of the Church. So he lost no time in setting joyfully to work to preach penitence.

To everyone he met he now gave the Gospel greeting: "The Lord give you peace!" Coming from a man whose voluntary poverty permitted him to enjoy this supreme benefit, these words were not without effect, for many to whom they were addressed made peace with their enemies and with their own conscience.[8]

It was at this time that Francis gave his first sermon in the church of San Giorgio, [where he had gone to school and in which he would at first be buried]. "He began," continues Thomas of Celano, "by wishing peace to the congregation, speaking without affectation, but with such enthusiasm that all were carried away by his words."

From now on the mockers held their peace. The influence of the Poor Man of Jesus Christ and God's Troubadour was spreading. People began to listen to this sunny prophet who preached redemption to sinners and to sad hearts the secret of regaining joy and gladness.

Unlike the lay reformers who swarmed through Europe in those days, he hurled no anathemas at the times and inveighed against no one. He limited himself to relating the Gospel with such humility, charm, and assurance that he gave it back its effectiveness and freshness. After all, this time the disciple reminded men of the Master, and the virtue of the preacher lent credence to his message. Had they not seen him for [over two] years living like the least of the poor and devoting himself to the relief of the lepers?

All this burst upon men in those days as a kind of revelation. Certainly it was an awakening and a new beginning. And as the habit St. Francis wore designated him as a guide, some thought that a new form of religious life had been born; and disciples eager to follow it soon presented themselves.

* * *

In a few months, they were eleven.

"The first was a man from Assisi, simple and good," of whom nothing else is told us and who disappears at once, like a wraith.[9]

The second was Bernard of Quintavalle;[10] the third, Peter Catanii; the fourth, Giles. Then, in uncertain order, come Morico, the Crosier from the leprosy hospital of San Salvatore;[11] Barbaro, Sabbatino, Bernardo Vigilante, John of San Costanzo; Angelo Tancredi, the knight; Philip, who "preached admirably, and interpreted the Scriptures perfectly without having studied in the schools"; and, finally, the Judas of the new apostolic college, that [Giovanni della Cappella, later known as] "John of the Hat," who, according to the *Fioretti*, "apostasized, and hanged himself by the throat." He was, it appears, very disobedient; he flatly refused to go without a hat, whereas the other brothers were content with their hoods.[12]

Bernard was a rich and important citizen of Assisi, thoughtful and of exemplary conduct. Greatly impressed by young Bernardone's conversion, he began to consider following his example and leaving the world. Meanwhile, to test him, he often received him as a guest in his home.

One night when both were sharing the same room, Francis promptly pretended to be sound asleep. Bernard, likewise feigning sleep, began to snore loudly — though he kept one eye open. He soon saw his companion rise cautiously, kneel down, and begin to pray. And all night, he could hear Francis, on his knees, with loving sighs, conversing with God. Bernard was now completely won over. In the morning, he asked his guest, "What would you say a man should do who wanted to get rid of his money?"

"It would seem to me that he ought to give it back to the Master he received it from."

"Well, then, I've decided to follow your advice!" replied Bernard.

"In that case," said Francis, "we shall go and consult the Gospels to find out what Christ's will is for you."

At daybreak they set out for the Church of San Nicolò to hear Mass, taking with them Peter of Catanii, who had likewise resolved to leave the world. They opened the missal three times at random. The first time, their eyes fell on these words: "If you will be perfect, go, sell what you have, and give to the poor." The second time, they read: "Take nothing for your journey"; and the third time: "If anyone wishes to come after Me, let him deny himself, and take up his cross, and follow Me."[13]

"Here," said Francis, "is what we are going to do, and all those who shall afterwards join us."

We do not know if Peter of Catanii, who was a jurist, had means; and if so, how he got rid of them.

As for the wealthy Bernard, of whom Thomas of Celano

declares that he "made haste to sell his property down to the last penny" the *Fioretti* depict him stationed in front of his door, distributing his possessions to the poor who rushed up for the handout. Even so, he seemed in more of a hurry to get rid of his money than the poor to receive it. Like a farm woman in the midst of the hen yard, he tirelessly reached into the folds of his cloak and gave fistfuls of money to every comer. Standing beside him, Francis helped to hurry things along.

While this was going on, a priest named Sylvester squeezed through the crowd, and going up to Francis, reminded him of an old overdue bill. "By the way," he said, "there are still some stones you bought from me to repair your churches that have never been paid for."

"That's quite possible!" replied Francis, "but never mind!" And plunging both hands into Bernard's cloak, he gave him a handful of silver. "Here you are!" he said. "If you want more, you have only to say the word!"

But it must have been the right amount, for the avaricious priest asked no more and left — greatly embarrassed.

Shortly after, renouncing his stones and other goods, Sylvester the priest also embraced the life of poverty.[14]

*   *   *

Peter and Bernard were persons of too much prominence for their vocation not to be heralded abroad. Seven days later, Giles heard of it from his kinsfolk, who, it seems, were farmers in the outskirts of Assisi. As for a long time he had been greatly concerned with his soul's salvation, he was delighted to learn that Francis was receiving companions. The next morning — April 23, 1208 — he said farewell to his family and went to hear Mass in the Church of Saint George on its titular feast day. Then he proceeded to the Portiuncula. A little way past the San Salvatore lazaret, he met Francis coming out of the woods. Running up to him and throwing himself at his feet, he begged him to receive him.

"Dear Brother," said Francis, raising him up, "it is a great favor that you have received today! If the Emperor, coming to Assisi to choose a knight or a chamberlain, had let his choice fall on you, you would feel proud, and rightly so! Well, it is God himself who invites you to His court, by calling you to serve Him in our little band."

Taking Giles by the hand, Francis led him to the hut where Bernard and Peter were. "Here," he said, presenting him, "is a good brother God has sent us! Let us sit down to table to celebrate his coming."

After the meal, he took him to Assisi to find something with which to make him a habit. On the way, a beggar woman asked for charity. Francis said to his companion, "Give her your fine cloak." Brother Giles obeyed, and afterward related that "his alms had appeared to fly up to Heaven," and himself with it, so happy he felt. But his happiness "grew still greater" when, shortly afterward, he saw himself "wearing the coarse tunic" in which Francis had clothed him.[15]

* * *

The four new apostles lost no time in trying out their strength, and went forth in two groups for their first mission. Accompanied by Giles, Francis reached the March of Ancona[16] and the others went in a direction not disclosed to us.

The crowds had not yet started to run after the Little Poor Man. So he limited himself to singing songs — like the minstrels — in the public squares; and to recommending to the few listeners gathered to hear him to love God above everything else and to repent of their sins. Never being much gifted in public speaking, Brother Giles kept still, and intervened only to applaud his master's speech. "Do everything that my spiritual father tells you to do," he would say. "For you can believe me, he is quite right, and no one could tell you anything better."

According to the *Three Companions,* our missionaries did not enjoy great success at this time. Their strange garb did not add to their prestige. What did these ragamuffins want with their ragged clothes, their sermons, and their songs? People generally took them either for fanatics or fools. Young women fled at sight of them, as if they had the evil eye. "They are either madmen or saints," thought the wiseacres, not venturing to express an opinion.

As for Francis, he radiated hope, and already saw himself at the head of a great army, made up of the flower of chivalry. He confided to Brother Giles: "Like the fisherman who, hauling up all kinds of fish into his nets, throws out the little fish and keeps only the big ones, so we should choose and keep only the best."[17]

* * *

Back at the Portiuncula once more, Francis received four new brothers, equally natives of Assisi: Philip; the Crosier, Morico, whose Order ministered to the San Salvatore leprosarium; Sabbatino; and [probably] Giovanni della Cappella.

The people of Assisi did not take kindly to this increase in the brotherhood. They forgave Francis, so long as he was one of a kind; but when they saw that he was gathering recruits, they anxiously asked themselves where it would all end, and also how many of these healthy men — who so often came begging to their doors — they would have to feed. "If they had held onto their own property," people grumbled, "they wouldn't be reduced to eating other men's bread."

Thus the penitents of the Portiuncula now received more insults than alms.

Things had come to such a pass that Bishop Guido thought it his duty to intervene. He too, when he had encouraged Francis, never dreamed that the latter would gain adherents. "Your way of life appears too hard and impractical to me," said he, wishing to induce Francis to give up so radical a poverty.

But Francis replied: "My Lord, if we owned property, we should need arms to defend it. Besides, property engenders many disputes and lawsuits harmful to love of God and neighbor. That is why we do not want to have anything of our own here below."

Unless he was prepared to say the Gospel was wrong, there was nothing to reply; and Bishop Guido, who sometimes lost his lawsuits,[18] declared himself convinced. Doubtless, to completely satisfy the bishop, Francis explained to him that, far from being idle, his followers would busy themselves in earning their living and have recourse to public charity only when absolutely necessary.

Our penitents strove, then, not to be a burden to anyone. Some of them hired themselves out as laborers in monasteries and private homes. Others helped farmers in the field,[19] and still others took care of victims of leprosy in the neighboring lazar houses. But the demands made by the common life and the apostolate, the needs of the sick, and the fact that Francis, in conformity to the Gospel, was "opposed to receiving money and thinking about the morrow" — all these things made mendicancy inevitable.

Now unless he is born a slave, what man does not have a horror of a state wherein one receives without giving and must accept insult and injury without repaying in kind?

The brothers would gladly have dispensed themselves from begging, and at first Francis tried to spare them. Every day, notes *The Three Companions*, it was he who, despite his frail constitution and impaired health, took the bowl and went out begging.

But he finally succumbed at the task, and as no one stepped forward to take his place, he said to the brothers: "My little children, you must make up your minds to go out begging, since, following the example of our Lord and of His most blessed Mother, you have chosen the way of perfect poverty. And do not believe that it is so difficult and humiliating. You have only to say, 'Charity, for the love of God.' And since, in exchange for what they give you, your benefactors will receive the incomparable blessing of God's love, you will therefore be in the position of someone who offers a hundredfold for one. So be not ashamed, but go forth with joy."

The brothers were not yet numerous enough to go out two by two (which would have made them bolder). So each went alone. But everything went along famously; and when the brothers returned at night, there was not one of them who did not declare himself satisfied with his daily "stint." They also amused themselves by comparing results — those having the fullest sacks were, naturally, the proudest. Their father congratulated them; and from that time onward, the brothers vied at being the ones to receive permission to go out begging.[20]

* * *

Francis spent the summer and fall of 1208 at St. Mary of the Angels, devoting himself to his spiritual family.

By making the brothers poor and destitute, he had constrained them to trust in God and to seek Him alone. But he still had to form them in the spiritual life and show them the special way whereby he wished to lead them. So he instructed them, encouraged and corrected them, teaching them to pray,[21] exercising them in humility and penance, training them in perfection; and — like those artists to whom one gives a good model so that they may paint a good picture — he continually placed before them the person of our Lord. "When

the Lord gave me brethren," he declares in his Testament,
"no one save the Most High taught me what I must do." By
this, we see that the founder of the Franciscans did not feel
that he owed anything to the doctors and founders of Orders
who had preceded him.[22]

* * *

When winter came, he decided to undertake a new crusade
with his sons. Calling them together, he said to them: "Since
it is God's will for us to work, not only for our own salvation,
but also for the salvation of others, we will go all over the
world to preach — by example, even more than in words —
penitence and peace. Among those whom you will meet, some
will give you a good reception and will listen to you; but the
greater part will reject you and revile you. Reply humbly to
those who question you; and as for those who shall persecute
you, show them your gratitude."

At these words, which reminded them of their unpleasant
experiences and predicted more to come, the brothers began
to tremble so much that their father had to reassure them. "Do
not feel sad at my ignorance and your own," he said to them.
"God will keep His promise and speak by your mouth. Besides, the time is at hand when wiser men will come and help
us. And do not be discouraged any more about your small
number. There is something of which I should not speak to
you, if charity did not oblige me. But I can tell you confiden-
tially that the Lord has revealed to me in a vision that our Order is to spread over all the earth. And even yet there rings
in my ears the sound of the footsteps of men hastening from
France, from Spain, from England, and from Germany, to
join up with us." This talk restored their courage.[23]

Francis divided them, then, into four groups of two. It was
agreed that Bernard and Giles should go in the direction of

St. James of Compostella. He himself with a companion would go as far as the Valley of Rieti.[24] As for the others, other regions were assigned to them.

All dropped to their knees. Francis blessed them and tenderly embraced them, saying to each: "Dear brother, put your trust in the Lord, who will take care of you." He then dismissed them.[25]

*   *   *

The brothers kept the recommendations made to them as best they could.

When they passed near a crucifix, they would kneel down and say a *Pater*. When they entered a church, they would say the following prayer: "We adore You, O Lord Jesus, here and in all the churches of the entire world; and we bless You, because by Your holy Cross You have redeemed the world." They greeted all whom they met with their usual, "God give you peace!" letting it be understood, no doubt, that they themselves possessed this peace and found it good.[26]

But some surly folk, displeased at this salutation, replied, "What are these new manners? Why can't you greet people the way other religious do?"

They were so gruff that a timid brother asked St. Francis not to have to greet people in this way. But the Saint said to him, "Let them be, as these men do not discern yet what comes from God. For the Lord Himself revealed this greeting to me. And it is the Lord, too, who has raised up our little brotherhood, which is bound to distinguish itself from others in this — that all its wealth must consist in possessing Him alone."[27]

If well-disposed listeners consented to hear more, the brothers would address this short sermon to them, known as the "exhortation to repentance":

"Fear and honor, praise and bless, thank and adore the Lord God Almighty, in Trinity and Unity, Father, Son, and Holy Spirit, Creator of all things. Do not put off any longer confessing all your sins, for death will soon come. Give and it will be given you; forgive and you will be forgiven . . . Blessed are they who die repentant, for they shall go to the Kingdom of Heaven! But woe to those who are not converted, for these children of the Devil will go with their father into everlasting fire. Be watchful, therefore. Shun evil, and persevere in well-doing unto the end."

An enemy of verbosity, and knowing what danger and uselessness for his brethren lay in long sermons on apologetics and dogma, Francis had prudently enjoined his friars to stick to this little speech.[28]

Here again, they had more opportunity for practicing patience than eloquence.

People had never seen men dressed that way before. So sometimes they were taken for savages, and sometimes for sneak thieves in disguise who ought to be driven off with clubs. Many wondered where they came from, and if they were not dangerous heretics. People kept asking them who they were. "We are Penitents, from the city of Assisi," they would reply. This was their first name, a fact which reassured no one. And they made them repeat it so often, writes the biographer, that this was not the least of their fatigues. Some threw mud at them. Others, grabbing them by their hoods, dragged them behind them like so many sacks. In some places they were disrobed in public. But they did not resist, refusing — so as to keep the Gospel — to resist evil, and waiting for people to have the charity to give back their clothes.[29] Brother Giles once gave his cowl to a pauper and traveled without it for twenty days.[30]

* * *

Brother Giles, as we have said, set out toward St. James of Compostella with Brother Bernard. In the course of this journey, they passed through Florence, where they met with the worst possible reception.

It was in the dead of winter, and night had fallen before they could find shelter. They finally prevailed on a pious lady to let them sleep in the bake-house under the porch. But when her husband came home, he was very annoyed. "Why," he demanded, "did you let those low fellows spend the night under the porch?"

The woman replied that at any rate she had not been so imprudent as to let them in the house; and as for whatever wood was left in the bake-house, it would be no great loss if they walked off with it.

"In any case," replied the husband, "I forbid you to give them any blankets."

Now it was very cold, "so that the slumbers of Brother Bernard and Brother Giles were quite light that night, they having only the garments of Lady Poverty to cover themselves and the zeal of their devotion to warm them."

The next morning, as the pious lady entered a church, she found the two brothers deep in prayer. "If they were thieves as I thought," she said to herself, "they would not pray so well." Continuing to observe them, she saw a man named Guido go up to them to give them alms. They refused.

"Why don't you take money like other beggars?" he inquired.

"Because we have embraced poverty voluntarily," replied Bernard.

"You had means before?"

"Oh yes! A great deal!" responded Bernard, speaking mostly for himself. "And if we have no money left now, it is because we gave it away for the love of God."

The lady, who had heard the entire conversation, now approached, this time to offer them decent hospitality in her home. But as they had just accepted the same invitation from the charitable Guido, they thanked her humbly and followed their new friend. They spent several days with him, and so thoroughly edified him that after their departure, people noticed that he gave still more alms than before.

* * *

But, according to *The Three Companions*, the adventures of the brothers rarely turned out so well; and one should say rather that they failed all along the line.[31]

As for Francis, he had better success in the Valley of Rieti, where entire populations who had become almost pagan were converted by his words. There, [now or later], in the person of the knight Angelo, he made one of his best recruits. "You have worn," said he to him, "the belt, the sword, and the spurs of the world, long enough. Come with me and I will arm you as Christ's knight."

The ex-warrior obeyed. Within the Order, where he was called Brother Angelo, his refined courtesy remained proverbial; and after the death of his master, he formed — together with Brother Leo and Brother Rufino — the group known as the "Three Companions."[32]

It was at that time that Francis had the consolation of knowing that his sins were forgiven.

For long hours he prayed near Poggio Bustone, in a grotto far above the valley — trembling with anguish at the thought of the sinful years of his youth. "Lord, I beseech you," he would repeat weeping, "have mercy on me, a sinner!"

Suddenly an immense sweetness filled his soul and he swooned from happiness. When he came to, his darkness and anxieties had vanished. He had become a new man; and from that time onward, he possessed the certainty of having been restored to God's grace.[33]

But this sentiment of his justification never prevented him from considering himself a great sinner. Just as the true artist sees better than all others the distance separating him from absolute beauty, so did he measure only too well the depth of the abyss separating the divine perfection from our human misery to cherish any thoughts of vain glory. And such was his eagerness to excuse others that he adjudged all to be better than himself. Men could not humiliate him — he humiliated himself.

* * *

After having preached for some time in the Valley of Rieti, Francis felt a great longing to see his brothers again and prayed the Lord to bring them back to him. His prayer was answered; for with no signal having been given, all soon regained the Portiuncula.

Great was their joy at seeing their father again. They related to him the blessings with which God had favored them, made accusation of their faults, and humbly accepted needed admonitions.

Four new recruits, "virtuous men full of merit," now brought the number of the growing brotherhood up to twelve. The Saint then disclosed to them his plan to write a Rule and to seek its approval by Pope Innocent III.[34]

- 5 -

Before Pope Innocent III

To those who consider the thirteenth century the "great Christian century," and the age in which St. Francis lived "one of the finest types of human civilization," it is natural that the pontificate of Innocent III should appear as "one of the most glorious in history."[1]

No Pope was ever closer to making the "theory of the two swords" a triumphant reality. This doctrine maintained that the Church having received power in Heaven and on earth, God had given it at the same time jurisdiction over all earthly sovereigns and authority to depose them if they so deserved.[2]

There was, so to speak, no country in which Innocent III had not succeeded in imposing his will. In Italy he ousted the emperor and drove his officials from the pontifical states. In Sicily he received the homage of the regent, who entrusted to him the tutelage of her son, the future emperor. In Germany he dethroned Philip of Swabia and gave the crown to his rival, Otto of Brunswick, next excommunicating the latter to enthrone Frederick II in his place. In England, John Lackland became his vassal, as were already the kings of Hungary, Aragon, and Castile. France alone attempted to resist him in the person of Philip Augustus.

This glorious picture of pontifical policy had its counterpart, however, in the scandals then desolating Christianity. For without speaking of the princes who, contesting the theory of the two swords, braved excommunication, warred against the pope, and taught their people to despise the spiritual prerogatives of the Bishop of Rome, truth compels one to confess that many clergy at this period afforded a most afflicting spectacle.

Living under the regime of landed property, the clergy were absorbed in the management of temporal affairs, to the neglect of their priestly ministry. Priests preached little, studied not at all, practiced simony, and lived loosely and lazily — having, it would seem, no other concern than the exercise of power and the possession of honors, pleasure, and money. Many prelates made a display of unheard-of luxury, and had recourse to traffic in church benefices to maintain it. They would even sell these benefices at public auction; as for example Ralph, Bishop of Liége, who had them sold by a city butcher along with his meat.[3] As for the people, their moral and religious status was on a par with that of their pastors.[4]

In brief, the evil was so serious and so widespread that Innocent III himself said that it "would take fire and sword to cure it,"[5] and everywhere men talked of reform. Never had one seen so many self-styled "prophets" and "reformers" as at this period.

* * *

Prophets and prophetesses foretold purifying chastisements and the coming of a better age.

"Woe to all nations!" cried St. Elizabeth of Schönau (1126-1164), "for the world has become darkness! The Lord's vineyard has perished; the Head of the Church is sick and his members are dead! Do you sleep, shepherds of the flock? But I know how to awaken you!"[6]

"God's justice is about to strike!" prophesied St. Hildegard (1098-1179). "His judgments shall be accomplished; the empire and the papacy have fallen and shall go down together. But from their ruins, the Holy Spirit will cause a new people to rise. All men shall be converted, and the angels shall return in confidence to dwell among the children of men."[7]

The most extraordinary of these prophets was Joachim of Fiore (1145-1202), who had an enormous influence, notably on the Spiritual Franciscans. His exegesis and calculations led him to announce that the existence of the human race on earth was divided into three periods, over which presided respectively the Father, Son, and Holy Spirit. The first period is that of the Mosaic law, of servile obedience and fear. The second period is that of grace, of filial obedience and faith. As this period has been far from perfect, and even ends badly, a third period would succeed it in 1260, inaugurating the reign of the Spirit, of liberty and of love, and would last until the end of the world.

But all was not raving on the part of the Calabrian Cistercian. This pure and gentle man had a burning love for Christ. He had a deep love for and feeling of kinship with nature; he tenderly rested the faces of the dying against his breast to warm them and so make dying easier; he lived in destitution, professing that nothing brings man close to God like voluntary poverty; and he showed much distaste for useless learning. "Dialectics," he wrote, "closes what is open, darkens what is clear, and engenders idle speech, rivalries, and blasphemy; as is proven by those arrogant scribes, who by dint of their reasoning, founder in heresy."[8]

* * *

The reformers, for their part, wanted to go back to the Gospel. Unfortunately, many among them who aspired to instruct the Church fell into heresy or schism. However, the Vaudois, or "Poor Men of Lyons," had started out well.

Their founder, Peter Valdes, a rich merchant of Lyons who had given up his property to practice and preach the Gospel, had gained a number of adherents, attracted by his ideals and virtue. These lived in poverty, penance, and perfect equality, and from time to time met in chapters.

When they began to lash out against the laxity of the clergy, the Archbishop of Lyons excommunicated them. They appealed to the Pope and were received at the Vatican. Alexander III embraced Peter Valdes, congratulated him on his vow of poverty, and authorized him and his followers to address moral exhortations to the people, wherever the bishops permitted, on condition that they should not attempt to interpret the Scriptures or teach theology. The fault of the "Poor Men of Lyons" lay in their overstepping these orders.

As all roads lead to Rome, and these penitents always declared that they were on their way to the tomb of the Apostles, they soon spread all over Europe, reading the Gospel to the people in the vernacular and seasoning it with commentaries displeasing to the clergy. The prelates wished to impose silence on them; but they continued to preach more than ever, and Pope Lucius III finally condemned them in 1184, including them in the same anathema as the Cathari. It is not certain that Peter Valdes was still their head at this time.

What we do know is that the greater part of his disciples, out of hatred for the teaching Church, became heretics (known as Waldenses), placing the authority of the Bible above that of the Pope, affecting to confess to virtuous laymen rather than to priests of evil life, and rejecting Purgatory, indulgences, and the veneration of the saints, on the pretext that these things were profitable to the clergy.

Many, however, submitted in an exemplary manner, some acting under the influence of the German, Bernhard Prim, and others under that of the Spaniard, Durando of Huesca. Durando's disciples took the name of "Poor Catholics," and one might almost look on them as pre-Franciscans.

In 1208, they went to Innocent III, promising him to obey their bishops and to preach only with their permission. They likewise agreed to receive the Sacraments from any priest with faculties to administer them and to stop discouraging the faithful from paying the tithes required by the Church. The Pope then permitted them to keep on with their way of life. They proposed to follow the Gospel counsels as if they were precepts, to despise gold and silver, and take no thought for the morrow. The clerks gave themselves over to study and engaged in polemics with the heretics, and the laymen did manual labor. All wore the religious habit with sandals, kept two Lents a year, and said a certain number of Paters and Aves seven times daily at the canonical hours.

As the bishops, however, continued their opposition, the "Poor Catholics" were finally obliged a few years later to become absorbed in the Augustinian Order.[9]

* * *

Let us likewise mention the "Humiliati," who took their rise in Lombardy, and in 1216 had up to a hundred and fifty communities in the Milan diocese alone. Their name came from the ash-grey habit they wore. Because they resembled the Waldenses and Cathari they were looked on at first with suspicion until Innocent III approved them in 1201.

The Humiliati were made up of three orders, one of brothers, one of sisters, and a "third order" composed of seculars. The members of the third order remained in their state of life and with their families; but professed to avoid immodesty in dress and all disputes, to assist the poor and the sick, to listen to a pious exhortation on Sunday, to fast twice a week, and to say seven Our Fathers during the day.

As for the religious, they lived in convents, dividing their time between manual labor and the chanting of the Divine Office. If the product of their labor was insufficient for their needs, they went out begging. If it was more than sufficient, they gave the surplus to the poor. As their rule did not forbid them to own property in common, they wound up in most comfortable circumstances, and even with a monopoly on the woolen industry in Lombardy.

* * *

Among the malcontents of the period, there assuredly were very holy souls who thought only to follow the example of Christ and the Apostles. There were likewise a goodly number of utopians and stiff-necked persons, who were still more insufferable than the ones over whom they set themselves as censors. Some there were who, under the cloak of reform, were literally leading the world into chaos. Such were the Cathari, called in Italy the Patarini, in France the Albigensians, in Eastern Europe Bogomiles, and in the northern countries Bulgars or Bulgarians.

Born or resurrected no one knows where, but probably imported from the Balkans, their doctrine was allied to that of the ancient gnostics. Like them, the Cathari believed in the existence of two creative principles.

One of these principles is good, and is God, Author of all good, and in particular of spiritual souls which exist since time immemorial. The other is evil, and is Satan or Jehovah, author of evil, suffering, and all material objects. Man is their common work, since he owes his soul to God and his body to Satan. And as the flesh comes from the latter, it is clear, for example, that Christ's body was only an appearance. Jesus assumed human form merely to incite us to revolt against Satan and against the Church of Rome, his representative here below, and to invite us to belong to the church of the Cathari.

This church, moreover possessed everything needful to lead man to Heaven. It had its priests or "perfect," its faithful or "believers," its liturgy, its grace, its parishes, its schools, and even a number of convents.

The "perfect" were those who had received the *consolamentum* or laying on of hands, and who, in order to keep themselves thereafter from all stain, had renounced marriage and all property, enfeebled themselves with fasting and mortification, refusing in addition to use meat, milk, butter, or cheese, claiming that the souls of sinners accomplished their time of expiation in the bodies of animals before ascending to Heaven.

It devolved on the "perfect" to administer the *consolamentum* to the "believers," and to restore to them the Comforter, the Holy Spirit, who had left them at their birth and was to take them back to Heaven after death. For greater safety, the majority of "believers" did not receive this sort of baptism until the hour of death. Meanwhile, the priests urged them frequently to formulate a desire to receive it, and to come every month to pray with them, promising them that thanks to these desires and prayers, the grace of the *consolamentum* would not be refused them.

The Cathari apostles displayed an extraordinary zeal, becoming merchants in order to frequent the fairs and preach to the people, schoolmasters for the formation of youth and, above all, doctors in order to assist the sick and dying. People admired their austerity and enjoyed their diatribes against the laxity of the clergy. The nobility in particular flattered themselves that they would inherit the riches of which they proposed to despoil the Church. Many people were overjoyed to hear them say that receiving the *consolamentum in extremis* was sufficient to save their soul; and when they denounced marriage as an invention of Satan to perpetuate suffering and the world, all those who preferred license to the duties of domesticity could not be otherwise than grateful.

Along the way, the Cathari absorbed the disciples of Arnold of Brescia, who denied the validity of sacraments administered by bad priests. Together they spread all over Italy.[10]

From Lombardy they entered the Papal States and made their way as far as Calabria. In Rome itself, in 1209, when Otto IV came to receive the imperial crown, he discovered a school where Catharism was publicly taught. Neither repressions nor excommunications succeeded in reducing these stubborn men. They triumphed at Ferrara, Verona, Rimini, and Treviso. At Piacenza they drove out the Catholic clergy and prevented their return for three years. At Viterbo, where they had many consuls, Innocent III had to tear down their houses to obtain their submission. In 1203, the city of Assisi itself had a Patarin for podestà.[11]

As for the heretics of Languedoc, it is well known only the massacres of the Albigensian War of 1209 subdued them.

*   *   *

Such was the assortment of reformers and rebels with which the Roman Curia was at grips when Francis presented himself to obtain the approval of his Rule. The time was [probably April or May, 1209].[12]

The twelve "Penitents of Assisi" set out from the Portiuncula. "Let us choose a leader whom we will obey as to the Lord," said Francis as they were leaving. "We shall take the roads he points out and lodge in the places he designates." They elected Brother Bernard, and the journey went off well.

Every night they found charitable people to give them lodging. Every day they went happily on, assured of success, for Francis had divulged a recent vision to them. He had dreamed that, coming across a great tree with an immense number of branches on his way, he had stopped to admire it. Suddenly a supernatural force had made him grow as tall as the treetop. Effortlessly, he put out his hand and bent the tree to the ground.[13] To him, this was a presage of the ease with which — by God's grace — the mighty Innocent III would let himself be swayed. And then, was not the Gospel Rule he was going to show him the charter of his alliance with the Lady Poverty? And since she was Christ's spouse, Christ's Vicar could not fail to recognize and receive her.

The reception was, at first, very chilly, if we are to believe Matthew of Paris. This contemporary chronicler relates that going into the Lateran Palace, Francis walked in unceremoniously and went up to where the Pope was. But he looked so shabby with "his poor tunic, his tangled locks, and his great black eyebrows," that Innocent III pretended to take him for a swineherd.

"Leave me alone with your rule!" said he. "Go find your pigs instead. You can preach all the sermons you want to them!"

Francis did not wait to be told twice. He dashed to a pigsty, smeared himself with dung, and reappeared before the Pope.

"My lord," he said, "now that I have done what you commanded, please be good enough to grant me my request."

The Pontiff had to admit that this petitioner did not appear to be a rebel. So, "thinking it over," writes Matthew, "he regretted having given him so ill a reception: and after sending him away to wash up, promised him another audience."[14]

Is the anecdote true? At any rate, it offers nothing improbable, either on the part of Francis, who sought out humiliation, or on the part of Innocent III, who sometimes used strong words when he was angry. Did he not write in 1205 to Tignosi, the administrator of Viterbo: "You fear neither God nor man. Wallowing in your sins like an ass in its dung, you stink so that everything around you smells, and God himself is nauseated."[15]

We shall soon see what the Pope decided to grant to the Little Poor Man, but it is fitting at first to know what this Rule was that he was asked to approve.

Very short it was, we are told, and made up of a series of Gospel texts and of some regulations needed to guide the life of the friars.[16] It is true that we no longer have it in its original form, but the scholarly reconstructions which have been made of it,[17] permit us to summarize it as follows:

Preamble. Francis and his successors promise obedience to Innocent III and to succeeding popes, and the Brethren were to obey Brother Francis and his successors.

What the Rule is. It obliges the friars to conform to the kind of life imposed by Christ on His Apostles, i.e., the integral practice of the Gospel. In this lay its great and complete novelty, for never before had a monastic rule made the Gospel taken literally the foundation of the religious state. Certain of these rules, by imposing the vow of stability on the monk and diverting him from preaching, even prevented him from leading the apostolic life.[18]

How new Brethren are to be received. All those whom God shall induce to enter the brotherhood are to be affectionately received; but they are to be admitted only after they have abandoned all their goods, and, if possible, distributed them to the poor.

The habit. They are to wear a tunic with hood, a cord and trousers. The place for men in rich clothing being, according to the Gospel, in kings' palaces, the Brethren are to wear mean clothing, which they can mend by sewing on coarse pieces, with God's blessing.

Of precedence. Our Lord having declared that it is for heads of State to act as masters and for the great to give orders, the Brethren, for their part, are not to have any authority over one another; and he among them who would be first, shall place himself in the lowest place, making himself servant of all.

Of charity and humility. Let no Brother cause pain to another. Let all avoid anger, calumny, detraction, and murmuring. Rather than dispute with any man, they will keep silent or else humbly reply, "We are useless servants." Instead of judging or condemning anyone, let them rather consider their own faults. Let them show great condescension and meekness toward all men, and let even thieves and robbers be kindly received by them. If a Brother fall ill, the others shall take care of him; and all shall show the same love and care toward one another as a mother has for her child.

Of work and poverty. If possible, the Brethren shall follow their former trade. If they are in the service of others, they shall not fill the position of treasurer or of other employments of a nature to harm their soul or scandalize their neighbor. In exchange for their labor, they shall be content with food and clothing. If necessary, they will beg alms, but they are never to receive money.[19] It also forbidden for them to have animals for hire or anything else whatever save their tools. They shall not even appropriate their hermitages for themselves, or defend them against anyone to keep them.

How they are to behave in the world. The Brethren are to carry nothing with them for the road, neither sack nor provisions. Their greatest joy shall be to mingle with victims of leprosy, beggars, and other wretches. When they enter a house, they shall say: "Peace be to this house!" and shall eat whatever is set before them.

Of preaching. The Rule inserts here the little penitential exhortation that we quoted above, and which Francis bids the Brethren to address on occasion to the people.

Orthodoxy. Let the Brethren, under pain of being expelled from the fraternity, always conduct themselves as good Catholics. Let them follow the customs and usages of the Church of Rome, and defer to the teachings of the secular and regular clergy in everything that is not contrary to their Rule; and if they go to confession, let it be to whatever priest is approved by the Church.[20]

* * *

The reader, like the Roman Curia of the time, will not fail to note the analogies offered by this Rule with the program of the Reformers of the period. Are these chance resemblances, the result of inevitable influences, or genuine borrowings? We should like to discuss this question if only the necessary documents were not entirely lacking. All that we could do, then, would be to build up vain hypotheses. So, as things stand now, the problem cannot be solved.

Certainly, it is unlikely that Francis would not have heard of Joachim of Fiore and of Peter Valdes, since everybody was talking about them;[21] or that he never came across any Cathari, since these were everywhere, even in Assisi and Spoleto. But the fact is that he never mentioned the names of these people, and that unlike the "Poor Catholics," the Cistercians, and St. Dominic, he never disputed with heretics.

He evidently knew of the way of life and evangelical tendencies of the former, and he was not ignorant of the ranting and ravings of the others, but was he influenced by them?

All that we are able to say is that Francis declared that the Lord alone had shown him what he must do, that his Rule resolved in an orthodox manner those difficulties to which his contemporaries often presented heretical solutions, and that he himself seemed to take from the reformers of the time whatever they had that was good, conducting himself as if he wished to render them all useless and harmless.[22]

Meanwhile, as we have said, he was obliged to enter into contact with the Roman Curia and obtain the approval of Innocent III.

* * *

Again, it was the Bishop of Assisi who came to his assistance. It so happened that the bishop was in Rome. Surprised at meeting some of his flock there, he anxiously asked himself if the Brothers had left his diocese for good. They reassured him and informed him of the purpose of their journey. Guido presented them to his friend, Cardinal John of St. Paul, who offered them hospitality.[23]

This prelate was a man of God whose piety was outstanding even among the most virtuous members of the Sacred College. It was he who had been charged the previous year with preparing the case against the Waldensians. The bishop vouched for the Penitents of Assisi as having only deference for the clergy, and the cardinal himself was able to appreciate the fervor and humility of his guests. He nonetheless sought to dissuade Francis from founding anything new and counselled him instead to enter one of the old Orders with his followers.

Such a solution was prudent and shrewd, but Francis remained unconvinced. He defended his Rule so persuasively that he brought the cardinal over to his way of thinking. John of St. Paul spoke about the matter to the Pope, and the young founder had an audience at which he could put forward his plans.[24]

Now the prodigious sagacity of Innocent III has never been called in question; but his detractors have claimed that, absorbed in his great temporal plans, he was somewhat lacking in a Christian outlook. Thus St. Ludgard (1182-1246) is said to have seen him condemned to Purgatory until the Last Judgment.[25] But the holiest of women are not infallible. The fact is that the conduct of Innocent III was always exemplary; the reform of the Church was the thing he had most at heart; and on this occasion he conducted himself with wholly supernatural wisdom.

The cardinals cried out in protest when they heard Francis explain his program. No doubt they wondered if he were not some new "poor man" from Lyons or elsewhere, come to have some supposedly evangelical rule approved, so he could go out and stir up the people against the prelates. Besides, it seemed impossible to them for a religious institute to subsist without property or revenues.

Thus all were of the opinion that so literal an interpretation of the Gospel went beyond human strength, and the Pope himself declared, "Although your zeal, my dear sons, reassures Us, We must nevertheless think of your successors, who may find the path you wish to follow too austere."

But the Cardinal of St. Paul replied, "If we reject this poor man's request on such a pretext, would not this be to declare that the Gospel cannot be practiced, and so to blaspheme Christ, its Author?"

These words made so strong an impression that Innocent said to Francis, "My son, pray God to manifest His will to Us. When We know it, We shall be able to give you an answer with perfect surety."[26]

This second interview with the Pope already was a great step forward over the first one — if there was a first one.

The third was a complete success. For this Francis prepared himself by beseeching God to touch the heart of the Pope. Thereupon, Christ (so say the biographers) sent a dream to his earthly Vicar and inspired the Saint with a parable. It was this parable that Francis recounted to the Holy Father when, a few days later, he reappeared in his presence.

"Your Holiness," he began, "once upon a time in the wilderness, there was a very poor, but very beautiful woman, whom the king had loved, and who had had many sons by him. When these sons had grown up, their mother said this to them: 'My sons, do not be ashamed to be poor, for you are the king's sons. And addressing the eldest sons, she said, 'Go to your father, who will not fail to recognize you and take care of you.'

"As soon as they arrived at the court, the king, struck by their handsome appearance, discovered that they resembled him. 'Who is your mother?' he asked. They replied that she was a poor woman living in the wilderness. Filled with joy, the king pressed them to his heart.

"'Do not be afraid,' he said, 'for I am your father. And if I receive so many strangers at my table, how much more reason have I not to admit my sons!' And he asked the mother to send him his other sons also, so that he could lodge them all in his palace."

"Your Holiness," continued Francis, "the wilderness is this world, barren of virtue. This poor woman whom the king made fruitful is I, to whom Christ has given sons who strive to reproduce the features of their father by imitating his poverty. Finally, the sons who sit at the king's table are my brothers, whom the Lord will never leave in need, He who so bounteously feeds all His creatures, even sinners."[27]

If he had any of the poet about him, Innocent must have been won over by this troubadour in tatters who sang with such gusto the joy of being poor. At any rate, he realized that this reformer was not dangerous. He was no Cathar cursing a wicked god for having inflicted life on him, nor some other zealot drawing from his gloomy virtues the right to demand perfection of all men and to hurl invectives at the whole world. This was a humble child of God who condemned neither clerics nor laymen, and whose sole ambition was to share his inner joy with those who wished to possess it.

The great statesman likewise realized the assistance that Francis could bring to the Church. He was reminded of a dream he had had a few nights previously. He had seen, writes Thomas of Celano, the Lateran basilica — head and mother of all churches — leaning to one side, ready to topple over. Suddenly, a little religious ran up, who with a simple push of his shoulders raised it and straightened it once more. The Pope now recognized the providential man of his dream in this hum-

ble suitor who simply sought, without wishing to disturb anyone, permission to live according to the Gospel.[28]

He verbally approved the Rule, and, after numerous com-
mendations, charged Francis with the direction of the brotherhood. The brethren made a vow of obedience to Francis, who,
in turn, promised to obey the Pope. Those among them who
were still laymen received the small tonsure; and all were given
the right to "preach penitence," i.e. to address moral exhortations to the people. It is thought that it was then that Francis was ordained a deacon.[29]

So the Franciscan Order was attached to the Church of
Rome. She did not give it a definite approval, but she did give
it a chance to win its spurs. "Go, brethren," said the Pope,
dismissing the twelve Penitents, "and may the Lord be with
you! If it please Him to increase you, come and tell me about
it. And I shall see then about granting you more numerous
favors and entrusting you with a more important mission."[30]

The mission that the Pope had in mind was probably that
of preaching the crusade against the Saracens or the heretics,
as others already were doing. As for the "favors" he held out,
they would consist of a Bull giving the Rule its official consecration.

Being no stickler for formalities, Francis felt no regret at leaving without anything in writing. The Pope's word was enough
for him. His dearest wish having been fulfilled, he thanked
God, prayed before the tomb of the Apostles, then left the
city with his companions.[31]

* * *

Along a dusty and monotonous road, the little group went
up the Tiber to Orte. There they entered the wooded ravine
along which coursed the turbulent waters of the Nera.

The Brothers interrupted their journey, writes Thomas of Celano, to stop not far from Orte in a complete wilderness.[32] There they spent two weeks with Holy Poverty, tasting such delights that they resolved never more to leave her chaste embrace. Their destitution was total, and no man came to interrupt their prayer. While part of them went into town to beg from door to door, the rest prayed and waited for them. Then all ate together the collected food, thanking God for treating them so well. If there was anything left over and no one was found to give it to, it was put away in an old Lombard tomb for the next day. The friars came to prize this solitude so much that they feared lest they become too attached to it, and so miss their vocation.

For some of them were strongly attracted to the solitary life and did not want to go back among men. But Francis reminded them that in imitation of Christ, they were to win souls for God. And he set off with them on the road to Assisi.[33]

- 6 -

Rivo Torto

On their return, the Brothers settled in a place called Rivo-Torto.[1] The "crooked stream" from which this spot derived its name has disappeared; and topographers argue as to whether Rivo Torto was located near the old Santa Maria Maddalena leprosarium about 1500 yards from the Portiuncula, or if it occupied the site of the present church of Rigobello, a mile farther on, in the direction of Foligno.[2]

It would seem that the Brothers passed the autumn and winter there. They made good use of an abandoned hut which could serve as a shelter when it rained. It was hardly big enough to hold them all; but Francis used to say that a man gets to Heaven more quickly from a hovel than from a palace. He wrote their names with chalk on the beams so that when they wished to pray or rest, each might find his place without letting their being cramped disturb their quiet peace of mind.[3]

* * *

Rivo Torto is the brief and wonderful springtime in which the fairest Franciscan virtues flourished — those virtues which God's troubadour praised in the following Salutation:

117

"Hail, O Wisdom, Queen! May the Lord keep you, and your sister, pure and holy Simplicity!

"Hail, O holy lady Poverty! May the Lord keep you, and your sister, holy Humility!

"Hail, O holy lady Charity! May the Lord keep you, and your sister, holy Obedience!

"For it is from the Lord, most holy virtues, that you proceed. And there is not one among you that one may practice without being dead to self; and whoever possesses one of you, possesses all; and who offends one of you offends all."

Francis shows next how holy Patience foils the wiles of the Devil, how holy and pure Simplicity confounds the wisdom of the world and of the flesh, and, how finally, holy Obedience disposes the body to obey the spirit and men to obey their neighbor.

"And it is not just men," he adds, "that the true Christian obeys, but also animals, so that even fierce beasts may do with him whatever God wills."[4]

* * *

Of all these virtues, poverty is the one that was to impart its originality to the Franciscan Order and constitute its "true foundation."[5]

Voluntarily poor one may be from philosophy or asceticism, for reasons of zeal, of charity, or others still.[6] But Francis was poor from love. He made himself poor because his beloved Christ had been poor. He espoused Poverty because she had been "the inseparable companion of the Most High Son of God," and because for twelve centuries she has wandered about forsaken.[7]

In truth, it was a wonderful union. Never was a loved woman the object of a more chivalrous and loyal cult, of more impassioned and more charming homage.

It is to the *Sacrum Commercium* rather than to the biographers that we shall go for the story of the espousals of the Little Poor Man. No document so well expresses his sentiment or better reproduces the way in which he spoke of the chosen lady of his heart.[8]

This little song of chivalry opens with the questing of God's servant: "I pray you, point out to me," he said to two old men encountered in the country, "the dwelling place of Lady Poverty, for I faint with love for her."

The old men disclose to him the place of her abode, but they add, "A man must be naked and free of every burden if he would attain the mountain top where she has taken refuge. Take also with you companions who will help you in your painful ascent. But woe to him who is alone, for if he chances to fall, he has none to aid him."

Francis then chooses a few faithful friends, and with them, presents himself to the forlorn princess:

"We come to you, O Lady, because we know that you are the Queen of the virtues; and prostrate at your feet, we beseech you to join with us and become our way leading to the King of Glory, as you were the way for Him when He came to help those sitting in the shadow of death.

"For, leaving His royal abode, the Son of the Most High sought you whom all men flee. Enamoured of your beauty, it was you alone whom He desired to wed on earth. You had prepared for Him a fitting throne within a most poor Virgin; from which throne He came forth to manifest Himself to the world. It was you again who provided Him an abode in that miserable stable when at His birth there was no place for Him in the inn. There, you became, His whole life long, His inseparable companion. For the foxes have holes and the birds of the air their nests, but He had no place to lay His head. Again, when He who had once opened the lips of the prophets opened His own mouth, it was to praise you, saying:

"Blessed are the poor in spirit for theirs is the Kingdom of Heaven.' And it was for love of you that instead of rich merchants He chose poor fishermen as ministers and witnesses of His preaching.

"And you, most faithful spouse and sweet lover, never left Him for an instant, and were never closer than when you saw Him despised by all men. Had you not been with Him, He would never indeed have been so contemned by all. You were at His side when He was outraged by the Jews, insulted by the Pharisees, derided by the princes of the priests. You were with Him at the buffeting, the spitting, and the scourging; and when He came to die — naked, arms outstretched, feet and hands pierced — you were His only companion and went up with Him on the Cross. At last, before He returned to Heaven, He left you the sign of the Kingdom of God with which to mark the elect; so that whoever seeks after the kingdom everlasting must needs come to you.

"O Queen, have pity on us! Mark us with the sign of your favor! For love of Him who loved you so much, despise not our prayers, but deliver us from every danger, O Virgin filled with glory and with blessing."

At these words, the Lady Poverty thrilled with happiness, and in a voice filled with sweetness, bade her visitors to listen to her long tale.

How many vicissitudes in her life, from the Garden of Eden where she kept Adam company as long as he stayed naked, and whom she left when she saw him prefer the pursuit of earthly goods to the service of God! "As Abraham, Isaac, and the other patriarchs likewise loved riches, I wandered on earth for centuries, sad and solitary, until that day when the Son of God came to fulfill those things which you have brought to mind."

Here Poverty quotes the "covenant" and "immutable decree" which Christ left His disciples before he ascended again into Heaven: "Take nothing with you, neither gold nor silver. ... Do not resist those who would take away your goods ... Do not be anxious about tomorrow." She celebrates the heroism of the first faithful, "who sold their goods, had all things in common and lived in perfect equality." Then she adds something of her later history:

"So long as the blood of the Crucified Poor Man was fresh in their memory, and the chalice of His Passion inebriated their heart, Christians practiced poverty. But then came peace, which for me was worse than war and renewed my sufferings. Once more all forsook me, including those so-called religious who had promised me to be faithful. How many there are among them who, in the world, lived poor, hungry, and lean, lacking even lowly bread, and lodging 'neath the sweet-briar, and who, once united to me, have grown fat in their cloisters, have sought to appear great in men's eyes, and have come and spat in my face."[9]

These complaints bring tears to the eyes of Francis and his followers, who swear eternal fidelity to the forlorn and lovely lady. She consents to follow them to their hermitage.

"Let me first visit," she says upon arrival, "your cloister, your refectory, your kitchen, your dormitory, your stables, your fine furniture and magnificent establishment; for thus far I have seen only your radiant and friendly faces."

"Dear Lady and Queen," they replied, "your servants are weary from our journey, and you too must be tired. So with your kind permission, we shall begin to dine. When we shall have recovered somewhat, we shall carry out your wishes."

"Gladly, but I must first wash my hands."

They went and fetched — for want of better — a chipped earthen pot, filled with water. She asked for a towel, but when they did not find any, one of the friars offered his tunic instead.

They then led the princess to the table, i.e., before a few

pieces of barley bread spread out on the grass. Everyone sat down on the ground; and after giving thanks to God, the Lady Poverty pretended to wait for cooked food to be served up on plates. But only a bowl of fresh water was brought in, in which everyone dipped his crust.

"Don't you have some fresh vegetables to top off our menu?" she inquired. The Brothers excused themselves for having neither a gardener nor a garden and they went off to gather some wild fruits and herbs in the forest.

"Don't you have at least a little salt to season these bitter herbs?"

"Lady," they replied, "we should have to go to the city to get some."

"Then salt is not necessary. Please pass me a knife to cut this bread with, for it is really quite dry."

"Alas, dear Lady, we have no maker of knives at hand. Meanwhile, we pray you to use your teeth."

"Will you not let me taste of your wine?" she asked.

"O Queen! We never use it, and it seems to us that Christ's spouse as well ought to shun wine like poison."

After they were thus satisfied, all rose, and joyously intoned their thanks anew. As the Lady Poverty expressed the desire to rest a few moments, they showed her the bare ground. And when she asked for a pillow, they slipped a stone under her head, then withdrew so she could sleep. When she awoke, the fancy took her to visit their cloister. So they led her up a hill, and pointing to the horizon with a sweeping gesture, as if the whole world were theirs: "There, Lady, is our cloister!"

The fair visitor declared herself perfectly satisfied. "Truly, today I believed myself in Paradise," she said. And after another long discourse, she took leave of them.

*   *   *

As will have been seen, holy poverty made harsh demands and life was hard at Rivo Torto. We must believe that the farmers and leprosy patients among whom the first Franciscans labored were either poor or stingy; for the Brothers often had nothing to eat except scraps begged from door to door. It even happened that for lack of bread they had to eat turnips left in the fields.[10]

They would have overdone their penances if their Father had permitted them. One night the sleepers in the hut were awakened by groans.

"I'm dying! I'm dying!" moaned a voice.

"Get up, brothers! And make a light!" ordered Francis. He asked who was dying.

"Me!" said the voice.

"What are you dying of, Brother?"

"Of hunger!"

At once, the saint had the table set, and so that the "dying one" should not feel ashamed at eating alone, they all ate with him willingly.[11]

Francis profited by this opportunity to enjoin upon them less severe fasting, urging them not to try to imitate him in this.

"For," he explained, "I who am at the head of the brotherhood have duties that the rest do not have. And besides I am so made that I need only a little coarse food to live."

Francis was also accustomed to sprinkle his food with ashes or cold water. This especially distressed Brother Buonaparte, the convent cook.

"Why shouldn't I feel sad," he complained one day to the Saint, "when I see you spoil my dishes I have so carefully prepared, hoping they would do you good!"

"Brother Buonaparte," replied Francis. "Since we both have good intentions, I, in acting the way I do, and you in cooking as well as you can, God will surely not fail to reward us."[12]

But the indiscreet zeal of his sons compelled him many times to come back to this subject. He made it a rule for them not to chastize their bodies except when the body persisted in its laziness and negligence. "In this case," he said, "like well-fed donkeys who refuse to bear their burdens, it must be made to feel the stick."[13]

Unlike the Cathari who received the *consolamentum* and then starved themselves to death to keep from sinning any more, Francis held life to be a gift from God. "In sickness as in health," he declared, "a religious ought humbly to ask for what he needs. If his request is not granted, let him then patiently bear his infirmities for the love of God. This will be his way of winning a martyr's crown."[14]

But the youthful founder was so solicitous of his children's welfare that they all considered him as their "beloved mother" — *mater carissima*.[15] One day Brother Sylvester looked very ill; but no one — so great was the general austerity — noticed it. Francis saw him and said to himself: "I think that some grapes eaten on an empty stomach would do him a great deal of good." And the next morning, rising before dawn, he awakened Sylvester; and while the rest were still asleep, they went to breakfast on fresh grapes in a nearby vineyard.[16]

Another time, it was Brother Leo who felt ill along the way. As a vineyard was close at hand, Francis went and gathered a few clusters of grapes, which quickly restored his friend. But the owner came out from the hedge and began to beat the thief with a stick. As usual, the Saint thanked God. However, during the rest of the trip, he would sometimes turn toward his companion and hum the following refrain:

> *Frater Leo est bene refectus,*
> *Sed Frater Franciscus est bene percussus;*
> *Frater Leo bene comedit,*
> *Sed Frater Franciscus suo corpore bene solvit.*

Brother Leo had grapes to eat,
But Brother Francis he was beat;
Brother Leo had a choice tidbit,
But Brother Francis smarted for it![17]

The Saint was always preaching to his disciples of the good to be drawn from those mortifications that are profitable to the soul without harm to the body. Thus he urged them not to bother about political or scientific news which turns the mind away from more useful preoccupations. When on [going to Rome where he was to be crowned], the German Emperor Otto IV passed by Rivo Torto in September, 1209, the Saint shut himself in the hut, enjoining his companions to do likewise. One of them was assigned to place himself in the path of the procession, to remind the new emperor that all earthly glory is fleeting and that his own would not last long. This was a prophecy whose fulfillment was hastened as we know by Innocent II. [In January, 1210, he denounced and the following year] excommunicated Otto IV, substituting the young Frederick II, his protégé, as head of the Empire.[18]

*   *   *

Among the virtues forming the train of Holy Poverty, the *Salutation* particularly mentions humility, patience, and simplicity.

"Oh holy Lady Poverty!" sang Francis. "May God keep you, with your sister, holy Humility."[19]

He who was proud by nature and had once made so many ambitious plans, now deemed himself the meanest of men and aspired to nothing more than to be treated as such. "I am the greatest of sinners," he told Brother Pacifico, who asked him what he thought of himself, adding that if God had granted the same graces to the lowest criminal, he would have profited by it ten times more.[20]

To be sure, many servants of God have talked like this, but Francis really wished to be taken at his word. He was seldom happier than the day when the Bishop of Terni, to congratulate him for his apostolate in the city, publicly declared that once more God had drawn good out of evil, by bringing forth fruits of salvation by so poor and miserable a man, who besides was not uneducated. Delighted to hear things so well put, Francis rushed to the prelate's knees: "How wisely Your Excellency has spoken!" he exclaimed. "You, at least, have given God His due, while leaving me what belongs to me, and of which others unjustly desire to despoil me."[21]

The name which Francis gave to his friars indicated the rank to which he destined them in the world and in the Church. It was the very lowest. In his eyes, their humility ought to equal their poverty. He wanted them to share Christ's humiliations as well as His destitution. "What is the use," he would say to them, "of renouncing the riches of earth, if you intend to keep those of self-love?"

The idea of naming them Friars Minor came to him one day when someone read in his presence the passage of the Rule in which it is said that "the brethren ought to become very little, *minores*, and hold themselves to be inferior to all." Interrupting the reading, he declared that this was the very vocation of his followers and that from then on this is what they would be called. And they well deserved their name, says Thomas of Celano, speaking of the first friars, "for they were truly very little people, humbling themselves before all, and seizing every opportunity for self-abasement and for receiving insults."[22]

If such occasions were lacking, they tried to make them, as did Brother Juniper who went walking in Assisi half naked, his clothes rolled in a bundle on his head.[23] To be sure, such "follies" did not last; but they were so much to St.

Francis' taste that he would have liked to have had many Brother Junipers in his Order.[24]

* * *

Soon holy patience, as Francis understood it, likewise appeared to be beyond human strength.

It was the Savior, immolated like an obedient Lamb, who was his model; and it was in the Gospel that he had found the formula: "Blessed are you when men shall reproach you and persecute you. . . . I say to you not to resist the evildoer. If someone strikes you on the right cheek, turn to him the other also. If anyone would take your tunic, let him take your cloak as well."[25]

Giving what you have to someone who wants it, looking on persecutions as blessings, and with no escape from them by recourse to the protection of Rome and ecclesiastical privileges — such was the Little Poor Man's norm of conduct. This it was likewise that he attempted to impose on his whole Order, though in such an undertaking he certainly could not succeed. But Bernard, Giles, Juniper, and a number of others (as we shall see), nevertheless continued to practice "holy patience" according to their Father's intention and the letter of the Gospel. "They sought," says Celano, "those places where their reputation for holiness had not yet penetrated, where they hoped to receive much ill-treatment. And how many times did they see themselves insulted, despoiled, scourged, and cast into prison! But, far from defending themselves, they endured it all, thanking God and blessing their tormentors."[26]

* * *

The first Franciscans likewise practiced "pure and holy simplicity," which imparts such charm to everything about the Poverello and his companions.

The simple man is he who never dreams of deceiving and

who has no fear of being deceived. "I would be a hypocrite," said Francis, "if I did not always act as if I were being watched by the whole world." Fearing to pass for an ascetic, he never failed, when he had been received in a well-to-do home, to enumerate when he left all the dainties he had been served.[27] It was this same scruple about sincerity which led him to accuse himself before his hearers in Poggio Bustone of having used lard in Lent, failing to add that his weak stomach refused everything cooked in oil. Along about this time, his superior made him wear a fox skin over his chest. So he sewed a second skin outside his tunic, so that no one would fail to know how he "pampered" himself.[28]

Himself the soul of honor, Francis was suspicious of none. No man ever honored his fellow-man more, trusted men more, nor believed more fully in the given word. "So you are going away thus, you simple man, without anything in writing?" "Do I not have your word, Holy Father?" he replied to Honorius III, who had verbally granted him the Portiuncula Indulgence.[29]

This same childlike candor was to be found among the Franciscans of Rivo Torto. No more could they — so great was their purity of soul — believe in man's malice. They had a licentious priest for confessor, writes Thomas of Celano. But there was no use pointing out his infamy. They did not want to hear anything about it, and continued to address themselves to him more respectfully than before. But when the priest told one of them to beware of hypocrisy, the latter was so distressed that he could not sleep. The others tried in vain to reassure him. "A priest cannot lie," he kept repeating, "so I must be just a hypocrite." And it took Francis to restore his peace of mind.[30]

*   *   *

You recall how the *Sacrum Commercium* disavowed the kind of servants of God who, after promising poverty, lived slothfully within their comfortable monasteries.

But the new "poor men" of Rivo Torto observed the great and holy law of labor. All of them devoted themselves to some form of manual labor.[31] An idler, whom Friar Thomas assures us ate enough for four men, did attempt to sneak into their little band, but he did not stay long. When Francis saw that this big eater refused to go begging, he told him, "Go your way, brother drone! You are good only at eating the honey gathered by the busy bees."

And the parasitic drone left the Order.[32]

We know that Francis himself sometimes hired himself out as a day laborer. Since time immemorial, the people of the valley of Rieti boast that he kept goats in their district.[33] Perhaps he also did carpentry and made household utensils. For St. Bonaventure tells us about the wooden bowl he was working at from the beginning of Lent, and how thinking of it distracted him while he was saying Tierce. Although he had put his heart into this task, he did not hesitate to sacrifice it, and threw the vase in the fire to atone for his distraction.[34]

The favorite occupation of the first friars, however, was the care of victims of leprosy. "All, whether commoners or nobles, had been told by Francis on their entry into the Order that they would have to work in the lazarets."[35] For no unfortunates on earth were dearer to him. He called them his "Christian brothers," to show that he treated them as equals and as honorable members of the family of Christ.

Francis punished himself once for having humiliated a patient who was particularly repulsive. It was Brother James the Simple who had again brought the man among the friars. "Didn't I tell you," observed Francis, "that it wouldn't do to bring our Christian brothers here?" Scarcely had Francis uttered these words, when fearing to have offended the sick man, he went to the guardian, Peter Catanii. "Give me a stiff penance," he said, "for the fault I have committed."

"Choose your own penance," was Peter's reply.

When mealtime came round, Francis made his "Christian brother" sit down in the place of honor, while he himself drank from the cup which the afflicted man had touched with his suppurating lips and ate from the bowl in which he had dipped his fingers eaten away by ulcers.[36]

The *Fioretti* likewise mentions a certain Brother Bentivoglio who, not to be separated from his patient, put him on his back, and walked at night thus burdened fifteen miles on foot.[37]

The same collection tells the story of a patient believed to be possessed by the Devil because of the way he insulted and beat his nurses. To add to this, he cursed dreadfully all the time. The brothers rejoiced to be treated in this way, but finally wound up wondering if it was right for them to take care of such a blasphemer. So they came to consult Francis, who went with them to the lazaret.

"May God give you peace, dear brother!" said he by way of greeting.

"There is no peace for me," replied the sick man, "since I am nothing more than a mass of suffering and rotting flesh."

The Saint explained to him that we can turn bodily evils to the saving of our soul by bearing them with resignation.

"How can I stand pain," retorted the despairing man, "that never stops day or night? And that isn't all! For not one of the friars you sent me is any good."

"Well, then! I'll take care of you myself," said Francis.

"All right. But what can you do better than they?

"I'll do whatever you want me to do."

"Then begin by bathing me, for I smell so, I can't stand myself."

Francis put some water on to heat in which he had steeped some fragrant herbs. Then undressing the patient, he began to rub him gently while a Brother poured the perfumed water over his body. Now as the water poured over him, not only did the leprosy disappear, but the man's soul was restored to health. This fellow who always went to extremes began to weep so hard, imploring forgiveness for having blasphemed God and beaten the Brothers, that for a fortnight the whole neighborhood rang with his acts of contrition.

But the improvement did not last; and the sick man having received the Last Sacraments, died a holy death, and afterward appeared to St. Francis to announce that he had been saved.[38]

* * *

Should we be surprised to learn that happiness reigned among the denizens of Rivo Torto? No longer tormented by vain wishes and desires, and enjoying a pure conscience, these Poor Men "lived perfectly happy, and none of them would have dreamed of complaining," writes Thomas of Celano.[39] For did not their Rule say, "Wherever they may be, let the brethren refrain from murmuring. Let them not appear sad and gloomy like hypocrites; but let them show themselves joyous in the Lord, pleasant and cheerful, as is fitting."?[40]

Pleasant and habitually cheerful, Francis certainly was by nature; and so he always remained, despite the troubles and disappointments he was to encounter. Conforming to the knightly code which insisted on gaiety, [later on Mount La Verna] "this brave knight of Christ thrilled with joy at the thought of being able to partake of his Master's Passion.[41]

Faithful to the Gospel, which bids the persecuted man to rejoice in the midst of trial, he sang when at the beginning of his conversion the robbers dumped him into a snow-filled ditch.[42] He sang all his life, declares the *Speculum*, as if his chief concern were to cultivate happiness within and scatter it around him.[43] And when, in his last months of life, he felt himself growing blind, it was again with transports of joy that he welcomed this final trial.[44]

"O sublime martyr!" exclaims Thomas, "How could you do it, when others found the mere sight of your sufferings a thing almost unbearable?"[45]

This spiritual gladness which feeds on self-denial and voluntarily ignores disappointments, this joyous knightly enthusiasm whose happiness it is to serve the best and most powerful of Kings — nothing pleased the Little Poor Man more than to see his friars acting in this way. A Brother came back from begging with a song on his lips. Francis ran to meet him, took his sack, kissed him on the shoulder, then grasping his hand, cried, "Blessed be that brother who goes forth to beg without being urged and comes back home in such good spirits!"[46]

"Since they are God's troubadours and minstrels," he continued, "is not the role of the Friars Minor to comfort their neighbor and move him to spiritual gladness?"[47]

Francis said that "spiritual joy is as necessary to the soul as blood is to the body."[48] A gloomy man for him was hardly a citizen of the city of God. Melancholy he dubbed "the Babylonian evil, which plays the devil's game, and renders us vulnerable to his shafts. But for the servant of God who strives to live in joy, the devil's pains go for naught; and he leaves him, finding no entrance to his soul."[49]

This was one of the reasons why he turned his followers away from exaggerated corporal austerities. "Our brother the body," he said to the Penitents of Rivo Torto, "needs a certain ration of food and sleep. If you refuse him this, he will also refuse to serve you, and discouraged, reply, 'How can you expect me to give myself up to vigils, prayer, and good works, when because of you, I am too weak even to stand?' "[50]

So the Saint did not want to see long faces. Taking a leaf from St. James, he said that a man must pray when he is sad, and then make haste to become happy again. One day he sent a glum-faced Brother back to his cell. "If it is your sins that are troubling you," he told him, "that is something between God and you. Go then and ask His forgiveness, and then come back to us with a smiling face."[51] The case of this gloomy friar was an exception.

The ideal Franciscan is "Brother Juniper, *egregius Dei joculator*, that excellent *jongleur* of God who always had words burning with divine love on his lips."[52] The ideal again is the austere and silent Brother Giles who, we are assured, was always cheerful. When spiritual joy flooded his soul, he would even pick up blades of grass and stones and kiss them. He likewise loved music, and following the example of his blessed Father, he would accompany himself — for want of a viol — on two pieces of wood which he rubbed together. To those who expressed astonishment at this, he exclaimed, "Tongue cannot say, nor writing express, nor the heart of man conceive the happiness that God reserves for his friends."[53]

So they were happy men, those first disciples of St. Francis; and that is why the *Fioretti*, which recounts their life, is such a joyous book. It may even be that it is the only masterpiece of world literature devoid of all bitterness, in which man truly appears to have found happiness.

*   *   *

As soon as he had returned from Rome, Francis resumed his apostolic activity. Every Saturday night, he walked to Assisi, spent the night in a hut in the Canons' garden, and preached Sunday morning in the Cathedral of San Rufino.[54] As was his custom, he began by wishing peace to his hearers; and often he preached on the union of hearts and the pardon of offenses.

The topic was timely, for more than ever, Assisians were at one another's throats and at sword's point with their neighbors.

It will be recalled how the lords of Assisi, threatened in their privileges, had sought help from Perugia; and that after the battle at St. John's Bridge in which Francis had been taken prisoner, they had refused every attempt at reconciliation. Thereupon the Emperor, to keep it on his side, had granted autonomy to the commune of Assisi; and Innocent III, whose vassal Perugia was, had laid its rival under interdict and excommunicated its podestà. But strong in the support of the Emperor and loyal to their first magistrate, the citizens of Assisi had only become more adamant toward the exiles and the Perugians. Hostilities had then broken out again, fiercer than before, resulting in general misery in the region. The conflict had gone on for a decade.[55]

On November 9, 1210, the nobles and citizens of Assisi signed a treaty which, in part, read as follows:

"In the name of God and with the grace of the Holy Spirit, in honor of our Lord Jesus Christ, of the Virgin Mary, of the Emperor Otto and of Duke Leopold, the *majores* and *minores* of Assisi pledge themselves by these presents never (except for a previous agreement) to contract any alliance with the Pope, the Emperor, or anyone whatever, and to agree to act together in the future for the best interests of the commune."

In other clauses, the nobles renounced their feudal rights in return for a quit rent; the inhabitants of surrounding villages were added to the citizenry; the tax rate was fixed; and from that time onward everyone could go peacefully about his business. Nothing, however, was done for the serfs. Still, the effect of this treaty was to bring back the exiles, and so [internal] peace was restored to the city.

[Modern biographers have attributed to St. Francis a major pacifying role in this event. However, Arnaldo Fortini, the leading authority on the history of Assisi, insists that the pact of 1210 was merely a political truce between the upper and middle classes aimed solely at pursuing the war against Perugia still more effectively; consequently he denies the Saint's influence on the pact.][56]

* * *

The sojourn at Rivo Torto ended on a singular note. One day the friars were assembled for prayer, when a peasant strolled up to the hut with his donkey.

"In with you! In with you!" he yelled, pushing the donkey ahead of him. "You can see that we couldn't find a better place anywhere than this!"

The peasant made a feint of talking to his beast, but it was plain that his words were directed to the occupants of the shelter. Francis was distressed at such rude behavior and especially deplored the troubling of the community's prayer. But it never occurred to him to resist. He limited himself to remarking, "Truly, brethren, our God-given vocation is not to play the host to donkeys, but to pray and to teach men the way of salvation!" And he left the hut with his companions.[57]

- 7 -

The Portiuncula and the
Life of the First Friars

Driven away from Rivo Torto, the friars had to start looking for other quarters. "Dear children," said Francis to them, "since God seems to want to increase our numbers, we must find a little church to say the Office in and bury our dead, and a little house of earth and wattles for us to be together in. So, if it seems good to you, I will go see the bishop about it."

All approved, and Francis set off for the bishop's palace.

Bishop Guido replied that, unfortunately, he had nothing he could give him. The Canons of San Rufino gave the same answer, adding that the best thing for the friars to do was to keep on working in the lazarets, where they were short of nurses. It was the Benedictine Abbot of Mount Subasio who met the desire of the Little Poor Man by giving him the Portiuncula chapel and the plot of earth around it. Francis would not consent to take it as a gift; and to make it clear that it was a loan, every year by way of rent, the friars brought the monks a hamper of loaches that they had caught in the stream.[1]

At the Portiuncula, Francis believed he would really be

able to carry out his dream of living the Gospel.[2] Located in the midst of a wood, the hermitage was made up of the chapel of Our Lady of the Angels, a large thatch-covered cabin which served as the community house, and as many huts as there were religious. The large cabin was of puddled clay; the huts were made of wattles; and the whole was surrounded by a hedge. And that is the way the Saint would have liked to see all his residences. Even the churches he always wanted to have "small and built of earth or wood."[3]

As for the kind of life first lived in the brotherhood, whether at the Portiuncula or elsewhere, it can quite well be depicted by sketching the portraits of Brothers Bernard, Rufino, Giles, Masseo, Juniper, and Leo. To speak of these first disciples, who all received their formation from Francis and tried to conform their lives to his example, is to demonstrate what Francis' ideal was, and at the same time evoke the golden age of the Franciscan epic.

We have told of the vocations of Bernard and Giles. The others entered the Order in 1210.[4] All merited to be set up as models for all the Brethren. "The good Friar Minor," said Francis, "ought to love poverty like Brother Bernard and prayer like Brother Rufino, who prays even when he is asleep. He ought to be lost in God as Brother Giles, as courteous as Brother Angelo, and as patient as Brother Juniper, that perfect imitator of Christ crucified. He ought to possess the purity and innocence of Brother Leo, the good manners and common sense of Brother Masseo, and finally, by his charity and detachment from the world, resemble Brother Lucido who never stays more than a month in the same place, asserting that we have no lasting home on earth."[5]

* * *

The superior of the brotherhood was, of course, Francis. "His orders were not disputed," wrote Thomas of Celano.

"Scarcely had he expressed them, when all rushed to carry them out."[6] But Francis did not spend all his time giving orders. He delegated a part of his authority to a friar who bore the name of "mother," and, like a mother, looked out for the community's needs. The "mother" played the role of Martha and led the active life. Thus the others could, like Mary, give themselves to the contemplative life. From time to time — to reverse the roles and even things up — the "children" became "mothers," and the latter became "children."

This arrangement was kept up for a time in the hermitages, where the number of religious was limited to three or four.[7] But the "mothers" were soon replaced by the "guardians" or local superiors. Their name [perhaps] came from the fact that they "guarded" the door and watched over their brethren.

* * *

The *Fioretti* shows us two guardians, Brother Masseo and Brother Angelo, exercising their charge. A handsomer man or one with a more pleasing personality could nowhere be found than Brother Masseo da Marignano, who, it seems, always brought back the best morsels from the begging tours. Thus he sometimes needed to be humiliated. One day Francis made him whirl around with arms flung wide, until he became dizzy and fell full length on the ground.

Another time he said to him before the assembled community: "Brother Masseo, if the brothers here possess the grace of prayer, you have received the gift of eloquence and know how to talk to people. So to let us practice contemplation, you are to have charge of the door, give out alms and do the cooking. While we eat inside, you will eat outside; and if visitors come, you will be there to say some good words to them without our having to be disturbed."

Brother Masseo bowed his head and drew back his hood in sign of obedience; and for several days he was cook, porter, and alms giver. But the others soon began to feel remorse to see all the burden of the work fall on Brother Masseo's shoulders, and they came and begged their Father to release him. "Until you have done so," they said, "we feel that we will be lukewarm and distracted in our prayers."

They got their request; for, judging that the trial had lasted long enough, Francis restored things as they were before.

But if we are to believe the *Fioretti*, Brother Masseo was again porter and Brother Elias the superior on the day that a youthful pilgrim of a marvelous beauty came to the door of the hermitage and knocked so loud and so long that all in their huts wondered what was going on.

"Young man," said Brother Masseo, "evidently, this is the first time you have come here, or you wouldn't knock that way."

"And how should I knock?" inquired the stranger.

"Like this! First, you knock calmly three times with a little pause between each rap. Then, after the space of an Our Father, if you see that I am not coming, you can knock again."

"But I am in a great hurry," replied the visitor. "Could I speak to Brother Francis?"

Masseo explained that Francis was praying in the woods, and that it was not customary to disturb him when he was receiving such great graces from Heaven.

"Then call Brother Elias, who they say is so learned. I should like to ask him something."

But Brother Elias refused to be disturbed, and this put Brother Masseo in an embarrassing position. What was he to say to the stranger? If he told him Elias could not come, that would be a lie, but telling the truth would scandalize the visitor. So while he was debating what to do, the caller pounded louder than ever at the door. Masseo came running. "You didn't pay any attention to what I said," he complained to the angel, who soon afterward vanished.

For the visitor was an angel who, under color of asking Elias why he had banned the use of meat, had come to congratulate the friars for their observance of the Gospel, which, as everyone knows, does not breathe a word of any such prohibition.

For a long time, Brother Masseo prayed God for the gift of humility. "Lord," he prayed constantly, "make me humble, even at the price of losing my two eyes." He was finally heard, without losing his eyes; and ever thereafter so great was his happiness that he expressed it in prayer by a gentle moaning, always the same. When Brother James of Falerone, whom this "cooing" wearied slightly, remarked to him that it was a most monotonous sound, Brother Masseo replied:

"Does a man who has found happiness think it necessary to change his tune?"

Brother Masseo, born in Marignano, near Assisi, lived to be very old, and only died, says Wadding, in 1280. Unlike Brother Lucido, Brother Giles, and so many of the first Franciscans, he did not care for traveling and preferred the society of certain of his brethren even to pilgrimages. "I find I gain more," he said, "associating with living saints than with dead ones. For the latter are silent; whereas the others can talk and tell us of the temptations they have overcome, thus forewarning us against the perils that threaten us."[8]

* * *

We have seen that the Rule commanded the friars to welcome all visitors, "including thieves and robbers." Now along about the year 1213, Brother Angelo Tarlati, who like his namesake, Angelo Tancredi, was a former knight, was living at the hermitage of Monte Casale. As porter, he one day received a visit from three notorious robbers who, lacking travelers to rob in the neighboring woods, had come to the convent to beg alms. He gave them a very poor reception:

"What? Murderers like you? Not satisfied with robbing honest folk of the fruit of their toil, you want to take the little belonging to God's servants! You, who have no respect for God or man and don't deserve that the earth should hold you! Get out of here, and don't let me see you again!"

Perhaps the fiery guardian called on his sword which in former days he used to thrust through rascals like them. Be that as it may, the robbers withdrew in high anger. But scarcely had they left when Francis returned, laden down with the bread and wine which he had collected as alms. Learning what had happened, he reproached the porter:

"You have behaved like a man with no religion!" he said. "Does not the Gospel which we have promised to follow declare that it is the sick and not the well who need the doctor? Take this bread and this wine in the name of obedience, and go and find those robbers! Run up hill and down dale until you find them; and as soon as you see them, shout, 'Come, brother robbers! Come and eat the good things Brother Francis begs you to accept!'

"And they will come. Then spread a cloth on the ground and put this bread and this wine on it, to which you will add some eggs and cheese. And serve these unfortunate men with humility and good humor until they are satisfied. Then, and not until then, ask them not to kill anybody any more, adding that serving God is not nearly so hard as their profession. And I do not doubt that the Lord in His mercy will inspire them with better sentiments."

Nor was their conversion long delayed. For from this time on, says the chronicler, they were to be seen every day at the hermitage, bringing on their backs the firewood needed by the friars. And not only did they pledge themselves to gain their living from then on by honest toil, but all three ended up by entering the Order, in which they died the death of saints.[9]

*   *   *

The growing brotherhood thus excluded no one; and like our Lord, Francis received sinners gladly. Did he not have the power to turn dross into gold?

Even eccentrics were kindly received by Francis, and his affection for John the Simple and Brother Juniper is well known.

John the Simple was a ploughman, and is believed to have lived in Nottiano, eight miles from Assisi [east of Mount Subasio]. While tilling his field, he learned that Francis was sweeping a church in the neighborhood. Leaving his oxen, he went off to find him, took the broom out of his hands and finished the cleaning. Then he sat down beside him by the side of the road and opened his heart to him:

"I have been hearing about you for a long time," he said, "and wanted to meet you. But I didn't know where to find you. Since God has permitted this meeting, what do I have to do to enter your company?"

The Saint decided at once that this simple-hearted man would make an excellent friar. "If you want to come with us," he said, "you must first forsake your lawful possessions and give them to the poor, as my other friars have done."

John hastened to unyoke one of his oxen and brought it to St. Francis. "Here," said he, "is my lawful portion of the inheritance; for since the time I have been working for my parents, it seems to me that I have earned this ox. So I want to give it to the poor the way you told me to do."

Now John's parents, poor themselves and with children to take care of, were appalled to learn of their double loss and began to utter cries of distress. Francis took pity on them.

"I do not want to see you weep any more," he said. "Prepare a good meal. We will eat together; and while we are eating, I will tell you something that will make you happy again."

They sat down to table, and presently the Saint began to speak to the parents: "It is a great honor for you to have your son decide to enter God's service, for to serve God is to reign. It also means that you will truly become rich, for all the brothers John will find in the Order will become in a sense your own children. You must then be very happy. But to make you still happier, you will do me the favor of keeping, in memory of your son, this ox which according to the Gospel he ought to have given to the poor?"

Now as Francis talked, their tears began to stop, and when the parents learned that John was not going to take his ox when he went away, it was such a relief to them that they were completely consoled.

On receiving the habit, John also took the resolution to imitate his spiritual father in everything. Did Francis stop to pray? At once, Brother John stopped short and began to pray. When Francis knelt, he knelt, and sighed, wept, and raised his arms to heaven the same time St. Francis did, coughed when he coughed, and, in a word, copied his slightest movement. Puzzled, the Saint asked him one day the reason for all this.

"Father," he replied, "I have resolved to become holy by following your example in everything. And that is why I wouldn't, for anything in the world, let a single action of yours go by without imitating it."

Francis felt a special affection for John and frequently took him along as his companion. John died early; but often afterwards the Saint used to speak of him, and always called him "our brother St. John," so sure was he that John was in Heaven.[10]

*   *   *

No less edifying and still more picturesque was the famous Brother Juniper, who entered the Order in 1210, was present at the death of St. Clare in 1253, and died in Rome five years later.

St. Clare, who loved and understood him, had dubbed him "God's *jongleur*," *Domini joculator.*[11] As for Francis, who did not require everyone to be like everybody else, he replied to those who considered Juniper's whimsies out of place, "O brothers! I wish I had a whole forest of junipers like him!"

Brother Juniper enjoyed such a reputation for sanctity that we are told possessed persons would flee across fields to avoid meeting him. Francis himself, when he had to deal with some especially recalcitrant demon, had only to say to it, "I am going to call Juniper," for the demoniac to be immediately delivered.

They tell how, in order to observe the rule of "not resisting evil," Juniper once let himself be taken for a spy at Viterbo and condemned to death without protest. Tied to a horse's tail, they were already dragging him to the gallows, when at the last moment his guardian rushed up and managed to clear up the confusion and rescue the alleged traitor.

It is also reported that in order to practice recollection, Juniper once went six months without saying a word. The first day he kept silent in honor of God the Father, the second day in honor of God the Son, the third in honor of the Holy Spirit, the fourth for love of the Blessed Virgin, and so on. Every day he kept silent in honor of some new saint.

But Juniper when he did speak, expressed himself with deep wisdom, if we are to judge by the two following examples: "Do you know any noblemen whose nobility would keep them from hauling dung, if that would enable them to win a houseful of gold? Then why should we be so hard to please, and why refuse little humiliations that can gain eternal happiness for us?"

To his fellow friars who were discussing how to repel impure thoughts, he indicated his own method: "As for me, as soon as I sense the tempter's approach, I shut myself up in my heart with holy thoughts. Then I shout to the devil who knocks at the door, 'Begone! The inn is full and we're not opening up to anyone!' And when the devil hears this, he at once goes away in defeat."

Juniper was not a man to wish for honors here below, content, like so many others, to give the glory to God. Some devout Romans learned this at their expense the day they set forth to meet him as he was approaching the Eternal City. Seeing some children playing seesaw, Brother Juniper made a show of entering into their game; and with great seriousness, as if he had nothing better to do that day, he began to seesaw until his disappointed admirers withdrew.

The early Rule, following the Gospel, said: "Let the Brethren give to all who ask; and if someone takes away their garment and tunic, let them be stripped without protest."[12] Such precepts made Brother Juniper commit not a few excesses. Like his blessed father, he could not stand seeing a poor man worse clad than he; and sometimes he would give the needy great pieces of cloth cut out of his habit, and sometimes his whole tunic.

His guardian had just reprimanded him about this, when he met a beggar shivering in his rags. "You've come at a bad time," said Juniper to him. "My superior has just forbidden me to give away my tunic. But if you want to take it away from me, I won't stop you."

The beggar needed no second invitation; and lifting up the charitable friar's habit, he pulled it off wrong side out, so that Juniper had to return home in his drawers. Since much fun was made of him on this occasion, he wanted to repeat the experience so as to acquire new merits.

After another such "folly" in which he walked naked from Spoleto to Assisi, the exasperated guardian exclaimed: "O

Brother Juniper! I really don't know what penance to give you this time for such scandalous conduct!"

"Father, I'll tell you," replied the culprit. "Just command me to go back where I came from in the same regalia."

After the death of St. Francis, Juniper's charity took a special turn, and the idea often came to him of distributing to the poor the books and other objects that he deemed superfluous in a Franciscan house. The friars had to put their things under lock and key or else have them disappear.

Now how was it, with a reputation like that, that Juniper was entrusted on a feast day with the care of the altar of the Basilica of Assisi? The fact remains that he profited by his charge to detach some costly silver ringlets from the altar-frontal and give them to a beggar woman. Furious, the Minister General stormed so at Juniper that he almost lost his voice. That night, hearing a knock at the door, he opened it to see Brother Juniper standing there with a candle in one hand and a dish in the other.

"Father," said he, "you shouted so a while ago that I thought you must be hoarse. So I've brought you some buttered gruel which will do your throat and chest a lot of good."

The superior refused the remedy and curtly invited Juniper to stop his silly pranks.

"Very well," replied Juniper. "Since you scorn my gruel, which was not made to be thrown away, then please hold the candle for me, and I'll eat it."

Before such simplicity, the Minister was disarmed, and the two religious feasted fraternally together.

Assuredly, this was a superior after St. Francis' own heart. For did not the Rule prescribe that superiors were to be servants to the other friars and take delight in washing their feet?[13] While we are not told that Brother Juniper demanded that particular service, his actions often proved even more embarrassing.

The *Fioretti* tells us that a friar was sick in bed at the Portiuncula.

"What can I do for you?" Brother Juniper asked him.

"I think," replied the patient, "that I would feel much better if only I could eat a bit of pigs' feet."

"Nothing to it!" replied Juniper. "I'll get you some in no time."

Running to the kitchen, he took a large knife, rushed toward a corner of the woods where the pigs were munching acorns, pounced on the finest pig, straddled it, cut off a foot, came back to the convent, and put the foot in a stew. He then carried it to the sick friar, who ate it with much relish and at once felt better.

But soon the owner of the pig arrived, breathing forth fire and brimstone. Even St. Francis was unable to calm him. So he sent for the friar whom he suspected of the crime.

"Was it you, by any chance, who cut off the foot of a pig in the woods?"

"Certainly, Father," replied Juniper triumphantly. "Didn't God create pigs for man's use? And this stew did our patient so much good that if I had had to take the feet off a hundred pigs to cure him, I assure you that the Lord would have been pleased!"

This speech added fuel to the flames of the farmer's wrath, and he went off swearing that they would be hearing from him soon.

"Brother Juniper!" exclaimed Francis. "This time you have really gone too far, and it is up to you to make amends. Go then, and try to calm this man who is beside himself."

"Gladly, Father!"

Brother Juniper caught up with the farmer, threw himself on his neck, pressed him to his heart, fell on his knees, and begged his forgiveness. He spoke to him of the sick friar who was now getting well; and finally got him to agree — to straighten everything out — to sacrifice the rest of his beast and to think no more about it. And all this with so much exuberance, grace, and tears, that the farmer wound up weeping himself, agreed to butcher his pig, and soon after, brought it, with apologies, to the Portiuncula.

Brotherliness flourished in these Franciscan hermitages, as the friars remembered to practice the Rule's advice: "If a mother loves her son according to the flesh, with how much greater reason ought brothers according to the spirit to love one another."[14]

One day when a band of cruel boys were chasing two friars with stones, far from thinking about warding off the blows, each man tried to draw the stones toward himself by placing himself as a shield in front of his companion.[15]

Juniper, we are told, particularly loved Brother Tendalbene, whom he could make laugh or cry at will, and who, in addition, was so patient that he would have let himself be beaten all day without a murmur. When his friend died, Juniper's grief knew no bounds. "Nothing on earth interests me any more," he would go around saying. "Everything else can perish now that my dear Tendalbene is gone."

And as if to destroy this useless world, Juniper took up a stick and began to smash everything in his path. "If I followed my own idea," he would say, "I would take the skull of my dear Brother Tendalbene and divide it in two. One half would make me a bowl to eat from, and the other half a cup to drink from. But my brothers would not be able to understand me, and would probably protest."

Let no one be surprised that we devote so much space to Brother Juniper. We have simply imitated Brother Leo and his friends in their accounts from which all these little stories are taken. Evidently, Juniper was amusing and of a nature to arouse their enthusiasm. But Leo and his partisans had other good reasons for exalting "God's *jongleur*," whom Francis himself had, as it were, canonized. And was not singing the praises of Brother Juniper to condemn at the same time those friars whose books Juniper stole, and whose conduct resembled less and less the way of life of the first friars?[16]

* * *

But it is in Brother Giles that everybody sees the purest example of the primitive Franciscan. "That man is truly my knight of the Round Table," said Francis of him with pride.

Giles lived for a few years at the Portiuncula; then at Cetona, and from about 1234 until his death in 1262, on the outskirts of Perugia, in the hermitage of Monte Ripido.

Giles had at first loved to travel, and had made pilgrimages to Rome, Compostella, and the Holy Land. For Francis had started out by letting those travel whose vocation was not to remain always at home. But whether in the convent or elsewhere, Brother Giles put a quiet fearlessness into observing the Rule — working with his hands, heedless of worldly events, and constantly absorbed in God.

He changed his occupation according to time and place. Sometimes he would hire himself out as a day laborer on farms and in monasteries. At other times he was a scullery assistant in the palace of a cardinal at Rieti. At [Acre] in the Holy Land, he became a water carrier, going through the city with a pitcher of water on his shoulder and shouting: "Who wants fresh water? Who wants my good water?" Elsewhere he made rush baskets and transported the dead to the cemetery.

Not only did Brother Giles always refuse money for his trouble, but according to the usage then in force at the Portiuncula,[17] he even refused to accept in kind anything he could not use that day. "Like the birds of the air, I have no barns in which to store my wheat," he replied to a farmer who, seeing him glean, offered him a few sheaves. "God preserve me from falling into avarice!" he exclaimed to a woman who, because he was a religious, wanted to pay him more for his faggots than the price agreed upon. At Rome, a man could not find anyone to gather his nuts because the tree was so high. Giles offered to knock them down and go halves. He made the sign of the cross and trembling with giddiness climbed up the tree. When evening came, he had so many nuts that he had to make a sack out of his tunic to carry them away and give them with much joy to the poor.

Little gifted for preaching, Giles liked to keep silent and recommended the practice to others. "The true religious," he declared, "ought to be like wolves, which never show themselves in public unless necessary." He himself sought the solitude of caves and woods and professed that it was better to act than to talk. "Isn't there more merit," he would ask, "in going to St. James of Compostella than in showing others what road to take?" He thought it unfortunate that men did not have long, curving necks like cranes. "Then," he would say, "many words would stick in their throats because of the difficulty they would have getting out."

It is fortunate, though, that the solitary of Perugia sometimes stepped out of his habitual silence. Otherwise, posterity would have been deprived of that little masterpiece, *The Golden Sayings of Brother Giles*.

If, by their pithy form and keenness of observation, these sayings are related to the *Imitation of Christ* and to the *Maxims* and *Thoughts* of the great French moralists, they are nonetheless original by their note of optimism, their humor, and the feeling for nature which pervades them. We are astonished that this humble lay brother who called himself "ignorant" should have possessed such gifts of discernment and of reading men's hearts and the ability to express himself in such precise and familiar terms. He was furthermore a great mystic, who after undergoing mysterious and cruel inner sufferings,

was favored by God with graces of a very high order. St. Bonaventure therefore considered him a master of the interior life
and drew inspiration from him in his writings on mystical theology.[18]

When people came to consult him, Giles' reply was sometimes brutally frank. To a mother who bewailed the loss of
her son, a canon, he said, "Which did you prefer in him, the
body or the soul?"

"Alas, it was his body," she replied, "for I had threatened
to curse him if he ever became a Friar Minor."

"Then go to the cemetery," Giles retorted, "and find his
body you loved so much, and you will see what has become
of it."[19]

To two cardinals who requested his prayers, he observed,
"Assuredly your Eminences have no need of them, for you
have a thousand times more faith and hope than I have."

"And how is that, Brother Giles?" asked one.

"It is," he replied, "because with all your riches and honors
you believe and hope to be saved, whereas I, in spite of my
poor and despised life, am so afraid of being damned."

He sometimes gave unsolicited advice. Thus it was that he
got a certain priest of Perugia to add this little couplet to his
sermon: *"Bo! Bo! Bo! Molto dico e poco fo."* ("Too-rah-loo-
rah-loo! Much do I say, but little do I do!")

He also possessed the gift of repartee. One day when he
was speaking of the dangers of incontinence, he was interrupted by a married man. "All this does not concern me," he remarked with a smug air, "for I have my wife, and know no
other woman."

"Doesn't a man ever get drunk on the wine from his own
cask?" retorted Brother Giles.

He had the greatest admiration for his blessed Father Francis. Following his example, he composed verses, sang and
danced, and like him played the viol; and he declared that

no one should utter Francis' name without licking his lips for joy. "And truly, he had only one defect," he would add, "and that was his poor health. If Francis had been as strong as I am, for instance, no one — not even the whole world taken together — would have been able to keep pace with him."

He regretted that so many of his sons had degenerated. He burst into tears when Brother Leo came to Perugia to tell him about the great convent that Brother Elias was building on the Hill of Hell:

"Let him build it even bigger if he likes! Let him make it as long as from Assisi to Perugia if he insists! I'll never live there! I'll be glad to stay in my own little corner!"

Brother Giles had a chance to give brutal vent to his opinion of the building when he went to Assisi to venerate the relics of St. Francis.

"Really!" he declared to the religious of the Sacro Convento. "Now all you need are wives!"

"Brother Giles! What do you mean by saying a thing like that?"

"I mean that since you have forsaken holy poverty, all that you need to do now is to abandon chastity. You made a vow about that, too!"[20]

* * *

When Francis left the Portiuncula to retire into solitude, his choice usually fell on Brothers Angelo, Rufino, Masseo, and Leo and his companions. With one or more of them he would climb to the Carceri, or go to Sant'Urbano near Narni, Fonte Colombo near Rieti, Monte Casale near Borgo San Sepolcro, Le Celle near Cortona, Sarteano near Chiusi, and finally La Verna in the Casentino, where the great miracle of the stigmata took place. These hermitages, situated among lovely landscapes, are the high places of the Franciscan saga.

The Carceri in particular still shows evidence of the life lived there by its first guests. These little "prisons" are caverns in the heart of the forest, on the flanks of Mount Subasio, [eighty minutes' walk] above Assisi. One may see there, on the brink of a chasm, the grotto where St. Francis prayed and the one where he slept on a tiny stone bed. A little higher up in a cleft in the rock is the one where Brother Sylvester withdrew; he who, "like Moses, knew the happiness of speaking to God like a friend to his friend." A hundred yards away, separated by the torrent, are to be found the grottos of Brothers Rufino and Bernard.[21]

*   *   *

We know that Brother Bernard was sent to Bologna in 1211 to found a convent. At first he was greeted with stones; and to obey the Rule, he would stay for hours to be jeered at on the public square. It was a rich magistrate who was the first to recognize the missionary's holiness and help him carry out his plans. Soon the entire city began to show him marks of veneration. But as nothing could be more displeasing to Bernard, he hurried back to the Portiuncula. "Father," said he to Francis, "you will have to send someone else to Bologna, for it is a place where I myself have more to lose than to gain."

Francis always showed special consideration for his "first-born son." When he was dying, he blessed him with a special blessing, recommended him to the affection of all, and begged the superiors to let him live wherever he wished. "Of all the brethren," says the *Fioretti*, "none was so humble as Brother Bernard. He excelled in understanding the most difficult passages of Scripture, and like St. John, merited to soar like an eagle to the very light of divine wisdom."

Once Brother Bernard was rapt in ecstasy and remained motionless, his eyes fixed, from Matins to Nones — even neglecting at the Elevation of the Mass to draw back his hood. He would also forget about mealtime, and stay for days at a time on the mountain conversing with God, causing Brother Giles to say that only swallows and Brother Bernard could live in the air and find their food so far from the earth.

Bernard is believed to have died between 1240 and 1246. When his fellow-friars knew that the end was near, many of them hastened to his bedside. Entering his cell, Brother Giles called out to him, "*Sursum corda!* Lift up your heart, Brother Bernard!"

As this old friend wished to remain until the end, Brother Bernard requested that a hut should be built for him in the garden, where, as was his custom, he could indulge in contemplation. A little before breathing his last, this firstborn son of St. Francis raised himself up in bed and said to those around him: "I am not able to speak to you at length. But remember that where I am, you will soon be also; and I tell you that for nothing in this world, or for a thousand worlds like this, would I wish to have lived otherwise than I have done, nor have served any other master than our Lord Jesus Christ."[22]

*   *   *

Brother Rufino, a cousin of St. Clare, belonged to the first nobility of Assisi.[23] Timid, retiring, silent, and perhaps with a slight stammer, he had a horror of speaking in public; and he lived so lost in God that he would often speak incoherently, for instance when he was called away from his prayers to collect alms.

St. Francis, to try his virtue, sent him one day to preach in Assisi. "You will only have to say what God inspires you to say," said the Saint.

Rufino declared that not having received the gift of eloquence, he preferred to stay home.

"Since you have not obeyed promptly," said Francis, "I command you, under holy obedience, to go without your habit."

But as soon as Rufino had left, the Saint reproached himself for having been so harsh. "What right have you," he thought, "a common Bernardone, to order Brother Rufino, a noble citizen of Assisi, to do outlandish things that will make people think he is crazy? I am going to teach you to perform yourself the things you make others do!"

And removing his tunic, he called Brother Leo and set off with him for the city. When people saw him coming in this outfit, the ridicule that had greeted Rufino broke out afresh. "Their austerities have made them all lose their minds!" people muttered, shaking their heads.

Brother Rufino was just saying the little penitential exhortation of the Rule, when Francis entered the church in which he was preaching. The poor fellow was attempting to shout in order to be heard; but the louder he shouted, the more people laughed. Judging that his punishment had lasted long enough, Francis took his place in the pulpit. Half-clad as he was, he began to picture the Savior's nakedness on the Cross in words so pathetic that the laughter of the congregation soon gave way to tears. "And I do not know," adds the author of the *Actus*. "whether so many tears were ever shed before in Assisi as on that day." Putting on their tunics again (which Brother Leo had been careful to bring), Francis and Rufino went back down to the Portiuncula, thanking God for having been associated with the sufferings of His Divine Son by this victory over themselves.

The following anecdote, likewise taken from the *Actus-Fioretti*, contains a vulgar word, for which we apologize, but whose efficacity Rufino proved in his struggles with the devil.

For it was the devil who, appearing to him at the Carceri in the form of Christ, had been tormenting him for some time about predestination. "Everything that you have done as a Friar Minor is a total loss," said he. "Besides, this Francis you are taking for a guide is damned himself, and my advice to you would be not to have anything more to do with him and to change your state of life."

And Rufino, who did not enjoy either preaching or begging, began to wonder if his vocation were not to become a hermit; and for a time, he avoided St. Francis. But the latter sent Brother Masseo to fetch him. Brother Masseo had a hard time trying to get him to come. As Rufino arrived grumbling, the Saint, who had divined everything, caught sight of him and sang out: "Rufino, you dear idiot, just whom have you been trusting?"

Then Francis unmasked the devil's plot and showed Rufino how to get rid of him. "If the devil comes back again, you have only to say 'dung' to him, and he'll leave you alone."

When the devil reappeared, Brother Rufino obediently tossed this simple word at him, and that was all that was needed to put him to rout. And so great was his pique, says the *Fioretti*, that he unleashed a terrible tempest in his flight. Mount Subasio was shaken to its foundations. Stones torn out of the ground were shattered in fragments in the the air, and chunks of flaming rock rolled with a terrific roar down the valley. The Brothers rushed out of their caves to see what was going on; and so it was that they witnessed the cataclysm, "whose traces" (says the narrator) "are still visible today."

Rufino's peace of soul was definitely restored, and till the day of his death at Assisi in 1270, he never again despaired of his salvation. Francis venerated him so highly that he often called him "St. Rufino," and would say, "If it were up to me to canonize him, I would not hesitate to do so right now, so certain am I of his salvation."[24]

*   *   *

Of all the friends and companions of the Poverello, Brother Leo was perhaps the favorite. As he was a priest, the saint chose him as his confessor and secretary.[25] He had dubbed him the *Frate pecorella di Dio*, because of his meekness and candor; and Brother "God's Little Lamb" followed the Saint like his shadow, carrying out his slightest wish.

When he was disobedient, says the *Fioretti*, it was because God Himself prevented him from obeying by a miracle; as happened in a hermitage wherein the poverty was so great that the friars did not have breviaries. Now Francis wanted to say Matins with Brother Leo.

"Since we have no books," said Francis, "here is the way we will chant the Office today. I will be the first choir, and you will be the second and repeat whatever I say."

"Very well, Father. Let us begin in God's name!"

The Saint intoned: "Brother Francis, you have done so much evil and sin in the world that you certainly deserve Hell."

"And God will perform so much good through you that you will surely go to Heaven."

"What? That isn't right at all! Brother God's Little Lamb, you must repeat my words without any change!"

"Very well, Father! Let us begin again in God's name!"

His voice choked with sobs, and beating his breast, the Saint resumed: "Brother Francis, the iniquities of which you have been guilty against the Master of Heaven and earth are so great that you deserve to be cursed for all eternity!"

"And you will make, thank God, such progress in virtue that you will merit to be blessed for all eternity!"

"But why don't you say it the way I do?" asked Francis. "God's Little Lamb, I command you under obedience to repeat my exact words. When I say, 'Wicked Francis! Tremble lest you do not find grace before God, you who have so gravely offended the God of goodness and the Father of all consolation!,' then you must reply that it is perfectly true that I am unworthy of pardon."

"Very well, Father!" agreed Brother Leo. "I shall reply then that God, whose mercy is still greater than our sins, will surely show mercy to you."

At these words (we read in the *Fioretti*), Francis became a little angry, without, however, losing his patience.

"But, Brother God's Lamb, what has got into you, to be so disobedient and to insist on the very opposite of what I say?"

"Father, God is my witness that I try to repeat your words, but He Himself puts other words on my lips."

This admission disconcerted the saint, who again implored his friend to cry shame on his sins and to threaten him with God's punishment. So Brother Leo attempted an all-out effort to give him satisfaction, exclaiming:

"Brother Francis, not only will God spare you His punishments, but He will shower down His graces upon you and will glorify you for all eternity. For he who humbles himself shall be exalted .... And there is no use in my trying, for I can never say anything else. For the Lord is Truth itself, and He it is who compels me to speak as I do."

It was reserved to Brother Leo to become, together with Thomas of Celano, the great evangelist of St. Francis. As he had been his closest confidant, those zealous for the primitive observance eventually saw in him the only perfect interpreter of the Franciscan spirit. It has been claimed that Brother God's Little Lamb played this role with less serenity than was fitting, and no doubt there is some truth in this. For he did turn into a furious sheep when it came to defending the spiritual heritage of his venerated Father. Thus it was when, learning that a marble poor box had been placed in the Basilica of Assisi, he confided to Brother Giles his intention of smashing it.

"Brother Leo," replied the wise Brother Giles, "you had

better keep still, if you love life, for Brother Elias is capable of anything."

But Leo set off for Assisi and smashed the famous poor box with a mallet. His reward was to be whipped and imprisoned on orders from the builder of the Sacro Convento. But this treatment must have been sweet to the man who had learned from Francis himself that perfect joy consists in being persecuted.

From that time onward, giving up trying to do battle with too powerful an adversary, Brother Leo, during the long years of life still remaining, limited himself to telling and writing of the wonders he had witnessed. He lived until 1271, and like his friends, Bernard, Rufino, Angelo, and Masseo, was buried in the Basilica of Assisi.[26]

- 8 -

St. Clare and the
Order of the Poor Ladies

It was [nearly] six years after his conversion, says Thomas of Celano, that Francis founded the Order of "Poor Ladies."

A woman is usually worth what the ideas of the man she admires are worth; and her capacity for sacrifice enables her to attain the heights of heroism when that man has shown her the way. So it was with St. Clare, who, better than anyone else in the world, and nearly as well as the Poverello, himself, realized his ideal.[1]

Born in 1193 or 1194, she belonged to the rich and noble house of the Offreduccio. She had two younger sisters, Agnes and Beatrice, who both became nuns of San Damiano. Her father was named Favarone di Offreduccio. Among her paternal uncles were Monaldo, feudal chief of the house, and Scipione the father of Brother Rufino of Assisi.[2] Her mother, Ortolana, must have been an unusual woman to have made — at a time when traveling was fraught with danger — three pilgrimages: to the Holy Land, to Rome, and to San Michele on Mount Gargano. When she was pregnant and praying for a happy delivery, a mysterious vision assured her that her child would be a light for many souls; and that was why Ortolana named her daughter Clare at baptism.

We are told that Clare understood and wrote Latin, that she loved music, and took a special delight in well-turned sermons. She had doubtless had a chance to hear minstrels in her father's house and to read romances of chivalry, for her language likewise is colored by the vocabulary of the literature of chivalry. The white alb which she made for St. Francis and which we see today at Santa Chiara in Assisi attests her skill as a seamstress; and her *Legend* tells how, old and infirm, Clare was propped up by the sisters with cushions so that she could still spin and sew.

Clare possessed a great deal of common sense, a loving and loyal heart, a gentle and prudent persistence, and an unflinching courage. She had the art of making herself loved, and was so persuasive that Francis, the cardinals, and the popes themselves always came round to her way of thinking. Sanctity aside, she was assuredly one of the most noble and charming women known to history.

As a little girl, Clare showed that her thoughts were turned toward God. Hearing her mother tell how the hermit Paul in the desert counted his three hundred daily prayers with pebbles, she began to tell off in the same way the many Our Fathers she prayed.

Clare was very beautiful, and when she was twelve her parents wanted to marry her, but she obtained a delay that she meant to use to prepare other plans. Meanwhile, she wore a cruel hair shirt under her rich clothing, despised money, dearly loved the poor, and deprived herself of the choicest morsels to give them to the needy. When the masons recruited by Francis repaired the Portiuncula, she dipped into her own purse to pay for meat for them, so that they might have more heart for working.

* * *

The Friars Minor soon became dear to her, and Francis was to be her guide and model. She had been impressed by the conversion of the "king of youth"; she was thrilled by the knightly bearing of God's songster; and when she attended the services in San Giorgio Church and the Cathedral of San Rufino, what must have been the effect on her — who enjoyed beautiful sermons — of the fiery improvisations of this poet inebriated with God's love! Going to him in secret, she confided to him that her parents were urging marriage upon her, and was encouraged by him never to have any other Spouse but Christ.

But the time came when it was evident that further family discussions were useless and that no one would give in. So it was decided that she should take the initiative and flee from her home on Palm Sunday night.[3]

*   *   *

In this year of 1212, Palm Sunday fell on March 18.[4] In the morning, Clare, adorned like a bride, went with her family to San Rufino; but when it came time for the distribution of the palms, her heart failed her. Here she was about to leave her mother and sisters forever, and this was the last time that she would pray with them in the church where she had been baptized. It almost seemed to Clare as though her secret would suffocate her. She could not stir from her pew and the bishop had to descend the sanctuary steps to place the blessed palm in her hands.

That night, with her cousin Pacifica di Guelfuccio won over to her plans, Clare, without so much as farewell left her home. The two accomplices hastened to the Portiuncula, where, before the altar of Our Lady of the Angels, Francis cut off their hair and clothed them in a coarse habit like his own. Then he led them to the monastery of San Paolo belonging to the Benedictine nuns, two miles away in the marshlands of the Isola Romana.[5]

Let it be said in passing that the circumstances of this entry into religion have been censured, and that after seven centuries an English lady of letters is unrelenting toward St. Francis and St. Clare:

"This is an incident which we can hardly record with satisfaction," she writes, deploring that so fair a career should have been begun by this sort of elopement.[6] But if elopements which end in happy marriages are rarely condemned, why not admit that divine love also has its rights, being just as much a reality as human love? And whether the union contracted by St. Clare that night was a happy one, the continuation of this history will permit you to determine.

The young girl's flight stirred up her relatives, who the following day went to the Isola Romana in an attempt to bring the fugitive back home. Clare received them in the chapel, clinging to the altar-cloth and showing them her shorn head. The relatives realized that they would not succeed in changing her mind and did not insist. They would at least have liked to keep in the family the property that the girl wished to give to the poor, and they offered to redeem it at the highest rate. But not wanting to have the air of being dispossessed only in appearance, Clare rejected their proposals and the inheritance passed into the hands of strangers.

*   *   *

Upon learning that Agnes was getting ready to imitate her sister, did the nuns of San Paolo fear the renewal of the scenes they had just witnessed? At any rate, accompanied by Brothers Bernard and Philip, Francis hastened to entrust his spiritual daughters to more intrepid Benedictines, taking them to Sant'Angelo Abbey on the slope of Mount Subasio, below the

Carceri. It was there a week after Easter that Agnes joined her sister and her friend.[7]

At the flight of this child of fifteen, the family's wrath boiled over, and the uncle Monaldo set off at the head of a dozen horsemen to storm the monastery. To gain admittance, says the *Legend*, he at first showed himself conciliatory. But as soon as he was in the presence of his nieces, he brutally ordered the younger girl to follow him at once. As Agnes refused, one of the horsemen pounced on her and dragged her by her hair to the door. Others came to his assistance and carried her off in their arms by the narrow path winding down the mountain. In her struggles, the poor child left pieces of her dress and locks of her hair on the briars as they went. "Help, dear sister! Help!" she sobbed.

At this appeal, Clare fell to her knees, imploring God to help one who wanted to belong to Him. And that was all that was needed, according to the *Legend*, for the girl's body suddenly became so heavy that she seemed fastened to the ground. "Anyone would think she had eaten lead all night!" exclaimed one of the abductors. Then, insane with rage, Monaldo tried to strike her a brutal blow in the face with his fist. At once a horrible pain gripped his arm so that he screamed in agony.

Meanwhile, Clare, running up, confronted these barbarians and commanded them to release her sister. And these ravening wolves, who an instant before were so bloodthirsty and attempting to snatch the pious virgin from the arms of the Lord, became as gentle as lambs, abandoned their prey, and returned peacefully to their homes.

*   *   *

Just as he had done for Clare and Pacifica, St. Francis cut off Agnes' hair with his own hands and received her profession. She now belonged to the jurisdiction of the Church and it was to the Bishop of Assisi that Monaldo would have to appeal to recover his ward. But he probably desisted, for Bishop Guido approved the two sisters and four months later generously gave them San Damiano as a refuge. Here it was that the Order of "Poor Ladies" or "Poor Clares" was born.[8]

We can imagine Clare's happiness at being able to settle in the shadow of the poor shrine recently restored by her friend. She lived there until her death. Agnes spent seven years there, after which she was sent to the monastery of Monticelli near Florence. Her sister, Beatrice, and their mother, Ortolana, also became nuns at San Damiano, and likewise their cousins Balvina and Amata, daughters of Martino di Corano.

Francis always watched affectionately over his "dear little spiritual plant." Chivalrous as always, he had promised never to forsake her, as Clare herself recalled before her death. "When the Blessed Father saw that we feared no poverty, toil, sorrow, humiliation, or the contempt of the world, but rather that we held these in great delight, moved by love he wrote for us a form of life as follows:

" 'Since by divine inspiration you have made yourselves daughters and handmaids of the Most High and Sovereign King, the Heavenly Father, and have espoused yourselves to the Holy Spirit by the choice of a life according to the perfection of the Holy Gospel: I will and promise for myself and my Friars always to have for you as for them the same diligent care and special solicitude'."

Afterwards, not only did the religious of the Portiuncula minister to the nuns of San Damiano, but they also shared with the Poor Ladies whatever they collected by begging.

The day came when on the strength of a pontifical decree rightly or wrongly interpreted, the Minister General John Parenti forbade them to preach to the nuns or to hear their confessions. But Clare did not see things that way; and when the collecting friars came back with their loaded sacks, she went to meet them and said, "Go back to your Minister, and tell him from me that since you can no longer feed our souls with your spiritual conferences, it is useless for you still to nourish our bodies with your alms." When Pope Gregory IX heard about this, he revoked the aforesaid decree.[9]

* * *

Only one of the sermons preached by St. Francis at San Damiano has come down to us, and it is a sermon without words. It was in 1221. Clare and her community, assembled in choir, were awaiting their blessed Father. Francis knelt down, and his eyes raised to heaven, prayed for a while. He then had ashes brought, put part of them on his head and sprinkled the rest around him in a circle. Again he paused, recited the *Miserere*, and then left. And that was his whole sermon.[10]

What were the Poverello's reasons for acting in this way? Perhaps, not being in the mood for words that day, God's *jongleur* thought that such a pantomime would be the best possible instruction on the last end of man. Or, perhaps also, feeling his death to be near, he wanted to teach Clare gradually to do without him, and her nuns not to measure their spiritual advancement by the number of sermons they heard.

The fact is that in his eyes the zeal shown by certain friars in recruiting nuns and in assuming their spiritual direction could give rise to abuse. He also feared for them the danger sometimes incurred by familiarity with even the most devout women. He himself, writes Celano, declared that he knew only two women in the world by sight.[11] These were apparently Sister Clare and Brother Jacopa. The fact remains that he did not like to have the name of "Sisters Minor" given to the Poor Ladies, and to those who displayed an exaggerated zeal toward them he said, "The Lord has preserved us from taking wives, but who knows whether it is not the devil who sent us sisters?"[12]

If, for some years, the saint climbed less frequently the path leading from the Portiuncula to San Damiano, it was especially for his own friars' instruction. "Do not believe," he said to those who reproached him, "that my love for Clare and her companions has diminished. But I have tried to be an example to you. Only those ought to minister to the sisters whom long experience has shown to have the Spirit of God." And to get his thought across, he told them the following parable:

"A king had sent two ambassadors to the queen. When they returned, he asked them what they thought of the queen.

"Sire," replied the first ambassador. "You have a very beautiful wife. Happy indeed is he who possesses her like!"

"And what do you think of the queen?" he asked the second.

"I admired," he replied, "the attention with which she listened to your instructions."

"You did not find her beautiful?"

"Sire, it is for you to judge of her beauty. My part was to transmit your message."

The king then gave judgment as follows: "You, whose eyes are chaste" (he said to the one who had just finished speaking), "I will reward you, and you shall ever remain in my service. As for you," (he said to the indiscreet ambassador) "whose unchaste eyes have rested on the queen, go! And never come again to defile my palace with your presence!"

"And if earthly kings are so exacting," added Francis, "what modesty of the eyes does Christ not have a right to expect of those whom He sends to His spouses!"

Apparently, the Saint did not mortify his daughters more than strict necessity required. The *Fioretti* relates that he consented one day to invite Clare to dinner at St. Mary of the Angels.[13]

This was a favor that the Abbess of San Damiano had long sought in vain. So she got some mutual friends of the Saint and herself to intercede for her. These came to St. Francis and said, "It is too harsh and contrary to divine charity for you and not to fulfill the desire of a virgin so holy and dear to God. Remember that after all she is your little spiritual plant and that it was your exhortations that took her away from the vain illusions of the world."

"Then you think I ought to eat with her?"

"Certainly! And even if she were to ask more, you ought to grant it."

"Well, since that is your opinion, it will be mine, too. And so that she may really have reason to be happy, it will be here at the Portiuncula that we shall dine. For it is a long time that our sister Clare has been a recluse at San Damiano, and nothing could afford her greater pleasure than to see the place once more where she gave herself to the Lord as His spouse."

On the appointed day, Clare arrived, accompanied by a Sister. With deep humility, she first venerated the image of St. Mary of the Angels over the altar where she had taken the veil and had her hair cut off. She then employed the time before dinner in visiting every nook and cranny of the hermitage. Francis, who following his usual custom, had had the food served on the ground, sat down beside her. The others took their respective places, and all made ready to dine. But scarcely had they swallowed the first mouthfuls when Francis began to speak of God, and all fell into an ecstasy.

Soon, however, a crowd came rushing to the convent. It was the inhabitants of Assisi and Bettona and the surrounding district, who, seeing flames over the forest and believing that a great fire had broken out at St. Mary of the Angels, were coming to put it out. But they could see that no damage had been done; and when, entering the "banquet hall," they found Francis and his guests with their hands joined and eyes raised to heaven, they realized that the flames they thought they had seen were the flames of divine love with which these holy persons burned. And they withdrew as edified as they were reassured.

As for Francis, St. Clare, and the other guests, adds the *Fioretti*, they scarcely touched the food at all, being sufficiently nourished by the spiritual consolations they had experienced; and many among them ate nothing at all.

*   *   *

The way of life of the nuns of San Damiano was inspired by the letter of the Gospel and by the Rule of the first Franciscans. The Sisters recited the canonical hours, worked with their hands, cared for the sick, and practised penance and poverty, just as the friars did at the Portiuncula.

Never was there a closer and more harmonious union than that existing between St. Clare and St. Francis. Never were two souls in more perfect accord in their way of looking at things of earth and heaven. One sometimes wonders which of the two copied the other. One would say that there was a kind of spiritual kinship, so like were their characteristic features and reactions. The Poverello's ideal remained always pure in the heart of this daughter who kept unchanged the deposit of his fairest inspirations and who, like a limpid mirror, reflected his best image. Thus in hours of discouragement and darkness, we sometimes see him coming back to the poor walls of San Damiano — the cradle of his vocation — to seek from his spiritual daughter the comfort and assurance of which he stood in need.

Like the Poverello, Clare was humble, merciful, charming, optimistic, and courteous. At San Damiano, she cared at first for the sick, as Francis had done at the start of his religious life. Later on, in 1220, learning of the martyrdom of the Franciscans in Morocco, and longing to shed her own blood for the Faith, she would have gone to the Saracens if she had not been hindered.[14]

She blessed the Creator for having made the world so entrancingly beautiful.[15] She cultivated flowers, loved animals, and counseled the [extern] Sisters to admire the trees when they went outside the convent.

Clare was also a great contemplative, constantly conversing with God, and every day from noon to Nones, experiencing — from meditating on the Savior's Passion — mysterious torments which filled her eyes with tears. Once, from Thursday to late Friday in Holy Week, she remained so ravished out of herself that a Sister had to pluck her by the sleeve to remind her that Francis had forbidden her to pass more than twenty-four hours without taking at least an ounce and a half of food.

The slightest word sufficed to transport her into supernatural realms. One Sunday in Eastertide, she was so struck by the antiphon *Vidi aquam* that she spent the whole day sprinkling her companions with holy water to remind them of the water that flowed from the Savior's side.

Excessively hard on herself, fasting perpetually, rejecting all cooked food, and sleeping on boards, Clare was a mother to her daughters. "Our flesh is not of bronze, nor is our strength that of stone," she wrote in 1229 to Agnes of Bohemia, Abbess of Prague. "So I urge you to be less strenuous in your fasting, so as to render reasonable worship to the Lord, and to season your holocausts with the salt of prudence."

So long as she was not totally incapacitated, she took care of her sick daughters, even of their humblest needs. When her Sisters came back from begging, she washed their feet and kissed them reverently. In the winter, she would get up in the middle of the night and tuck in their bed clothes; and in the morning, it was often she who, the first one up, rang the bell and lit the lamps, so as to give extra rest to the nuns who had this duty.

The *Process of Canonization* relates a charming miracle, which shows how quick God was to answer her slightest prayer and also how kind Clare was.

There was a sick nun at San Damiano who was visibly wasting away from lack of appetite. Distressed, the Saint asked her if there were not something that she would like. "Oh!" exclaimed the nun, who apparently cherished some pleasant memories of her secular life, "I would like to eat some trout from the Topino and some hearth-cakes from Nocera, if I had some! But where are they to be had?"

Clare dropped to her knees, and hardly had she begun her prayer when a knocking was heard at the door. It was a fair youth carrying two packages wrapped in napkins containing the delicacies the sick nun desired. As the hour was late and the weather bad, the Sisters invited the youth to spend the night at the guest house used by the Friars Minors. But he refused, and vanished like a phantom.

Painters have popularized this other miracle which is believed to have occurred on a Friday in September, 1240, when the Imperial Army had invaded Central Italy, "burning cities, cutting down trees, laying waste vineyards, and torturing women and children."

For Frederick II had enrolled Saracens among his troops, who little heeding the Church's excommunication, fought with no inhibitions against the Pope's soldiers, and showed little respect for the nuns who fell into their hands.

Already, declared the *Legend*, this band of ruffians had scaled the walls of San Damiano and entered the cloister, when Clare had the Blessed Sacrament brought, and going toward them, made this prayer: "Lord Jesus, do not permit these defenseless virgins to fall into the hands of these heathen. Protect them; for I, who have nourished them with Your love, can do nothing for them."

She likewise prayed for the city of Assisi, nearly all of whose inhabitants were saved.

Then, continues the biographer: "immediately the boldness of those dogs was changed into fear and they quickly clambered over the walls they had scaled, being routed by the power of her prayers." Not only the Sisters but the people of Assisi itself owed their safety to the prayers of St. Clare.

*   *   *

In the first of three letters that she wrote to Agnes of Bohemia, who before becoming Abbess of Prague had been betrothed to Frederick II, Clare exclaimed: "O blessed Poverty, to those who love and embrace her she bestows eternal riches! O holy Poverty, to those who possess and desire her God promises the Kingdom of Heaven! O Poverty, beloved of God, which our Lord, the Creator of the world, has deigned to embrace so completely on earth!"[16]

These accents are less spontaneous and sublime than those of the Poverello, and Clare may not have spoken so well of poverty as St. Francis did. But it can be said that she loved it no less and that she fought as hard as he to be true to it.

At this period nothing was more opposed to the usages of the Church than to authorize nuns to do without revenues. Especially for recluses, it was thought that it was tempting God to aspire to live by alms from day to day. In 1215 or 1216, however, Clare obtained from Innocent III what has been termed the *Privilegium paupertatis*, i.e., the canonical right to possess neither property nor revenue. Gregory IX attempted to withdraw it, when in 1228, he came to Assisi for the canonization of St. Francis. The former Cardinal Hugolin said to her:

"If it is your vow which prevents you from accepting revnues, I can release you from it."

"Holy Father," she replied, "absolve me from my sins, but from following Christ I have no desire to be dispensed."[17]

Instead she implored the Pope officially to recognize for her the right never to have revenues. At this request, Gregory began to laugh. These were not, he observed, the kind of privilges people were accustomed to demand from him. But he finally yielded; and as the formulary of the Pontifical Chancellery possessed no model of similar acts, he himself drew up the original Bull, *Sicut manifestum est.* "As it is manifest," we read in it, "that to be deprived of necessary things does not frighten you . . . and that He who feeds the birds of the air and clothes the lilies of the field will not fail you in both food and clothing . . . We accede to your supplication and authorize you by apostolic favor to live in highest poverty. Likewise by these presents it is granted you never to be constrained to receive possessions."

However, the majority of then existing convents of Poor Ladies renounced the use of this privilege; and others founded afterward imitated them. Thus there were in the Order two observances: that according to which the nuns lived on uncertain alms, and that according to which they lived from assured revenues. Deeming this diversity undesirable, Innocent IV, after deliberation, decided to put an end to it; and by his Bull of August 6, 1247, he imposed a new Rule on the Poor Clares in which the right of all to property and revenues was recognized.[18]

* * *

Ill for twenty-nine years, Clare had only six more to live. Her infirmities, arising from her excessive penances, had made her a permanent invalid, nearly always bedfast. But her soul was as serene and ardent as on that night in her youth when Francis received her first vows. She dragged herself to the offices of the community whenever she could; and she enjoined her nuns to remain united to the Friars Minor, and the friars to obey their ministers while practicing the most absolute poverty. Half-helpless, but faithful to the law of labor, Clare continued to make corporals or altar linens for needy priests.

Among the friars who came to see her, the most regular and most welcome visitors were those who preserved the Franciscan spirit of the first days. Like her blessed Father, Clare was especially fond of Brother Juniper, of joyous and happy mien, of Brother Leo who had copied out a breviary for her,[19] and of Brother Giles whose improvised sermon one day afforded her so much pleasure.

It was on a day when a great doctor in theology — [Adam of Oxford, *not* the famous Alexander of Hales] — was preaching at San Damiano. Was it to put an end to too learned considerations or simply to test the preacher's virtue? Whatever it was, Brother Giles interrupted him in the middle of his sermon. "Silence, Master!" he shouted. "That's enough! It's my turn to speak!"

The theologian did not wait to be told twice — and never, it would seem, was Brother Giles so sublime. As for St. Clare, she said to those around her, "How happy our Father Francis would have been to see a master in theology bow thus to a simple lay brother!"[20]

*   *   *

The nearer she came to death, the more was she surrounded by universal veneration. High personages in the Church hastened to her bedside.

The eighth of September, 1252, witnessed the arrival of Cardinal Rainaldo of Segni, protector of the Order, at San Damiano. Clare submitted a Rule of her own to him, which clashed with Innocent IV's Rule. Chapter eight, among others, copied the very words of the Rule of the Friars Minor: "The Sisters," we read, "are to take nothing as their own, whether it be a house, or a place, or anything at all. Instead, they are to be as pilgrims and strangers in this world; and as those who serve the Lord in poverty and lowliness, let them send for alms with full hope in Him. Nor should they feel shame thereby, since for our sakes the Lord Himself came into this world as a poor man. Such indeed is the greatness of this perfect poverty, that it makes you, my dearest Sisters, heirs and queens of the kingdom of heaven, so that though you are in want of this world's goods, you are made rich in virtues. Let this always be your 'portion' here below . . . and desire never to have aught else under heaven."

Clare won over Cardinal Rainaldo, who promised to interest the Holy Father in her project. Soon Innocent IV himself came twice to visit the sick abbess. He made no attempt to conceal his love and admiration for her. When the invalid besought him to absolve her from her sins, he exclaimed before giving the absolution, "Would to God that I had as little need of it as you!"

The saint now waged her final combat. We can guess with what ardor she implored Christ's Vicar to grant to her and her daughters "the privilege of most high poverty." Innocent IV allowed himself to be persuaded; and the ninth of August, 1253, (likely a few days after his second visit), he signed at Perugia the Bull *Solet annuere* which approved the new Rule. The next day a friar hurried from Perugia to San Damiano to bring Clare the longed-for Bull. This was Clare's last joy on earth, for she died the next day.

Although for three weeks she had been unable to take any nourishment whatever, her presence of mind and spiritual strength remained intact. To her sister Agnes who had just returned to San Damiano, she said, "Do not cry, dear Sister. I am not leaving you for long, for you will soon rejoin me." And Agnes did die three months later.

When Brother Juniper approached her bed, Clare asked, "Do you bring me good news from God?" Juniper thereupon began to speak words so burning with divine love that it was like flames leaping up from a burning heart. And his words were a great consolation to the dying Clare.

Also at her bedside were her faithful friends, Leo and Angelo. She asked them to read to her the Passion of the Lord. Upon Brother Rainaldo exhorting her to bear her infirmities with patience, she replied, "Dearest Brother, ever since I have known the grace of my Lord Jesus Christ through His servant Francis, no suffering has troubled me, no penance has been hard, no sickness too arduous."

Clare's daughters gathered round her couch sobbing. She spoke tenderly to them to console them, blessed them for the last time, and enjoined them to walk in the path of holy poverty. She was heard to murmur, "Depart in peace, for thou wilt have a good escort on thy journey. Go forth confidently to Him who has protected thee and loved thee as a mother loves her child."

Sister Anastasia asked her whom she was addressing.

'I am speaking to my blessed soul, and he who has been its guide is not far distant." (Doubtless this was St. Francis come to take her to Heaven.) "Lord God," spoke Clare again, "blessed be Thou for having created me!" Then she breathed her last.

The funeral took place the next day in the Church of San Damiano [with burial later that day at San Giorgio]. Innocent IV and numerous cardinals were present. Instead of the Office of the Dead, the Pope proposed that the Office of Virgins should be sung in her honor, which would have meant canonizing her before her burial, says the *Legend*. But the Bishop of Ostia, more of a stickler for formalities, protested that it was more seemly to sing the customary Mass of Requiem and to wait a little before placing Sister Clare on the altars. So they waited [two months before opening the formal Process]. The canonization took place two years later, [August 15, 1255, at Anagni].

- 9 -

From the Clothing of St. Clare to the Lateran Council 1212-1215

   A period opens here in which precise dates are scanty. But we do find two sure landmarks — the deed of gift of Mt. Alverna, which will be mentioned later on, and St. Francis' two unsuccessful attempts to go to the infidels.

It was after the victory of Las Navas that he attempted for the first time to carry out his plan. Never, perhaps, until this year 1212, had men lived in such dread of seeing the Saracens overrun Europe. Already master of Morocco and a part of Spain, did not the Moorish chieftan, En-Nazir, boast that he would soon push on to Rome "to purify" — as he put it — "the Church in a blood bath?" Innocent III ordered universal prayers and processions and called on all Christendom to take up arms. But many Christians at that time were warring among themselves and others turned a deaf ear, so on July 14, 1212, the Spaniards were alone at Las Navas to wage battle. They won a brilliant victory which stirred all Europe to enthusiasm, and after which men imagined that the Moorish peril had been turned aside forever.

The situation appeared no less favorable in the East, although the crusaders occupied themselves mostly with commerce and with the petty kingdoms they had founded for their own profit. But since the Pope had excommunicated them all in a body to bring them to order, people everywhere began to realize once more that the object of the crusade was to deliver the Holy Places; and everybody — even the children — wanted to share in what appeared to be the forthcoming victory. We are told that thirty thousand of these innocents did set out from Touraine and twenty thousand from the Rhineland to recapture the Savior's Tomb, and that they all perished on the way or else fell into the hands of slave merchants.[1]

Were the dwellers in the Portiuncula seized by the general enthusiasm, and did Francis believe the moment ripe for going to preach Christ's peace to those whom Christian arms had been unable to conquer? What is certain is that he did decide to leave for the East. Adventure and the unknown were to his liking and the prospect of shedding his blood inflamed his knightly zeal. Besides, had not his recent experiences shown him that with God's help all things are possible to man? Since, following his example, so many Christians had forsaken all in imitation of Christ, why should he not succeed in having the infidels likewise open their hearts to the Gospel?

It was likely toward the close of the year 1212 that Francis embarked with a companion on a boat bound for Syria. Unfortunately, contrary winds landed our passengers on the Dalmatian coast. As no further opportunity offered itself that year for continuing their voyage, the two friars determined to return to Italy. They wanted to board a ship about to sail for Ancona, but were barred because they had no money to pay for their passage. So they had to slip secretly on board with the connivance of an obliging sailor. Thomas of Celano gives us to understand that they would have fared ill if a tempest had not suddenly broken out, forcing the overtasked rowers to use up their own provisions faster. The famished sailors were thus only too glad to have recourse to the charity of the two missionaries, whose little store of food had miraculously multiplied.[2]

About two years later, Francis renewed his plans for a spiritual crusade in Moslem lands, choosing this time Morocco. "He dreamed of nothing less," writes Celano, "than of converting the Miramolin and his satellites." Accompanied by Bernard of Quintavalle, he headed for Spain, "walking so fast," (so great was his haste to reach his destination) "that his companion often had trouble keeping up with him. But God intervened, and sickness compelled him to give up his journey."

Friar Thomas adds in passing that at this time he himself entered the Order, but he tells us nothing more of this second abortive expedition. According to well-founded local tradition, we may believe that on this occasion Francis made a pilgrimage to St. James of Compostella and returned to the Portiuncula by way of France.[3]

* * *

Before embarking for the East, however, Francis had undertaken several apostolic missions in the north of Umbria and in Tuscany. These had resulted in recruiting a goodly number of new friars. At Pisa he received Brothers Albert and Agnello who later on filled important offices in the Order. At Florence he received John Parenti, who was to become Minister General from 1227 to 1232. The latter discovered his vocation in a most curious manner. A former student of law at the University of Bologna, now a judge at Civita Castellana, [from a window one day he observed a swineherd having a hard time getting his pigs to enter a city-gate, and he heard the man shout at them: "Go through the gate, pigs, the way judges go into hell!"]

These words set John Parenti to thinking, and he lost no time in abandoning a profession so generally looked down upon.[4]

It is not known whether it was before or after Francis left for Syria that he spent a Lent in an island of Lake Trasimene. He insisted on staying there alone, eating only half a loaf of bread. He would have preferred to eat nothing at all, remarks the *Fioretti*, if out of humility he had not wished to leave to the Savior the glory of having gone without any food for forty days.[5]

When this Lent was over, Francis passed through the neighboring regions. [It was probably at] Cortona that he enrolled in the brotherhood a man of gentle birth who extended hospitality to Francis and his companion one day, and whom the Saint praised for his courtesy.

This Messer Guido, says the *Fioretti*, could have done no more were he entertaining angels from Heaven. He warmly embraced the two friars, washed and kissed their feet, caused a great fire to be lit and an excellent repast brought to them, and as they ate served them himself with a beaming countenance. He then said to Francis, "Father, from now on I want to provide for your needs, for God has given me great wealth. I must show Him my gratitude by sharing it with the poor. So now whenever you need cloaks or tunics, do not think of buying them, for I will pay for them."

When alone again with his companion, Francis said to him, "I tell you I have rarely seen so courteous a man, and nothing would please me more than to have him as a friar. He is grateful to God for his blessings, generous to the poor, and most courteous to others. Now courtesy, brother, is one of God's finest attributes; for God makes His sun to shine and His rain to fall on sinners and just alike. And courtesy is truly the sister of Charity, for it extinguishes hatred and maintains love among men. So we must come back this way again some day, in case the Lord should inspire this perfect gentleman to join with us in His service."

And Messer Guido did enter the Order. He spent all his life at Le Celle, near Cortona, in a cave in a valley by a stream, only leaving this retreat from time to time to preach penitence to the people of the neighborhood.[6]

From the Cortona country, Francis went through the region extending to the southwest of Lake Transimene, founding among others the hermitages of Cetona and Sarteano. [On a journey through the Marches of Ancona, he received as many as thirty recruits at once in the city of Ascoli Piceno.]

*   *   *

So the friars increased rapidly. Before the close of 1215 they had spread over not only north and central Italy, but to Southern France and Spain.

They were to be met along the road, walking two by two, recollected and joyful, while their little hermitages were found on the outskirts of the towns or in the surrounding mountains.[8] They did not live withdrawn from the people, since it was from them that they received their subsistence. The people on their part loved the friars for their voluntary destitution, as one loves children for their weakness. They were edified by the spectacle of their life in which religion appeared devoid of ambition and greed, and they did not stint their friendship or their bread.

As the friars furthermore proved to be good and obedient Catholics, and never preached without the permission of the parish priests, and practiced poverty for its own sake and not to fight the Church or recall simoniacal priests to their duty, the clergy likewise favored them.

Only the Bishop of Imola, it would seem, refused Francis

permission to preach. "Brother," he replied curtly. "I am here for that purpose, and I don't need anyone to tell me what to do."

With a courteous bow, Francis withdrew — but he was back an hour later. "Are you back again?" boomed the bishop. "What do you want now?"

"Your Excellency," replied Francis, "when a father drives his son out the door, there is nothing left for him to do but to come back in through the window. So I, as your loving son, have not hesitated to come back to see you."

Deeply moved, the bishop embraced him, and gave him and his friars permission to preach in his diocese as often as they wished.[9]

The time of ridicule and insult was over. From now on the Little Poor Man stole all men's hearts. Instead of sowing — like so many of the reformers — the seeds of rebellion and hatred, he built up, showed the tasks that needed to be done, and nourished souls eager for perfection and holiness. Men blessed this herald of a spiritual springtime. Even robbers, touched by his respect and trust, were friendly inclined. As for the Patarini and other heretics, he did not try to win verbal victories over them; and these disputers usually left him in peace. Often his arrival in a town resembled a triumphal entry. The church bells were rung and people went to meet him shouting, *"Ecco il santo!"* (The saint is here!)[10]

Enthusiasm like this, comments the *Fioretti*,[11] astonished good Brother Masseo, who one day expressed his thoughts to the Saint in this way: "Why after you? Why after you, rather than another?" he kept repeating.

"What do you mean, Brother Masseo?" asked Francis.

"Father, there's something I don't understand."

"What is it, Brother?"

"I was wondering why everybody runs after you, trying to

see and hear you, and have you direct them, when you are neither handsome, nor learned, and not even of noble birth. Why you, rather than others?"

At these words, the *Fioretti* tells us, Francis could not conceal his joy. At first, he stood motionless, his face upturned to heaven. Then, falling on his knees, he thanked God and explained: "Why me? Why me? Do you want me to tell you, Brother Masseo? Well, know that all this comes from the All-seeing God who, looking down and finding nothing viler on earth, quite naturally fixed His gaze on me. For to make His work shine forth in men's eyes, the Lord takes what is ignorant, weak, and despicable, in preference to what is learned, strong, and noble; so that the creature may have no cause to glory, but the glory may go to the sole Author of all good."

When people insisted on touching Francis' garments in veneration, he would say, "Don't canonize me too soon, for a 'saint' like me might still bring sons and daughters into the world!"

At the hillside hermitage of Sarteano, he suffered, according to Thomas of Celano, "violent temptations in the flesh." He was praying one night in his cell when the devil suggested that he ought to give up his austerities. The tempter said that God did not ask men to destroy themselves, and that it was therefore better for him to lead the common life and have a home and family, rather than to keep on with so miserable a life as a celibate. At once, the Saint arose and laid aside his garment, saying:

"Since the tunic belongs to the Order and does not deserve to be torn, I will respect it. But you, brother ass," he continued, addressing his body, "are going to be whipped to teach you better behavior." And he began to scourge himself with a rope. As the temptation did not go away, he went outside, took some snow, and began, in the bright moonlight, to make seven snow figures in a row in front of him. Then going from one to the other, he said to himself aloud, "There you are, Francis! The family you want to raise is complete. This one here is your wife. These four smaller ones are the children she has given you, two sons and two daughters, as you see. These two big ones are your servant and your maid. And now it is to you, the father, that they all look for support. So hurry and get them something to wear, for they are all naked and are going to freeze to death in this bitter cold . . . . What? . . . . You hesitate? . . . You think there are too many of them? . . . Then remain in God's service, friend, and don't think about anything else!"

Meanwhile the devil had fled and the temptation vanished. So Francis, thanking God, returned to his cell. But a friar who had been praying that same night on the mountain in the moonlight had seen and heard everything, which greatly vexed the Saint when he learned of it. So Francis forbade the friar ever to speak of this scene to anyone.[12]

* * *

Toward the end of spring in 1213, Francis went to Romagna and reached the foot of the castle of Montefeltro (now San Leo) perched on a spur of the Apennines near San Marino.

Now on this day, the *Fioretti* reports, a relative of the lord of the place had been made a knight and a number of noblemen were present at the ceremony. When Francis heard of the festivities, he decided to attend with his companion. On his arrival he went into the square where all the noblemen were assembled. Climbing up on a little wall and beginning to speak, he took as his theme a couplet from a poem of chivalry:

> *Tanto è il bene ch'aspetto*
> *Ch'ogni pena m'è diletto.*
> I aspire to so great a treasure
> That all pain for me is pleasure.

Using these verses, he pictured the suffering that the apostles, martyrs, virgins, and confessors had endured to obtain an eternal reward, and developed thoughts so sublime that he stirred the enthusiasm of the knights present.

But the most deeply impressed of them all was Count Roland, lord of Chuisi-in-Casentino, who was inspired with a generous plan which he wished to tell Francis about at once. Francis tactfully protested that "politeness required Roland first to dine with his hosts and friends."

When the banquet was over, Roland told the Saint of his plans. A mile and a half from his castle at Chiusi, atop Mount La Verna, he possessed an ideal site for the practice of contemplation and penance. "If you are willing to accept it for yourself and your friars," he added, "I freely and gladly offer it to you."

Unfortunately, Francis could not go there at the moment. "But as soon as I get back to the Portiuncula," said he, "I will send my friars, and if they find the place suitable, we will build a hermitage there in God's name."

And everything went as Count Roland wished; for an authentic deed signed by his sons in 1274 states that the gift of Mount La Verna was made to the brothers on May 8, 1213.[3]

*   *   *

Did the Little Poor Man see something supernatural in this acquisition? Did Providence, which had not permitted him to land in the territory of the Saracens, mean for him to forsake the active ministry for prayer and contemplation? This is the question that Francis now asked himself once more and for which he sought guidance and light.

He called Brother Masseo, according to the *Fioretti*,[14] and said to him, "Go to Sister Clare, and ask her to pray to God to know whether I should preach part of the time, or spend all my days in prayer. Then go and ask the same thing of Brother Sylvester."

Brother Masseo went first to San Damiano where he transmitted Francis' message to Clare. Then he climbed up to the Carceri where Brother Sylvester was leading a hermit's life. Sylvester had a reputation for always getting a prompt answer to his prayers; and indeed, Heaven let him know at once that it was Francis' vocation to be occupied both with his own salvation and with the sanctification of others. Sylvester told this to Brother Masseo, who at once started back to San Damiano, where St. Clare informed him that she had received the same reply from God.

Brother Masseo then went down again to the Portiuncula where Francis was waiting for him. After washing his feet, the Saint had a good meal served him, and only afterward, kneeling bareheaded, his arms stretched out cross-wise, he asked him, "What does my Lord Jesus Christ desire of me?"

The faithful messenger then disclosed his twofold and identical message. "Good! Let us go forth in God's name!" exclaimed Francis, rising. And taking with him Brother Angelo and Brother Masseo, he headed for Cannara, two leagues distance from Assisi, and began to preach.[15]

*   *   *

Of all the sermons that St. Francis preached on this journey, the one to the birds is certainly one of the most beautiful ever preached on earth.

"Because everything comes from the same source," writes St. Bonaventure,[16] Francis sensed the kinship which exists between men, animals, plants, the sea and the stars. And is not the outlook of him who takes no thought of the bonds linking all creatures together and themselves to God most incomplete? Did not Christ Himself speak of the goodness of the Heavenly Father who gives the sparrow its food and the lily of the fields its brilliant garb? And before sin came into the world, did not men, beasts, and the elements live in harmony? But no one in the West ever experienced or expressed as did St. Francis such a feeling of the universal brotherhood of all creation. His heart is the way one pictures Adam's in the Garden of Eden; and it is to be believed that the very beasts perceived it, for they always showed such gratitude for the honor he paid them.

So, with his companions, Francis went beyond Cannara and going toward Bevagna, he reached — after a half an hour's walk — the place known today as Pian dell'Arca. "There were some trees there," relates the *Fioretti*, "so filled with birds that never had the like been seen in these parts; and there was likewise a multitude in the neighboring field."

Marvelling at this spectacle and filled with the Holy Spirit, Francis said to his companions, "Stay here by the road and wait for me, while I preach to our sisters, the birds."

He entered the field, and scarcely had he commenced his sermon, when all the birds clustered round to listen. They remained motionless, even though the Saint's habit brushed against them lightly as he passed.

"My little sisters, the birds," he said to them, "many are the bonds which unite us to God. And your duty is to praise Him everywhere and always, because He has let you free to fly wherever you will, and has given you a double and three-fold covering and the beautiful colored plumage you wear.

"Praise Him likewise for the food He provides for you without your working for it, for the songs He has taught you, for your numbers that His blessing has multiplied, for your species which He preserved in the ark of olden time, and for the realm of the air He has reserved for you.

"God sustains you without your having to sow or reap. He

gives you fountains and streams to drink from, mountains and hills in which to take refuge, and tall trees in which to build your nests. Although you do not know how to sew or spin, He gives to you and your little ones the clothing you need.

"How the Creator must love you to grant you such favors! So, my sister birds, do not be ungrateful, but continually praise Him who showers blessings upon you."

At these words, all the birds began to open their beaks and spread their wings; and stretching out their necks, they reverently bowed their heads, showing by their songs and actions the great joy they felt. Francis rejoiced with them, charmed and delighted at their numbers, their variety, and the loving familiarity they showed. At last, he made the sign of the cross over them and dismissed them. Then all the birds rose together and fled off, in the form of the cross he had made over them, in four groups toward the distant horizon.[17]

*   *   *

The Poverello's whole life is filled with similar incidents. The theologian St. Bonaventure reports no fewer than fifteen of them, according special mention to the hare of Greccio which followed Francis like a little dog, the kingfisher and the fish in Lake Rieti which came regularly to ask his blessing, the pheasant of Siena that refused to eat for sorrow after its friend died, that cicada at the Portiuncula that came at his call and, lighting on his hand, sang God's praises with him, and finally the devoted sheep that also lived at St. Mary of the Angels, accompanying its master to the Office, prostrating itself at the Elevation, and saluting with its gentle bleatings the statue of the Blessed Virgin.[18]

Other biographers of the Poverello revert continually to this feeling he had for the beauty of the world and for the love he bore toward every living creature.[19] "How are we to express," exclaims Celano, "the tenderness he showed as he discovered in them the Creator's power and goodness! How are we to depict the joy he felt at seeing the sun, moon, and stars, and the pleasure he took in contemplating the beauty of the flowers and inhaling their fragrance!"

To the gardener of the Portiuncula he recommended taking part of the space devoted to vegetables for flowers; and when he came across flowers growing in the fields, he would stop for a while and talk to them. "One could say that his heart, by a unique privilege, had penetrated the secret of all things created."

When he walked on stones, he did it with a kind of reverence, thinking of Christ whom St. Paul compares to a rock. When he washed his hands, he would choose a place where the water would not be trampled underfoot afterwards. Out of regard for his "brother fire," he would not let still smoking firebrands be tossed aside, candles snuffed, or lights and hearth-fires extinguished. He forbade his friars who went to the woods to chop down trees, wishing to give every growing thing a chance to live out its life.

Francis cherished the tiniest forms of life. He would pick up worms lying on the road and put them to one side to keep them from being crushed. In the winter he had warm wine and honey brought to the bees to help them through the cold months. He built nests for doves so that they might increase and multiply; and one day in the March of Ancona he gave his new cloak to redeem two lambs being carried off to the butcher.

But Francis had his preferences, so Brother Giles informs us; and he did not quite forgive the ants for what appeared to him their feverish haste and exaggerated foresight. His unstinted praise went to the birds, who took no thought for the mor-

row but trusted from day to day in Providence. His favorite
bird was the crested lark, called *lodola capellata* in Italian.
"Sister lark with her little hood," he would say, "looks a little
like us, and with her earth-colored plumage, she urges us to
be satisfied with our poor and coarse habits. She is humble
enough to seek her food in dust and dung. Soaring high (as
she usually does) and praising the Lord with her song in the
air, she teaches us to despise earthly things and to make our
dwelling even now in Heaven."[20]

* * *

Now of all the beasts that have had a place in the Franciscan legend, there is none more famous than the wolf of
Gubbio, whose edifying history is related by the *Fioretti*.
While his "conversion" may have taken place in the last years
of the Saint's life, the reader will permit us to anticipate events
a little and report it here.

Once Francis had stopped for the night, at the monastery
of San Verecondo north of Assisi. Next morning when, mounted on a donkey, he was preparing to set off for Gubbio, the
peasants warned him that the country was infested with fero-
cious wolves. But the Saint replied, "What have my donkey
and I done to my brother wolves for them to seek to devour
us?" And he started off.[21]

When he arrived at Gubbio people could talk of nothing
else but the wolves. There was one wolf especially that claimed
their attention. Of an extraordinary size and ferocity, always
famished and furious, it ate not only animals, but men and
women. People were so terrified that they went out from town
armed from head to foot. But this fierce brute was accustomed to dining on the best armed people, and the time came
when hardly anybody dared venture outdoors. Now God, in

order to make manifest His servant's sanctity, inspired him to confront the raging wolf; and although everyone implored him not to, Francis set forth with his companion.

The people of Gubbio climbed up on roof and rampart to see what was going to happen. Terrified, they soon saw the wolf lunging toward St. Francis with gaping jaws! But with the sign of the cross, Francis stopped it. "Come here, brother wolf!" he ordered. "In Christ's name, I forbid you to be wicked."

At these words, the wolf put its head down, and came and lay at Francis' feet.

"Brother wolf," continued the Saint. "I am very sorry to hear of the dreadful crimes you have committed in these parts, going even so far as to kill creatures created in God's image. You deserve death by torture like the worst of murderers, and I understand why the people of Gubbio detest you. But I want to reconcile you with them, so that they will not be afraid of you any more and you will not have to fear anything from them or their dogs."

The wolf made signs to show that these words were most pleasing to it. St. Francis continued: "If you agree to make peace, brother wolf, I will tell the people to feed you as long as you live, for I know that it was hunger that drove you to commit so many crimes. Do you promise never to harm man or beast again?"

The wolf bowed its head to show that it agreed, and to seal the pact, placed its right paw in the Saint's outstretched hand. Francis then led the animal into town. The wolf followed its benefactor like a lamb. The pair halted on the public square where the people of Gubbio were gathered.

Francis then preached a fine sermon in which he showed how our sins draw down God's punishment in this world and plunge us into Hell in the next — a fate much more fearful than the jaws of the fiercest wolf. He urged his hearers to do penance, adding: "My brother wolf here promises never to harm you again, if you will promise to feed him as long as he lives. I have received his pledge and I stand surety that he will keep his word."

As one man, the assembly swore that it would take care of the wolf. Again the wolf knelt, bowed its head, wiggled its ears and wagged its tail, and by placing its right paw in the Saint's hand, once more indicated that it would keep the pact.

And this it never failed to do during the two years that it continued to live. The town took care of it, and the wolf came and went freely without molesting anyone, and without even the dogs barking at it. It died of old age, and the *Fioretti* declares that grief was universal at its death. For the people had become attached to it, and when they saw it peacefully trotting around town, they thought of St. Francis whose memory was so dear to the inhabitants of Gubbio.[22]

- 10 -

The Lateran Council and the
Meeting with St. Dominic

Although the early biographers make no mention of it, historians generally admit that Francis was present at the Fourth Lateran Council.[1] The assembly opened on November 11, 1215, at St. John Lateran, before a huge gathering. Representatives of the spiritual and temporal powers of the whole of Europe and of the Near East were present; and it was before four hundred bishops and archbishops, eight hundred abbots and prelates, besides the ambassadors from all ruling sovereigns, that Pope Innocent III pronounced the opening address.

Did the Pope have a feeling that only a few months remained to him for carrying out the great idea of his reign? Certainly, His Holiness spoke as if he were soon to appear before God, declaring in particular that it was for no temporal ambition that he had convoked the Council, but moved by the sole desire of reforming the Church and recovering the Holy Land from the infidels.

In his eyes the two enterprises were indissolubly linked. Since Christians at that time still looked on the repossession of Christ's tomb as a point of honor, the Pope hoped that a victorious crusade would somehow restore Europe to a state of grace and renewed fervor, thanks to which the abuses favorable to the success of the heretics might be abolished and the reform of the Church brought about.

After depicting the profanation of the Holy Places by the Saracens, the Pontiff deplored the scandals dishonoring Christ's flock, threatening it with God's punishments if it did not reform. He recalled Ezekiel's famous vision in which the Lord God, His patience exhausted, cries out in a loud voice: " 'Approach, you who watch over the city, every one of you with his weapon of destruction in his hand.' And I saw six men approaching from the upper gate which faces the north, every one of them with his deadly weapon in his hand. In the midst of them stood a man clad in linen with a writer's inkhorn at his belt . . . . And the Lord said to him: 'Go through Jerusalem and mark with the sign of the TAU the foreheads of all those men who weep and lament over the abominations which are done in it.' And He said to the others: 'Pass through the city after him, and smite. Let not your eyes spare, nor show any pity. But spare and slay not those upon whom you shall see the TAU.' "[2]

"And who are," continued the Pope, "the six men charged with the divine vengeance? They are you, fathers of the Council, who with all the arms at your disposal — excommunication, depositions, suspension and interdict — shall smite without pity those unmarked with the atoning cross who persist in dishonoring the city of Christendom."[3]

These words inspired the deliberations and resolutions of the Council. After condemning the errors of the Cathari and pantheists, the assembly decreed the establishment of schools of theology to remedy the ignorance of the priests, and commanded the faithful to confess and receive Communion at least once a year. It compelled Jews to wear a distinguishing badge, and strengthened the decrees against heretics and other unbelievers. Lastly, it enacted measures designed to curb the greed and ambition of the Roman prelates, measures whose benefits would, it was hoped, extend to the lower ranks of the clergy. But, as we know, these decrees remained a dead letter. Almost the same is to be said of the crusade set for the year 1217, but which lacking the support of the monarchs of Europe, had no important result.

Did the Pope foresee these failures? It would seem so, to judge from the disillusioned tone of certain passages in his discourse.

How is it, then, that men date from his pontificate the religious reform destined to stave off for a few centuries the already menacing schisms and secessions? It was because this reform, given legal status in the canons of the Council, was instituted and implemented from this time onward, thanks chiefly to the Dominican and Franciscan Orders, both beneficiaries of papal favor and officially recognized at this time.

The Friars Minor obtained a stronger legal status during the Council. The latter having decreed that every new Order must adopt either the Rule of St. Benedict or St. Augustine, Innocent III declared that this measure did not include the Franciscans whose Rule he had approved five years previously.[4] The Dominicans, however, adopted the Rule of St. Augustine and the Constitutions of Prémontré and were approved the following year.[5]

*   *   *

Some writers believe that it was the Council that persuaded Francis that he had a role to play in the reform of the Church.[6] In support of this thesis, they allege the cult given by the Poverello from that time on to the letter TAU.

"The TAU," the Pope had said, "has exactly the same form as the Cross on which our Lord was crucified on Calvary. And only those," he added, "will be marked with this sign and will obtain mercy, who have mortified their flesh and conformed their life to that of the Crucified Savior."

Could one better preach the return to the Gospel demanded by contemporary reformers or more clearly condemn the lust for gold, honors, and pleasure with which they reproached the clergy? Incontestably, these words and many others manifest the Church's willingness for self-regeneration, and for absorbing the reform movements of the period.

How could Francis, who saw God's hand in everything, be other than impressed by this proclamation which expressed so well his ideal of life and his dream of an apostolate?

The fact is that the TAU, which the Pope made the emblem of the reform, became from then on Francis' own blazon. He used it as a signature, painted it on his door, and placed it on his writings. Even his friends, it would seem, noticed the new use that he made of the saving talisman. For instance, there was Brother Pacifico who, before the Council, had seen his venerated father in a vision, pierced by a cross with four arms, and who in another vision after 1215 saw him marked with a TAU on his forehead.[7]

We can hardly say that all this merely proves the Poverello's devotion to the Savior's Passion. Others have seen in it the proof that Francis felt as though the Pope's appeal had been meant for him personally, and considered himself from that time onward as officially enrolled among the knights of the penitential crusade. Henceforth, he would be one of the scribes with the inkhorn charged with marking the foreheads of the elect, and his disciples would be invested with a sort of ecclesiastical ministry — to the point that instead of following their evangelical vocation as wandering penitents, these *jongleurs* of God would henceforth heed and obey the directives of the pope and Roman Curia.[8]

*   *   *

It was perhaps his meeting with St. Dominic that served to confirm Francis in such sentiments.[9] Twelve years older than the founder of the Franciscans, the Spaniard Dominic de Guzman had been until past forty a canon of the cathedral of Osma in the kingdom of Leon. He had always been devoted to study and to the practice of virtue. His true vocation was born in the course of a journey made to Rome in 1205 in company with Diego, his bishop. Innocent III, who had just appointed the Cistercians to convert the Albigensians, invited the two Spaniards to join them. The Cistercian methods had small chance of success. The people, seeing the papal legates appear with great pomp, followed by a train of mules loaded with baggage, had all the more reason for admiring the austerity of the Cathari apostles and for letting themselves be indoctrinated by them. The Cistercians soon gave up the attempt. The Bishop of Osma died in the midst of his labors, and it was Dominic who then became head of the mission. He recruited a few priests who were determined to make their doctrines their rule of life, and with them he continued his preaching. These "preachers" practiced rigorous penance, went barefoot, and organized debates sometimes lasting several days.

As we know, the Cathari refused to listen to reason; and as they were deemed to be endangering the whole social structure, it was decided to settle the affair by force of arms, and in 1209 to organize against them the famous crusade known as the Albigensian Crusade. In 1215 St. Dominic momentarily left the theater of war to attend the Council; and it was apparently on this occasion that he met for the first time the young founder of the Friars Minor.

In a dream, according to the Dominican chronicler, he had seen himself presented by the Virgin to our Lord, accompanied by a stranger who, like himself, was charged with converting the world. When the next day he perceived Francis in a street in Rome, he recognized in him the unknown man of his dream. He stopped Francis, narrated his vision to him, and embracing him, said, "Let us be comrades, and nothing on earth can prevail against us."

Unlike the Poverello, who knew nothing of what men learn in schools or of administration, Dominic was as endowed with a genius for organization as he was able in explaining the doctrine of St. Paul and in learnedly refuting heretics. His plans were in complete harmony with the Pope's program; and in founding an Order which overcame the ignorance of the people by preaching, and that of the clergy by the establishment of schools of theology, he fully realized the views of Innocent III, if, indeed, he was not simply carrying out his instructions. Moreover, he enjoyed the entire confidence of Cardinal Hugolin, the most influential man of the Curia, and it was at the latter's residence that his most important interview with Francis took place.

*   *   *

A word must be said of this prelate whose influence was exercised in the Church for more than half a century, and whom we shall see appearing again on every page of this biography. A relative of Innocent III, to whom he owed his career, and whose ideas he had embraced, Hugolin became in 1216 the collaborator of Honorius III until the day when he himself, under the name of Gregory IX, was in turn elected pope. His pontificate, which lasted from 1227 to 1241, is one of the most amazing in history. The inflexible old man still led the fight in person aginst Frederick II, perhaps the most dread adversary the Roman Curia has ever known.

Handsome, brave, robust and eloquent, possessed of unparalleled energy and skill, a great traveler and a scholar, this statesman was likewise a man of God.[10] He seemed happy only in the society of monks, on whom he chiefly counted to reform the Church. His life was austere and his soul open to mystic inspiration; and in his decisions, the latter frequently outweighed the calculations of human policy.

Hugolin had a warm and faithful heart. "Dearest sister in Christ," he wrote to St. Clare, "ever since I have been compelled to leave you, I have been so sad and weep so much that I should die of grief, if prayer, my habitual remedy, were not my consolation."[11]

He had no less affection for St. Francis, whom he venerated as one sent by God, and to whom he tried always not to cause pain. If he did not hold all Francis' views as capable of realization, he did at least, as long as the Saint was alive, unceasingly seek with great tenderness to adapt his ideal to whatever he judged to be in the best interest of the Church and of souls.

*   *   *

Thus it was at the residence of Cardinal Hugolin and evidently in accord with him, that St. Dominic made the following proposition one day to the Little Poor Man. "Brother Francis," said he, grasping his hands, "I would like to see your Order and mine combined and living under the same Rule in the Church."

The administrative advantages envisaged by the papal statesman and by the perspicacious founder of the Preaching Friars are readily divined. Besides, they doubtless were able to observe some of the lack of organization in the Franciscan brotherhood, and foresaw that its leader might soon be out of his depth. Thomas of Celano does not tell us how Francis got out of this proposition, but it was skillfully evaded.

Francis likewise rejected another proposal the Cardinal made to the two Saints in the same interview. "Since," said he, "the pastors in the early Church were poor and consumed by charity rather than by greed, why shouldn't we choose bishops from among your friars?" Here again it was his interest in church reform that inspired the collaborator of Innocent III.

The two founders vied with each other, to let the other have the honor of replying first. Finally, Dominic spoke up. "My Lord," he said, "the dignity of their state should suffice my friars, and for my part I will not permit them to seek any other."

Francis then replied: "Your Lordship, my brothers are called *Fratres minores*, that they may not attempt to become *majores*. Their vocation teaches them ever to remain in a humble condition. Keep them in it, even against their will, if you would have them be useful to the Church. And never, I beg of you, permit them to become prelates."

Such was the way the Saint conceived of the cooperation of his friars in the task of restoring the Christian spirit.

Before separating, writes Thomas of Celano, Dominic and Francis affectionately recommended themselves to each other. Dominic begged Francis to give him his cord as a souvenir. He obtained it only after much urging and put it on under his second tunic. As the Little Poor Man withdrew, Dominic said to those around him, "I tell you truthfully that there is not a religious who would not profit by following in the footsteps of so holy a man."[12]

The two saints sometimes saw each other after that and continued to love each other.[13]

But as soon as they were dead, their sons became bishops just like other priests; and it is plain that in Friar Thomas' eyes, some were too eager to do so, for he does not spare his reproaches. "Sons of saints!" he exclaimed in 1245. "How can you unblushingly give full rein to ambition and turn aside from the road leading to the eternal city? You whose fathers wished only to know the path of humility!"

He likewise chided the jealous and the quarrelsome: "If the honors you run after show that you are bastard sons," he wrote, "the envy that you bear one another shows the depth of your degradation. Whereas your fathers tenderly loved one another, you cannot even bear the sight of one another. Why do you not turn your arms against the demons, instead of biting and devouring one another? Your sermons would surely bear more fruit if people knew you to be more charitable, and they would have more faith in your words if they did not sense the hate with which your hearts are filled." But the writer, realizing that his rhetoric has carried him away, adds, "There are friars here and there who do edify, and these words are not addressed to them. I mean to speak only of bad religious, who, to my way of thinking, ought to be expelled from their Order before they corrupt others."

In conclusion, he turns to God, imploring Him to make Dominicans and Franciscans "kindly disposed toward each other."[14]

Certainly, in the main, one can say that his prayer has been heard and that, to borrow Lacordaire's oratorical style, "the kiss of Dominic and Francis has been transmitted from generation to generation on the lips of their posterity."

There was a time, however, in which questions of scholasticism or prestige incited some of these religious to such rivalry that the popes themselves were obliged to intervene.[15] But today when everybody yields the pleasure of solving the unsolvable to everybody else, and zeal for God's glory rarely moves people to annoy their neighbors, Preachers and Minors are united in fellowship. And the memory of the ancient quarrels is so blotted out that [a century ago] Father Lacordaire was able to pen in good faith that "never has the breath of jealousy sullied the spotless crystal of their centuries-old friendship."[16]

- 11 -

The Indulgence of the Portiuncula

On Saturday, July 16, 1216, Jacques de Vitry arrived in Perugia where the Roman Curia was then in residence.[1] Newly named Bishop of St. John d'Acre, he was about to take possession of his diocese and had therefore come to receive episcopal consecration, only to learn on arrival that Innocent III had died that very morning.[2]

Men's manners were rude in those times, and the ambitious acted undeterred by convention. "There is no one who dies as solitary and forsaken as a pope," remarks the contemporary Thomas of Eccleston. Innocent III had indeed barely entered his death agony when all his courtiers forsook him to go off to their own affairs. But Francis, declares the same chronicler, had hastened from Assisi to pay final homage to the great pontiff who had understood his vocation and approved his work.[3]

The Pope's body was borne in an open coffin to the cathedral where the funeral was to take place the next day. "That was the day," writes Jacques de Vitry, "when I really understood the nothingness of earthly grandeur. Incredibly, the preceding night, thieves had entered and stripped the Pope of everything of value he had on. With my own eyes I saw his half-naked body lying in the middle of the church, already smelling."

He then describes the impression made on him by the Roman Curia the few weeks he was there. "The members are so taken up by temporal affairs and by lawsuits," he writes, "and so preoccupied by everything having to do with kings and states that one can scarcely touch upon questions pertaining to religion. All this caused me much grief.

"Happily," he continues, "I found in my travels one spectacle of quite another sort." And he goes on to describe to his correspondents in Lorraine the things he has just seen in Umbria six years after the journey to Rome of the first Friars Minor and four years after the clothing of St. Clare. We should give full weight to this unique on-the-spot evidence (in October, 1216) of a traveler who had no reason for embellishing Franciscan origins. Nothing better confirms the writings of Thomas of Celano and the Three Companions.

"The thing that has consoled me," declared Jacques de Vitry, "is the sight of so many men and women who have abandoned their wealth and forsaken the world for love of Christ. These men, who bear the name of Friars Minor, are held in highest esteem by the Pope and cardinals. Utterly uninterested in temporal concerns, they devote all their efforts to withdrawing from the world souls in danger and inducing them to follow them. By the grace of God they have already achieved great success and made numerous converts; for their followers recruit others, and their hearers increase of themselves. As for their mode of life, it is that of the primitive Church, where, as the Scripture says, the multitude of believers had but one heart and soul. During the day they are to be found in the cities and villages, preaching or working. At night they return to their hermitages or retire into a solitary spot to pray.

"The women dwell together in refuges near the cities, living by the work of their hands without accepting any gifts. And they are so humble that any veneration shown them confuses and displeases them."

The new bishop next describes the Chapters of the Friars Minor: "Once a year the men of this Order assemble at a place agreed upon to rejoice in the Lord and to eat together. There, taking counsel of upright men, they adopt and promulgate holy laws which are then approved by the Pope. Then, separating for another year, they scatter throughout Lombardy, Tuscany, and even to Apulia and Sicily.

"Recently Brother Nicholas, a holy and religious man, and compatriot of the Pope, left the Curia to join them. But he was recalled by the Supreme Pontiff who could not get along without him. My own opinion is that God has determined to make use of these poor and simple men to save a multitude of souls before the end of the world, and to denounce by their example the remissness of our prelates, who like dumb dogs refuse to bark."

*　　*　　*

The vacancy of the Apostolic See lasted only two days. "It is true," says Ciaconius, "that to hasten the election, the Perugians had decided to lock up the members of the Curia and to progressively decrease their rations."[4] Of the nineteen cardinals present, two were apparently going to cause a stalemate: Guido, Bishop of Palestrina, and Hugolin dei Conti whom we know already. To hasten matters, the electors charged these two favorites with the task of electing a candidate. They chose Honorius, a man of advanced age and in poor health, but who nevertheless lived until 1227. "An excellent and pious old man has just been elected pope," wrote Jacques de Vitry, "and he is furthermore a plain and benevolent man who has given almost all his fortune to the poor."

Francis must have thrilled with joy at learning of the election of a pope so filled with love for God and the poor. The Lord Himself, he thought, has taken in hand the cause of the holy Gospel; the great projects announced by Innocent III would now be realized; the new crusade already being preached would restore Christ's tomb to Christians; and prospects for the reform of the Church appeared most bright.

Did these fair hopes play a part in determining the extraordinary step that Francis made a few weeks later? For it was at this time that he came to ask of Honorius III the famous Indulgence of the Portiuncula or Great Pardon of Assisi.[5]

In his Lateran discourse, Innocent III had pointed out as marked with the TAU three kinds of predestined men: those who would consent to take the cross, those unable to go on the Crusade who would busy themselves at combating heresy, and, finally, those sinners who would work at the task of self-reform. Did these words stir up a desire in St. Francis to put the whole world in the state of grace, by making it easy for those who could not set out for the Orient or who were too poor to gain an indulgence, to share in the universal redemption? Whatever it was, on a summer's day in 1216, he took Brother Masseo with him and set out for Perugia.[6]

"The previous night," writes Bartholi, "Christ and His Mother, surrounded by heavenly spirits, had appeared to him in the chapel of St. Mary of the Angels."

"Francis," said the Lord, "ask of Me whatever you will for the glory of God and the salvation of men."

"Lord," replied the Saint, "I pray You by the intercession of the Virgin, Advocate of mankind and present here, to grant an indulgence to all those who visit this church."

The Blessed Virgin bowed before her Son to show that she seconded the request, and her petition was granted. Christ next bade Francis to go to Perugia to obtain the desired favor from the Pope.

As soon as he was in Honorius' presence, Francis said to him: "I recently repaired for Your Holiness a church dedicated to Mary, God's Blessed Mother. I now come on behalf

of those who shall visit this church on the day of its dedication, to solicit an indulgence which they may be able to gain
without an offering."

"It is fitting that those who desire an indulgence should
make an offering," observed the Pope. "And how many years'
indulgence do you desire? One year? Three years?"

"Holy Father, what are three years?"

"Do you want six years? Seven years even?"

"It is not years, but souls I desire!"

"What do you mean by 'souls'?"

"My meaning is that everyone who shall enter this church,
confessed and absolved, should receive remission of all his
sins, both as to their guilt and penalty."

"But this is a thing unheard of, and quite contrary to the
usages of the Roman Curia!"

"But, Holy Father! It is not of myself that I speak, but I
have been sent by Jesus Christ our Lord!"

"Well, then! I grant it to you. In the Lord's name let it be
done as you desire!"

At these words the cardinals present begged the Pope to
take back his words, pointing out that such a favor would be
hurtful to the indulgences of the Holy Land and Rome, which
from then on would be counted as nothing.[7] But the Pope
refused to recall his words. His counsellors besought him to
at least restrict as much as possible this unheard-of favor.

Addressing himself to Francis then, Honorious said, "The
indulgence is granted in perpetuity, but only once a year; that
is, from the first vespers of the day to those of the following
day."

Promptly withdrawing, Francis bowed and was already
starting for the door when the Pope recalled him. "So you are
leaving, simple little man, without any document?"

"Your word is enough for me, Holy Father! If this indulgence is willed by God, He will manifest it Himself. My char-

ter is the Virgin Mary, my notary is Christ, and the holy angels are my witnesses."

So he set out with Brother Masseo for the Portiuncula.

The travelers had been walking for an hour when they came to the village of Collestrada, above a knoll halfway between Assisi and Perugia. There Francis, worn out with fatigue, fell asleep. When he awoke he received a revelation which he disclosed to his companion. "Brother Masseo," said he, "know that what has been granted me on earth has just been ratified in Heaven."

The dedication of the chapel took place on the following second of August. Borrowing the words used by Solomon at the inauguration of the Jerusalem temple, the liturgy of the feast seemed chosen for the occasion. "Lord God," it reads, "is it to be thought that You should indeed dwell on earth? Behold, the heavens themselves cannot contain You, and how much less this house which I have built! Let Your eyes, however, be open day and night upon this house. And when strangers come from distant lands to pray there, listen to them, O Lord, and send them away forgiven."[8]

Before the bishops of Assisi, Perugia, Todi, Spoleto, Gubbio, Nocera, and Foligno, Francis, looking down at the crowd from a wooden pulpit, told them the great news.

"I desire to send you all to Paradise," he cried, "by announcing to you the indulgence which has been granted me by Pope Honorious! Know then that all those present, and those who shall come in the future to pray in this church, will receive the remission of all their sins. I should have liked to have had this indulgence granted for a week, but I have only succeeded in getting it for one day."[9]

* * *

Such is, according to the documents to be considered presently, the origin of the famous Pardon of Assisi. We must confess that the indulgence aroused strong opposition.

Things were not like they are now, when every Catholic can gain plenary indulgences without loosening his purse-strings or going outside his parish. At this period, only pilgrims to the Holy Land, to Rome, and to St. James in Galicia could obtain such favors. However rich they might be in relics, other shrines were infinitely less well endowed, having only a few days or few years of indulgences to offer visitors.

Placed thus on the same footing with the three most celebrated pilgrimages in Christendom, the Portiuncula promptly lowered the status of those innumerable sanctuaries from which monks and clergy derived fame and subsistence. That they should have exerted every effort to fight it is understandable. Do we not see them — on the roads or at the ports — going out to meet pilgrims bound for Assisi, to "prove" to them that the Franciscan privilege was false and urge them to go back?[10]

Today the only moot question is no longer whether the indulgence be valid — for this the Church has many times confirmed — but if it owes its origin to the initiative of St. Francis.[11]

For some critics the saint's trip to Perugia with the verbal concession wrung from Pope Honorious is a legend. For others it is a proven historical fact.

The first group allege the silence of the ancient biographers, who they say would not have failed, had the story been true, to report so glorious a fact. Neither Thomas of Celano, St. Bonaventure, nor the Three Companions make any mention of it. It is only some fifty years after the event that testimony in its favor appears. What credence then is to be placed in evidence so tardy?

The advocates of authenticity reply that the silence of the first biographers was necessary; and that therefore it has no weight against evidence which, for all its lateness, is no less conclusive. If these early authors remained silent, say they, it was because they had every reason to do so.

It must be recalled that Francis had obtained the indulgence against the wishes of the cardinals, who considered it harmful to the success of the crusade; and had the indulgence been noised abroad, these prelates would most assuredly have had it revoked. The saint knew it; and with his horror of entering into conflict with the clergy[12] and of soliciting privileges of the Roman Curia, religiously refrained from requesting confirmation from the apostolic chancery. Furthermore, according to Coppoli, he forbade Brother Leo to mention it, leaving its later revelation to God.[13] It is germane to add that the Franciscans themselves, charged with collecting crusade funds, were opposed to any mention of a favor capable of jeopardizing the effects of their preaching. Were not these sufficient reasons for the silence of biographers writing at that time?

But time marched on; the era of the crusades had closed; and the Friars Minor had become powerful enough in the Church to shout from the housetops a secret already out. In 1277, acting on orders from Jerome of Ascoli, Minister General and future pope, Brother Angelo, the Provincial of Umbria, began to collect notarized testimony capable of confounding the adversaries of the Great Pardon.

Among the witnesses named, we find Benedict and Rainerio of Arezzo, Pietro Zalfani, and Giacomo Coppoli.[14] The two friars, Benedict and Rainerio, testified that Brother Masseo had told them the history of the indulgence many times in the words we have reported above. Signor Pietro Zalfani of Assisi, who had been present as a youth at the dedication of St. Mary of the Angels, gave a summary of St. Francis' address on this occasion. Signor Giacomo Coppoli of Perugia attested that he had heard from the lips of Brother Leo the story of the circumstances under which the indulgence had been granted.

It is noteworthy that at the period of these depositions the Great Pardon had already become very popular, and soon pilgrims from all over Italy were converging on St. Mary of the Angels. It was at this time, around 1308, that owing to redoubled attacks from the enemies of the Portiuncula, Teobaldo Offreducci, Bishop of Assisi, had a solemn diploma drawn up, with the idea of putting an end to objections.[15]

This official act was evidently most vexing for the adversaries of the indulgence, as it still is for modern critics who deny its authenticity. The document reports in detail how the great favor was obtained. It reproduces the sworn testimony of those witnesses already named, to which is added that of Brother Marino, a nephew of Brother Masseo. Then it inveighs (with a bit of name calling) against the envious, the jealous, and the ignorant, who "with their foul mouths" dare to impugn a privilege recognized in Italy just as much as it is in France or Spain; a privilege which for so many years (the document continues) has been openly preached before the Roman Curia, to which Pope Boniface VIII has just shown himself favorable anew, and of which the cardinals themselves are eager to avail themselves to obtain pardon for their sins.

Teobaldo Offreducci's diploma did not reduce the diehards to silence. But their attacks were unavailing, since from this time onward, August second of every year brought to St. Mary of the Angels a multitude of pilgrims from all over Europe to obtain "without having to make an offering, the remission of the penalty due to their sins."

Later on, as we know, the popes generously extended the same favor to many churches in the entire world; and since that time only the learned continue to dispute the Franciscan indulgence.

- *12* -

The Chapter of 1217 and Missions In Christian Lands

Following the example of King Arthur, who every year at Pentecost assembled the Knights of the Round Table in chapter, Francis early formed the custom of holding capitular assemblies. These took place at the Portiuncula,[1] giving Francis an opportunity to see his first companions again, to become acquainted with friars who had recently entered the Order, to give paternal advice to all, and to add to the Rule, after a general consultation, some new regulation deemed necessary.

In the beginning, these meetings were quite closely spaced. They were held at Pentecost and Michaelmas; but in time they took place less frequently; and commencing with 1221, they were held only every three years.[2]

The most celebrated of them all is the "Chapter of Mats," described by the *Fioretti*.[3] Present were five thousand friars divided in the plain around St. Mary of the Angels into silent groups of sixty, a hundred, or three hundred men, whose sole occupation was prayer, charitably rendering service to each other, or conversing of spiritual things, a group so disciplined that it could have been taken for an army encamped. As it was summer, some of the friars slept outdoors, others in huts of reed, and all of them slept on the bare ground or on straw, with a stone or piece of wood for a pillow. It was these many temporary shelters set up in the fields that gave this famous chapter its name.

Hugolin, affirms the *Fioretti*, came every day without fail to St. Mary of the Angels. We can picture the immense procession of Friars Minor going to meet the prelate. From Perugia, where the Curia was staying, a brilliant escort of clerks and nobles, in addition to St. Dominic and seven Friars Preachers, accompanied him. Hugolin was moved to tears at sight of the Poverello and his thousands of sons, their ascetic faces beaming with virile joy and zeal. Recalling, perhaps, the Pope's words at the Lateran Council, he explained, "Here is the army of Christ's knights all ready for battle!"

Then, with one of those instinctive gestures of the born leader, the cardinal dismounted, and casting aside his sumptuous cloak and his shoes, walked barefoot to the chapel to say Mass. Francis preached the sermon, taking as his subject these verses he knew so well:

> *We have promised great things,*
> *And still greater have been promised to us.*
> *Let us keep the promises we have made;*
> *Let us long for the fulfillment of those made to us;*
> *Pleasure is fleeting, but its punishment eternal;*
> *Suffering is light, but the glory to come is infinite.*

The Saint exhorted his friars to obey the Church and to pray for all Christendom. He urged them to be patient in adversity, pure as angels, to live at peace with God and man, and be humble and gracious toward all. He moreover counselled them to despise the world and to love the poverty taught by the Gospel. In conclusion, he said, "I command all of you here present to be diligent in prayer and praise to God without care for your bodily nourishment, for Christ has expressly promised to provide for you." The order was immediately carried out, and one and all went off to pray.

St. Dominic did not fail to observe that all this was most imprudent, and he expected disaster to befall these thousands of hungry and heedless men. But the Lord showed that feeding His poor belonged to Him; for a long procession of donkeys and mules was soon seen arriving at St. Mary of the Angels, laden with bread and wine, beans, cheese, and all sorts of victuals that the inhabitants of Perugia, Spoleto, Foligno, Assisi, and the surrounding regions were bringing to Francis and his sons. They even brought plates, goblets, and all other necessary dishes. Not only did no one go hungry, but when the chapter was over, a number of friars had to stay at the Portiuncula to finish the food that remained.

Meanwhile, Dominic had recognized the intervention of Providence in all this; and after apologizing for having taxed Francis with blundering, he promised to observe evangelical poverty henceforth himself and to make its practice mandatory on his sons.

"Now the zeal of the Friars Minor," declares the *Fioretti* in conclusion, "incited them to too many corporal austerities. Some of them who wore hair shirts and iron chains about their waists had become unable to pray; some friars had even died. When Francis heard about these things, this most mild and prudent father commanded those using such instruments of penance to take them off at once and put them in a pile. And no fewer than five hundred of these instruments were counted — a great heap which the Saint ordered to be left there.[4] After which, encouraging his sons once more in good works and telling them to pass through the world without stain, he sent them back to their provinces filled with joy, with God's blessing and his own."

*   *   *

If we cannot identify this "Chapter of Mats," of which the account in the *Fioretti* is confusing and full of errors,[5] we do have four General Chapters for which we have accurate information. The first two were held in 1217 and 1219 and decided upon the establishment of foreign missions. The two others took place in 1221 and 1224, and coincided, as we shall see, with the most painful period in the life of the Little Poor Man.

The rapid extension of the Brotherhood called for the introduction of the elements, at least, of organization. With this the Chapter of 1217 was concerned. It divided the Order into "provinces." These took the name of the region in which they were established and had a "Minister Provincial" at their head. In the course of time, certain important provinces were subdivided into "custodies" presided over by a "custos." On the lowest level were the residences, hermitages, and friaries, under the jurisdiction of the "guardians."[6]

Those innovations did not prevent the founder from wishing to preserve in his religious family the spirit of quasi-equality which had prevailed in the beginning. Nothing in the titles of the superiors was to include the idea of authority or ambition. Avoiding the designations of "masters" or "priors" so as not to give the impression that they were above the others, Francis had given them the name of "ministers," "custodians," or "guardians," to indicate that they were at the service of the friars rather than at their head. In his eyes, as we have seen, their role was that of a mother caring for her children. "I have chosen him as mother," he said of Brother Elias, named Minister General. "He is the pious mother of the Province of France," he said in the same way of Brother Pacifico, designated as Minister Provincial in that country.

And this is the way in which the superiors were pledged to justify their titles. "Let them remember," said Francis, "the words of the Lord, 'I am come not to be served, but to serve.' They ought, then, to be the servants of the other friars, visit them frequently, instruct, encourage, and watch over them, like a shepherd over his sheep. And let the Brothers obey them in all things not contrary to our vocation. And in their actions, let all be inspired by the holy Gospel, which commands us not to do to others what we would not wish done to us, and to do to others what we would wish them to do to us. In fine, let the Minister remember that the souls of the Brothers have been entrusted to him, and that if one of them should perish by his fault, it is of him that our Lord will demand an accounting."[7]

* * *

It was following the Chapter of 1217 that the first departure of the friars who were to establish the Order outside of Italy took place.[8] In calling for volunteers for this knightly expedition, Francis had not concealed its dangers. No one, for example, had either sent for them or was expecting them in the lands where he was sending them; they themselves were ignorant of the language and customs of those far-off regions; they were going forth without money and without authorization to receive it; and in accordance with their father's will, they were likewise leaving without letter of recommendation from pope, bishop, or prince — a factor laying them wide open to suspicion.

As was his custom, the Saint had resolved to set the example. "As it is not fitting," he said, "for me to send you into privation and insult without exposing myself to them also, I beg of you to ask God which direction I ought to take for His greater glory." When he was enlighted on this point, he told them his decision: "In the name of our Lord, Jesus Christ, of His glorious Mother, and of all the saints," said Francis joyously, "I choose the province of France. For the French are especially dear to me, because they have a greater reverence than other people for the Holy Eucharist."[9]

As the volunteers who had responded to his appeal stood before him, Francis enjoined them: "Always go two by two, walk in all humility and modesty, praying much, and refraining from vain speech and observing silence from sunrise to Terce. Even while traveling, behave as if you were in your hermitage and carry your cell with you. For your cell is your body which goes with you everywhere, and the hermit who occupies it is your soul, whose constant care should be to remain united to God in thought and prayer."[10]

With these words, he blessed them, and then with Brother Masseo set out toward the north.[11] The author of the *Fioretti* gives us a poetic account of the incident which marked the beginning of the journey:

"Arriving at some village along the road, they were hungry and so separated to beg their bread. To those who did not know him, Francis was of unassuming appearance, so that all that he collected that day were a few old crusts. Brother Masseo, meanwhile, with his more impressive appearance, had received some large pieces of fresh bread. When the two travelers, who had agreed to meet near a fountain, compared their collection, Francis could not contain his joy at his companion's success:

" 'Brother Masseo! Brother Masseo!' he exclaimed, 'Truly we are unworthy of such abundance and of such a treasure!'

" 'But dear father, how can you speak of abundance in the face of such poverty? Not only do I see here neither table nor servants, but we lack even a bowl and a knife!'

" 'Our incomparable wealth,' replied Francis, 'consists precisely in our not owing to man's ingenuity but to God's providence alone this alms of bread, this fine stone which serves as our table, and this clear fountain where we may quench our thirst. So we ought to pray God to love ever more the noble treasure of holy poverty.'

"Joyfully they ate their bread and drank from the fountain. Then, singing hymns, they arose and went on their way. Suddenly, Francis was inspired to change their itinerary, 'Dear beloved Brother,' said he to his companion, 'let us first go to Rome and pray the Apostles Peter and Paul to obtain for us the inestimable grace of holy poverty.'

"They turned back, and once more Francis began to sing the praises of his beloved lady:

" 'It is blessed Poverty, Brother Masseo, who makes us trample under foot earthly and transient things. She it is who removes the obstacles which prevent us from attaining God. It is she again who permits us even on earth to converse with angels; and finally, it is she who unites us to the risen Christ returning to His Father, raising us up to Heaven even in this life.

" 'Truly, Brother Masseo, coarse vessels like ourselves are unworthy to contain such divine riches. So let us go and pray the holy Apostles, perfect lovers of this Gospel pearl, to obtain the favor we desire. And by their intercession, may Christ, the teacher and most exalted example of holy Poverty, vouchsafe to make us true observers and humble disciples of this dear and most loveable virtue.' "

Perhaps the *Fioretti* was right when it says that the Little Poor Man wanted to go to Rome before setting out for France. For he had often gone and knelt at the tomb of the Apostles when on the eve of making an important decision.[12]

In any case, it was at Florence that he met Cardinal Hugolin who was preaching the Crusade in Tuscany. The cardinal, knowing the opposition which the brotherhood still aroused and the inner perils threatening it, said to his friend:

"You must not cross the Alps while there are prelates in the Curia who persist in looking with disfavor on your Order. Do not go, if you want cardinals who, like me, are favorable to it, to be able to defend it successfully."

"But would it not be shameful to send my friars far off, and to stay here myself sheltered from the perils they must face?"

"You were wrong to let them go off to those distant regions where they risk starving to death."

"My Lord," replied the Saint, "God wants my friars to spread out over the whole world; and not only will Christian lands give them a good reception, but even infidels will receive them and be converted by their words."

If the cardinal, says the *Speculum*, did agree that this was the vocation of the Friars Minor, he none the less persuaded Francis not to leave Italy.[13] Instead, it was Brother Pacifico who introduced the Franciscan Order in France.[14]

* * *

Brother Pacifico was a former troubadour who had been crowned poet laureate by the emperor, and had ever since borne the name of the "King of Verses." "A poor strayed soul," writes Celano, "the king of those who compose light songs, attached to the chariot of iniquity by the thongs of vanity, he walked in darkness until that day wherein Divine Goodness deigned to bring him back to righteousness."

He had gone to visit one of his relatives in religion at a convent [of former Benedictine nuns who became] Poor Ladies near San Servino [in the March of Ancona], when he heard St. Francis preach. At once he was conquered by the seraphic poet, and as Francis continued to exhort him to do good, "A truce on words!" cried the poet laureate. "What I ask of you is to take me away from men immediately so that I can belong to the Great Emperor!"

Francis gave him the habit of the Order and called him Pacifico because of the peace which from that moment filled his heart.[15] Pacifico was to have much to do to preserve this peace in the trials that awaited him in Paris.

There the friars who were lodging in a dependency of the Abbey St. Denis were taken at first for Albigensians with subversive designs. Unfortified by references, all that they could show was their Rule, which they presented to Bishop Peter of Nemours and to the theologians of the Sorbonne. These conceded the Rule to be Catholic, but wrote to the Pope, nevertheless, for further information. The 11th of June, 1219, Honorious replied that the Franciscans were excellent Catholics, deserving to be well treated.[16] This attestation did not prevent certain bishops from continuing to harass them, and a Bull of May 29, 1220, was required to proclaim anew that the friars offered no danger to public security.[17]

The King of Verses left France in 1223 or 1224,[18] and was succeeded by Gregory of Naples. The latter undertook to build on the place called "Vauvert" (on the present site of the Luxembourg) a vast and beautiful convent, little in keeping with holy poverty. Francis learned of his ostentatious dwelling and ordered it destroyed. He was not obeyed; but in 1229 the barely finished building collapsed; and as Hell was held responsible, the demon who carried on operations there was thenceforth held in horror by the Parisians. Later on, the "demon Vauvert" became by corruption the *diable vert*. The convent itself, rebuilt larger than before, soon sheltered men like Alexander of Hales, St. Bonaventure, Roger Bacon, Duns Scotus, and Occam; and for a century, together with the rival convent of the Dominicans, was the most important intellectual center of Christianity.

*   *   *

It is especially to the contemporary chroniclers Jordan of Giano[19] and Thomas of Eccleston[20] that we owe our knowledge of the fate of the friars sent to other countries.

Those who went inside Portugal were treated as undesirables up to the time the Royal Family granted them their protection. Queen Urraca saw at once that they were good servants of God; and, thanks to her, King Alfonso II permitted them to settle in Lisbon and Guimarrens. The Infanta Sancia was no less favorable to them. She made them welcome in her own district of Alenquer; and such was her solicitude for them that she always kept a few spare habits in her palace for friars returning from travel who needed a change.

It was at the convent of Alenquer that a very recollected friar was living whom the noble Maria of Garcia desired to have as her spiritual director. But he fled her with as much obstinancy as she put into pursuing him.

"Bring me," he said to her one day, "a bundle of straw and we will set it on fire." (The unduly devout lady would have brought him the moon.)

When the bundle had been reduced to ashes, the friar said to her, "Know that God's servant gains no more from consorting with women than straw does from consorting with fire." And this ended their relations.[21]

Directed by Elias, the friars also set out for Syria. [This, according to Jordan, took place in 1217. Few details are given, beyond the entry in Syria of Caesar of Speyer.][22]

The mission to Hungary is described more at length. The friars had embarked with a Hungarian bishop returning to his homeland; but he apparently abandoned the mission too soon to its fate, for our missionaries were cruelly treated in that land. Apparently, they were taken for religious charlatans, come in penitential garb to exploit the devotion of the people. They were driven from the cities; and in the country, farmers set their dogs on them, and herdsmen chased them, jabbing them in the back with their pointed sticks.

"Perhaps it is our clothes they want," said one of the friars, and to obey the Gospel, they took off their cloaks. As people continued to beat them, they took off their habits. Evidently, this too was not enough, for they had to give up their breeches.

"I know one of them," writes Jordan, "who lost his breeches

fifteen times. The idea finally came to him of smearing them with cow dung. Only then did the disgusted shepherds leave them alone." Understandably, all were in a hurry to leave this inhospitable country.[23]

Still worse was the reception accorded the friars in Germany. They arrived, says Jordan, under the leadership of John of Penna, to the number of about sixty, none of whom knew German. Having learned the word "Ja," they answered "Ja" the first night when people asked if they were hungry; and this time they were well fed. But the trouble was that they likewise replied "Ja" the next day when people inquired if they were those cursed heretics who, after corrupting Lombardy, had come now to infect Germany. The rumor spread that the plague of the Cathari was invading the Empire. So the friars were arrested, imprisoned, bound naked to the pillory, and flogged until they bled. They speedily agreed that this country was no place for them; and leaving hurriedly, they went back and told the Italians that no people in the world were more dreadful than the Germans, and that anyone returning to them was plainly hankering for martyrdom.

As Jordan notes, the missions of 1217, "thus came to naught." It is true, he added with the author of Ecclesiastes, that the hour of success had not yet come and that there was a time for everything under the sun.[24]

*   *   *

The moment soon came for Germany to show herself more merciful toward the Friars Minor.

"I was present at the Chapter," writes Jordan, "in which a few years later [1221], Francis, seated at the feet of Brother Elias and too feeble to speak himself, plucked Elias by his habit and whispered something in his ear. 'Brethren,' said Elias, 'the Brother (for Francis was so called in the Order) wishes to observe that we have forgotten to mention the Germans. There are, he says, many good Christians among them, like those we often see pass by here with long staffs and big boots, going to the tomb of the Apostles. The Brother is aware that those among you who went to Germany a while back were harshly treated; so he does not want to force anyone to go there. But if there are any who desire to go of their own free will, he will bless them more than if they were to set sail for missions beyond the seas. Let those, then, who want to go to Germany step to one side.' "

At this appeal, about ninety friars took seats apart, to await further directions.

"I recall," continues Jordan, "that at this period there were two things for which I especially prayed God daily; first, not to fall into the Albigensian heresy, and secondly, not to die a victim of Teutonic fury. A witness to the courage of these ninety heroes, I, who regretted failing to make the acquaintance of the Brothers beheaded at Morocco, did not wish to miss the opportunity of seeing the future martyrs.

"So I went up to them, and going from one man to another, I asked them their names. One of them told me that he was Brother Palmerius, adding, 'You are coming with us too!' and laughing, made me sit down beside him. He was a deacon, a native of Monte Gargano, a pleasant fellow, who later on became guardian of the friary of Magdeburg. I thought this one of his usual jokes. 'No! No!' I replied, 'I just came over to make your acquaintance.' But my struggles were in vain, and Palmerius and his friends kept me in their midst.

"They were just finishing reading the list of religious, divided by provinces, and I had just learned that the provincial of Germany was Caesar of Speyer, when the latter approached our group to choose the men he was going to take with him. His attention was called to me. 'Not at all!' I protested. 'I have never wanted to go to Germany! Besides, it's a cold country and bad for my health!' These protests made an impression on the new provincial and on those around me. So they took me to Brother Elias to have him settle the matter. 'Brother,' said the Minister General, 'I command you under holy obedience to make up your mind and tell us whether or not you want to go to Germany.'

"On hearing holy obedience mentioned, great was my perplexity. On the one hand, I did not want to say 'No,' and thus follow my own will. On the other hand, I feared by saying 'Yes' to expose myself rashly to martyrdom and to deny the Faith under torture. So I went to consult my friend, that holy friar I told about above who had lost his breeches so many times in Hungary. He advised me to tell Brother Elias that I had no preference, and that I would obey whatever he commanded. This I did; and Brother Elias ordered me to accompany Brother Caesar. We set off to the number of twenty-seven, twelve clerics and fifteen lay brothers; and that is how I was one of those who introduced the Order in Germany."

The travelers were soon enroute by way of Trent, Bolanzo, Sterzing, and Mittenwald. They went in small groups, so as not to give the impression of an invasion. Among them were John of Piano de Carpine who later went to Central Asia, our friend Thomas of Celano, who seems to have returned very soon to Italy, and several eloquent preachers. Sometimes the missionaries were hospitably received by prelates; and at other times they were met at the door by an evasive *God berad!* ("May God provide"), which reduced them to eating forgotten turnips in the fields.

Eventually, they became most successful, however, in their enterprise, won the friendship of the people, made many recruits, and founded friaries all over Germany, emigrating into Bohemia, Poland, Romania, and as far as Norway.

It would appear that Brother Juniper had some imitators among them; for one day in the year 1222 the religious of

Salzburg, on receiving a letter from Brother Caesar directing them to be present at the provincial Chapter, "if they wished," they were plunged by these last words into deep consternation. Did their superior doubt their obedience and had he lost confidence in them? So, by common consent, they set out and walked two hundred and fifty miles on foot to Speyer to clear up this mystery and protest their submission. The Minister Provincial, delighted to see them again, smilingly promised to write more clearly in future.

Brother Jordan likewise frankly admits his own troubles and blunders. At Erfurt, where he was guardian, and where for a number of years the community was living in what had been an abandoned church and nunnery, the magistrates came to him and offered to build a cloister. "A cloister?" replied Jordan. "I have never seen one. I don't even know what it is. But if you want to do us a favor, just build us a little house near a stream where it will be easy for us to wash our feet every day."

A few years later, returning from Italy where Thomas of Celano had presented him with some relics of St. Francis, he had to stop at the friary of Eisenach. The porter surprisingly refused to let him in and told him to go to the door of the church. As he was waiting outside in some astonishment, he finally saw his fellow-friars arriving, who then escorted him into the church with candles and hymns. Unable to comprehend why he had merited such a reception, he suddenly remembered the relics he was carrying. "And I," he writes, "who up till then had not been such a great admirer of St. Francis, was compelled to admit that if people arranged ceremonies like that in his honor, then he really must be a saint."

Finally, Jordan's *Chronicle* relates the journey he made with a companion to Rome to bring the grievances of the Saxon friars against Brother Elias to the Pope.

This was in 1238. Gregory IX had not yet risen when the

two friars unceremoniously burst into his bedchamber. The Pope ordered them to leave. But rushing up to his bed, Jordan began burrowing under the bedclothes, and, extracting the Pope's foot, covered it with kisses as he murmured, "Oh, Holy Father, do not drive us away, I beg of you, for we do not have any such precious relics in Saxony!"

The former Cardinal Hugolin, who knew his Friars Minor, could not help laughing. "He sat up in bed," writes Jordan, "listened to us kindly, and after saying that we did well to appeal to him, he promised to put a stop to the actions of Brother Elias." The latter was removed from office the following year.[25]

* * *

The establishment of the friars in England encountered fewer difficulties than elsewhere. It is true that it took place somewhat later, after the Chapter of 1223; so we are anticipating a little in speaking of it here.

The *Chronicle* of Thomas of Eccleston describes the beginnings of this English province, whose fervor brought so much joy to St. Francis. The founders were nine in number, including their head, Blessed Agnellus Pisa, who all embarked on a boat belonging to the Benedictines of Fécamp, landing at Dover on September 10, 1224. Some settled at Canterbury, and others at London, and still others at Oxford, where a number of students and illustrious professors soon joined them. All showed as much zeal for study as for holy poverty.

They took a hand themselves in the construction of the friary at Oxford; and some high prelate or other, who had recently entered the Order, could be seen carrying stones and mortar like a mason's apprentice. Those taking courses at the university had to walk a long way through the snow barefoot and wade through swamps up to their knees.

The chapel of the friary of Canterbury was done by a carpenter in a day. At first, only three friars were in residence, one of whom was so crippled that the other two had to carry him to the choir at night to chant Matins. But so merry were they in their extreme poverty that the Office was sometimes interrupted by the infectious gales of laughter that would sweep over them.

Eccleston speaks at length of Brother Solomon, the first novice recruited in England. This young man, who up to then had been noted for his elegance, took the bowl and went begging according to the Rule. When he knocked at his sister's door, she herself opened it. She handed him some bread, turned her face away, and exclaimed: "Cursed be the hour I ever saw you thus!" But he took the bread with great joy and went off.

Brother Solomon was happy at being treated by his family as St. Francis had been. Entrusted with the care of the sick, he begged for them flour and figs which he put in his hood, and faggots which he carried under his arm. Once, in winter time, he took so ill that the other friars feared he would die. To add to their distress, they had no wood for a fire to warm him. Then, writes Eccleston, holy charity suggested to them the same strategem used by pigs in a like extremity. They clustered close around him and rubbed themselves against him until they succeeded in reviving him.

The old chronicler also holds up as an example the holy friar Geoffrey of Salisbury to whom Lord Alexander of Bassingbourn came one day for confession. As the latter rattled off his sins without compunction, Brother Geoffrey began to weep so much that Lord Alexander was also moved to tears, became genuinely converted, and finally decided to enter the Order.

The Franciscans prospered wonderously in England. Less than ten years after their arrival, they had in their ranks men like Adam Marsh, John of Reading, Haymo of Faversham, and Richard of Cornwall; and twenty years later, they possessed no less than forty-nine friaries in the country. They were known at first by the name of "Brethren of the Order of the Apostles," so greatly did their way of life evoke in the eyes of the people that of the humble founders of the Church.[26]

- 13 -

The Chapter of 1219
and Missions In Pagan Lands

It is plain that toward the year 1219, where we are now, the relations of the Little Poor Man with his followers were no longer the same. Up to this time, almost everyone had followed him as a venerated father and infallible oracle. But from now on, many would oppose his ideal and attempt to evade his authority.

It was inevitable that, growing and spreading as it did, the Brotherhood should become less homogeneous and less fervent. The friars who had received their training at Rivo Torto were now submerged in the mass. The immense majority of the Order was composed of religious who had not been formed by St. Francis. A great many hardly knew him. The superiors or ministers were recruited for the most part among the outstanding and influential clerics, to many of whom it was repugnant to be led by "a man without learning," a man indeed considered an impractical and even dangerous visionary by some prelates in high places.

Certainly, in coming to the Chapter of 1219, these ministers did not bring with them a definite reform slate; but they nonetheless made no effort to conceal their dissatisfaction and their own inclinations. What they wanted, in fine, was for the Order to bear a closer resemblance to other religious congregations, to be able to devote themselves to study, to practice a poverty less strict, and to profit by ecclesiastical favors.

They had a good opportunity, for instance, to show how the friars, for lack of official references, had been expelled from countries of the Empire and were threatened with a similar fate in France. Now, if Francis did not reproach others for having recourse to Bulls, exemptions, and privileges, he himself would have none of them. It was not his idea to be either protected or preserved. Had not his beloved Christ been compelled to flee before His enemies? Had He availed Himself of immunity and protection at the scourging and crucifixion?

So, far from displeasing him, persecution which made him like to our Lord delighted him. This was the concept he instilled into Brother Leo, giving him the most astounding definition of perfect joy that men had heard since the Gospel passage: Blessed are they who suffer persecution. The famous dialogue must have taken place about this time. Together with the *Canticle of the Sun*, it constitutes St. Francis' masterpiece. To the religiously-minded of all time, the Poverello repeats that it is not in performing wonders, but in sacrifice and suffering that man's true nobility and earthly happiness consist.[1]

* * *

"Brother Leo, God's Little Sheep, take your pen. I am going to dictate something to you," declared Francis.

"I am ready, Father."

"You are going to write what perfect joy is."

"Gladly, Father!"

"Well, then, supposing a messenger comes and tells us that all the doctors of Paris have entered the Order. Write that this would not give us perfect joy. And supposing that the same messenger were to tell us that all the bishops, archbishops, and prelates of the whole world, and likewise the kings of France and England, have become Friars Minor, that would still be no reason for having perfect joy. And supposing that my friars had gone to the infidels and converted them to the last man . . . ."

"Yes, Father?"

"Even then, Brother Leo, this would still not be perfect joy. If the Friars Minor had the gift of miracles and could make cripples straight, give light to the blind and hearing to the deaf, speech to the dumb, and life to men four days dead, if they were to speak all languages and know the secrets of men's consciences and of the future, and were to know by heart everything that has been written since the beginning of the world until now, and were to know the course of the stars, the location of buried treasure, the natures of birds, fishes, rocks, and all creatures, understand and write it on your paper, Brother Leo, that this would still not be perfect joy."

"Father! For the love of God, please tell me then just what is perfect joy?"

"I'll tell you. Supposing that in the winter, coming back from Perugia, I arrive in pitch darkness at the Portiuncula. Icicles are clinging to my habit and making my legs bleed. Covered with mud and snow, starving and freezing, I shout and knock for a long time. 'Who is there?' asks the porter when he finally decides to come. 'It is I, Brother Francis.' But he doesn't recognize my voice. 'Off with you, prankster!' he replies. 'This is no time for jokes!' I insist, but he won't listen. 'Will you be off, you rascal? There are enough of us without you! And there is no use in your coming here. Smart men like us don't need idiots like you around. Go, try your luck at the Crosiers' hospice!'

"Once more, I beg him not to leave me outside on a night like that, and implore him to open up. He opens up, all right.

'Just you wait, impudent cur! I'll teach you some manners!'
And, grabbing a knobby club, he jumps on me, seizes me by
the hood, and drags me through the snow, beating me and
wounding me with all the knobs in his cudgel .... Well, Leo,
if I am able to bear all this for love of God, not only with
patience but with happiness, convinced that I deserve no
other treatment, know, remember, and write down on your
paper, God's Little Sheep, that at last I have found perfect
joy."

*   *   *

Among the friars present at St. Mary of the Angels in 1219,
there were a certain number who would have preferred joys
less perfect, convents less poverty-stricken, and in general more
comfort and security. Was it this year that Francis, on arriving at the Chapter, was surprised to discover a stone edifice
suddenly sprung up alongside St. Mary of the Angels? At any
rate, he was indignant. What? In this dear Portiuncula which
was to serve as a model to the whole brotherhood, they had
dared to make a mock of holy poverty? It was in vain that
the culprits explained that this new building was owing to
the solicitude of the Assisians. Climbing at once on the roof,
and calling on his friars to help, the Saint began hurling down
the tiles. It was plain to be seen that this was only the beginning; and to keep the whole building from being torn down,
the friars shouted to the knights of Assisi, who stood close
by, ready to intervene.

"Brother," they remonstrated. "In the name of the commune we represent, and which is the owner of the building,
we implore you to stop!"

"Since this house belongs to you," Francis replied, "I have
no right to touch it." And sick at heart, he broke off his work.[2]

A still more painful scene occurred one day when "several

wise and learned friars got Cardinal Hugolin to urge Francis to be guided by the wiser brethren." To their way of thinking, it was from the way of life of Saints Benedict, Augustine, or Bernard that inspiration for revising the statutes of the Brotherhood should be taken. The cardinal carried their request to the Saint. Francis made no reply, but taking the prelate by the hand, he presented himself with him before the Chapter.

"Brothers! Brothers!" he cried, overcome by emotion, "the way that I have entered is one of humility and simplicity! If it is a new way, know that it was taught me by God Himself, and that I will follow no other. So do not speak to me about the Rules of St. Benedict, St. Augustine, or St. Bernard. The Lord wishes me to be a new kind of fool in this world, and will not lead me by any other way. As for you, may He confound you with your wisdom and learning, and make the ministers of His wrath compel you to return to your vocation, should you dare to leave it!"

These maledictions terrified the assembly and even the cardinal; and this time, at least, no one dared to insist.[3]

*   *   *

The Chapter of 1219 maintained the decisions relative to the division of the Order in provinces. Their number was even increased, since France from then on had three provinces.[4] Friars were appointed to go to Christian lands where they had not yet penetrated or to return to those from which they had been driven. But the great innovation of this Chapter was the creation of missions in pagan lands.

Brother Giles left for Tunis, where the Christians of the city, fearing that his zeal might compromise them, thrust him in a boat to force his return. Great was his disappointment at seeing the crown of martyrdom escape him; but he consoled himself when it was given him to realize that certain vexations of the Devil outdid all other tortures in cruelty.[5] Other friars, whom we shall meet soon again, headed for Morocco. Francis himself, ever eager to shed his blood for Christ, chose to go to Egypt.[6]

*   *   *

After appointing two vicars to replace him at the head of the Brotherhood, Francis left the Portiuncula at the beginning of June and went to Ancona to take passage on one of the ships conveying crusaders to the East.

A large number of friars accompanied him, but not all of them could be accommodated. Francis said to them, "Since the sailors refuse to take all of you, and since I, who love you all equally, haven't the heart to make a choice, let us ask God to manifest His will to us." Calling a young boy who was playing on the wharf, he asked him to point out twelve friars at random, and it was with them that he embarked.[7] Among them were Peter Catani, the former jurist, Illuminato of Rieti and Leonard, two former knights, and Brother Barbaro, one of the first disciples.[8]

They set sail on June 24, 1219, St. John's Day, and first put into port at the island of Cyprus. They reached St. John d'Acre about the middle of July, and a few days later Damietta [in the Nile delta], which had been under seige by the crusaders for a year. Duke Leopold of Austria, their leader, had all sorts of men under his command. If some had taken the cross out of holy zeal, many were mere adventurers, attracted to the Orient by the hope of pillage and pleasure. The license and disunity reigning in this army was sufficient explanation of its previous failures.

When, on the morning of the 29th of August, Francis learned that the army was going to attempt a decisive assault, he said to his companion, "The Lord has revealed to me that the Christians are running into a new defeat. Should I warn them? If I speak, they will call me crazy. If I keep still, my conscience will reproach me. What do you think, Brother?"

"The judgment of men matters little!" replied his companion. "After all, this will not be the first time you have been taken for a madman! Unburden your conscience then, and tell them the truth!"

The leaders mocked at Francis' warnings and the attack took place. The result was, as we know, a disaster in which the crusaders lost over four thousand men, killed or captured. Francis had not the heart to witness the battle; but he sent messengers three times for news. When his companion came to him to announce the defeat, he wept much, says Thomas of Celano, especially over the Spanish knights whose bravery had led nearly all of them to their deaths.[10]

*   *   *

The Saint remained there for several months. At first, his apostolate among the crusaders had marvelous results. He was hailed as a prophet ever since, in opposition to the leader, he had dared to predict defeat. His courage and knightly bearing filled the warriors with admiration and his guilelessness and charm won their hearts. "He is so amiable that he is venerated by all," wrote Jacques de Vitry to his friends in Lorraine.

The celebrated chronicler who at that period occupied the episcopal see of St. John d'Acre and made frequent visits to the crusaders' camp, added that many abandoned the profession of arms or the secular priesthood to become Friars Minor. "This Order which is spreading through the whole world," he wrote further, "imitates the primitive Church and the life of the Apostles in all things. Colin the Englishman, our clerk, has entered their ranks, with two others, Master Michael and Dom Matthew, to whom I had entrusted the parish of the

Holy Cross. Only with difficulty do I hold back the Chanter and Henry and others." Jacques de Vitry also announced to his correspondents that "Brother Francis has not feared to leave the Christian army to go to the enemy camp to preach the faith."[11]

The idea of converting the Saracens must have appeared singularly fantastic to men who up to then had thought only of cutting their throats. It is true that the Moors asked only to do likewise; for, quite apart from an eternal reward, every Moslem who brought a Christian head to the Sultan received a golden bezant from him.[12] Cardinal Pelagio, who now arrived in Damietta with reinforcements, was far from encouraging Francis in his project.[13] If not actually forbidding the undertaking, he at least declined all personal responsibility, charging Francis not to compromise thereby the Christian name and Christian interests.

The Saint took Brother Illuminato with him and set out toward the enemy lines, singing, "Though I walk in the midst of the shadow of death, I will fear no evil, for Thou art with me."[14] To comfort his less reassured companion, Francis showed him two ewes peacefully grazing in this perilous spot. "Courage, Brother!" he cried joyously. "Put your trust in Him who sends us forth like sheep in the midst of wolves."

However, the Saracens appeared, jumped on the two religious, and began to beat them. "Soldan! Soldan!" shouted Francis as long as he was able. The soldiers thought that they were dealing with envoys and brought them in chains to their camp. Francis explained in French that he desired to see the Sultan and convert him to the Gospel.[15] Had he said this anywhere else, it would have meant instant death; but the court of Al-Malik al-Kamil included skeptics who liked to discuss the respective merits of the Koran and the Gospel, and who likewise were chivalrous in their deportment.

The Sultan also doubtless saw in the arrival of the Friars

Minor an opportunity for diversion and ordered the evangelizers to be shown in. It is said that in order to cause them embarrassment, he had a carpet strewn with crosses laid down in the room in front of him. "If they walk on it," he said, "I will accuse them of insulting their God. If they refuse, I will reproach them with not wishing to approach me and of insulting me."

Francis walked unhesitatingly over the carpet, and as the prince observed that he was trampling the Christian cross underfoot, the Saint replied: "You must know that there were several crosses on Calvary, the cross of Christ and those of the two thieves. The first is ours, which we adore. As for the others, we gladly leave them to you, and have no scruples about treading on them, whenever it pleases you to strew them on the ground."[16]

Al-Malik al-Kamil soon conceived a warm friendship for the Poverello and invited him to stay with him. "I would do so gladly," replied the Saint, "if you would consent to become converted to Christ together with your people." And he even offered, writes St. Bonaventure, to undergo the ordeal by fire in his presence.

"Let a great furnace be lit," said he. "Your priests and I will enter it; and you shall judge by what you see which of our two religions is the holiest and truest."

"I greatly fear that my priests will refuse to accompany you into the furnace," observed the Sultan.

And indeed, at the simple announcement of this proposal, the venerable dean of that priestly group hastily disappeared. "Since that is the way things are," said Francis, "I will enter the fire alone. If I perish, you must lay it to my sins. But if God's power protects me, do you promise to acknowledge Christ as the true God and Savior?"

The Sultan alleged the impossibility of his changing his religion without alienating his people. But as his desire to keep this charming messenger at his court was as strong as ever, he offered him rich presents. These were, as we may well imagine, refused. "Take them at least to give to the poor!" he urged. But Francis accepted, it appears, only a horn which later on he used to summon people when he was about to preach.

He departed very sad as soon as he perceived the uselessness of his efforts. The Sultan had him conducted in state back to the Christian camp. "Remember me in your prayers," he begged as Francis left, "and may God, by your intercession, reveal to me which belief is more pleasing to Him."[17]

*   *   *

Thanks to the reinforcements of Cardinal Pelagio, Damietta fell on November 5, 1219. Francis was present at the taking of the city; but this victory of the crusaders drew more tears from him than did their recent defeat. The streets were strewn with corpses and the houses filled with victims of the plague. The captors fought like wolves over the immense booty, selling the captives at auction, except the young women reserved for their pleasure.

When Francis saw that Damietta had become a pandemonium in which his voice was lost in the clamor of unleashed instincts, the Saint left the country and took ship for St. John d'Acre.[18] There he met Brother Elias, Provincial of Syria, and among Elias' recruits, Caesar of Speyer who had fled Germany to escape the relatives of those whom he had enrolled in the crusade and the husbands of the women he had converted.[19]

It was also at St. John d'Acre that Francis learned that five of his sons had just shed their blood for the faith. They were Brothers Otho, Berard, Peter, Accursus, and Adjutus, who had left the Portiuncula at the same time he did; and who, as we have seen, set out for Morocco by way of Spain.[20]

Truly these five had left no stone unturned to obtain the grace of martyrdom. Arriving first in Seville, which was still in the power of the Moors, they had entered the mosque and began to preach against the Koran. It was a good place to meet Moslems, but a bad one in which to insult Moham- med. They were hustled out and beaten by the followers of the prophet. They then went to the royal palace.

"Who are you?" the king asked them.

"We belong to the regions of Rome."

"And what are you doing here?"

"We have come to preach faith in Jesus Christ to you, so that you will renounce Mohammed, that wicked slave of the devil, and obtain everlasting life like us."

The prince, beside himself with fury, ordered them to be beheaded; but seeing the joy his sentence caused them, he took pity on them and attempted to win them by presents. "May your money go to perdition with you!" they replied.

They were taken in chains to the summit of a tower, from which they shouted down to the passers-by that Mohammed was an imposter. They were then shut up in the public prison where they still attempted to convert their jailors and fellow- prisoners.

They were again brought before the king, who gave them the choice of returning to Italy or of being deported to Moroc- co. "Do whatever pleases you," they replied, "and may God's will be done!" It was decided that they should go to Morocco.

Shortly after their arrival, the Amir al-Muminin Yusuf, who commanded in Africa in the king's name, had them brought before him, half naked and in chains. "Who are you?" he asked.

"We are disciples of Brother Francis, who has sent his friars throughout the world to teach all men the way of truth."

"And what is this way?"

Brother Otho, who was a priest, began to recite the Creed;[21]

and he was starting to comment on it, when the Miramolin stopped him, saying, "It is surely the devil who speaks by your mouth." He thereupon handed them over to his torturers.

These used their cruelest devices against their victims. All night long the poor friars were flogged until they bled, dragged by the throat over pebbles, and doused with boiling oil and vinegar, while, their hearts failing them, they exhorted one other in a loud voice to persevere in the love of Christ.

The following day, January 16, 1220, the Miramolin summoned them at dawn to learn if they persisted in despising the Koran. All proclaimed that there is no other truth than the holy Gospels. The prince threatened them with death. "Our bodies are in your power," they replied, "but our souls are in the power of God."

These were their last words, for Abu-Jacob thereupon had his sword brought and cut off their heads in the presence of his women attendants.

When these facts were reported to Francis, he is said to have exclaimed, "Now I can truly say that I have five Friars Minor." But when the account of their martyrdom was read before him, he interrupted the reading as soon as he perceived that a few words praising him had been inserted.[22]

* * *

Syria, at this period, was partly Christian and partly Moslem. Thanks to a permit received from Conradin, Sultan of Damascus and brother of Al-Malik al-Kamil, Francis could travel anywhere in the country without paying tribute. He made use of this privilege, says Angelo Clareno, to visit the Holy Places.[23] How we would like to have a contemporary account of those who saw him or accompanied him to Palestine — showing us the Little Poor Man celebrating Christmas in Bethlehem, weeping on Good Friday at Gethsemani and Calvary, and communicating on Easter morning at the Holy Sepulchre! But, unfortunately, the records are silent about these months in the life of St. Francis.

They only break the silence again to state that during the summer of 1220, an emissary from the Portiuncula named Brother Stephen arrived in Syria bearing bad news. His message was that the vicars were leading the Order to ruin, and that the faithful friars implored their father, if he was still of this world, to come back at once and save his work.[24]

- *14* -

Crisis in the Order and the Rule of 1221

A crucial period now faced the Brotherhood of the Little Poor Man, which was rife with every kind of dissension and dispute. Among the causes of such a crisis must be emphasized the lack of organization in the Order and the increasing diversity of aims of its members.

Inspired by the three Gospel texts in the missal of Assisi: "If you would be perfect, renounce all that you possess. Take nothing with you for your journey. Let him who would be My disciple deny himself and carry his cross," the Rule of 1209, taken as it stood without authorized commentary, was less a piece of monastic legislation than a code for spiritual living. Thus the friars had at first enjoyed great freedom, some living as hermits, others as pilgrims, day laborers, nurses, or wandering preachers. Moreover, their vow of obedience was somewhat unique, since any precedence among them on a stable basis simply did not exist; and their superiors were as likely to be recruited from illiterate laymen as from clerics versed in canon law.

If such a way of life proved agreeable to a few heroic penitents stimulated by the presence of the most radiant of the saints, it could no longer be so to thousands of widely-scattered religious, among them a number of clerics and scholars who found too hard or too narrow the primitive ideal of Rivo Torto. Thus the fire had long been smouldering under the ashes, and already disunion reigned in the Order when Francis embarked for Egypt.

His extended absence had permitted the fomenters of new ideas to push their advantage, especially since they could count on the compliance of the two vicars. For those to whom the Saint had turned over his powers were definitely their men. Their names were Matthew of Narni and Gregory of Naples, one of them charged to remain at the Portiuncula and receive new friars, and the other to go from friary to friary to settle problems that arose. Of the first we know nothing, except that he thought as did his colleague. As for Gregory, an ardent advocate of studies and a great friend of brother Elias, he was according to Eccleston, a good preacher and administrator. Later, however, [as Minister of France (1223-1233)], he showed himself to be so cruel and authoritarian that he was removed and condemned to imprisonment.[1]

Meanwhile, the task of both was a thorny one. For how were they to govern an Order in which independence and even vagabondage were so esteemed? To be sure, it was often for reasons of piety that the "Lord's wandering minstrels" were moved to travel about. We see one of them, among others, who garbed himself as a pilgrim, resolved to play the madman for the rest of his life, and so reap a rich harvest of insults.[2] But some among them showed themselves less edifying on their travels; those, for instance, who sought the society of women, "eating with them out of the same bowl," not to speak of greater familiarities.[3] There were also those who followed weird impulses which had no relation to their vocation. Such was one John Capella (if it were really he) who set off for Rome with a band of leprosy patients of both sexes, proposing to unite them in a mixed congregation and already soliciting papal approval for his scheme.[4]

These abuses and many others evidently gave the vicars cause for intervention. As the rumor of Francis' death spread, they further imagined that it was up to them to impart to the Brotherhood the organization it lacked, and they seized this opportunity to make their own views prevail.

Having called together a chapter composed of the most influential friars, they promulgated constitutions inspired by the legislation of other Orders. They tightened up on discipline, multiplied fasts, and prescribed many privations foreign to the Rule. These measures were [owing perhaps to the desires of many well-meaning clerics who clamored for a more regulated life]. Here and there in guise of residences, vast and solid buildings were seen to rise. The Provincial Peter Staccia established a house of studies in Bologna like the one possessed by the Dominicans. Finally, in order to be less hampered in their apostolate, the friars solicited favors from the Roman Curia. Thus it was that the missionaries to France received papal letters commending them to the bishops of the country, and Brother Philip, the visitor of the Poor Ladies, obtained a bull of excommunication against anyone attacking his protegees.[5]

All this, so contrary to the intentions of the founder, transformed the character of the Brotherhood too radically not to call forth protests from the earlier friars. Many among them revolted. They had cause to rue it, however, for Gregory of Naples was firm and meant to be obeyed. "Certain recalcitrants were afflicted with unjust penances, others were driven from the community like men of evil life, and still others, in order to flee from the wrath of their persecutors, escaped and wandered hither and yon, bewailing the absence of their beloved shepherd and guide."

Then it was that one of these unfortunates escaped unbeknown to the vicars and had the good fortune to meet Francis in Syria. He handed him a copy of the new ordinances and implored him to hasten to the rescue of his perishing Order.

The Saint was at table with Peter Catani when Brother Stephen appeared. Meat was being served. Now according to the new constitutions it was a day of abstinence.

"Master Peter," inquired Francis, "what are we to do?"

"Master Francis," replied Peter, "we shall do whatever pleases you, for it is up to you to command."

"Then let us eat meat, in keeping with the liberty given us by the holy Gospel."

Francis left at once, taking with him Caesar of Speyer, Peter Catani, the friend of his early days, and Brother Elias, who had just revealed his talents as Provincial of Syria. These were three superior men who would, he believed, assist him in restoring the unity of his religious family.[6]

At Venice, where they disembarked, the travelers separated. Francis, who had acquired new infirmities in the Orient, wanted to take a few days rest before returning to the Portiuncula.

One might have said that even the wild creatures in his country were glad to see him again. A flock of larks, singing loudly, flew about him in a thicket. "Brother," he remarked to his companion, "since our sisters the larks praise their Creator so gladly, let us join them." And they paused to recite their hours. But as if anxious to emulate the friars, the birds made such a racket that they could not hear each other pray. "Sister larks," said the Saint, "would you have the goodness to stop a moment?" And the birds stopped their concert until Francis and his companion had finished reciting their breviary.[7]

The Saint headed for Bologna. Being ill, he rode astride a donkey that Brother Leonard was leading by the bridle. Now, tired himself, Leonard who, as we have seen, was born of a noble family, had an inner moment of bad humor. "Some things are very queer on this earth!" he thought. "For instance, who would have thought that I, whose parents would not have dreamed of associating with the Bernardones, would one day be walking along on foot, while their son rides at ease?"

"You are quite right, brother," observed Francis, dismounting. "It is plain that since you are a nobleman, it is not right that I should ride the donkey and you go on foot."

Surprised at being found out, Leonard fell at Francis' feet and begged his pardon.[8]

The Saint could soon gauge for himself the importance of the revolution under way. As he neared Bologna, he learned that the friars were occupying a great house belonging to them — the one where Peter Staccia had established his convent of studies. He summoned the minister and said to him: "Are you trying to destroy my Order, forgetting that it is my will that the friars spend less time in study than in prayer?" And having compelled all the religious, even those who were sick, to vacate their property on the spot, he imposed a curse on Peter Staccia and withdrew. It was in vain that Peter ran after him to have him take back his curse. He replied that it was too late, and that it had been confirmed by Christ himself. And this was so true, writes the author of the *Actus*, that the guilty friar "soon surrendered his soul to the devil in the midst of a horrible stench."[9]

*   *   *

When the faithful friars learned of their Father's return, "joy filled their hearts, as though a new light shone upon them." They came out of hiding, thinking all would now be straightened out.[10] But the Saint judged otherwise. What had happened showed that the innovators were supported by those higher up, and that he alone would be unable to restore peace.

In a dream, he saw a black hen no bigger than a dove, with many more chicks around her than she could shelter under her wings. "This hen," he said to himself on awakening, "is certainly me with my short stature and dark skin. The dove she resembles is a symbol of the simplicity I must practice to obey the Gospel. The chickens are my virtuous friars whose number is now too great for a little man like me to defend. So I am going to entrust them to the Church of Rome, which is alone able to protect them."[11]

Without going near the Portiuncula or wishing to encounter the rebels, he went to Rome. Refusing out of humility to knock at the Pope's door, he waited for a long time on the threshold. When the Pope appeared, he threw himself at his feet, saying, "God grant you peace, Holy Father!"

"God bless you, my son," replied Honorius III.

"Your Holiness," continued Francis, "your dignity is too great and you are too absorbed in great matters for the poor to have recourse to you as often as they would like."

Doubtless, the benevolent Pontiff remarked that there was no lack of cardinals to whom one could address himself at need.

"Exactly! There are too many of them, Holy Father! Please designate just one of them for me to take your place and to treat with me about the interests of my Order!"

"Whom do you want me to appoint?"

"The Bishop of Ostia," replied Francis, who had complete confidence in the friendship and piety of the powerful cardinal. For had he not, to show his sympathy for the friars, even doffed the purple sometimes and put on their habit?

The Pope agreed to the Little Poor Man's request, and Hugolin, named "protector, governor, and corrector of the Brotherhood," became the representative of the Holy See for the business of the Order.[12] From that time onward he became the Saint's permanent advisor as well as the supreme arbiter between the rival parties of his religious family; and it was he, who after trying to restore peace, helped to give it its definitive statutes.

* * *

The skill and authority of the man whom Francis now called his "apostolic lord" soon made itself felt; and this in a way to reassure the founder without at the same time discouraging his adversaries.

Brother Philip had to give up visiting the Poor Ladies, and the letters of excommunication he had obtained were annulled. John Capella was obliged to dissolve his mixed congregation of leprosy patients and return to his convent. A Bull of September 22, 1220, forbade the lovers of travel to circulate in future without letters of obedience; and as much to weed out undesirables as to form the rest to discipline, a year's novitiate was required of those desiring to enter the Order.[13] Finally, it was decided to prepare without delay for the Chapter of 1221, while Francis was to busy himself with working out a new Rule which would — so it was hoped — meet with general approval.

Meanwhile, the rebellious vicars, dismissed from office, had had to give way to Peter Catani, who had already replaced Francis on many occasions in his absence. Unfortunately, Peter died prematurely on March 10, 1221.[14] And his death can be said to have been an event with far-reaching consequences, when we consider that this old and loyal disciple of the Poverello was succeeded by Brother Elias, the least Franciscan of men, who governed the Brotherhood for thirteen years. Except from 1227 to 1232, Elias Bombarone exercised the functions of Minister General from 1221 to 1239.[15]

* * *

Despite all the research that has been made about him, Brother Elias remains a mysterious figure.[16] Born, it would appear, in or near Assisi, he had been by turns a mattress-maker, school teacher, and notary before entering the Order. Ambitious and charming, a man of universal talent, he was born to be outstanding in the highest offices. Although a simple lay-brother, he was reputed to be very learned, and "no one," says Eccleston, "was more famous in his time in all Christendom." We see the Bishop of Lincoln, the famous Robert Grosseteste, seeking his friendship, Italian cities asking him to arbitrate their conflicts, and Bela IV, King of Hungary, sending him a golden cup to win his favor. Enjoying the confidence of the two masters of the world, the Pope and the Emperor, he long played the role of peacemaker between them, and St. Clare herself was attached to him.

He doubtless had his virtuous moments, since Francis and Hugolin had placed him at the head of the Brotherhood, and he always had a goodly number of partisans. It may also be said to his credit that he loved and venerated the Poverello, that he did everything possible to alleviate the sufferings of his last years, and to glorify him after his death.

The two superimposed churches that he erected on the rock of Mount Subasio to enclose the Saint's tomb constitute one of the architectural marvels of Europe. He flanked them with a sort of convent-fortress, which he made his general headquarters and which he offered as a refuge to the popes in case of need; and they did sometimes store their treasures in it. And when we consider that less than twelve years were required to complete all these works, we must agree that Brother Elias was a remarkable man indeed.

We have seen that Brother Giles, Brother Leo, and their friends looked upon the basilica and the Sacro Convento of Assisi as a complete betrayal of the Franciscan ideal. But in the eyes of the Vicar General and his party these glorious edifices were to be symbolic of the role and status to which the Friars Minor could aspire in future. Elias, for his part, constantly worked at increasing vocations to the Brotherhood. He divided the Order into seventy-two provinces, allegedly to honor the seventy-two disciples of our Lord, but with an eye to humiliating the Dominicans whose manpower was less. He multiplied missions in pagan lands, promoted study, and urged the friars to mix in politics, and to establish important foundations everywhere.

Evidently, it was only gradually that Elias was able to reveal his characteristic role and to carry out his plans. In the first years of his generalship he was still restrained by filial piety and prudence. But with Francis dead, he threw off all reserve. He never went anywhere save on horseback, dined at a separate table, ate choice viands, kept a special cook for his own use, and a dozen servants, dismissed and replaced provincials according to his good pleasure, scattered and persecuted those religious faithful to the spirit of the Portiuncula, and, too occupied with his building projects and embassies to visit the transalpine provinces, he sent substitutes charged with imposing his will with an iron hand and carrying out his vengeances. Supine submission was the only road to his favor. By his orders, Caesar of Speyer, his former disciple and companion in the Holy Land, was thrown in a dungeon where he succumbed to ill treatment. Even Brother Bernard of Quintavalle had to flee to Assisi to escape the same fate.

From 1235 on, the friars of Germany, France, and Italy beseeched Cardinal Hugolin, now Pope, to put an end to this insufferable dictatorship. But Gregory IX waited until 1239 to give them satisfaction. It is true that at this date his own dealings with the Emperor were irreparably ruined and that Brother Elias inclined too much to the Ghibelline side to be of further service to the Holy See.

The former General was formally excommunicated when he

took refuge with Frederick II who continued to make use of him. In 1244, under Innocent IV, he tried to re-enter the Order and regain his power, but his attempt only netted him an additional excommunication. Elias lived for some time longer at the imperial court; then with a dozen faithful followers he retired to the humble and charming hermitage of Le Celle near Cortona. The entire city was devoted to him and venerated him as a saint. Elias built a new church in honor of St. Francis at Cortona, and died on April 4, 1253, reconciled at the last moment with the Church [by a secular priest].

* * *

Although Francis had abandoned the charge of Minister General to Brother Elias, he nonetheless remained for all the true father and lawgiver of the Brotherhood. It was as such that, assisted by Caesar of Speyer,[17] a man well versed in the Scriptures, he revised the Rule for the Chapter of 1221. It comprised twenty-three chapters interspersed with numerous texts taken from the New Testament and inspired (as we shall see) by the purest spirit of Rivo Torto.[18]

It naturally took into account the Bull *Cum secundum,* which had inaugurated a year's novitiate (chap. III), and proscribed the practice of vagabondage (chap. V). It likewise profited from the experience acquired in the course of the preceding ten years, and here and there alluded to the abuses revealed by recent events. Thus chapters III and IX condemn all distinction between permitted and forbidden food; chapter XII forbids the friars unchaste looks and association with women; and chapter V authorizes disobedience to superiors whose orders run contrary to the Franciscan vocation.

But for the rest, far from mitigating the text of 1210, the Rule of 1221 merely reproduced, developed, and commented on it in the sense of a perfect and literal observation of the Gospel.

Neither in common nor as individuals are the friars to own anything. They are to have no beasts of burden at their convents or elsewhere (chap. XV). They are not "to claim or defend" their tiny hermitages against "anyone whatever" (chap. VII). As for money, it is not only forbidden them to possess it, but even to make use of it in any way: "They are not to value it any more than pebbles," and if (which God forbid) one of them should transgress the prohibition, let him be considered by all as a false friar, a thief, a traitor, and a Judas carrying the purse (chap. VIII).

Their social rank is that of the poor, and they shall hold to it in imitation of our Lord, His Mother, and His disciples, who lived (Francis assures us) on public charity.[20] Their habit is to consist of a tunic that can be patched, a hood, a cord, and drawers (chap. II). They are not to travel on horseback but on foot (chap. XV), carrying nothing with them, neither sack nor wallet, nor bread, nor silver, nor staff; and they are not to resist evil, but let themselves be despoiled without protest (chap. XIV). Chapter VII recalls the obligation of manual labor and the comportment of religious in domestic service. Chapter IX treats at length the solicitation of alms to which the friars will be obliged to resort, since it is forbidden them to lay up anything in store, and because their labor will not always suffice for their living. Let them not be ashamed to beg, since, following our Lord's example, they have voluntarily embraced poverty, and alms are a right and a legacy acquired by Christ's merits for all the poor. But let them rejoice to find themselves in the company of those whom men despise, the poor, the weak, the infirm, the victims of leprosy, and the beggars by the wayside.

The Rule also mentions the Chapters of Pentecost (chap. XVIII), the ministers whom it constantly calls the servants of the other friars (chaps. IV, V, XVI, XVIII), the superiors who are forbidden to take the name of prior (chap. VI), the preachers and the exhortation to penance which each may make when and wherever he pleases (chap. XXI); those who go to the Saracens and other infidels, who have two ways in which to do good: the first, by comporting themselves as Christians without arguing or quarrelling with anyone, and the second, by preaching the word of God (chap. XVI). Finally, the friars are commanded to confess to each other if there are no priests, while waiting to do so to an approved confessor (chap. XX); and all are to behave in word and in deed as good Catholics, under pain of being driven from the Brotherhood (chap. XIX).

All this let us note, was required of clerics as well as of laics;[21] for, except for the Divine Office, for which the former were to recite the Breviary, and the latter to say Pater Nosters, the legislator made no distinction between them. And it was in referring to the Divine Office that he forbade clerics to have any books except those needed to recite their hours.

The tone of the Rule recalls that of the Gospels, wherein precepts and prohibitions are mixed with love-inspired encouragement and counsel. Here is Chapter Ten, "Concerning the Sick Brethren":

"In whatever place a Brother shall fall sick, the others shall not leave him without taking care to have one of the friars or more, if need be, appointed who will serve him as they would wish to be served themselves. But in case of great necessity, they can entrust him to some other person who will assume his care. And I ask the friar who is sick to give thanks to the Creator for all things, and to desire to be whatever God wills for him, whether healthy or sick, because all whom God has predestined to eternal life He prepares by the goad of suffering and infirmity and the spirit of compunction, as the Lord says: Those whom I love I rebuke and chastise (Apoc. 3, 19). But if the sick friar lets himself be troubled or angered wheth-

er against God or the other friars, or is too demanding of medicines in the vain desire of saving the flesh which is soon to
die and which is the enemy of the soul, this comes to him
from the evil one; and he is a carnal [self-centered] man and
is acting no more like one of the friars, since he loves the
body more than the soul."

The last two chapters alone make up a third of the Rule.
There is first of all a long "admonition" (chap. XXII), made
up almost entirely of Gospel texts, in which the Little Poor
Man warns his children never to look back. He says:

"Consider this word of the Lord, 'Love your enemies and
do good to them that hate you.' It is because our Lord Jesus
Christ called a traitor 'friend,' and of His own free will gave
Himself up to His executioners that we must, in imitation of
Him, look upon as friends those from whom we have received
suffering and injustice, humiliations, torments, martyrdom,
and death. We ought to love them with our whole heart, for
they obtain for us everlasting life.

"The only thing that remains for us to do, now that we have
forsaken the world, is eagerly to do God's will and please Him
. . . Let us not then be one of those stony places where the
divine seed falls without bearing fruit. . . . Let the dead bury
the dead. Let us beware of the wiles of the devil, who by the
affairs and cares of this life desires to stifle in our hearts the
Lord's words and precepts . . . In the name of that holy charity which is God, I beseech all the brethren to lay aside every
obstacle, every care and encumbrance, that they may serve,
love, honor, and adore God with pure hearts and minds. . . .
Let us build within a tabernacle and dwelling for Him. . . . Let
us pray: Our Father who art in Heaven. Let us have recourse
to Christ, the Shepherd and Bishop of our souls . . . who Himself vouchsafed to pray to His Father for us, saying, 'Holy Father, keep in Your name those whom You have given Me. I
do not pray that You take them out of the world, but that

You keep them from evil . . . for where I am, Father, I will that they may be with Me and behold Your Glory in Your kingdom.' "

The twenty-third and last chapter is a long prayer, a sort of heavenly hymn as worthy of admiration as the most beautiful prefaces of the ancient liturgy. It constitutes perhaps the most perfect example of the way in which Francis spoke to God and of God when he let his heart speak. We must be content to quote only a few extracts:

"Almighty and Sovereign God, holy and just Father, King of Heaven and earth, we give You thanks because by Your only begotten Son and in the Holy Spirit You have created all things spiritual and corporal, and have made us in Your image and likeness . . . . We thank You that, having created us through Your Son, You caused Him to be born of the glorious and blessed Virgin Mary, and willed that we poor captives be redeemed by His Cross, blood, and death.

"And because we all, miserable sinners, are not worthy to name You, we humbly pray that our Lord Jesus Christ, Your beloved Son, may give You thanks, together with the Holy Spirit the Comforter, for all Your benefits. Alleluia. And you, glorious and blessed Mary, Mother of God, ever Virgin . . . and all saints present, past, and to come, we humbly beseech you to give thanks to God most high, to His most dear Son, our Lord Jesus Christ, and to the Holy Spirit, the Paraclete, forever and ever. Amen! Alleluia!

"And all those who would serve Almighty God in the Holy, Catholic, and Apostolic Church, the priests, deacons, subdeacons, acolytes, exorcists, lectors, porters, and all clerics, and all religious both men and women, kings, princes, workers, tillers of the soil, servants, masters, virgins, the chaste, married people, laymen, men, women, babes, youth, old people, the sick and the well, the humble and the great, all people, families, tribes, and nations, all men on earth present and to come, we humbly beg and beseech them — all of us Friars Minor, useless servants — humbly beg and beseech them to pray for us the grace of perseverance in the true Faith and in penitence, without which no man can be saved.

"Let us all love with our whole heart, powers, and strength the Lord God who has given us our bodies, our souls, and our lives. Let our one desire and purpose, then, be to seek to love and enjoy our Creator and Savior, alone true God, complete and perfect good, alone merciful and mild, from whom comes all forgiveness, grace, and glory . . . May nothing cause us to turn aside from these things . . . Let us love, honor, adore, serve, praise, bless, glorify, exalt, extol, and give thanks to the Most High God, Father, Son, and Holy Spirit, Creator of all things, the Savior of those who believe, hope, and love Him, God unchanging, invisible, unutterable, ineffable, incomprehensible, unfathomable, blessed, laudable, glorious, exalted, great, sublime, clement, lovable, delectable, wholly and absolutely desirable forever and ever."[22]

This long document closed with this supreme adjuration:

"In the name of the Lord I ask all the friars to know the tenor and meaning of these words and to recall them often. And I pray all in deep humility, to cherish, observe and keep this Rule of Life. And on behalf of Almighty God and of our Holy Father the Pope, I, Brother Francis, formally prescribe and ordain that no one shall add to or take away from it anything whatever, and that the Brethren shall never have another Rule . . . . *Amen.*"

*   *   *

Such is the Rule that Francis brought to the Chapter of 1221. There was in it, as we see, none of the compromises hoped for by the ministers. Rather, it seemed to be a veritable challenge. The Little Poor Man did not expect approval for it to come without a struggle; but at this period he was still hopeful and willing to fight, as is proved by the text which served as the theme of his opening sermon: *"Benedictus Dominus Deus qui docet manus meas ad proelium.* Blessed be the Lord, my God, who teaches my hands to make war."[23]

The Chapter, which united at least 3000 friars and lasted seven days, was presided over by Cardinal Rainerio Capocci, replacing Hugolin, unable to attend. And the Cardinal must have congratulated himself on his inability to be present; for his attempts at arbitration, brought out into the open, would have had no chance of success. Carried away by the holy founder, the majority of the friars would have rallied to his intransigeance, while the opposing party would not have consented to disband. And thus the gulf separating the adversaries would have been widened still more.

The documents make no mention of the discussion which took place on the Rule. If there was any, there is no doubt that the ministers and Brother Elias were agreed not to push matters to a conclusion. For it was better to separate with nothing decided, and to leave it to the Cardinal-Protector to prepare — by private negotiations — a satisfactory solution. And so it was done.

But before seeing how Hugolin resolved the conflict, we must first relate in chronological order the institution of the Third Order, which was in part his work, and the founding of the first Franciscan school, to which he likewise gave his support.

- 15 -

The Third Order

It almost began to look as though Francis was going to transform Umbria into a second Egypt of the Desert Fathers. He made God so lovable and the spiritual world so real that there were times when all his hearers wanted to forsake the world to assure their salvation.

Jacques de Vitry was alarmed at this epidemic of vocations: "There is a great danger," he wrote in March, 1220, "in thus accepting pell-mell the perfect and the imperfect. The latter should at least go through a trial period before being admitted into religion." The Saint himself complained of the quantity of his new candidates. "There are too many Friars Minor!" he murmured. "May the time come when the people instead of meeting them at every turn may complain that they see too few of them!"[1]

It was both to divert the stream of candidates and to permit lay men and women to live in a holy way in the world that he instituted the Order of Penance.

"Do not be in such haste," he said [probably in 1209] to the people of Cannara who wanted to leave everything to follow him. "I promise to provide something for you."

For already he was thinking of the Third Order, if we are to believe the *Fioretti*.[2] The new institution did not receive its canonical statue until 1221, but many lay people had not waited until this date to lead a Franciscan life. Among these early tertiaries may be mentioned Count Orlando of Chuisi, the donor of Mount La Verna, Praxedis, the Roman recluse to whom Francis gave the habit and cord,[3] and, finally, the Lady Jacopa de' Settesoli, widow of the knight Graziano Frangipani.[4]

* * *

It was apparently in 1212, a few months after the clothing of St. Clare, that the Poverello made the acquaintance of "Brother Jacopa," who became his great and faithful friend. Jacopa, who was then about twenty-two years of age, belonged to high-ranking Roman nobility, descending on her father's side from the Norman knights who had invaded Sicily, and allied on her husband's side [according to legend], to Flavius Anicius, who [in 717] saved the people of Rome from famine by giving them bread: hence their name of *Frangens panem*. The name of Settesoli came from the domain of Septizonium which the Frangipani had acquired [in 1145] from the Camaldolese monks.

On becoming a widow, Jacopa would no doubt have embraced the religious life, if the guardianship of her two sons and the safeguarding of their patrimony had not prevented her. A deed of May 13, 1217, shows her generously renouncing a claim against the Holy See in order to put an end to a lawsuit pending between the papal steward and her minor children. She was an able woman, well deserving, because of her virile energy, the name of "Brother Jacopa" by which Francis made her famous in history.

The Poverello was often her guest during his visits to the

Eternal City; and at her house he used to eat a tasteful con-
fection called *"mostacciuoli,"* which he asked for again (as
we shall see) on his death bed. This mixture of almonds, su-
gar, and other ingredients crushed in a mortar was perhaps
what we call today "sugared almonds." Jacopa also appears
to have seen to renewing the Saint's wardrobe.

In gratitude for her loving care, Francis made her a present
of a lamb "that he used to let follow him," says St. Bonaventure, "in honor of the most meek Lamb of God." And the
amiable Doctor adds that this "lamb seemed to have been
formed by him to the spiritual life," so pious had it become
and solicitous of the perfection of others. "It would follow its
mistress to church, stay near her while she prayed, and go back
home with her. If Jacopa forgot to wake up in the morning,
the lamb would come and give her little butts with its head
and bleat in her ear to constrain her to go to her devotions."[5]

When the Poverello was about to leave this world, he expressed the desire that Clare and Jacopa might see him for the
last time. After Francis' death, the noble Roman lady went back
to Assisi to reside, to be near those who had known him,
and to relive past memories with them.

As ever it happens to those whom death seems to forget,
Jacopa knew the sorrow of surviving those whom she loved —
her two sons and all her grandchildren. She also knew other
sufferings, for she saw the Frangipani allied to the enemies
of the Papacy and persecution raining down upon the most
faithful followers of holy poverty. Her brightest hours were
assuredly those she spent conversing with Brother Leo, Brother Rufino, and their friends. She also used to visit Brother
Giles, the hermit of Monte Ripido. Once she was a witness to
the way Giles refuted the paradoxes proposed to him one day
by a theologian on the subject of predestination. Drawing
from his sleeve a tiny zither with willow strings, Brother
Giles began to reel off in verse — as he scraped away at his

instrument — a dozen syllogisms whose conclusion was always the same, namely that man either freely saves himself or freely damns himself. Then, having sung enough, the holy *jongleur* went into one of his habitual ecstasies.

Some historians believe that Brother Jacopa [died in 1239, while others hold she] was still living in 1273 and that she died past ninety. She was buried in the basilica of Assisi, not far from her master. The following epitaph was inscribed on her tomb: HIC REQUIESCIT JACOBA SANCTA NOBILISQUE ROMANA; and on the half-effaced fresco surmounting the tomb we still see her, led by an angel and bringing the dying Francis the hair-cloth garment in which he was buried.

* * *

By common consent, the "Letter to all the Faithful," written about 1226, constitutes a sort of rough sketch or draft of the future Third Order Rule. It is a circular addressed to the whole world, urging all men to a better practice of the Gospel.[6] It begins:

"To all Christians, religious, clerics and laymen, men and women, to all inhabitants of the earth, Brother Francis, their servant and subject, offers respectful greeting, and desires for them the true peace of Heaven and sincere charity in the Lord."

The Saint first declared his intentions: "Since I am the servant of all, I am obliged to serve all and to communicate to all the sweet smelling words of my Lord. So, since I cannot visit each of you because of my infirmities and bodily weakness, I have purposed to repeat to you in this letter — which will be my messenger — the words of our Lord Jesus Christ, who is the Word of the Father, and the words of the Holy Spirit, which are spirit and life."

Next follow several pages containing, along with nu-

merous Gospel texts, the favorite themes developed by the
Saint in his sermons; which may be paraphrased as follows:
It was for the salvation of us all that the Word of God became incarnate in the womb of the Virgin Mary, and that after
having lived in poverty with His Mother, He offered Himself
as a Victim on the Cross. Yet few, alas, consent to taste and
see how the Lord is sweet and His burden light, and many
prefer darkness to light. But they deserve to be called blessed
who love the Lord and do what the Gospel teaches. And what
does it teach? To love God with a pure heart, to worship Him
in spirit and in truth, and to pray without ceasing, preferring
for this the Lord's Prayer, and to receive the Lord's Body and
Blood in Communion. We ought, moreover, to be good Cath-
lics, to visit churches, and to confess our sins to the priests,
who though sinners themselves, are nonetheless God's ministers and deserving of our respect. The Gospel likewise commands us to love our neighbor as ourself. Let us then do good
instead of evil to our brothers. If our function be to judge,
let us judge mercifully; if it be to command, with indulgence,
deeming ourselves the servants of others. If our role be to
obey, let us obey humbly, unless the thing commanded should
be a sin. Let us avoid excesses of the table; let us do penance;
let us give generously to the poor. In fine, let us be simple,
humble, and pure, rather than wise and prudent according
to the flesh.

Here is an eloquent passage:

"And upon all those who shall have done these things and
persevered in them, the Spirit of the Lord will rest and live
and dwell within them; for they shall be the sons of the Heavenly Father, whose works they do, and the spouses, brothers,
and mothers of our Lord Jesus Christ. We are His spouses
when the faithful soul is united to Jesus Christ by the Holy
Spirit. We are His brothers when we do the will of His Father who is in Heaven. We are His mothers when we bear Him

in our heart and body by charity and the sincerity of our conscience and bring Him forth by holy deeds, meet to enlighten our neighbor. Oh, how glorious, how holy, how grand it is to have a Father in Heaven! How holy, how beautiful, and how sweet it is to have a spouse in Heaven! How holy and how blissful, pleasing, and humble, peaceful and sweet and heart-warming and supremely desirable it is to have such a Brother who has given His life for His sheep!"

As for those who do not live according to the Gospel, they are blind men who shun the light and lose their souls. To arouse them, Francis depicts vividly the story of a miser's death:

"The body is sick, death draws near, while the friends and relatives of the sick man urge him to make his will. His wife and children make a show of tears. The sick man, seeing their tears, is moved. 'All I have,' he sighs, 'I leave to you.' Truly, is he not cursed who entrusts his soul and body, and all he has to such hands? Cursed is he who puts his trust in man, says the Lord. Now the heirs call a priest who says to the dying man: 'Do you wish to receive a penance for your sins?' 'Yes,' he replies. 'Do you agree to make reparation with your money for the wrongs and injustices you have committed to the detriment of others?' 'No,' he replies. 'How so?' 'Because I have given everything I have to my friends and relatives.' Whereupon, he becomes unable to speak and dies that way, the poor wretch! The devil tears his soul from his body with such cruelty that you would have to be that man to have any idea of it. Everything that he thought he possessed in power and resources is taken away from him. His relatives and friends divide up his fortune, while cursing him for not leaving them more. And already the worms have begun to devour his flesh; and thus does he succeed in ruining himself body and soul in this short life and in gaining hell, where he will be tormented forever."

The Saint ends with these words:

"To all those who receive this letter, I, Brother Francis, your little servant, most humbly beg and beseech you in the charity which is God, to receive humbly and lovingly these sweet words of our Lord Jesus Christ and to keep them perfectly. Let those who are unable to read, have these words read to them frequently, and remember them and devoutly practice them until death, for they are spirit and life. If they do otherwise, they must render account thereof before the judgment seat of Christ. But those who receive them gladly and delight to meditate on them and to copy them to help others, if they persevere therein till the end, may they be blessed by the Father, Son, and Holy Spirit. Amen."

*   *   *

Was this letter to all the faithful especially addressed to tertiaries? Certainly Orlando, Praxedis, and Jacopa might find in it a sort of reminder composed for them by their spiritual father. The people of Cannara could likewise believe that their beloved preacher was keeping his promise to think of them, when he sent them so beautiful a sermon. It was no less true, however, that for seculars desirous of living the Franciscan life something more was needed. They required a real Rule and special statutes, like those of the Friars Minor and the Poor Ladies they desired to resemble.

No one could better satisfy their aspirations than Cardinal Hugolin, always ready to promote the ideas of St. Francis in the interests of the Church. As a papal legate in Lombardy, he had seen the work of the Humiliati, who teemed in those regions and had, as we have said, a third order whose members lived like real religious.

It was from these Lombard tertiaries, it would seem, that the cardinal took his inspiration for drawing up, with St.

Francis, the Third Order Rule of 1221.[8] While it is true that the original text is lost, critics agree in finding the exact reproduction of it in documents dating a few years later.[9] It consisted of thirteen chapters, part of them dealing with the personal sanctification of tertiaries, part with their social life, and the rest with the organization of fraternities.

Of the personal sanctification of the tertiaries. The Brothers and Sisters, says the Rule, ought to dress modestly, in keeping with the state of penance they have embraced. Chapter I determines the material, form, color, and cost of this clothing. Fur worn by the penitents is to be modest lambskin; their wallets and belts are to be made of plain leather without silk bindings. Avoiding banquets, spectacles, dances, and other too worldly amusements, they are to be content with two meals a day, observe abstinence four times a week, and fast every Friday and sometimes on Wednesday, besides the Lent before Easter. The "visitator" will grant dispensations, however, to the feeble, to laborers, and to pregnant women.

If they know how to read, the tertiaries are to recite daily the seven canonical hours. If not, they are to say fifty-four Our Fathers and Glorys, and during the Lents, unless prevented, all are to assist at Matins. They are to examine their conscience every night, confess and receive Communion three times a year; and every month they are to meet to attend Mass, listen to a sermon, and take part in prayers said in common.

Social life. The penitents are to take care to pay the prescribed tithes, to pay the debts they have contracted, and to make restitution for goods unjustly acquired. They shall be obliged to exhort members of their families to serve God, to urge the sick to repent, and to denounce to the ministers or the visitator any members of the fraternity who may cause scandal. They will attend the funerals of fellow tertiaries and recite for them a certain number of Psalms or Our Fathers with the *Requiem aeternum*. At each monthly meeting they are to contribute a sum for the poor and the sick. These are not to be neglected, for the ministers are to see that they are comforted with visits and receive all necessary assistance.

It is further incumbent upon each tertiary to make his will within three months of his profession, to become reconciled with his enemies, and not to make new ones. Finally, the brothers are forbidden to bear arms or to take any solemn oath without the consent of the Pope.

Organization of the fraternity. This is directed by a visitator, two ministers, and several minor officers. The visitator possesses supreme authority. He shall be told of infringements of the Rule, grant necessary dispensations, and expel incorrigibles. Both ministers are elected annually by the outgoing ministers with the advice of the members. They shall make inquiry as to the orthodoxy of postulants, and shall pledge the newly professed before a notary to observe the Rule faithfully until death, shall convoke the penitents to the monthly meeting, distribute the alms and take care of the sick.

Finally, the minor officers are brothers whose role it is to assist the ministers, collect monthly dues, assist the poor, and act as messengers and secretaries.

*   *   *

Such in substance were the statutes of the new institute. The text itself was a simple statement of regulations and of prohibitions, in plain words and without Scripture references, very similar in form to the constitutions drawn up by Hugolin for the Poor Clares. It contained none of that enthusiasm and idealism that Francis brought to everything he did and said; and it is evident that he took little part in drawing up this canonical and administrative document — he who could not open his mouth without quoting the Gospel and uttering the Savior's name.

The article which best revealed the intervention of the future Gregory IX was assuredly the one referring to the oath. Already the great statesman Innocent III had inserted it into the Rule of the Lombard tertiaries. It was without doubt a revolutionary feature in that period of history.

The whole political structure of the Middle Ages rested on the oath. A man swore an oath to his suzerain or to his commune. Then whatever happened, however unjust or arbitrary the war in which the suzerain or the commune was involved, he was bound to take up arms and espouse their quarrel. Thus, to have control of the oath meant that the Holy See could wield an unhead-of power against its adversaries. In that way, by opposing wars which it judged to be unjust and by favoring the others, it could break the resistance of the communes, resist the civil power, and hold the Emperor himself in check. And that is what happened, as soon as the tertiaries spread throughout the peninsula. Thanks to them, the papacy found everywhere valuable auxiliaries, whose help enabled it to drive the Ghibellines to the wall.[10]

Great also were the social consequences of the new institution. The obligation of its members to make their will deprived the suzerain of the benefits of intestate successions. The establishment, in each fraternity, of a common treasury facilitated the redemption of the tallage and the emancipation of the serfs. The fraternal mingling within the penitential communities of peasants and nobles brought the various classes of society closer together. All this, without taking into consideration the canonical immunity which freed the tertiaries from lay jurisdiction, and the voting system whereby they named and replaced their superiors — all this gradually undermined the feudal order and tended at the same time to better the poor man's lot.[11]

It is almost impossible to know the exact extent of Francis' awareness of all these novelties.[12] Apparently, it was enough for him that the Rule prescribed and promoted the observance of the Gospel for it to be according to his own heart. Likewise, it was doubtless enough for those to whom it was addressed to know that it came from him for them to be eager to receive and obey it. So they put on the cord, placed Franciscan visitators at their head, and considered themselves henceforth sons of the Poverello.

It was in Florence, in 1221, during a sojourn of Francis with Hugolin, that the first fraternity was canonically erected.[13] And wherever Franciscans and Poor Clares were to be found, the Third Order was set up. Its members soon spread all over the world, either grouped in fraternities or keeping their Rule as isolated tertiaries. In the course of centuries, the Church raised a hundred and twenty-nine of them to her altars. Among them, we find kings like St. Louis of France and St. Ferdinand of Castile, princesses like St. Elizabeth of Hungary, former sinners like Margaret of Cortona and Angela of Foligno, innocent children like St. Rose of Viterbo, numerous popes, simple priests like the Curé d'Ars, a merchant of combs like Blessed Peter of Siena who died a centenarian in 1289 and merited a place in the *Divine Comedy*, and men still more illustrious, such as Petrarch, Raphael, Michelangelo, Murillo, Galvani, Volta, Christopher Columbus, Palestrina, and Liszt.[14] Fifty-three members of the Third Order Secular of St. Francis are canonized saints, and seventy-six have been formally beatified by the Church. Of the latter, eleven are being considered for canonization, while an additional thirty-seven tertiaries are candidates for beatification.

* * *

Among these holy personages, it is fitting to mention here especially the one who is their common patron, Blessed Luchesio, the first tertiary. Perhaps a boyhood friend of St. Francis, he went at first into business and politics at San Casciano in the region of Siena. His life at that period cannot be said to have been of the most edifying; for as a wheat merchant, he hoarded grain in times of plenty for resale at a high price in times of scarcity. Politically, he was active in the Guelf faction. Buona Donna, his wife, as beautiful as she was intelligent, shared his ambitions and tastes. But when Siena fell into the hands of the Ghibellines, they both fled to Poggibonsi in the territory of Florence, where the adherents of the Pope were still masters. There, Francis' exhortations completed the conversion of this couple, whom the blessings of exile had already visibly transformed.

After distributing their goods to the poor and reserving for themselves only four acres of land, they put on the penitents' habit, and from then on their lives were dedicated to the poor. They received them into their home and shared the vegetables from their garden with them. If the sick were too feeble to come, Luchesio cared for them in their own houses. He brought some of them home with him; and often his neighbors would see him coming back with a couple of them, one perched on the back of his donkey and the other one on his own back. He went to the Maremma (the marshes between the mountains and the sea) and as far as the Tyrrhenian seashore when malaria was raging in those districts. And if his own resources were exhausted, he would appeal to public charity, begging from door to door for his protegés; and because of the charm of his personality, generally obtaining all that he asked.

God permitted that this couple, who had been one in life, should not be separated in death. When, in April, 1260, Buona Donna fell ill, Luchesio was so affected that the malady from which he himself was suffering suddenly grew worse. He still kept on his feet to assist his wife to receive the Last Sacraments. Then he clasped her hand, saying: "Dear wife, we have always loved each other on earth. So why don't we go to Heaven together? Just wait for me a little, Buona." Going back to bed, he called back his friend, Father Hildebrand, who gave him the last Sacraments. Then seeing that Buona Donna had expired, he made the sign of the cross, pronounced the names of our Lady and St. Francis for the last time, and surrendered his soul to God.[15]

- 16 -

The Founding of the
First Franciscan School

Some recent writers have advanced the thesis that Francis encouraged his sons to study; but this idea appears to many as somewhat startling, and in general it is the opposite opinion that has prevailed.[2]

Yet let no man believe that, following the envious and the ignorant, the Poverello despised learning and scholarship.[3] On the contrary, he had such a reverence for books that if he saw a scrap of writing on the ground, he would pick it up and put it in a safe place. "Who knows," he would say, "whether this paper does not have God's name on it or some praise addressed to Him?"

To those who observed that this was not usually the case with pagan writings, he would reply, "I pick them up, because even they contain letters that can spell the Creator's glorious name. Whatever is good in them does not belong to the infidels any more than to other men, but to God, the only Source of good."[4]

As for the scholars, the courteous Little Poor Man asked nothing better than to bow before their superiority and to show his esteem for them. He would have us venerate the

271

theologians who dispense God's word to us;[5] he dubbed the illustrious Anthony of Padua his "bishop";[6] he called the Doctor of Laws, Peter Catani, "messere";[7] and was so devoid of prejudice with regard to the erudite that he called upon some of them — such as Elias, Pacifico, Peter Staccia, and Gregory of Naples — to fill the highest positions in his Order.

Nevertheless, regardless of how noble and beneficial learning appeared to him, Francis did not consider it useful for his friars. In vain would one have objected to him that it was a necessity for whoever would scan God's mysteries. Francis knew that man is incapable of solving the unsolvable, and that it is by prayer and humility alone that he merits the supernatural light which permits him to draw near to God. "I used to be tempted myself," he would say, "to have books. But the Gospel showed me God's will. I opened it and came upon these words: 'To you it is given to know the mystery of the kingdom of God; but to the rest, all things are revealed in parables.' "[8]

He had also observed that scholars, never being done with their studies, devoted time to them that could be better employed elsewhere. "In the Day of Judgment," he would declare, "they will present themselves empty-handed to the Supreme Judge."[9] He added that it was better to practice virtue than to be able to talk about it. "It was for shedding their blood fighting against the infidels," he liked to repeat, "that the Emperor Charlemagne, Roland, Oliver, and the other paladins deserved to live in men's memories. But today's heroes would rather gain glory by telling of such deeds than in trying to imitate them."[10]

Especially did he see in learning a stumbling block to the poverty and humility of his Order. If he knew some modest and reserved scholars, he no doubt knew still more whom self-esteem had made obstinate and proud; and this made him say that "there are many whom learning makes so puffed-up and proud that they are utterly incapable of humble submission."[11] He knew likewise that comfortable buildings were needed to house libraries and men of study. Now how could Francis, who wanted only "little houses made of branches and mud," reconcile these requirements with the cult of holy poverty?[12]

With the satisfaction of self-love and the public esteem it generates, together with the expense involved, Francis feared, then, lest study should imperil the vocation of his friars and raise them above the rank in which he had placed them. His intention was that they should forego study just as they had renounced large churches, beautiful monasteries, and ecclesiastical honors — that they should leave to others the more appealing ways of being useful to one's neighbor.[13] Besides, as he said to a novice, "there are so many who seek to become scholars" that the friars for their part can very well do without this, since "God will bless them for making themselves sterile out of love for Him."[14]

As this novice had been authorized by Elias to have a psalter, he came to Francis to have the permission confirmed. "Once you have a psalter," replied Francis, "you will want a breviary. And when you have a breviary, no longer deigning to disturb yourself, you will say haughtily to your brother, 'Brother, please fetch my breviary!'" Then taking up a handful of ashes, he began to rub his head with them, saying: "I — a breviary! I — a breviary!"

A few months later, the novice came to him again to talk about the longed-for book. "Go and do as the minister says!" exclaimed Francis, exasperated. At once repenting, he ran after the novice. "Come back, brother, and show me the place where I spoke to you!" Then, throwing himself on his knees and beating his breast, he said to the novice, "*Mea culpa!* Forgive me for answering you as I did; for according to the Rule, a real Friar Minor ought to be content with his habit, cord, and drawers, and possess nothing else."[15]

So to the friars who were unlettered, Francis recommended that they should not seek schooling.[16] But many educated men had been admitted to the Brotherhood and continued to flock in. Now, must these, for lack of books, forget what they had learned and become ignorant once more?

Francis would have liked that the learned sacrificed their learning, just as the nobles renounced the privileges of birth,[17] so that ridding themselves of every trace of superiority, both should strive to acquire "holy simplicity, the daughter of grace, sister of wisdom, and mother of justice."[18] Nothing, writes Thomas of Celano, was dearer to him than this virtue, "which, content with its God, despises everything else," and is therefore greatly superior to learning. The Saint explained his meaning by the following parable:

"Once upon a time there was a great assembly, to which the religious of the whole world were convened to hear two sermons. The first was to be preached by a scholar, the second by an ignorant man. Before opening his mouth, the scholar said to himself: 'This is not the time to show off what I know; for there are men here who know more than I do, and whom I shall not be able to astonish. So I shall speak simply.' Garbed in sackcloth, he ascended the pulpit and humbly limited himself to a few maxims on the brevity of life, the utility of patience, and the everlasting happiness promised to the elect in Heaven.

"The assembly found this discourse perfect and was deeply edified by it. Only the unlearned man, whose time had come to speak, was a trifle disappointed — the only sermon he felt capable of preaching had just been stolen from him. 'Well!' he said to himself, 'if the savants are now going to speak like simple men, then I shall adopt the style of the savants, and like them, give a brilliant commentary on the Scriptures.' He knew a few verses of the Psalms. He chose one of them, relying on divine inspiration to explain them. And

God came so mightily to his aid that his hearers were filled with admiration by his eloquence."

And Francis added: "This assembly is our Order, whose variety is pleasing to our Heavenly Father. In it the learned and the ignorant alike ought to share of their best with one another: the first, by placing themselves like the simple in the one school of the Holy Spirit; the second, by imitating the humility of the learned, who have forgone places of prominence in the world to share our despised state."[19]

* * *

But, you may ask, without study, how could the friars be expected to give themselves to preaching and the apostolate? Wasn't St. Francis contradicting himself here and demanding the impossible?

Not at all! To grasp this point we must recall the way Francis understood the apostolate; and let us especially consider what distinguished his Brotherhood from that of the Friars Preachers.

To be sure, Francis' Order, like that of St. Dominic, was an apostolic Order. But his methods for converting souls were not at all like those used by his friend. For Dominic had founded an Order corresponding to the need of the Church at that time for preachers versed in dogma and the Scriptures.

The monks of those times did not preach; and the bishops and parish priests whose office it was to do so, generally refrained: the first because they [were cloistered or] too busy with their temporal concerns, the second because they were too ignorant, and both of them were too often discredited by their conduct from preaching effectively about virtue. Here and there bishops farmed out the preaching to laymen, who turned over to them part of the proceeds. But these substitutes were not trustworthy, and were rightly discredited by the hierarchy.

They likewise deplored the scarcity of professors of theology, since too many clerics preferred to devote themselves to jurisprudence, which opened up to them more lucrative careers. Even the great University of Bologna had no chair of Sacred Theology at this period. In vain, the Third Lateran Council in 1179 had ordered that there should be a professor of grammar in every diocese, and in every archdiocese a professor of theology, to instruct the clerics; but this decree, as to the second part at least, remained a dead letter.

It was the Friars Preachers who supplied the Church with the preachers and doctors she lacked. They were authorized to "recite the canonical hours in a brief and rapid manner, so as to allow more time for study;" and were obliged, "whether travelling or at the monastery, to study day and night." And Dominic succeeded so well in his purpose that half a century after his death his Order possessed around seven hundred doctors of theology; whereas in 1220 one could not have found more than a hundred in all Christendom.[20]

Quite other was to be the type of activity of the Franciscans. Their very name defined their role. Far from entrusting to them the influential mission of teaching alongside the bishops, Francis had called them "Minors" to indicate that they were to remain in the lowliest place, to imitate the crucified life of the Savior and observe the Gospel literally. For occupations, he assigned them manual labor and the care of lepers; and in the conversion of sinners, it was on their prayers and their example that he counted most. "Many," he declared, "are the friars who, devoting their energies to study rather than to prayer, attribute the good they do to the sermons they preach. They thus appropriate to themselves what belongs to others. My true knights of the Round Table are those who weep in solitude for their own sins and the sins of others. To them the Savior will show on the Last Day all the souls saved by their prayers."[21]

Let us add that as a good troubadour, Francis also trusted in poetry and music to "touch men's hearts and bring them to spiritual joy." We shall see later that after composing the *Canticle of Brother Sun*, "he taught it to his companions and dreamed of sending them all over the world with it. The most eloquent among them would speak first; then all the rest would begin to sing the Praises of the Lord. Finally, their leader would say to the audience: 'Since we are God's *jongleurs* and deserve a reward for our songs, the one we ask is that you live from now on as good Christians.' "[22]

* * *

Naturally, the Friars Minor had to preach too. We recall how their father had bidden them greet everyone they met with "God give you peace!" He soon permitted them to say more, and to recite a little exhortation to penance already mentioned, and which was less a sermon than an edifying refrain. Later on, those authorized by the Minister General could preach; but here again (let us insist), these were purely moral and practical exhortations, since Innocent III had forbidden the Franciscans to touch on dogmatic and biblical subjects; and the definitive Rule itself bade them to confine themselves to speaking "of vice and virtue, of punishment and glory, and not to preach long sermons, in imitation of our Lord who always spoke briefly when here on earth."

So Francis was not being inconsistent when he urged his friars to lay aside their books and to rely on the inspirations of grace to touch men's hearts. It was likewise the way Francis himself preached.

"Speaking from the heart," says Thomas of Celano, "avoiding all the apparatus of distinctions, of sounding words, and the subtleties of rhetoric, he expressed the inexpressible in a few words, and with flaming gestures rapt his audience to

Heaven. If he ran out of words, he simply told his hearers that he could not recall what he had prepared. In this case, either the inspiration came back and he was more eloquent than ever; or else, not finding anything to add, he would dismiss the people with his blessing."[23]

Laying aside the sermon "aids" and the dialectics so dear to pulpit orators of the period, his preaching was simple and clothed with mysterious power. We have contemporary accounts of two of his sermons. The first was given at Rome before Honorius and his court:

"After asking the Pope to bless him, the Little Poor Man began without the least timidity. He was so full of his subject that he began to gesticulate and to dance, if not like a tumbler, at the very least like a man intoxicated with divine love. No one thought of laughing; on the contrary, all were so moved that they could not restrain their tears — in admiration for the workings of divine grace in such a man. It was Cardinal Hugolin who had proposed that Francis should preach; and he was so fearful lest the thing should not go off well that he prayed all the time for God to help his friend."[24]

The other sermon was the one the Poverello preached at Bologna on August 15, 1222:

"I was studying in that city," writes Thomas of Spalato, "when I had an opportunity of hearing Francis preach on the square of the Public Palace, where almost the whole population had assembled. He preached of angels, men, and demons with such eloquence and precision that the most learned were amazed that an untutored man could express himself so well. His discourse had nothing of the tone or mannerisms of the preacher. Rather it was like a conversation whose sole object was to extinguish hatred and restore peace. The orator was wretchedly garbed, his appearance frail, his face without beauty; but this did not hinder his words from reconciling the Bolognese nobles who had been slaughtering one another for generations. And so great was the enthusiasm that men and women rushed up to him to tear his garments to shreds and make off with the pieces."[25]

*   *   *

Certainly, to find God and communicate Him to others, Francis himself had no need to study. The current teaching of the Church, joined to meditation on the Gospels and liturgical texts, was sufficient for him. This inspired man found richer nourishment in the songs of birds and streams than in the laborious cogitations of the learned. And when God in addition communicated Himself to his soul in prayer, what need had he of books?

To convert souls the way the Poverello did, no school was necessary. But on one condition — that of being as great a poet and as great a saint as he. Was it an illusion on his part to believe that his example could be followed [by many]?

How could one require of scholars sufficient heroism to close their books, forsake their beloved studies, and, in the words of Pascal, "consent to grow stupid"? This was no more to be expected than to see them continue to live in wattle huts.

And how could anyone make these eloquent men — once in the pulpit — "speak briefly of virtue and vice," foregoing all doctrinal instruction and the confounding of heretics? If a man needs to be instructed himself in order to teach others, where is he to find the true doctrine if not in the masters and in their works? Besides, was not the example of the Fathers of the Church and of St. Dominic there to show the possibility of allying theology and sanctity?

So thought a number of friars burning to widen the scope of their zeal and to follow in the footsteps of the Dominicans. Resistance was all the more vain, since the Roman Curia itself supported them, only too glad to have such valuable auxiliaries for its reform of ecclesiastical studies and in its battle against heresy.

It was Cardinal Hugolin who, with his customary skill, made Francis listen to reason. We do not know how he went about it and to what extent he really convinced his friend. The fact is that he did bring him to authorize the reopening of the great convent of Bologna and the resumption of the courses inaugurated there by Peter Staccia.[26]

Now, since it was necessary for members of the Order to study, no one was better fitted to instruct them than Brother Anthony, who had just revealed his learning and sanctity in Lombardy. So it was he who was assigned to teach.

* * *

Born in Lisbon in 1195, Anthony of Padua was a canon regular at Santa Cruz in Coimbra, when in 1220 the remains of the first Franciscan martyrs were brought back from Morocco for burial in the church of the canons.[27] Burning to follow in the footsteps of these heroes, he left his Order to enter that of the Friars Minor and set off for Morocco. However, almost immediately he fell ill. He re-embarked to return home, but was cast by a tempest off the coast of Sicily. He there joined some friars of Messina who were going to the General Chapter of 1221. At the Portiuncula nobody paid any attention to him; and the superiors would have even forgotten to give him an obedience, had it not been for Brother Gratian, Provincial of Lombardy, who agreed to take Anthony with him.

At the hermitage of Montepaolo, Anthony lived at first in a cave, which he left only to assist at the offices and to keep the house clean. His theological lore and his oratorical talents, however, were made manifest on an ordination day at Forli. When others refused to preach because unprepared, Anthony was bidden by his superior to preach extemporaneously. Thereafter, except for the time devoted to the lessons which he gave at Bologna, Toulouse, and Montpellier, he preached the rest of his life: in the Lombard region where he combated the Cathari with his great learning; in France, where he preached in Brive, Arles, Bourges, and Limoges; and, finally, in Padua, where he died at the height of his fame at the age of thirty-six. He was canonized less than a year after his death, and was named a Doctor of the Church in 1946.

This prodigious orator, who has become Christianity's most popular saint, is said to have spoken all languages. Even the fishes (the *Fioretti* assures us) heard him gladly.[28] The fact is that immense crowds assembled to hear him and merchants closed their shops when he preached. He confounded the most learned Patarini, and excoriated from the pulpit the immoral lives of prelates, a proof that the saints of the second Franciscan generation no longer had, as did their Father, a horror of disputes and of attacks against individuals.

It is thought that it was in the winter of 1223 that St. Anthony inaugurated his lectures at the Bologna friary.[29] At once, as at a given signal, schools were established in every province of the Order; and twenty years later, the Franciscans possessed chairs at Oxford, Paris, Cologne, and elsewhere, whose renown soon became universal. In them flourished those famous geniuses whose doctrines and works have been studied and republished for centuries: Alexander of Hales, the "Irrefragible Doctor"; St. Bonaventure, the "Seraphic Doctor"; Roger Bacon, the "Admirable Doctor"; Ockham, the "Invincible Doctor"; and Blessed Duns Scotus, the celebrated rival of St. Thomas, who caused the doctrine of the Immaculate Conception to triumph in theology.

We may also be sure that Franciscan preaching was not long in liberating itself from every impediment; and in 1230, Hugolin, now Pope, officially abolished the prohibition forbidding the friars to comment on dogma and the Scriptures from the pulpit.

*　*　*

Far from these famous universities, however, where Franciscans and Dominicans vied with each other in learning and eloquence, the humble "school" of Rivo Torto still endured, where Brother Leo and Brother Giles meant to preserve, with their disciples, the spirit of simplicity of the early days. It was this "school," as we know, that produced the *Speculum Perfectionis*, the *Sacrum Commercium*, and those incomparable *Fioretti*, so much appreciated by those who profit very little (alas) from the *Summas* and *Commentaries* of Oxford or Paris.

The simple brethren held that the friars did wrong in wanting to become scholars and have themslves talked about. "Ah, Paris, Paris!" exclaimed Brother Giles. "It is you who are ruining the Order of St. Francis!" Later on, the Franciscan poet Jacopone da Todi likewise accused Paris of having brought about the ruin of Assisi.[30]

While venerating the theologians, Brother Giles sometimes found them tedious: "Of all your treatises, there are only two that I judge worthy of constant study — the first which teaches me to praise God for his benefits, and the second which teaches me to repent of my sins." He also counseled them to waste less time trying to explain the unexplainable, and said in regard to predestination: "Those who claim to know everything that the sea contains have only to jump into the water after it, if they so desire. For my part, I'll stay on shore where I can wash my hands and feet, or all of me if I like. Once I have learned how I ought to behave, why should I weary myself learning more?"[31]

One day the ecstatic of Monte Ripido began to needle St. Bonaventure. "When one thinks," said he, "of the light that great doctors like you receive from Heaven, how do you expect ignoramuses like us to be saved?"

"The all-important-thing for salvation," replied Brother Bonaventure, "is to love God."

"You're not trying to make me think that an illiterate man can love Him as much as a learned man?"

"Come now, Brother Giles! Not only as much, but sometimes more. Why, one sometimes sees old women surpassing the greatest theologians in this respect."

At that very moment an old beggar woman was coming down the road. Giles rushed to the garden and shouted to her over the hedge: "Rejoice, old lady! For I have just learned that if you will, you can love God even more than Brother Bonaventure does!"

Thereupon he fell into an ecstasy in which he remained for three hours.[32]

- 17 -

The Final Rule
and the Temptation of St. Francis

We have seen that the Rule of 1221 was unable to restore harmony among the friars. Obviously, its greatest defect was its attempt to maintain the primitive characteristics of the Brotherhood and to conform to an outmoded state of things. But there was still another defect on which the party of Elias, upheld by Hugolin, could more honorably insist — the lack of definiteness and precision needed in a legislative document, a factor which consequently gave it no chance of securing Rome's approval.

Aided by the Cardinal-Protector, the Ministers persuaded Francis to elaborate a new text. Taking with him Brother Leo and Brother Bonizzo, a learned jurist, the Saint climbed the wooded heights of Fonte Colombo near Rieti; and there in a cavern in the wilds above a narrow valley through which flowed a mountain stream, he set to work once more.

We know nothing of the Rule he then composed. Nevertheless, it is probable that it likewise was not pleasing to the opposition; for when the time came for discussion, Brother Elias, to whom it had been entrusted, declared that he had lost it.[1]

284

If one way for a diplomat to achieve his ends is often to gain time, one may ask whether this loss was really involuntary. Was there some hope of exhausting the Saint's patience? Or, knowing him to be ill, did the opposition count on his death before he had confirmed his intentions in writing?

Again accompanied by Brother Leo, Francis repaired once more to the hermitage of Fonte Colombo, where, fasting, praying, and lamenting before God, he attempted anew to draw up the Gospel code which he desired to bequeath to his sons.[2] He passed through fearful hours of discouragement. The task to which the attitude of the dissenters condemned him seemed beyond his strength.[3] How could their human views be harmonized with God's own demands? How was he to let his heart speak, and appeal from it to the hearts and loyalty of his friars, in a dry administrative ordinance in which he was no longer permitted to quote from the Gospel? Especially now when he had so much to say and insist on, when he sensed his authority reduced, his adversaries become more and more powerful, and his ideal less and less followed. And perhaps — poet that he was — he suffered additional pangs at the difficulty he had to be brief and to condense his thought.

Yet as the guide and father of an immense religious family, he could not abandon those loyal men whom he had induced to follow him.

One night he saw in a dream some famished friars who begged him for food. He attempted to gather up some crumbs which he saw scattered on the ground; but like dust, they sifted through his fingers. "Francis," said a voice, "make a loaf from these crumbs, and in this way your friars can eat them."

Francis obeyed. Among the religious present, some eagerly ate of this mysterious bread; others, refusing, were immediately covered with leprosy. The Saint understood that the crumbs were the words of the Gospel, that the loaf represented the Rule which he must continue to draft, and that the rebels were harming themselves and incurring God's punishment. This dream encouraged him to complete his task.[4]

Meanwhile the ministers were anxiously wondering what the new text would be like. Some of them even went to Fonte Colombo to declare that they would never accept a rule which ran counter to their desires. Francis replied that he was writing under God's dictation and sent them away with his curse.[5]

[Not all the ministers were of this sort, for one wrote to Francis of the trials his office brought — so great that he longed to abandon his charge and take himself to a hermitage.] To him Francis wrote:

"I do my best to reply to you on the state of your soul, to bid you not to be disturbed any more by the difficulties you are encountering, which (you say) keep you from loving the Lord God. Do not be afflicted by what it does not please God to grant you. Even if the brothers should beat you, you ought to look on all such treatment as a grace. Prefer, then, the duties of your charge to the life you might live in a hermitage.

"If one of your brothers should have committed all the sins in the world, so act, if he comes to you, that he shall not leave without having read forgiveness in your eyes and received from you some kind word. By this I shall know that you love the Lord and that you love me, His servant and yours. If the culprit does not come to you, then go to him yourself and ask him if he desires to be forgiven. And should he come to you a thousand times, you must love him more than you love me, to win him to God. Let the guardians know, when you are able, that you are fully resolved to act thus.

"At Pentecost, with God's help and with the common consent of the brothers, we shall endeavor to bring together in one, all the chapters of the Rule relative to mortal sin. It will be worded something like this: 'If a brother fall into mortal sin, he must go to his guardian, and then to his custos, who will receive him mercifully, dealing with him as he would wish to be treated himself. And if the other friars learn of his fault, let them not shame or reproach the guilty one, but show great mercy toward him and carefully keep his secret . . . . And the confessor shall say to him, 'Go and sin no more,' and this shall be all the penance he shall impose."[6]

In closing, Francis counseled the minister to think over the things still lacking in the Rule, and arranged to meet with him at the Chapter of Pentecost, where he hoped that everything could be peacefully settled.

Contrary to his expectations, the hoped-for agreement was arrived at only at the price of new and difficult negotiations. The documents are lacking which would permit us to describe them. [Nevertheless, I surmise] that they were long drawn-out, often stormy, and fraught with immeasurable suffering for the Little Poor Man.

In May, 1223, Francis attended the General Chapter of the Portiuncula. A few months later, he left for Rome, where his Rule, already so much worked over, received from Hugolin its definitive form. The 29th of the following November, Pope Honorius approved it by the Bull *Solet annuere*; and ever since it has constituted the official legislation of the Friars Minor.[7]

*   *   *

This Rule differs entirely in its makeup from the previous plan. Three times as short as the Rule of 1221, quoting only ten verses from the Gospel, (whereas the other contained a hundred), it consists of twelve short chapters from which every prayer and effusion of the heart have almost disappeared. The words are chosen with great care, with the double intent of not wounding the susceptibilities of the intransigents nor of discouraging the demands of the moderates. But whereas the Rule of 1221 constituted — in a blending of lyrical prayer and touching supplication — a detailed description of Franciscan life as dreamed of by its founder, and was so worded that no learned commentaries could dilute it, that of 1223 on the contrary is a canonical text to be interpreted by jurists — a series of prescriptions and prohibitions for them to decide whether they oblige *sub gravi* or *sub levi*, and in which they would later find matter for twenty-seven mortal sins.

If, fundamentally, there is no glaring contradiction between the two documents, still we cannot affirm that the rule of 1223 perfectly expresses the intentions of the founder.[8] This is especially apparent in the suppressions and omissions to which he was obliged to consent.

For example, Francis desired to insert the following clause in his text: "If, in the course of their travels, the friars shall find the Blessed Sacrament reserved in unseemly vessels or places, they shall urge the priests to remedy matters; and if they refuse, they shall do so in their stead." This was an ordinance which would have been certain to engender conflicts with the clergy, and which the wise Hugolin ruled out.[9]

It was doubtless the same hand that struck out the dangerous and anarchistic article authorizing the friars to judge the conduct of their superiors and to disobey any who would prevent them from observing the Gospel literally (Chapter V).

Equally suppressed was the passing reference in the Rule of 1221 to the care of leprosy patients. An outstanding suppression was those words so characteristic of the first Franciscans: "And when they shall go through the world, they shall take nothing with them, neither wallet, nor bread, nor staff; and they shall not resist the evildoer, letting themselves be despoiled without resistance."[10] In short, almost everything was done away with that commanded the Friars Minor to remain in the ranks of the truly poor.

From this time on, in fact, the friars were engaged in elevating themselves to the social rank of other clerics and religious. First, by means of study, of which, to be sure, the new Rule makes no mention. But it should be noted that it no longer forbids the friars to have books.[11] Next, by means of favors gradually obtained from the Roman Curia and by the increasingly lenient interpretation of their vow of poverty.

It was Hugolin who discovered the legal formula permitting them to occupy suitable buildings from which it would no longer be possible to dislodge them. He already had this in mind when, in order to get Francis to let his friars go back to their convent at Bologna, he declared, as we have seen, that the building belonged to the Holy See.[12] Extended to all conventual property, such an interpretation would do away with every type of difficulty and would render incalculable service in the future.

It was also thanks to the "governor, protector, and corrector of the brotherhood" that the friars obtained the Bulls which rapidly improved their status in the world and in the Church. For they soon had no further cause to envy the other mendicant orders on this score.

Already prior to 1221, pontifical letters recommend them to foreign prelates;[13] in March, 1222, they obtained permission to officiate in their conventual churches in times of interdict;[14] in 1225, they were authorized to celebrate Mass on portable altars without the bishops being able to object;[15] in March, 1226, friars going to Morocco received permission to use money;[16] and Francis was hardly dead before Friars Minor were elevated to the episcopate. Finally, as soon as he became Pope Gregory IX, Hugolin granted two extremely important Bulls to the Franciscans: the one confers the privilege of exemption on them and withdraws them from that jurisdiction of and dependence on the bishops in which their Father desired them to remain;[17] and the other removes all force of law from the Testament of the Saint.[18]

*   *   *

These accommodations and mitigations, profoundly modifying the physiognomy of the Brotherhood, have been held by many against the authoritarian and powerful prelate. The Rule of 1223, privileges and exemptions, the abandonment of manual labor, the encouragement given to study, the prestige accorded clerics and the possibility of their being admitted to ecclesiastical dignities, the partial abandonment of the original Gospel program — all this is in great part his work. Hence, some have accused him of "utterly disorienting the Franciscan movement in order to turn it completely to the profit of the Church."[19]

Evidence is lacking, however, for so flat a condemnation. If we are to judge Hugolin fairly, it behooves us not to lay more responsibility at his door than is rightly his. Was it his fault if the ideal of the Little Poor Man could be entirely realized only by a few exceptional souls? The moment that this ideal became the common property of several thousand men, it had to be watered down, as it were, in order to remain accessible to all. Who could possibly make heroism and holiness the common law of this world?

The difficulties in which Hugolin soon found himself enmeshed stemmed from the fact that some, like Brother Giles and Brother Leo, looked on the primitive ideal as a thing realizable and not to be touched; while others, led by Brother Elias, held it to be slightly utopian and utterly impracticable.

These difficulties could only be aggravated by the growth of the fraternity, by the entry of learned men into the Order, and by the different ways in which the friars conceived of the apostolate: some wishing to exercise it only in strict fidelity to the spirit of Rivo Torto, and the rest thinking it should be revamped to adapt it to the requirements of study and to current conditions of apostolic effort.

Such was the conflict which the Cardinal Protector was called upon to resolve.[20] This he did, to be sure, in accordance with his personal opinions and with an eye to furthering the reforms of Innocent III, but not without entering as fully as possible into the sentiments of St. Francis. His arbitration therefore was a meritorious compromise between the demands of the two parties involved.

As the official representative of the Church to which belongs the right to regulate the statutes of religious orders, it would have been easy for him — relying on Brother Elias and the papal authority — to crush the zealots of the primitive observance. Yet he always treated them with consideration. Later on, when he had become Pope, far from seeking to destroy the writings from which their intransigeance drew its support, he eulogized the Testament of St. Francis and assigned Thomas of Celano to relate the humble chronicles of Rivo Torto. And when Brother Elias had almost brought to triumph in the Order those tendencies capable of utterly destroying the Franciscan spirit, he removed him from office, covering him with ridicule in the eyes of Christendom.[21]

Thus it was that in everything practicable the work of St. Francis was able to continue; the sons of the Poverello remained in possession of their Father's heritage; and down through the centuries men have seen his sublime and inaccessible ideal, like a ferment of "holy discontent" laid in the hearts of his children, ceaselessly impel them onward to new and more holy reforms.[22]

To be just toward Hugolin, in fine, we must remind ourselves that he always defended Francis against those prelates who desired to put a speedy end to the Franciscan adventure. And what would have become of the Poverello without the prudence of this great cardinal? When we realize that the Saint's fate might otherwise have been settled like that of some Waldensian, that this extraordinary figure of history might thus have been lost in the crowd, and that nothing of him would have come down to us, we cannot do otherwise than honor the memory of his powerful friend.

*   *   *

Few men have suffered more than St. Francis. In addition to the infirmities due to his continuous state of poor health and the mysterious tortures of the stigmata, he constantly afflicted his body with fasting and vigils, with fatigue, penances, and mortifications of every sort.[23] He habitually treated "brother ass" with such harshness that before leaving it, he felt the need of a reconciliation. "I bear it witness," he said, "that it has shown itself obedient in every circumstance, and has not pampered itself. I must acknowledge that it and I have always been of the same mind to serve our Lord."[24]

Of all the Poverello's sufferings, the most dreadful was that which marked the period we have just studied. It was the one referred to by his biographers when, without being more specific, they speak of St. Francis' "great temptation."[25] This was a unique trial, a torture particularly long and cruel, a distress of conscience so serious and so profound that divine intervention was necessary to deliver him from it.

It was a sort of intense anguish in which the Little Poor Man, almost abandoned by God, walked in darkness, a prey to indecision and doubt, almost, it would seem, to the point of despair.

Reduced to powerlessness ever since Elias and the other superiors of the Order loom between him and his friars, he sees the ministers and learned brethren resisting him, Hugolin enjoining him to make concessions — and so his work seems irreparably compromised. What is he to do? Was it not from the Lord that he received this form of life that he practiced and desired to transmit to his sons? Could he have been deceived? Under color of following the Gospel, had he been merely chasing shadows, deluded by self and the devil? Is it for the sins of his youth that God has forsaken him?

And so this Heaven-inspired man, finding Heaven now mute, is troubled in spirit. His assurance and optimism vanish. He is obsessed by fears of evil and devoured by scruples.

Many are the manifestations of this state of soul as reported by his biographers. For months, writes one of them, he refused to visit the Poor Ladies. It was Sister Clare, we know, who saved him from himself this time, succeeded in seeing him again and even in eating with him. "Do you believe," he observed afterward to his friars, "that I do not cherish with all my heart our Sisters of San Damiano? It would be cruel and sinful to abandon them."[26]

Another time, he seems to reproach himself for defending his ideal against Hugolin; and the man who held obedience to be a joy and knightly service now goes to extremes and speaks of it in a macabre style: "The obedient man ought to be like a corpse which lets itself be placed anywhere and does not protest. If men clothe it in purple, it appears the more livid. If they seat it on a platform like a doctor, instead of raising its head, it will let it fall on its breast."[27]

His moods shift like those of a soul that has lost its moorings. At times he is animated by holy wrath: "Let them be accursed by You, O Lord, those men whose evil example shame the good friars of the Order and destroy by their conduct what it has pleased You to build up."[28] Then, indignation giving way to discouragement, he confines himself to pitying those faithful religious whom the reformers may drive some day from the Brotherhood, reducing them to life in the woods.[29]

This man who was so clear in his thinking and so assured in his progress has suddenly become unsure of his way, uncertain of his duty, troubled in spirit, entangled in the most contradictory resolutions. One day he dreams of authorizing the partisans of the primitive observance to leave the perjured community.[30] Does he fear lest this will soon be his own fate? "Supposing," he says, "that the friars, ashamed of an unlettered superior like me, shamefully expel me from the Brotherhood. I tell you that I would not be a true Friar Minor if I did not rejoice to be treated that way."[31]

But he soon reconsidered, recoiling before schism, and counseling submission. "Should a superior command something contrary to their spiritual good, though the friars should not obey him, let them never separate themselves from him, and let them love him in proportion to this persecution of them."[32]

Finally Francis adopted for himself a middle course. Increasingly avoiding the society of the friars, he chose to withdraw with a few faithful friends to secluded hermitages. He would even have liked to go back to his first way of life and the care of lepers.[33] From time to time he still wanted to fight. "If I go to the Chapter," he would shout, "I'll show them who I am!"[34]

But these were only passing moods. Harshness was not his forte. "I am no executioner," he would say.[35] The more often, he sadly resigned himself; and to those who reproached him for forsaking his friars, he replied that he loved the brothers "with all his heart." "But," he would add, "I would love them still more, and I would not be as a stranger among them, if they would follow in my footsteps and stop citing examples of what the other Orders do."[36]

His distress at this period is evident — and what it cost him to witness the collapse of his dream. This martyrdom was prolonged up to Rome's approval of the Rule. God then made this obedient son of the Church realize that his role as founder was definitely over. "Poor little man," said our Lord to him, "Why are you so sad? Is not your Order My Order? Is it not I who am its Chief Shepherd? Cease to be afflicted then, and take care rather of your own salvation."[37]

To this man stumbling in the night, distressed at no longer knowing God's will, these words brought back the light. And when, thereafter, the friars came to him to speak of books, of mitigations of the Rule, and of the practice of the older Orders, he would only say: "Do what you will. I am no longer obligated to do anything except pray for my friars and give them a good example."[38]

The biographers relate the way in which this "great temptation" ended. One day [at the Portiuncula] when the Saint was praying in tears, crushed by the weight of his responsibility and grief, a voice was heard saying: "Francis, if you had faith like a grain of mustard seed, you would say to this mountain, 'Be removed,' and it would obey you."

"What mountain, Lord?" asked Francis.

"The mountain of thy temptation," continued the voice.

"Lord," replied Francis, "let it be done to me according to Your word." And at once the temptation vanished.[39]

Thereafter the conscience of the Little Poor Man was limpid and calm once more like a fair lake, and a great peace again filled his soul.

- 18 -

Christmas at Greccio

The steps preliminary to the approval of the Rule had compelled Francis to prolong his sojourn in Rome [in November, 1223]. On this occasion he no doubt saw Brother Jacopa. Certain dignitaries of the curia also came to show him their veneration.

One day on returning to Cardinal Hugolin's palace at the luncheon hour, he drew from his sleeve the pieces of black bread he had just begged and offered them to the other guests. The prelate was very embarrassed, writes Thomas of Celano, for it was a state dinner, at which foreigners were being received by him for the first time. However, everyone was openly glad to share the Little Poor Man's quest and many kept their pieces as a souvenir.

When the meal was over, the cardinal drew his friend aside: "Brother," he asked, "why do you humiliate me by begging alms when you are my guest? Don't you know that my house and everything in it is yours?"

"My Lord," replied Francis, "since nothing is more pleasing to God than holy poverty, far from shaming you, is it not rather an honor for you to honor in your home our common Master, who deigned to live poor on earth for love of us? I must also think of my present and future friars, who would otherwise scorn to go out begging. I must act in such a way that there will be no excuse for them before God in this world or in the next at being ashamed to humble themselves."

Deeply moved, Hugolin embraced him, saying: "Son, do as you like, for it is plain that the Lord is with you and inspiring you."[1]

At Rome, Francis had found Brother Angelo, one of the Three Companions, staying with Cardinal Brancaleone; for the first friars, as we have seen, often hired themselves out as domestic servants to earn their living. Giles himself lived for a while in [Rieti] in the house of Cardinal Niccolo di Chiaramonte. Evidently this custom was found to be edifying by the princes and prelates, since for a time it was quite the thing for them to have a Franciscan among their household servants. Some of the friars, however, began to grow overfond of living in palaces; and Thomas of Celano, in his *Vita secunda*, does not spare these degenerate Penitents, who, "because of laziness, ambition, and a love of ease," preferred the dwellings of the great to their own wooden huts.[2] One of these *Palatini*, as they were dubbed, who lived at the court of the King of England, came to a very bad end, according to Eccleston.[3]

Brother Angelo, to be sure, did not deserve any such reproach. Having come to Rome no doubt on pilgrimage, if he was staying with a cardinal, it was only temporarily; and he was meanwhile living according to the Rule, by the work of his hands.

As nothing detained Francis there any longer, he decided to return to Umbria with Angelo. Cardinal Brancaleone, however, was most desirous to welcome Francis first at his palace. As it was winter and the weather was very bad, Francis surely could wait a little, it would seem, before starting home! "Besides," added the prelate, "you can live with me in as much

seclusion as you like; and if you wish, you will be at liberty
to take your meals with my poor." Joining his pleas to the
cardinal's, Angelo offered to prepare for him a cell in a solitary
tower at the foot of the garden where he could live as in a
hermitage.

Francis accepted, on condition that he need not leave the
tower or receive anyone there. But the first night he received a
visit from the devil, who beat and harassed him in every way.
Calling his companion, he said to him, "The demons are the
constables and seneschals of the Most High, charged either
with making those whom He loves expiate their former sins,
or with compelling good religious who sin through ignorance
to examine their consciences better. Since I do not recall any
sin I have not confessed and done penance for, it must be that
there is something else and that God does not want me here.
And indeed, when my friars learn that I am staying with a
cardinal, they will surely say, 'Well, there is a fellow who is
taking his ease, while we are fasting and doing penance in
our poor hermitages.' So I must leave here."

In the morning he climbed down from the tower and told
the cardinal what had happened in the night, adding as he
left: "My Lord, the man you took for a saint deserved to be
driven from your house by fiends."[4]

*   *   *

Leaving Rome, where he was never to return again, Francis
set out for the Valley of Rieti. Freed from all responsibility,
now that the Bull of November 29 had given definite status to
the Order, a new era opened before him. He was nearing the
final stage of his career, in which, while waiting for death,
his one desire would be to live in peace, close to Christ. Apparently, he went back once more to the hermitage of Fonte
Colombo which had recently witnessed his great trial; and as

Christmas was approaching, he wanted — this year, at any rate — to celebrate it his own way.

Of all religious feasts, writes Thomas of Celano, Christmas was for Francis the most beautiful. For him it was the feast of feasts, the one that reminded him (he would say) of the day when God, become a little Babe, was nourished by a woman's milk. The picture of Jesus in His Mother's arms made him stammer with emotion. Sometimes he would begin to weep at the thought of the destitution of the Crib. One day at table, when a friar depicted the dire distress of the Virgin and her Son at Bethlehem, he got up at once from the table, shaking with sobs, and finished the rest of his meal on the bare ground in honor of their "royal poverty." "For," he explained, "is not this virtue of which Christ the King and the Virgin Queen wished to give us an example of royal virtue?"

Nevertheless, it was joy that predominated in him at the approach of the Savior's birth.[5] One year, when the feast fell on a Friday, Brother Morico, the former Crosier, asked if the friars had to abstain from meat.

"Abstain!" exclaimed Francis. "Why, it's a sin to call that day Friday on which the Child was born to us! The very walls should have a right to eat meat today! And if that is impossible, we ought to rub them with fat, at least, so that they can eat meat their way." Asses and oxen, he said, ought to have a double ration of hay and oats in memory of the ox and ass that warmed Jesus in the Crib with their breath. Another time he said: "If I saw the Emperor, I would ask him to scatter grain on the highways on Christmas for our brothers the birds, and especially for our dear sister larks."[6]

* * *

So a fortnight before the Nativity of 1223, Francis sent for his friend, John Velita, the lord of Greccio, who had apparently forsworn the profession of arms to enter the Order of Penance.[7] Opposite Greccio, which rises on a rocky shelf bordering a spacious valley, John possessed a steep hill, honeycombed with caves and surmounted by a small wood. The Saint judged this site proper for the setting he had in mind. Since this was a novelty in the liturgy of the period, he had submitted the idea before quitting Rome to Pope Honorius, who had approved it.[8]

"I should like," said he to his friend," to celebrate the coming feast of the Savior with you. And I should like to commemorate His birth at Bethlehem in a way to bring before me as perfectly as possible the sufferings and discomforts He endured from infancy for our salvation. That is why I want you to set up a real manger on this mountain spot, with hay, and to bring in an ox and an ass like those that kept the Infant Jesus company."

John Velita was only too happy to lend a hand to this project; and Francis dismissed him, recommending him to hurry so that everything would be ready when he came.

It is from Thomas of Celano's *Vita Prima* that we shall paraphrase the account of the feast. It is almost contemporary, for he wrote it only four or five years afterward.

The people of the country had joined with the friars of the surrounding hermitages, bearing torches and candles to lighten the darkness of this night which, like a star, has shone for centuries and will shine forever. Winding up the mountain, the procession wended its way toward the spot where — between a great ox and a little donkey — the Crib was set up. Under the great trees it was as light as day, and from rock to rock the echo reverberated of the chanting of the friars, mingled with the pious refrains of the crowd. Standing before the Crib, torn with compassion and filled with unspeakable joy, the Poverello, sighing deeply, awaited them.

The Mass commenced, at an altar placed in an overhanging

niche. Never, the celebrant himself confessed, had he experienced such consolation while offering the Holy Sacrifice. Vested in the dalmatic, Francis assisted as deacon. At the proper moment, he intoned the Gospel in a sonorous voice; then he preached a sermon to proclaim the joys of Heaven to those men of good will who had flocked to his appeal. In words honey-sweet he spoke of the poor King who twelve centuries before, on such a night, was born in the little town of Bethlehem, calling him either "Jesus" or the "Babe of Bethlehem," and pronouncing the word "Bethlehem" like a bleating lamb. And whenever one of these divine names occurred in his sermon, he would pass his tongue over his lips that he might longer taste their sweetness.

Thus it was a night marvelous above all other nights; and we must not be surprised that God afterward wished to shower down His blessings upon his blessed spot. Many sick folk recovered their health there and even domestic animals who ate a few stalks of hay from the Crib were cured. For it is true that on this hay the Savior of the world had miraculously rested.

John Velita in fact reported that he saw the little Jesus asleep on it, and that there was a moment when the Divine Infant awakened, opened His eyes, and smiled at St. Francis.

This stupendous vision, according to Thomas of Celano and St. Bonaventure, rewarded the zeal of the pious lord of Greccio; but it likewise symbolized the admirable work accomplished on earth by him who reawakened the faith slumbering in men's hearts — faith in Jesus Christ our Lord, who lives and reigns with the Father, in the unity of the Holy Spirit, world without end, amen. Alleluia! Alleluia![9]

- 19 -

The Stigmata

Francis passed the rest of the winter and the following spring at the hermitage of Greccio. From time to time he preached in the surrounding villages, but on Easter Day it seemed to him that he owed a lesson to the friars themselves.

On the occasion of their minister's visit, they had procured tablecloths, glasses, and other fine things to adorn their table. The meal was underway when a knock was heard at the door: "For the love of God," came a quavering voice, "an alms for a poor sick pilgrim!"

And they saw a little beggar come in, wearing an old hat and leaning on a staff. It was Francis who had disguised himself to remind his friars of their vocation. He held out his bowl, received a piece of bread, and sat on the ground before the hearth to eat it. "Since your table is too fancy for the poor who go begging at people's doors and who, more than other religious, are bound to imitate the Savior's humility," said he, "permit me to sit here like a real Friar Minor."[1]

Thus, without seeking any more for opportunities, but taking them as they came, Francis continued to protest against the inroads made on his evangelical ideal.

Far from departing from it himself, he daily came closer to it. "Those who lived with him," wrote Thomas of Celano, "know that his mind dwelt constantly on Christ. Jesus filled his heart, was on his lips, and before his eyes; his bodily members, like the powers of his soul, were as though marked with the seal of Christ."[2] His friars likewise admired his increasing resemblance to his divine Model. Everything in his life now recalled the life of the Savior. Under the garb of the pilgrim who had presented himself to them, wrote Friar Thomas, the religious of Greccio had immediately recognized the image of the Pilgrim of Emmaus.[3] But what was this distant resemblance compared with that soon to be his?

Francis went from Greccio to the General Chapter of June, 1224. It was the last one he attended.

* * *

A few weeks later, he left the Portiuncula for La Verna, a hundred miles north of Assisi.[4] In his choice of this solitary summit for a residence, was there a presentiment of the sublime favor awaiting him there? We know only that he chose to take with him a few friars according to his heart: Leo, Angelo, Illuminato, Rufino, and Masseo, the faithful companions of so many other journeys.[5]

They set out at the beginning of August, and Brother Masseo, who was good at meeting the public, was put in charge. "You shall be our guardian," said Francis. "We will sleep wherever you say; at mealtime we shall beg our bread; and the rest of the time, faithful to our custom, we shall recite our hours, speak of God, or else walk along in silence."[6]

The region of Casentino, toward which the little caravan was headed, forms a broad and imposing valley, filled with meadows, vineyards, and forests, with castles and charming villages perched on the hills. It is watered by the upper Arno, and hemmed in on all sides by the inaccessible summits of the Apennines. Among them, Mount La Verna rises, abrupt and isolated, about four thousand feet high, a lofty and solitary plateau.[7]

Already it was visible, though doubtless still far away, when after one or two days of hiking, Francis became so exhausted that it was necessary to find a mount for him. A villager lent his donkey for the rest of the trip. He must have been an honest fellow, but with a dislike for being fooled, and he meant to have the saints repay any favor he did for them. As he followed his beast, he felt a desire to know God's servant better. Going up to him, he asked:

"Tell me, are you really that Brother Francis of Assisi people talk about so much?"

"Yes," replied the Saint.

"In that case, I want to give you some advice, and that is to be as good as people say you are, for you have a great reputation for holiness among us."

"Instead of taking offense at this lesson," writes the chronicler, "and saying (as some proud friars I know would have said), 'What a nitwit he must be, to preach to me like that!,' Francis dismounted and knelt before the rustic, and, kissing his feet, thanked him for his charitable warning."

The heat became stifling. As they were climbing a very rugged slope, the peasant, who increasingly lagged behind, declared that he was dying of thirst. "Either you find me something to drink," said he, "or I'll die here!"

Again St. Francis dismounted, and raising his arms to heaven, prayed until a spring was discovered near a neighboring rock.[8]

They arrived at the mountain which was to become the Saint's Calvary and Tabor. After ascending the first escarpments, and before starting on the last incline, they paused a moment for breath. Francis sat down under a great oak, which lived, we are told, until 1602, and which a tiny chapel has since replaced. He was gazing at the beauty of the place and the countryside, when hundreds of birds flew down around him, fluttering and singing loudly. In a moment his head, shoulders, arms, and legs were covered with them. Francis thereupon said to his companions: "Dear brothers, I believe that our Lord Jesus Christ is pleased to have us settle here, since our brothers and sisters the birds are giving us such a joyous welcome."

In fact it was there that, by the impression of the Stigmata, our Lord was about to complete his resemblance to Him.

* * *

The summit of La Verna is an uneven plateau, supported by titanic rocks and covered with pines and beeches, where even today legions of familiar birds are loud in their song. A hermitage was built there for the Saint by the Count of Chiusi, and also a little oratory [which was dedicated in the late sixteenth century] to St. Mary of the Angels. From this vantage point the eye takes in an immense panorama. On a clear day one may [catch a glimpse of the Adriatic from La Penna, the summit of the mountain, nearly an hour's walk from the shrine].

As soon as Count Orlando learned of the arrival of Francis and his companions, he came from his castle to welcome them and bring them some provisions. Francis asked him to build him a hut "cell" under a large beech tree a stone's throw from the hermitage. When it was done, Orlando said to his guests: "Dear brothers, I do not mean to have you want for anything on this mountain wilderness, so that you may not be hindered in your spiritual exercises. So I say to you once and for all, feel perfectly free to come to me for anything you need. And if you do not come, I shall be very displeased."

Then he departed with his retinue.[9]

The day was at its close. On Mount La Verna the late afternoons of summer are of surpassing beauty. Nature, which has lain prostrate under the burning sun, seems to take on new life. A thousand voices awaken in the branches of trees and in the clefts of the moss-covered rocks, forming a sweet and melancholy symphony; while for hours the sun still illumines the distant peaks of the Apennines with its iridescent afterglow, filling the heart of the laggard contemplative with what a Franciscan poet terms "the nostalgia of the everlasting hills.[10]

Francis bade his companions to be seated and instructed them how friars living in hermitages should comport themselves, counselling them not to abuse the generosity of Count Orlando but to remain ever true to Lady Poverty. Speaking to them also of his end which he saw approaching, he said to them: "Because I see that I am drawing near to death, I wish to dwell here in solitude and bewail my sins before God. So if any lay people come here, you are to receive them yourselves, for I do not want to see anyone except Brother Leo."

He then blessed them and retired into his hut of branches. From time to time, he would come out and sit down under the beautiful beech to admire the magnificent scenery.

One day when he was thus engaged, his eyes fixed on the gigantic cliffs huddled there before him, towering above the great chasms, he wondered what could have caused such a upheaval in the earth's surface. Then as he prayed, it was revealed to him that these huge crevices had been opened at that moment when the rocks on Mount Calvary, according to the Gospel, were rent. From that time onward, La Verna was for him a witness and constant reminder of Christ's Passion. His love for the crucified Savior increased, his prayer became continuous, and God now favored him with extraordinary mystical graces.[11]

*   *   *

"With the best of intentions" (continues the chronicler), and with that biographer's indiscretion for which posterity will ever be grateful, "Brother Leo diligently spied on his spiritual father."

Sometimes he would hear him lamenting over his Order: "Lord," he would say, weeping, "what will become of this poor little family that You have entrusted to me, when I am gone?" But more often he surprised him in loving colloquy, or crying out for very love, or rapt in ecstasy. Thus it was, we are told, that he saw Francis lifted up several yards above the ground, sometimes even to the top of the great beech. Then he would silently draw near, and when the feet of the ecstatic were within reach, he would embrace them, saying, "Lord, be merciful to me a sinner. And by the merits of this blessed Father, may I find grace in Your sight!"

Meanwhile the Assumption drew near in which Francis had decided to begin a lent which would last until the feast of St. Michael the Archangel. Resolved to keep his too curious observer away, he enjoined Brother Leo to station himself at the door of the hermitage, saying, "When I call you, you are to come."

Then going some distance away, he called to him in a loud voice. Brother Leo came running. "Son," said Francis, "I am still not far enough away. We must find a place where you cannot hear me."

Finally they found the right spot. On the mountainside, hollowed out in the stone, there was a sort of ledge overhanging a chasm some hundred and twenty feet deep. The friars had to place a log as a bridge over the chasm to reach this ledge and erect on it a little hut of reeds. When this was done, their Father dismissed them, saying:

"Return to the hermitage; for with God's grace, I desire to live here in absolute silence and not be disturbed by anyone. You, Brother Leo, may come only twice a day, the first time to bring me bread and water, then about midnight to recite Matins with me. But before crossing the bridge, you are to take care to announce yourself by saying: *Domine, labia mea aperies.* And if I answer, *Et os meum annuntiabit laudem tuam,* you are to pass over. But if I do not, you are to go back at once."

When the Feast of the Assumption came, Francis commenced his great fast.[12]

*   *   *

We are approaching the truly seraphic period in the life of the Poverello, days when, as if lost in God, his soul consummated its final alliance with and conformity to the very soul of Christ.

As the history of mystical phenomena offers nothing similar, and no one has ever been able to claim that he has drawn aside the veil from such mysteries, it is here especially that the historian must limit himself to reproducing the statements of authoritative witnesses. For us these are principally Brother Leo, the Saint's confessor; St. Bonaventure, the Seraphic Doctor; and the author of the *Considerations on the Most Holy Stigmata* — himself dependent [in part on the *Actus beati Francisci* and Thomas of Celano, and in part of the tradition of the friars residing at La Verna].

They report that at this time the Poverello's fervor and austerities were redoubled, that he suffered dreadful pain, and was horribly tormented by the Evil One. "Oh," he would sometimes say to Brother Leo, "if the Brothers only knew what I have to endure from the devil, there is not one of them who would not have compassion and pity for me."[13]

Nevertheless, in the midst of this painful purification, God still sometimes sensibly visited his heart. Thus it was — to console him and give him a foretaste of Heaven — that He sent him an angelic musician. Once and only once, the celestial spirit passed the bow over his viol, but "the melody that came forth was so beautiful," declared the Saint later, "that I almost swooned: and if the angel had drawn his bow a second time, I know that my soul would have left my body, so boundless and unbearable was my joy."

Francis also enjoyed the friendship of a falcon that nested near his cell. Every night before Matins, this affectionate creature would beat its wings against the walls of the hut. But if the Saint was too ill or too tired, the compassionate bird would let him rest and not waken him until later.[14]

Likewise Brother Leo, no less charitable, did not insist when the Saint did not reply to his *Domine, labia mea aperies.* Once, though, he crossed the bridge anyway.

Not finding Francis in the hut, he started out in the moonlight to look for him in the woods. He found him in ecstasy, conversing with someone invisible. "Who are You?" the Saint was saying, "and who am I, Your miserable and useless servant?" Leo also saw a ball of fire descend from Heaven and return almost immediately.

Seized with awe at this supernatural spectacle, and fearing lest his curiosity might lead St. Francis to dispense with his services, the indiscreet friar attempted to flee, but the rustling of the leaves betrayed him.

"Who is there?" cried Francis.

"It is I, Father: Brother Leo."

"Didn't I forbid you, dear little Sheep, to spy on me this way? Tell me under obedience, did you see or hear anything?"

Brother Leo confessed what he had seen and heard and asked for some explanation. The Saint admitted to his friend that our Lord had just appeared to him and he told Leo that something wonderful was going to happen soon on the mountain.[15]

* * *

What was this wonderful thing? As was his habit, Francis wanted to consult the Gospels about it. In the hermitage chapel where Brother Leo said Mass, he asked his friend to

open the missal three times at random, and each time it opened
at the story of the Passion. "By this sign," writes St. Bonaventure, "the Saint understood that, having imitated Christ
in his life, he was also to imitate Him in the sufferings that
preceded His death. So, filled with courage, despite his ruined
health and physical exhaustion, he made ready for martyrdom."[16]

The feast of the Exaltation of the Cross had come. It com-
memorated the victory which had permitted Heraclius to regain the Savior's Cross from the infidels; and no feast was more
popular at that time among Christians, who were continually
being called on to take the cross in the Crusades. It was probably on this day, September 14, 1224, that the miracle of the
Stigmata took place.[17]

In that hour which precedes sunrise, kneeling before his hut,
Francis prayed, his face turned toward the east. "O Lord," he
pleaded, "I beg of You two graces before I die — to experience in myself in all possible fullness the pains of Your cruel
Passion, and to feel for You the same love that made You sacrifice Yourself for us."[18]

For a long time he prayed, his heart aflame with love and
pity. Then "suddenly," writes St. Bonaventure, "from the
heights of Heaven a seraphim with six wings of flame flew
swiftly down." He bore the likeness of a man nailed to a cross.
Two of his wings covered his face, with two others he flew,
and the last two covered his body. "It was Christ Himself, who
had assumed this form to manifest Himself to the Saint. He
fixed his gaze upon Francis, then left him, after imprinting the
miraculous Stigmata" of the Crucifixion on his flesh.

"From that moment," continues the Seraphic Doctor,
"Francis was marked with the wounds of the Divine Redeemer. His hands and feet appeared as though pierced with nails,
with round black heads on the palm of the hands and on the
feet, and with bent points extruding from the back of the

hands and the soles of the feet. In addition, there was a wound in the right side, as if made by a lance, from which blood frequently flowed, moistening his drawers and tunic."[19]

There had been no witnesses to the prodigy, and although it had left visible marks, the Saint's first thought was to keep it secret; then, after much hesitation, he decided to ask counsel of his companions. "So he asked them in veiled words if they thought that certain extraordinary graces ought to be kept secret or revealed."

Brother Illuminato, who well deserved his name, remarks St. Bonaventure, divining that something out of the common order had occurred, spoke up:

"Brother Francis, it might be wrong for you to keep for yourself that which God has given you to edify your neighbor."

Timidly, then, the Saint told what had happened; but without showing his wounds, which he always took care afterwards to cover up with bandages. He even formed the habit of keeping his bandaged hands in the sleeves of his habit.[20]

However, as the Stigmata never disappeared, a number of persons were able to see them. Among them were Brother Leo, whom Francis took as his nurse and who regularly bathed the oozing wound in the side; Brother Rufino and several others who gave sworn testimony about them; and all those present at the death of the Saint or who were able to venerate him in his coffin, especially Brother Jacopa and her sons, and Sister Clare and her daughters. In addition, Pope Alexander IV, who in a sermon heard by St. Bonaventure, averred that while Francis was still alive he had seen the miraculous marks with his own eyes.[21]

Some rationalist scholars have indeed attempted to impugn their existence, although the presence of "nails embedded in the flesh," proved most vexing to them. But their opinion bears no weight; and while waiting for them to furnish proof, we may refer to the judgment of the Holy See which, [by a favor not granted to any other Saint and by the advice of St. Robert Bellarmine, extended to the whole Church the annual observance of the feast of the Stigmata of St. Francis at the time of Pope Paul V (1605-1621); and although the changes made in 1960 reduced this feast to a commemoration, the feast is still observed by the Franciscan Order, to which it was granted by Pope Benedict XI (1303-1304)].[22]

* * *

In addition to his habitual maladies and infirmities, the Little Poor Man now experienced an increase of mysterious inner torment. No doubt he also continued to suffer from the betrayal of some of his own sons, but his soul was overflowing nonetheless with happiness and serenity. What other saint had ever received such proof of God's love and assurance of salvation? The litany that he wrote soon after the great miracle expresses the fullness of his joy. It is the *Magnificat* of the stigmatized Poverello:

> You are the Holy one, the Lord.
> You alone are God. You alone do wonders.
> You are mighty and great.
> You are the Most High.
> You are King omnipotent, O Holy Father, King of Heaven
> and earth.
> You are three and one, the Lord God, every good.
> You are good, every good, the highest good,
> The Lord God, living and true.
> You are charity and love.
> You are wisdom, humility, patience, tranquility, happiness
> and joy.
> You are justice, temperance and all-sufficient riches.
> You are beauty and mildness.
> You are our protector, defender, and guardian.
> You are our strength and our refreshment.

You are our faith, hope, charity, and our infinite sweetness.
You are our life eternal, Lord wonderful and great;
God omnipotent, Savior most merciful![23]

Now while Francis thus sang of his happiness, Brother Leo had become depressed. He was a victim, as he himself tells us, "of the most painful of spiritual trials." Perhaps he had begun to despair of his salvation. Be that as it may, so great was his distress that nothing would have induced him to speak of it to anyone. "Oh, if only," he thought, "my blessed Father would write me a few words of encouragement in his own hand, it would comfort me, or perhaps even cure me!"

Francis divined the spiritual anguish of his beloved companion and condescended to his desire. He took the sheet of paper with his *Laudes* on it and wrote on the back these three scripture verses: "May the Lord bless you and keep you! May the Lord show His face to you and be merciful to you! May the Lord lift up His countenance upon you and give you peace!", adding in his large handwriting, "God bless you, Brother Leo!" Sketching a crude head which some suppose to be that of Brother Leo, he drew a letter TAU over this portrait, then handed the parchment to his friend, saying: "Take this, Leo, and keep it as long as you live."

We can imagine the surprise and joy of Brother Leo, and the happiness he felt at seeing himself marked on the forehead with the sign of the elect. On the instant, he was freed from his obsession, which never troubled him again. And for the forty remaining years of his life, he always carried the beloved talisman on his person.

That is why the priceless autograph, preserved at the Sacro Convento of Assisi, is so worn and dim today. The paleographers, however, have deciphered it perfectly. In addition to the phrase mentioned, it contains fifteen handwritten lines by which Leo himself takes pains to authenticate it. We read, among others, these words under the blessing: *Beatus Fran-*

ciscus scripsit manu sua istam benedictionem mihi frati Leoni; and under the man's head traversed by the TAU: *simili modo fecit istud signum tau cum capite manu sua* ("This blessing was given to me, Brother Leo, by Blessed Francis who wrote it in his own hand, and it is also his hand that drew the head and the T").[24]

*　*　*

The feast of St. Michael had arrived, and the Saint's fast came to an end. Already the snow was beginning to fall on the mountain tops, and soon the hills that Francis must cross to get back to the Portiuncula would be impassable.

[An apocryphal] document attributed to Brother Masseo relates how the Little Poor Man took leave of La Verna: "The morning of September 30, 1224, Francis assembled us in the chapel where, following his custom, he had heard Mass. After commanding us always to love one another, to apply ourselves to prayer, and to take great care of the oratory, he commended the holy mountain to us, and ordered that friars present and future were to hold it in veneration. 'Brother Masseo,' said he, 'my desire is for the superiors to send only God-fearing religious here, chosen among the best in the Order.'

"He then said, 'Farewell, farewell, Brother Masseo! Farewell, farewell, Brother Angelo!' And in the same way he took leave of Brother Sylvester, and of Brother Illuminato, adding, 'Live in peace, my dear children. Farewell! For I return to the Portiuncula with Brother God's Little Sheep, never to return again. My body goes away, but I leave you my heart. Farewell, farewell to you all! Farewell, Mount La Verna! Farewell, Mount of the angels, beloved mountain! Farewell, Brother Falcon: once more I thank you for your kindness to me. Farewell, great rock, I shall see you no more. Farewell, St. Mary of the Angels! Mother of the Eternal Word, to you I entrust these children of mine.'

"We all broke into sobs. He went away, weeping, bearing our hearts with him."

Accompanied only by Brother Leo, Francis took the path [over the nearby Monte Casella and then down to Mont-auto and Borgo San Sepolcro]. When they reached the last peak from which Mount La Verna is still visible, the Saint dismounted, knelt down, and blessed it for the last time: "Farewell, mountain of God, holy mountain, *mons pinguis, mons in quo beneplacitum est Deo habitare.* May the Father, Son, and Holy Spirit bless you, Mount La Verna! Peace to you, beloved mountain, which I shall never see again."[25]

- 20 -

The Canticle of Brother Sun

The return to the Portiuncula was by way of Borgo San Sepolcro, Monte Casale, and Città di Castello. Francis was obliged to ride on a donkey, so painful had walking become for him. And it was this way that he traveled in future, although St. Clare had made special shoes for him to ease his wounded feet.[1]

Apparently, Brother Leo had not denied himself the pleasure of telling about the miracle that had just occurred, for their way was marked by popular demonstrations and by miraculous cures. Everyone wanted to see and touch the stigmatic of La Verna, who had become as a living relic, endowed with supernatural virtue. Even his donkey's bridle was believed to help mothers in difficult childbirth obtain a happy delivery.

Francis, meanwhile, humble and absorbed in God, did not hear the murmurs of veneration by which he was accompanied. Pulling the sleeves of his habit over his bandaged hands, he extended only his finger tips to be kissed by his admirers, not even looking around him.

"Shall we reach Borgo San Sepolcro soon?" he inquired, long after they had passed the town.[2]

They made a short halt at the hermitage of Monte Casale, where he restored an epileptic friar to health. Stopping also at Città di Castello, he delivered a possessed woman who "barked like a dog," and cured a young boy "whose wound healed over in the form of a red rose."

Already the first snows had made their appearance on the mountains. One night when our travelers, prevented by a storm from reaching shelter, had been forced to take refuge under an overhanging rock for the night, they were unable to light a fire — a thing which put the muleteer in a bad humor. "It is all Francis' fault," he grumbled, "that we are in this fix and liable to freeze to death."

The Saint touched the grumbler on the back, and (writes St. Bonaventure) the mere touch of his stigmatized hand made the shivering man warm again. A few minutes later he dozed off, and as he himself related later on, he never slept better in his life.[3]

* * *

No sooner had Francis arrived at the Portiuncula than, as though filled with new zeal, he wanted to resume his apostolic tours. But the aggravation of his gastric disorders and the pain caused by the stigmata and his weakness from the loss of blood, troubled the friars. They begged him to seek medical treatment, but he gaily calmed their fears. Did not his honor as Christ's knight require him to die in harness? And throughout that winter and the following spring, mounted on a donkey, Francis continued to go about Umbria, preaching in as many as three or four villages in a day.[4]

At Foligno, Brother Elias told him of a dream he had had about him: an old priest all in white appeared to him, warning him that Francis would die in two years.[5] This announcement filled the Poverello with joy, but his infirmities soon increased to the point that the friars feared lest he should suc-

cumb before that date. He became almost blind and suffered
from excruciating headaches.

As Honorius III and the Curia, driven from Rome by a popular uprising, were lodged in Rieti, Cardinal Hugolin urged
Francis to consult Teobaldo Saraceni, the Pope's physician.
Now the Saint had a horror of doctors, and in order to get
him to agree to treatment, Elias had to appeal to his spirit of
obedience and quote this Scripture verse: "The Most High
hath created medicines out of the earth, and a wise man will
not abhor them." (Ecclus. 38:4)[6]

It was in the summer of 1225 that Francis consented to go
to Rieti. Taking with him those who remained his nurses to the
end — Brother Masseo and the three Companions — he decided first to take leave of St. Clare, whom he feared never to
see again. Upon his arrival, his condition became so grave that
he had to give up going any farther. He stayed about seven
weeks at San Damiano, where St. Clare had the consolation
of caring for her spiritual father. She had a hut of reeds built
for him [between the chaplain's house and the convent], like
the one he occupied at the Portiuncula; but before getting any
rest there, he spent some dreadful hours.

One would have thought that, "summoned by the devil,
all the mice in the country had met there to torment him."
The wattles of his cabin were full of them, and the ground was
covered with them. They climbed up on the table where he
ate and into the bed in which he was attempting to sleep,
and scurried squeaking over his face. One night, his patience
exhausted, and tempted to despair, the Poverello cried out to
God who seemed to have forsaken him. It was then that a
familiar voice was heard:

"Francis, if in exchange for all these evils, you were to receive a treasure so great that the whole earth — even if it were
changed into gold — would be nothing beside it, would you
not have reason to be satisfied?"

"Certainly, Lord!"

"Then, be happy, for I guarantee that one day you shall enjoy the Kingdom of Heaven, and this is as certain as if you possessed it already."[7]

What did they matter now — after such an assurance — the mice, the suffering, and the other inventions of the Evil One? The divine words filled Francis with heavenly joy; the cabin of torments became a place of delight; and this malefic night inspired the invalid, overwhelmed by every ill, with the most optimistic song ever to spring from a human heart.

* * *

We like to think that it was at San Damiano that the Poverello composed it.[8] For did not everything in this place which had seen the birth of his vocation, recall God's mercies toward him? The cave in which he had hidden to escape his father's "prison." The stone bench where the old priest had sat and talked to him. The miraculous crucifix that had shown him his way. And this chapel rebuilt by him, whence in the silent night he could hear the chant of the Poor Ladies. No doubt, the thought of Sister Clare — the perfect incarnation of his ideal — the nearness of the four good Brothers who cared for him with such tender devotion, and the thought of so many more of his sons who followed the Gospel so well in their poor hermitages, were added consolations.

So Francis blessed his fruitful and beautiful existence. He blessed all nature and life, victorious over death and evil; he blessed the sun which illumines man's joys and sorrows, his struggles and triumphs; he blessed the earth, where man may merit Heaven; and he thanked God for having created him.

When the sun had risen, he called his companions and said to them: "The Lord has deigned to assure me that I shall one day enter His Kingdom. So to show Him my gratitude, I desired to compose this new song which you are about to hear."

And the blind Saint, for whom the least ray of light was a torture, sang to them what he called *The Canticle of Brother Sun:*[9]

> Most High Almighty Good Lord,
> Yours are praise, glory, honor and all blessing.
>
> To You alone, Most High, do they belong,
> And no man is worthy to mention You.
>
> Be praised, my Lord, with all Your creatures,
> Especially Sir Brother Sun,
> Who is daylight, and by him You shed light on us.
> And he is beautiful and radiant with great splendor.
> Of You, Most High, he is a symbol.
>
> Be praised, my Lord, for/by Sister Moon and the Stars.
> In heaven You have formed them clear and bright and fair.
>
> Be praised, my Lord, for/by Brother Wind
> And for/by air and cloud and clear and all weather,
> By which You give Your creatures nourishment.
>
> Be praised, my Lord, for/by Sister Water,
> For she is very useful, humble, precious and pure.
>
> Be praised, my Lord, for/by Brother Fire,
> By whom You light up the night,
> For he is fair and merry and mighty and strong.
>
> Be praised, my Lord, for/by our Sister Mother Earth,
> Who sustains and rules us
> And produces varied fruits with many-colored flowers and
> plants.
> Praise and bless my Lord
> And give Him thanks and serve Him with great humility.

Such is the hymn that won for the Poverello the title of

the "Orpheus of the Middle Ages," the incomparable psalm which Renan considered the "most beautiful piece of religious poetry since the Gospels." Sister Clare probably was the first to hear it, she who loved poetry and music and who also showed herself so grateful to God for the gift of life. Francis dictated it in Italian, such as we still have it; then had it sung by his companions to a melody he had adapted for it. And he himself was so pleased with it that for a moment he thought of sending Brother Pacifico through Europe to sing it to everyone.[10]

An occasion did come soon to call on the talents of the former troubadour.

*   *   *

A violent quarrel had once more set the civil and religious authorities of Assisi at loggerheads. Bishop Guido had excommunicated the podestà Oportulo who had countered by forbidding all relations between the bishop and the officials. Nothing could be more painful to the Saint than to see his fellow-citizens at odds. Immediately adding a new stanza to his poem, he called Brother Pacifico and said: "Go find the podestà for me, and invite him with his worthies to come to the bishop's palace to hear my song."

There was a great crowd in the bishop's courtyard when the King of Verse appeared with his musicians: "You are about to hear," he announced, "the 'Canticle of Brother Sun' which Francis has just composed to the glory of God, and for the edification of his neighbor. And he himself asks you through me to hear it with great devotion." Brother Pacifico then intoned:

Most High Almighty Good Lord,
Yours are praise, glory, honor and all blessing.

To You alone, Most High, do they belong,
And no man is worthy to mention You.

Be praised, my Lord, with all Your creatures,
Especially Sir Brother Sun,
Who is daylight, and by him You shed light on us.
And he is beautiful and radiant with great splendor.
Of You, Most High, he is a symbol.

Alternating with their leader, the friars repeated the stanza in unison. Meanwhile the podestà, writes the author of the *Speculum*, "had risen, and, with hands joined and tears in his eyes, was listening with reverent attention." The entire audience imitated him, moved by these accents of a beloved voice and at hearing their dear Saint singing the beauties of a world he could no longer see.

Be praised, my Lord, $_{by}^{for}$ our Sister Mother Earth,
Who sustains and rules us
And produces varied fruits with many-colored flowers and
                                                                                    plants.

It was at this point that Francis had introduced his plea for pardon and peace, his true heart's message to his fellow-citizens:

Be praised, my Lord, $_{by}^{for}$ those who grant pardon for love
                                                                                    of You,
And bear sickness and tribulation.
Blessed are they who shall bear them in peace,
For by You, Most High, they shall be crowned.

At these words, the emotion of the assemblage was at its height, and sobs choked them as the podestà turned toward the bishop. Falling on his knees before him, he said: "Even if he had killed my own son, there is not a man in the world that I would not want to forgive now, for love of God and His servant Francis. With much greater reason, my Lord, I am ready to make whatever satisfaction you may desire."

Bishop Guido was no less prompt to admit his own errors. Raising the podestà to his feet and warmly embracing him, he said: "I likewise ask your forgiveness. Pardon me for not fulfilling my charge with proper humility and for having yielded once more to anger."

They separated completely reconciled; and, thanks to Francis, charity and peace won out once more among the people of Assisi.[11]

* * *

As soon as he was able to be moved, the Saint left Sister Clare, whom he was never to see again, and with his companions, headed for Rieti, fifty miles away. They passed near Terni, then along the winding course of the Velino, coming at last into a lovely plain at the end of which was to be seen — etched against the somber mass of Monte Terminillo — the smiling city where the papal Curia was staying.

Rieti was preparing a triumphal welcome for the stigmatized Saint of La Verna. To avoid it, or because of his exhausted state, three miles before reaching his destination Francis asked hospitality of the parish priest of San Fabiano. He was a poor priest whose income was derived from a vineyard. He gave Francis and his escort a warm welcome, but was soon to repent having a saint in his home. For his house was invaded by crowds of pilgrims. The horses of the prelates of the Curia trampled down his garden, and the thirsty throngs picked his choicest grapes and ravaged his vineyard.

As he was blustering against the people who had ruined him, Francis observed: "Father, there's no use in crying over spilled milk. But tell me, how much does your vineyard bring you in the best years?"

"Fourteen measures."

"Well, then! If you will agree not to call people names any more, I'll guarantee you twenty from this vintage. And if you fall short, I promise to make up the difference."

But the Saint did not have to make up anything, for when the grapes were harvested, the priest had his twenty measures. And this was a real miracle, for his vineyard had never yielded more than fourteen before.[12]

The arrival of Francis at Rieti gave full scope to the popular devotion. The bishop's palace, where Hugolin installed him, was the scene of sometimes stormy demonstrations. People fought over his garments, his combings, and even his nail parings. A farmer who had collected the water in which Francis had washed his hands, sprinkled his sick flock of sheep with it and they were immediately healed.[13] The case is also told of a canon named Gideon, who was also sick, but as a result of his debaucheries, and who came up to Francis weeping and asking him to bless him.

"How can I make the sign of the cross over you," Francis asked him, "a man who lives only for the flesh? I will bless you, though, in Christ's name; but know that evil will befall you again, if you ever return to your vomit."

And the prediction came true; for when the cured canon went back to his sinful life, he alone was killed when the roof fell in at the house of a fellow canon where he was passing the night.[14]

Meanwhile, the Saint's condition grew steadily worse. His stomach, liver, and spleen were seriously affected, while he continued to suffer horribly in his head and eyes. At that time, wishing to hear some music, he summoned a friar who had been a troubadour in the world, and begged him to borrow a viol and give him a little concert. "It would do Brother Body so much good," he remarked, "to be a little distracted from his sufferings."

But the former troubadour, who believed that a saint ought to stay in character, observed that some people might be scandalized.

"Then let's not say any more about it," replied Francis, "for we do have to make concessions to public opinion."

But the next night, a mysterious visitor came and played the viol under his windows. In the morning, Francis sent for the scrupulous friar. "God consoles the afflicted," he observed. "Last night, to make up for the concert you refused me, He permitted me to hear one infinitely more beautiful than all the music of earth."[15]

* * *

Not wanting, however, to tarry longer in the palace of the Bishop of Rieti, he asked to be taken to the hermitage of Fonte Colombo. It was there that he underwent treatment by a doctor.

The treatment consisted in cauterizing with a red hot iron the flesh around the more affected eye, from ear to eyebrow. The sick man shuddered at the sight of the preparations, then addressed the glowing iron: "Brother Fire, the Most High has made you strong and beautiful and useful. Be courteous to me now in this hour, for I have always loved you, and temper your heat so that I can endure it."

"We fled," confessed his companions, "so as not to witness his sufferings. But our Father said to us: 'Men of little faith, why did you run away, when I did not feel anything at all?' Then turning to the doctor, he said: "If it wasn't done right, you may do it again!' "

And this the doctor did, for he opened the veins over Francis' temple, after which another physician thought it his duty to pierce both ears with a red-hot iron.[16]

With all this, Francis enjoyed great spiritual happiness. Sometimes the Brothers heard him singing new hymns, whose words and music he had composed. Some of them he sent to St. Clare, who was also ill and much worried about him.[7] His heart was more eager than ever, and his head teemed with impossible projects. "Brothers," he would say, "let us start serving our Lord, for so far we have done nothing."

For Francis would have liked to live his life over again, seeking new apostolic and knightly adventures.[18] Since this was impossible, he began to dictate letters, two of which, at least, have come down to us.

In one, addressed to the "rulers, consuls, judges, and governors of all countries," Francis urged these highly-placed personages to "think of death which waits for no man, not to transgress God's Commandments, and to receive frequently our Lord's sacred body and blood." Then perhaps recalling what he had seen in Moslem lands, he begged them to "appoint a public crier or other means to invite the people every night to praise and thank the Lord."

In the other letter, addressed to all the guardians of his Order, he asked them to urge clerics and bishops to venerate the Body and Blood of Jesus Christ above everything else, and to use only proper chalices, corporals and linens at the altar.[19]

And so it was that the Little Poor Man spent his last winter on earth.

* * *

When spring came again, Elias and Hugolin had Francis taken to Siena, where it seems there were also some very celebrated physicians.[20] It was during this journey in the plain extending south of San Quirico d'Orcia, that a meeting occurred that has become legendary.

Francis saw three poor women coming toward him, so perfectly alike in age, height, and features, that one would have thought them triplets. As they passed him, they bowed reverently and greeted him: "Welcome, Lady Poverty!" "Never," writes Thomas of Celano, "did a greeting give so much pleasure to St. Francis." Believing them to be beggar women, he requested the doctor who accompanied him to give them something. Dismounting, the latter gave each of them some money. Thereupon the three sisters disappeared so suddenly that our travelers, who had turned around almost at once, were unable to see what had become of them. "It was doubtless a celestial vision," writes St. Bonaventure, "symbolic of the virtues of poverty, chastity, and obedience, to which Francis had always been so faithful. But as poverty," he adds, "was incontestably his chief title to glory, it was natural that it was this virtue these mysterious virgins wished especially to honor in him."[21]

The reception Francis received at Siena was no less enthusiastic than that of Rieti. Clergy and laity vied with one another in their display of both curiosity and veneration. The biographers tell us that a knight made Francis the gift of a pheasant that did not want to leave him and that refused to eat whenever it was separated from him. They also speak of a learned Dominican who came to propose to him a theological difficulty from which he extricated himself with honor. They further declare that it was there, with the connivance of Brother Pacifico, that a friar of Brescia succeeded in seeing the sacred stigmata. "I forgive you," said the Saint later to the King of Verse, "but you have caused me much pain."[22]

As for the doctors of Siena, their efforts were as ineffectual as those of the Pope's physician. One night the Saint vomited such a quantity of blood that the friars believed his last hour had come. Gathered round his pallet, they were inconsolable: "What is to become of us," they mourned, "poor orphans that we are, abandoned by him who was father, mother, and good shepherd to us?"

They besought him to leave them a written testimony of his last wishes, to guide them in the future. Francis had Brother Benedict of Pioraco, who had celebrated Mass several times at his bedside, summoned. "Write," he said, "that I bless all my friars present and to come. And as I am not able to speak longer, here, in a few words, is what I want them to know: In memory of me who have blessed them, let them always love and honor one another. They must ever love and honor our Lady holy Poverty, and they must ever humbly and faithfully obey the prelates and clergy of our holy Mother the Church."[23]

* *

Meanwhile, Brother Elias, who had been alerted, hastened to the invalid to take him "home" to die. Francis himself desired to breathe his last at the Portiuncula; while his fellow-citizens, who had just been despoiled by the people of Bettona of the body of St. Crispolto, did not intend to be dispossessed this time.[24]

Assuredly, it is rather painful to observe the preoccupation of Elias and the Assisians during the last months of the Poverello's life. But we must remember that the people of the Middle Ages were a little less hypocritical than we; and we should likewise recall the development that the cult of relics had taken on at this period. Nothing outweighed for a city the advantage of possessing the body of a servant of God to place on its altars. Piety, patriotism, and self-interest were here in accord; and men were as willing to shed their blood then for holy relics as they have since been for assuredly more futile motives.

Led by the Minister General, the cortege wended its way toward Cortona; and the invalid stopped for a few days at the hermitage of Le Celle, a league from the city. There, a poverty-stricken man who had just lost his wife and had several children to care for, came to Francis to ask for alms. Francis gave him his cloak, saying, "It is very fine, as you see. That is why, if you dispose of it, be sure to make whoever wants it pay you well."

It was a new cloak, for it replaced the one the Saint had taken off on the same trip to give another poor man. The Brothers lost no time trying to get it back; but the beggar held on to it so stubbonly that they had to hand him a good sum to make him give it up.[25]

[Some time after returning to the Portiuncula, with the onslaught of the summer heat, they decided to take Francis up to the healthier air of the hermitage of Bagnara, in the mountains east of Nocera. Later, while there, the Saint seemed at death's door.] The swelling of his legs had gone up to his abdomen, and he could not take any nourishment. Fearing the worst, the municipality of Assisi dispatched its men at arms to meet the cortege. Thus escorted, the group reached the village of Satriano in the mountains. There, driven by hunger and thirst, the knights and their retinue attempted in vain to procure some provisions. "It's up to you, then," they said laughingly to the friars, "to feed us, since the people here refuse to sell us anything whatever."

"You should have gone about it differently," replied Francis, "and put your trust in God and not in flies." By flies he meant their money. "Ever since man sinned, all earthly goods are alms that God gives with equal kindness to good and evil men. So go to them and ask them for what you need for the love of God." They obeyed and this time obtained all they desired.[26]

The arrival at Assisi was in the nature of a triumph. "Everybody exulted," writes Celano; "for they hoped that the Saint would soon die, and they blessed God for bringing him back to their city." However, as the Portiuncula was in the open, exposed to an enemy raid, Brother Elias — for greater surety — had Francis carried inside the ramparts. He installed him in the bishop's palace, and the municipality posted armed men about it to forestall a kidnapping.[27]

- 21 -

The Testament and Death

Nothing was to be lacking in the life of the Poverello to make it a perfect masterpiece, and his death was the
harmonious culmination of his life. His last weeks on earth are
like the close of a beautiful day, wherein the setting sun seems
to shed on the world all its remaining splendor. Thus, before
leaving his friars, Francis expressed to them once more his
most intimate thoughts, poured out upon them all his tenderness, and then, serene and filled with gratitude, went home to
God.

* * *

Regardless of what one thinks of Brother Elias, we do well
to recognize the loving care with which he surrounded St.
Francis till the end, imposing no restrictions on his liberty or
choice of companions. Assuredly, he is not without merit, for
he could not help reflecting that what was said and written
at the invalid's bedside might tend to be unfavorable to him.

It was apparently to his faithful attendants that Francis drew
the portrait of the ideal head of the Brotherhood. Uneasy

over what was to become of it, and themselves too, once Elias had a free hand, one of them urged Francis to designate someone to fulfill the post of Minister General after he was gone.

"I do not see anyone capable of being the shepherd of so great a flock," he replied, "but I shall enumerate, nonetheless, the qualities he ought to have.

"The head of the Order ought to be a very austere and pious man, sympathetic and discerning, loving all his friars without acceptation of persons, a man of prayer. I should like to have him rise early in the morning, placing Holy Mass at the beginning of his day and praying at length for himself and his flock. Then let him put himself at the disposal of all, answering all requests pleasantly and kindly, receiving both the learned and the unlearned, and letting himself be despoiled, if I may so speak, by all those needing him.

"If he is a scholar himself, far from priding himself on his learning, let him be diligent above all to be humble and simple, endeavoring to preach by example rather than by word. And let him not be a collector of books, lest study make him neglect the duties of his office. As the head of a family of poor men whose model he is to be, let him hate money, convinced that there is no greater corrupter for us, no deadlier foe. Thus he will never wrongly use money-boxes. Let him limit himself to having for his own use one habit and a little copy of the Rule, with writing materials and a seal for the service of the brethren.

"He will also be the one to console the afflicted, restore hope to the despairing, humble himself to bend the incorrigibles, and sometimes forego his own rights to gain souls for Jesus Christ. He will show mercy to deserters of the Order, reminding himself how terrible must have been the temptations capable of bringing about such falls and that he himself would surely have succumbed to them if God's grace had not preserved him. Finally, he will close the mouths of tattlers and beware of talebearers, deeming himself under obligation to find out the truth for himself. However, let this leniency not go so far as to favor laxity; for it devolves on him to make himself feared as well as loved. Let him not be a man whom a selfish desire to remain in office would keep from a manly enforcement of justice; instead, he must be one to whom such a high office is rather an onus than an honor.

"The brothers, for their part, are to honor him as Christ's vicar; charitably providing for his needs, and procuring for him such supplements of nourishment as may be required by his weakness and fatigue. In such case, the minister shall not eat secretly, but in public, for the encouragement of those who are ill, that they may not be ashamed of letting themselves be cared for. "Let him take no pleasure in his prerogatives, and let him take as much pleasure in receiving insults as praise. Finally, I desire his helpers and companions likewise to give an example of every virtue, and to receive gladly all those who resort to them."[1]

* * *

Understandably, Francis was unable to attend the Chapter of Pentecost in 1226. To make up for his absence, he dictated the *Letter to the General Chapter and to all the Brothers*.[2] In this long epistle, the Saint reverts to the reverence due to God's Word and to the Holy Eucharist.[3] Addressing himself especially to the priests of the Order, he says:

"Listen, my Brothers. If the Blessed Virgin Mary is justly honored for having carried the Lord in her most chaste womb, if St. John trembled at baptizing Him, not daring, as it were, to place his hand on God's Chosen One; if the tomb wherein Jesus reposed for a few hours is the object of such veneration; then how worthy, virtuous, and holy ought he to be who touches with his fingers, receives in his mouth and in his heart, and administers to others, Christ, no longer mortal, but eternally triumphant and glorious! Let every man tremble, let the whole world shake and the heavens rejoice, when upon the altar the Son of the living God is in the hands of the priest!"

Fearful lest familiarity should dull reverence and holy poverty be endangered, Francis urged the friars to celebrate only one mass a day in their friaries.[4]

He next begged forgiveness of God and of his brethren for having sometimes "through negligence or infirmity or simplicity, sinned against the Rule," commending to them the exact observance of its prescriptions, saying: "Those who do not recite the office as prescribed by the Rule, or who go about as they please and care nothing about observing the Rule, I do not consider Catholics. For this reason, until such time as they mend their ways, I refuse to see or speak to them."

* * *

The *Testament* which the Poverello dictated at the approach of death is too important a document not to be reproduced in its entirety.[5] The Saint begins by telling the origin of his vocation:

"This is how the Lord gave me, Brother Francis, the grace to begin a life of penance: when I was yet in my sins, it seemed to me unbearably bitter to look at victims of leprosy. And the Lord Himself led me among them, and I showed kindness towards them. And when I went away from them, that which had at first seemed bitter to me was now changed for me into sweetness of soul and body. And then I tarried but a little while, and left the world."

Here Francis' thought turns toward Him whom he loved, served, and did his best to imitate: toward our Lord living among us in the Eucharist and still manifesting Himself in the Scriptures:

"And the Lord gave me such a faith in the churches, that in simplicity I would thus pray and say: 'We adore Thee, O Lord Jesus Christ, here and in all Thy churches which are in the whole world, and we bless Thee, because by Thy holy Cross Thou hast redeemed the world.' Then the Lord gave me, and gives me now, towards priests who live according to the law of the Holy Roman Church, so great a confidence, by reason of their priesthood, that even if they sought to persecute me, I would nonetheless return to them. And if I were to have as great a wisdom as Solomon possessed, and were to meet with poor priests of this world, I do not wish to preach without their consent in the parishes in which they dwell. And these and all others I desire to reverence, love and honor as my lords. And I do not wish to discover if they are sinners, because I behold in them the Son of God, and they are my lords. And for this reason I do this: because in this world I see nothing with my bodily eyes of Him who is the most high Son of God except His most holy Body and His most Blood, which they receive and which they alone minister to others.

"And these most holy mysteries above all else I desire to be honored and adored and kept in precious places. Whenever I shall find writings with His most holy names and words in unbecoming places, I wish to gather them up and I ask that they be gathered up and laid in a more worthy place. And all theologians and those who impart the most holy words of God, we must honor and reverence as those who minister to us spirit and life."

Going back to the past, the Poverello then tells of his life with his first companions:

"And after the Lord had given me brethren, no one showed me what I was to do, but the most High Himself revealed to me that I should live according to the pattern of the Holy Gospel. And I caused it to be written in few words and simple manner, and the Lord Pope confirmed it to me. And those who came to us to accept this way of life gave to the poor whatever they might have had. And they were content with one habit, quilted inside and out if they wished, with a cord and breeches. And we had no desire for aught else. The clerics among us prayed the office like other clerics, while the laics said the Our Father. And quite willingly we would live in poor and abandoned churches. And we were simple and without learning, and subject to all.

"And I was wont to work with my hands, and I still wish to so do. And I earnestly wish that all the friars be occupied with some kind of work, as long as it becomes our calling. Those who do not know how should learn, not indeed out of any desire to receive the pay which the work may bring, but to give a good example and to avoid idleness. And if there are times when no pay is given for our work, then let us have recourse to the table of the Lord, and beg alms from door to door. As for our greeting, the Lord revealed to me that we were to say: 'The Lord give you peace!' "

After these reminiscences of the life led by the first Franciscans, the Saint speaks out for the last time against the changes some would force on his work. A paragraph forbids the friars "to receive churches, houses and all else built for their use, unless these are truly in keeping with holy poverty," and bids them "consider themselves simply as guests therein," since they are but strangers and pilgrims on earth. Another reminds them of their duty of non-resistance and of not seeking papal favors: "I firmly command all the friars by obedience that, wherever they may be, they do not dare to ask for any letter of privilege at the Roman Curia, either directly or through intermediaries, whether concerning a church or any other place, or under the pretext of preaching, or even as protection against persecution. Rather, if they have not been welcomed in one place, let them depart to another and there do penance with the blessing of God."

Then comes a personal protestation of obedience and ortho-doxy, with the sanctions to be enforced against friars suspect-ed of insubordination to the Church:

"And it is my firm desire to obey the Minister General of this brotherhood, as likewise the guardian whom it has pleased him to give me. And I wish to be as a prisoner in his hands, that I can neither move nor act apart from obedience to him and without his consent, because he is my master. And though I am simple and ailing, I wish always to have a cleric who may recite the office with me, as it is prescribed in the Rule. And all the other friars are to be bound in like manner to obey their guardians and to say the office in the manner prescribed by the Rule. And should some be found who are not saying the office according to the prescript of the Rule but are trying to introduce some other form of it, or who are not Catholics, all the friars, wherever they are, are to be bound in obedience to present any such, wherever they may find him, to the custos nearest to the place where they have found him. And the cus-tos is to be firmly bound by obedience to guard him day and night as a prisoner, so that he cannot escape his hands, until he shall in his own person deliver him into the hands of his minister. And the minister is to be firmly bound by obedience to send him by such friars who will day and night guard him as a prisoner until they bring him before the Lord of Ostia, who is the master of this whole brotherhood and has it under his protection and correction."

The *Testament* closes with these lines: "And the friars should not say 'This is another Rule,' because this is a re-minder of our past, an admonition and exhortation, and my testament, which I, the little Brother Francis, am making for you, my blessed brothers, to this end, that we may observe in a more Catholic manner the Rule we have promised the Lord. And the Minister General and all other ministers and custodes shall be bound by obedience not to add to these words or take away from them. And let them always have this writing with them together with the Rule. And in all the Chapters they hold, when they read the Rule, let them read these words also. And all my brothers, both clerics and laics, I firmly charge by obedience not to make any explanations on the Rule or of these words and say: 'Thus they are to be understood.' Rather, as the Lord has granted me simply and plainly to speak and write the Rule and these words, so simply and without gloss you are to understand them, and by holy deeds carry them out until the very end."

Next comes the blessing: "And everyone that shall observe these things, may he be filled in Heaven with the blessing of the most high Father; and may he be filled on earth with the blessing of His beloved Son in fellowship with the most Holy Spirit the Comforter and all the powers of Heaven and all the Saints. And I, Brother Francis, your little servant, as much as I can, confirm to you within and without this most holy blessing. Amen."

Such was the Last Will and Testament of St. Francis, and the way he interpreted the Rule of 1223. But, as we have seen, the Order had evolved too far for it to be still possible to take his intentions into consideration. Thus in 1230, Hugolin, having become Pope, gave to that Rule the interpretation for which many of the friars had been waiting, at the same time declaring that the *Testament* was not legally binding. This intervention was not immediately decisive. The struggle between the intransigeants and the moderates continued and grew; and it took a century, as we know, to eliminate the "Spirituals" from the Brotherhood.

As for Francis, now that, following the example of the knights and martyrs, he had once more testified to his faith and said his *Credo* before dying, there remained nothing more for him than to await the hour of death.[7]

* * *

A doctor friend from Arezzo came to pay him a visit. His name was Buongiovanni or "Good John"; but in obedience to the Gospel, wherein Jesus says that "God alone is good,"[8] Francis always called him "Finiatus" or "Bembegnate." He asked him, "What do you think of my dropsy, Bembegnate?" "Brother," replied the physician guardedly, "I think that with God's grace, all will be well."

"Please tell me the truth! For whether I live or die makes no difference to me. My great desire is to do God's will."

"In that case," replied the doctor, "I shall tell you that according to medical science, your disease is incurable; and my opinion is that you will die either at the end of September or the beginning of October."

Raising his arms to heaven the happy invalid exclaimed; "Welcome, Sister Death!"[9] Then addressing a brother, he said, "Call Brother Angelo and Brother Leo so that they can come and sing by my bed."

Despite their sobs, the pair intoned the Canticle of Brother Sun; but this time, before the final doxology, the invalid stopped them and added the following verses:

> Be praised, my Lord, for/by our Sister Bodily Death,
> From whom no living man can escape.
> Woe to those who die in mortal sin.
> Blessed are they whom she shall find in Your most holy will,
> For the second death shall not harm them.

And it was this new stanza that his companions sang him the Canticle of the Creatures from that time onward. "They sang it several times a day to comfort him, and even in the night to edify and entertain the armed guard in front of the palace."

But was it seemly for one of God's servants whose relics they would soon be venerating, to behave thus in the face of death? Some people, and among them Brother Elias (who doubtless already was thinking about his basilica), did not think so.

"Dear Father," said he to the Saint, "I am glad to see you so merry. But in this city, where people look on you as a saint, I fear lest they be scandalized at seeing you prepare for death this way."

"Leave me be, Brother," replied Francis. "For in spite of all that I endure, I feel so close to God that I cannot help singing."[11]

The ravages of the disease now spread all through him. The dropsy had been followed by extreme emaciation; and the doctors were astonished that this "skeleton" still lived. His sufferings were atrocious. To a brother who asked him if he would rather be executed than suffer such dreadful pain, he replied: "My choice is whatever God sends me. But I must admit that the cruelest martyrdom would be easier to bear than three days of pain like this."[12]

There was an alarming moment, when believing he was about to die, the friars knelt round his bed to receive his final blessing. Unable to see, Francis asked if it was on Elias's head that his right hand was placed. Being assured that it was, he then said, "My blessing on you, my son. I bless in you, as much as I am able, all my friars and my dear sons. My children, always live in the fear of God, for great temptations threaten you and the time of tribulation is near. But I am hastening to the Lord, and I go full of trust to Him whom I have desired to serve with all my heart."[13]

It was a false alarm — the Poverello was not to die in a palace.

*   *   *

In accordance with Francis' wishes, Brother Elias decided to move him to the Portiuncula.[14] To this the magistrates of

Assisi gave their consent, provided that he was accompanied by an armed escort. The procession went through [nearby Porta Moiano] and wended its way to the plain along a path lined with olive trees. When they reached San Salvatore delle Pareti near the Crosiers' leprosarium, Francis asked them to set down his litter and turn his face toward Assisi.

At that spot the whole city is to be seen, with its ramparts and towers, its winding streets and storied houses, and a little to the right, the tiny convent of San Damiano. Higher up, rises the bare [Rocca] with the ruins of its demolished castle at the summit; while afar off in the rear the heights of Mount Subasio appear, marked by the ravine in which the hermitage of the Carceri lies hidden.

Francis had himself raised to a sitting position, and for a long time he seemed to gaze upon the familiar landscape that his blinded eyes could no longer see. Then, painfully raising his hand, he made the sign of the cross: "God bless you, dear city," he murmured. "You that were once a den of robbers, have been chosen by God to become the dwelling place of those who know Him and who will pour out upon the people the fragrance of their pure lives. Lord Jesus, Father of mercy, remember, I entreat You, the abundance of good things that You have shown it, and may it ever be the dwelling place of those who will glorify Your blessed name forever and ever. Amen."[15]

The procession, now midway to its destination, resumed its course and soon reached St. Mary of the Angels.

* * *

The invalid was settled in a hut a few feet from the chapel. This wooded solitude, so often visited by the Spirit of God, assuredly supplied an appropriate setting for his death — a death of radiant beauty. Francis took leave of the world with the same simplicity and courtesy that had marked every act of his life. He forgot nothing. His sons and daughters, the places he loved, the lady of his thoughts, all living creatures, his brothers who had been so close to him, all shared in his farewells and blessings.

He commended his beloved Portiuncula to his disciples. "This place," he said to them, "is holy. Always hold it in veneration and never forsake it. If men drive you out one door, come back in by the other; for it is here that the Lord has increased our numbers, illumined us with His light, and set our hearts on fire with His love."[16]

In honor of his lady, Poverty, he had himself placed naked on the ground, and covering his wounded side with his hand, he said to his friars: "My work is done. May Christ teach you to do yours!"

He waited until — like a final alms — a few garments were given him for the little time that remained to him. His guardian brought them to him, and, in a voice choked with sobs, said: "I lend you these breeches, this tunic and hood. And to keep you from thinking that you are the owner, I forbid you, under obedience, to give them away to anyone at all."

At these words, the poor blind man with his fleshless body and head marked with fearful wounds, trembled with joy. Then they put him back in his bed.[17]

Those present then asked his forgiveness for the pain they had caused him, and implored anew his blessing. Laying his hand on the head of each in turn, he declared that he forgave them their faults and offenses; and, addressing himself to Bernard of Quintavalle, he added: "I also absolve and bless, as much as I am able, and even more than I am able, all my absent brothers. Tell them what I have said and bless them in my name."

Rightly fearing lest his oldest comrade, the veteran of his knightly band, might soon undergo persecution, he continued:

"I ordain that in the Order special affection shall be shown to my dear brother Bernard, who was the first to give his goods to the poor and to enter with me upon the Gospel way."[18]

Francis took care not to forget Sister Clare, whom they had just learned was in tears at the thought of the coming loss of her Father and supporter. He had the following message brought to his dear "little spiritual plant":

"I, little brother Francis, desire to follow to the end the life and poverty of our Lord Jesus Christ and of His most holy Mother. And I entreat you, my Ladies, whatever advice you may receive in future, never to depart from it. And you are to tell the Lady Clare," he added, addressing the messenger, "that I forbid her to give way to grief, for I promise her that she and her Sisters shall see me again."[19]

He likewise thought of his friend Jacopa in Rome. "It would sadden her too much," he observed, "to learn that I have left this world without telling her beforehand." And he began to dictate for her the following letter:

"To the Lady Jacopa, servant of God, Brother Francis, Christ's little poor man, greetings and fellowship of the Holy Spirit in our Lord. Dearest friend, you must be told that the end of my life is at hand, as our Blessed Lord has shown me. Come at once, if you want to see me alive. Bring haircloth with you to wrap my body in, and whatever is necessary for my burial. And please bring with you some of the good things you gave me to eat when I was ill in Rome."

The dictation had reached this point and the messenger was waiting for it, ready to set off on horseback, when the sound of a cavalcade was heard. It was the Lady Jacopa arriving from Rome with her two sons and her retinue. God himself, as she declared later on, had inspired her at prayer with the resolve to start at once for Assisi. A Brother rushed up to the invalid's bedside. "I bring you good news," he whispered, without saying what.

"God be praised!" murmured Francis. "Open the door for her, for the ban on women entering here is not for Brother Jacopa."

Jacopa had brought everything necessary for the Poverello's burial — a veil to cover his face, the cushion in which his head would rest in his bier, the haircloth shroud, and all the candles required for the wake and the funeral. She also brought some of the almond pastry he loved; but he could only taste a morsel, and so he asked Brother Bernard to eat it. As Francis' condition suddenly improved, the Lady Jacopa thought of returning to Rome; but Francis begged her to stay until Sunday, assuring her that he would not last longer than then.[20]

*   *   *

"When I am dying," he said, addressing himself to those around him, "lay me on the ground the way you did three days ago; and when I am dead, leave me there for the space of time it takes to walk a mile."

More and more frequently now, the strains of the Canticle of Brother Sun rose from the hut, with the stanza of praise to Sister Death. On Friday, October 2, Francis had bread brought, blessed it, and like Christ in the Upper Room, distributed it to the Brothers present.[20]

The following day, which was to be his last, the Passion according to St. John was read to him at his request. "The guest to whom no man willingly opens his door," did not come until twilight. As soon as the Little Poor Man saw her enter, he greeted her courteously, 'Welcome, Sister Death!" And he asked the doctor to announce, like a herald-at-arms, the solemn arrival of the expected visitor, "for," he added, "it is she who is going to introduce me to eternal life."

The friars laid him on the ground on a coarse cloth; and to honor his dread guest, he had them sprinkle him with dust and ashes. Then in a barely perceptible voice, he intoned the one hundred and forty-first Psalm, which those present continued with him:

"*Voce mea ad Dominum clamavi.* I cried to the Lord with my voice: with my voice I made supplication to the Lord . . . . In this way wherein I walked, they have hidden a snare for me . . . . There is no one that hath regard to my soul. I cried to Thee, O Lord: I said: Thou art my hope, my portion in the land of the living . . . . Deliver me from my pursuers . . . . *Educ de custodia animam meam.* Bring my soul out of prison, that I may praise·Thy name: the just wait for me, until Thou reward me."

Then in the darkling cell there was a great silence. Francis lay motionless, and the Brothers who bent over him saw that he had ceased to breathe. He died singing, in the forty-sixth year of his age, and the twentieth of his conversion.

*   *   *

At this very instant, a great flock of larks alighted on the roof of the hut, their twitterings a mixture of sadness and great jubilee. In the same hour, a holy friar saw a flaming star borne on a white cloud over the waters, ascending straight to Heaven. It was the Poverello's soul winging its flight to the regions of eternal bliss.

As for Francis' body, it was as though transformed. His limbs, which had been long contracted by suffering, became supple like those of a child; his face was as beautiful as an angel's; the wound in his side appeared of a rosy red hue; and on his once swarthy flesh — now white as milk — the stigmata of his hands and feet stood out like black stones on white marble. One might have thought, [as Brother Leo said later,] that it was the Divine Crucified taken down from His Cross who lay there.

All night long the great forest resounded with the chanting of Psalms by the friars, mingled with the murmur of the voices of the throngs who had flocked there. At dawn on Sunday, October fourth, a procession formed to conduct the mortal remains of the Saint to Assisi. The Friars Minor, singing hymns, were joined by the neighboring populations, bearing palm branches and candles. They were in haste to cross the ramparts, for a surprise attack by the Perugians was always to be feared.

At a given point, however, the procession turned, and, to fulfill the dead Saint's wish, went on to San Damiano. The open bier was brought inside the cloistered nuns' chapel; and so it was that Clare could see the face of her beloved Father once more. She bathed the holy corpse with her tears and covered the sacred stigmata with kisses.

Then the cortege resumed its march toward the Church of San Giorgio, where the first interment of the Poverello took place. About four years later, May 25, 1230, the body was transferred to the crypt of the basilica being erected by Brother Elias.[22] And it is in this grandiose monument — so unlike Francis — that men continue to come to venerate his dust.

THE END

Appendix I
The Sources of the Life of St. Francis

The sources of the life of St. Francis can be divided into four categories:

I. The Saint's own writings.

II. Writings of Franciscan origin: (a) early biographies; (b) compilations; and (c) chronicles.

III. Writings of non-Franciscan origin.

IV. Diplomatic sources.

I
Writings of St. Francis

It is in his writings that the personality of the Poverello finds its best expression. Nothing gives us a more intimate knowledge of it, and the best guarantee of the authenticity of the early documents is their agreement with Francis' own testimony about himself.

There exist two critical editions of the Saint's works, both first published in 1904: the edition of the Quaracchi Fathers (A28) and that of H. Boehmer (A27). They agree in almost every particular and comprise the following writings:

1. The Rule of 1221 (*Regula prima* or *non bullata*). Drawn up from 1210 to 1221, it did not receive the written approval of the pope.

2. The Rule of 1223 (*Regula secunda* or *bullata*). Approved by Pope Honorius in 1223.

3. The Testament. Made by the Saint in 1226, shortly before his death. [See Esser's definitive study (A62).]

347

4. Two texts addressed to St. Clare.

5. Of the Manner of Life of Religious Living in Hermitages (*De religiosa habitatione in eremo*). [Critical text edited by Esser (A61).]

6. Of the Veneration of Christ's Body. [Studied by Cornet (D48).]

7. Admonitions. There are twenty-eight of these, of which it has been rightly said that they constitute St. Francis' "Sermon on the Mount."

8. The Blessing of Brother Leo. The autograph given by St. Francis to his friend after the Stigmatization. [See A53 and A54.]

9. The Letter to all the Faithful.

10. The Letter to the Friars in General Chapter assembled.

11. A letter to a Minister.

12. A letter to all the guardians. (Held for doubtful by Goetz).

13. A letter to Brother Leo. ["Probably authentic." Cambell (E44).]

14. A letter to those who govern. (Considered doubtful by Boehmer [and Cambell] and authentic by the Quaracchi Fathers).

15. A letter to St. Anthony of Padua. (Generally considered substantially authentic, it has long been a moot point whether it was authentic as to form. It has recently been proved that both substance and form are equally by St. Francis). [See A55 and A56, and Ch. 16, Note 28.]

16. The Lauds or Praises. A sort of paraphrase of the Pater in the style of the Middle Ages, followed by a long doxology.

[Jacques Cambell (A44:258; A44a) reduces the paraphrase of the Our Father to the category of an unauthentic work, on the basis of manuscript studies. The long doxology, which begins: *Sanctus, sanctus . . .* he considers as a genuine work of Saint Francis. It seems likely, as the Assisi ms. 338 would indicate, that St. Francis prefaced this doxology with the Our Father (perhaps adding an adjective or two; e.g., *Sanctissime Pater noster*) and the *Gloria Patri*; some scribe then inserted a paraphrase which came to be attributed to the Saint. Boehmer had already rejected the paraphrase not only because of the elegance of style it manifests, but also because of certain phrases that seem to imply a more formal theology than Francis possessed. I. B.]

17. The Salutations of the Virtues and of the Blessed Virgin. Some manuscripts separate these two salutations; others combine them.

18. *Laudes Creatoris* (Praises to God). Composed by St. Francis on La Verna, after the stigmatization.

19. The Office of the Passion. (With the exception of Boehmer, universally considered authentic). [See A57-A60.]

20. The Canticle of Brother Sun. This is the only one of St.

Francis' writings that has come down to us in Italian, the language in which it was composed. The Quaracchi Fathers have not inserted it in their edition, but its authenticity is uncontested today, both by them and by other authorities. [See C144-C186 and Appendix VIII.]

The letters mentioned here are not the only ones written by St. Francis. We know that he addressed several to Cardinal Hugolin, one to the friars of France and another to those of Bologna, all of which have been lost. He also composed other canticles and poems in both Italian and Latin, and perhaps, even in French; but these have not been preserved.

II
Writings of Franciscan Origin
A. Biographies

The principal biographies of St. Francis are those of Thomas of Celano and St. Bonaventure.

1. The *Vita prima* of Thomas of Celano (A65)

A native of Celano in the Abruzzi, received into the Order about 1215, Thomas of Celano was sent to Germany in 1221, became custos of the Rhineland in 1223, and later returned to Italy. In 1228 he was in Assisi, where he was present on July 16, at the canonization of St. Francis. He was again in Assisi in 1230; and again from 1246 to 1247 to write his *Vita secunda*; and then from 1250 to 1252 to write his *Tractatus de miraculis*. He is believed to have passed his last years in his native district as spiritual director to the Poor Clares of Tagliacozzo. His remains have rested there since his death about 1260; and his body is exposed yearly to public veneration on August second. See a résumé of his life and a study of his writings in A64:iii-xlii. [For recent studies, see A90, A93-A103.]

The presumed author of the *Dies irae* [cf A95], Celano is one of the most elegant Latin writers of the Middle Ages. It was because of his talents as an author that Gregory IX designated him to compose the Legend of St. Francis. Finished in 1228, the *Vita prima*, as Thomas himself admits, did not aim at completeness, but rather, as the pope desired, to glorify the newly canonized Saint. The thing expected of the man officially charged with this task was a book of edification, such as those composed by Sulpicius Severus and Gregory the Great on St. Martin and St. Benedict. Any allusion to the opposition encountered by Francis on the part of his own friars would therefore have appeared out of place.

In his prologue, the biographer declares that the truth will ever be his guide and master—*veritate semper praevia et magistra*; that everything he reports has been gleaned from the lips of the Saint or that he has received it from witnesses of authority and integrity. He has divided his work into three books and forty-six chapters in order "that the order of events may not be confused by differences in time and that their authenticity may not be impaired."

The First Book relates the conversion of St. Francis and the edifying life that followed upon it, together with some of the miracles he worked during his life. Book Two covers the last two years of his life and his glorious death. Book Three "contains an account of the many miracles he continues to work from Heaven and which have just been confirmed by the papal authority itself."

Does the author always follow the chronological order that he has mapped out for himself? Doubtless, the events reported in Book I are all (as announced) prior to the last two years of his hero's life, and the principal ones among them occurred in the order given. However, a concern for literary composition sometimes leads him to substitute a systematic order for the chronological, i.e. to link up episodes really belonging to different periods. He likewise draws inspiration from previous hagiographical texts and even borrows some fine literary flourishes from Seneca. Such procedures were common to the time.

However, the chronology of the *Vita prima* has been shown to be of indubitable historicity, and no critic has attempted to substitute a better order. [See Appendix II on Chronology].

The author has been reproached with giving too fine a role to Brother Elias and passing over some of the Saint's closest companions. It is true that in 1228 Brother Elias, as a favorite of the Pope and the Emperor, was one of the most outstanding personages in Christendom, and that Brother Leo and his friends were beginning to be cold-shouldered. It is equally true that Celano, somewhat the courtier by nature, let himself be dazzled by official titles and success. Later on, he was almost cured of this failing which, no more than his literary flourishes, seems not to have made him alter the truth.

2. The *Vita secunda* of Thomas of Celano (A67)

We must never, in dealing with these early Franciscan documents, lose sight of the troubled conditions in which they appeared.

During the first century of its existence, the Order was sadly divided. Three tendencies in it divided men's minds: the lax, ultra-conservative, and moderate interpretations. Those favoring relaxation were nearly eliminated by the sensational excommunication of Brother Elias. The ultra-conservatives or "Spirituals," who demanded strict observance of the Rule and Testament, appealed to Brother Leo for support. They soon clashed with the Roman Curia, which condemned and finally liquidated the party (1313-1317). Their suppression was the triumph of the moderates, whose most illustrious representative was St. Bonaventure. Among the Ministers General who governed the Order between Brother Elias (1221-1227 and 1232-1239) and St. Bonaventure (1257-1274), it is well to recall that Albert of Pisa, Aymon of Faversham (1240-1244), and Crescentius, belonged to the Moderates, whereas Blessed John of Parma upheld the "Spirituals" (1247-1257). On this period, see Jordan (E29), Gratien, *Histoire* (E23), [and especially Brooke (E3); also D62].

It was Crescentius who in 1244 ordered Thomas of Celano to take up his pen once more; and, to assist him, urged those friars who had known St. Francis personally to put their recollections of him into writing.

Was the *Vita prima* considered faulty? Not at all. The point then at issue was not one of suppression, but of completion. Certainly, one might be shocked at seeing Brother Elias—who had now become by his rebellion the scandal of Christendom—so favorably presented in the volume. It was also well to put an end to the many motivated tales beginning to circulate about the Poverello. But the main reason was that the *Vita prima*, designed for the general public, did not sufficiently satisfy the pious curiosity of many friars, who desired a deeper knowledge of Francis' interior life and of what he required of them.

Clearly, no one knew as much about St. Francis as did Leo, Angelo, and Rufino, who had long been so close to him. Brother Leo, his confessor, especially, had been with him since 1221. Together, the Three Companions drew up voluminous memoirs which they addressed to the Minister General. Their covering letter read as follows:

"Having been, like all the brethren, commanded to impart to your Paternity what we know of the examples and miracles of our blessed Father, we who have lived so long with him, have decided—taking truth as our guide—to bring to the notice of Your Reverence a small portion of the many wonders we ourselves have seen or that have been related to us by trustworthy witnesses, particularly by Brother Philip, Brother Masseo, and Brother Illuminato, as well as by Brother John, the companion of the venerable Brother Giles and confidant of the saintly Brother Bernard.

"Instead of relating miracles, which in truth do not constitute sainthood but only manifest it, we have preferred to endeavor to make known the godly life and real intentions of our blessed Father. Equally, rather than add a new biography to those which have already appeared, and to relate facts already told with such charm and exactness, we have culled, as in a fair meadow, some of the flowers that seemed most beautiful to us; and which may—if it appears good to you—be added to the earlier Legends. For we believe that their venerable authors would not have failed to include them, had they known them; for assuredly, nothing would deserve more to be set forth by their talent, and thanks to them, to come down to posterity. Written at Greccio on August 11, 1246." (Latin text in A281:733 and A143:375.)

As we see, the Three Companions esteemed the author of the *Vita prima* most highly, and hoped that he would add their memoirs to his work. Their suggestion was not followed as such; for instead of completing his first Legenda, Celano wrote a new one in which the "flowers" of the Three Companions had the special place.

Twice as long as the *Vita prima*, the *Vita secunda* comprises 224 paragraphs divided into two parts, of which the First is six times shorter than the Second. The whole is preceded by a Prologue (1-2) and followed by a Prayer (221-224).

In the Prologue, Celano and the Three Companions together address the minister Crescentius, presenting to him their work, and emphasizing the difficulty they encountered of discovering the truth among so many obliterated memories and contradictory information.

In the final Prayer, the Companions speak to St. Francis, praying to him to bless all his children and especially those who dedicate this new book to him.

The First Part (3-25) is almost a chronological account, going from Francis' birth to the nomination of Hugolin as Protector of the Order. It completes, sometimes repeats, and sometimes also corrects, the *Vita prima*.

Part II, however, except for its final paragraphs (214-220a) relative to the death, canonization, and translation of the Saint, constitutes a complete break with the chronological order. It is a sort of systematic tableau, filled with discourses and anecdotes, in which the author passes in review the virtues and unveils the ideas of the saintly Founder. It speaks of his spirit of prophecy and of divination (27-54), his cult of poverty (55-64,69-70), his contempt of money (65-68), his temptations (115-124), his piety and the efficacity of his prayers (94-101), his love of the poor (83-93) and of all creatures (165-171), his humility (140-150), his simplicity (189-195), his ideas about begging (71-79), about consorting with women (112-114) and nuns (204-207), about sloth (159-162), and joy (125-134), etc.

Such is the plan of the *Vita secunda*, whose historical value is incontestable, in spite of some traces of literary embellishment that are to be found in it.

As for the sources from which the author has drawn, the principal is evidently the notes of the Three Companions, which were so extensively used that the latter averred themselves to be collaborators of Celano and stood guaranty for his work. But under what form did these memoirs find their place in the new Legend? Were they added to its first part, unchanged in form and substance, as a common compilation; or did Celano, like the true writer he was, adapt them as he did other material?

For his sources could not have been limited to the "flowers" of the Three Companions. Ever since the publication of the *Vita prima*, Celano, far from losing interest in his subject, must have taken pains to assemble all available information. And besides those writings which were perhaps already in circulation before 1244 (with an aim to filling out the omissions and silences of the *Vita prima*), was it not likely that the invitation of the General Chapter and of the Minister Crescentius would have redoubled the literary activity of those friars who believed themselves to be well informed? For the appeal of 1244 was addressed to all; and nothing would indicate that the Three Companions were the only ones to respond.

Thus everything would lead to the belief that Celano had abundant source material at hand for his writing of the *Vita secunda*. What he did with the writings he had at his disposal, what he took from them and what he discarded, and what happened to them afterward, are problems hotly debated and to which we shall return later on.

The *Vita secunda* was generally well received within the Order and approved by the General Chapter of 1247.

3. *The Treatise of the Miracles* by Celano (A68)

Meanwhile devotion to the Little Poor Man was increasing daily and the number of miracles attributed to his intercession grew accordingly.

As the *Vita secunda* had given very little space to them and many new ones had taken place since the publication of the *Vita prima*, it was deemed necessary to put out a special work which would celebrate the wonder-working powers of the Saint. Again it was to Thomas of Celano that John of Parma, the successor of Crescentius, entrusted the task. The aged writer took pen in hand once more, and in 1253 the *Tractatus de miraculis* was completed.

It consists of 198 paragraphs divided into 19 chapters, of which one, the 16th, is devoted entirely to the famous "Brother Jacoba." The rest, except for a few interesting biographical details, relate only miracles, of which a third were already known to us.

4. The *Legend* of St. Bonaventure (A74)

The *Vita secunda* derived too much of its inspiration from the Three Companions for the intransigents not to use it against their adversaries. However, with the support of Pope Alexander IV, the latter had their revenge when they obtained the dismissal of John of Parma. His successor, St. Bonaventure, felt that a good method of appeasement would be to publish a Life of St. Francis that would please everybody; and he permitted the writing of this life to be entrusted to him by the General Chapter of 1260.

Of the fifteen chapters in the Legend of St. Bonaventure, the first four give the Poverello's life from his birth to the official approval of his Rule, the eight following pass his virtues in review, and the last three deal with the end of his life and the honors accorded him by the Church after his death. The volume is followed by a long Appendix enumerating the miracles obtained by his intercession.

This biography is edifying and at the same time precise and purposeful. It is edifying throughout, and nowhere else has the working of grace in the life of St. Francis been better described. The exactness of the author comes from the fact that after gathering information from the survivors of the first Franciscan generation, he finally decided that he could do no better than to condense or even to copy Celano. For the historian, the main defect of the work lies in its voluntary omissions. Since the past could not be brought back, and recalling it spread dissension, and since the only policy judged desirable and possible was to bring about a union of minds within the observant group in power at this period, no mention must be made of the Founder's Testament; and any reminder of his personal ideas on the nature and activity of his Institute, on learning, manual labor, the care of lepers, the poverty of dwellings, etc., must be avoided. It was this reason that led the Seraphic Doctor to limn a portrait of St. Francis that, while admirable, is not adequately faithful.

His Legend was considered capable of obtaining the expected results; for not only was it approved by the Chapter of 1263; but the General Chapter of 1266, over which he presided, forbade the friars to read any others in future and commanded them to destroy everything that had been published before about St. Francis [cf A248].

The importance of this decree on the history of Franciscan sources cannot be overemphasized. For its execution was more thorough than those analogous measures to which all threatened governments are reduced. Barely a few copies of the condemned writings escaped destruction; and the Spirituals were obliged to conceal these so carefully that it has taken more than six centuries to discover part of them.

The *Vita secunda*, for example, was not found until 1798. Even in our time, the Quaracchi Fathers possessed only two complete copies of this document for their critical edition, whereas they had hundreds of manuscripts of the Bonaventurian Legend at their disposal. The *Treatise on Miracles* was not unearthed until 1899. As for those writings inspired by Brother Leo, like the *Speculum perfectionis* and the *Legenda antiqua* of Perugia, 1898 and 1922 respectively mark the dates when they were first published.

5. The Other Biographies

1. The *Legenda chori* (A66) is a resumé of the *Vita prima* that Celano made in 1230 for readings at Matins. The *Legenda minor* (A75) of St. Bonaventura is also a series of liturgical lessons composed for choir use about 1261. It replaced the *Legenda chori* of Celano when the decree of proscription was promulgated in 1266.

2. The *Vita sancti Francisci* by Julian of Speyer (A69) is a beautifully written and extensive summary of the *Vita prima* by a German friar who had been choir master at the court of the kings of France and had entered the Order during St. Francis' lifetime. He wrote between 1232 and 1239. At about the same time, Julian, who was also a poet, composed the verses and probably the music of the *Officium rhythmicum* (A70), of which large portions, of great beauty, are still chanted by the Friars Minor.

3. The *Legenda versificata sancti Francisci* by Henri d'Avranches (A71). Born in Germany of a Norman father he was an itinerant clerk, half-troubadour, half parasite, who made endless rhymes on everything for everybody. One encounters the "arch-poet" Henri d'Avranches at the court of Gregory IX and again at the court of his enemy, Frederick II. He bore the title of official "maker of verses" for the king of England and he wrote verses for King Louis. He was likewise a canon of Avranches and dean of the chapter of Maestricht—a tragic death shattered his career and his lyre in 1272. Toward 1232-34, he had composed, based on the *Vita prima* of Celano, an epic poem of 2,589 hexameters in honor of the newly canonized Saint. It is a sort of *Francisciade*, displaying the same kind of inspiration and talent as the *Henriade* of Voltaire; [cf A71a].

4. *De laudibus beati Francisci* by Bernard of Besse (A77), St. Bonaventure's secretary, is a little treatise whose interest consists chiefly in the light it sheds on the problem of Franciscan sources.

5. The *Legenda santae Clarae virginis* instructs us concerning the relations of Francis with his spiritual daughter. It was written in 1256 by command of Pope Alexander IV. [Modern scholars attribute it to

Thomas of Celano; for recent editions, see E170, E191, E210, E211, E211a; only the last includes the Latin text.]

   6. We must also make mention here of the *Life of St. Francis* (A76) in *The Golden Legend* of James of Varazze (1265-1280), and several other short Legends, such as the *Legenda choralis Umbra* of about 1250-1252 (A73), the *Legenda monacensis* of about 1263-1283 (in A64), all of them rewritings of Celano or St. Bonaventure.

B. Compilations

A compilation is a work made from extracts by various authors. The writers here referred to appropriate either in whole or in part the work of others, improving what they consider good and correcting what they deem defective, sometimes copying faithfully, and scarcely ever indicating their sources.

Of these numerous compilers, of especial interest are those who have transmitted to us the texts of Brother Leo or of other witnesses going back to the first Franciscan generation.

It is certain that Brother Leo, for his part, did not limit himself to the documents of 1246. Thirty years after his death, rolls of parchment were still in circulation containing some of his other writings in his own hand. He wrote a (lost [?]) life of Brother Giles (A136: 322). For other writings of his—though perhaps not the exact text —see A123. The more attempts were made to water down the Poverello's ideas, the more did Brother Leo strive to recall and defend them. A number of his friends did likewise, especially the Spirituals, who claimed to be the true repositories of the Franciscan spirit. It was from them that certain of the compilations, chronicles, and apologies which follow are taken:

   1. The *Legenda trium Sociorum*, or Legend of the Three Companions, is no longer considered to be the work of the said Companions. It opens with the letter addressed by them to the Minister Crescentius; then, contrary to what is set forth in the preface — "*per modum legendae non scribimus*" — there follow some eighteen chapters forming a veritable Legend, rather similar to Part I of the *Vita secunda*, [as they deal mostly with the Saint's youth and conversion.] It is thus a sort of literary forgery, which aside from chronological confusion, does report events with exactitude, including some then unpublished. Scholars have concluded that the compiler [perhaps] possessed some of the documents utilized by Celano, including omitted portions. [Today nearly all] consider the Pseudo-Legend of the Three Companions to date from the first years of the fourteenth century. [Some] believe that it [may] contain nine paragraphs (15, 46, 47, 48, 49, 50, 51, 52, 56) bor-

rowed from Brother Leo's original text. [For editions and studies, see A83a, A87, A143-A147, especially the work of Abate, summarized at the end of this Appendix.]

2. The *Speculum Perfectionis* or "Mirror of Perfection of the State of the Friar Minor," of which we possess several versions, is not (as Sabatier believed) an authentic work by Brother Leo, but a compilation made after his death, and drawing its inspiration from him. Anachronisms and interpolations abound. In a number of incidents and stories, the *Speculum* is closely allied to Part II of the *Vita secunda*; but the sources utilized are more literally followed in the *Speculum*, in addition to many authentic incidents of which Celano either was ignorant or which he did not dare report. [For editions and studies, see A83, A85-A87, A124, A151-A155.]

Of all these primitive compilations, the most valuable is perhaps the so-called *Legenda antiqua* of Perugia of which [two] mutilated copies have been discovered. As we have it, it contains forty-eight chapters, all of which have their counterpart either in the *Speculum* or in Celano's *Vita secunda* and *Tractatus de miraculis*. The compiler however, seems very often to give the original, which would lead us to believe that we possess here [some of] the most important fragments of the authentic writings of Brother Leo. [For editions and studies, see A148-A150; FNV II, 479-485; C160:348-353; esp. A249: 461-496 and 194-200.]

4. The *Philipps* or *Little Manuscript* is noteworthy for its more complete version of the *Actus* than that utilized by Sabatier for his 1902 edition; and nine paragraphs (153*b*, 154, 155, 164, 179, 194, 197) belong, according to some critics, to the original text of Brother Leo; [see A156, A157, and A249:3-19 and 182-194].

5. The *Codex S. Antonii de Urbe* (A220) and the *Liber exemplorum* (A221) likewise contain several anecdotes apparently borrowed from the memoirs of St. Francis' confessor. The latter is a compilation of 146 "Examples" for sermons, probably written between 1268 and 1273. [Regarding its author, See Appendix V, Part 6, "The Fortini House."]

6. With the *Sacrum Commercium* and the *Fioretti* we touch on writings in which literature and legend overlay strictly factual data.

The *Sacrum Commercium beati Francisci cum Domina Paupertate* is a little [allegorical] epic. It relates the spiritual marriage of Francis and his companions with the Lady Poverty. [Oliger (A271: 39) considers the date 1227 in some manuscripts "inadmissible" and ascribes it to John of Parma, ca. 1260-1270. For eds., see A82, A83a, A112-A119.]

The *Fioretti* is a collection of translations made in the 14th century of Latin texts, almost of all of which have been recovered today. [Many modern editions have] six parts: the *Fioretti* proper, the *Considerations on the Stigmata*, the *Life of Brother Juniper*, the *Life of Brother Giles*, the *Sayings of Brother Giles*, and "Additional Chapters." (These have little of interest for us.) The *Life of Brother Giles* and the *Life of Brother Juniper* are [adapted] from the *Chronicle of the Twenty-four Generals*, to be mentioned later. It is to Brother Leo and to two disciples of Brother Giles that we owe the collection of the latter's sayings. The six *Considerations on the Stigmata* are borrowed from Celano, St. Bonaventure, and unknown sources, in a few of which legendary accounts are reproduced. It is the only part of the work considered at the present time as constituting, not a translation, but an original work.

The *Fioretti* proper consists of fifty-three chapters, to be found in a fourteenth century compilation entitled the *Actus beati Francisci et sociorum eius* (A158). The principal author of the *Actus*, Ugolino of Montegiorgio, had known the disciples of the first Franciscans. His collection is apparently designed to illustrate by example and "acts" the maxims set forth in the *Speculum*. Perhaps the translator borrowed his title from the letter-preface of the materials utilized by Celano.

Contemporary critics are much less disdainful of the *Fioretti* than were their predecessors. Granted that the author has added his own contribution to it, that the painter has stylized his picture, that the orchestra leader has brought in variations of his own, and that the masterpiece, containing so much that is historic, contains some more that is legendary. Yet [in the chapters dealing with St. Francis] there are no false notes; the tone rings true; the themes are those that only the Poverello could invent; the atmosphere wherein the Franciscan adventure develops is incomparable; the portrait of St. Francis has never been painted elsewhere in so lifelike a manner. Legend, which so often is bigger than its hero, merely keeps pace with him here. Thus, just as the Lord's Prayer was not written by the Evangelists, neither are the "sermon to the birds" and the "dialogue of perfect joy" the work of the compiler of the *Actus* or of the translator of the *Fioretti*. [For editions and studies, see A158-A186, with bibl. and notes in A166; see also the end of this Appendix.]

C. Chronicles

[See A130-A142]

1. *The Chronicle of Jordan of Giano* (A133). In 1221, Jordan left the Portiuncula with Celano and eighty other religious for Germany. The memoirs which he dictated in 1262 are of considerable value. They deal with the first chapters of the Order, with the troubles

that broke out in the brotherhood during Francis' voyage to the Far East, and with the establishment of the friars in Hungary and Germany.

2. The *Chronicle of Thomas of Eccleston* (A135), completed around 1260, narrates the history of Franciscan foundations in England, at the same time giving us information about Brother Elias, and in general helping us to understand the Poverello's extraordinary influence over his disciples.

3. The *Chronicle of Salimbene* (A136-A137). Born in Parma in 1221, entering the Order in 1238, Fra Salimbene was in contact with several of the first friars. He wrote his memoirs between 1282 and 1287. He loved to travel and to take in everything of interest. A great talker, he possessed common sense and the ability to write vividly. One would have preferred to see him more entranced with the mighty figure of his father, St. Francis, and to have had him write more about him. What he says concerning the early years of the Order confirms what we know from other sources. [See A138-A142 for studies, & A130, A131 for French & English annotated excerpts.]

4. Although often inspired by passion, the works of the Spirituals P. J. Olivi (d. 1298), Angelo Clareno (d. 1337), and Ubertino of Casale (d. after 1328), are valuable for reference. To these zealots, Brother Leo was a fifth evangelist, and they make frequent appeal to him. [See E47-E73.]

5. The *Chronicle of the Twenty-Four Generals* (A191) [by Frère Arnaud de Sarrant or Samatan in Aquitaine] is an immense compilation made in the second half of the fourteenth century. It contains much information on Brothers Bernard, Giles, Leo, Masseo, Juniper, and Rufino, taken from documents since lost.

6. The *Book of the Conformities* (A193) of Bartholomew of Pisa is a still more monumental compilation, which was approved by the Chapter of 1399. Its very title expresses the object of this celebrated work. A man of prodigious learning and of no less marvelous credulity, Bartholomew quotes his sources exactly and is familiar with some no longer available to us. [His correct name is Bartolomeo Rinonichi or Rinonico, *not* Albizzi; cf AFH 50 (1957) 462. See Goyau's work on his book (A195).]

7. The *Chronicles* of Mariano da Firenze (A230-A235), of Nicholas Glassberger (A134a), of Mark of Lisbon (A236), and of Wadding (A240-A245), are most useful to students of the Franciscan Order; but the biographer of St. Francis finds in them mostly traditions whose accuracy he must check.

[8. *La Franceschina* (A229) is an invaluable 15th century compendium of early Franciscan biographies.]

III
Writings of Non-Franciscan Origin

Among non-Franciscan authors giving us first hand information are:

Jacques de Vitry, an impartial eye-witness whose testimony is of inestimable value. He speaks of St. Francis and his companions in two letters, one written in 1216 and the other in 1220, as well as in his *Historia orientalis*, and in one of his sermons. [See A128, A129, and Ch. 11, Note 1.]

Thomas of Spalato, who on August 15, 1222, was present at a sermon preached by St. Francis in the Piazza of Bologna (A80:9-10).

The author of the *Legenda de passione sancti Verecundi*, who mentions two visits of the Poverello to the monastery of San Verecondo in the diocese of Gubbio (A80:10-11; & F292).

Their testimony, as well as that of Ernoul, Burchard, of the author of the *Life of Gregory IX*, of Eudes de Châteauroux, etc., were published by L. Lemmens, *Testimonia minora saoculi XIII.* (A80); G. Golubovich, *Biblioteca bio-bibliografica della Terra Santa e dell'Oriente franciscano* (C94); Gratien de Paris, *Sermons franciscains du cardinal Eudes de Châteauroux* (A215a).

IV
Diplomatic Sources

Official contemporaneous documents of value as source material on the life of St. Francis are as follows:

1. The circular letter written by Brother Elias announcing his death (A72; cf C196).

2. The registers of Honorius III (F81) and Gregory IX (F88, F89), which permit us to follow Hugolin in his journeys and to fix the dates when he met St. Francis.

3. A score of Bulls promulgated by the Roman Curia between 1218 and 1230 (F109).

4. The Act of Donation of Mount La Verna (in F109, F380, F383).

5. A number of official acts concerning the community life of Assisi, of the Bernadone family, etc., are published or summarized by Arnaldo Fortini [in his 1959 *Nova Vita di S. Francesco* (A296)].

* * * * *

[Without duplicating the coverage in the "Guide to Research on St. Francis of Assisi 1939-1963," we must add to Englebert's survey of the Sources a few comments on several outstanding contributions to that subject in those years.

[The latest available comprehensive study dates from 1940: *The*

Sources for the Life of S. Francis of Assisi (A268) by the Anglican Bishop of Ripon, John R. H. Moorman, who has recently been "in the news" as an observer at the Second Vatican Council. This book remains today an extremely useful compendium of information about all major and most minor sources, from the Writings to the *Actus-Fioretti.* Its value as a practical handbook is only slightly decreased by Michael Bihl's having "confuted convincingly" (Brooke E3:66) its two theories regarding the origins of the so-called Legend of the Three Companions (A247): a) that it was compiled soon after 1247 from several earlier documents, of which the principal was a proto-biography of the Saint extending only to 1215 which had been written just before 1229 and used in *I Celano;* and b) that part of Julian of Speyer's Legend was taken from a "Lost Document" also used by *I Celano* and perhaps written by Brother Giles. After refuting these two hypotheses as *"nimis arbitrarias,"* Bihl gave the book a lengthy objective abstract rather than review in the AFH, in which, unfortunately, he did not analyze but merely described Moorman's most valuable section: his attempt in Chapters V & VI to identify the elusive *Scripta Leonis* as reflected in *II Celano,* the *Speculum Perfectionis,* the *Legenda Antiqua* of Perugia, and the Little Manuscript. Similarly, we can also regret that Moorman did not give his readers a critical analysis of Bihl's masterly study of the last two sources in his fundamental "Disquisitiones Celanense" (A249), which Moorman of course used.

[However, Moorman was not able, due to the times of publication and World War II, to make use of two equally basic studies which appeared, respectively, in 1941 and 1939 in Italy. They are the final form of the Quaracchi editors' *Praefatio* to AF X, and the apparently definitive study by Abate of the so-called Legend of the Three Companions. As the first is well known and generally available, but the second has been almost completely ignored, for some unknown reason — and still is! — we shall give the reader a translated synopsis of its contents in the pithy words of the author, Padre Giuseppe Abate, Conv, one of the greatest and most perspicacious Franciscan scholars of our times (A143 & A147).

[In the little town of Sarnano in the Marches (the area of Chapters 41, 46, & 47 of the *Fioretti;* cf F132:56-65 & F32:262-269), he discovered a codex written partly in the late 13th and partly in the early 14th century which turned out to be a typical Franciscan compilation containing, among other items, substantial portions of the *Tres Socii* and the *Legenda Antiqua* of Perugia. Hoping to print some of the rest in an appendix (which has not yet appeared!), Abate published in the 1939 MF the Sarnano *Tres Socii* text (completed from other manuscripts) and a treatise of over 100 pages, which he summarized thus in his table of contents: (L3C: Legend of the 3 Companions):

The L3C in the judgment of Sabatier. The Portiuncula the "holy fortress" of the *zelanti?* Alleged dissensions in the Franciscan Order have been over-dramatized. Thomas of Celano and the 3C were not partisans. Crescenzio of of Iesi was not a relaxed friar and did not mutilate the L3C. Variety of opinions of the 3C. The "complete" L3C of Da Civezza & Dominichelli (A219) was an unsustainable experiment. The 3C & Thomas of Celano. Throughout the 13th century no mention was ever made of a Legend spe-cifically called "of the 3C." Rather than a life of SF, the L3C is a history of the foundation of the Franciscan Order. The Letter of the 3C is not an enigma nor a forgery; it is an authentic document that has no connection with the Legend. Chapters 17 & 18 of the L3C are not an interpolation. The L3C was not written by Brother Leo, neither alone nor collaborating with others. The so-called L3C is the work of a single author. It is not the one written by Giovanni the Notary. The *Anonymus Peruginus* and its sources. Bernard of Bessa did not know the L3C. Where is the true L3C? Value of the 3C. Manuscripts of the 3C. Various versions. The L3C is a late compila-tion made from the *Anon. Per.* and the two Legends of Thomas of Celano The compiler's method in editing or reworking. To his verbal reworking of the sources, the compiler often adds that of the facts; a typical example; the abandoning of Rivo Torto.

[This carefully reasoned and extensively documented treatise must be studied by all who write on the Sources of the life of St. Francis. Unfortunately very few have yet done so — "*proh dolor parum cog-nita,*" one lamented in 1959 (CF 29, 1959, 515). Only Ezio Fran-ceschini has dissented from Abate's conclusions (MF 47, 1947, 615-617), but has failed so far to explain why (Ant 32, 1957, 475). Until the Quaracchi editors publish a critical edition and study in AF XI — and perhaps even then — Abate may well have said "the last word" on this controverted Legend. However, Clasen has announced a new study (WW 27, 1964, 122).

[In this connection, the Franciscan historian of the Abruzzi Province Aniceto Chiappini, OFM, has thrown an important new ray of light on the identity of the Apostolic Notary Giovanni. Since the 16th century the latter has been consistently called Giovanni da Ceper-ano and known as the author of a lost life of St. Francis. Zefferino Lazzeri (A145) and Otto Karrer (A86 & A85) have claimed without success that it is really the so-called Legend of the Three Com-panions. But only a few years ago Chiappini noted that in Angelo Clareno's *Chronicon* (E57:20; cf 9) John is mentioned as "*sanctus vir frater Ioannes de Celano.*" Having studied some sermons by a friar of that name (A256), Chiappini concluded that this was in fact the author of the lost Legend, the Ceperano in late works being a misreading for Celano. Fra Giovanni da Celano was a brother of the famous Thomas, was also a Friar Minor as well as a Curia notary, and died about 1270. His *Legenda,* beginning "*Quasi stella matutina,*" was probably written between 1230 and 1245 and based primarily on *I Celano.* Though lost, a Dominican liturgical adaption survives (AF X, 533-535; cf lvi-lvii).

[Important new research by Giacinto Pagnani, OFM, librarian and archivist of the Province of the Marches, has brought out hitherto unknown information about Fra Ugolino di Montegiorgio (or Monte Santa Maria), the talented author of the *Fioretti's* Latin original, the *Actus* (A178; & A166:20; & especially A162:16-21 & 210). Pagnani has cleared up the confused identification of this Ugolino with another friar, Ugolino son of Rinaldo Brunforte, ex-bishop of Teramo, who was provincial when he died in 1384 — or with an earlier Ugolino, son of Buonconte Brunforte, probably a layman, who died about 1248. In 1957 Pagnani discovered archival documents of 1319 and 1342 which mention "frater Ugolinus Boniscambii de Monte Sanctae Mariae," making him a member of a well-to-do family of that town. Another significant fact about him is the testimony he gave in Naples in 1331 against Fra Andrea da Gagliano, who was accused of favoring the excommunicated former Minister General Michele da Cesena, a leader of the Spirituals (E50 & E56). The stand taken then by the author of the *Actus,* which has often been charged with being a Spiritual pamphlet, reveals that he sided with the other saintly friars of the Marches whom he venerated, such as Blessed John of Alverna and Conrad of Offida, in seeking to reform the Order from within rather than leave it. Consequently, the *Actus-Fioretti,* despite several partisan chapters, should be classed as a powerful proto-Observant rather than a Spiritual book (see A166:21-26; & E53). In the absence of documents, Pagnani believes that Ugolino died about 1345. (For other recent studies of the *Actus-Fioretti,* see our "Guide.")

[In conclusion, let us record a few desiderata regarding the problem of sources from the special point of view of the biographer. While of course recognizing that the professional responsibility of the paleographer and textual critic is to trace (if possible) an error-proof genealogy of the earliest documents, the biographer must in addition have as a working tool basic equipment which will supply: 1) *all* extant versions of each separate incident or pericope, critically evaluated as to their relative authenticity; and 2) all major comments or studies of those texts by the foremost experts. It is indeed regrettable that today very few examples of such an approach to the life of St. Francis of Assisi are available, though much of the preliminary spadework has been done, even decades ago.]

Appendix II
Chronology

Note: Capital letters in parentheses refer to items in the list of chronological references in *I Celano* below. Arabic numbers in parentheses *without* a capital letter refer to paragraphs in *I Celano* (A65). References like this (A65) are always items in the Bibliography.

1. Preliminary Note

"The chronology of the life of St. Francis is enough to make one despair" — such is the mature judgment expressed orally by a scholar who has studied the problem for over twenty years. Even today some of the most critical publications still give "1209(1210)" as the year of the approval of the proto-Rule in Rome. Among the various complicating factors often mentioned are the two medieval Italian methods of reckoning the calendar year (the Pisan with the year beginning on March 25 before a Christmas or the Florentine, beginning after that Christmas). To these, Terzi (C9:ix) adds an important variant: in the *calculus pisanus*, 1206 plus 3 gave 1208, or 1226 minus 2 gave 1225. However, Fortini, from his exhaustive study of Assisi archival documents, insists (FNV II, 503) that they do not follow the Pisan system. It should also be stressed that most such documents are very explicitly dated, with several built-in counterchecks, as they usually include not merely the calendar date, but also the years of reign of both pope and emperor, plus the complex Roman indiction. Nevertheless, cases of falsely dated documents are frequently found.

However, despite the medieval hagiographer's deplorable prejudice against specifying any date except that of his subject's death or birth in heaven, Friar Thomas of Celano in his *Vita Prima* (*I Cela-no*), written only two years after the death of St. Francis, was exceptionally generous in providing more or less clear chronological clues. As will be seen from the List below, he supplied no less than twenty in the 118 numbered paragraphs of the actual biography (excluding the canonization and miracles). After running through his List (arranged chronologically, with known or probable years supplied), we can set up a Chronological Chart, with other known data, and then analyze it in an attempt to discover the system, if any, which he used, consistently or not. Such a study, which has not yet been made — and which must still be developed in greater detail — will throw some important light on the half a dozen major chronological problems in the life of St. Francis, which we will then examine separately.

Part 15 of this Appendix is a Chronological Table which contains the principal conclusions reached.

2. List of Chronological References in *I Celano*

(A) "... *fere usque ad vigesimum quintum aetatis suae annum tempus suum... perdidit.*" He wasted his time until almost the twenty-fifth year of his age. (2) Born in 1181 or 1182?

(B) "*Factum est autem, cum iam dictam ecclesiam* [Portiuncula] *reparasset, conversionis eius annus tertius agebatur.*" It happened that when he had already repaired that church, the third year of his conversion had begun. (21) Early 1208 or 1209?

(C) "... *illo tempore Oddo imperator, ad suscipiendam coronam ... transiret... pater... iuxta viam... in praedicto existens tugurio* [Rivo Torto] ... *Apostolica in eo vigebat auctoritas.*" At that time the Emperor Otto was traveling through on his way to receive the crown, the Father was living in that hovel... The authority of the Apostles was growing strong in him [Francis]. (43) Sept., 1209.

(D) "... *ecclesia Sancti Damiani ... est locus ... in quo ... ordo pauperum Dominarum ... a conversione beati Francisci fere sex annorum spatio iam elapso... exordium sumpsit.*" The Church of San Damiano is the place in which the Order of (Poor Clares) originated when a period of nearly six years had passed from the conversion of St. Francis. (18) Spring, 1212.

(E) "*Sexto... conversionis suae anno, ... in partibus Sclavoniae... se invenit.*" In the sixth year of his conversion he found himself in the region of Slavonia. (55) 1211 or 1212?

(F)   "*Post non multum. . . temporis versus Marrochium iter arripuit.*" Not long afterward he set out for Morocco. (56) 1213?

(G)   ". . . *tertio decimo anno conversionis suae ad partes Syriae pergens* . . . Proceeding to the region of Syria in the 13th year of his conversion . . (57) June, 1219.

(H)   ". . . *tertio anno ante. . . obitus sui diem apud. . . Graecium . . . in die natalis Domini . . .*" In the third year before the day of his death at Greccio on the Lord's Nativity." (84) December 25, 1223.

(I)   "*Superiore quidem tractatu . . . vitam . . . Francisci usque ad octavum decimum conversionis suae annum ennarando . . .*" In the Part above narrating the life of Francis up to the 18th year of his conversion. (88) 1223/24; i.e. between Greccio and La Verna.

(J)   "*Reliqua. . . gesta ipsius a paenultimo vitae suae anno. . . adnectemus.*" We shall add the rest of the things he did from the next to last year of his life. (88; cf Prol. 2) From La Verna until death: 1224-1226.

(K)   ". . . *cum videret sibi imminere diem extremum, quod etiam per revelationem divinam ante duobus annis ei fuerat indicatum. . .*" When he saw that his last day was imminent, which had also been indicated to him by a divine revelation two years earlier. (108) July or November, 1224?

(L)   "*Nam cum ipse beatus pater et frater Helias tempore quodam apud Fulgineum morarentur nocte quadam. . .adstit . . .Heliae sacerdos quidam. . .dicens:'. . .dic fratri Francisco, quoniam expleti sunt decem et octo anni ex quo mundo renuntians, Christo adhaesit, et duobus tantum annis dehinc . . .viam universae carnis. . . introibit.'*" For when at a certain time the blessed Father and Brother Elias were staying in Foligno, one night a certain priest stood before Elias, saying: 'tell Brother Francis that eighteen years have passed since he abandoned the world and adhered to Christ, and only two years from now he will enter into the way of all flesh.' (109) July or November, 1224?

(M)   "*Faciente ipso moram in eremitorio, quod. . .Alverna nominatur, duobus annis antequam animam redderet caelo, vidit . . . Seraphim. . .*" While staying in a hermitage called Alverna two years before he gave his soul back to Heaven, he saw a Seraph. (94) September, 1224.

(N)   ". . . *per decem et octo annorum spatium, quod tunc erat expletum, vix aut numquam requiem habuerat caro sua. . .*" For a period of eighteen years, which was then over, his body had hardly ever or never had any rest. (97) End of 1224.

(O) "*Haec fere per duos annos. . . sustinuit.*" He endured these things for almost two years. (102) End of 1224 until October 3, 1226.

(P) "*In mense. . . sexto ante obitus sui diem, cum esset apud Senas. . .*" In the sixth month before the day of his death, when he was in Siena. . . (105) April, 1226.

(Q) ". . . *cum videret sibi imminere diem extremum . . . Erat tunc temporis manens in palatio Assisinati episcopo, et propterea rogavit fratres, ut eum ad locum.. . Portiuncula citissime transportarent.*" When he saw that his last day was imminent.. . He was at that time staying in the palace of the Bishop of Assisi, and therefore he asked the friars to take him to the Portiuncula without delay. (108) September, 1226.

(R) "*Anno. . . Dominicae Incarnationis millesimo ducentesimo pletis viginti annis ex quo perfectissime adhaesit Christo, Apostolorum vitam et vestigia sequens, egressus de carnis ergastulo. . .*" In the year of the Lord's Incarnation 1226, on October 4 [actually the evening of the 3d, the day being counted from sunset to sunset] Francis, twenty years having passed since he had adhered in a most perfect way to Christ, following the life and footsteps of the Apostles, going forth from the prison of the flesh. . . (88) October 3, 1226.

(S) "*Conversionis suae tempus iam erat viginti annorum spatio consummatum. . .*" A period of twenty years had now passed since the time of his conversion. (109) September, 1226, after moving from the Bishop's palace to the Portiuncula.

(T) ". . . *vicesimo conversionis suae anno, feliciorem finem felici connectens principio, felicissime caelo spiritum commendavit.*" In the 20th year of his conversion, adding to a happy beginning an even happier end, he most happily commended his spirit to Heaven. (119) Early October, 1226.

Saint Francis of Assisi: A Biography

3. Chronological Chart

YEARS	KNOWN DATA	I CELANO REFERENCES (abbreviated; cf List)	(a)	(b)	(c)	YEARS
1205	6 G. de Brienne dies	usque ad 25m annum tempus perdidit (A)				1205
1206				1		1206
1207			1 – – –	2	1	1207
1208		cum iam reparasset, conv. ann. 3s (B)	2 – X –	3 $\checkmark$	2 X	1208
1209	4? Approval in Rome 9 Otto to Viterbo	Apostolica in eo auctoritas (C) via Rivo Torto (C)	3 – – –	4	3	1209
1210			4 – – –	5	4	1210
1211		6c conv. anno Sclavoniae (E)	5 – – –	6 X	5	1211
1212	5? Clare to S. Dam.	a conv. fere sex (D)	6 $\checkmark$ –	7	6 X	1212
1213	5 S. Leo	Post non multum versus Marocchium (F)	7 – – –	8	7	1213
1214			8 – – –	9	8	1214
1215	11 IV Lateran Council		9 – – –	10	9	1215
1216	7 Inn. III/Hon. III		10 – – –	11	10	1216
1217			11 – – –	12	11	1217
1218			12 – – –	13 X	12	1218
1219	6 Francis to Egypt 11 Damietta taken	13o anno conv. (G)	13 $\checkmark$ –	14	13 $\checkmark$	1219
1220			14 – – –	15	14	1220
1221			15 – – –	16	15	1221
1222			16 – – –	17	16	1222
1223	12 Greccio Christmas	3o anno ante ob. (H)	17 – – –	18 X	17	1223
1224	9 La Verna Stigmata	usque ad 18m conv. ann. (I) paenult. anno (J) cf (M); tunc	III $\checkmark$ 18 $\checkmark$ II $\checkmark$ 19 $\checkmark$	III X 19 X	III X 18 $\checkmark$	1224
1225		18 ann. spatium explet. (N) cf (L)	II X 20 $\checkmark$	II X 20 X	II X 19 X	1225
1226	10/3 Francis dies	expletis 20 ann. (R) conv. tempus 20 ann. consumm. (S)	I 20 $\checkmark$ –	I 21 X	I 20 X	1226
		20o conv. suae anno (T)				

(a) July 1206/July 1207 as first year of conversion;
(b) calendar year 1206, (c) calendar year 1207 as same.
I, II, III years preceding death.
short line after or before year is midyear (July 1).

4. The Chronological System of *I Celano*

From these twenty references it should be possible to determine: a) whether Thomas of Celano used a particular system of chronology in his Vita Prima; b) what it is; and c) whether he adhered to it consistently.

Naturally we must begin with several undisputedly certain facts, which are: the Saint's death on October 3, 1226; the Greccio Christmas on December 25, 1223; the stigmatization in September, 1224; and the journey of the Emperor Otto IV through Italy to Viterbo for his coronation in Rome by Pope Innocent III on October 4, 1209. To these can be added, from non-Franciscan Crusade sources, the presence of Francis at the siege of Damietta from the summer of 1219 until after its capture on November 5, 1219.

Combining those dates with the data in our List, we find that.

the 20th year of his conversion fell in 1226 (R) (S) (T);

   18th   1224 (I) (N);

   13th   1219 (G).

Presumably, then, the trip to Slavonia in the sixth year fell in 1212 (E), and the conversion of St. Francis was in the winter of 1206/1207. So perhaps there is really no problem after all. Was Friar Thomas simply using calendar years throughout, as these indications seem to imply? In other words, is his system of an elementary and obvious simplicity? What then is the problem?

A systematic and thorough attempt to harmonize all the major chronological references in *I Celano* with all the known data will result invariably with a number of agreements (marked √) combined with one or more conflicts (marked X) — hence the students' despair.

Let us begin with the simple calendar system, starting from the verified trip to Egypt in 1219, in the 13th year of conversion. We then follow column (c), with the first year falling in 1207 and the 20th in the calendar year 1226. This is Fortini's system (C3). But right there we encounter the first conflict: how could Thomas of Celano stress that by October 3, 1226, twenty years of conversion had passed (R) (S). True, in (T) he places the death in the 20th year — perhaps just to demonstrate that he is not always perfectly consistent. However, with (c) an apparently insuperable obstacle (ignored by Fortini!) arises in 1212 (or 1211) with the vocation of St. Clare and her settling in San Damiano "nearly (or about) six years after the conversion" (D). As will be explained in Part 9 below, the year 1212 is disputed by some who place the event in 1211; however, most scholars today accept 1212. The exact month when Clare moved from Panzo to San Damiano is not known, but generally thought to be May or June. But how could Friar Thomas call the spring or summer of the year "nearly (or about) six years" from the conversion if he sets the latter around December or January? And Fortini's system, with Francis' conversion early in 1207 and her vocation in the spring of 1211, yields almost four years!

That Thomas does not use the calendar year system throughout is shown clearly in his terms for the last three years (I, II, III). He places the Greccio Christmas in the third year (H), but December, 1223, falls in the fourth calendar year; and he has the stigmatization (1224) "two years" (M) before the Saint's death, but 1224 is the third from last calendar year. So it would seem clear that at least in these cases he is not using the calendar years.

A glance at column (b) with 1206 as the first year of conversion will show that the calendar year system results in no less than eight conflicts.

So a 12-month year of conversion independent of the calendar year must be devised — one that will fit into the data with a minimum of conflict. The two principal ones have been worked out by Leon Patrem (C7), based on February 1206/February 1207 as first year of conversion, and by Terzi (C9) with mid-March of the same years. Fortini's five volumes do not include a study of chronology, and he supplied some notes on the subject in a brochure (C3); based on Salimbene's reported *magna nix* on February 5, 1207, he places the bishop's trial about then. But the Chart will show that these three systems have the same faults as (b) and (c). Patrem has to explain away the trip to Egypt falling three to four months after the end of his 13th year of conversion; Terzi denies the conflict by calculating 1219 minus 13 gives 1206. For Fortini, as with (c), there is no conflict in 1219, but as we have seen, in 1212 (or 1211) with St. Clare's vocation, and another in 1226, as for Fortini the 20th year of conversion would not be completed until December 31, 1226, or even February, 1227.

5. Conversion and Year of Conversion

We must therefore try to ascertain as closely as possible what Thomas of Celano meant when he used the terms conversion and year of conversion, and specifically when the first year of conversion began.

Working backward with his guideposts, we find that the first year of conversion began:

twenty years before Francis died (R) (S) (T);

eighteen years before the stigmatization (L) (N) — whether the vision of Brother Elias at Foligno in 1224 occurred before or after the stigmatization will be studied in Part 3 below;

thirteen years before the trip to Egypt (G);

nearly or about six years before St. Clare went to San Damiano (D);

a little over two years after Francis repaired the Portiuncula (B).

The Chart shows that the concatenation of these specifications requires the first year of conversion to begin in the summer of 1206 — more exactly not before June (for then the departure for Egypt in June, 1219, would not fit into the 13th year) and not later than September or perhaps even August, depending on the Foligno vision (for the eighteen or twenty years of (R) (S) and (L) (N) must extend until then).

With the first year beginning around July 1, 1206, we have in column (a) seven agreements and only two potential conflicts; (B) in 1208 (to be analyzed in Part 7) and the problematic (T) in 1226 — both probably inconsistent momentary reversions to the calendar years.

What Thomas of Celano meant by the phrase "year of conversion," which he used six times (B) (E) (G) (I) (S) (T), is obviously what we would render by year of apostolate, year of new life, or year *after* conversion. Undoubtedly in his mind it was a logical hagiographical counterpart of the familiar *annus pontificatus*, which is still used to designate the non-calendar years beginning on the day of election of a pope; for instance, the second year of the pontificate of Pope Paul VI extends from June 21, 1964, to June 20, 1965.

Now we are in a position to clarify what Thomas of Celano meant when he used the word conversion, for we know that in his judgment it was completed by the summer of 1206.

Just what was the "conversion" of St. Francis? Was it the "Go — rebuild My Church" message of the San Damiano Crucifix, as some have thought? Or was it the decisive break with the world at the bishop's trial which Patrem, Fortini, and Terzi consider the decisive turning point that marks the beginning of the first year of conversion?

What does Thomas of Celano himself have to say? From his several chronological hints in the *Vita Secunda* (*II Celano*) and Treatise on Miracles (*III Celano*), it is clear that for him the conversion was a gradual process extending over a number of months: *"paulatim de carne transiturus ad spiritum"* (*II Celano*, 11.) It began with the vision at Spoleto (omitted in I *Celano*), after which Francis *"incipit transformari in virum perfectum"* (began to be transformed into a perfect man) (*II Celano*, 7). Even the San Damiano experience was still "*in principio suae conversionis vitae*" (*III Celano*, 2), though Francis was then "*mutatus perfecte iam in corde,*" (*II Celano*, 10.)

Did Friar Thomas consider the bishop's trial the end of the process? The answer probably is: yes and no. Yes, because (as we shall see in Part 7) he apparently places the end of the repairing of the Portiuncula just over two years later, at the beginning of the third year of conversion; evidently in this instance he simply meant the third calendar year: 1206/1207/ early 1208. Yet no, since he repeatedly dates the beginning of the first year of conversion, as we have seen, in the summer of 1206.

We must therefore study closely all available clues regarding the months between the bishop's trial — presumably in January, February, or even March, 1206 — and the following summer. What did Francis do during those months? Was he still not completely converted? Is there some factor which, in the mind of Thomas of Celano, would mark the definitive beginning during that summer of the new life, the years after conversion?

After the trial Francis had a cold reception by the robbers and then by the monks of the Priory of Valfabbrica (not Valingegno; see Ch. 3, Note 15). We must now carefully note his clothing. He left Assisi dressed in "a rough and mean tunic of a farm servant of the Bishop" (*Bonaventure*, II, 4), which Thomas calls a ragged shirt (16). The monks refused to give him even an old garment. But his friend in Gubbio made him a present of a small tunic. Bonaventure shows Francis nursing the victims of leprosy in Gubbio before returning to Assisi, presumably still wearing the tunic he acquired in Gubbio. But when the Saint sets about repairing San Damiano — which Friar Thomas calls "the first work that (he) undertook after having won his liberation from the hand of his materialistic father" (18) — we are informed that he had changed clothes again (*mutato habitu*) and was wearing a kind of hermit's habit, with leather belt, staff, and shoes (21). It need not be stressed that in the Middle Ages a man's status was clearly indicated by his clothing, and that the numerous hermits of those times wore a kind of standard garb, as just described, which was universally recognized as a religious habit.

We can therefore venture to conclude that the event in the summer of 1206 which in the mind of Thomas of Celano marked the formal end of the process of conversion and the beginning of the first post-conversion year was the deliberate assumption by Francis, on his return to Assisi from Gubbio, of the standard hermit's habit, as he set about repairing San Damiano, his "first work" for God. Probably concurrently he became formally enrolled as an "oblate" of the Church — a distinct ecclesiastical status stressed by Fortini (FNV II, 223) as the basis of Francis' appeal to the bishop's court.

We can now proceed to examine briefly the principal remaining chronological problems "*seriatim*" — in consecutive order, as Thomas stresses that he wrote the *Vita Prima* (Prol. 1).

6. Year of Birth 1181 or 1182?

When Thomas of Celano in (A) says that Francis wasted his time until nearly or about the 25th year of his age, exactly what does he mean: until the youth was, in American parlance, 23 going on 24, or 24 going on 25? Taking *fere* as "approaching," was he about the age of 23 and 10 months or a year older? On his 24th birthday he would begin his 25th year. Scholars have argued for both interpretations, but only a few of them, and none conclusively, with an exhaustive analysis of Thomas' vocabulary in all his extant works.

And when did Francis stop wasting his time "*miserabiliter*"? Here the answer seems clear: when his process of conversion began with the Spoleto vision. But exactly when did that take place? All we can say is that it had to be before Gautier de Brienne died in June, 1205. But it could have been in the spring or late winter of 1205 or even in the second half of 1204, depending on how slowly or rapidly we guess the process evolved between Spoleto and the bishop's trial in early 1206.

Most scholars place the birth late in 1181 or early in 1182. With the latter, 23 full years bring us to early 1205. So if we choose to read the phrase in (A) as until Francis was about 23 years and 10 months old (as Patrem does), then going back from May, 1205, would yield a birthdate of around August 1, 1181. Incidentally, in the 17th century the Saint's birthday was celebrated in Assisi on September 26 (C13:371).

Regarding the month or season of the year, a determining factor which has not been explored is the time of year when the Saint's father would normally travel to France and the number of months the journey would normally take. Fortini (FNV I/1, 102) has him leave in July. More light will have to be shed on this question by experts on the medieval French fairs, such as Dr. Face (C30).

7. First Disciples & First Missions 1208/1209

Although several leading biographers of St. Francis place the coming of his first followers in 1209 and the approval of the Order by Innocent III in 1210 — or both in the same year — a careful analysis of all relevant early texts (and not just the incomplete data of *I Celano*) will show that a full year had to elapse between those two events. With the bishop's trial early in 1206, the first disciples' vocations must be placed somewhat over two years later, in April, 1208, and the trip to Rome in the spring of 1209, as we shall see, because Thomas of Celano specifies that it occurred before September, 1209, and he has not been proved wrong.

In addition to later texts reporting that the Saint wore his hermit's habit for two years (AF III, 2 & 3) and that the first followers joined him two years after his conversion (*Tres Socii*, 27), we have a rather cryptic sentence in *I Celano*, 21 — our (B) — which, when interpreted correctly and fitted into otherwise verified facts, has the same meaning, even though it makes Friar Thomas use a calendar-year calculation in this instance, instead of his usual summer-to-summer years of conversion. First, how should his words be translated? Certainly not: "It was the third year of his conversion when he began to repair this church." Grau's German version (A90:91) is correct, and can be rendered literally in English as follows: "When he had repaired that church, one was in the third year of his conversion." The "*cum iam reparasset*" definitely means "when he had fiinished repairing." And the sense of the "*annus tertius agebatur*" is simply that the third year was at that time running its course. The month which the writer had in mind could be any of the twelve. But it is clear that in this case Thomas of Celano could not have had in mind the twelve months from July, 1208 through June, 1209 — unless he had been seriously misinformed about the events of those months. As shown below, the time in question — running between the end of the Portiuncula repair and the St. Mathias Mass on February 24 — has to be the days or weeks between that day and January 1, if Thomas was thinking in calendar years, or between February 24 and some unknown day in January or early February, 1206, when the bishop's trial marked the end of the process of conversion. But since we have seen that placing the start of the years of conversion there only leads to conflicts in 1219 and 1226 and other years, according to the system Thomas followed throughout the rest of his *Vita Prima*, it would seem more likely that in this instance he simply adopted the calendar-year calculation — as he apparently also did with (T) in 1226.

Regarding the St. Mathias Mass, some clarification is still needed. Some writers claim the Gospel was then in the Mass of the Vigil. But no one has yet described, in connection with this crucial event in the Saint's life, a contemporary Umbrian — or better yet an Umbrian Benedictine missal. The text of *I Celano*, 22, combines elements from several Gospels. A minority opinion that the Mass was that of St. Luke on October 18 is chronologically untenable.

Now, after April, 1208, with the arrival of Bernard, Peter Catanii, and Giles — to say nothing, as usual, of the unknown first disciple — we come to the vexed and still unclear problems of the first disciples and the first missions preceding the trip to Rome a year later. The questions involving the identity of the individual men will be treated in Appendix VII on the Companions. Here only the numbers of followers participating in each mission is important. Though only one pre-Roman mission is mentioned by Thomas of Celano and St. Bonaventure, later more or less reliable sources such as the *Tres Socii* and *Anonymus Perusinus* indicate that between the reception of the first three friars in April, 1208, and the journey of Francis and his first eleven companions to Rome in the spring of 1209, the first Franciscans undertook three distinct minor mission tours. Their order and chronology were first noted by the Quaracchi editors in 1897 (AF III, 713), then clarified by Patrem (C7), and have recently been re-emphasized but somewhat confused by Terzi (C9 & F59). As Brother Giles took part in all three, in *Franciscan Mystic* (E121: 20-38), I tried to arrange them in proper sequence, despite conflicting evidence.

The first mission, probably only a few weeks after April, 1208, saw Francis and Giles make a short tour in the Marches of Ancona, with Bernard and Peter going elsewhere. The two principal sources are the *Tres Socii*, 33-34, and *Anon. Per.*, 15-16; but other bits appear in AF III, 76; Codex S. Antonii, 71; & Minocchi's *Legenda Antica*, 4; compiled materials are found in *La Franceschina* (A229:I, 56-58),& E121:20-25.

It is the second and third missions that are difficult to distinguish clearly. Between the first and second, three more followers joined Francis, making a total of seven Franciscans, including the Saint. Then, according to a probably reliable text quoting Brother Giles in the *Liber exemplorum*, n110 (also in AF I, 418, & F59:244), Francis summoned the six into the woods near the Portiuncula and suggested that they set out on a preaching mission. This second mission of the seven is also reported by *Tres Socii*, 36, and *Anon. Per.*, 18, but with a significant difference: whereas in all three texts Francis' exhortation to his companions is similar, in the first he says *dividamur in gentes*, while in the other two he says *eamus per mundum*. It would seem probable that this time they traveled together.

It must have been on this mission that the seven friars came to the hermitage of Poggio Bustone in the Rieti Valley, where the Saint had a mystical experience in which he was assured that his sins had been remitted and that men from many nations — French, English, Spaniards, Germans — would soon hasten to join the little new Order. Thomas of Celano (26-28) mentions this revelation (without naming Poggio Bustone) and has Francis, "at that same time," after another disciple had joined them, send forth all eight (including himself) "two by two" on a third mission to preach peace and penance.

Terzi in his monumental *Memorie* (F59:207-253) has made much of this "Peace Mission" starting from Poggio Bustone. The first specific identification of that place as the site of the remission of sins occurs in the generally unreliable *Actus Sancti Francisci in Valle Reatina* (A222:52), written by a local friar in 1416, probably reflecting a valid local oral tradition. But while he mentions both the sins and the great number of soon coming friars, he does not refer to the mission of peace. Therefore we can consider the former as authenticated in Poggio Bustone, but until further evidence is forthcoming it remains possible that Francis sent forth the seven from some other place.

Incidentally, Terzi seeks to strengthen the case for Francis' stay in Poggio Bustone at this time, the winter of 1208/1209, by stressing another incident which certainly occurred there: at the end of a St. Martin's fast in winter, the Saint disclosed to the people that he had been using lard with his food. For Terzi, 1208/1209 is proved by the words *"in exordio praedicationis"* in the Lemmens *Extractiones* text (A125:39), which would date the incident "at the beginning of the preaching" of St. Francis. But it happens that the same story is reported in the *Legenda Antiqua*, 40 (which Terzi uses for another detail), with the words *"in primo verbo suae praedicationis."* So stronger support will have to be found for the early date. The context referring to the Saint's inability to digest oil in his "illnesses" suggests a later year. This example demonstrates the absolute necessity of always studying carefully every word of *all* extant versions of each incident for important variants.

To his enduring credit, Msgr. Terzi has also made significant archaeological discoveries at Poggio Bustone and there, as at La Foresta, Fonte Colombo, and Greccio, he has arranged notable works of restoration and improvement.

The mission of Bernard and a companion (probably Giles) to Florence is assigned by *Tres Socii* and *Anon. Per.* to the second mission, but can be taken as identical with the one in *I Celano*, 30, in which Bernard and Giles "set out toward" St. James of Compostella in northwestern Spain. That Thomas' words *"versus. . . iter arripuit"* should not be translated as "made a journey to," is shown by his using the same expression (55) when St. Francis "set out for" Morocco, which he did not reach — just as Bernard and Giles did not reach Spain on this trip, though both went there later, Giles alone and Bernard with Francis.

But now, "within a short time," as Thomas repeats three times in four lines (30), all eight friars reassembled — no doubt early in 1209. And with the coming of four more, they were ready for their momentous petition to the Holy See.

8. Rome & Otto 1209 or 1210?

The year when Pope Innocent III granted his approval to Francis and his first eleven companions remains one of the most difficult yet important problems in the chronology of the Saint's life. Again here is another regrettable instance of a major question which has not yet been given the thorough attention which it merits.

What are the basic facts? In a word, they can be summed up thus: Thomas of Celano, writing only nineteen years later, declares that the approval in Rome occurred before September, 1209, when the German Emperor Otto IV traveled through Italy on his way to meet Innocent in Viterbo and be crowned by him in Rome on October 4 (C). Moreover, Thomas specifies that Otto passed by Rivo Torto (43). A few modern scholars have given a superficial study to Otto's itinerary and have concluded that Friar Thomas must have been misinformed, as they claim that Otto did not go near Assisi on his way to Rome, but visited the Valley of Spoleto only in December, 1209; January, and November, 1210. Without further or adequate analysis of all relevant data, biographers have consequently concluded that Thomas of Celano was not only mistaken in placing Otto at Rivo Torto in September, 1209, but also in writing that the approval of the Order in Rome had then already taken place. Here, with Patrem and Terzi, we must emphasize that Thomas gives these two cogent chronological guideposts: 1) in his *seriatim* (chronological) narrative he inserts the Otto incident among the anecdotes of the early days at Rivo Torto, after the return from Rome; 2) he describes Francis as meditating on the *"ingens negotium quod habebat in manibus,"* with the *"Apostolica auctoritas"* strong in him. The latter expression is literally repeated from (36): *"auctoritatae apostolica sibi concessa,"* and of course refers to the formal authorization of the Holy See to preach (33).

Fortini represents most outstandingly today the defenders of the Rome-in-1210 and no-Otto-in-Assisi-in-Sept.-1209 thesis. But unfortunately in all the wealth of material which the great historian of Assisi amassed in his five volumes, he did not include a study of chronology. Now in that new edition (FNV I/1, 370: II, 192) and in a 1959 brochure (C3:13-14), he refers to a new element which, he claims, proves that the only documented visit of Otto to Assisi was on November 4, 1210. With his chronological system based on the bishop's trial in February, 1207, Fortini assigns the vocations of the first three companions to April, 1209, and the departure of the twelve for Rome "at the beginning of the summer of 1210" (FNV I/1, 367), though in the brochure (C3:15) the approval in Rome is assigned to the spring of 1210.

It is therefore obvious that a careful study of the itinerary of Otto, both in September, 1209, and throughout the rest of 1209 and the year 1210, becomes essential in order to clarify this important problem in the chronology of St. Francis and of the history of the Order of Friars Minor. We must try to answer two questions before we can convict Thomas of Celano of error. First, is it a fact that Otto did not go near Assisi on his way to Rome in September, 1209? And second, is it true that his only visit to Assisi must be dated November 4, 1210?

For his journey to Rome, let us see first what the contemporary 13th century chroniclers reported; then we can follow the evolution of modern scholars' opinions on the subject. According to the former, his arrival in northern Italy in the summer of 1209 "with an unusually large army" (MGH-SS XIX, 298) made "all Italy tremble with exceeding fear" of what even then was called the "*Theutonicus furor*" (*ibid.* 150 & 316). Incidentally, that year also brought several major earthquakes (*ibid.* 315), while the winter was very harsh and the summer stormy with much thunder, lightning, and rain (MGH-SS XVII, 824).

Presumably the chronicler closest in time to 1209 would leave us the most accurate report of Otto's itinerary. The German Benedictine Abbot Arnold of Lübeck's *Cronica Slavorum* (MGH-SS XXI, 248) and the *Continuatio Sanblasiana* of Otto of Freising's Chronicle (MGH-SS XX, 333) both state that after crossing the River Po, Otto went through Milan and traveled south through Tuscany, Arnold specifying Genoa, Lucca, Siena, and Bolsena as stopping points on the way to Viterbo. As a result, even such a scholar as E. Winkelmann in his *Philipp von Schwaben und Otto IV von Braunschweig* (Leipzig 1878) II, 192, had Otto pass through Siena; others, such as Luchaire and Caggese, thought that he traversed Tuscany after crossing the Apennines south of Bologna or Faenza. However, the leading modern historian of Florence, Robert Davidsohn, in his *Geschichte von Florenz* (Berlin 1896) I, 658, showed (without documentation) that for political reasons Otto "avoided the way by Florence, which was hostile to him."

It was only when scholars began to study the official imperial documents, published or abstracted in the invaluable *Regesta imperii* (B11) that the real itinerary came to light, as far as it could be traced. Yet even here, too many writers (like Schnürer) used only the first of the editors' three expert comments (B11:95, 268, 2165) on the relevant documents in their collection. Those documents, prepared and dated by imperial notaries in the German camps, proved that on his way to Rome in August and September, 1209, Otto did not visit either Milan or Florence or Lucca or Siena. As the editors commented, the Siena and Tuscan itinerary was "certainly incorrect, like nearly all early sources on the journey" (B11:-96), adding: "It is most probable that Otto did not touch Tuscany at all, but like Frederick II in 1220 followed the Via Emilia to the neighborhood of Rimini, and then in the direction of the Via Flaminia came to Viterbo through the March [of Ancona] and the Duchy" [of Spoleto] (B11:96). Again on p. 268 they listed as the probable route: Fano, Cagli, Nocera, and the Duchy. Finally, on p. 2165, in their "Verbesserungen und Zusätze," they suggested that Otto might have followed the route mentioned by Salimbene (A136:308): "*Urbinum civitas est in montibus, per quam itur ad. . . Callium, que est clavis marchie Anconitane, per quam itur Assisium ad vallem Spolitanam,*" i. e. Urbino-Cagli-Assisi. So we find that back in 1901 leading German historians, far from flatly denying that Otto passed near Assisi on his way to Rome, actually wrote that his passage through the Duchy of Spoleto was "most probable" and that he "could" have gone by Assisi. It is noteworthy that none of the editors' comments on the itinerary so much as mentions Thomas of Celano's testimony — still another remarkable example of the absence of communication between secular and religious historians.

The *Regesta imperii*, however, could trace Otto only as far as San Procolo, 10 kms. from Imola, near the present Pieve del Ponte, where the Via Emilia crosses the Senio River (B11:96), in a document dated only September. But in 1938 Wolfgang Hagemann in his study of the archives of Gubbio, "Kaiserurkunden und Reichssachen im Archivio Storico von Gubbio," QF 29(1938/39) 150, mentioned a hitherto unknown document he had discovered which was dated September 8 in Otto's camp near Forlì. This confirms that he was traveling toward Rimini.

But from Forlì to Viterbo, the only clue remains *I Celano*, 43, except for a reliable contemporary report (B11:95; RIS VIII/4, 15) that he did not go by way of Ancona. Friedrich Ludwig's basic study (F6:48) — which was probably used for the *Regesta*, p. 2165, comment — points out that Otto would have saved 50 out of 200 kms. by not going so far east as Ancona. Ludwig also shows that the famous Via Flaminia had been used by five other German kings bound for Rome: Otto I in 962; Otto III in 996, 998, & 101; and Henry IV in 1084.

Another significant clue pointing toward the Duchy of Spoleto is the fact that on March 22, 1209, while still in Germany, Otto sent orders to Italy that transit facilities and supplies be prepared there as well as in the March of Ancona (B11:96). Our foremost authority today on the history of central Italy in those years, Prof. Daniel Waley, states in his *Papal State in the Thirteenth Century* (B13:58) that Otto "took the Via Emilia and Via Flaminia."

So now we have Otto within ten (not 20-25) miles of Rivo Torto in September, 1209, for the Flaminia enters the Valley of Spoleto at Foligno. We might leave Friar Thomas with a ten-mile topographical error and assume that his informants were mistaken in specifying that the emperor passed right by the hovel of Rivo Torto: *iuxta viam*. But perhaps in this detail too *I Celano* is correct. From Foligno to Viterbo (*not* Rome) there are three possible routes: either Foligno-Spoleto-Terni-Narni-Orte-Viterbo; or Foligno-Massa Martana-Todi-Orvieto-Viterbo; or Foligno-Rivo Torto-Ponte S. Giovanni- (or Bettona) -Todi-Orvieto-Viterbo (favored by Terzi, F59:248n61). The last route has the serious advantage for an army of following the level Topino and Tiber valleys as far as Todi. The main question here is perhaps a political one: did Otto have reason to visit or avoid Spoleto? For if he arrived on the Flaminia in Foligno and wished to go through Spoleto, he would not have passed by Rivo Torto. On the other hand, for some reason such as a temporary obstruction — a broken bridge or a landslide — his army might have had to make a detour coming south along the Flaminia, perhaps via Gubbio and Ponte S. Giovanni or Petrignano, and once there, if he wanted to enter Spoleto, he would have passed by Rivo Torto going east rather than west. Still another possible if not probable route would be Forlì-Cesena-Bagno-Borgo S. Sepolcro-Assisi-Spoleto. It is necessary to list all these conjectures to show that, since he was almost certainly passing through the Duchy of Spoleto, there actually existed *three* alternate routes which would have taken him past Rivo Torto. Incidentally, Fortini's map of the Assisi district has no road passing right by Rivo Torto, but the map accompanying the Umbrian *Rationes Decimarum* (F1) shows the Perugia-Foligno highway running right past it, as it does today. On Fortini's *Strada francesca*, see Part 14 below. See also the Maps in this book.

Finally, let us note that early Franciscan sources contain still another significant anecdote connecting Otto with St. Francis at this same time, when the emperor was traveling to Rome. According to a Fra Elemosina di Assisi, who flourished in 1293-1339 (cf FNV II, 72) and who declared that he had heard the story as true and reliable from some elderly friars, Otto, hearing about the Saint, stopped a while at Rivo Torto and had a conversation with Francis, in the course of which the Poverello assured him that even if the road from there to Rome were covered with gold coins, he and his friars would not touch a single one (GBB II,106 & 119). A little reflection shows that though this late source cannot be considered of primary historical value, nevertheless it does not actually, as might at first appear, contradict the account of Thomas of Celano. While Francis refused to watch the emperor and his army march by, after the lone friar-envoy had warned Otto that his glory would not last long, the latter may well have stopped and insisted on having an interview with the Saint. So both accounts may be true, though of unequal value; but the late text certainly serves to strengthen the total evidence for Otto's presence in Rivo Torto in September, 1209.

Now we are in a position to take up Fortini's document which is said to prove that Otto was in Assisi only once, on November 4, 1210 (FNV II, 192; C3:13-14). The document in question, however, has not been published. So far all we have is an Italian abstract, first printed in L. Jacobilli's *Cronica della Chiesa e Monastero di Santa Croce di Sassovivo nel territorio di Foligno* (Foligno 1653) 62, with the reference "Lib. Regest sign. † fol. 279." The sole mention of Otto on the *Cronica's* p. 62 or adjoining pages reads as follows: "*L'anno 1209 adi quattro di Novembre, Indict. 12; Ottono quarto Imperadore per suo privilegio dato in Assisi, l'anno primo del suo Imperio, ad instanza di questo Nicola Abbate del Monastero di Sassovivo, prese sotto la sua protettione la Chiesa di San Liberato nel Territorio del Castello di Muggiano, con le sue possessioni e beni, ordinando ad Enrico Tedesco, Castellano di detto Castello, che la difendi, e protegga in suo nome.*" Fortini (FNV I/1,389-90) identifies the Chiesa di San Liberato as that of Orte and the Castello as that of Mugnano near Perugia.

Thus we see that the document is actually dated 1209 and not 1210. In 1881 already, the editors of the *Regesta imperii* (B11:126) had studied this text of Jacobilli and concluded that the date 1209 could not be correct, because Otto was in Tuscany in October and November, 1209, and because Mugnano was only occupied by Otto's forces in September, 1210; therefore they assigned the document tentatively to November, 1210, while pointing out that there is no proof that Otto was in Assisi then, but that he may have been there on October 4, 1210. However, they identify Mugnano as the castle of Mugnano on the Tiber northeast of Viterbo and near Orte. Obviously further study and clarification of this quite uncertainly dated document is needed before it can be used as evidence.

As regards Otto and St. Francis, however, a few observations are in order: first, it remains a fact that Otto was in Foligno and the Valley of Spoleto in December, 1209, and January, 1210 (B11:103-106; AF X, 34n5). Now Fortini in his new biography (FNV1/1,370) states that the refusal of Francis to watch Otto pass by Rivo Torto happened in mid-December, 1209, adding that Thomas of Celano merely meant it took place during the emperor's journey in Italy on the occasion of his coronation. Yet in his 1960 brochure Fortini (C3:13-14) insists that Otto was in Assisi only on November 4, 1210. Does he now hold that the Rivo Torto incident occurred then? The effect of such dating would be to reduce the interval between Francis' prophecy and its first fulfillment from over a year to only a fortnight, as Pope Innocent III excommunicated Otto for his depradations in the States of the Church on November 18, 1210 (B11:127); actually the Pontiff had already denounced him to the world the previous January (B13:60). Subsequently Otto lost the title of Emperor to the young Frederick II in 1212, was decisively defeated at Bouvines in 1214, failed to secure a rehabilitation at the Lateran Council in 1215, and died in Germany on May 19, 1218, absolved of his excommunication.

A last note on the Roman trip of Francis and his friars: contrary to some statements of defenders of the 1210 date, the Praemonstratensian Abbot Burchard never wrote that he saw Francis in Rome in 1210. What he wrote was that he saw there some of the Poor Men of Lyon, and it is known from a bull that he was there in 1210. He added that the Pope had granted his approval to the Friars Minor rather than to the Poor Men of Lyon (A80:17-18).

In conclusion, until further studies clarify the facts, it appears very probable that Thomas of Celano was correct in stating that the Emperor Otto passed by (or near) Rivo Torto in September, 1209, after St. Francis had obtained the approval of Pope Innocent III in Rome. That approval must have been granted in the spring of 1209, before May 25, when the Pope left to spend the summer in Viterbo.

9. The Vocation of St. Clare — 1211 or 1212?

Today only three advocates of March 27, 1211, as the date of the reception of Clare by Francis are left: Lazzeri (AFH 13, 434),

Franceschini (E89), and Fortini (FNV II, 344), but the last two have not analyzed the problem. In the anniversary year 1953, Cresi (E164) and more critically Hardick (E184) contributed two studies of the chronology of the life of St. Clare, based largely on data from her sources rather than those of St. Francis, and both concluded that the Palm Sunday in question fell on March 18, 1212. The confusion arises not only from the various datings of Francis' conversion, but also from the conflicting testimony of several elderly Poor Clares in the Process of Canonization in 1253 that she lived in San Damiano for about or more than 42 or about 43 years (E197:35).

But probably the significant little word *fere* in *I Celano*, 18 (D), when taken with the July, 1206, beginning of Francis' post-conversion years, is the key to this conundrum. The first point is: when did St. Clare move to San Damiano? She spent only a few days at San Paolo and then an undetermined number of weeks at Panzo. It is generally agreed that she settled in San Damiano in May (E170:160n18), whatever was the year. Now according to Thomas of Celano, the Order of Poor Ladies had its beginning there *fere* (almost or about) six years' time after the conversion of St. Francis. Since, as we have shown, those six years began in the summer or July of 1206, the six full years would be over in July, 1212, and so May, 1212, would be "almost six years" or "about six years," i. e. five years and ten months. Often *fere* meant almost, in the sense of nearly, approaching, well nigh. In fact this is probably the sense in which Thomas also uses it in both (A) and (O). It is clear too from the Chart that placing the first year of conversion at the bishop's trial in January-March, 1206, would make the winter of 1211/1212 nearly or about six years later, or with the trial in February, 1207, as Fortini has it, the six years would end in the winter of 1212/1213 — yet Fortini places Clare in San Damiano in the spring of 1211, reducing Thomas' six years to four! But in both cases the season is impossible for the move to San Damiano. Thus it can well be said that Thomas of Celano's use of the single word *fere* in this passage provides us with the confirmation for his system of chronology, since it requires a summer at the end of a year of conversion falling in 1212. At the same time it delivers a fatal blow to the 1211-Clare-to-San-Damiano thesis, because that would not only set the beginning of the first year of conversion back to the summer of 1205, but it would make June, 1219, fall in the 14th year of conversion instead of the 13th, and it would bring the 20th year of conversion to an untimely end in the summer of 1225.

The same passage (D) throws some light on the abortive trip to Dalmatia-Sclavonia, which must now be fitted into the year running from the summer of 1211 to the summer of 1212 — the sixth year of conversion, at the end of which six years would have passed from the conversion. Since Francis was in Assisi in March and again in May for St. Clare's reception and move to San Damiano, the Dalmatian journey must have been either in the late summer of 1211 or in June, 1212, assuming that sailings for Palestine were unlikely during the winter. Would Francis have left Italy, seeking a martyr's death, right after founding a second Order? Again Friar Thomas has a probably decisive clue: the Saint decided to return to Italy "since in that year hardly any ship could sail to Syria" (55). The implication is that it was then too late in the year, i. e. 1211, to take another ship, as sailings were normally in the spring. A careful examination of contemporary chronicles and shipping records might confirm that unusually bad weather forced the cancellation of many sailings in 1211.

The next long journey of St. Francis, to Spain and back, cannot yet be dated accurately, but probably began in 1213, "*post non multum temporis*" (F), since we find him at San Leo near San Marino on May 8 of that year receiving the offer of Mount La Verna from Count Orlando. The Via Emilia, leading to Piacenza and the roads through the Alps into France, runs by the foothills ten miles beyond San Leo. However, some writers assign the Spanish trip to 1214/1215 (cf CF 30, 369).

10. The Return from Syria

A definitive clarification of the events in 1220 is still much needed, despite the pioneering work of Fischer, who places the return to Italy in January, 1220 (C2:42), a month now considered too early. Brooke (E3:65-66) favors September. But it is certain that a thorough study of the various complex factors involved must still be done. Among those factors are the length of the Saint's stay in Damietta and Palestine, his itinerary on landing in Venice, the date of the Bologna studium closing, his meeting Pope Honorius in Rome or Orvieto, and the several Chapters (September 1219 & 1220, and May, 1220 & 1221). Terzi (C9:88) brings Francis to Orvieto in the summer of 1220; Fortini (FNV I/2, 107) has him leave Acre in the fall sailings, rest in Venice, stop over in Bologna, then still meet the Pope in Orvieto, and hold the Chapter at the Portiuncula on September 29, 1220 (FNV I/2, 130).

11. The General Chapters 1217-1223

Again it must be regretted that so far no scientific and complete monograph has definitively settled the several still uncertain questions regarding the series of General Chapters in the years 1217-1223. It is now commonly accepted that the Chapter of 1217 sent forth the first missions beyond the mountains, e. g. to France, and beyond the seas, i. e. Elias to Syria and Giles to Tunisia; that of 1219 saw the first martyrs leave for Morocco via Spain and Francis set out for Egypt; and that of 1221 marked the first successful mission to Germany. But apart from the relative obscurity still enveloping the one or two assemblies in 1220, the fundamental question as to which General Chapter saw the Founder resign his office has now been re-opened by Brooke (E3:76ff & 106), who rejects the usual 1220 or 1221 in favor of 1217 or 1218.

Marinus von Neukirchen's excellent dissertation on the history of the legislation of the Franciscan General Chapters (E76) does not undertake to analyze in any detail the conflicting early texts dealing with the meetings in those crucial years which marked the reorganization of the Order, culminating in the Rule of 1223.

12. The Two Last Years 1224-1226

We have now reached the period in the life of St. Francis about which there has been more extensive controversy in recent years than any other, if we exclude the 1000-page argument over the *casa paterna* which does not directly involve the chronology of his life. In this Appendix only the strictly chronological aspects of the great San Damiano-vs-Rieti-Valley Cantico dispute will be treated, leaving the textual and topographical problems to the second Part of Appendix VIII on the Cantico.

Actually the present disagreement between Fortini and Terzi does not cover all the 24 months from October, 1224, to October 3, 1226, but only the year running roughly from November, 1224, to the winter of 1225/1226. Once Francis reaches Siena in March or April, 1226 (P), there is harmony. But every month of 1225 is today a scarred battleground. Deplorable as such tempests-in-scholars'-tea-pots may seem, especially if they undermine popular faith in genuine shrines or build untenable cases for unauthentic ones, the literature produced in this case (see C144-C186) demonstrates the need for a more critical study of the documents involved, which will surely in the end effect those objective re-evaluations and revisions which are clearly necessary on both sides.

To gain a little perspective on the issues, let us briefly summarize the serene view of this period as reflected in the biographies of Cuthbert and Joergensen. In November, 1225, the stigmatized Saint returns to Assisi from La Verna and undertakes a preaching tour. During the spring of 1225 he is treated for his eye-sickness in Assisi under Brother Elias' supervision. In June he receives a letter from Cardinal Hugolin in Rieti summoning him to be treated by doctors there. Bidding goodbye to St. Clare at San Damiano, he is stricken with a 50-day illness culminating in his composing the Canticle of Brother Sun at San Damiano. Cuthbert adds here the reconciliation of the bishop and podestà, while Joergensen incorrectly places it during the Saint's stay in the bishop's palace in September, 1226, when we know now that Bishop Guido was absent on a pilgrimage to Monte Gargano. In September, 1225, Francis is well enough to travel to the Rieti Valley, where he arrives when the poor priest's trampled grapes are ripe. There follow the several incidents known to have happened in the fall and winter in Fonte Colombo and Rieti, such as the cauterizing and the unconverted canon.

Now let us see what has happened recently to this untroubled narrative. As a direct result of the intense argument over Terzi's claim that the Saint composed his Cantico at La Foresta in the Rieti Valley in the autumn of 1225, we now find Fortini insisting that Francis lay ill in the chaplain's house at San Damiano from December, 1224, or January, 1225, until August, 1225 — not two months or less, but eight or nine months — and for Fortini this "is the only conclusion to which a study of the sources leads us" (FNV II,513). On the other hand, according to Terzi, on returning to Assisi Francis undertook a long journey, despite his stigmata and the winter weather, as far south as Subiaco, east to Celano, and north through the Marches, arriving back in Assisi only in the spring; then, after ineffective treatment of his eyes by Elias' doctors in Assisi, the Saint went to San Fabiano-La Foresta in the Rieti Valley early in September, stayed there about four months, and submitted to the cauterizing in Fonte Colombo in mid-January (C9:151).

It is to such astounding and partly absurd conclusions that scholars arrive when, in their righteous desire to defend beloved shrines, they stubbornly seek to re-interpret and adjust a set of early texts of seriously differing authenticity which very evidently cannot be reconciled. Obviously a good measure of critical objectivity in evaluating those texts is indispensable, but unfortunately lacking.

The basic texts are the following. First, the most authentic: those of Thomas of Celano. After receiving the Stigmata, though suffering more seriously from various illnesses than before, Francis traveled around the country riding on a donkey in order to preach. When his eyes became severely afflicted from lack of care, Elias compelled him to have them treated, presumably in or near Assisi. Then as no remedy was found, he went to a doctor in Rieti and was welcomed there by Cardinal Hugolin and the Curia. At the Cardinal's urging, he submitted to having his temples cauterized (*I Celano*, 98, 99, 101, *II Celano*, 166). One night after receiving the Stigmata, he was given a divine promise of eternal life, and in gratitude composed the Canticle (*II Celano*, 213).

Next, texts of somewhat less reliability. Two years before his death, while staying in a little cell at San Damiano, Elias ordered him to have his eyes treated, but it was agreed to postpone the treatment because the weather was very cold then. After suffering there for 50 days, unable to bear any light and overrun by fieldmice, Francis received the promise of eternal life and composed the Canticle, and while still there added a few lines to reconcile the feuding bishop and podestà. Then, the time being right for medical treatment, he left San Damiano for Fonte Colombo near Rieti, where at first he wanted to postpone the treatment until Elias arrived, but finally submitted to the cauterizing, at the insistence of Cardinal Hugolin. Other doctors pierced his ears (*Legenda antiqua*, 42-48; *Speculum*, 100-101). The incident of the poor priest's vineyard took place while the Saint was staying at San Fabiano near Rieti because of his eye-sickness (*Legenda antiqua*, 25; *Speculum*, 104).

And third, the last or probably least reliable version: Cardinal Hugolin wrote to Francis to come to him in Rieti and have his eyes treated. On setting out, the Saint went by way of San Damiano to greet St. Clare, but that night his eyes became so much worse he could not leave. St. Clare had a special cell made for him, in which he stayed for fifty days, tormented by fieldmice day and night. One night he received the Lord's promise of eternal life, and left the next morning for Rieti after saying goodbye to St. Clare. On arriving near Rieti he saw a crowd coming to meet him and so turned aside to the poor priest's church two miles from the town; it was then vintage time (*Actus*, 21; *Fioretti*, 19).

Now we are in a position to identify the irreconcilable statements in these texts which, as Fortini and Terzi have shown involuntarily, make a sensible and coherent narrative impossible. Two relevant background factors must also be taken into consideration: 1) the papal court resided at Rieti from June 25, 1225, to February 3, 1226; and 2) Fortini (FNV II,511-513) places the excommunication of the podestà by the bishop late in July, 1225; while the first is a fact, the second is a supposition. A third point: as will be shown in Appendix VIII, Part 2, the whole case for the Cantico's being composed at San Fabiano is absolutely untenable on grounds of textual criticism; consequently we disregard it in this attempt to clarify the chronology of events having at least some probability on textual grounds.

So we have Fortini trying to reconcile all the texts by putting the Saint in San Damiano in winter, the earlier the better for the "two years before his death," and then being obliged to leave him there all through eight or more long months. And why: first in order to have him still there when Fortini thinks, but cannot prove, that the podestà was excommunicated; and second, in order to have him arrive in the Valley of Rieti in September, when the grapes are ripe. In so doing, he has to ignore the text in the second group which says clearly that Francis went to Fonte Colombo when the season or weather was right for medical treatment — so too Terzi, for other reasons, paradoxically claims that that season was in January, 1226. No wonder that Bigaroni (C163:98) felt obliged to cut this knot by postulating two different trips by Francis from Assisi to the Valley of Rieti in 1225: one in February or March, for the cauterizing in Fonte Colombo, and another in September for those ripe grapes. But this unconvincing Solomonic splitting of the trips into two suffers from the same basic malady as the theories of Fortini and Terzi, and only serves to confirm the fundamental error of their whole approach, which is, at any cost, uncritically to reconcile all the texts among themselves, no matter what might be their relative degree of reliability or how flagrantly they contradict and undermine one another.

Let us for a change apply a sound principle of historical investigation and classify our alleged facts into groups according to the probable degree of authenticity of their sources.

Thus in the first group of thoroughly reliable data we have, from Thomas of Celano: the preaching tour on the donkey after the stigmatization; the severe eye-trouble treated in vain by Elias' doctors; the welcome in Rieti by Hugolin; the cauterizing; and at some unspecified time after the stigmatization the promise of eternal life followed by the composition of the Canticle.

Next, as probably more or less reliable data we have: Elias' ordered treatment postponed owing to cold weather, Francis being then in the special cell at San Damiano; 50 days later, still there, the promise of eternal life, the Canticle, and the reconcilation of bishop and podestà. When the weather is warmer, the Saint goes to Fonte Colombo, postpones the cauterizing, then submits to it. Later other doctors pierce his ears; all in vain. In September, when the grapes are ripe, he is at San Fabiano because of his eyesickness.

And now, disregarding completely for the time being the third and most unreliable source, the *Actus-Fioretti*, let us construct a tentative chronology of these much-disputed months which will at least have the crucial advantage of being based exclusively on thoroughly reliable and probably reliable data. It runs as follows:

Mid-November, 1224: Francis returns to the Portiuncula from La Verna, and soon afterward

December-February, 1224/1225, undertakes a relatively short preaching tour, riding on a donkey.

March, 1225, returns to the Portiuncula. Visits St. Clare at San Damiano; a crisis in his eye-sickness develops and he is obliged to stay there. Elias persuades him to be treated, but treatment is postponed due to cold weather.

April-May, still at San Damiano, suffering, nearly blind, as weather improves he undergoes treatment by Elias' doctors without improvement; composes Canticle after receiving promise of eternal life.

June, reconciles bishop and podestà and leaves for the Valley of Rieti. After Hugolin's welcome in Rieti, on to Fonte Colombo, where he probably stays through

July and August, first postponing and then submitting to the cauterizing, despite Elias' continued absence, on the insistence of Cardinal Hugolin.

September, moves to San Fabiano when the grapes are ripe, in order to be treated by other doctors, who pierce his ears. Restores the poor priest's trampled vineyard.

October through March, either in Rieti or Fonte Colombo until the departure for Siena. For numerous incidents in this period in both places, see Ch. 20 of this book and Terzi's *Memorie* (F59), Parts 1 & 2.

Thus, proceeding by sound critical methods, we have chosen to accept the second group's cold weather at the beginning of the stay in San Damiano even though it involves rejecting the late texts' departure in September. Similarly, we have accepted the second group's Fonte Colombo destination — after a brief stop-over passing through Rieti for Hugolin's welcome in *I Celano*, 98 — and have rejected the *Actus'* first stop at San Fabiano; as between the two, the least reliable has to be sacrificed. We have had Francis stay at San Damiano about three months, from about the end of March until the end of June, as our second group specifies 50 days (40 or 60 in some manuscripts) only up to the Canticle, but several weeks more must be allowed to include the bishop-podestà reconciliation as well. Though our better sources will not let the Saint arrive in Rieti before June 23, Hugolin could have written him from Tivoli (where the papal court moved in April), to meet him in Rieti toward the end of June. So of the *Actus-Fioretti* late data, typically telescoped for narrative purposes and authentic in substance but inaccurate in various details, only the plausible Cardinal's letter need be retained. All the rest must be completely and ruthlessly set aside in the interest of scientific history.

If and when Fortini succeeds in proving beyond all doubt that the bishop excommunicated the podestà at the end of July, then the chronology outlined above would have to be modified to that extent, placing the departure for Rieti and Fonte Colombo at the end of July or early in August, but a good month before the grapes get ripe.

Other important elements in the problem of the Cantico, such as Abate's theory favoring the bishop's palace in Assisi as the site of composition and the Terzi-Sacchetti-Sassetti debate over the location of San Fabiano, will be analyzed in Appendix VIII, Part 2.

13. The Foligno Vision

As a postscript to this study of the years 1224-1226, a few words should be said about the question of the month in which Brother Elias in Foligno was given notice that Francis had only two more years to live; see texts (K) & (L). Did this incident happen before the Saint went to La Verna or on his return, in other words around August 1 or mid-November, 1224? Obviously it could not have taken place during September or October, because Francis was on the mountain throughout September and slowly traveling back to Assisi during October. So the divine warning came either 26 months or about 22 1/2 months before his death. Which was it?

A clue is supplied in *I Celano*, 108-109 (L) & (S): in September, 1226, while staying in the bishop's palace, the Saint saw that his last day was approaching and therefore hastened to return to the Portiuncula to die, because his twenty years of converted life were then already (*iam*) over. A relevant background factor (recorded in *Speculum*, 122, but not by Thomas of Celano) is the doctor's then prognosticating the Saint's death late that month or early in October.

Some light is supplied by one early secondary source and two late ones placing the Foligno vision before the stigmatization. Henri d'Avranches (AF X,478) inserted it in his narrative poem just before the journey to La Verna. That this dating became accepted in the 14th and 15th centuries is indicated by *The Second Consideration on the Stigmata* (E166:179) which, without mentioning the prophecy at Foligno, has Francis tell his companions on arriving at La Verna: "I see that I am drawing near to death." And in reporting the dream or vision of Brother Elias the late Italian compendium which Marcellino da Civezza and Dominichelli took for the complete *Tres Socii* (A219:205) adds: "And he had himself taken to La Verna."

Following Papini, Faloci Pulignani in his excellent study of St. Francis and Foligno (F290) gives the end of July as the time of the incident and tries to identify the venerable priest who appeared to Elias as the martyr bishop and patron of Foligno, San Feliciano, who died about 254 at the age of 94.

Modern writers place the incident either before or after Foligno. Perhaps, with the evidence outlined above, the final argument might be that Divine Providence, when notifying a Saint that he would die in two years, would be more likely to give him in actuality somewhat longer rather than six weeks less than promised. Hence too Francis' question to the doctor and his haste to return to the Portiuncula: in September, 1224, he realized that he was "living on borrowed time."

If, therefore, the month really was July or early August, this would be still another precise confirmation of Thomas of Celano's dating the beginning of the first year of conversion in July, 1206.

14. Fortini's *Strada francesca*

Further study is also needed on the *Strada francesca* running along the plain below Assisi, which is mentioned in a document of 1070 (FNV III,70-71). According to Fortini (*ibid.*), this road between Perugia and Assisi "had throughout the Middle Ages national and international importance, as it united Rome with France. After ascending along the Tiber, from Orvieto it turned toward Assisi; it ran along Lake Trasimene, and went on through Arezzo, Bologna, Modena, along the ancient Via Emilia, whence passing across the plain of the Po, it joined the passes of Grand St. Bernard, Mont Cenis, and Tenda. The road followed the remains of the ancient Roman highways and was indicated on relevant maps, together with the cities or *stationes* where the travelers stopped for rest. It also served — besides merchants — pilgrims, ambassador, and condottieri with their armies."

Now a road with the name *Strada francesca* is well documented in the archives of Assisi. The only questions which arise are: 1) was it so named because it was an integral part of the famous highway used by the pilgrims traveling from France to Rome and back? And 2) did that pilgrim route actually follow the itinerary given above? A careful study of available literature leads to these conclusions: apart from the presence of the name in Assisi documents, there is no evidence that Assisi was located on the main France-to-

Rome pilgrimage route; but there is proof that pilgrims from Germany passed by Assisi on their way to Rome. Perhaps, therefore, the origin of the name of the Assisi highway must be sought elsewhere.

First, let us turn to the two works to which Fortini refers as authorities in a footnote appended to the statement quoted above. They are Albert von Hofmann's *Das Land Italien* (F5) and Jules Bédier's "Les chansons de geste et les routes d'Italie" in his *Les légendes épiques* (C54). For the first, the reference given is pp. 3ff, but that is the title page; after the "Einleitung" on pp. 13-45, the author takes up the several regions of Italy, reaching Umbria on p. 299. Nowhere in his 458 pages did I find a mention of an important pilgrimage highway passing by Assisi; in fact the only passages relevant to our subject and area occur on p. 195: Chiusi was a road center on the highways from Florence, Perugia, Siena, and Rome; on p. 231: the famous swamps of the Chiana (mentioned by Dante in *Inf.* 29:46, & *Par.* 13:23) made a detour by Arezzo and the Upper Tiber Valley necessary; and on p. 303: those swamps drove traffic west by Siena and east by Todi until the later draining of the swampland gave back to the Arezzo route its former prominence.

Bédier's text on p. 145 and map between pp. 146-147 shows two main routes for the French pilgrims: 1) the well-known Via Cassia, generally called the *Via Francigena*, which ran as follows: Pavia-Piacenza - Borgo S. Donnino - Pontremoli - Fucecchio - Siena - Montepulciano-Viterbo-Roma; and 2) Piacenza-Bologna-Faenza-Forlì Bagno - Arezzo - Castiglione del Lago - Orvieto - Montefiascone-Viterbo-Roma, going no closer to Assisi than the western side of Lake Trasimene.

That the Cassia, as described in 1) just above, was the true *Via Francigena* is fully confirmed by Konrad Schrod's *Reichstrassen und Reichsverwaltung im Königreich Italien* (754-1179) (F12:27-29), and by Michael Bihl, OFM, in his study "De nomine S. Francisci" (C35:494-498). It too ran far west of Assisi, between Siena and Acquapendente. See also E. Martinori's basic histories of the Via Cassia (F7) and Via Flaminia (F8).

However, our witness testifying to the German pilgrims passing by Assisi is unimpeachable: none less than St. Francis himself, as relayed by Brother Elias and quoted by Brother Jordan of Giano (n.17). At the General Chapter of 1221, Jordan heard Elias transmit a plea from the Poverello, who was too weak to deliver the speech himself, for volunteers to undertake another mission to "Germany, where," said Elias, "there are devout Christian people who, as you know, often pass through our country, perspiring under the heat of the sun, carrying long staffs and wearing big boots, singing praises to God and the Saints. . . ." Evidently those pilgrims were following this route: Via Emilia to Cesena-Bagno-Borgo San Sepolcro-Assisi-Spoleto-Terni-Narni-Roma. But of course the vague expression "through our country" could also apply to other routes, such as the detour from the Flaminia via Cagli and Gubbio mentioned by Salimbene.

Perhaps further research in the archives of other Umbrian towns will yet prove that French pilgrims passed between Perugia and Assisi and gave their name to the road in question. Certainly the evidence presented here does not support such an origin of the name. Some writers have therefore suggested, with Leone Bracaloni, OFM, and Edouard d'Alençon, Cap (cf EF 50,1938,396n3), that the name came rather from association with the visit or visits of Charlemagne to the area (see Ch. 1, Note 19). This would account for the *pons Gallorum* and *hospitale Gallorum* also mentioned in the medieval archives of Assisi (FNV III,134-135).

15. Chronological Table

1181, summer or fall (?) — Born in Assisi (App. II, 6). Baptized Giovanni di Pietro di Bernardone, renamed Francesco by father. (App. III, IV, V).

1198, January 8. — Innocent III elected Pope.

1198, spring. — Duke Conrad of Urslingen's Rocca fortress besieged, taken, and razed by people of Assisi, as he yields Duchy of Spoleto to Innocent III (App. VI,1).

1199-1200. — Civil war in Assisi; destruction of feudal nobles' castles; families of later St. Clare & Brother Leonardo move to Perugia (App. VI,2).

1202, November. — War between Perugia & Assisi. Latter's army is defeated at Battle of Collestrada. Francis spends a year in prison in Perugia, until ransomed by father as ill (App. VI,3 & 4).

1204. — Long illness.

1204 end, or spring 1205 (?) — Francis sets out for war in Apulia, but returns the next day, after a vision and message in Spoleto. Beginning of the gradual process of conversion (App. II,5; & VI,5).

1205, June. — Gautier de Brienne dies in southern Italy (App. VI, 5).

1205, fall & end. — Message of the Crucifix of San Damiano. Conflict with father.

1206, — Jan. or Feb. — Bishop's trial (App. II,5).

1206, spring. — Francis in Gubbio, nursing victims of leprosy (App. II,5).

1206, summer, probably July. — Returns to Assisi, assumes hermit's habit, and begins to repair San Damiano (App. II,5): end of conversion process; beginning of Thomas of Celano's "years of conversion" chronology (App. II,5).

1206, summer, to Jan. or early Feb. **1208**. — Repairs San Damiano, San Pietro, and Portiuncula (App. II,7; Ch 3, Note 1-2; Ch. 4, Notes 1, 3).

1208, Feb. 24 . — Francis hears Gospel of St. Mathias Mass. Changes from hermit's habit to that of barefoot preacher; begins to preach (App. II,7).

1208, April 16 — Brothers Bernard and Peter Catanii join Francis. On April 23 Brother Giles is received at the Portiuncula (App. II,7).

1208, spring. — First Mission: Francis and Giles go to the Marches of Ancona. (App II,7).

1208, summer. — Three more, including Philip, join them (App. VII,1).

1208, fall & winter. — Second Mission: all seven go to Poggio Bustone in the Valley of Rieti (App. II,7). After being assured of the remission of his sin and the future growth of the Order, Francis sends the six, plus a new seventh follower, on the Third Mission, two by two. Bernard & Giles go to Florence (App. II,7).

1209, early. — The eight return to the Portiuncula. Four more join them (App. VII,2).

1209, spring. — Francis writes brief Rule and goes to Rome with his eleven first companions. There he obtains the approval of Pope Innocent III. (App. II,8; Ch. 5, Notes 23 & 28). On the way back, they stay a while at Orte, then settle at Rivo Torto.

1209, Sept. — German Emperor-elect Otto IV passes by Rivo Torto (App. II,8).

1209 or **1210**. — The friars move to the Portiuncula.

1209-1210 (?) — Possible beginning of Third Order.

1211, summer (?) — Francis goes to Dalmatia and returns.

1212, March 18/19. — On Palm Sunday night, reception of St. Clare at the Portiuncula (App. II,9).

1212, May (?) — After a few days at S. Paolo and a few weeks at Panzo Benedictine convents, Clare moves to San Damiano (App. II,9).

1213, May 8. — At San Leo, near San Marino, Count Orlando offers Mount La Verna to Francis as a hermitage.

1213/14 or **1214/15** (?) — Francis travels to Spain and back.

1215, November. — Fourth Lateran General Council. Francis in Rome (Ch. 10, Note 1).

1216, July 16. — Pope Innocent III dies in Perugia. July 18: Honorius III elected. French Archbishop Jacques de Vitry at Perugia (Ch. 11, Note 1).

1216, summer. – Francis obtains the Portiuncula Indulgence from Pope Honorius in Perugia (Ch. 11, Notes 6 & 15).

1217, May 5. – Pentecost General Chapter at the Portiuncula. First missions beyond the Alps and overseas. Giles leaves for Tunis, Elias for Syria, & Francis for France, but Cardinal Hugolin meets him in Florence & persuades him to stay in Italy (Ch. 9, Note 9).

1219, May 26. – Chapter. First martyrs leave for Morocco. On June 24, Francis sails from Ancona for Acre and Damietta.

1219, fall. – Francis visits Sultan. November 5, Damietta taken by Crusaders.

1220, Jan. – First martyrs killed in Morroco.

1220, early. – Francis goes to Acre & Holy Land.

1220, spring or summer (?) – Francis returns to Italy, landing at Venice (App. II,10). Cardinal Hugolin appointed Protector of the Order.

1220, (or **1217, 1218**) (?) – Francis resigns (App. II,11). Peter Catanii vicar.

1221, March. – Peter Catanii dies.

1221, May 30. – Chapter. First Rule. Elias vicar.

1221. – Rule of Third Order approved by Honorius III.

1221/1222 (?) – Francis on a preaching tour in southern Italy.

1222, Aug. 15. – Francis preaches in Bologna.

1223, early. – At Fonte Colombo Francis composes Second Rule. Chapter on June 11 discusses it. Fall: further discussion in Rome.

1223, Nov 29. – Pope Honorius III approves Rule of 1223.

1223, December 24/25. – Christmas Crib Midnight Mass at Greccio.

1224, June 2. – Chapter sends mission to England.

1224, end of July or early August (?) – In Foligno, Elias is given message in vision that Francis has only two years to live (App. II,13).

1224, Aug. 15-Sept. 29 (Assumption to St. Michael's Day). – Francis fasts at La Verna, receiving the Stigmata about Sept 14.

1224, Oct & early Nov. – Francis returns to the Portiuncula via Borgo San Sepolcro, Monte Casale, & Città di Castello.

1224/1225, Dec.-Feb. (?) – Riding on a donkey, he makes a preaching tour in Umbria & the Marches (App. II,12).

1225, Mar. (?) – On a visit to St. Clare at San Damiano, his eye-sickness suddenly turns much worse. Almost blind, he has to stay there in a cell in or by the chaplain's house. At the insistence of Brother Elias, at last consents to receive medical care, but weather is too cold and treatment is postponed.

1225, Apr.-May (?) – Still at San Damiano, undergoes treatment without improvement. Receives divine promise of eternal life and composes Canticle of Brother Sun.

1225, June (?) — Adding to the Canticle, reconciles feuding bishop and podestà of Assisi. Summoned by a letter from Cardinal Hugolin, leaves San Damiano for Rieti Valley.

1225, early July (?) — Welcomed in Rieti by Hugolin and papal court (there from June 23 to February 6). Goes to Fonte Colombo to undergo eye treatment urged by Hugolin, but has it postponed owing to absence of Brother Elias.

1225, July-Aug. (?) — Doctor cauterizes the Saint's temples at Fonte Colombo, without improvement.

1225, Sept. — Francis moves to San Fabiano near Rieti to be treated by other doctors, who pierce his ears. Restores the trampled vineyard of the poor priest.

1225/1226, Oct.-Mar. (?) — In either Rieti or Fonte Colombo.

1226, April. — Francis is in Siena for further treatment.

1226, May or June (?) — Returns to the Portiuncula via Cortona.

1226, July-Aug. — In summer heat, he is taken to Bagnara in the hills near Nocera.

1226, late Aug. or early Sept. — His condition growing worse, he is taken via Nottiano to the palace of the bishop in Assisi. Bishop Guido is absent on a pilgrimage to Monte Gargano.

1226, Sept. — Knowing that his death is imminent, Francis insists on being carried to the Portiuncula.

1226, Oct. 3. — He dies there. Sunday, Oct. 4, is buried in San Giorgio Church.

1227, Mar. 19. — His friend Hugolin becomes Pope Gregory IX.

1228, July 16. — In Assisi Gregory IX canonizes St. Francis.

1230, May 25. — Translation of the Saint's remains to his new basilica, San Francesco.

Appendix III
The Family of St. Francis

The 1000-page controversy over the *casa paterna* of the Poverello (treated in Appendix V), while no doubt confusing and unedifying for visitors to Assisi, has produced some good fruit in its related research and debates regarding the Saint's family. This Appendix will summarize the information now available on the following topics: his father (ancestors, trade, wealth, personality); the mother (name, French origin (?), time of death); the brother Angelo and his two sons and their descendants (with genealogical chart); and lastly the question of the family's nobility. Closely related to these topics, in addition to the home (Appendix V) are the Saint's birth and baptism (see Appendix IV), the wars of Assisi during his youth (Appendix VI), and the chronology of his early years (Appendix II).

1. Father

Despite his exhaustive research in the archives of Assisi, Fortini has not succeeded in finding much definite information about the ancestors of Pietro di Bernardone. As with all his numerous genealogical reconstructions and charts, Fortini is obliged to do a great deal of guessing as to family relationships, because surnames were not used in Italy until later in the 13th century. In the 12th century a man was known only by his first name and that of his father (or after the latter's death, that of an uncle). Fortini lists several references to a Bernardone and his sons, but hesitates to identify him as the Saint's grandfather in the text, while including him in the family chart without question-marks (FNV II,93 & 100); see our chart below.

The long debate over the possible origin in Lucca of the paternal line has been closed since Bracaloni's 1933 article (C17), though it is worth noting that the first mention of a Luccan Moriconi link appears in a very unreliable *Vita e Fioretti de Sancto Francesco* printed in Milan in 1477, which has been studied in recent years because it mentions the *stalletta* birth (cf Appendix IV). However, at that time the old European sport of connecting rich families with great heroes and saints by means of elaborate (and expensive) fabricated genealogies was beginning its centuries-long vogue. In the case of the Little Poor Man of Assisi this fashion reached an absurd peak in the 17th century, with the publication of a forgery tracing his ancestors back for 23 generations and linking him with the Emperor Justinian and with St. Benedict (C18:11). As recently as 1960 Bracaloni (C20:24-26) had to clarify a non-existent but alleged connection between the prominent 17th-century Bini family of Assisi and that of Francis.

In recent years secular historians have increased our knowledge of medieval Italian merchants and French fairs, thus filling in the background of the life and trade of Pietro — though without once mentioning him as a notable case study (another instance of the sorry lack of communication between secular and religious scholars). Describing typical Florentine merchants of the 13th and 14th centuries, Sapori (C32:xi-xii) seems to be drawing a profile of Pietro di Bernardone: often they were quarrelsome in temperament, vehement in language, calculating, skilled in writing and accounts, haughty and touchy for the honor of the family firm, even on occasion hard-hearted toward their own children. He cites this relevant passage in the will of Simone di Rinieri Peruzzi, whose son had taken some money from the paternal coffer and compromised the family's political position: "May my son be cursed forever, both by myself and by God! Amen. And if, after my death, he is still living and I cannot punish him as much as he deserves, may the justice of God chastise him as a criminal and traitor!" Henri d'Avranches, the contemporary poet, paints a strikingly similar picture of Pietro (AF X, 408-409). One naturally wonders whether Francis ever heard this lapidary quotation from Gratian's *Decretum*: "*Mercator vix aut nunquam potest placere Deo*" (RHE 49/1,1954,77n4).

Face has shown in his thorough study of *The Caravan Merchants & the Fairs of Champagne* (C30) that by 1180 (shortly before the birth of Francis) the cloth merchants of Genoa had developed such a sophisticated system of partnerships, agencies, freighting services, and regular rapid courier communications with their French colleagues that they normally arrived only when the fair was half over, after the close of the period for Flemish cloth sales.

In the archives of Assisi, Fortini has found records showing that Pietro di Bernardone invested the substantial profits from his trade primarily in real estate, as did other members of the rising bourgeoisie. Significantly, the *patrii agri* (AF X,411), the fields belonging belonging to his father where Francis enjoyed taking walks, were located along Monte Subasio near the Benedictine convent of Sant' Angelo di Panzo, in which Francis placed Clare, and on the plain between Rivo Torto and the chapel of San Pietro della Spina, which he repaired after working at San Damiano; moreover the direct path from Assisi to the latter fields went past San Damiano (FNV II, 102-112).

Some confusion still exists regarding the time when Pietro di Bernardone died. In 1215 a document lists his son as Angelus Pice, Angelo son of Pica, implying that the father was then dead. However, in 1926 Fortini referred to a Petrus Bernardi in documents of 1228 as probably the Saint's father, without discussing the contradiction (FNV 42). Attal (A265:90) denied that Pietro was living after 1215. In 1959 Fortini did not treat the question.

Just as the puzzling figure of Brother Elias has recently been re-assessed (see Ch. 14, Note 16), so at least one writer, Attal (C34: 59-96), has entered a strong plea for a more sympathetic understanding of the personality and tragedy of the Saint's father. The gist of his interesting psychoanalysis of Pietro is that he loved his son with an all-too-human affection which, with his materialism, made him completely incapable of understanding a Saint.

2. Mother

Thanks to Abate's pugnacious defense of the *stalletta* birth legend (see Appendix IV), we have had an intensive discussion of the meaning and origin of her name Pica. For he has claimed that it was actually only a nickname given her by the people of Assisi when Francis was born, because she insisted on being taken to the stable. The Italian word denotes either a magpie or a morbid appetite. By extension, he claims it was applied to her as a result of that apparently capricious and bizarre quirk of a pregnant woman. As supporting evidence he stresses two facts: 1) his search of the Assisi archives from the 12th through the 15th century disclosed no other instance of a woman named Pica, though he found numerous nicknames (Sfasciata - impudent; Fresca - fresh!); and 2) her name is given as Johanna in the late *Vita S. Francisci Anonyma Bruxellensis*

(A215), which includes the *stalletta* legend. Abate therefore concludes that her baptismal name was Giovanna, as was that of her great-granddaughter (not daughter, as he has it; see chart). For this "*non intempestiva digressio*" of Abate, see A33:535-542.

Fortini (FNV II,94) rejects the connection of Pica with the stable birth nickname, and claims that it derives rather from Picardy, the supposed home of the Saint's mother, between Champagne and Flanders, which the Italian merchants probably also visited. Thus we now have a second theory on the possible French origin of Pica, in addition to the no longer accepted Bourlémont-Grancey-of-Burgundy genealogy (C39). Fortini gives the following reasons for considering Picardy "anything but improbable" as her home: her husband's frequent trips to France; the name Francesco which he gave his son; Francis' "good" knowledge of the French language (actually not good); and his love for France. Terzi (C28:5-6) accepts Giovanna as her baptismal name and Picardy as her home on the grounds that her son Angelo named his two sons Giovanetto and Piccardo. Bracaloni (C20:24) rejects the Picardy origin, without analysis. Abate (C12:503) holds there is no evidence of a non-Assisi origin of the Saint's family.

When did Domina Pica die? Did she live to see her Francis canonized? Though some 18th and 19th century works gave 1236 or 1222 as the year of her death (C38:298-299) and Fortini (FNV II,69) hopes she lived until 1240, there is no evidence at all.

3. Brother

Was Angelo the only brother of Francis? Some discussion of this question has arisen from the phrase in *Tres Socii*, 3: Pica *ipsum* (Francis) *prae ceteris filiis diligebat.* As there are no references in any documents to other brothers, Bracaloni (C18:17), Bughetti (C21:452), and Fortini (FNV II,95) consider the phrase generic; the latter stresses the *frater eius carnalis* of *I Celano*, 16, as implying the existence of no more than one brother.

We do not have much information about Angelo. Fortini found his name as witness in two documents of 1215 (FNV II,51, 95, 167; & III,589). For another possible mention as seneschal of Assisi in 1221, see Ch. 13, Note 2.

However, Fortini (FNV II,96-101) has supplied numerous mentions in archival sources of Angelo's two sons, Giovanetto and Piccardo. The latter was a devout bachelor *continens* or *penitens* (tertiary) who served for many years as procurator of the friars at the Sacro Convento. He is named in wills and other legal documents from 1256 to 1284, the approximate year of his death. His brother

Piccardo made a will in 1261 and probably died soon afterward, leaving a wife Bonagrazia and two children, Ceccolo and Giovanella. The former had six children and two grandchildren, with whom, according to a genealogical note of 1381 (C28:32), "*ulterius non processit genealogia S. Francisci, deficiens in mortalite.*" Wadding (*Annales* 1182n3) quoted a document of 1534 naming two paupers Antonio and Bernardone as descendants of St. Francis, but Fortini (FNV II,49-50) traces their ancestry in a family which he supposes intermarried with that of the Saint, while Abate (MF 40,504; MF 46,188) declares that the line stopped with the two grandchildren.

It is not clear whether Piccardo was older than Giovanetto. On their houses and complicated real estate dealings, see Appendix V.

4. Nobility?

Again buttressing his determined defense of the *stalletta* legend, Abate used in 1948/49 a rather surprising argument which had not been included in his 450-page work of 1940. He claimed that none less than Francis himself (quoted by Thomas of Celano) had referred specifically to the stable birth in this phrase in *I Celano*, 53: "*nativitatis suae humilia primordia recolebat.*" But in order to make these words refer to the actual circumstances of the birth rather than to the humble social rank of the parents, Abate went to some length to demonstrate that the latter belonged to the nobility, even if only the lower nobility. However, the decisive words on this subject seem to have been written in two 13th-century texts: 1) *natus parente mediocri* (A80:57; AF X,533); and 2) *modicus quidem fuit, non multum nobilis* (C33:137). Several 13th-century references to Pica as *Domina* imply a degree of upper-class rank. But Pietro di Bernardone was definitely of the new *mercator* bourgeoisie. As the contemporary Dominican Bartholomew of Trent put it, "*Franciscus... tantae fuit vanitatis, ut vellet militare, cum esset mercator*" (A80: 63). Fortini, with his expert knowledge of the social history of Assisi, rejects Abate's nobility thesis (FNV II,197). Abate's discussion appears in C33:518, 123-127, 132-137.

5. Chart

(FNV II, 100)

Note: years are not of birth and death,
but as found in documents.

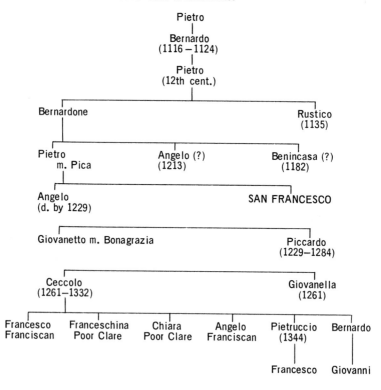

Appendix IV
Birth, Baptism, & Name

The extended controversy over the *casa paterna*, being closely connected with the *stalletta* birth legend, has necessarily supplied several useful analyses of the early texts and later legends clustering around the birth and baptism of St. Francis. The principal studies abstracted in this Appendix are those of Abate (C33), Bracaloni (C18:147-163), and Golubovich (C24). For the history of the house of Piccardo which became San Francesco Piccolo, see Appendix V, Part 3.

1. Birth

Except for the statement that Francis was born in Assisi, none of the first authentic sources provide any details about his birth. But a text in the *Liber exemplorum*, written before 1273 (see Appendix V, Part 5), and therefore generally considered relatively reliable, narrates the following significant anecdote (Latin text in A221:262-263; FNV II,59): according to a Frater Nicolaus de Assisio, whose home adjoined the Saint's, his mother used to say that when Pica was resting in bed after the birth, a pilgrim knocked on the door and begged for alms. He accepted part of a chicken (still a traditional gift to Umbrian mothers; cf F203:28) and then insisted on seeing the baby. When she agreed, he embraced the child and said: "Two boys have been born on one day on this street (or neighborhood). One – this one – will be one of the best in the world, the other the worst." Note that this story does not mention the stable, and that the incident occurs after the birth. Naturally the identity of the bad boy intrigued later writers: the author of the *Vita anonyma Bruxellensis* (A215; cf MF49,359) described him as "*iniquissimus et perversissimus sicut judas. Credo fuit frater iohannes de capella.*" Mariano da Firenze, early in the 16th century, specified in his (unpublished) life of St. Francis (FNV II,53) that the evil man's name was Azolino de Navata, an otherwise unknown person. This anecdote was transmitted in the 14th century by Arnaud de Sarrant (A213:125) and by Bartholomew of Pisa in his *Book of Conformities* (A193:IV,108). The latter added these details: the pilgrim was an angel, he impressed a cross on the baby's right shoulder, and predicted that the devils would prepare many snares for him.

Meanwhile the "conformities with Christ" had been developing. Yet none of these 14th-century works which used it mentioned the stable: the *Actus-Fioretti*, Arnaud de Sarrant, and Bartholomew, though the latter made the pilgrim-angel a "conformity" with the aged Simeon and with the Magi. Bartholomew's devastating silence lead Abate to write a fascinating but unconvincing piece of dialectical argumentation (C33:520-526), concluding that he may have known of the stable birth but have omitted it as alien to his selection of (forty!) conformities. To that, all we can say is that Bartholomew omitted it either because he never heard of it or because he knew the story but considered it unauthentic.

As Papini asked about the Wolf of Gubbio (cf Ch. 9, Note 22), "who said it first?" The first document to mention the birth in the stable is the *Vita anonyma Bruxellensis* (A215:122), which its editor Fierens assigns to the 14th or 15th century, but which Abate (C33:519) believes was written at the same time as Bartholomew's *Conformities*, around 1385-1390. In this late account, Pica, finding her labor difficult, remembered the Nativity and humble place of birth of Christ, and so went down to the stable, had an ox and ass lead in, and there gave birth to her child with little pain. By the middle of the 15th century this legend had become so popular that Benozzo Gozzoli painted the stable birth in his series of splendid illustrations of the life of St. Francis in the Franciscan church in Montefalco (see C247). Incidentally the Bruxelles *Vita* — and Abate — also claim that Pica went to the Holy Land; actually Clare's mother did so.

A few years later, in 1477, the legend reached its ultimate stage of embellishment in the Milan *Vita e Fioretti de Sancto Francesco,* written by an imaginative Venetian — reprinted in 1495 and translated into French in 1947 (A169) — which invents its own fictional version of the pilgrim and stable stories.

Today, all scholars except Abate and Attal reject the stable birth but tend to accept the *Liber exemplorum* pilgrim anecdote. It is worth noting that Giacomo Oddi in 1477 omitted the former but included the latter in his compendium *La Franceschina* (A229:I,6).

2. Baptism

Where was Francis baptized? Visitors to Assisi are shown the medieval baptismal font in the Duomo of San Rufino which was used at the baptism of both Francis and Clare (cf C37). But scholars do not agree as to whether in 1182-1193 it was in San Rufino or in the older Cathedral, Santa Maria Maggiore. In recent years Fortini and Abate have engaged in still another erudite dispute, this time over the location of Clare's home, i. e. whether it was the first or second house on the left as one faces San Rufino. Their writings on this topic (E214-E218) differ regarding the time when the new San Rufino was completed or first open for ceremonies, after being rebuilt in enlarged form over the 11th century Ugonian structure. Abate (MF 49,362) holds that the font was probably still in Santa Maria Maggiore in 1182, while Fortini (FNV I/1,106) places the Saint's baptism in San Rufino.

From his expert knowledge of medieval church history, Abate (*ibid.*) supplies some interesting background data: baptism was then by immersion and always in the cathedral (except in rural areas and emergencies), and was customarily administered on the vigil of Easter or Pentecost.

Later legends connected with the baptism are recorded in the 1477 Milan *Vita*, but can be ignored (C18:154).

However, statements often found in modern works that the famous (or infamous) Emperor Frederic II, variously called *Stupor Mundi*, Anti-Christ, or the first modern man, was either born or baptized in Assisi or both, require a definite clarification, but unfortunately have not so far received one. Even Fortini, the great historian of Assisi (FNV I/1,135; F233:157), does not reject the birth in his city, as he should. Among others, Wolfgang Hagemann has shown, in his article on "Jesi im Zeitalter Friedrichs II," QF 36 (1956)142, that Frederick was unquestionably born in Iesi in the March of Ancona on December 26, 1194. The Emperor himself called Iesi "my Bethlehem." Therefore the 13th-century German Franciscan Albert of Stade was certainly mistaken in stating in his Chronicle (MGH-SS XVI,352) that Frederick was born *"in valle Spoletana in civitate Asis."* But could his understandable confusion of *Asis* for *Aesis* be due to his knowing that it was in Assisi that the royal child was baptized (as he states in the same sentence) in the presence of 15 bishops and cardinals? Unfortunately, neither Hagemann nor Kantorowicz nor any biographer of Frederick has tried to determine as precisely as possible where and when he was baptized — a question of minimal importance in his life, but of major interest for the history of Assisi. In the absence of a scholarly monograph, here are the relevant facts.

Frederick's mother, Queen Costanza, soon after the birth, hastened to rejoin her husband Henry VI in the Kingdom of Sicily early in 1195, and left the infant in the care of the wife of the Duke of Spoleto, who brought him to Foligno, and he spent his first years there (Hagemann, 143). For the deplorable confusion in modern lives of St. Francis of this Duke Conrad of Urslingen with Count Conrad of Luetzelhard (nicknamed *Mosca-in-cervello*), see Appendix VI, Part 1. Again Frederick himself wrote: *"In Fulginio fulgere pueritia nostra incepit."* We know that owing to political considerations, his baptism was delayed for several years, until 1196 or 1197. The author of the *Gesta Innocenti III* (cXIX) reports that he had not been baptized when at the age of two he was elected King of the Romans. The Italian medievalist Salvatorelli (B11:398; no source given) thinks that he was baptized at Tivoli in 1197. But Fortini (F233:158) quotes a passage in the *Annales Ecclesiatici* of Cardinal Cesare Baronio (d. 1607) stating that, according to an ancient document dealing with the life of Innocent III found in the archives of Avignon, Duke Conrad, who was also Count of Assisi, had Frederick baptized there at the age of three, i. e. in 1197; cf *Ann. Eccl.* (Lucae 1746) XIX,71, sub 1197. May some Frederickian expert finally solve this puzzle!

3. Name

Bihl (C35) made a masterly study of the name Franciscus (Francesco), which showed that despite Thomas of Celano's calling it "rare and unusual" (*II Celano*, 3), in a list of Pistoia names in 1219 thirteen out of 4000 were Francis. Fortini also found several in Assisi before the Saint's time (FNV I/1,107). De Beer has an interesting page (A97:104) on the sources of the attributes of Franciscus for Friar Thomas.

Novel yet late is a statement in a sermon by Jacobus de Padua on St. Francis, delivered in Paris in 1345, that Pietro di Bernardone was also called *franciscus"* as a nickname, owing to his trips to France. In editing the text (AFH 44, 1951, 472), Victorien Doucet, OFM, comments that this opinion is novel but quite plausible.

Abate (C33:364-370) has a section on the two names, Francesco and Giovanni, and stresses that the latter remained the Saint's legal, baptismal name. Unfortunately, baptismal records were not kept until the Council of Trent made them obligatory.

On Francis' fervent devotion to his patron, St. John the Baptist, see D130 & AF X,132.

Appendix V
The Home of St. Francis

For the last 350 years visitors to Assisi have been shown the Chiesa Nuova, near the Piazza del Comune, with the remnants of the house in which St. Francis is said to have spent his childhood and youth. And about 50 yards beyond, they visit the small Oratorio di San Francesco Piccolo where, according to a late thirteenth-century legend, he was born in a stable. The Chiesa Nuova site has belonged to the Order of Friars Minor since 1615, while the Conventual Franciscans of the Sacro Convento have owned the Oratorio in recent times.

Such was the generally accepted situation regarding the *casa paterna* or the home of the Poverello's family until 1939 when the learned Conventual historian, Father Giuseppe Abate, announced that he had found important archival documents proving that the Saint had in fact been born in the Oratorio house (C11). Thus began the most impassioned and extensive of a dozen modern controversies about disputed points of fact in the life of St. Francis of Assisi. In the last 25 years, over 1300 carefully documented pages have been written on "this bitterly vexatious problem." Among the picturesque features of the many complex major and minor arguments and counter-arguments one encounters allegedly disappearing manuscripts and pillar stones, the birth of one of the worst men in the world, a Neapolitan filibusterer, generations of Assisi butchers and Jewish money-lenders, and a rix and knifing.

The deplorable result of this unedifying controversy is that today visitors to Assisi may be shown not just two but three or even four different sites which various scholars claim to have been the home of Pietro di Bernardone. In this Appendix we shall summarise briefly the history of the controversy and the most important evidence and arguments for each site. Then we will record certain conclusions which indicate that the whole problem needs to be thoroughly re-studied, with further research on several still obscure points, by a qualified and independent medievalist. We are confident that such a study would go far toward the final resolution of the present deplorable disagreement of experts, which only produce scandal and disillusion among the public.

1. The Controversy

Developing his 1939 brochure into a 550-page book, published first in the Conventual Friars' *Miscellanea Franciscana* in 1940 (C12), Abate analyzed over 200 archival deeds and documents which, even to his own surprise, led him to these sensational con-clusions: (1) that the Oratorio of San Francesco Piccolo was not merely the site of the Saint's birth but was also the one and only genuine *casa paterna*, i. e. his birthplace and the family home in which he spent his childhood and youth; and (2) that as from 1229 until 1615 not a single document indicated a connection between the Saint or his family and the site of the Chiesa Nuova, the latter was based on a fraud!

Naturally the indignant Friars Minor hastened to prepare elabo-rate refutations of such shocking and to them "absurd" charges and to strengthen the historical documentation of the Chiesa Nuova, while also stressing the legendary origins of the so-called Stalletta or stable at the Oratorio site. In 1940 Girolamo Golubovich, OFM, the distinguished historian of the Franciscan missions in the Near East, made a preliminary reply to Abate (C24). In 1940-41 Ben-venuto Bughetti, OFM, a leading medievalist of the Franciscan Col-legio di San Bonaventura at Quaracchi near Florence, wrote two strong articles in its *Archivum Franciscanum Historicum* (C21). But the major defense of the Chiesa Nuova was prepared by Leone Bracaloni, OFM, the venerable artist-historian who has resided at San Damiano since 1911, in a 325-page book published in 1943 (C18). Five years later Abate buttressed his arguments with two long articles in the *Miscellanea* (C13).

Then, in 1959, with neither side yielding an inch, Arnaldo Fortini, the former mayor of Assisi and expert on its archives and history, devoted seventy pages of his monumental five-volume *Nova Vita di San Francesco* (C23) to an entirely new thesis: he claimed that the *casa paterna* was neither at the Oratorio nor the Chiesa Nuova, both east of the Piazza del Comune, but rather between the churches of San Nicolò and San Paolo, west of the Piazza.

Finally in 1960, after Bracaloni published two brochures criticizing Abate's and Fortini's conclusions (C19, C20), Msgr. Arduino Terzi, OFM, of Rome, the historian of the Franciscan shrines in the Valley of Rieti, announced in a booklet that he agreed with the late Father Bughetti in placing the *casa paterna* at the Chiesa Nuova but at a slightly different site from Bracaloni, facing north rather than east (C28). Significant minor contributions to the debate were made by several other experts; for a complete list of writings on the subject since 1939, see the Bibliography, C11-C28.

2. The House of the Sons of Angelo 1229-1253

In 1229 the municipal government of Assisi undertook to enlarge the Piazza del Comune. As a result the owners of the condemned buildings were granted financial compensations that were paid in part by the owners of nearby buildings which increased in value, and among the latter were listed the *filij angeli piche*, the sons of Angelo (son) of Pica, who paid 6 Lucca pounds *pro eorum domo*, for their house. The two sons of Angelo (brother of St. Francis and son of the widowed Pica) were Giovanetto and Piccardo. As Bughetti insisted, this basic document suggests that that house close to the Piazza was the *casa paterna* of the rich merchant Pietro di Bernardone, in which the young Francis "was used to seeing stocks of cloth to be sold" (*I Celano*, 5). For it is known that the merchants of Assisi had their stores on the Piazza, also called Mercato or Forum, and it was usual for the shop to occupy the ground floor of the medieval merchant's home. Of course we would expect that this public document written less than a year after Assisi's most famous son had been canonized would have specified that the house of his nephews had been his home. But unfortunately not a single one of the half dozen extant notarial documents referring to the several houses that certainly belonged to Angelo's descendants between 1229 and 1398 mentions the Saint.

3. The Oratorio House

A second fundamental document indicates that in 1253 Giovanetto and Piccardo jointly owned two houses located on the sites east of the Piazza del Comune which in later centuries became the shrines known, respectively, as the Oratorio di San Francesco Piccolo and the Chiesa Nuova. For in that year the two brothers signed a notarial agreement dividing their inherited property, which also included numerous lots of land near Assisi. This document, however, describes only Piccardo's share. Which of the two sites was henceforth his? The Oratorio, unquestionably, declares Abate; the Chiesa Nuova, demonstrably, replies Bracaloni. Among the pieces of evidence invoked by both scholars are the concatenation of successive neighbors listed in numerous notarial documents over the next three centuries, the specification of a *formello* (an open gutter between two houses) on one side of the building, an arch mentioned in 1281, and above all the names "House of St. Francis," "House Where St. Francis Was Born," and "Chapel or Oratory of St. Francis" which were commonly applied to that house in numerous documents between 1398 and 1544. Bughetti, Fortini, and Terzi agree with Abate that Piccardo's house became the Oratorio, which was also called (after 1452) "the Church of San Francesco Piccolo." Prof. P. Perali of the Vatican Archives published in 1941 (C26) an important tax list of 1395 which clearly shows in the vicinity of the Oratorio certain neighbors that Bracaloni nevertheless claims were near the Chiesa Nuova site.

Bracaloni's principal argument, the *formello*, is seriously undermined by the fact that all the documents except that of 1253 show the same house as having two adjoining houses on each side; consequently either the *formello* disappeared after 1253 or it was not on the side but in the rear, as in reality it is at the Oratorio. A careful study of all the complex evidence has convinced me that Abate's documented chain of successive neighbors of the Oratorio site is substantially unbreakable.

In 1281 Piccardo was living in this house, though he owned two other houses in Assisi. A year later he and Ceccolo, the son and heir of the now deceased Giovanetto, signed an agreement by which Ceccolo granted the Oratorio house to Piccardo in exchange for a house in the San Rufino-Porta Perlici district northeast of the Piazza del Comune. According to Fortini's research, Ceccolo moved to that house for some time, but returned to the Chiesa Nuova site by 1335. Several explanations have been suggested for the puzzling fact that Ceccolo granted to Piccardo in 1282 the same house as the latter had acquired in 1253 when he and Giovanetto divided their property: either Piccardo had sold it back to his brother or nephew in the meanwhile, or perhaps the agreement of 1253 lapsed with the death of Giovanetto, who made a will in 1261 leaving an unspecified house to his wife. Though no document so states, probably Giovanetto was the elder of the two brothers and it was he who retained the family home and store near the Piazza in 1253.

A century of silence envelops Piccardo's house between 1288 and 1398. Perhaps, as Bughetti suggested, Piccardo himself, who was a devout (and unmarried) Franciscan Tertiary, erected in it a private altar in honor of his canonized uncle, but the first evidence we have that such an altar existed there during the 14th century is a will of

1400 stipulating that "the image of St. Francis above the altar in the house where St. Francis was born be painted the way it is." The will does not give the house's location, but must refer to the Oratorio because the same expression was applied to that house by the same notary in 1412, 1414, and 1419; and incidentally, a daughter of the testator was married to one of the house's neighbors. Consequently this will of 1400 tends to confirm the dating of some faded art work on the right wall of San Francesco Piccolo as of the first half of the 14th century. Two years earlier, in 1398, a notarial document clearly identified this house as "the House of St. Francis." From then until 1429 it is described in several documents by that name, often with the qualifying words *que vocatur*, "which is called," suggesting that the name as such was then still somewhat novel. It was described as a Chapel for the first time in 1429, and in 1452 as a Church. In only one document of 1481 is the famous stable mentioned: "*Oratorium Stabuli S. Francisci*."

This brings us to the problem of the stable legend, which is first recorded in the late 14th-century *Vita Sancti Francisci Anonyma Bruxellensis* edited by Alfons Fierens (A215). It is obviously a product of the conformity-with-Christ theme which was given a powerful impulse by the Saint's stigmatization, then by the Latin *Actus Beati Francisci* and its popular Italian translations *I Fioretti di San Francesco*, culminating in Friar Bartholomew of Pisa's monumental *De Conformitate Vitae Beati Francisci ad Vitam Domini Jesu*, which was published in 1399. Abate, trying with all his argumentative skill to strengthen the case for the Oratorio house, attempted the impossible: to explain why Bartholomew did not mention the birth-in-the-stable as one of the most striking of his forty Conformities. It remains evident that his reasons for not mentioning it were either that he had never heard of it or that he considered it a fable. In both cases, the story stands condemned. However, its legendary character should not necessarily eliminate all claim of the Oratorio house to some connection with the Saint in view of the rich documentary evidence which Abate has discovered establishing the following facts: (1) a year before the stableless *De Conformitate* appeared, a notarial document described that house as "the House of St. Francis," (2) throughout the 15th century it remained known as such in Assisi, and (3) it certainly belonged before 1253 to the Saint's family. These significant facts suggest that the late-fourteenth century tradition in Assisi which explicitly connected his house with St. Francis, and specifically with his birth, has a strong right to acceptance by critical historians today.

4. The Chiesa Nuova Site

Now what about the other house of the sons of Angelo near the Piazza del Commune? Is Abate right in asserting that it had no claim whatever to association with the Saint until the Friars Minor acquired the site and built the Chiesa Nuova on it in 1615, describing it as the traditional *casa paterna*? He is correct insofar as none of the numerous notarial documents dating from 1398 to 1567 which he analyzed in 1940 refers to the Saint or to his brother Angelo's descendants.

But Abate began by misreading the important 1229 document, concluding that the sons of Angelo had *received* compensation and hence that their house was among those *destroyed* when the Piazza was enlarged. In a definitive study of that document, Perali in 1941 (C26) demonstrated that they *paid* and therefore that their house remained intact, though he suggested it may have belonged to Pica's family or may have been bought by Angelo — interesting suppositions for which there is no evidence. We agree with Bughetti that this house was probably Pietro di Bernardone's store and residence, which the two sons of Angelo continued to own jointly until they divided their inheritance in 1253. At that time, presumably, Giovanetto (probably but not demonstrably the elder) continued to occupy it, for we know that he was also a merchant. Upon his death some time after he made his will in 1261, his son Ceccolo inherited the house, though Fortini has shown that he moved to the Porta Perlici house for some years after 1282.

Until 1959, no document was known which clearly mentioned this house near the Piazza del Comune between 1229 and about 1575 (not 1615). But fortunately for the historical tradition of the Chiesa Nuova site, Fortini discovered in the communal archives of Assisi and printed in his 1959 *Nova Vita* brief excerpts from a decisive notarial document of 1335 which places the house of Cicchus Piccardi close to the Platea Comunis and the nearby Macello or butchers shops, and next to a house owned by Vanne di Battaglione. It is in the form of a complaint lodged with the city authorities by Vanne's brother Nicoluccio against two men who attacked and wounded Vanne in front of the latter's house. However, though the far-reaching significance of this crucial document has been acknowledged by Fortini, Bracaloni, and Terzi, no one has yet given it and its ramifications the thorough analysis which they merit. Its major importance of course lies in the fact that it shows the Piazza house still in the possession of the Saint's family in 1335. Its reference to the Platea Comunis also confirms the proximity of that house to the Piazza, which has been questioned by Abate and Attal. Just three years later the topography of this site was substantially modified by the addition of a large eastern wing to the nearby Palazzo dei Priori, cutting the Chiesa Nuova site off from the Piazza del Comune and creating the Plateola Macelli, now (after later changes) called the Piazza della Chiesa Nuova.

Unfortunately the mention of Nicoluccio and Vanne di Battaglione in this basic document of 1335 has resulted in needless confusion, for in notarial documents of 1398 and 1410 a Benedetto di Vanne appears as a neighbor of the Oratorio of San Francesco Piccolo. While Fortini is probably right in assuming that Benedetto (or Betto) di Vanne is a son of Vanne di Battaglione, he is certainly in error in stating that the two houses are the same.

Perali's valuable tax list of 1395 can no doubt shed a clarifying light on this confused situation, for it shows in the Capudicina Strate Nove S. Clare (the Oratorio section) two tax payers named Farolfus Vannis and Salutius Vannis, whereas in the Macello section it lists a Nicolaus Vannutij. It is indeed regrettable that the family of Vanne di Battaglione is not among the leading families of Assisi whose genealogies have been extensively traced (despite the frustrating lack of surnames) by Fortini, Abate, and Bracaloni. Research on this family now becomes only one of several new studies that must still be made for a definitive clarification of the *casa paterna* problem; others will be indicated below. In this case, we believe it will confirm our hypothesis that in the 1335 and the 1395-98 documents, two houses belonging to different members of one family are involved, just as in 1615 two branches of the Bini family owned, respectively, a house near the Oratorio and another on the site of the Chiesa Nuova.

What happened to the house of Angelo-Giovanetto-Ceccolo after 1335? For 240 years the documents are discouragingly silent, except for a frustrating false reference and a mystifying hint. Ceccolo had six children who might have inherited the house, but four of them became friars or nuns. Two other sons, Pietruccio and Bernardo, married and had a son each, Francesco and Giovanni, respectively. Now the tax list of 1395 shows a Bernardus Ciccholi residing in the Macello or Chiesa Nuova section; and a notarial document of 1412 mentions the *res olim Bernardi Ciccoli* in the same neighborhood. Even Abate thought this was Ceccolo's son Bernardo — until he discovered another document of 1406 in which the same notary described the same house quite unmistakably (in the photocopy) as *res olim Bernardi de Napoli.* Consequently the house-owner was a notorious Neapolitan filibusterer Bernardo di Ceccolo da Napoli who was banned from Assisi in 1401; here too more research is desirable to ascertain exactly how he was named in the ban and other extant documents.

The mystifying hint is an all-too-vague document of 1507 (found by Abate, but not used by Bracaloni) which states that the Friars Minor of Santa Maria degli Angeli and San Damiano had purchased a house tantalizingly described only as *quadam domus*, a certain house, from the Ciminelli family, with a reference to another (now lost) deed recorded by a notary named Maghetti. Here the suggestive hint lies in the facts that the Ciminellis owned the Chiesa Nuova site and that Maghetti was an immediate neighbor. Again further research might throw more light on this strange transaction which implies that the Order of Friars Minor in 1507 had reason to take a special interest in acquiring a house in the Chiesa Nuova area; but for reasons unknown they seem to have relinquished it, only to buy it again in 1615.

The next evidence we have of this continuing though tenuous tradition of a house connected with St. Francis on the Chiesa Nuova site is found in the first guidebook to Assisi, written by the Conventual Fra Ludovico di Città di Castello (or Pietralunga), who died in 1580 (DSPU 28,1926,74). On and near the Piazza del Comune he noted two alleged sites of stores of Pietro di Bernardone. Then, when one leaves the Piazza by a street on the right, he wrote, "at a stone's throw, there is the house of St. Francis. Nearby on a certain small street there is at a corner a small street, and there is a small church called S. Francesco piccolino." Although Abate insists that this somewhat ambiguous text refers only to the Oratory site, by its two sentences it obviously differentiates "the house of St. Francis" from the small church "nearby." Fra Ludovico's reference marks the beginning of a new interest in this site. However, the fact that it had undeniably fallen into almost general disregard is proved by a striking panoramic map of Assisi drawn (not without some errors) in 1599 by Francesco Villamena which lists 66 points of interest there, including S. Francesco Piccolino but omitting the house near the Piazza. Similarly the municipal Statutes published in 1469 mention "the Church in which St. Francis was born" but not the Piazza home.

The first decades of the 17th century witnessed a rebirth and intensification of popular devotion to the Franciscan shrines of Assisi. In addition to the Conventual and Observant Friars, the newer branches of the Order such as the Riformati and Capuchins and Third Order

Regular were acquiring or building churches there. Thus it is note-worthy that about 1615 the Observants made an unsuccessful effort to buy the Oratory of San Francesco Piccolo (which was evidently not owned then by the Conventuals), and both the Observants and the Capuchins sought to purchase a certain dilapidated house on the Chiesa Nuova site. The former bought it from the Bini family on May 2, 1615, and proceeded to build a large new church called at first San Francesco il Converso and later La Chiesa Nuova. The sales deed de-clared that the house "by ancient tradition was that of the former Pietro Bernardone, and as such in Assisi it has been considered and is openly and publicly considered by tradition by all the inhabitants." In-side the house were shown the iron ring which the Saint's father used to bind his son, as well as the closet in which the boy was imprisoned by his father. Significantly, the Observant Friars of the Chiesa Nuova also showed to visitors the door at which the pilgrim or angel was said to have knocked and announced that the mother should go to the sta-ble to give birth to her son. Unfortunately only a few parts of the walls of the original structure were preserved. Subsequently, adjoining properties were also acquired by the Franciscans; a study of these sales deeds is needed in order to clarify the still confused history of this site and its successive neighbors.

Henceforth Assisi had two houses of St. Francis. During the next three centuries various writers accepted the authenticity of one or the other or both, but gradually the Chiesa Nuova came to be generally looked upon as the "traditional" *casa paterna*, while the Oratorio of San Francesco Piccolo was considered, by those who accepted the sta-ble-birth legend, as merely the site of the Saint's birth. Hence the consternation and disbelief which greeted Abate's announcement in 1940 that the latter was the *only* authentic *casa paterna*.

5. The Fortini House

It is paradoxical that the great historian of Assisi, Arnaldo Fortini, discovered one of the strongest testimonies for the Chiesa Nuova site in the document of 1335, yet he came to the conclusion that the true *casa paterna* was really at the other end of the Piazza del Comune, be-tween the churches of San Nicolò and San Paolo.

The fulcrum or cornerstone of his thesis lies in another fundamental early document: a passage in the *Liber exemplorum* (A221,n.116) published by Livarius Oliger, OFM, in 1927, in which a Fr. Nicolaus de Assisio narrated the story of the pilgrim who came to the home of St. Francis a few hours after his birth and predicted that of the two boys born on that street (or in that neighborhood) on that day, one would be among the best men in the world and the other among the worst (cf Appendix IV). Fra Nicola stated that his mother used to tell that story, and he introduced it with these memorable words: "The house of my father adjoins the house of St. Francis."

It is evident that those words would identify beyond all doubt the *casa paterna* — if the house of Fra Nicola di Assisi could be located. So the all-important question is: who was he, and when and where did he live before becoming a Franciscan? Fortini is convinced that he was a prominent notary of Assisi named Nicola di Giacomo di Ranuccio who was born about 1240, was a municipal counselor in 1283, procurator and syndic of the Friars Minor in 1291, joined the Order about 1304, and died after 1326. As a layman and father of a family he lived in one of two houses just west of the Piazza del Comune, between the churches of San Nicolò and San Paolo.

A second cornerstone of Fortini's thesis is the striking fact that the Saint's devout nephew Piccardo took a strong interest in the house next to Nicola di Giacomo's. In March, 1280, the now elderly Piccardo bought for a high price a two-third ownership of that house and then leased it to Nicola for a token payment to be paid yearly on October 4; the notary owned the third part. But in 1282 Piccardo granted his rights to the Benedictine superiors of the adjoining Priory of San Paolo and the Abbey of San Benedetto on Monte Subasio. Both contracts included clauses forbidding alienation of the property for 29 years (but made no mention of St. Francis). On this nexus of apparently convincing evidence rests the case of the Fortini *casa paterna*.

However, neither Bracaloni nor Terzi have accepted his conclusions, though unfortunately they have not given his claims a thorough scientific analysis. As the former insists, the fulcrum is the identity of Fra Nicola, and there were probably several other Fra Nicola di Assisi in the Umbrian Seraphic Province which numbered 800 friars in the mid-14th century; for instance, a saintly laybrother of that name, according to Bartholomew of Pisa (1399), had died "recently" in Perugia (AF IV, 202). But neither Bracaloni nor Terzi has challenged Fortini's novel attribution of the authorship in 1318-19 of the *Liber Exemplorum* to Maestro Fra Francesco di Bartolo della Rossa of Assisi, the author of a *Tractatus de Indulgentia* defending the Portiuncula Indulgence, who flourished between 1298 and 1334. Fortini's reasons for this attribution are the style and the suggestive fact that both the *Liber*'s author and Fra Francesco evidently lived for a while in Paris and Cologne and were acquainted with a Frater Nicolaus Teutonicus. But Fortini does not deal with Oliger's assigning the date of writing of the *Liber exemplorum* from internal evidence to the years 1268-1273. This book of anecdotes mentions the death of Conradin (1268) and refers to Pope Gregory X (1271-76), but calls Pope Innocent V only by the name which he had as a Dominican priest before his election in 1276; and its frequent references to St. Bonaventure as Minister General never give him the rank of Cardinal which he received in 1273. Consequently Oliger explicitly doubted that the two German friars named Nicholaus could be the same. Therefore, although the only extant codex of the *Liber* dates from the late thirteenth or early fourteenth century, it must be a copy of an original written around 1270 by some unknown friar, and not by Fra Francesco di Bartolo about 1318.

For the *casa* problem the main point is of course that the Frater Nicolaus of Assisi whose home adjoined that of St. Francis, according to the *Liber exemplorum* written about 1270, cannot be Fra Nicola di Giacomo di Ranuccio who, though living then, became a Franciscan only about 1304. Consequently, with this essential cornerstone removed, the house west of the Piazza takes on a much more limited significance as merely a fourth house in Assisi in which the prosperous Piccardo had a temporary though puzzling interest. Another major objection to this site as the *casa paterna* is that it would make the Saint a member of San Nicolò Parish, whereas his attendance at school and especially his funeral at San Giorgio strongly suggest that his home was in the latter parish east of the Piazza.

Possibly more extensive research may uncover decisive data concerning Fra Nicola d'Assisi and his home. He certainly cannot be the already-mentioned Franciscan of that name who, according to Bartholomew of Pisa, was a saintly laybrother infirmarian, because that friar died in Perugia not long before Bartholomew wrote his book in the 1390's; that author specifically states that a son of a (widower) Frater Valentinus de Narnia whose vocation in the Order was saved by this Nicola's prayers was still living then. The same writer clearly distinguishes the two Nicolas and also supplies the valuable additional information that the 13th-century Nicola's mother was named Margaret and that he later became guardian of the friary in Spoleto (AF IV, 108). Several friars named simply Frater Nicolaus are mentioned as witnesses in Assisi documents of the years 1247, 1276, and 1278 published in Fortini's FNV (III, 464, 476-477), though regrettably not included in its incomplete index. Disagreeing with Oliger, I believe that our Nicola d'Assisi may well be the Frater Nicolaus mentioned in another anecdote of the *Liber exemplorum* (n.111) as the uncle of a Fra Bentevenga, both of whom died, presumably in Assisi, before the *Liber* was written. (The nephew was perhaps the questing brother of that name at San Damiano in 1214 who is mentioned in St. Clare's Canonization Process.) Further archival research might confirm the identity of these friars and locate their family and all-important home among the immediate neighbors in 1229-1253 of the house of the sons of Angelo near the Piazza.

6. Conclusions and Suggestions

Summing up the facts which we have discussed, we can rejoice that the controversy over the *casa paterna* of St. Francis during the last twenty years has resulted in the discovery and publication of many hitherto unknown documents concerning four houses in Assisi more or less directly connected with his family, but unfortunately much confusion still exists in the interpretation of those documents.

Our study has led us to the following conclusions: (1) the notarial documents published by Abate demonstrate irrefutably that the house accepted by Piccardo in 1253 became the Oratorio di San Francesco Piccolo; (2) an altar with an image of St. Francis existed in that house for some years before 1400; (3) that house was called "the House of St. Francis" in 1398, at a time when the legend of the stable birth was either not known or not accepted in Assisi by Bartholomew of Pisa; (4) that house was generally considered in Assisi throughout the fifteenth century as "the House of St. Francis" and "the House Where St. Francis Was Born," and after 1452 as "the Church of San Francesco Piccolo."

Turning to the house near the Piazza del Comune, we find that: (5) the two sons of the Saint's nephew Angelo owned it jointly until 1253; (6) Giovanetto and then his son Ceccolo continued to own it until after 1335; (7) the popularity of San Francesco Piccolo during the fifteenth century caused this site to lapse into general disregard: (8) it was perhaps bought before and sold after 1507 by the Observant Friars Minor; (9) about 1575 it too was called "the House of St. Francis"; and (10) in 1615 it was acquired by them as the *casa paterna* and made into the Chiesa Nuova.

In the light of those facts and probabilities we have reached this tentative conclusion, based not on any documentary proof but merely on obvious possibilities: *the strong evidence for the persistent tradition of both San Francesco Piccolo and the Chiesa Nuova site suggests that the Saint's father Pietro di Bernardone owned both houses, and consequently that both houses have justified claims to the title of "house of St. Francis."*

This solution to the vexed problem of the *casa paterna* is far from original, as it was first advanced in 1768 by the Bollandist Constantin Suyskens, S. J. In the *Acta Sanctorum*, he suggested that San Francesco Piccolo was perhaps the home of the Saint's family when he was born, but that they moved to the other house when he was a boy or a youth (converso). In 1933 the Conventual Luigi Manconi came to the same conclusion (cf CF 5,1935,147*). Now, however, after the publication of a wealth of new documentary material which was unknown to them, it must be emphasized that *the weight of the evidence in favor of this hypothesis has increased enormously.*

Therefore, in the interest of historical truth and in order to bring to a pacific end the "cold war" that has been loyally waged between the defenders of each shrine as the single exclusive *casa paterna,* we strongly recommend that a definitive new study of the whole problem be undertaken by an independent medievalist, covering especially those points which we have shown to require further research. We are confident that such an objective study will result in a much-needed clarification and vindication of the provable claims of *both* shrines, to the advantage of historical science and to the edification of all friends of St. Francis and all visitors to Assisi.

Appendix VI
Wars

This Appendix will present an abstract of the rich data which Arnaldo Fortini and others have disclosed in recent works concerning the several wars of Assisi during the youth of St. Francis.

Part 1, "The Two Conrads," clarifies — for the first time in any book on St. Francis — the confusion of Duke Conrad of Urslingen and Count Conrad of Luetzelhard, known as *Mosca-in-cervello* (fly-in-brain). It also sketches the background of the popular uprising in Assisi in 1198 against the former.

Part 2, "The Civil War," describes the class war in the next few years between the feudal nobility (including the families of St. Clare and Brother Leonardo of Assisi) and the rising burgher class — the *majores* and *minores*.

Part 3, "The Perugia War," summarizes the ten-year warfare between Assisi and Perugia, in which Francis fought at the Battle of Collestrada in November, 1202.

Part 4, "The Prisoner," deals with his year as prisoner-of-war and several post-mortem miracles which he performed for prisoners.

Part 5, "The War in Apulia," attempts to clarify the confusion in early texts and modern biographies regarding a Count Gentile.

1. The Two Conrads

It is indeed surprising that Fortini (FNV I/1,134, 151) perpetuates Muratori's mistaken identification of Duke Conrad of Spoleto as "Conrad of Lutzen," with the comical nickname *Mosca-in-cervello* (fly-in-the-brain, i. e. mad). But a glance at the indexes of several turn of the century editions of relevant 13th-century chronicles would

show that actually two different persons are involved. In 1940 Salvatorelli (B11:410) complained that this confusion, dating back to Muratori (d. 1750), should cease. Unfortunately, no complete biographical
sketches of either man have yet been compiled.

The following information has been culled from relevant medieval
sources and modern studies listed by Van Cleve (C68) and Waley
(B13). Among perhaps more than a score of prominent Germans
named Conrad late in the 12th century, the two who concern us led
parallel careers as generals and local rulers in the areas of central
Italy occupied by the Hohenstaufen Emperors Frederick I (Barbarossa) and his son Henry VI, roughly in the years 1175-1200.

(1) COUNT CONRAD OF LUÉTZELHARD came from a cas-
tle near Seebach and the Lahr River in Swabia, served in Italy first
under the infamous warrior and excommunicated Archbishop Christian
of Mainz beginning in 1172; by his belligerent personality soon earned
the nickname *Mosca-in-cervello* (which even Pope Innocent III used
in referring to him); participated in the unsuccessful siege of Ancona
in 1174; after the Pact of Venice in 1177 was appointed Markgraf of
Ancona; led the imperial troops in Abruzzi-Molise until defeated at
Capua in 1191; two years later returned and took and slew all the
inhabitants of Monteroduni; at least twice arrested and imprisoned
high prelates: in 1172 the French Bishop Gerald of Cahors and in
1192 Cardinal Ottaviano of Ostia; in the years 1191-95 served as Markgraf of Tuscany and Romagna; led an imperial army in Sicily before
dying about 1197, leaving a son of the same name who served under
Frederick II thirty years later. This Conrad was also called "*bellicosus
marchio*" and "*patriae fulgor*" (the fighting marquess and the lightning
bolt of the land). He did not rule over Assisi or Spoleto.

(2) CONRAD OF URSLINGEN, DUKE OF SPOLETO AND
COUNT OF ASSISI AND NOCERA, also came from Swabia, probably arrived in Italy in 1172 with Christian of Mainz; was present at
the capture of Assisi in 1174; appointed Duke of Spoleto by Barbarossa
in 1777, as well as Count of Assisi and Nocera; in Assisi with the Emperor at Christmas 1177; so oppressed the clergy in his Duchy that some
were reduced to begging; with his wife (probably a native of Nocera)
served as guardian of the infant Frederick II for three years, 1195-97
(see Appendix IV, Part 2); after the death of Henry VI in September 1197, offered to serve under Innocent III; in April 1198 at Narni
yielded the Duchy to the Pope's envoys and returned to Germany; in
1202 went to southern Italy or Sicily to replace the deceased imperial
general Markward, but died before November 1202. In 1219 his wife
was living in Nocera. His two sons, Berthold and Raynald, later used
the title "Dukes of Spoleto" and served Frederick II in Tuscany and

Umbria. Pope Gregory IX excommunicated Raynald in 1229. A descendant, Werner von Urslingen, became a famous *condottiere* in central Italy a century later; by 1442 the family was extinct. Its arms were: silver, three shields gules. It was of course this Conrad who ruled over Assisi from 1177 to 1198, often residing in its Rocca during the youth of St. Francis.

To understand the explosion of anti-German feeling which swept across Italy after the unexpected death of Henry VI in September, 1197, we need only recall the liberation of Italian towns from Nazi control by the Allies in 1944-1945. A few months later, in January, 1198, a forceful 37-year-old cardinal became Pope Innocent III and set about recovering the States of the Church in central Italy from the now weak Hohenstaufens. In March, Conrad of Spoleto tried to offer his duchy to the Pope together with a substantial payment and military support. Innocent rejected the offer, and in April at Narni, Conrad unconditionally surrendered his duchy to two papal legates, one of whom was the Cardinal Ottaviano who had been imprisoned by Mosca-in-cervello. Before meekly obeying the Pope's order to retire to Germany, Conrad also handed over three major fortresses in the duchy, those of Cesi, Gualdo, and Assisi. But the citizens of Assisi had laid siege to Conrad's Rocca dominating the city, and refused to let the papal envoys have it until it had been captured and thoroughly razed as a symbol of oppression. For these events, see FNV I/1,152, and Waley's *The Papal State in the 13th Century* (B13:30-37). The only documented data on the Urslingen family appears in C. von Stälin's *Wirtembergische Geschichte* (Stuttgart 1847) II,586-594; cf 109 on Luetzelhard.

2. The Civil War

In describing the bitter conflict in Assisi in the years 1198-1202, Fortini (FNV I/1,157-164; II,131-161) duly stresses the underlying social and economic factors, showing clearly that as in so many other Italian cities at that time, the struggle for power was not — as often depicted in turn of the century writings — between the upper and lower classes, the aristocracy and the masses of little people, but rather between the feudal nobility and the new burgher class of merchants and artisans. Also involved inevitably were natural conflicts of interest between the empire and the papacy (Ghibellines and Guelfs), the traditional rivalry and hostility between neighboring towns (Perugia was Guelf, so Assisi must be Ghibelline), and the emancipation of the newly independent commune or city-state from its previous subjection to emperor or feudal duke or relatively dominant local bishop (on the latter, see F191).

Inside the city of Assisi, the feudal nobility — the *boni homines* or *maiores* — resided in the neighborhood of San Rufino and to the west around the church of San Giacomo de Murorupto. Their town houses were equipped with tall, square towers for defense — those same towers which have made San Gimignano famous but which dominated the skyline of every medieval Italian town almost like the skyscrapers of lower and central Manhattan.

It was those towers that were now leveled in the civil war in Assisi. At the same time their rural counterparts, the great feudal castles of Sasso Rosso on the slopes of Monte Subasio beyond San Benedetto, Monte Moro, Bassano, and above all the fortress-tower of San Savino on the plain, whose owners exacted tolls from passing merchants, were attacked and destroyed or damaged. Here Fortini surmises: "naturally we cannot think that Pietro Bernardone, his sons, and relations failed to respond to the consuls' summons on the day when iron and fire assailed the towers that were suffocating their lands on the plain and barring their trade-routes. . . . There is no doubt that (Francis) participated intensively in all these events" (FNV I/1,162,164).

Among the leading families of the feudal nobility of Assisi were two which have a special link with the life of St. Francis; from one he called to the service of God St. Clare and Brother Rufino and from the other Brother Leonardo of Assisi.

Fortini (FNV II,315-317, 327-348; chart 349) corrects — let us hope definitively — the modern errors that Clare's family was named Scifi and that they were lords of Sasso Rosso or Coccorano. The following genealogical chart (condensed from his) shows at a glance the principal relationships:

THE FAMILY OF ST. CLARE

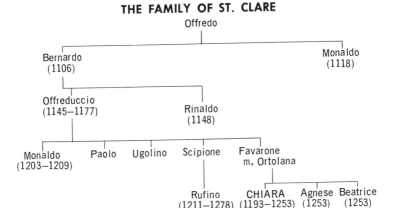

Offredo

Bernardo (1106)   Monaldo (1118)

Offreduccio (1145–1177)   Rinaldo (1148)

Monaldo (1203–1209)   Paolo   Ugolino   Scipione   Favarone m. Ortolana

Rufino (1211–1278)   CHIARA (1193–1253)   Agnese (1253)   Beatrice (1253)

Thus her father was Favarone; her uncle Scipione was the father of her cousin Rufino; another uncle Monaldo, lord of Coriano (not Coccorano), was the head of the family around 1210; and her grandfather was Offreduccio di Bernardo, also a leading *bonus homo*. Their home was close to San Rufino. Incidentally, Agnese was called Caterina before becoming a Poor Clare.

Although none of the early Franciscan sources so state directly, it can be deduced from the testimony of Sister Filippa in the Process of Canonization of St. Clare that both families — Clare's and Filippa's — were among the feudal aristocrats whose castles and homes were destroyed and who therefore took refuge and sought help in Perugia, Assisi's traditional enemy. From archival documents Fortini has fully proved the presence in Perugia in the years around 1202 of Clare's uncle Monaldo and Filippa's father Leonardo di Gislerio; and Filippa testified that she knew Clare during her childhood. Also Sister Benvenuta said the same thing, and her family resided in Perugia. Consequently Fortini concludes that Clare was living in Perugia, in exile, at the age of ten, when the troops of Assisi, including young Francis, fought a bloody battle against those of Perugia. And among the latter were no doubt Clare's uncle Monaldo and Filippa's father Leonardo. Just when Monaldo, Favarone, and Clare returned to Assisi cannot be specified, but Fortini believes it was probably in 1205. Favarone was perhaps still alive in 1229. For the Battle of Collestrada, see below; for the career of Leonardo, see Appendix VII.

3. The Perugia War

In Perugia the exiles from Assisi succeeded in persuading the consuls and city fathers to launch a war against Assisi. Alliances were made by both cities with towns that were friendly or hostile toward the enemy. In October, 1201, Perugia made a pact wih Foligno. Assisi sought and obtained arms and soldiers from Bevagna, Spello, Nocera, and Fabriano. Naturally Assisi rejected Perugia's demand that the exiled noblemen's property be restored and damages paid.

Fortini (FNV I/1,190-194; II,171-178) confirms that the decisive battle took place in 1202, and supplies background from local documents and especially from the Chronicle of Bonifazio di Verona which celebrates in verse the history of Perugia from 1150 to 1293. The forces of Assisi took the initiative and advanced to the Ospedale di Collestrada, on a wooded hill a mile or two east of Ponte San Giovanni but only 600 yards from a bend in the Tiber River. The Perugian army crossed the river, attacked, and won a smashing victory.

4. The Prisoner

Fortini (FNV II, 178) flatly denies the statement in *Tres Socii*, 3, that Francis and the other prisoners returned to Assisi a year later because of a truce or peace pact between the two cities, for he finds no documentary evidence of any truce before August, 1205. He therefore believes that Pietro di Bernardone ransomed his son when the latter fell sick in prison, as there existed in Perugia (in 1164) a *congregatio et societas captivorum amalatorum*. Actually, the war between Perugia and Assisi, though temporarily suspended in 1205, did not end until 1210. They entered into other pacts in 1223 and 1228, but renewed their wars in the next century, with Perugia taking and sacking Assisi in 1321 and 1332 (C63).

Fortini rightly notes (FNV I/1, 202) that among the miracles attributed to Francis after his death, the number of dramatic liberations of prisoners reported by Thomas of Celano and St. Bonaventure is striking and implies a certain personal sympathy on the part of the Saint; see the seven instances in *III Celano*, 88-94, "De carceratis et vinctis."

On this theme Felice M. Rossetti has written a whole book, *San Francesco e i carcerati* (D176).

5. The War in Apulia

A typical example of the confusion often arising from an uncritical acceptance of texts appears in the several attempts that have been made to identify the so-called Count Gentile involved in Francis' desire to be knighted in Apulia, while other writers compound the error by applying his name to the nobleman of Assisi with whom the Saint set out.

Using the Papini "Who said it first?" rule, however, we discover the following basic facts: 1) neither *I Celano*, 4, nor *II Celano*, 6, mentions a count, the first speaking only of the Assisi nobleman; 2) *Bonaventure*, I, 3, is the first to bring in an unnamed count in Apulia: *in 'Apuliam ad quemdam liberalem comitem*. Next the *Anonymus Perusinus*, 5, changes this to read *ad comitem Gentilem*, and the final state is reached in *Tres Socii*, 5, which specifies *ut a quodam comite Gentili nomine miles fiat*. So only the last two late sources name the count. Did they simply change Bonaventure's *liberalem* into the synonymous *gentilem*, to which some scribe then gave a capital G? Or were they referring to an actual Count Gentile fighting for the Pope in southern Italy around 1205, and if so to which one? Sabatier, *Vie* (A305:25), found no less than three. Ottavio da Alatri, *Cap*, who has studied this question most thoroughly (C67), believes it was Conte Gentile della Pagliara (Palear), conte di Manupello, brother of Walter of Palear;

on him see also Professor Thomas C. Van Cleve's definitive study of *Markward of Anweiler and the Sicilian Regency* (C68:index). Perhaps it was, but Bonaventure's *quemdam liberalem comitem* might well have been the most famous "noble-minded count" then in southern Italy; Gautier de Brienne (on him, see C66a). Fortini (FNV III, 178-182, 205-207, 228-232, 244-246) elaborates on the romantic appeal of that valiant knight who had rescued an Italian queen and her beautiful daughters from custody in an Alsatian abbey and whose exploits in war were being sung by wandering minstrels. Though he died in June, 1205, not long after Francis had been told in his vision at Spoleto to serve God rather than man, his brother Jean de Brienne no doubt met the Poverello at Damietta in 1219 and became both King of Jerusalem and a Franciscan tertiary, with a tomb in the Saint's Basilica in Assisi (on him, see C80; on his tomb, C82; cf FNV 1/1,246, on the discovery of Gautier's tomb in 1937).

At any rate, there is no justification for seeking the elusive count in Assisi or anywhere but Apulia.

Appendix VII
Companions

In this Appendix we shall briefly survey the problems arising from confusion in the early sources and modern research concerning the identity of the first companions of St. Francis. A recent controversy between Fortini and Terzi regarding the place of origin of Brothers Illuminato, Philip, and Angelo — Assisi or Rieti Valley — has produced contradictory data about those three. Fortini (E111) has also provided considerable background information about several other companions. After a list of the Saint's favorite companions, we will examine the unclear problem of the ecclesiastical status of the first companions: were they clerics or lay brothers? Lastly, Part 4 of the Appendix will present brief biographical sketches of 16 principal companions.

1. The First Companions

In 1912 Oliger (E61:3-5) showed conclusively that the number of companions accompanying St. Francis to Rome in 1209 is eleven in the earliest sources, but twelve in later texts. Grau (E112) has recently restudied this question, reaching the same conclusion. However, the exact identity of the eleven is still under discussion, as confusion has resulted from several causes. The first of these is the anonymous *"quidam de Assisio, pium ac simplicem spiritum gerens"* of I Celano, 24, who joined the Saint even before Bernard and Peter Catanii and who was also one of the eleven with Francis in Rome: *"omnibus dictis fratribus"* (I Celano, 32) — a point often overlooked. Since this anonymous first companion is not included in any other source, it is inevitable that there be conflicts between them.

To have a clearer grasp of these contradictions, we list here the first companions in three principal sources:

Total incl. Francis	No.	I CELANO	BONAVENTURE (III)	TRES SOCII....
2	1	*quidam* (24)	Bernardus (3)	Bernardus (28)
3	2	Bernardus (24)	*quinque* (4)	Petrus (28)
4	3	*vir alter* (25)	*tertiu(s)* Aegidius (4)	Aegidius (32)
5	4	Aegidius (25)		Sabatinus (35)
6	5	*alio uno* (25)		Moricus (35)
7	6	Philippus (25)		Ioannes de Capella (35)
8	7	[*certitudo remis-.. sionis...; veniunt... Hispani* (26-27)] *alio bono viro* (29) [*ite...bini et bini* (29)]	*alio bono viro* (7)	*illis undecim*
9-12	8-11	*alii quatuor* (31)	*quatuor* (7	*ipse duodecimus* (46)

The only fact which all three lists have in common is that the Saint had eleven companions when he went to Rome. A point of prime importance for the identity of Philip is the correct translation of the reference to him in *I Celano*, 25: "His autem alio uno apposito, frater Philippus septenarium numerum adimplevit." From the context it is certain that Thomas of Celano meant: after another had joined them, Philip also joined and brought the total number (including Francis) to seven. But Terzi founds his argument for the Rieti Valley origin of Philip on an erroneous reading; see Philip in Part 4 below. Note too that the late *Tres Socii* list does not include Philip among the first six, and in fact does not even name him.

Another source of misinterpretation lies in the difficult distinction between the number of companions and the total number of friars including the founder; for instance, the *septenarium* and *octonarium* of *I Celano*, 25 & 29, refer to the total, whereas the *senarius* and *septenarium* of Bonaventure, III, 4 & 7, explicitly denote only the *filiorum numerus* and *soboles*, i. e. the companions. Translations must be carefully doublechecked on these points, as several contain mistakes, which become evident when one numbers each friar in the margin by hand, adding the successive totals including the Saint.

The names of three of the four last disciples are given only in later sources (AF III,4; MF 8,57): Giovanni di San Costanzo — a locality near the Portiuncula (FNV II,286); Bernardo di Vigilante — Fortini found his father in a document of 1186, and a brother Bonaventura in one of 1235 (FNV II,287); and Barbaro, of whom practically nothing is known (E100: 180n4; cf Ch. 13, Note 9).

The last of the eleven (or twelve in later lists) is variously given as Angelo Tancredi or Sylvester or Morico; see their biographical sketches below.

On all the early companions, apart from Grau's basic study (E112), the new editions of the *Martyrolgium Franciscanum* (E100-E102) contain useful references to sources. It is indeed a pity that the new Italian edition of Léon de Clary's *Auréole séraphique* (E108) is already out of print and has not been translated into any other language.

2. The Favorite Companions

It is an interesting fact, not often brought out, that of the eleven or dozen first companions, only one or two came to rank among the favorite associates of the later years of St. Francis.

Though the *primogenitus* Bernard was certainly a favorite companion, the Poverello found himself obliged quite unwillingly to forego his presence after Bernard had commanded him under holy obedience to scold and correct him harshly whenever they were together (*Fioretti*, III). Peter Catanii was undoubtedly a close friend, but more than once served as the Saint's vicar and hence did not accompany Francis; moreover, he died five and a half years before the latter. Giles, the third of the first identifiable three, was a perfect solitary and is rarely mentioned with Francis after the first year or two.

The four (not three) special or favorite companions were Leo, Rufino, Angelo, and Masseo, whose tombs fittingly cluster around that of the Saint. They probably joined the Order within the first year or two after the approval in Rome in 1209. To them can be added Brothers Pacifico and perhaps Leonardo and Illuminato. On all of them, see the biographical sketches.

Of all the first and favorite companions, only one has been beatified: Blessed Brother Giles. On a movement to beatify the four favorites, see E114.

3. Laicus-clericus

St. Bonaventure (III,10) states that after Pope Innocent III approved the proto-Rule, "*Laicis fratribus omnibus qui servum Dei fuerant comitati fecit coronas parvulas fieri, ut verbum Dei libere praedicarent.*" That sentence has been generally taken to mean that all the non-clerics among the companions were given the clerical tonsure and made clerics. It does not necessarily specify that all eleven companions were lay brothers when they came to Rome; grammatically, it could imply that one or more were already clerics.

The main question, however, is this: was the small tonsure or crown that of clerics; were they really made clerics? The problem arises because there are eight 13th and 14th century texts which describe Brother Giles as *laicus*. Unfortunately this is still another puzzle which has not yet been carefully studied.

Since it is largely a problem in semantics, it must be made clear at the outset that the medieval Latin *clericus* and *laicus* each had two different meanings. The former meant either cleric or educated, while the latter meant either layman or lay brother — or illiterate or uneducated. The situation with regard to the varying types of tonsures used in the Middle Ages is even more confusing; I have yet to find a clear and compete list. But the Cistercian Colomban Bock (E93:398, 406) distinguishes the small crown mentioned by St. Bonaventure from the clerical and the monastic tonsures, which in turn had a variety of sizes and forms in different centuries and countries.

Therefore, while one hesitates to question the opinion of such writers as Van Ortroy (AB 19,1900,133), Paschal Robinson (*The Golden Sayings of Blessed Brother Giles*, p.xx), Abate (MF 60,1960,63-64), and especially the outstanding historian of the Franciscan lay brotherhood, Alessandro da Ripabottoni (E92:232,234), it seems worthwhile to raise the question, in order that it may receive the thorough analysis which it merits (cf E121:48).

Thomas of Celano (*II Celano*, 193) reports that St. Francis instructed the brother who cut his hair not to give him the major clerical crown which as a deacon he would normally wear, because he wanted his simple (lay) brothers to have a share in his head. This seems to imply that they had the *corona parvula* mentioned by St. Bonaventure. (On Francis as deacon, see D97.)

The first text to specify clearly that the companions in Rome were given the clerical tonsure (*clerica*) is a passage in Salimbene's *Chronicle* (A136:289-290): "*Papa Innocentius tertius beato Francisco et sociis suis XII* [sic!] . . . *clericas fecit.*" His testimony certainly carries a heavy weight of authority and could even be considered decisive, since he personally knew at least one of those companions, Brother Bernard (*ibid.* 39); moreover, Fra Salimbene was particularly sensitive on the whole topic of lay brothers, whose dominance when he joined the Order in 1238 he resented bitterly and criticized scathingly over forty years later (*ibid.* 99-104).

The next text affirming the clerical status is found in *Tres Socii*, 52: "*datisque tonsuris beato Francisco et fratribus aliis XI . . . ut scilicet omnes essent clerici dicti fratres XII.*"

If those two texts are correct, how is it then that the following could describe Brother Giles as *laicus*? (1) St. Bonaventure, *Opera Omnia* IX,269. (2) *Chronicle of the 24 Generals*, AF III,81 & (3) AF III, 253. (4) Bartholomew of Pisa, AF IV,213, (5) Little Mss.,

A157:110n219. (6) Thomas of Eccleston, A135:51-52. (7) *Vita B. Aegidii*, in *Acta Sanctorum* (P 1866) XII, Apr. III, p.241: *"fuit enim laicus vel conversus."* (8) Sacro Convento 1350 inventory in F275: III,31. (9) *La Franceschina*, I,262-263: *"non sapeva lettera."* And a 10th text, *ibid.* I,103, calls Bernard *laico*. No doubt some of these texts may have the sense of *"uneducated."* But not all, e. g. those that merely mention his place of burial. They prove that in the 14th century Brother Giles was widely thought of as a lay brother. Hence the problem, which must still be clarified.

4. Biographical Sketches

NOTE: Detailed and complete biographical information about the companions of St. Francis is generally lacking. Years of birth and hence ages at death, and sometimes even date and place of death are often not available. The day given in parentheses is the date of commemoration in the *Martyrologium Franciscanum* (E100).

ANGELO TANCREDI: In 1926 Sacchetti Sassetti, a historian of Rieti, first disclosed some data in 13th-century documents concerning the prominent noble family of Dominus Tancredus and his son Rainaldus (F58:35-38). But Fortini (FNV II,287-296) has discovered in the archives of Assisi documents proving the existence there at the same time of an equally prominent nobleman named Tancredi di Ugone di Tebalduccio; he traces in considerable detail the genealogy of this Tancredi, his four brothers, and their eleven sons and daughters. One of the latter joined the Poor Clares and in 1253 became Abbess of San Damiano. In assuming that Tancredi of Assisi had a son named Angelo, Fortini stresses a list of first friars made by Fra Paolo da Venezia, Bishop of Pozzuoli, who died in 1344 (on him, see CF IX,251). This list (MF 8,57) includes Angelus Tancredi as the eleventh companion and then adds: *"omnes de Asisio."* Then, among other companions such as Rufino and Leo, it mentions Angelus de Reate, *homo curialis*. Consequently, Fortini insists that actually there were two different early friars named Angelo. Moreover, he claims that they are clearly differentiated in the early sources and only confused and combined in later texts, beginning with the *Actus*.

The basic factor which makes this typical conundrum difficult to solve is the complete absence in the archives of both Assisi and Rieti of a single document which explicitly connects the Franciscan Angelo with either Tancredi. And just as Terzi in defending the Rieti tradition (F59:37, 433; C185:29-31) can point to several obvious errors of Fra Paolo, so Fortini can attack the authenticity of that tradition insofar as it relies on the 15th-century *Actus Sancti Francisci in Valle Reatina*

(A222:21, 45). The last reference therein has an interesting original account of Angelo's vocation which quotes St. Francis in the first person, with this unique detail: "*Cum enim semel ad presentiam summi Pontificis vellem accedere iter per civitatem Reate accepi.*" This perhaps valid local tradition, taken with the texts specifying that the knight Angelo was one of the first eleven or twelve companions, suggests the possibility that on their way to Rome in the spring of 1209, Francis and the eleven passed through Rieti and the Saint "drafted" Angelo into God's service then. But in this connection Terzi (F59:252) believes that Angelo joined Francis when the latter, with one companion, preached in the Rieti Valley early in 1209, during the third mission (two-by-two; total eight friars) described in Appendix II, Part 7; thus Terzi rejects this plausible testimony of the local *Actus*.

Pratesi (E117) does not accept Fortini's Assisi Angelo or two Angelo's, and Cambell (A210:414n55) considers Fortini's grounds for the distinction "of small weight." Again a new scientific study of all extant texts will be needed to clarify the probabilities; with the two Tancredi, certainty may be unattainable. Meanwhile, disregarding Angelo's origin and assuming that only one friar is involved, the principal items in his career can be summarized as follows:

Brother Angelo was present at the Sermon to the Birds; visited Cardinal Brancaleone with Francis in Rome in 1223; was with the Saint at La Verna in 1224; accompanied him, perhaps even as personal guardian (F59:439n54), during the stay in Fonte Colombo and Rieti in 1225, and during his last days in Assisi in 1226, when the Saint often had Angelo and Leo sing the Canticle of Brother Sun to him. He recorded his memories of Francis with Leo and Rufino in Greccio in 1246. Was present at the death of St. Clare in 1253. Died about 1258 (February 13); buried near the Saint's tomb. The latter praised the kindness and courtesy of this favorite companion. (See references above and in A210:77; E117; E100:59n4; E112:144.)

BERNARDO DI QUINTAVALLE: Fortini (FNV II,273-276) found documents of 1188 mentioning a Quintavallis Berardelli and of 1204 with a Ioannes Quintavallis, whom he identifies as, respectively, the father and brother of Bernard, proving that the Quintavalle was in this case a personal rather than a place name. A brother Marzio appears in a document of 1232. Bernard's house is first described only in the 16th century.

One of Assisi's leading citizens, he joined Francis on April 16, 1208; accompanied Giles on an early mission to Florence; was appointed leader of the journey to Rome in 1209; founded the first Franciscan house in Bologna; was with Francis when he took Clare to Panzo, and on his trip to France and Spain; remained in or returned to Spain. Primarily a great contemplative, he spent much time in a grotto at the Carceri. Received a special blessing from the dying Francis, who praised his perfect love of poverty. Later reproved Elias for his Cadillac-type palfrey, and to escape persecution spent two years (1238-39) in an isolated hut on Monte Sefro between Camerino and Nocera. Was visited in Siena by Fra Salimbene in 1241. Died at San Francesco in Assisi between 1241 and 1246 (July 10); buried there. (FNV II,273-276; E100:257n7;E112:137.)

ELIAS — ELIA DI ASSISI: Though Salimbene (A136:96) claimed that Elias' father was from Castelbrizi near Bologna and only his mother from Assisi, Fortini (FNV II,300; F233:81) insists that the famous friar came from Brittignano near Assisi; yet Lorenzo di Fonzo (E158: 169) retains Beviglie near Assisi as his place of birth. Born about 1170-1180; served as *scriptor* (notary) and probably studied law in Bologna, after teaching Latin and grammar to boys in Assisi and working at his father's mattress-maker craft. Fortini accepts — and di Fonzo does not reject — his identification as the first consul of Assisi Buonbarone in 1198, and perhaps of Ancona in 1199, as rendering more plausible his later prestige and administrative ability. Fortini (FNV I/1,154) even suggests that Elias was married and father of a son.

Joined the Order between 1210 and 1215. Di Fonzo assumes that he was a cleric. Appointed minister of Syrian Province in 1217; founded friaries in Acre and Damietta; received Caesar of Speyer; returned to Italy with St. Francis in 1220.

Succeeded Peter Catanii as Vicar, 1221-1227; active in shaping the Rule of 1223; promoted missions to England (1224) and Morocco (1227), and developed studies. The dying Founder gave him a special blessing. During John Parenti's generalate 1227-1232, built the Basilica of San Francesco, and completed it during his own generalate 1232-1239, with the first Sacro Convento (only 1/3 the size of the complete structure). Ruled despotically and oppressed several of the Saint's companions (see Bernard above). Re-organized provinces, often dispatching laic visitators to collect funds; favored lay brothers' vocations.

Deposed by Gregory IX in 1239 on complaint of many superiors, retired to Hermitage of Le Celle di Cortona, but soon joined the excommunicated Emperor Frederick II in Pisa. Was twice excommunicated while serving as the latter's advisor 1240-1250; after Frederick's death in 1250, withdrew to Cortona and built the Church of San Francesco there. Died in Cortona on April 22, 1253, reconciled to the Church but not the Order. A little known 13th-century Cortona document claims he was from Orsaia near Cortona (E126:2). (See Ch. 14, Note 16; D62, E3, E154-E167.)

GILES — EGIDIO DI ASSISI: Born of a peasant family about 1190. Joined Francis on April 23, 1208; went with him on the first mission to the Marches of Ancona; to Florence with Bernard; and to Rome in 1209. Then undertook pilgrimages to St. James of Compostella and the Holy Land. Spent about a year alone in Rome. Lived in a grotto at the Carceri. In 1215 assigned to Favarone Hermitage near Perugia. Went on brief, frustrated mission to Tunis in 1217. Was in Rieti in 1225; present at the death of St. Francis, who praised his perfect spirit of contemplation. Retired to Cetona, then in 1234 to Monteripido Hermitage near Perugia. Was visited there by Pope Gregory IX (1234-36) and St. Bonaventure (1260). A great mystic and contemplative, his pithy "Golden Sayings" were collected. Deplored relaxation in the Order. Died at Monteripido on April 22, 1262; buried at San Francesco al Prato in Perugia; but after several moves, since 1937 in the Oratorio di San Bernardino. Cult approved by Pius VI in 1777 (April 23). (See E119-E121; A210:395-410.)

ILLUMINATO: Another case of confusion triply compounded! To an older dispute over the identification of the Illuminato who was with Francis in Egypt and La Verna with a secretary of Brother Elias from Chieti in the Abruzzi who became Provincial of the Umbrian Province and then Bishop of Assisi in 1273-1282 — now disproved — another minor tug-of-war has lately arisen between Fortini and Terzi over the region of origin of the first Illuminato: Assisi or Rieti. Fortini (FNV II,303-306) claims that the *ab* Arce in some texts proves that the friar's home was the district of Arce on the plain near the Portiuncula where the leprosarium of San Rufino d'Arce was located. But Terzi (C59: 431, 437; C185:31-32) stresses the other texts which have *de Reate*; insists that even the Arce derives from the Rocca Accarina (Arx - Arce) near Terni where the friar's family owned land, though residing in Rieti, as proved by the latter's Porta Accarana; and finally he asserts that a man from near Assisi would not be identified by the name of a mere tract inhabited only by persons afflicted with leprosy. Involved in the dispute is also a purported document of 1238 said to be signed by Brother Elias which Fortini considers a 16th-century "sophistication." Whether from Assisi or Rieti, Brother Illuminato supplied St. Bonaventure with valuable information about the visit of St. Francis to the Sultan and about the Stigmata. But where and when he died is uncertain: in Assisi or Mirepoix near Toulouse, France, about 1266 (March 5). (See the references above and E100:168n3.)

JOHN OF CAPPELLA – GIOVANNI DELLA CAPPELLA: As
the traditional Franciscan Judas, he soon acquired an expanding legend which makes it almost impossible to distinguish fact from fiction
(E112:140). Fortini (FNV II,283) believes that he belonged to the
same noble family as a notary Dominus Petrus Iohannis de Cappella
of Assisi mentioned in a document of 1297. But Abate (E215:12n2)
connects the name rather with the place of origin of the architect of
San Francesco in 1253 Filippo da Campello. Brother Jordan of Giano (Giano, n13; A133:13) also has de Conpello, i. e. the village of
Campello a few miles north of Spoleto, across the valley from Giano.
No one seems to have brought out the fact that Thomas of Celano
indirectly identifies the infamous Giovanni as the *alio uno* or fifth
companion in *I Celano*, 25 (see the list in Part 1 above), for that
"other one" is the only one of the first eleven whom Thomas fails to
characterize as good or holy. As to his sad career, we can, only list uncritically the principal charges against him appearing in later sources.
He was a procurator, dealt too much with seculars, became relaxed in
discipline, was often reproved by St. Francis; was the first to wear a
hat and to leave the Order. He then founded his own Order of men
and women, including leprosy patients, sought but failed to obtain the
Holy See's approval; contracted leprosy, bore it without patience, and
before dying by hanging like Judas, stole the balsam set aside to em-
balm the body of St. Francis. (AF I,5; AF II,6; AF III,4, 668; AF
IV,178, 193; 440; AF V,176; AFH 1,101; *Actus*, XXXV; A229:I,50;
II,377.)

JUNIPER – GINEPRO DI ASSISI: Joined the Order about 1210.
Sent by St. Francis to found friaries in Gualdo Tadino and Viterbo.
Accompanied him on a journey to Rome and Naples. Had an almost
Slavic cult of the humiliated Christ after a decisive mystical experi-
ence reported only in *La Franceschina* (A229:II,201; English tr. in
A166:230). Francis praised his perfect patience and self-contempt
and desire to imitate Christ "*per viam crucis*." Consoled St. Clare
when she was dying. Died in Rome in 1258 (Jan. 4). (AF III,54-67;
A210:410-414; A229:II,197-208; E100:7n7; E127-E129.)

LEO – LEONE DI ASSISI: Ordained priest probably just before or
after joining the Order in 1210. Became the confessor, secretary, and
constant companion of Francis in his last years. The Saint praised his
great simplicity and purity of soul, calling him Frate Peccorella or
Pecorone, perhaps partly because Leo's head was surprisingly large; cf
report of examination of his remains in 1755 in E114:644.
    In 1246 at Greccio recorded his memories with Rufino and Angelo.

Also wrote lives of Giles (E166:241-258, 348) and Bernard. Probably wrote or inspired the oldest parts of *The Mirror of Perfection* and the *Legenda Antiqua* of Perugia. Was sent by the Poor Clares of San Damiano with a message to St. Bonaventure at La Verna in 1259(?). Spent his last years in Assisi; was visited by Salimbene, James of Massa (a principal source of the *Actus*), and the Spiritual leader Angelo Clareno. Died in Assisi in 1278? (November 15); buried near the tomb of St. Francis. (AF III,67-74; A210:78; E100:441n4; E130.)

LEONARDO DI ASSISI: According to Fortini (FNV II,137-146), this friar was, as a layman, Leonardo di Gislerio, one of the lords of the castle of Sassorosso, who is mentioned, with his brothers, father, and uncles, in many documents in the Assisi archives showing that their aristocratic family, like that of St. Clare (see Appendix VI, Part 2), took refuge in Perugia in 1200, when the people of Assisi destroyed their feudal castles and city homes. Consequently it would appear probable that Leonardo in November, 1202, fought in the Battle of Collestrada against Francis and his fellow-soldiers. Leonardo di Gislerio was the father of three sons and one daughter, Filippa, who joined St. Clare at San Damiano in about 1215. As her father's name is not mentioned in archival documents after February, 1215, he may have become a Franciscan in that same year or soon afterward. Apart from the significant anecdote stressing his noble rank in the world (see p. 245-246), we know only that this mature knight was one of the friars chosen by the Saint to travel with him to Egypt, and that Leonardo testified at his spiritual Father's canonization and is our source for the more authentic version of the famous anecdote of the Perfect Joy (see Ch. 13, Note 1). He died about 1230 (June 2). (E100:204n5; AFH 20, 107; FNV II, 137-146.)

MASSEO DI MARIGNANO: Though Ubertino da Casale who knew him (AFH 1,267) calls him a *"miles de Perusio,"* Fortini (FNV II, 298-299) insists that the Marignano was a now forgotten locality near Assisi. Tall and handsome, Masseo joined Francis about 1210 and often traveled with him. Was present in Perugia at the granting of the Portiuncula Indulgence in 1216. Francis praised his pleasant demeanor, common sense, and inspiring speech. He spent much time in a grotto at the Carceri and at the Hermitage of Cibòttola west of Perugia. Author of some prayers and reflections discovered but not yet published by Abate (MF 56,344n2; cf A189:112-114). Died in Assisi in 1280 (Nov. 17); buried near the tomb of St. Francis. (AF III,115-121; E100:444n5; FNV II, 298; III, 461.)

MORICO: Fortini (FNV II,282) distinguishes between the frater Moricus parvus who was among the first companions and the Morico mentioned in *Bonaventure, IV,* 8 as being a former Crosier and apparently joining the Order after the vocation of St. Clare. This distinction is also made in AF III,252-253. According to *La Franceschina* (A229:I,64; II,274), combining the two, Morico became the twelfth companion at Rivo Torto when Francis and the eleven returned from Rome. He may have been from Spello (MF 17,156). One Moricus is said to have died in Orvieto, while the other – or the same? – died in Assisi about 1236 (March 30). (E100:118n3.)

PACIFICO: Was *not* named Divini; not to be confused (cf F132: 72n239) with the Brother Pacifico of *Fioretti,* XLVI; and of course not with the Franciscan St. Pacifico Divini of San Severino who died in 1721. Of his origin we know only that he was from the Marches. Cosmo (E131) stresses the immorality of the *giulari;* but did not use the useful materials on the troubadours in the Marches listed by Vitaletti in *Archivum Romanicum* 3(1919)434; cf Ch. 1, Note 21. Historians cannot ascertain whether Pacifico was "crowned king of verses" by Henry VI, Otto IV, or Frederick II, as no non-Franciscan source mentions him. An identification with a Guglielmo di Lisciano is tenuous (F132:73).

Converted by St. Francis while visiting a relative at the Benedictine convent of San Salvatore di Colpersito on a hill close to San Severino, whose nuns became Poor Clares. According to *II Celano,* 106, the Saint "had come there to visit his daughters." But the conversion of Pacifico must be assigned to not later than 1215 because of his presence at San Pietro di Bovara near Trevi with Francis (in connection with the empty-throne-of-Lucifer vision) before Trevi was rebuilt in that year (cf A249:482; F313). Thus Thomas of Celano is saying that the nuns were already Poor Clares in 1215, only three years after St. Clare's vocation; but the first archival document referring to them as such is dated 1223; here is another early Franciscan conundrum.

Pacifico must have been quite mature, if not elderly, when converted, because in 1217 Francis appointed him first Provincial in France, where he served until 1223 (AFH 10, 290-294). He was perhaps in Rieti in 1225 (E131a; disputed by Terzi, F59:25); was with the Saint in Siena in 1226, while serving as Visitator General of the Poor Clares (AFH 15, 75). In 1227 Gregory IX commended him to the Poor Clares of Siena. Soon afterward he returned to France and died at Lens in Belgium about 1230 (July 10). (Besides above references, see E100:257n6; F132:69-73; FNV 1/2,33-38; MGH-SS XXII, 492.)

PETER CATANII – PIETRO DI CATANIO: Fortini (FNV II, 276-280) has traced the family of a Catanio di Guiduccio in the Assisi archives; so Faloci Pulignani (MF 14, 12-14) probably erred in identifying Peter with the Pecciaroni family of Gualdo Cattaneo near Bevagna. However, the historian of Assisi has not eliminated all the confusion surrounding the question as to whether Peter was a canon of San Rufino. Jordan the chronicler, who knew him (Giano, n11), calls him a doctor of law, and reports that St. Francis addressed him as *dominus*, thus refuting the statement in *Anonymus Perusinus*, 11, that neither Bernard, Peter, or Francis knew how to read well, changed in *Tres Socii*, 28, to "not knowing how to find in the Gospels the passage about renouncing the world." Peter is called a canon of the cathedral in Assisi by the *Chronicle of the 24 Generals* (AF III,4) and the Codex S. Antonii de Urbe (A220:378), both late sources. But he is also described as *Sancti Rufini canonico* in an important early 14th-century lectionary of the Duomo Chapter containing a 13th-century Passion of St. Rufino describing the translation of his remains from the old to the new church of that Saint in 1212. Now although Fortini demonstrates conclusively that its references to many contemporary persons are authentic, he claims that the mention of Peter Catanii as a canon was interpolated, because his name is not found in lists of the canons (FNV II,278-279, 367-368; III, 34-35, 234-237). Moreover, no doubt by oversight, in his new biography (FNV 1/2,107) Fortini also calls him a former canon of San Rufino. Obviously, the lectionary needs a thorough scientific study, as it is also a basic source for the legend of St. Rufino and the history of the cathedral, and the latter in turn is decisive for the problem of the home of St. Clare (cf Ch. 8, Note 2).

Peter Catanii joined Francis with Bernard on April 16, 1208. He served as vicar during the Saint's early absences, and accompanied him to Egypt and Syria in 1219/20. Appointed vicar when Francis resigned his office in 1220 (or 1218?; cf Ch. 14, Note 17). Died at the Portiuncula on March 10, 1221. (E100:91n4; E112:138; & above refs.)

PHILIP – FILIPPO LONGO: The major recent controversy involving the companions has been one between Fortini and Terzi regarding Brother Philip. To understand it, the reader must note carefully that in our list of first companions at the beginning of this Appendix Thomas of Celano clearly specifies that Philip was the *sixth* to join Francis, making a total of seven friars including the Saint, and also that Philip joined *before* the *certitudo remissionis*; after which another good man became the seventh disciple (total eight), and then the eight set out on a mission two by two.

Unfortunately, Terzi (F59:223-225, 245, 248-251, 429-430; C185: 27-29; F60:108-109; C9:46-47) has misread *I Celano*, 25 & 29, and claims that Philip was the seventh disciple who joined Francis between the remission of sins at Poggio Bustone and the mission of the eight, and therefore that Philip came from the Valley of Rieti (see Appendix II, Part 7 for the sequence of the three early missions and for the stay at Poggio Bustone). Wadding (*Annales*, 1209n28) has the same error, perhaps from Henri d'Avranches (AF X, 438) and Bernard of Bessa (AF III,668), both of whom count Philip as the seventh disciple, perhaps induced into confusion either by the forgotten unknown first follower of *I Celano*, 24, or by a careless reading of Friar Thomas' text. But until proved wrong, the order of the *Vita Prima* must obviously be accepted as the primary authority, and it definitely specifies that Philip joined the Order before the remission of sins, which means before the mission to the Valley of Rieti. Consequently Brother Philip did not come from that Valley, but almost certainly from Assisi, as stated by the 14th-century text of Fra Paolo da Venezia (MF 8, 57). A minor argument against the Rieti Valley origin of Philip is that the 15th-century *Actus S. Francisci in Valle Reatina* (A222) fails to claim him as a native son.

Fortini (FNV II,283-285) insists on the Assisi origin of Philip, and despite the fact (stressed by Terzi) that the word *longus* or *Longus* is added to his name only in later texts, claims that he was the son of a man named Longus, whose two other sons, Blasius Longus and Iohannes Longus appear, respectively, in documents of 1201 and 1215, with a grandson Ugo in 1233. But, as usual, there is no document explicitly linking the friar with the family. The nickname *longus* became a surname during the 13th century, but the small "l" in several codices suggests that it may in this case have still been an adjective, as with *Moricus parvus*. The late *Chronicle of the 24 Generals* (AF III,632) Appendix II, quoting the Portiuncula Indulgence testimony of Michele Bernarducci, lists *fratrem Philippum Longum de costa sancti Savini* (Severini in the earlier *Tractatus*, F247:lxxxii), which Fortini identifies as a section of the commune of Assisi along the slope of Monte Subasio near San Benedetto. Terzi, however, retorts that it was the village of Castro San Savini near Rieti. The Brother Philip of Adria (Atri) or Andria mentioned in the Legend and Process of St. Clare may have been from the Abruzzi or Apulia, unless the word was Antria near Perugia or Mandria near Fortini's Costa San Savini (FNV II,284).

After joining Francis as sixth companion in the summer or fall of 1208, Philip accompanied him to the Rieti Valley and in 1209 to Rome. Preached in the Marches around 1213 (*Fioretti*, XLV). Served as Visitator of the Poor Clares in 1219/20 and again 1228-1246. Died in Perugia (rather than at Cahors in France) about 1259 (March 14). (E100:96n5; E112:142; FS 35, 202n117; A229:I,478n1; & refs. above.)

RUFINO: First cousin of St. Clare (see Chart, p. 423), small & delicate, joined Francis about 1210. A great contemplative, he had a grotto at the Carceri. The Poverello praised his constant spirit of prayer and considered him a saint. Was at La Verna with Francis in 1224, as one of his favorite companions. In 1246 at Greccio recorded his memories with Leo and Angelo. Was still living in 1278; died soon afterward (November 14); buried near the Saint's tomb. (FNV II,383-387; E100:440n4; AFH 46, 20.)

SYLVESTER — SILVESTRO: Elderly canon of San Rufino when he joined Francis in 1209/10, after the return from Rome, as the first priest in the Order. Also a contemplative with a grotto at the Carceri, to whom (with Clare) the Saint turned for divine guidance as to living a life of prayer or preaching. Accompanied Francis to Arezzo in 1217. Died in Assisi about 1240 (March 4). (FNV II,280-281; E100:83n5.)

Appendix VIII
The Canticle of Brother Sun

Apart from the colossal controversy over the Home of St. Francis (treated in Appendix V), no other subject has aroused so much debate in recent years as the famous Canticle of Brother Sun. As Sabatelli has pointed out in his excellent survey of literary studies of the poem (C157), this extraordinary interest proves that the living influence of the Canticle is more effective in our times than ever, because it is a lyrical expression of a profound mystical experience of one of the most appealing and popular Saints "in the state of poetic grace."

The authenticity and authorship problems have long been settled. And so are those of textual criticism and philology after Branca's edition in 1948 (C146). The thoroughly biblical sources or *humus*, deriving from the liturgy and especially the breviary, have been explored and listed· obviously the principal models are the Canticle of the Three Youths (Daniel 3:52-90) and Psalm 148, as well as numerous passages in Ecclesiasticus and a few in the Apocalypse (see Branca's Appendix 1; cf Getto, C150:38-41).

Apparently no one has yet noticed a possible indirect liturgical source in a remarkable 11th-century Advent hymn beginning *Jubilemus omnes* which urges all men to rejoice over all God's creation, specifying the sun, moon, stars, air, winds, etc. This "proto-Franciscan" hymn is found in some old Roman-French missals and is quoted in Dom Prosper Guéranger's *L'Année liturgique, L'Avent* (P 1900) 237.

The two main points of contention regarding the Canticle today are: the precise meaning of the often repeated *per*, on which depends the religious and psychological essence of the whole poem; and the time and especially the place of its composition. The principal arguments

441

on both sides of these two controversies will be summarized and ana-
lyzed in this Appendix. For the Bibliography of the first, see C144-
C159, and of the second C160-C186. An English translation of the
Canticle appears on p. 321, and Branca's Italian text in Part 3 of this
Appendix.

1. Meaning

Here the question at issue is simple and basic: did St. Francis mean:
"Be praised, my Lord, for Brother Sun... for Sister Moon... for
Brother Wind . . . for those who forgive . . . for our Sister Bodily
Death," or did he mean: "Be praised, my Lord, by Brother Sun . . . by
Sister Moon. . . by our Sister Bodily Death. . . "? Or was his mean-
ing: "Be praised . . . through Brother Sun . . . through Sister Death
. . ."? All three senses of the Italian *per* have been proposed and de-
fended by various scholars. All agree that in the early thirteenth cen-
tury *per* was used in Italy as the equivalent of the French *par* and
pour; at the end of the century Dante used *per* in both senses.

The traditional meaning for the last several centuries had been *per-
for*, with very rare exceptions (cf CF 3,453*). Luigi Foscolo Benedetto was the first modern critic to make a serious plea for *per-by*, in
his article in Pegaso in 1930 (C144) and then in his important book
(C145) in 1941, thus starting a controversy which has involved over
a score of scholars during the past twenty years.

To clarify frequently used terms, we must note that *per-for* (or on
account of, *propter*) is called the causal sense, *per-by* the sense of
agent, and *per-through* the instrumental sense; in Italian: *causale,
agente, strumentale*.

The reader may also note that the *per* in question is found in seven
lines of the Canticle: lines 10, 12, 15, 17, 20, 23, & 27. But *per*
also appears in three others lines; in lines 7, 14, & 18, it has the meaning "by" or "through." The argument concerns only the first seven instances.

Turning to the early sources in seeking the meaning in the poet's
mind, we find that they give substantial grounds for both interpretations, i. e. *per-for* and *per-by*.

First of all, the Saint himself wrote in his Letter to All the Faithful
(*Opuscula*, 94-95): "Let every creature which is in the sky and on
earth and in the sea and in the depths render praise . . . to God,"
which is adapted from Apocalypse 5:13. So too these words at the beginning of Chapter 23 of the Rule of 1221 remind us of the Canticle's
first lines: *Omnipotens, altissime . . . Domine . . . propter temetipsum
gratias agimus tibi"* (ibid, 57). Incidentally, Benedetto found the *al-
tissimus* repeated 23 times and the *omnipotens* 19 times in the Opus-

cula (C145:55). But no one has yet made a scientific study of the use of the Latin *per* in the two *Legendae* of Thomas of Celano and the two other fundamental sources for the Canticle: the *Speculum Perfectionis* and the *Legenda Antiqua* of Perugia. In this connection too the use of the Latin *per* in the liturgy needs a more systematic study. Pagliaro (C154), followed by Monteverdi (C153), favors the instrumental per-through of the Preface of the Mass, but pays no attention to the other relevant per-by examples that appear in the Creed and the two Prayers of Blessing just before the Our Father.

Friar Thomas of Celano is the principal authority for the per-by thesis. It is perfectly clear from the following passages that he interpreted the Canticle's *per* in that sense. The only question is whether Thomas' interpretation was the same as the Saint's. According to the first biographer, when Francis "found an abundance of flowers, he would invite them to praise the Lord. . . Likewise he would urge. . . earth and fire, air and wind to love God and serve Him willingly" (*I Celano*, 81). Referring more specifically to the Canticle, Thomas wrote: "For he invited all creatures to praise God, and by means of certain words which he had once composed, he used to exhort them to love God. And even death itself . . . he would urge to give praise . . ." (*II Celano*, 217). And after describing the mystical experience of the promise of eternal life, Thomas added: "It was then that he composed certain Praises of the Creatures and incited them to praise the Creator" (*II Celano*, 213). In general terms, St. Bonaventure (IX,1) also reports that Francis urged all created things to praise the Lord.

Two minor arguments for the per-by interpretation are the facts that St. Francis used to express himself in (imperfect) French in moments of exaltation (hence per-par), and that the friar of Rieti who wrote the *Actus S. Francisci in Valle Reatina* (A222:60) in 1416 substituted *da* for most of the *per* in his transcription of the Canticle (which incidentally ends with five lines that do not appear in any other text).

Owing to his eminent authority as our earliest and most reliable source, the testimony of Thomas of Celano would be conclusive if we did not happen to have two other works claiming to originate with Brother Leo and the favorite companions of the Saint's last years which not only provide clear textual evidence in favor of the per-for thesis, but also supply a plausible psychological-religious motivation and background for it.

The *Speculum Perfectionis* of Sabatier and Delorme's *Legenda Antiqua* of Perugia, usually in almost identical words, refer to the Canticle in no less than six different passages. Scholars agree today that these two works, though actually compiled around 1310-1320, contain some texts which, despite later editing, can with probability be traced back to Brother Leo, either in his old age or to his memories and those of Brothers Angelo and Rufino recorded at Greccio in 1246. Consequently, the authority of these passages for the origin and meaning of the Canticle must be considered almost equal to that of Thomas of Celano from the point of view of source criticism, and definitely superior, insofar as authentic, from the point of view of intimate knowledge of the events and the mind of Francis.

Concerning the Saint's motivation in composing the Canticle, they state (*Speculum*, 100; *Legenda Antiqua*, 43; quoting the latter) that on the morning after he had been told by God to rejoice in his sufferings over the great treasure of eternal life "as though you were already in My Kingdom," the Poverello said to his companions: "I must now rejoice very much . . . and always give thanks to" the Holy Trinity for that grace. "So for His praise and my consolation and the edification of others I wish to make a new Praise of the Lord concerning His creatures, which we use every day and without which we cannot live and in which the human race greatly offends the Creator, and every day we are ungrateful for such a grace, because we do not praise our Creator and the Giver of all good things for it as we should."

This crucial passage unquestionably shows that for the writer the entire Canticle was meant to be a song of praise to God in gratitude for His gifts to man, i.e. for the sun, the moon, the stars, the wind and air and weather, for water and fire and the earth with its flowers and plants. This sense of per-for is moreover explicitly specified a few lines later (*Legenda Antiqua*, 43; but *Speculum*, 119): "For to the Praises of the Lord which he made, that is, *Altissimo, omnipotente*. . . he gave a title, calling them the Canticle of Brother Sun, which is more beautiful than all other creatures and can better be compared to God. So he used to say: 'In the morning when the sun rises, every man should praise God who created it, because it brings the light of day to our eyes; and in the evening when it is dark, all men should praise God on account of (*propter*) that other creature, Brother Fire . . .' " Obviously this sense of *propter* corresponds to our "for," and not to either "by" or "through."

Furthermore, the idea that the creatures rather than men are called to praise God in the Canticle is contradicted by this passage (*Speculum*, 118; *Legenda Antiqua*, 51): "On account of the many consolations which he had and used to have from the creatures of God, a short while before his death he composed and made certain Praises of the Lord in order to inspire the hearts of people who heard them to praise God and in order that God be praised by all (or by men) for (or in) His creatures."

The other three passages (*Speculum*, 101, & *Legenda Antiqua*, 44 – on the bishop and podestà; *Speculum*, 123, & *Legenda Antiqua*, 100 – on Sister Death; and *Speculum*, 90, & *Legenda Antiqua*, 45 – a passing mention) do not help to clarify the meaning of *per*.

Thus we find Brother Leo and his friends (as reported in these relatively late and somewhat rewritten sources) specifying that Francis meant: "Be praised, my Lord, for Brother Sun," etc.; while their contemporary Thomas of Celano clearly understood the same words to mean. "Be praised . . . by Brother Sun" Both interpretations, therefore, can be based on more or less equal authorities. The weight of textual authenticity may favor Friar Thomas, but the intimacy of Leo and his friends with the Saint tends to guarantee the correctness of their interpretation, especially inasmuch as it supplies the basic motivation of the mystical experience underlying the Canticle's creation, which Thomas, incidentally, corroborated in a few words (*II Celano*, 213).

The important point to note, therefore, is that *both* interpretations were current in the 13th century, just as the word *per* then had both meanings. And while modern scholars have argued for one meaning or the other – and some have elaborated still a third sense: the instrumental *per*-through – more than one has come to the conclusion that St. Francis, as a poet and a mystic, may well have had both senses in mind, and that all three senses can be harmonized with his spiritual outlook.

Such being the case, the English translation in this book simply incorporates both the "by" and the "for," leaving the reader free – as does the evidence – to choose the interpretation which he prefers.

For indications of the opinions of some leading scholars, see the indispensable article by Sabatelli (C157), the reviews in CF XI, 63-68, and the brief annotations in the Bibliography, C144-C159. Fortini (FNV II,542) does not analyze the problem and does not express a preference.

2. Where Composed

Just as the visitor to Assisi today may find three different sites pointed out as that of the home of Pietro di Bernardone – two of which may be correct, as shown in Appendix V – so too the traveler in Franciscan Central Italy may be told that the Canticle of Brother Sun was composed by St. Francis at San Damiano near Assisi or at Santa Maria Maggiore, the Vescovado or palace of the bishop of Assisi, or 50 miles to the south at La Foresta in the Valley of Rieti; and to make matters still more bewildering, in Rieti he may be informed that the vineyard and church of San Fabiano was not, as claimed, at La Foresta four miles away, but on a hill just outside the city.

The first attack on the traditional identifications of these sites came in 1926, when Prof. Angelo Sacchetti Sassetti of Rieti in his *Anecdota franciscana reatina* (C173; F58) denied the claim of La Foresta as San Fabiano, in favor of Campomoro on the hill near Rieti. However, the subsequent argument over La Foresta (C166; C174) did not involve the Canticle until Benedetto in 1941 (C162) first advanced the novel suggestion that it was composed not at San Damiano but at San Fabiano. That surprising claim was to find its most eloquent and tenacious advocate in the retired Bishop Arduino Terzi, OFM, a native son of the Rieti area, who in 1953 devoted almost 150 pages in his monumental *Memorie* (C181; F59) to it, and has now written about 500 pages in all on this subject (C181-C186).

While Sacchetti Sassetti continued to study the history of La Foresta and Campomoro in six brochures (C175-C180), Fortini of course came to the defense of San Damiano (C167; C168). And in 1956 Abate increased the general confusion by contributing an 85-page article (C160) which claimed that the Canticle was probably composed neither at San Damiano nor in the Valley of Rieti but in the bishop's palace in Assisi. Since then, both Terzi (C183) and Fortini (C169; C170, the latter repeats and extends C167-C169) have criticized Abate's hypothesis. Marino Bigaroni, OFM, also wrote a book (C164) in defense of San Damiano against Msgr. Terzi's claims, but he does not deal with Abate's work as the two were writing at the same time.

We shall now summarize only the principal arguments put forth by these scholars in their nearly 1000-page controversy over one of the most important incidents in the life of St. Francis. But first we must refer the reader to the analysis of the chronological aspect of the problem which was treated in Appendix II, Part 12, and which is essential to an understanding of the events.

(a) The Texts

Although Thomas of Celano mentions the actual composition of the Canticle (*II Celano*, 213), neither he nor St. Bonaventure specifies where Francis was at the time. Probably the earliest text giving that crucial detail is the title affixed to the Canticle in the famous Assisi Biblioteca Comunale Manuscript 338, which reads: *Incipiuntur Laudes creaturarum quas fecit beatus Franciscus ad laudem et honorem Dei, cum esset infirmus apud Sanctum Damianum.*" Naturally the disputing scholars have had a good argument over the date of this manuscript, or rather of this particular part of it; for their studies, see C160: 336-343 (Abate), FNV II,517-521 (Fortini), C183:159-174 (Terzi),

and C163:57-68 & 126-128 (Bigaroni); cf Esser's earlier monograph
A47. The dates range all the way from about 1250 to the first third
of the 14th century. Naturally the opponents of the San Damiano thesis, such as Terzi and Abate, favor the latest possible dating. Abate
also believes it was written by a foreigner, probably a German, because of its many *ka* and *ke*, but Fortini replies that those spellings are
often found in the archives and *laudesi* texts of Assisi in the 13th century. Only an expert paleographer can express an opinion on such a
technical question as the date of this text. But it would seem probable
that its reference to San Damiano can be taken as representing the
tradition current in Assisi in the second half of the 13th century.

   Apart from this codex, the only early texts specifying San Damiano
are those valuable yet relatively late compilations, the *Speculum Perfectionis* of Sabatier and the *Legenda Antiqua* of Perugia published
by Delorme. Whereas the former treats of the circumstances surrounding the composition of the Canticle in four chapters, of which only
two are consecutive (100, 101, 90, 115), the latter presents a unified
and organic narration in five consecutive chapters (42/2-46) covering
all the events involved: Francis is confined to a small cell near San
Damiano by quasi-blindness for over fifty days; Elias persuades him
to accept medical treatment, but at first it is too cold; the Saint is be-
set by hordes of fieldmice, receives the assurance of eternal life, and
composes the Canticle, then adds the verses which reconcile the feuding bishop and podestà; he also composes some other Praises of God
for St. Clare and her Sisters, whom he is unable to visit; and finally,
with better weather, he leaves on horseback for Fonte Colombo. Although most of these events are described in both works in almost the
same words, only the *Legenda Antiqua* contains some extremely important lines in ch. 42, second half (to be clearly distinguished from
the first half referring to the Saint's meeting with Cardinal Hugolin in
Rieti later that year), and in the first part of ch. 46. For the convenience of the reader, especially those who can only consult the *Legenda*
in the AFH edition with its different numbering of the chapters, we
append this outline of those chapters in the *Speculum* and both editions of the *Legenda*, quoting the latter's all important references to
time and place:

EVENT	SPECULUM (A151-A152)	LEGENDA AFH (A148)	ed. Paris
duobus annis ante obitum suum . . . valde infirmus . . . moraretur in cellula . . . apud Sanctum Damianum . . . magnum frigus . . .	—	77	42/2
ibi . . . 50 dies et plus . . . tot mures . . . 'Frater . . . iubila . . . ac si iam esses in regno meo' . . . mane . . . fecit . . . Canticum fr. solis	100	78	43
Eodem tempore . . . episcopus	101	79	44
illis diebus et in eodem loco . . . fecit . . . sancta verba cum cantu pro consolatione dominarum pauperum . . .	90	80	45
dum appropinquaret tempus congruum . . . discessit B. F. de loco illo . . . et perduxerunt eum socii . . . apud . . . Fon. Col.	— (cf 115)	81	46

Thus it is quite clear that, according to the *Legenda Antiqua*, the Saint resided over 50 days in a cell near San Damiano, composed the Canticle there, presumably added the verses for the bishop and podestà while still there, then wrote some verses there for St. Clare, and departed from there for the Rieti Valley. Another important detail which appears only in the *Legenda*, 43, is the description of the *cellula* as not only *facta ex storiis* (also in *Speculum*, 100, with *de* instead of *ex*), but as *facta . . . ex una parte illius domus*, i.e. the house of the chaplain and questing brothers. This matter of the house and cell will be treated below in connection with Abate's thesis favoring the bishop's palace. Incidentally, Abate's Sarnano manuscript (A147) contains most, but not this part of the *Legenda*.

Of course the direct dependence of the San Damiano thesis on the *Legenda Antiqua* and the *Speculum Perfectionis* has resulted in a welcome, though partisan, re-examination of their value as historical sources. The general tendency of each disputant is naturally to shape his appraisal to their relative degree of support to his particular thesis. Thus Fortini perhaps overstresses their authenticity, and Terzi and Abate, while making full use of their rich factual data, tend to discount their reliability.

Lastly, the visit of St. Francis to San Damiano and his stay there owing to illness is also described, without reference to the Canticle, in the *Actus*, 21 (and *Fioretti*, XIX). Despite the fact that this work is the latest in date and known to be inaccurate in specific details even when correct in substance, Fortini and Terzi persist in trying to reconcile its account with those of the *Speculum* and *Legenda Antiqua*. Abate (C160:361) and Bigaroni (C164:106) have noted that the *Actus* version is both confused and confusing.

(b) The Rieti Valley Thesis

Perhaps never before in the history of modern scholarship has an important event in the life of a major Saint been challenged with such a flimsy textual basis as the claim of Benedetto and Terzi that all the references to Assisi and San Damiano in the Codex 338, *Legenda Antiqua*, *Speculum*, and *Actus* in connection with the Canticle are nothing more than copyists' multiple errors which really should read in each case Rieti or San Fabiano. And what are their grounds for labeling all these passages as errors — in over twenty extant manuscripts of the *Speculum* and dozens of the *Actus*? The answer to that question is simply incredible, yet true: the textual foundation of their whole theory is a passing reference in an article by I. della Giovanna in 1895 to a reading of "*S. Fabiano*" instead of San Damiano in one passage in two manuscripts of an Italian translation of the *Speculum Perfectionis* dated 1503 (A208:529). In 1941, when Benedetto first advanced this insecure hypothesis, the manuscripts could not be examined owing to war conditions. But when they were checked, after Terzi in 1953 built his elaborate claim on them, in each case it was discovered that the reading was actually San Damiano! Facsimiles of the passages have been printed by Bigaroni (C164: opp. 64 & 128); for discussion, see FNV II,505, and C160:368.

Consequently, the whole case for the Rieti Valley origin of the Canticle simply has no textual basis whatsoever. And with it, Msgr. Terzi's complicated secondary topographical and chronological arguments concerning the Canticle's composition in his region inevitably crumble as well, leaving, however, a number of other points connected with the Saint's activities in 1225 still to be extracted from the murky chiaroscuro in which the recent controversies have enveloped them.

(c) The Problem of San Fabiano

Foremost among those points is the precise location of the small church of San Fabiano, where St. Francis restored the poor priest's trampled vineyard, as narrated in *Speculum*, 104; *Legenda Antiqua*, 25 (AFH n60); & *Actus*, 21 (*Fioretti*, XIX). Since his first book on the subject in 1926 (C173), Sacchetti Sassetti has insisted that the archives of Rieti mention only a church of San Fabiano (sometimes Flaviano) in the 13th and 14th centuries at a site known as Campomoro on a small hill, *collis S. Fabiani*, only a few hundred yards to the southeast of the city. Regarding the church of Santa Maria della Foresta, in a vale on a hill four miles north of Rieti, he has shown that the earliest documents mentioning it, at the beginning of the 14th century, do not refer to a church of San Fabiano. And whereas there was after 1280 a convent of Poor Clares at Campomoro, La Foresta was inhabited by a few hermits (not Clareni), was deeded by one of them in 1346 to the bishop, seems then to have been abandoned until some Clareni appear there in 1513; finally it was transferred to the Roman Province of the Order of Friars Minor by the bishop in 1584. The first writer to identify La Foresta as the site of the vineyard was the Franciscan Minister General Francisco Gonzaga in his 1587 *De origine Seraphicae Religionis*, followed by Wadding in his *Annales*. According to Sacchetti Sassetti, those historians were induced into error by the fact that in 1554 the Poor Clares abandoned their convent at Campomoro for a new one within the city, the chapel of which was also called San Fabiano. As the *Actus* gives the distance between Rieti and the vineyard church as *duo milliaria* (two leagues), whereas the other sources just have *prope*, perhaps Gonzaga and Wadding, seeing that La Foresta was about four miles away and the church of San Fabiano was in their time inside the city, assumed that the vineyard had been at La Foresta. For Sacchetti Sassetti's thesis as summarized here, see F58:7-32; for his later contributions, mostly on the subsequent history of both sites, see C174-C180. In 1962 he repeated his claim for Campomoro as the site of the vineyard in a letter-to-the-editor published in *Storia illustrata* 6(1962)n6. But since 1926, only Bughetti (AFH 20,425) among the OFM appears to have accepted his conclusion that La Foresta was not San Fabiano.

To prove that it was, one would have to find there a church or chapel dedicated to San Fabiano, the "incomparable" layman elected Pope about 236, who died as a martyr in 250 (January 20). When Sacchetti Sassetti first wrote in 1926 and when Benedetto claimed in 1941 that the Canticle was composed at San Fabiano-Campomoro, there was no explicit documentary or archaeological evidence of such a church at La Foresta. But Bishop Terzi has proved himself a master excavator and archaeologist in a series of discoveries at the four hermitages of St Francis in the Rieti Valley. And in 1947 at La Foresta, assisted by Padre Goffredo Ligori, OFM, he made an opening in the wall of the church of Santa Maria by the altar of St. Francis, and beyond the wall they found a chapel decorated by mural paintings, with a 12th-century altar, (F59:278). The central figure in the apse was clearly Christ seated on a throne, with two Saints on each side. According to Terzi (F59:262), they are: on the viewer's right, St. John the Baptist and (perhaps) St. Barbara, patron of Rieti; and on the left, the soldier martyr St. Sebastian, and in the place of honor under the Savior's right hand, the Pope and martyr St. Fabian, who is associated with Sebastian in the liturgy of January 20. Terzi believes that these paintings were made in the 14th cenury, with others on adjoining walls, including one of the Franciscan Bishop St. Louis of Anjou, who died in 1297 and was canonized in 1317. However, the identification of the mitered figure under Christ's right hand as San Fabiano has been strongly contested by Sacchetti Sassetti in several of his brochures (C176, C177, C179) and questioned by Abate (C160: 391n90), on the grounds that a pope should be wearing a tiara rather than a miter and a pallium rather than a casula, and that the soldier martyr is wearing a Roman toga and not a military *clamide*. Sacchetti Sassetti therefore concludes (C179:16) that the two figures represent a civilian and a bishop, both unidentifiable. Abate (*ibid.*) sensibly concludes that at present, until more valid and reliable evidence is available, the identification of La Foresta as San Fabiano may not merit a completely negative judgment, but that its description as a Franciscan "shrine" calls for very broad and necessary reservations.

For Terzi's description and history of La Foresta, see F59:261-273, & C183:7-20.

(d) The Bishop's Palace in Assisi

The thesis which Abate (C160) advocated in 1956 for the origin of the Canticle in the Vescovado rather than San Damiano contained such persuasive arguments that it has received a sympathetic if tentative acceptance by Fidentius van den Borne, OFM (A320:300) and two prominent Capuchin scholars, Mariano da Alatri and Quirinus van Alphen (RSCI 11,265). It is certainly far more plausible topographically than the Rieti Valley thesis, but it suffers from the same fatal absence of textual support. Abate is obliged to fall back upon the improbable supposition that copyists repeatedly wrote *Sanctus Damianus* when they should have written *Sancta Maria*.

Before constructing his own case, Abate tries to demonstrate the "probative inadequacy of the San Damiano thesis" by discounting the authority of the Assisi Codex 338, the *Speculum, Legenda Antiqua, Actus,* and Vatican Latin Mss. 4354, stressing their relative unreliability as late texts or compilations. Next he establishes the total inadequacy of the textual basis of the Reiti Valley thesis, before rejecting the chronology of Terzi for 1225. In this important section (C160: 373-383), he insists that if St. Francis undertook a preaching tour after returning to Assisi from La Verna, it must have been brief and confined to Umbria; the sudden intensification of his eye-sickness must have occurred that winter; the fruitless treatment in Assisi by Elias' several doctors must have covered several months; the trip to Rieti was probably soon after the end of June; Campomoro seems more plausible than La Foresta; the Saint did not stay at San Fabiano from September to January, as Terzi claims, but went from Rieti to Fonte Colombo for the cauterizing; the reconciliation of the bishop and the podestà took place in Assisi, not Rieti; the Saint went to Siena before April, 1226.

The Conventual historian then begins to present his own theory in a section (C160:383-392) devoted to the *domus* and *cellula* in which Francis was living when he composed the Canticle. Abate and Bigaroni (C164:123-126) have no difficulty in showing that the grotto a few yards below the double church at La Foresta could not possibly be described as a *cellula facta de* or *ex storiis,* i.e. a cell made of rush-mats. In defending his grotto, Terzi can only claim that it was covered with such mats, but its solid rock walls refute his theory. Much has been written by Terzi, Abate, and Fortini concerning the meaning of the word *domus* in the texts dealing with the Canticle, the first insisting that it must refer to the poor priest's home, while Abate claims that it was never used alone to designate a religious residence, but Fortini (FNV II,492-494) and Bigaroni (C164:122 & 135) cite decisive texts, e. g. *I Celano,* 10, and several references in the Process of Canonization of St. Clare, in which the San Damiano chaplain's house is called simply a *domus.*

Next, Abate submits his most valuable contribution: sources narrating the incident of the mysterious repulsion of Bishop Guido of Assisi when he boldly entered unannounced into the Saint's private room at the Portiuncula show clearly that Francis was then absorbed in prayer inside a *parva cellula de storiis* set up in a corner of his *cella* (C160:388, quoting the Little Mss. n162 (A157:84); also in *Legenda Antiqua,* 6 (AFH n46); cf, without the crucial *cellula, II Celano,* 100). Evidently, then for greater privacy and recollection, the Saint used to have a kind of screened alcove within a room. Bigaroni (C164: 124) also stressed this important text. It is therefore quite plausible that when Francis composed the Canticle, he was in such an inner cell inside a room of a house, which Abate believes was probably the bishop's palace, but which might still more plausibly have been the *domus* of the chaplain and questing brothers near the church and convent of San Damiano, as the sources clearly state. This cell within a room effectively eliminates the objection that the sick Saint would not have been left in a mat-cell outdoors during cold weather.

The *domus*, which has long since disappeared, was perhaps on the right side of the church, where the Chapel of the Crucifix now stands (C160:393). No doubt it was small and plain; large enough only to accommodate the chaplain, his *socius*, and two questing brothers (FNV II, 488, 492-494). In fact Terzi (C9:170n31) and Abate (C160: 363n6 & 365) claim it would have been too small for those friars and Francis and his three or four favorite companions. But we know that the early friars slept several per room, and we do not know that this house did not have an adjacent shed or barn. Moreover, the *socius* and questing brothers may well have moved back to the Portiuncula when the Saint's stay had to be extended.

In the third section (C160:393-402), Abate develops his strongest argument against San Damiano, contending that such a prolonged stay there on the part of Francis was "morally improbable" in the light of his stringent opposition to all but a bare minimum of necessary visits to the Poor Clares on the part of a few authorized friars. In this connection, historians who have recently treated the subject agree that the Sisters at San Damiano were under strict papal enclosure after 1218 (C160:394n5: BF I,263; C164:121), and that the romantic Victorian accounts (still echoed in later biographies) which have St. Clare personally nursing the Poverello in her little garden or making a cell for him there (cf the *Actus*) are to be dismissed as pure fiction.

As founder of the Second Order, St. Francis of course had full authority to visit San Damiano when he decided that such a visit was justified. But his extreme reluctance to do so is amply documented in the early sources. To those texts Abate has contributed (C160:399) a significant new addition which he discovered in a 14th-century Franciscan manuscript. It is another version of the incident narrated in *II Celano*, 207, in which the Poverello, instead of giving the Poor Clares a sermon as expected, simply sprinkled ashes on his head, recited a penitential psalm, and left. Abate's manuscript introduces that anecdote with this gem of a text: "Whenever St. Clare heard that St. Francis wanted to go away, she would send for him, saying, 'Go tell Brother Francis to come and talk to me,' because she thought otherwise she would not see him again." This supplies an illuminating background for his visit to San Damiano in 1225, as well as for Thomas of Celano's specifying that such visits were *coacta tamen et rara* (*ibid.*). Naturally Fortini and Abate have also had a lively argument over

Thomas's opening words in that paragraph: "...cum apud Sanctum Damianum faceret moram," the former interpreting them as meaning "while he was staying (there) for some time," whereas Abate and Terzi translate "while he was stopping off (there) for a short time" (FNV II,488; C160:398; F59:348). Incidentally, Abate's new manuscript adds that Elias accompanied Francis and first gave the nuns a sermon, but did not inspire devotion in any of them, and that after the Saint left, their lamenting was so loud it was heard outside the convent.

Also relevant is another late text (A207:30-31), quoting Brother Leonardo of Assisi and narrating a visit to San Damiano by Francis and Angelo, followed by a lunch (with the Sisters or in the chaplain's house?), during which Francis falls and lies on the floor in a prolonged ecstasy on hearing the Lord promise him eternal life; for the next eight days the Saint was so overflowing with joy that he could not recite his office, but kept repeating: "*Laudato sia il Signore!*" Bigaroni (C164: 96) connects this anecdote with the composition of the Canticle, but Bracaloni (in an article in *San Damiano* 15, 1948, n3) assigns it to some other time.

Besides stressing the moral improbability, Abate also argues that a long stay near San Damiano is implausible because it would have involved frequent, unwelcome visits by many seculars eager to see the Saint.

Abate then builds his case for the bishop's palace rather than San Damiano on the precedents of two little-known previous sojourns of the Saint in that palace while ill, and on the key word *veniat* in Francis' instructions to the companions whom he sent to the podestà: "*Vade, et dic Potestati ut veniat ad episcopatum.*" Abate claims that the *veniat* would be used only by someone speaking in the palace — otherwise he would say: "tell him to go to the Vescovado." Fortini (C168:17) replies with philological arguments and secondary senses in various dictionaries, but fails to point out the strong topographical case for *veniat*: the Vescovado lies in an almost direct line between San Damiano and the Palazzo dei Priori on the Mercato; on leaving the latter the podestà would actually come through the city streets in the general direction of San Damiano, toward someone there.

It may be a surprise to readers of this book that St. Francis was a guest of Bishop Guido during more than one illness, as the only instance which has been well known is of course that of September, 1226, before the Saint went to the Portiuncula to die. But Abate has found in the sources accounts of three other incidents occurring there during illnesses of the Saint, probably on two other occasions. It is therefore most important to analyze those incidents in order to determine when they took place.

The first and probably the earliest is recorded only by Bartholomew of Pisa in his *Conformities* (AF V,329; cf C160:409n18): once at the Portiuncula Francis fell ill and needed to eat meat, but such was his reverence for that *locus* that he would not break a then prevailing custom against eating meat there, and so he went to stay with the bishop until he recovered his health. The second case, according to Abate (*ibid.*) and Terzi (C183:112), may have happened at the same time; Wadding assigns it to 1212(n54): a rich young man from Lucca visits Francis, then ill and staying in the bishop's palace; while the Saint informs him he has no vocation, the youth's parents arrive and take him home (*II Celano*, 40; *Legenda Antiqua*, 28 (AFH n63); *Speculum*, 103). The early years are suggested by the expression: "at a time when no one was received without the permission of St. Francis."

The third incident is crucial for our subject, because the texts specify that it occurred during the winter, and Abate claims that the winter must have been that of 1224/25, when the Canticle was composed, two years before the Saint's death. Certainly the word *hiems* would not be applied to September, 1226 (cf C183:116). Just as in that last month of his life Francis had a desire to eat some parsley (*II Celano*, 51), so now, also in the palace, *valde infirmus*, the only food he wanted was a lake-fish called *squalus*, but none was available in Assisi in winter — when suddenly a messenger arrived, bringing three large *squalus* as a gift from Frater Girardus, minister in Rieti (*Speculum*, 111; *Legenda Antiqua*, 29 (AFH n64); AF V,427; *Actus S. Francisci in Valley Reatina*, A222:33 or MF 13,12; cf C160:410). Inasmuch as the gift came from the Franciscan superior in Rieti, the last account's unique ending, probably based on the tradition of the local friary, may well be authentic, and if so, of decisive importance: it adds (p. 34): "*et gustans de predictis, in paucis diebus fuit divina virtute sanitati pristine restitutus.*" Abate failed to mention this striking return to health. As we know, Francis never recovered good health after the sudden worsening of his eye-sickness in the winter of 1224/25. No doubt, the recovery is not found in the other three sources, but the fourth has the factor of local tradition in its favor, despite its late date (1409) and frequent errors. Incidentally, it does not contain a word about the Canticle having been composed in the Valley of Rieti, though Terzi replies that it may have said so in a lost continuation.

Since the *squalus* story forms the crux of Abate's thesis in favor of the bishop's palace, Terzi has given it a close and critical analysis in his *San Fabiano...*(C183:110-116) which is indispensable to an evaluation of Abate's case. Here Terzi's important contribution lies in pointing out that we have still another anecdote referring to an illness of St. Francis during a winter which is certainly not later than 1220/21: when the Poverello was recovering from *quadam maxima infirmitate*,

diagnosed as *febre quartana*, he made his Vicar Peter Catanii lead him
with a rope around his neck, wearing only his breeches despite the *mag-
num frigus et tempus yemale*, to the Piazza where he confessed to a
crowd of people that he had eaten meat during his illness (*Speculum*,
61; *Legenda Antiqua*, 39 (AFHn74); cf *I Celano*, 52, & *Bonaventure*,
VI,2). Although Wadding connects this story with that of the
boy from Lucca, the reference to Peter Catanii, who died in March,
1221, has led both Terzi (C183:115) and Sabatier (A151:111n1)
to date the incident in the winter of 1220/21, with the quartan fever
resulting from the Saint's sojourn in the Near East in 1219/20. Terzi
then insists that since this incident and that of the *squalus* both end
in a return to health, they can safely be assigned to the same winter:
that of 1220/21. No text of the piazza story mentions the bishop's
palace; in fact, Thomas of Celano refers to Francis and Peter entering
the city gate, implying that they came from the Portiuncula; but this
does not exclude the possibility that on recovering his health to some
degree in the bishop's palace (thanks to the *squalus*), the Saint returned to the Portiuncula and then decided to go up to the city square
and confess his meat eating — all during the same winter weeks of
1220/21. In my opinion, Terzi has thus definitely undermined, if not
demolished, the corner-stone of Abate's Vescovado thesis.

A hitherto unused minor criticism of the latter would be that it omits
a major circumstance in the standard accounts of the composition of
the Canticle, namely, the hordes of obsessing fieldmice, which form an
organic part of the rural environment of San Damiano, but are utterly
out of place, not to say embarrassing, in an episcopal mansion.

A secondary argument used by both Terzi and Abate against San
Damiano is the sending of the special Praises to the Poor Clares by
Francis after he had composed the Canticle. The sending, they claim
implies that he was then absent from San Damiano, either in the Valley of Rieti or in the bishop's palace (C160:414). But the basic texts
have an entirely adequate explanation: "cum *personaliter propter ip-
sam infirmitatem ipsas . . . visitare non posset*" (*Legenda*, 45).

Lastly, a late text in the *Codex S. Antonii de Urbe* (A220:387)
which has the bishop and podestà reconciled *coram*, "in the presence
of St. Francis," implying that he was then at the Vescovado, though
accepted by Terzi for Rieti (F59:401n284), is so obviously faulty —
a few lines above it also has the Saint "*eos visitans*" — that Abate
does not use it, though it favors his case.

(e) Conclusions

The basic texts narrating the composition of the Canticle of Brother Sun by St. Francis, as outlined and quoted in part in Section (a)

above, state unequivocally that he was at San Damiano when he did so, and this is confirmed by the weighty evidence of the Assisi Codex 338.

The thesis that this event took place rather in the Valley of Rieti, either at La Foresta or at Campomoro, literally does not have a text to stand on, and can therefore be completely discarded.

The claim that San Fabiano is to be identified with Campomoro has serious documentary evidence, while the claim for La Foresta still awaits definitive clarification of the subject and dating of the mural paintings in the chapel there.

The thesis that the Canticle was composed in the bishop's palace in Assisi is also completely lacking in textual evidence and is untenable for that reason. The *cellula* and *domus* mentioned in the sources denote a screened alcove in a room of the chaplain's house at San Damiano. Despite the proved opposition of St. Francis to visits by his friars to the Poor Clares, the sources indicate that he found himself obliged by a sudden almost complete blindness and acute illness to spend over two months confined to a room in that house in the first part of the year 1225. Modern accounts that describe St. Clare nursing him in a cell in her small garden within the papal enclosure are to be discarded as contrary to historical fact.

St. Francis accepted the hospitality of Bishop Guido of Assisi not only in September, 1226, but also during at least two other illnesses: once in his early years as a friar and again when he received a gift of fish from Brother Gerard of Rieti. As on both occasions he is reported to have recovered his health, the second stay in the bishop's palace did not take place in the winter of 1224/25, but in that of 1220/21, when it is known that he was also very sick and recovered.

Consequently, despite several attacks in recent years against the identification of San Damiano as the site of the composition of the Canticle, in favor of San Fabiano in the Valley of Rieti or of the Vescovado in Assisi, as of the present the conclusion is inescapable that there is no strong evidence for either of those theses, and that on the contrary the identification of San Damiano as the true site, as explicitly stated in the *Legenda Antiqua* of Perugia and in the *Speculum Perfectionis*, remains historically unimpaired.

3. Italian Text
Il Cantico di Frate Sole

1 Altissimo omnipotente bon Signore,
2 tue so le laude la gloria e l'onore e onne benedizione.

3 A te solo, Altissimo, se confano
4 e nullo omo è digno te mentovare.

5 Laudato sie, mi Signore, cun tutte le tue creature,
6 spezialmente messer lo frate Sole,
7 lo qual è iorno, e allumini noi per lui.

8 Ed ello è bello e radiante cun grande splendore:
9 de te, Altissimo, porta significazione.

10 Laudato si, mi Signore, per sora Luna e le Stelle:
11 in cielo l'hai formate clarite e preziose e belle.

12 Laudato si, mi Signore, per frate Vento,
13 e per Aere e Nubilo e Sereno e onne tempo
14 per lo quale a le tue creature dai sustentamento.

15 Laudato si, mi Signore, per sor Aqua,
16 la quale è molto utile e umile e preziosa e casta.

17 Laudato si, mi Signore, per frate Foco,
18 per lo quale enn' allumini la nocte:
19 ed ello è bello e iocundo e robustoso e forte.

20 Laudato si, mi Signore, per sora nostra matre Terra,
21 la quale ne sostenta e governa,
22 e produce diversi fructi con coloriti flori ed erba.

23 Laudato si, mi Signore, per quelli che perdonano per lo tuo amore
24 e sostengo infirmitate e tribulazione.

25 Beati quelli che 'l sosterrano in pace,
26 ca da te, Altissimo, sirano incoronati.

27 Laudato si, mi Signore, per sora nostra Morte corporale,
28 de la quale nullo omo vivente po' scampare.

29 Guai a quelli che morrano ne le peccata mortali!
30 Beati quelli che trovarà ne le tue sanctissime voluntati,
31 ca la morte seconda no li farra male.

32 Laudate e benedicite mi Signore,
33 e rengraziate e serviteli cun grande umilitate.

Notes

INTRODUCTION
by Omer Englebert

1. *Martinus Luther Werke* (Weimar ed.) VIII,579. [See A195.]
2. Sabatier, *Vie* (A305:565).
3. AF IV, xxiii.
4. Letter to Voltaire, Oct. 28, 1759, in *Oeuvres de Voltaire* (ed. Moland) XL, 205. [For 17th-century French works on St. Francis, see A290(b):14; & CF 20 (1950)127.]
5. *Encyclopédie d'Yverdon*, XX,553.
6. *Qeuvres*, X,380.
7. "He distorted facts, falsified them at will, and lied boldly, with the deplorable facility he had acquired." Sainte-Beuve, *Causeries du lundi*, (P 1853) VII,93.
8. *Oeuvres*, XII,338.
9. *Ibid.*, XXVI,331.
10. Lalande, *Voyage d'un Français en Italie* (P 1769) 299.
11. Stendhal, *Rome, Naples et Florence* (P 1927) II, 149-150.
12. For Senault, see Migne's *Orateurs sacrés*, VI,108 for Boileau, *ibid*, XXI, 778; for Lejeune, *ibid.*, IV,36.
13. Lebarcq, *Oeuvres oratoires de Bossuet*, I,189ff.
14. *Ibid.*, VI, lff.
15. Chateaubriand, *Oeuvres* (P n.d.) VI,285-288. First ed. 1850. [cf *The Memoirs of Francois René Vicomte de Chateaubriand* (L 1902) VI,143.
16. Michelet, *Oeuvres complètes, Histoire de France* (P n.d.) II, 402-408. [cf *The History of France* (L 1844) I,548-551.]
17. P, 1849. [cf *The Franciscan Poets in Italy of the Thirteenth Century* (L & NY 1914).]
18. P, 1848.
19. The Canticle of Brother Sun.
20. "He has been justly styled the second Christ, because he appeared like Christ reborn to his contemporaries no less than to later ages." Pius IX, in his Encyclical *Rite expiatis* (April 30, 1926) [in *The Franciscan Message in Authentic Texts* (St. Louis 1941) 44.]
21. Ernst Renan, *Nouvelles études d' histoire religieuse* (P 1884) 323-351 [cf *Studies in Religious History* (NY 1887) 306,310-312,315,320.]
22. H. Taine, *Voyage en Italie* (P 1914) II,25-28. [cf *Italy, Florence and Venice* (NY 1869) 21,23.]
23. Sabatier, *Etudes* (A307:69-70); & Maugain (A312:5).
24. [For Englebert's Bibliography, see A290:416-423, & A291:336-341; cf A5 & A6.]
25. Referring to his translation of the *Characters of Theophrastus*, La Bruyère wrote: "It was necessary to follow the spirit of the author and to translate in accordance with the nearest meaning of the Greek wording, and at the same time in accordance with the most precise conformity with the chapters — no easy thing — for frequently the meaning of a Greek word translated word for word into French is not the same in our language. For instance, "irony" is with us a mockery in conversation, or else a rhetorical figure; while for Theophrastus, it is

something between fraud and duplicity — without being one or the other." (*Discourse on Theophrastus*. It is the same with the word *consolatio*, for example, employed constantly by the author of the

Actus-Fioretti, which signifies, according to the case, joy, contentment, mitigation of pain, inner happiness, spiritual unction, etc.

1 ORIGINS AND LIFE IN THE WORLD

1. FNV 82, 112, 127. [FNV 1/1,67-69.]

2. A. Luchaire, *Innocent III, Rome et l'Italie*, 122. [cf. Waley, *Papal State* (B13:41).]

3. FNV 125.

4. Letter of Renan to Berthelot, May 11, 1850, in G. Faure's *Au pays de saint François* (Grenoble 1936) 74.

5. *Ibid.*, 47; Renan's expression. [On Umbria, see F162-F204.]

6. [See Appendix II on Chronology.]

7. The population of Assisi is about [9000. A census of 1232 listed 255 homes or about 22,550 inhabitants for the entire county of Assisi (FNV III,73).]

8. [For works describing Assisi, see F205-F228; for its history, F229-F245. On conditions around 1200, see F237 & F244. On various churches and monasteries of Assisi, F246-F286.]

9. *Tres Socii*, 9. [For the Saint's home, see Appendix V.]

10. [See Appendix III on the Saint's Family.]

11. *I Celano*, 53; *II Celano*, 31; *Bonaventure*, VI,1.

12. [See App. III.]

13. *Tres Socii*, 1.

14. [See Appendix IV on the Saint's Birth & Baptism.]

15. *II Celano*, 3.

16. *Tres Socii*, 1.

17. *I Celano*, 16; *II Celano*, 13; *Speculum*, 93.

18. It is a moot question whéther St. Francis spoke the *langue d'oil* or *provençal;* Sabatier, *Vie* (A305: 9,11).

19. *I Celano*, 23; & *Legenda . . . chori*, 13; AF X,20 & 124. [Fortini (FNV I/1, 120) states that the boy Francis must have received his first lessons in religion in his parish church, San Nicoló, which was located to the west of the Piazza del Comune, where Fortini claims to have identified the home of Pietro da Bernardone (see Appendix V). However, the historian of Assisi stresses that Francis attended the school conducted by the canons of San Rufino Cathedral at the church of San Giorgio (where he was first buried). At that time every cathedral chapter had charge of teaching grammar and rhetoric, while the parish priest-

teacher *(scholasticus)* taught reading (FNV I/1,116). A late text (C47) calls one of the Saint's teachers "maestro Alessandro da Foligno." J. W. Thompson has shown that the literacy of many of the laity in Italy in the 13th century was relatively high (C44). On education in medieval Italy, see C40a-C43. On San Giorgio, E220, F82, F83.]

20. *III Celano*, 3; AF X,273.

21. At that time everyone was familiar with the great epic legends, which had spread over all the West: the *geste* of Charlemagne, the stories of the Round Table, the Quest of the Holy Grail, whose themes were to be used in the *Chanson de Roland* and *Perceval* in France. Francis often alluded to them *(Legenda antiqua*, 71-72; *Speculum*, 4 & 72); and even the unlearned Brother Giles occasionally referred to them (in his *Dicta*, 63). [Unfortunately, no scholar has yet made a special study of the several Carolingian traditions that were current in Umbria during the youth of St. Francis. Fortini (FNV I/1,7 & 14; cf II,71) treats only one recorded in the unpublished *Liber Historiarum S. Romane Ecclesie* of Frate Elemosina, who lived in Assisi around 1300 and who narrated a siege of Assisi by Charlemagne. But Fortini does not mention the significant Umbrian romance dealing with the exploits of the famous knights Roland and Oliver at Perugia, which is summarized in *Franciscan Mystic* (E121:5) from Heywood's *History of Perugia* (F300:6-13), whose source was *L'Umbria* (Perugia) 1901, n. 13ff. For other materials, see C54, C56, and an important article by G. Vitaletti, "Tradizioni carolingie e leggende ascetiche raccolte presso Fonte Avellana," *Archivum Romanicum* 3(1919)409-510 & 5(1921)313-389; see esp. 415n1. Charlemagne passed through Central Italy eight times on his four journeys to Rome: in 774, 781, 787, 800; cf T. Hodgkin, *Italy & Her Invaders* (Oxford 1885-99) VI,373ff; VII,52ff, 68ff, 185ff, Oliger (C61a) has shown that Francis probably knew the popular Compostellan life of Charlemagne attributed to a Bishop Turpin of Rheims.]

22. *Don Quijote*, ch. 1.

23. Cf. M. Fauriel, *Dante et les origines de la langue et de la littérature italiennes* (P 1854); K. Bartsch, *Peire Vidals Lieder* (Berlin 1857), n. 41; Monaci, *Testi antichi provenzali* (R 1889), col. 67ff. [Cf. note 21.]

24. *I Celano*, 1 & 2.

25. *Bonaventure*, I,1.

20. In the Latin of the Middle Ages, "legend" does not mean "a legendary tale," but a "biography" or "work to be read," [and often an "official, authorized biography"].

27. *II Celano*, 3.

28. The Franciscan Rule was to bid the friars not to yield to the temptation "to judge and despise those whom they saw clothed in soft and colorful garments" (Rule of 1223, II).

29. N. Sormani, *La gloria dei santi milanesi* (Milano 1761) 215.

30. *II Celano*, 201; see Ch. 12, Note 9.

31. *I Celano*, 2.

32. *Ibid.*, 17; *Bonaventure*, I,1.

33. FNV 109-111, 114 [FNV I. 1.120-126,164-178; II,113-129. Fortini paints a vivid picture of the roistering in Assisi which the young Francis must have witnessed, if not participated in (on the latter, see n. 42 below). Yearly on December 6, the feast of St. Nicholas, patron of students, young and old celebrated the *Episcopello* or *Vescovino* by appointing a boy to act as a mock-bishop, dressed in episcopal robes, in grotesque, satyrical "ceremonies" in the church of San Nicolo, with processions through the streets. The irreverence and immorality of this bacchanalian festival obliged Innocent III to forbid it in 1207; nevertheless, it persisted in some Italian towns till the 17th century. On the parties and banquets described by Thomas of Celano and the *Tres Socii* legend, Fortini supplies additional data from the archives and statutes of Assisi and Perugia. In the city of St. Francis flourished a Compagnia di San Vetturino or del Bastone, a typical medieval *societas tripudantium* or sacred dancing society. Its meetings were held behind the altar-tomb of the early martyr bishop in the church of San Pietro. On June 13, the dancers, under the leadership of a chanting director, re-enacted on the city square the harrowing drama of San Vetturino's beheading. To celebrate the coming of spring on May-day or Calendimaggio, the same dancers enacted a worldly romance. Fortini assumes that Francis as a youth was a leader of this group on the basis of Thomas of Celano's statement that he carried the customary leader's staff at the last party he gave after his return from Spoleto. Fortini adds that in addition to the feasts and banquets which such *compagnie* organized, they also staged games, jousts, and tourneys, and even — in the first week of Advent — an informal bullfight. Often these events degenerated into acts of violence.]

34. *Tres Socii*, 2.

35. *Testament: "cum essem in peccatis."*

36. *I Celano*, 1-3.

37. Julian of Speyer, *Vita*, 1,1 (AF X, 336).

38. BF I,242.

39. Eudes de Chateauroux, Archbishop of Rouen, became a cardinal in 1245 and died in 1273. Among his sermons are ten on St. Francis and one on St. Clare. He refers many times to the sinful life of the young Francis: *"Tunc satiatus erat deliciis mundi et etiam delectationibus carnis"* (see A215a; Sermon 5); *Dominus fecit Franciscum sic inchoare sanctam conversationem ne peccatores . . . caderent in desperationem . . . Fuit enim magnus peccator* (Sermon 8); *Amplexus fuerat . . . immunditiam luxuriae. (Deus) Franciscum erexit . . . de immunditia luxuriae in qua lubricaverunt pedes ejus"* (Sermon on St. Francis, 4).

40. *Officium S. Francisci* (AFX,379).

41. [See C53.]

42. *Bonaventure*, I,1. Formerly, historians generally shared the latter's opinion; e.g. L. Lemonnier: "His flesh, which was one day to bear the sacred stigmata of the Savior, remained virginal" in his *(Histoire de saint François d'Assise* (P) 1891) 1,20; and Léopold de Chérancé: "Never did the breath of impurity tarnish the fair lily of his virginity. He remained ever chaste," in 1879 in his *Saint François d'Assise* (P 1933) 40. Later, some tended to resolve the question in an opposite sense; e.g. Beaufreton (A280:5-9), and among the friars themselves Father Gratien, for whom Francis' "moral lapses . . . however grave one might suppose them to be . . . never reached the proportions of making him a debauchee" (D 127:21); [see also C45-C53. Relevant to the problem is the vision of Brother Leo recorded in the Fourth Consideration on the Stigmata (A166:200) in which "he received assurance that St. Francis was truly a virgin in body." (Latin texts in AF III,68 & 676); this testimony is important for two reasons: Leo was the Saint's confessor for many years, and he reported the vision to an unspecified Minister General. The most thorough modern

study is that of the Capuchin Frédégand (Callaey) d'Anvers (C50 & C51), which favors the purity thesis; incidentally he reports that Sabatier wrote him in 1926 that he completely agreed. Fortini (FNV I/1,125) holds that despite all the immorality in Assisi at the time, Francis did not succumb. De Beer (A97:70) suggests that Friar Thomas meant that he was about to succumb when God saved him. Clasen (D156:152) believes that more careful study is needed.]

43. *I Celano*, 42.
44. *Tres Socii*, 3.
45. *Ibid.*
46. *Bonaventure*, I,1.

47. [On the confused identification of Duke Conrad by modern writers, see Appendix VI, Part 1.]
48. [On the civil war in Assisi between the feudal nobility (including St. Clare's family) and the rising middle class, see Appendix VI, Part 2.]
49. [For the important new data supplied by Fortini on the ten-year hostilities between Assisi and Perugia (1200-1209), see Appendix VI, Part 3. The battle in November, 1202, was at Collestrada rather than Ponte San Giovanni.]
50. [St. Francis as prisoner of war and patron of prisoners is treated in Appendix VI, Part 4.]

2 CONVERSION

1. E. Renan, *Nouvelles études d'histoire religieuse* (P 1884) 327; [cf *Studies in Religious History* (NY 1887) 308.]
2. J. Michelet, *Histoire de France* (P n.d.) II,403; [cf *The History of France* (L 1844) 1,549.]
3. *I Celano*, 83.
4. *Legenda antiqua*, 2 & 84.
5. *I Celano*, 3-4.
6. *Tres Socii*, 5.
7. *I Celano*, 5; *Tres Socii*, 5. [On the confusion in early texts and modern biographies regarding "Count Gentile," see Appendix VI, Part 5.]
8. *II Celano*, 5; *Bonaventure*, I,2.
9. *I Celano*, 5; *II Celano*, 6. [A careful analysis of the differences between Friar Thomas' two accounts is needed (D139:244n9).]
10. *II Celano*, 6; *Bonaventure*, I,3.
11. *II Celano*, 7. [On the banqueting, see Ch. 1, Note 33.]
12. *I Celano*, 7; *Tres Socii* 7.
13. *I Celano*, 6.
14. *I Celano*, 4; *II Celano*, 7; *III Celano*, 41; *Tres Socii*, 41; *Legend of St. Clare*, I.
15. *II Timothy*, 2:3.
16. St. Jerome, *Epistle* 22; St. Augustine, *De opere monachorum*, 18; *Prologue* of the Rule of St. Benedict.
17. Du Cange, *Glossarium mediae et infimae latinatis* (P 1766).
18. *Rolandslied* by the priest Conrad, 5159-5169, 5820, quoted by Felder (D 161b:311). [An extended study of Francis as "Christ's knight" appears in his *Knight-Errant of Assisi* (C58-C60).]
19. Wolfram of Eschenbach, IX; *Parzifal*, IX,888-890; *Chanson de Roland*, 1820, 3338ff; *Rolandslied*, 2378ff, 2398.
20. Several writers have tried to identify this "young man." Sabatier (A307:

163) wondered whether it was the future Brother Leo. [For Attal (E155:65), it was rather the future Brother Elias. As to the grotto, Fortini (FNV I/1,257; III.156-158) thinks it was the cave-cell of St. Francis at the Carceri, as a 15th century poem states that he "first did penance" there.]
21. *I Celano*, 6 & 7.
22. *Tres Socii*, 9.
23. *II Celano*, 8; *Bonaventure*, I,6; *Tres Socii*, 10. [Pilgrims in the medieval Basilica of St. Peter tossed alms through a grating down onto the pavement of the Apostle's tomb cell, under the altar (FNV I/1,263; II,222).]
24. *II Celano*, 9.
25. *II Celano*, 9; *I Celano*, 17. Sabatier (A307:158) quotes Jacques de Vitry as using the expression *Castrum dolorum omnium animae et corporis* to designate a leprosarium. [Fortini (FNV I/1, 266-273; II,257-266) supplies the stringent regulations of the medieval statutes of Assisi concerning the treatment of victims of leprosy. Among the half-dozen hospitals in the vicinity, he identifies the one mentioned here as San Lazzaro d'Arce (only later called Santa Maria Maddalena d'Arce) near the rural church of San Rufino d'Arce, halfway between Rivo Torto and the Portiuncula. Another well-known hospital was that of the Crosiers called San Salvatore delle Pareti on the site of present Villa Gualdi, on the road from Assisi to the Portiuncula. St. Francis healed a man afflicted with leprosy at the Ospedale of Collestrada between Assisi and Perugia (*Fioretti*, ch. 25; cf A166: 388). That disease, now often called Hansen's disease, was endemic in Europe until the Black Death of 1347. Before and after Francis, many Saints have given its

victims compassionate care, as have countless Catholic and Protestant missionaries in modern times. Today medical science considers Hansen's disease only mildly infectious, and recent International Congresses on Leprosy have recommended that the hated word "leper" be abandoned, as patients often suffer more from the cruel social stigma than from the bacillus. With his exquisite tact, St. Francis called them "brother Christians." cf Ch. 6, Notes 35-38 & relevant anecdotes.]

3 THE RESTORER OF CHURCHES

1. [The small church of San Damiano is first mentioned in a document dated 1030. Before the time of St. Francis, it was neither a parish nor a monastery. Probably about 1103 it was given to the prior of San Rufino by several families. It is not mentioned in a list of churches dependent on the bishop in 1198, but seems to have come under him soon afterward and was certainly his in 1253. The Poor Clares resided there from 1212 until a few years after the death of St. Clare in 1253, when they moved to the new Monastery of Santa Chiara on the site of San Giorgio. The first mention of the friars occupying San Damiano occurs in 1307. Throughout the 14th century it belonged to the Sacro Convento, passing in about 1380 to the Observant Franciscans and in 1604 to the Riformati. In 1867 an anti-clerical government expelled all but two caretaker friars, but in 1878 the British convert Marquess of Ripon, former Viceroy of India, "ransomed" the friary. In recent years it has been the philosophy seminary of the Umbrian province. See F262-F265 and Appendix VIII, Part 2.]

2. *II Celano,* 10 & 11; *Tres Socii,* 13-14; *Bonaventure,* II,1. [*The Anonymus Perusinus* (MF 9,1902,37) gives the name of the "poor resident priest" as Pietro. According to late sources, Francis recited this prayer before the Crucifix in San Damiano: "O great and glorious God, illuminate my heart. Give me steadfast faith, firm hope, perfect charity, and knowledge and understanding so that I may keep Thy commandments." Esser (C71) accepts its authenticity, though Cambell (A44:250-252; A43:203) considers it dubious. In a study of over a hundred Italian 12th-century painted crucifixes, Vavalà (C69c:624) describes the image of Christ as "an hieratic, sober, noble presentation, filled with spirituality . . . notable production . . . for the century and for the entire Romanesque output in Italy." For seven hundred years the Poor Clares kept it in their convent, but in Holy Week of 1957 it was placed on public display above the main altar in Santa Chiara, and in September 1958 installed above a new altar in the adjacent public chapel of San Giorgio (FNV I/1, 277-278). Rather than Byzantine, it should be described as Umbrian-Romanesque in style.]

3. *II Celano;* 11; *Tres Socii,* 13.
4. *I Celano,* 8; *Tres Socii,* 16; *Bonaventure,* II,1.
5. *I Celano,* 9; *Tres Socii,* 16; *Bonaventure,* II,1. [cf C71.]
6. *I Celano,* 10; *Tres Socii,* 16; *Bonaventure,* II,1.
7. *I Celano,* 11 & 12; *Tres Socii,* 17; *Bonaventure,* II,2.
8. *I Celano,* 13; *Tres Socii,* 18; *Bonaventure,* II,3.
9. *I Celano,* 13; *Bonaventure,* II,3.
10. *I Celano,* 14.
11. *Tres Socii,* 19.
12. *I Celano,* 14-15; *II Celano,* 12; *Tres Socii,* 19-20; *Bonaventure,* II,4. [Fortini (FNV I/1,286-294; II,223-237) shows that in accordance with the statutes of Assisi and other Italian towns the Saint's father could have had Francis condemned to prison or exiled. However, he also clarifies the youth's formal new status as a lay oblate in the service of the church of San Damiano which enabled him to appeal to the bishop's court.]
13. *Bonventure,* II,4.
14. *I Celano,* 16; *Bonaventure,* II,5.
15. *I Celano,* 16; *Bonaventure,* II,6; Henricus Abrincensis, *Legenda versificata,* liber IV. This verse text is graphically pictured by Henri d'Avranches who, after 1229, wrote St. Francis' life in 2589 verses. According to him, storm and flood prevented the Saint from leaving for several days: "What is to become of Francis without food or clothing? The monks will not let him stay; the weather will not let him leave. Poverty places him in a most painful dilemma. The harshness of his hosts overwhelms him, as much as does the fury of the elements. The hosts are more cruel, the elements more redoubtable. The prior of the convent, as one compelled to harbor an undesirable, tolerates him. He permits this wretched refugee whom the waters keep from leav-

ing, to wait in this place for the deluge to stop. However, as Francis, kept in by the storm, puts off his departure from day to day, his flimsy, threadbare garment falls in tatters. Thread no longer clings to thread — it is in shreds. Like a *jongleur*, he stays near the fire; but when he warms himself in front, he freezes in the back, and vice versa. But he is tortured by hunger even more than by the cold. All the bread that is given him for ten meals, he could eat in one. The monks refuse him a little broth to soften his old crusts — the pious monks would rather fatten their pigs. And how could you expect them to clothe the man to whom they refuse even the swill of the hogs?" — *Legenda versificata* (AF X, 429-430). [Of the two large Benedictine monasteries between Assisi and Gubbio, Fortini (FNV I/1,294-308; II,237-255) demonstrates that Francis stayed at the closer Priory of Santa Maria de Valfabbrica, rather than the more distant Abbey of San Verecondo di Vallingegno.]

16. *I Celano*, 16. [Fortini (FNV II, 256) assumes that this friend, who is named Federico Spadalunga in a reliable document of 1399, served with the troops of Gubbio in the battle against Perugia in 1202 and was perhaps imprisoned with Francis. His home on the market square in Gubbio became the church of San Francesco in the middle of the 13th century. See F293 and F492]

17. *Bonaventure*, II,6.
18. *I Celano*, 18; *Bonaventure*, II,7.
19. *Tres Socii*, 21.
20. *Testament of St. Clare* (E170: 82); *Tres Socii*, 21; *I Celano*, 18; Sabatier, *Etudes inédites* (A30:177-185).
21. *II Celano*, 14; *Tres Socii*, 22.
22. *Tres Socii*, 22.
23. *II Celano*, 13.
24. *II Celano*, 12.
25. *II Celano*, 12; *Tres Socii*, 23; *Anonymus Perusinus* (A126:37).

4 "DISCOVERY" OF THE GOSPEL AND FIRST RECRUITS

1. [Bracaloni (C70) has refuted the claims of Sabatier and Thode that St. Francis initiated a significant church building movement in Central Italy which introduced the pointed Gothic arch there. The related theory that the second church repaired by Francis was the large Benedictine Abbey of San Pietro, now inside but then just outside the walls of Assisi, has been slow to die out, though St. Bonaventure specified that the church was farther away from Assisi than San Damiano. Among half a dozen churches and chapels of St. Peter in the area, Fortini (FNV II,266-272) believes it was San Pietro della Spina (now in ruins) on the plain beyond Rivo Torto, close to some fields owned by the Saint's father.]

2. Thomas of Celano writes that "Francis loved the Mother of Jesus with an unspeakable love," because he saw in her "the one who gave us the God of majesty to be our Brother." The same author adds that "he chose her as the advocate of his Order, and placed under her wings the sons he was to leave behind, that she might cherish and protect them to the end" (*II Celano*, 198). His love for Mary was based not only on her divine maternity, but on the fact also that the Blessed Virgin had shared her Son's life of poverty, living like Him on alms and enduring with Him great privation (Rule of 1221, IX; *II Celano*, 200). He composed a charming Salutation in her

honor (*Opuscula*, p. 123), and an antiphon which accompanies each hour of the "Office" he wrote and which he recited daily (*Opuscula*, pp. 16-147). [On the simple yet profound Mariology of the Poverello, see Brown, *Our Lady and St. Francis* (D70) and "St. Francis of Assisi and Our Lady" (D72), as well as the fundamental studies of Esser (D73) and Oktavian von Rieden (D75).]

3. [Out of respect for historical truth, it is past time that the early history of the Portiuncula be definitively clarified even though this process requires a dose of "demythologizing." But in this case, it is interesting to note that the "myths" were created, not at the time by popular imagination, but four centuries after the little church was made famous by St. Francis, and they sprang from the fertile imagination of a single writer who was afflicted with an almost psychopathic disregard for historical facts. Sixty years ago the great Capuchin archivist Edouard d'Alençon (F251) proved that it was the totally unreliable Sardinian Fra Salvatore Vitale who in 1645 first wrote that the chapel had been built under Pope Liberius (352-366) by some hermits who came from the Holy Land and brought a stone from the tomb of the Blessed Virgin in the Valley of Josaphat, that they named the church St. Mary of Josaphat, and that in 516 St. Benedict enlarged it. As Vitale's only "documentation" was his

statement that an unknown and unnamed gentleman had loaned him a manuscript containing that information, we must agree that the complete silence of over a millennium outweighs his unacceptable evidence. This subject has recently been thoroughly re-examined by Luciano Canonici in his fundamental study of the history of the Portiuncula before and during the time of St. Francis (F248); cf D70:3-6. The first mention of the site in the archives of Assisi occurs in 1045, while the church is not listed until 1150, though it may have been built in the 10th century (F248:50; cf FNV III,92-99). Throughout the 13th century it was called Santa Maria della Porziuncula in official documents; later the earlier popular name, Santa Maria degli Angeli, returned to general use.]

4. For these dates, [see Appendix II on Chronology.[]

5. [*I Celano* 22, combines phrases from Matthew 10:5ff; Mark 6:7-12; Luke 9:1-6 & 10:1-16; cf AF X,19.]

6. *I Celano*, 22; *Tres Socii*, 25; *Bonaventure*, III,1.

7. *I Celano*, 22.

8. *I Celano*, 23; *Tres Socii*, 25; *Bonaventure*, III,2.

9. *I Celano*, 24.

10. [For biographical data about Brother Bernard and the other early companions, see Appendix VII.]

11. According to St. Bonaventure (IV, 8), St. Francis cured Morico when the latter was dying.

12. [See Appendix VII for the confusion between the early lists of eleven or twelve first companions.]

13. Matthew 19:21; Luke 9:3 & 23; Matthew 16:24; cf AF X,140.

14. *I Celano*, 24; *II Celano*, 48; *Bonaventure*, III; *Tres Socii*, 27-31; *Fioretti*, II.

15. *Legenda antiqua*, 55; *Vita fratris Aegidii*, AF III,75, & *Documenta Antiqua*, I,39.

16. The March of Ancona is one of the most beautiful regions in Italy. The Sibillini Mountains on the west rise to elevations of 7000 feet. This gardenland was the birthplace of the *Fioretti*, where the pure Franciscan spirit has been renewed from century to century. [See F130-F144.]

17. *Tres Socii*, 33; *I Celano*, 8; AF III,76. [Full accounts of this little-known first mission in the Marches are given in Pagnani's *Viaggi* (F132:7-33) and Brown's *Franciscan Mystic* (E121:20-25).]

18. *Horoy, Honorii III opera*, I,163 &

200. [cf FNV III,165.]

19. *Legenda antiqua*, 9.

20. *Tres Socii*, 35; *Legenda antiqua*, 3, 60.

21. "When they asked him how they should address God in prayer, he told them to say the Our Father ... and they began to sing it anywhere and everywhere in joy of spirit" (*I Celano*, 45-47). Francis was a great pray-er; but rather than multiply his devotions, "he never ceased to adore and contemplate the true and living God." He gave less the impression of being "a man praying, than of prayer incarnate." *Totus non tam orans quam oratio factus.* Admonition 16 (*Opuscula*, p. 14); *I Celano*, 95.

In addition to the Our Father, he made great use of the liturgy and the Psalms; not to speak of what no one could have knowledge, that is, the sublime soliloquies which his heart improvised in contemplation. Moreover, following the Gospel precept, he prayed in secret, taking care to comport himself like others, so as to avoid letting them see the fire that devoured him, going to bed when they did at the hour of repose, and rising while they slept to go and spend the night in prayer in the woods. *II Celano*, 94-101. [His "Paraphrase of the Our Father" is considered unauthentic by Cambell (A 44a), though included in the Quaracchi *Opuscula*.]

22. For the way in which Francis formed his disciples, see *I Celano*, 26, 30, 34, 35, 43, 51, 76; *II Celano*, 20, 21, 22, 28, 29, 129, 154, 182, 206; *Bonaventure*, IV,3: "Day and night they meditated on the book of the Cross, following the example of their Father, who constantly spoke to them of the crucified Christ." "Near the end, to a friar who wanted him to have the Prophets read to him, to alleviate his terrible sufferings, the Saint replied: 'I have read the Scriptures so often, that all I need now is to meditate them and go over them in my mind. I know Christ poor and crucified. Nothing more is needed, my son.'" *II Celano*, 105. [On Francis and the Bible, see D1-D5, D 77, D93.]

23. *I Celano*, 27; *Tres Socii*, 36; *Liber exemplorum*, 110.

24. After Assisi and La Verna, the Rieti valley was the scene of the most important events in the life of St. Francis. It has been studied in a remarkable way from this point of view by A. Terzi, O.F.M., *Memorie francescane nella Valle Reatina* (F59). [See also F57-F62, F350-F356, F359, F359a.]

25. *I Celano*, 29-30; *Tres Socii*, 36.
26. *Tres Socii*, 37.
27. *Legenda antiqua*, 67.
28. Rule of 1121, XXI.
29. *Tres Socii*, 37-38.
30. AF III,76.
31. *Tres Socii*, 39-40.
32. [For the controversy over Brother Angelo's place of origin, Assisi or Rieti,

see Appendix VII on the Companions. For the confused chronology of the first mission in the Valley of Rieti, see Appendix II.]
33. *I Celano*, 26.
34. *I Celano*, 30. For the way of life of these friars, see *I Celano*, 38-41; AF IV, 207-220; *Tres Socii*, 41.45.

5   BEFORE POPE INNOCENT III

1. H. X. Arquillière, *Histoire du moyen âge* (P 1939) 186, R. Morcay, *Nouvelle histoire de l'Eglise* (P 1937) 143.

2. This theory became a commonplace in Catholic preaching of this period. The famous Elinand (d. 1237), for example, said in the pulpit: "Every prelate is established by God above nations and kingdoms. From the beginning, God has willed that every secular dignity should be subject to ecclesiastical dignity, and should remain in the relation of the inferior to the superior, of the more base to the more noble." Tissier, *Bibliotheca Patrum Cisterciensium* (Bonnefontaine 1660) VII,303.

3. *Histoire littéraire de la France* (P 1864) XIV,402.

4. Excellent studies on this subject are found in Pierre Mandonnet, O.P. *St. Dominic and His Work*, tr. by Sister Mary Benedicta Larkin, O.P. (St. Louis 1944). [cf E255.]

5. Bull *Quamvis*, June 8, 1198, in F68. [For surveys of Innocent's reforming activity see F64, F72, F74.]

6. E. Roth, *Die Visionen der hl. Elisabeth von Schönau* (Brunn 1884) 115.

7. Quoted by Sabatier, *Vie* (A305) 68).

8. *Commentarium in Apocalypsim* (Ven. 1527) 70. On Joachim of Fiore, [see the comprehensive study by Bloomfield (E48).]

9. For the Waldenses, Humiliati, and "Poor Catholics," [see B30, B34, B35, B37, B39, B43-B4. Of prime importance on the relation of these sects to St. Francis: D198.]

10. For the Cathari, [see B29, B31, B40, B42, and especially Esser's study of St. Francis and the Cathari of his times: B32. On Arnold of Brescia: B33.]

11. [Sabatier and others assumed without documentary proof that this podestà was a heretic. However, Fortini (FNV II, 181) thinks it more probable that he had been excommunicated while podestà of Spoleto in 1201 for his political opposi-

tion to the papacy's moves to regain control of that part of the States of the Church. His name was Girardo di Giliberto. cf Waley (B13:48); AF X,447nl.]

12. [For the chronological problem (1209 or 1210), see Appendix II.]

13. *I Celano*, 32-33; *Tres Socii*, 45, 46, 53; *Bonaventure*, III,8.

14. *Chronica Maiora* of the Benedictine Matthew of Paris (d. 1259), quoted in A80:29. [The Pope's nephew told Friar Jerome of Ascoli (St. Bonaventure's successor before becoming Pope Nicholas IV) that Innocent "angrily rebuffed the servant of Christ as someone unknown," and Francis "humbly went out" (AF X, 570); cf MF 48(1948)525n5.]

15. A. Luchaire, *Innocent III* (P 1905) II,93.

16. I Celano, 32. [Testament of St. Francis.]

17. [On this *Regula primitiva*, as well as the Rules of 1221 and 1223, see my Guide, p. 11.]

18. See on this subject the study of Fr. Hilarin Felder, "Francis and the Gospel" in his *Ideals* (D161(b):1-18).

19. One case only was an exception, when the care of victims of leprosy required alms to be received in money: *Fratres tamen in manifesta necessitate leprosorum possunt pro eis [pecuniam vel] eleemosynam.* (Ch. VIII). But this exception was not retained later on.

20. Stirred up by the reformers of that era, many faithful affected the greatest scorn for the sacraments if administered by incontinent and simoniac priests. Some refused to assist at the Masses they celebrated; others trampled underfoot the Sacred Species which they consecrated; cf. Mandonnet, Vicaire and Ladner, *Saint Dominique* (P 1937) II, 188. Etienne de Bourbon relates that, confronted one day by one of these sectarians, Francis replied to his insidious questions as follows: "Whether the hands of this priest are what you say, I do not know. But even if they were, they could not alter the vir-

tue of the Sacraments. By these hands, God pours a multitude of graces upon His people. I kiss them in honor of the goods they dispense, and of Him whose instruments they are." Quoted by Lecoy de la Marche, *L'esprit de nos aïeux* (P 1888) 40; [cf. A80:93.]

21. The cloth merchants, among whom Francis grew up, were the greatest travelers and traffickers of ideas of this period.

22. According to Sabatier (A307:18, 20, 21), Francis never dreamed of posing as an innovator. He seemed not to see the heresy which attacks the Church and creates hate. Heresy, the crusades, and the Inquisition might have vanquished him, but Francis dispelled heresy the way light dispels darkness. If a St. Francis had lived in the sixteenth century, the voices of Luther and Calvin would have had only a passing importance.

The same author adds (A307:215-216) "Francis had been awaited, desired, longed for, and prepared for by the sighs of Christian humanity. All his ideas, borrowed from the Gospel, can be found again in a host of preceding or parallel efforts. Preached by others, they fall flat, spoiled by pride; but he had drawn from them a new spirit, a new soul. He made them come alive by humility, love, and obedience."

23. *I Celano*, 32; *Tres Socii*, 47-48. [Cardinal John of St. Paul was one of the most important curia cardinals in the two decades 1195-1215, yet we still lack a complete biographical study, and the several excellent brief articles on him remain almost unknown. Old errors, such as his being of the Colonna family, are still repeated. Though Msgr. Pio Paschini (F104) disproved it in 1940, Fortini, EC (VI,607) and DHGE (XIII,335) ignore Paschini's contribution. Before becoming a Benedictine of San Paolo fuori le Mura, John studied medicine at the famous college of Salerno and wrote a *Liber de simplicium medicinarum virtutibus*. In 1193 he was made Cardinal of St. Prisca, and during the last years of Celestine III became, with the future Innocent III, a leader of the activist group in the curia that advocated an increasingly firm opposition to the Hohenstaufen emperors. It was reported that he was favored by Celestine to succeed him in the papacy. Under Innocent III, he served as a legate to the German general Markward in southern Italy in 1198 and then in 1200-1201 in France, where he dealt with the problems of the Cathari in Provence and of

King Philip's attempt to obtain a divorce. He was appointed Bishop of Sabina in 1204, and strengthened that diocese between Rome and Rieti. He died some months before the Fourth Lateran Council met in November, 1215. See F102-F105.]

24. *I Celano*, 33; *Tres Socii*, 48. [A critical study of the exact sequence of events during this sojourn of the Saint in Rome still remains to be done. For recent works treating it, see F107-F122 & FNV I/1, 368-378; cf E121:40-49.]

25. Surius, *Vitae sanctorum*, VI,215 [from Sabatier, *Vie* (A305:122); cf ASS (P 1867) Jun. IV, 197 & 199. Our only source is the credulous Dominican Thomas of Cantimpré (d. ca. 1270), who wrote that the Pope said there were three reasons for his sentence, but Thomas would not specify them "out of reverence for such a great pontiff." To charges that the nun's vision was an illusion or a fable, the Bollandist editor replies that many judgments of God are mysterious to men. St. Lutgard reported many private revelations from souls in Purgatory. One that is especially relevant to a biography of St. Francis involved her friend Cardinal Jacques de Vitry (see Ch. 11, Note 1): four days after he died in 1240 he appeared to her and told her he had just been liberated from Purgatory (ibid. 203.)]

28. Bonaventure, III,9; *Tres Socii*, 49.

27. *II Celano*, 16-17; Bonaventure, III, 10; *Tres Socii*, 50-51.

28. Bonaventure, III,10; *Tres Socii*, 51-52; [*II Celano*, 17. Again a careful study is still needed of the various visions connected with this stay in Rome: the Saint's dream of the tall bending tree (*I Celano*, 33), later apparently transferred by mistake to Innocent (AF X, 570); and the Pope's vision of the falling Lateran, first recorded by Thomas of Celano about 1246, but simultaneously reported of St. Dominic: cf AF X, 141n8; Lemmens, *Test. Min.* (A80:67-70). Oliger (F118:69-70) quotes the significant inscription placed on the Lateran in 1290 by the Franciscan Pope Nicholas IV. Fortini (FNV I/1,375) considers the testimony of Brother Masseo in the *Liber exemplorum* decisive, though he was not present. cf F107.

29. Bonaventure, III,10; *Tres Socii*, 52. [For the problem of which tonsure the companions received and of when the Saint was ordained deacon, see Appendix VII.]

30. *I Celano,* 33; *Tres Socii,* 49.
31. *I Celano,* 33.
32. [In 1927 A. Camilli established that the site of the twelve friars' brief stay near Orte was not (as stated earlier —

and later) by the church of San Lorenzo, but by San Nicolao ad Scupulos; see F357, F358.]
33. *I Celano,* 34-35.

6 RIVO TORTO

1. Some writers think that before starting for Rome, the brethren had already moved from the Portiuncula to Rivo Torto; others, that from this time on, they occupied both sites alternately. Documents do not permit us to decide the question. [The problem arises from the fact that the *Speculum Perfectionis* of Sabatier shows St. Francis residing at Rivo Torto with Bernard and Peter Catani when Giles joined them, whereas other texts place this incident at the Portiuncula. Fortini (FNV II,307-314) and Canonici (F248) conclude that the latter is correct, since Thomas of Celano and St. Bonaventure stress that the Order actually began to exist there. Another problem is that of the precise location of Rivo Torto: Sabatier claimed it was contiguous to the lazaret of San Rufino d'Arce, but Fortini proves that the local archives clearly distinguish the two localities, which are 1514 meters (yards) apart. While Fortini (FNV I/1,365) has Francis and his first companions move to Rivo Torto before going to Rome, Canonici argues that they settled there only on returning from Rome. The site fell into neglect, until in 1491 a General Chapter of the Order resolved that the *"antiqua devotio Rivitorti"* be maintained, and in 1586 the foundations of the future (Conventual) Basilica with its palatial replica of the original delapidated shed were laid; the church was rebuilt in 1854 after an earthquake. cf F256, F257.]

2. [See Note above.]

3. *I Celano,* 42-44; *Tres Socii,* 55.

4. *Salutatio virtutum,* in *Opuscula.*

5. *Bonaventure,* VII,2; *Legenda antiqua,* 102.

6. Epictetus, incidentally, said to his disciples: "I have been sent to you by God as an example, possessing neither property nor wife nor children — no, not even a bed or tunic or piece of furniture" *(Discourses,* IV,8,31).

7. *I Celano,* 55; Rule of 1221, VI.

8. [For editions and studies of the *Sacrum commercium beati Francisci dum domina Paupertate,* see A82, A83a, A112-119. Though some manuscripts bear the date 1227 and Thomas of Celano's *Vita prima (I Celano,* 35) contains the words

(referring to the days spent near Orte) *"cum sancta paupertate ibidem habere commercium,"* Livarius Oliger, OFM, writing in 1950 (A271:39), accepts the attribution of *The Chronicle of the Twenty-four Generals* (AF III,283) of this literary and polemical masterpiece to Blessed John of Parma (d.1289), probably in 1260-1270, when he was living in retirement in Greccio.]

In 1305, in his *Arbor vitae crucifixae Jesu,* the Spiritual Ubertino da Casale composed and put in St. Francis' mouth an admirable "Prayer for Obtaining the Grace of Poverty," which likewise expresses the true sentiments of the Little Poor Man, and, like the *Sacrum Commercium,* doubtless reproduces formulas familiar to him. We give it here from the version of M. Beaufreton, *Anthologie franciscaine* (P 1921) 32-33:

"My sweet Savior, merciful Jesus, have mercy on me and on the Lady Poverty; for the love that I have for her has turned into anguish, and I cannot rest without her. You know, O Lord, if I love her; and behold her sadly seated, like a widow, rejected by all men. The queen of all peoples is considered vile and despicable; the queen of every virtue is seated on the dunghill and complains that all her friends have disdained her and are become her enemies; and that those even who have espoused her have long violated their pledged troth. O Lord Jesus! Remember that You descended to earth from the dwelling-place of angels to make this queen Your spouse, and to have of, in, and through her, perfect sons. Remember her fidelity and affection. Scarcely had Your soul become united to Your body in the Virgin's womb, when her tender care for You began. At Your birth, she received You in the stable and in the Crib; and accompanying You Your life long, she deprived You of all things so well that You had no place even to lay Your head. When you commenced the war of our redemption, she joined You like a faithful squire. She was by your side in the thickest of the battle, and did not withdraw when the disciples fled or else denied Your name. Finally, while Your mother, who followed You to the end and shared in all Your pains — while such a mother, because of the height of the Cross, could no longer reach You, in that hour the Lady Poverty embraced You more closely than ever and associated in Your crucifixion with eager zeal. She did not want Your Cross to be cunningly wrought, nor the nails to be in sufficient number, sharpened and polished. But of these she prepared but three; and she made them hard and blunt further to aggravate Your pain. And when You were dying of thirst, this faithful spouse took care to have men refuse You a little water; and, aided by impious satellites, she prepared You so bitter a draught that You must needs limit Yourself to moistening Your lips with it. Then it was that in the close embrace of this spouse You did expire; and she it was once more who paid You the last honors, watching jealously to see that You should have nothing that was Yours — no sepulcher, no ointments, no shroud even — so that all these must be borrowed. She was there at Your Resurrection; and while, amidst her embrace You gloriously lived again, she took care that You should leave in the tomb whatever had been lent. She ascended to Heaven with You; and You entrusted her with the seal of the Kingdom of Heaven, with which Your chosen must be sealed who would follow the path of perfection. Oh, who would not then love above all things the Lady Poverty! That is why I pray You in Your name, O Jesus most poor, as a special and perpetual privilege, to give to me and mine the grace to possess nothing under Heaven, and never to have, so long as we shall be in this miserable flesh, any other than the poor use of the property of others."

9. Here the author certainly does not report the words of St. Francis, for he never criticized monks any more than he did priests.

10. *Legenda antiqua*, 9; *I Celano*, 42.

11. *II Celano*, 2; *Legenda antiqua*, 1; *Speculum*, 27.

12. *Liber exemplorum*, 123.

13. *Legenda antiqua*, 96.

14. *Ibid.*

15. *II Celano*, 137.

16 *Ibid.*, 176; *Legenda antiqua*, 5; *Speculum*, 28. These authors speak of a "sick brother," without anything more specific. It is Wadding who declares that it was Brother Sylvester.

17. [A206:202.]

18. *I Celano*, 43. [See Appendix II on Chronology.]

19. *Opuscula*, pp. 20-21.

20. *II Celano*, 123, 133; *Bonaventure*, VI,6; *Speculum*, 60; *Legenda antiqua*, 3.

21. *II Celano*, 141.

22. *I Celano*, 38; *Legenda antiqua*, 67, 102; *Specuulm* 26. Francis said also: "We call ourselves Friars Minors, because we are obliged by word and example to be more humble than all other men."

23. *Vita Fratris Juniperi*, AF III, 54-64; and *The Little Flowers of St. Francis*, ed. R. Brown (A166:231 & 235).

24. AF III, 54; *The Little Flowers*, p. 222.

25. *Matt.* V: 11, 39-42. Toward the middle of the 13th century, Humbert de Romanis, the Dominican Master General, still considered the Friars Minor as bound to follow this precept to the letter. "Blessed Francis," wrote he, "wished his sons to observe the Gospel in all its rigor, even in its most heroic aspects. To turn the left cheek to the person who has struck on the right — this and other like prescripts, they are obliged to obey." *Maxima bibliotheca Patrum* (Lyon 1677) XXV,468.

26. *I Celano*, 40.

27. *Legenda antiqua*, 40.

28. *Legenda antiqua*, 40; *Speculum*, 61-62; *I Celano*, 52; *II Celano*, 130. This anecdote is certainly characteristic of Francis' chivalrous ways. "Knights have such a horror of lying," says Jacques de Vitry, "that they are not even capable of selling a mule at market. They would start by disclosing all his defects, which would scare off the buyers." Sermon of Jacques de Vitry, quoted by Lecoy de la Marche, *La chaire française au moyen âge*, 2e éd. (P 1886) 362.

29. Bartholi, *Tractatus*, VI.

30. *I Celano*, 46; AF III, 79. [It was Brother Giles; cf E121:89-90).]

31. Rule of 1221, VII; Rule of 1223, V; *Testament*; *Tres Socii*, 44.

32. *II Celano*, 75; *Legenda antiqua*, 62; *Speculum*, 24.

33. Sabatier, *Vie*, (A305:157).

34. *Bonaventure* X,6; *II Celano*, 97.

35. *Legenda antiqua*, 102; *Speculum*, 44.

36. *Legenda antiqua*, 22; *Speculum*, 27.

37. *Actus*, 53; *Fioretti*, XLII.

38. *Actus*, 28; *Fioretti*, XXV; cf. *The Little Flowers* (A166:138 & 388); cf Ch. 2, Note 25.

39. *I Celano*, 42.

40. Rule of 1221, VII.

41. *I Celano*, 93.

42. *Ibid.,* 16.
43. *Speculum, 95; I Celano,* 23, 26.
44. Bonaventure, *Legenda minor,* VII, 1-2.
45. *I Celano,* 107.
46. *Legenda antiqua,* 63; *II Celano,* 76.
47. *Speculum,* 95, 96, 100.
48. *Liber exemplorum,* 143.
49. *Legenda antiqua,* 97; *II Celano,* 125.
50. *Legenda antiqua,* 96.
51. *Legenda antiqua,* 96; *II Celano,* 128.
52. *Legend of St. Clare.* (E170:49)
53 *Vita fratris Aegidii,* AF III,106;
[quoting St Bernard.]
54. *I Celano,* 47; [*Bonaventure,* IV,4.]
55. Francis, who always preached peace, succeeded many times in procuring it. Without mentioning the wars that the foundation of the Third Order prevented since 1221, the saint ended civil wars in Arezzo and Bologna; cf *II Celano,* 108, and Thomas of Spalato in Lemmens, *Testimonia minora* (A80:9-10).
56. [See FNV I/1, 388-395; II,19-199; III,574-57 (corrected text of the pact); also Appendix VI, Part 3.]
57. *I Celano,* 44; *Tres Socii,* 55.

7   THE PORTIUNCULA AND THE LIFE OF THE FIRST FRIARS

1. Only the choir, the crypt of the church, and the guest house still remain of this Benedictine abbey, a few miles from Assisi on the slopes of Mt. Subasio. [See F258-F261; cf B81-B87 & F254.]

2. *Legenda antiqua,* 8; *Speculum,* 55; *Fioretti* (Bughetti & Englebert eds.) Additional chapters II and III. To the spiritual heirs of the Poverello, the Portiuncula became the mystical site where his spirit still breathed, the sanctuary wherein the flame which he had come to enkindle upon earth still glowed. Francis himself felt that he had nothing more precious to bequeath to his sons at his death. (*Legenda antiqua,* 9-10.)

"Holiest of holy places!" exclaimed the author of the *Speculum,* 84. "Of what veneration art thou not worthy!

"If thy first name, recalling the holy angels, is happily chosen, and thy second name, borrowed from the Blessed Virgin, no less so, thy third name of 'Little Portion' is a harbinger of countless blessings for the brethren.

"For here the broad road down which the world rushed to its destruction has become once more the narrow way of salvation.

"Here the narrow way has been made broad so that unnumbered elect may walk herein.

"Here the Rule was born. Here did Holy Poverty reappear, putting Pride to flight and raising anew the Cross among us."

3. *Legenda antiqua,* 14-16; *Speculum,* 11.

4. Wadding *Annales,* 1210.

5. *Speculum,* 85 [based on *I Celano,* 102; cf. AFH 20(1927)89-90.]

6. *I Celano,* 39.

7. *De religiosa habitatione in eremo* in the *Opuscula;* [cf A61.]

8. For Brother Masseo, [see Appendix VII.] Sources of these incidents: *Fioretti,* IV, XI, XII, XXXII.

9. *Legenda antiqua,* 90; *Fioretti,* XXVI; *Speculum,* 66. [A similar tradition is reported at Bellegra (F347).]

10. For John the Simple, see *II Celano,* 190; *Legenda antiqua,* 19; *Speculum,* 57; [FNV I/1, 403-405; II, 297.]

11. "The Lord's Jester" (*Domini joculator*) or "the Lord's bowman" (*Domini jaculator*), depending on the reading; cf. *Speculum,* (A151:168n4).

12. Rule of 1221, XIV.

13. Rule of 1221, V & VI. Francis also said: "Let those who are set over others glory in their office only as much as they would if it were their duty to wash the feet of the brethren." (*Admonition IV*).

14. Rule of 1223, VI.

15. *Tres Socii,* 42.

16. [On Brother Juniper, see Appendix VII.]

17. *Legenda antiqua,* 6.

18. See the preface of the Quaracchi Fathers to their edition of the *Dicta beati Aegidii Assisiensis* (E119).

19. *Liber exemplorum,* 76.

20. [On Brother Giles, see Appendix VII.]

21. For memories associated with the Carceri, see N. Cavanna, *L'Umbria francescana* (F30:119-133), [cf F384-F389.]

22. *Legenda antiqua,* 107-108; AF III, 35-45. [On Brother Bernard, see Appendix VII.]

23. Rufino's father was Scipione di Offreduccio, brother of Favarone di Offreduccio, father of St. Clare. [FNV II, 349.]

24. *Fioretti,* XXIX, XXX, XXXI; AF III,46-54; AF IV,192. [On Brother Rufino, see Appendix VII.]

25. As Brother Leo often interrupted his Mass to savor his happiness, Francis

said to him one day, "Son, I beg you to act as other priests do when you are at the altar. If God sends you some grace, wait until you have finished your Mass and then enjoy God's consolation in your cell. Unless you do this, vain glory could enter into it and the devil profit by it to take away your merit. Besides, those present might become wearied waiting for you." *Liber exemplorum,* 70 (A211).

At another time, Francis said this also about spiritual favors: "When God's servant receives His visit in prayer, before leaving his prayer, he ought to raise his eyes to Heaven and pray, hands joined: 'O Lord, who have vouchsafed to send sweetness from Heaven to me a sinner, I give it back to You to keep for me in Your treasury. For that is where it belongs and I do not wish to be a thief.'" *Liber exemplorum,* 17 (A211); *Bonaventure,* X, 4.

26. Analecta, III,65-74; *Fioretti,* VIII, IX; *Liber exemplorum,* 50, 67, 70, 72, 143 (A211). [On Brother Leo, see Appendix VII.]

8 ST. CLARE AND THE ORDER OF THE POOR LADIES

1. [On St. Clare, in addition to the biographies of St. Francis, see E168-E222, and especially E170 (Brady), E177 (De Robeck), E183 (Fortini), E187 & E189 (Franceschini), E191 (Grau), E196 (Hardick), E197 (*J'ai connu* . . .), E199 (Longpré), and the studies in E220. The Process of Canonization — of fundamental importance — is available in English only in E177, but without the very useful notes in E197.]

2. [On the family of St. Clare, see Appendix VI, Part 2. For the recent controversy regarding the site of her home — first or second house on the left when facing San Rufino — see E214-E218. This problem also still needs a thorough objective study by an impartial expert; the results would clarify the obscure history of the old and new San Rufino and its drastic reconstruction during the lifetime of Francis.]

3. [Here Englebert, following E. Gilliat-Smith's *Saint Clare of Assisi* (L 1914) 50, referred (in a paragraph which we have eliminated) to the so-called Porta dei Morti, alleged to be a door in medieval Umbrian houses through which only the corpse of the head of the family passed. But the art historian Mario Salmi (F197) has proved that such doors (now usually walled up) were used in the Middle Ages, with removable wooden steps, entirely for protection during the frequent streetfighting. He attributes the corpse legend to some romantic foreign tourist. cf C12:10; C18:127.]

4. [For the chronological problem, 1211 or 1212, see Appendix II.]

5. [Fortini (FNV I/1,425-430; II,388-396 documents the history of the rich Benedictine convent of San Paolo. In 1283 the nuns moved into Assisi; the community was suppressed in 1452.]

6. Mrs. Margaret Oliphant in her *Life of St. Francis* (L 1870), quoted by G. K. Chesterton in his *Saint Francis of Assisi* (L 1924) 127.

7. The Life of Bl. Agnes of Prague appears in *The Chronicle of the Twenty-four Generals* in AF III,173-182. [For a recent life, see E221; cf E222a. On Sant'Angelo di Panzo convent on the slope of Monte Subasio between Assisi and San Benedetto, see FNV I/1,430-434; II,396-402.]

8. [Englebert states that the official deed of donation was published in *In ricordo 1212-1912* (A 1913), but it is not extant; cf F265 for a document of 1253.]

9. Rule of 1253, VI, [English tr. in E170:74. For the Pope's decisions, *ibid.,* 165n71.]

10. II Celano, 207. [Abate C160: 399) has published a hitherto unknown 14th-century version of this incident, which describes the Sisters as unmoved by Brother Elias' sermon but so deeply stirred by the Saint's pantomine and departure that their sobs could be heard outside the convent. A quarter century has passed since Abate wrote that he would publish this entire manuscript "a suo tempo". . . .]

11. II Celano, 112. Thomas of Celano treats at length of Francis' comportment with regard to women and of the attitude he wished his friars to adopt in this respect:

"He strictly enjoined on them to avoid familiarity with women, since it was a honeyed poison which leads astray even men of sanctity. He feared lest the weak should fall and the strong become weak. To avoid evil for one who associates with women, he would say, is as easy as it would be to walk in the flames without burning one's feet . . . When he himself could not escape from their importunate chatter, he would humbly bow his head, say a few words, and then take refuge in silence. Only those who were inspired by a right intention and true devotion were able to obtain a few brief interviews with him. And even then he took care to speak loudly enough that everybody might hear what he said." *II Celano,* 112.

"One day, enroute to Bevagna, he thought he would faint, he was so exhausted from fasting. A devout lady, accompanied by her daughter, a virgin consecrated to God, brought him the food he needed, in exchange for which he nourished them spiritually by speaking to them of God. As he had not once looked at them, his companion said to him after they were gone, 'Why did you not so much as glance at this pious young woman who came to you with so much devotion?'

" 'Who would not fear to look upon a bride of Christ?' he replied. He often returned to this theme. "What business has a Friar Minor to transact with a woman," he would say, "except when she asks him for a penance in confession or for some brief counsel on a better life?" *II Celano,* 114.

12. *II Celano,* 204-206. Oliger, E201: 418.

13. *Fioretti,* XV. [Little progress has been made in clarifying the historicity of this incident in the last fifty years, since Paschal Robinson, OFM, write (AFH 5, 641) that its foundation "is likely to be the slenderest," while Father Cuthbert (AFH 6,670-680) regarded the meal as probable but the fire as an embellishment. The crucial point is whether St. Clare ever left San Damiano, where according to Thomas of Celano in her *Legenda* she "imprisoned" herself for forty-two years.]

14. [Process, Witness 7,#2; & 6,#6.]

15. Similar sentiments caused Brother Giles to say: "This world is a thing of horror to the wicked, but for the good a thing of wonder."

15a. [Franceschini's model study (E-

187) analyzes all aspects of the two attacks on Assisi in 1240 and 1241. The early texts, especially those of the eyewitnesses in the Process (E197:136), specify that the Blessed Sacrament was not carried by St. Clare but by someone who went before her (whether the chaplain or a nun is not clear), and that she prayed in the refectory and not upstairs in the dormitory. The legendary version that she carried a monstrance to an upper window seems to have originated, perhaps to satisfy the taste for drama of artists and local guides, after the 15th century; cf E17:401; E197:78; E170:163.]

16. [For the letters of St. Clare to Bl. Agnes, see E170, E208, E213 & E222a.]

17. The Franciscan Spiritual Ubertino da Casale reports this dialog in his *Arbor vitae crucifixae,* [Lib.V, c.V (cf E68: 155), but in direct discourse and he gives the Pope's name as Alexander, i.e. Cardinal Rainaldo who became Alexander IV; however, Casolini corrects him and identifies the Pope as Gregory IX. On St. Clare's Privilege of Poverty, granted first by Innocent III and confirmed by Gregory, see E170:12-13 & 103-104 (Engl. text); E172, E193, E198, & E204.]

18. [On the early history of the Order of St. Clare, see E174, E193, E194, E-201, E205, E206, E219, E220, & E222.]

19. [On the Breviary of St. Clare, see Van Dijk's article (D67) and his *Origins* (D60:135-144). He claims that the identification of its copyist as Brother Leo is traceable to the early 17th century, and demonstrates (D67:44-46) that it is not in Leo's handwriting.]

20. AF III,81. [V. Doucet has proved in his Prolegomena to the *Glossa* of Alexander of Hales (Q 1951) I,35°-38°, that the theologian was Adam of Oxford and not Alexander of Hales.]

21. Rule of 1253, VIII. [Engl. tr. in E-170:75. For studies of the Poor Clare Rule, see also E194 & E206.]

9 FROM THE CLOTHING OF ST. CLARE TO THE LATERAN COUNCIL 1212-1215

1. "Some historians have contested the reality . . . of the children's crusade in 1212. But research has proven the historicity of this strange episode." A. Luchaire, *Histoire de France* (P 1911) III/I, 310 [For a masterful summary of recent research, see C89.]

2. *I Celano,* 55; *III Celano,* 33; *Bonaventure,* IX,5; [cf C74; no early

sources specify the Dalmatian port.]

3. *I Celano,* 56; *III Celano,* 34; Bonaventure IX,6. [On St. Francis in Spain, see C76-C79.]

4. [AFV III, 210.]

5. *Fioretti,* VIII; *I Celano,* 60. St. Bonaventure (IX,3) declares that Francis observed four supernumerary Lents a year: one after Epiphany, another before

the Feast of Ss. Peter and Paul, a third before the Assumption, and a fourth in preparation for the Feast of St. Michael. If one adds to this the Lent of the Church and that of the Rule (from All Saints to Christmas), as well as the Friday fast, (1223, III), it is evident that the Poverello fasted on an average of five days out of seven. [See also Jordan J. Sullivan, Cap, *Fast & Abstinence in the First Order of Saint Francis; A Historical Synopsis and a Commentary* (Wa 1957) 1-4; rev: MF 58(1958)585.]

6. [On Bl. Guido of Cortona, see E-124-E126 & F154.]

7. *I Celano*, 62; [cf Pagnani in F132: 49-53.]

8. Wadding, *Annales*, 1212.

9. *II Celano*, 147.

10. *I Celano*, 62.

11. *Fioretti*, X.

12. *II Celano*, 116-117; *Bonaventure*, V,4.

13. *Actus*, 9; *First Consideration on the Stigmata*, in *Fioretti*. The Latin text of the deed of donation, dated July 9, 1274, which the sons of Count Roland of Chiusi caused to be drawn up, [has been published by Lazzeri (F383:7-29) and Mencherini (F380:38-39). On the St. Francis in San Leo, see F138, F141, & F144. The picturesque crag village of San Leo, with its medieval castle (in which the infamous Count Cagliostro died in 1795) and its two striking Romanesque churches, is far more worth visiting than San Marino.]

14. *Fioretti*, XVI.

15. *Bonaventure*, XII,2.

16. *Ibid.*, VIII,6.

17. *I Celano*, 58; *Fioretti*, XVI; *Bonaventure*, XII,3; [*Liber ex.* 69. On the Sermon to the Birds, see D26, D30, & D35.]

18. *Bonaventure*, VIII,6-10. [For a complete collection of early texts about St. Francis and animals, see D28-29; cf D25, D32, D33, & D36.]

19. *I Celano*, 58-61 & 77-81; *II Celano*, 165-171; *Legenda antiqua*, 48-51, & 84. [For studies of the attitude of St. Francis toward nature, see D24-D39.]

20. *Legenda antiqua*, 110; *Speculum*, 113.

21. Latin text in *Testimonia Minora* [(A80:10-11; also AFH 1(1908)69 & MF 10(1906)35. Engl. text in A166:321. On this Benedictine Abbey of San Verecondo di Vallingegno, five miles south of Gubbio, see FNV II,240-242.]

22. *Actus*, XXIII; *Fioretti*, XXI. [De-spite its worldwide fame, the wolf of Gubbio is still patiently awaiting a critical study that might establish its historical existence. In 1958 Abate was undertaking such a study, but it has not yet appeared. Modern would-be "demythologizers" have offered a variety of substitute "myths" of their own: the wolf must have actually been a bandit or a robberbaron or even an evil woman. The only one of these suggestions which has any plausibility is that (favored by Sabatier) of the bandit of La Verna (60 miles away) known as Fra Lupo and then as Frater Agnellus after being converted by St. Francis; on him see E283:270-274; cf Wadding, *Annales*, 1291n19. But what is the evidence for Gubbio's wolf? As the critical Conventual historian Niccolo Papini (cf A158:77) wrote over a century ago on the margin of an Assisi manuscript of the *Fioretti*, "*Chi la dice lo primo?*" — Who said it first? The earliest text appears in a third version of Henri d'Avranches' *Legenda Versificata* AF X, 521 & liv] rewritten in part by a French Franciscan after 1285: "*Unus praecipue lupus ipso fertur agente/Factus mansuetus villaeque reconciliatus*" (It is said that one wolf in particular was tamed and reconciled to a town by him). Thirty years of so later the story was recorded in detail in the *Actus*. In the late 13th or early 14th century the Franciscan Custody of Gubbio placed the image of a wolf on its seal, and in 1349 one of the town's districts took a wolf's head as an emblem. In 1503 the small church of San Francesco della Pace was built on the site of the wolf's grotto, near its traditional grave. Around 1900 a wolf's skull with teeth in its large jaws was discovered during alterations made on the site of the grave, according to Gubbio's British historian, Miss Laura MacCracken (F293a:83), who interviewed a cathedral canon who had examined the skull. In view of this evidence, Abate (A166: 322); and Ugolino Paris (F294:29-50) accept the basic historicity of the event, despite possible embellishment in the *Actus-Fioretti*. The undoubtedly authentic narration in the 13th-cenury *Legenda de Passione Sancti Verecundi* (MF 10,6; A-80:10; A166:321) has no direct connection with the wolf of Gubbio, though located a few miles away; for its importance in the chronological problem of the years 1224-25, see Appendix II.]

10   THE LATERAN COUNCIL AND
THE MEETING WITH ST. DOMINIC

1. They base their statements not only on probabilities, but also on the testimony of Angelo Clareno (d. 1336) and of Gerard de Frachet, author of the *Vitae fratrum ordinis Praedicatorum nec non cronica ordinis ab anno 1223 usque 1254* (Louvain 1896) 9ff. [Oliger in 1913 questioned (AFH 6(1913)341) Cuthbert's acceptance of St. Francis' presence at the Fourth Lateran Council in 1215; in 1926 (F38:71) he insisted that if Francis were there, it could only be unofficially; and in 1949 (A270:20) he wrote that "the matter is quite obscure, because the early sources are silent about it; nevertheless there are certain texts," with these references; AFH 6(1913)341; E61:16; *Legenda antiqua*, 67; AF III,9. Confusion arises from various sources having Innocent III announce his approval of the Order *in concilio* or *in concistorio*. To the argument that if the Saint had attended the Council some early source would surely have so testified, we who are living through a General Council must reply that the absence of the founder of a new Order at a Council which debated and forbade the creation of any more religious Orders is inconceivable; cf CF 27(1954) 214; CF 30(1960)22n54. See also F112, F113, F119, & esp. Grundmann (D199a; 136-156).]

2. [Literally, "with a tau." The tau was the last letter of the Hebrew alphabet. In old Hebrew script, its symbol was a cross. — Tr.]

3. Labbe, *Sacrorum Conciliorum collectio* (1778) XXII,968-973.

4. [See Note 1, above.]

5. On St. Dominic and the origins of his Order of Preachers, see the critical studies in *Saint Dominique, l'idée, homme et l'oeuvre* by P. Mandonnet & M.-H. Vicaire, O.P. (P, 1937. 2v.); [condensed English tr. by Sr. Mary Benedicta Larkin (St. Louis, 1944. 487p.); and the definitive biography by Vicaire (E255.)]

6. This is the thesis defended by Father Cuthbert (A88: 211ff) and opposed by Oliger (AFH 6,1913,8 & 341; Sabatier (A305:387n3) considered it plausible. [See Esser's studies, D125 & E16.]

7. *II Celano*, 106; *III Celano*, 3; *Bonaventure*, IV,9.

8. Cf. Fr. Cuthbert, *Life of St. Francis of Assisi* (A288:214): "This formal adoption of the Franciscan fraternity into the forces of the hierarchy will necessarily bring about wide-reaching results in its constitution and development; it will become more intimately associated with the general forward policy of the Church: a secluded growth will no longer be possible; its individuality must find its setting in the common life and system of the Catholic hierarchy, of which it now becomes a more intimate member. And of this too you may be sure, that the two fraternities of Francis and Dominic having thus formally been adopted by the Church, the orthodox penitential movement will gradually find itself entirely drawn within their enfolding organizations: and the fraternities will grow not merely from the vital force within them but by the shepherding care of vigilant authority: and that too will affect their ultimate history."

9. [Another problem awaiting a definitive solution is that of the times and places of the several meetings between Saints Francis and Dominic. Following Altaner (E248:22-23), Vicaire (E255a: II,20,219,277) considers their interview with Cardinal Hugolin, early in 1221, the only one with a serious historical basis, with a first meeting in 1215 "simply possible, nothing more." However, neither Vicaire nor Altaner seem to be aware of the important Olivi text regarding Dominic's presence at a Chapter at the Portiuncula, for which see Ch. 12, Note 5. Oliger (F38:73) accepts 1221 for the interview with Hugolin and from a document of 1222 locates the latter's home beside the Church of SS. Pietro e Marcellino on the corner of the Via Merulana and Via Labicana, across from the present Franciscan Collegio di S. Antonio.]

10. He had not always been perfect. Of a violent temperament, he was quick to anger, and when angered would use violent oaths. He corrected himself of this fault, he said, thanks to the intercession of Bl. Marie d'Oignies, whose relic had been given him by Jacques de Vitry. (*Acta Santorum*, Junii V,577); [cf AFH 19(1926)550.])

11. The letter is contained in *The Legend and Writings of St. Clare* (E170: 111); & in E206.

12. *II Celano*, 148-150; *Speculum*, 43.

13. [See Note 9.]

14. *II Celano*, 149.

15. The ancient chronicles and the Papal Bulls often show them in conflict. Besides the endless discussions on the relative merits of their Orders, they did

not agree on the stigmata of S. Francis (Bulls *Usque ad terminos* and *Non minus dolentes* of 1237), on the virtues of St. Clare (Bull *Profundi doloris* of 1260), on the Indulgence of the Portiuncula (Bartholi, *Tractatus*, pp. 35, 70), and on the Immaculate Conception. They even fought in churches (E. Gilson, *Les idées et les lettres*, P 1932, 228-29). It was in vain that in 1255 their major superiors signed a mutual letter beseeching them to live in peace. (AF X, 17n7). After St. Catherine of Siena, a Dominican tertiary, had likewise received the stigmata (though they were not outwardly visible), and plenary indulgences like that of the Portiuncula were to be gained everywhere, Dominicans and Franciscans already had less cause for strife. When, finally, belief in the Immaculate Conception of our Lady, extolled by the Scotists (disciples of Duns Scotus, a Friar Minor) and combated by the Thomists (partisans of St. Thomas, a Friar Preacher), was defined as a dogma by the Church in 1854, the last cause of conflict between the two Orders disappeared.

16. Lacordaire, *Vie de saint Dominique*, 6th ed. (P 1860) 254. Fr. Léopold de Chérancé, *Saint Francois d-Assise* (P 1933) 180, says the same thing in almost the same words. Fr. Cuthbert, a historian, highlights the differences: "Francis and Dominic are types of two spirits usually found amongst men in active opposition — the spirits of liberty and law. . . . Only the fanatic will deny that both spirits are of the very essence of life itself, whether it be found in religion or elsewhere, and therefore at all times in potential harmony. Yet it is only in the more exalted natures that this harmony is realized. . . . In after times something of this discord actually showed itself in the relations between the disciples of Dominic and those of Francis; though the greater spirits amongst them ever remembered the founders' friendship and were true to it." (A288:220).

11 THE INDULGENCE OF THE PORTIUNCULA

1. [The French prelate Jacques de Vitry is not only one of the most important reporters of the Franciscan movement in the years 1216-1221, but also one of the most interesting figures in the ecclesiastical hisory of Europe and the Near East in the 13th century. Born probably in Rheims between 1160 and 1170, he studied in Paris, became a canon regular, and served at Oignies in the ancient diocese of Liège from 1211 to 1216. There he was closely associated with the extraordinary lay mystic, Blessed Marie d'-Oignies, who died in 1213 (see Butler-Thurston-Attwater, *Butler's Lives of the Saints*, June 23). In 1213 and later he preached in France against the Albigensians and for the liberation of the Holy Land so effectively, using a rich collection of striking *exempla* or anecdotes, that in 1216 he was appointed Bishop of St. Jean d'Acre. After his visit to Perugia in the summer of 1216, he went to Acre, and in 1218-21 took part with the Crusaders in the siege of Damietta in Egypt, where he again encountered St. Francis. In 1225 he returned to Europe, resigned his difficult see in 1228, but the next year was made Cardinal-Bishop of Tusculum (Frascati) and served in the Curia until his death on May 1, 1240. In addition to his seven extant Letters (A128; A80:79-80), his *Historia Orientalis* and *Historia Occidentalis* and the *Exempla* from his sermons have been published; for eds. see A128:viii. On his spirituality as influenced by Bl. Marie d'Oignies, see A129. His significant longer text on the Franciscan Order in the *Historia Orientalis* (not quoted by Englebert) appears in A80:81-84.]

2. Innocent III had come to Perugia in May, 1216. He intended to travel on through Tuscany and Northern Italy to reconcile Pisa and Genoa and to hasten preparations for the Crusade which had been decided upon by the Lateran Council in November, 1215.

3. [Only Friar Thomas of Eccleston, writing forty years later, mentions that "St. Francis was present at the death of Innocent III" (A135:95). The scene has been dramatically evoked in fiction by Timmermans and by Federer; cf CF 5 (1935)175.]

4. Ciaconius, *Vitae Pontificium romanorum*, I,659.

5. Honorius III remained at Perugia until the winter of 1216-17. [On this Pope, see F78-F82 & F64 & F70.]

6. [Most of the documents dealing with the early history of the Portiuncula Indulgence have been published by Sabatier in his edition of Friar Francesco Bartholi's *Tractatus* (F247), including other materials used in this chapter. Fortini (FNV II,53-55) has supplied additional biographical data concerning Bartholi;

however, his attribution of the *Liber exemplorum* to that writer is rejected in Appendix V on "The Homes of St. Francis" (see section on "The Fortini House"). Sabatier did not use the important early text by Frater Andreas Bajuli (in F252 & A210:439-488) which appears in part in English in *Our Lady & St. Francis* (D70:48-56); it is also not mentioned in Fortini's five volumes. But Fortini (FNV II,427-445) has thoroughly documented the many references in the archives of Assisi to the witnesses and other persons mentioned by Bartholi. For a comprehensive bibliography of the indulgence through 1937, see F255.]

7. Witness the concern voiced in Canon 62 of the Fourth Lateran Council in 1215: "Since there are indiscretions and excesses in the indulgences which certain prelates have not hesitated to grant, and since because of this the keys of the Church tend to lose their value and penance becomes greatly diminished, we decree that in the dedication of basilicas indulgence granted must never exceed one year. We would even wish that it should always remain under that limit."

8. III Kings 8:27-29, 41-44.

9. [Here Englebert mentions the alleged repairs which St. Francis made in 1216 to the old episcopal Church of Santa Maria Maggiore in Assisi. But Bracaloni (C70:363-367) had shown in 1935 that an inscription of that year on the outside of the apse commemorating alterations made "*tempore Episcopi Guidi et Fratris Francisci*" had been misinterpreted in another inscription placed inside the church in the 14th century. It is high time that this modern error be eliminated; yet Fortini (FNV III,25) merely mentions the inscriptions in passing and does not explain them or allude to Bracaloni's article. See also Ch. 4, Note 1.]

10. Bartholi, xl.

11. In the first quarter of this century much was written for and against the authenticity of the Portiuncula Indulgence. Some who were at first opposed to it (including Sabatier and Joergensen) have passed into the other camp, while the contrary has never occurred. [Huber (F255) has supplied a documented history of the controversy.]

12. *II Celano,* 146: "Know, brothers, that it is better for the good of souls, which is so dear to God, to get along in peace with the clergy than to dispute with them."

13. Bartholi, li-liii.

14. Bartholi, xlv-xlix, liv.

15. Bartholi, lxix-lxxix. [While a strong case can be made for the historicity of the granting of the Indulgence by Pope Honorius in Perugia in July, 1216, the later controversies inevitably resulted in the creation of a number of probably legendary accretions. A critical analysis and clarification are also still needed here. Among these apocrypha must probably be included: the temptation of St. Francis by the devil and his throwing himself into a rosebush (but cf. F250); a second vision of Jesus and Mary in the Portiuncula with the message that Francis go to Rome to have the Pope assign a specific day for the Indulgence; the determination of the day by the Pope in Rome owing to the miraculous roses brought by the Saint in January; and an account of the promulgation of the Indulgence in which the seven attending bishops wish to limit it but cannot utter anything except what Francis announced.]

12 THE CHAPTER OF 1217 AND MISSIONS IN CHRISTIAN LANDS

1. One of the first chapters, however, was held near Gubbio in the monastery of San Verecondo whose abbot generously fed the three hundred friars present (A 80:10-11; MF 10,6-7). Bonin (RF mars, 1948) claims that it was the example of the Trinitarians and Cistercians which led Francis to inaugurate this type of reunions. [On the early Chapters, see E3, E75a, E76.]

2. "Francis decided that the friars should meet at the chapel of the Portiuncula twice a year, at Pentecost and Michaelmas. (*Tres Socii,* XIV). Soon, however, these Chapters were held less fre-

quently. We know from Jacques de Vitry that in 1216 the friars met once a year. This was still too often, especially after their subsequent diffusion and the organization of missions. The General Chapter of 1221 was the last gathering of all the religious, professed and novices...That year Francis inserted a new regulation in the *Regula Prima* (XVIII)... Each minister could in the future hold an annual chapter in his province at Michaelmas. Ministers of Italian provinces could assemble once a year at the Portiuncula for Pentecost. Finally, general Chapters uniting the ministers of all the provinces of the Order would thenceforth be held only triennially, at the Portiuncula for the Feast of Pentecost, unless the Minister General should decide otherwise." Gratien, *Histoire* (E23:43).

3. *Fioretti,* XVIII.

4. *Tres Socii,* 59; *Legenda antiqua,* 2.

5. The "Chapter of Mats" of the *Fioretti* is a "model Chapter" for which it is apparently futile to seek to determine the date. Taken separately, nearly all the features of the account are historical, but we are unable to assign them to the same meeting. It is certain, for instance, that the Order did not have 5000 members in 1216; yet it is in this year that it would be necessary to place this Chapter if the Roman Curia was to take part in it, since the Curia did not return to Perugia during the next ten years. If, on the other hand, in order to justify the figure of 5000 friars (attested by *Bonaventure,* IV,10; & *Speculum,* 68 [cf A135:32]), we choose the year 1221, we are then compelled to leave out Cardinal Hugolin, who at this period was in Northern Italy, and was replaced at the Portuincula by Cardinal Rainerio Capocci.

[The presence of St. Dominic at a Franciscan Chapter, as described in the *Actus-Fioretti,* has been dismissed as legendary by such eminent scholars as Altaner (E248:23) and Vicaire (E255a: 219), but they fail to take into account the striking testimony of Jean Pierre Olivi (Olieu), who wrote in his *Lectura super Lucam* that as a novice (in 1261) in Béziers he had twice heard an elderly Franciscan, Raymundus Barravus, formerly a canon regular of the cathedral at Caracassone, declare that as student of theology in Paris he heard St. Dominic state that he had seen Francis and thousands of his brethren unexpectedly receive provisions at a general chapter in Assisi. This incident merits a thorough analysis; see texts in A316(1960)582 & A80:97; cf E254 & E251.]

There was indeed a Chapter which was remarkable for the great number of reed huts set up around the Portiuncula, and which for this reason was dubbed the "Chapter of Mats." Only, historians do not agree as to the date. Cuthbert (A288. 259ff & 267) and Gratien (E23:14) place it in 1219; Facchinetti (A293:199), with Jordan of Giano, in 1221; [Moorman A268:29] in 1218, and Brooke (E2:287 in 1222; see Brooke's study, E74.]

6. "The friaries closest to each other were united under the direction of a superior dependent on the provincial su-

perior. Such a group made up a custody. As the number of religious and friaries continued to increase, the custody was later transformed into a province having like the others its minister provincial, and was in turn subdivided into custodies. The resident superiors whether of custodies or provinces were called indifferently either "ministers" or "custodes." In primitive documents these two names are synonymous. Later, each took on a particular signification: the superior of the province was called the minister provincial, that of the custody, custos, and that of the friary, guardian. The Rule of 1221 (Ch. IV) gave all superiors the title of ministers. The word custos appears in the Rule of 1223 in connection with the care of sick brethren (IV) and the election of the minister general (VIII), and that of guardian in the Testament of St. Francis. All . . . could be chosen from among the laics as well as from the clerics." Gratien, *Histoire* (E23:41).

7. Rule of 1221, IV.

8. [On the chronological problem, see C10 and Appendix II.]

9. *Speculum,* 65; *Legenda antiqua,* 79. [It has been generally stated, with reason, that in referring to the extraordinary respect of the French for the Eucharist, St. Francis had in mind the strong cult then flourishing in northern France and Liege, which has been described by Callebaut (F85:551-555), McDonnell (A129: 313ff), and Frédégand Callaey (D45, D46). The fervor of that cult, owing much to the influence of Bl. Marie d'Oignies (d. 1213), had been reported to the Curia in Perugia by her friend Jacques de Vitry in the summer of 1216 (cf Ch. 11, Note 1). However, another manifestation, which no doubt made a deep impression on Francis and which has not yet received the attention it merits, is to be found in a decree of the Bishop of Paris, in about 1215, obliging priests to elevate the Host after the Consecration of the Mass so that all the faithful present could see and adore it; cf D44, D47. In general, on the Saint's devotion to the Eucharist, see Esser's basic study (D49) and Cornet's important analysis of his letter on the subject (D48). Francis did not inaugurate, but stimulated the eucharistic cult promoted by Innocent III) cf D41, D51.]

10. *Speculum,* 65; *Legenda antiqua,* 80.

11. *Fioretti,* XIII; AF III,117-118.

12. See Cuthbert (A288:250).

13. *I Celano,* 74-75; *Speculum,* 65;

AF III,10; *Legenda antiqua,* 82. [Calle-
baut has made a definitive study of this
meeting (F85).]

14. *Speculum,* 65; [on Brother Pacifico,
see Note 18 below.]

15. *II Celano,* 106; *III Celano,* 3;
Bonaventure, IV,9; *Legenda antiqua,* 23.

16. Bull, *Cum dilecti;* BF I,2 (F109).
Giano, n4. [cf F79.]

17. BF 1,5 (F109).

18. [On Brother Pacifico, see Appendix
VII.]

19. [For editions and translations of

the Chronicle by Brother Jordan of Giano
see A130-A134 & A82. Englebert used
A133.]

20. [The best edition of the Chronicle
of Brother Thomas of Eccleston is that of
Little and Moorman (A135); for translations, see A130-A132.]

21. AF III,10.

22. Giano, n7.

23. Giano, n6.

24. *Giano,* n5, 8.

25. Giano, n17-24, 27, 43, 59, 63.

26. Eccleston, III (A135:12).

13   THE CHAPTER OF 1219 AND MISSIONS IN PAGAN LANDS

1. [Bughetti, the great expert on the
Fioretti, discovered and published in 1927
(A207:107) another version of this famous dialogue of "the perfect joy" attributed to Brother Leonard of Assisi, who
was one of the witnesses who testified at
the Saint's canonization process. This important text (English tr. in A166:319)
from an early 14th-century Latin codex,
because it is shorter and more realistic
than the *Fioretti* version, appears to be
older and more authentic. It is therefore
of major significance for two reasons: it
serves to confirm the general reliability of
Brother Ugolino of Monte Santa Maria
(author of the *Actus*) and his informants;
it throws new light on the psychology of
the Poverello during his "dark night of
the soul" by presenting him as rejected
by the cruel brother-porter not as a scoun-
drel, but because he is "a simple and uneducated fellow . . . We are so many and
so important that we don't need you!" A
relatively colorless echo of the story appears in *II Celano,* 145, and with more
detail in parallel texts (listed in A166:
320). Englebert paraphrases both the
Fioretti and the Bughetti versions.]

2. *Legenda antiqua,* 11; *II Celano,*
57 [Thomas of Eccleston (VI, A135:32)
quotes a Brother Martin of Barton, who
frequently saw the Saint, as reporting that
the seneschal of Assisi who asserted the
city's ownership of the building was *"frater suus secundum carnem."* Brooke (E3:
89) identifies him as Martin's brother,
but Fortini (FNV I/1,158) claims it was
Francis' brother Angelo; the context, using *ipse* and *ipsum* for Martin, seems to
favor Fortini's interpretation.]

3. *Legenda antiqua,* 114; *Speculum,*
68.

4. The Provinces of France (Paris),
Provence, and Aquitaine; [cf E23(a) 522
& 524.]

5. AF III,78. [For a detailed account

of Brother Giles' abortive mission to Tunis,
see E121:95-102.]

6. [The Saint's longing for martyrdom
has been thoroughly analyzed by the Capuchin scholar Oktavian von Rieden
(C120). For the rich literature available
on the Fifth Crusade, see C80-C89; Van
Cleve's account (C89) is by far the most
useful and up-to-date. For works on the
early Franciscan missions in the Near
East, see C91-C102, with Roncaglia (C97,
C98) supplying the best summary of
Golubovich's monumental collection of
documents (C94; cited GBB), supple-
mented by later studies. On the Poverello in Egypt and the Holy Land (C103-
C123): apart from the documents and
discussion in GBB I,1-128 & III,278-283,
corrected by his later article (C113), the
most important summaries are those of
Roncaglia (C12 & C98:26-30 and Ghinato (C112). Fortini's treatment (C108)
is the longest, but lacks objectivity. A definitive study of this crucial episode in the
life of the Saint has not yet appeared.
Useful monographs on particular points
will be indicated in the remaining Notes
of this Chapter.]

7. [Bartholomew of Pisa (AF IV,481)
is the first to specify that Francis sailed
from the port of Ancona. Fortini (C108:
43) suggests that he may have left from
Brindisi, as Giles did in 1215, for it was
then the standard embarkation port for
the crusaders in Central Italy. Pagnani
(F132:34-37) considers Ancona *"proba-
bilius."*

8. [For these companions, see Appendix VII.]

9. [Here Englebert and other modern
biographers of St. Francis mention an incident which, according to the sources
(including *II Celano,* 155), happened in
"insula Cypri" (or Cipri): a nobleman
was edified on seeing Brother Barbaro eat
some asses' dung as a self-imposed penal-

ty for having spoken angrily to another friar. But Fortini (FNV II,383-387), following Papini, claims that the place is not the Island of Cyprus but an Isola Cipii near Limigiano, south of Cannara, across the valley from Assisi, where Brother Rufino's father Scipione had a castle; moreover, he infers that the nobleman was none other than Rufino, who soon joined the Order and later reported the incident. In any case,] "Francis had a special horror of those whose tongue distilled venom and poisoned their neighbors." *II Celano*, 182.

10. *II Celano*, 30; *Bonaventure*, XI, 3. [On the Spanish soldiers, see C105. Incidentally, among the Italian troops at Damieta, there were some from Spoleo (C108:49).]

11. A80:80; A128:133.

12. *Bonaventure*, IX,7.

13. September, 1219. [On the Spanish Cardinal Pelagius, see the excellent studies of Donovan (C81) and Mansilla (C84).]

14. Psalm 22:4 (Vulgate).

15. *Bonaventure*, IX,8.

16. From the *Verba fratris Illuminati*, a 14th-century text in GBB I,36.

17. *I Celano*, 57; *Bonaventure*, IX,8-9; Giano, n10; *Fioretti*, XXIV; Jacques de Vitry; the continuator of William of Tyre; and other texts in GBB I. [A perfect example of the deplorable lack of communication between secular and ecclesiastical historians is the fact that a modern German Orientalist can write over 250 pages about Al-Malik al-Kamil (C83) without even mentioning St. Francis. Similarly, European historians until fairly recently wrote about the Crusades without studying Arabic sources. Yet it is important for us to learn that this Sultan had a passion for Sufi mystical poetry and especially for the works of the great 'Umar ibn-al-Farid (1181-1235), one of the finest Islamic writers on the very Franciscan subject of an intense personal love of God — no wonder the Sultan felt a warm affection for the Poverello! Did the compassionate, peace-loving Saint "approve" of the Crusades? The answer is yes, according to the *Verba fr. Illuminati* (GBB I,37; cf C112:174]: when the Sultan asked him whether, in view of Christ's teaching not to return evil for evil, Christians were morally right in invading Arab lands, Francis forcefully replied: "You do not seem to have read the whole Gospel, for it says, if your eye scandalize you, tear it out, by which (Christ) wished to teach us that no man should be so dear

to us that we should not separate ourselves from him, tear him away, and completely eradicate him if he tries to turn us away from the faith and love of God. So for that reason the Christians are rightly invading you and the land which you occupy, because you blaspheme the name of Christ and prevent from worshipping Him those whom you can. But if you wish to know, confess, and worship the Creator and Redeemer, they would love you as themselves."]

18. This is the way in which the author of the contemporary *Estoire de Eracles* sums up the voyage of St. Francis: "This man who started the Order of Friars Minor, Brother Francis by name, came to the army at Damietta and there did much good, and remained there until the city was taken. He saw the sin and evil which began to increase among the soldiers, and was displeased by it. For this reason he left there, stayed for a while in Syria, and then returned to his own land." — *Historiens des Croisades*, Vol. II, Bk. XXXII, Ch. 15; in GBB I,14-19.

19. GBB 1,117. Giano, n9.

20. The account of the sufferings of the martyrs was written on the day following their death by an eye witness belonging to the House of the Infante Don Pedro of Portugal [The Latin text appears in AF III,579-596; cf 15-22; cf C99, C100.]

21. "The prince said to them, 'What is the way of truth?' Brother Otto replied: 'The way of truth consists in your believing that the Father, Son, and Holy Spirit are three Persons and one God; in believing that the Son of God, Our Lord Jesus Christ, was born of the Blessed Virgin Mary, suffered, died, and was buried, arose from the dead and ascended into Heaven, whence He shall come to judge all men at the end of time.' Aborayde (Abu-Jacob) asked, 'Who taught you this?' Brother Otto, who was a priest, replied, 'We have learned it from many most holy witnesses, who are Abraham, Isaac, and Jacob, and the other patriarchs and prophets. The Incarnation of our Lord Jesus Christ then taught it to us, and afterward the Apostles, and finally the glorious martyrs and the saints of our own time," AF III,588.

22. Giano, n8, cf AFIII,21.

23. The text of Clareno is reproduced by Golubovich, GBB I,56; [with the key phrase ". . . *Sepulcro domini visitato . . .*" (p. 57) For the closest contemporary travel-account of the Holy Land at this time, see the report of the German priest-pilgrim Master Thietmar who was there

in 1217 (C87, C88; adapted in English in E121:77-81 for the 1215 journey of Br. Giles). On the evidence for the visit of Francis to the Holy Places, cf C112: 179.]

14   CRISIS IN THE ORDER AND THE RULE OF 1221

1. Eccleston, AF I,230 (A135:28-29). AF IV,242. [The English chronicler seems to play up beyond historical truth the role of his compatriot, Haymo of Faversham. Gregory died before 1258, and appears to have been released before then; cf A. Beguet, "Grégoire de Naples," AFH 4 (1911)621; and A. Sérent, "Bulla inedita Gregorii IX contra Fr. Gregorium Neapolitanum (28 Juni 1233)," AFH 27 (1933)3-28.]

2. *II Celano*, 32-33.

3. *Nullus . . . ad mensam in una paropside comedat.* Rule of 1221, XII; cf Sabatier, *Speculum*, p. 172n2.

4. [On Giovanni della Cappella, see Appendix VII.]

5. Bulls *Cum dilecti* (June 11, 1219), *Pro dilectis* (May 29, 1220), *Sacrosanta romana* (December 19, 1219), in BF I; [cf F79.]

6. Giano, n12; Angelo Clareno, in GBB I,56-57. [For the chronological problem, see Appendix II.]

7. *Bonaventure*, VIII,9.

8. *II Celano*, 31; *Legenda antiqua*, 30. [On Brother Leonard, see Appendix VII.]

9. *Actus* 61; *II Celano*, 58; *Speculum*, 6; [cf A166:349. Felder (E18(a): 127-131; (b):131-139) has an interesting analysis of this incident, in which he stresses the secular nature of the University of Bologna at that time as a center of juristic studies rather than theology; also that Friar Peter was a jurist. See also Abate's study of St. Anthony as the first Franciscan theologian of the Bologna studium (E150:275ff; cf Ch. 17, Note 29.]

10. Giano, n14-15.

11. *II Celano*, 24; *Tres Socii*, 63.

12. *I Celano*, 73-75, 99-101; *II Celano*, 25; *Tres Socii*, 64-65; Giano, n14; Glassberger, in AF II,17.

13. "Honorius Bishop, Servant of the Servants of God, to Brother Francis and to the other priors or custodes of the Friars Minor, greetings and Apostolic Benediction . . . We order you by these presents not to admit anyone to profession before a year's novitiate . . . We also forbid that friars should wander about without an obedience wearing the habit . . . Should any friars dare to do so, you are to in-

flict ecclesiastical censures on them until they repent." Bull *Cum secundum*, in BF I,6.

14. In the chapel of the Portiuncula, where he was interred, his epitaph reads: *Anno Domini MCCXXI id. Martii corpus fr.P.Cathanii qui hic requiescit migravit ad Dominum.* (AF III,30n8.)

The Chronicle of the Twenty-four Generals states that from the day after his death he performed so many miracles that people began to flock to his tomb with offerings. On hearing about this, Francis hastened to the Portiuncula and went to the miracle-worker's tomb. 'Brother Peter,' he said to him, 'you obeyed me so well while you were alive — obey me again now that we are being disturbed by all these seculars. I therefore order you under obedience to put an end to your miracles and let us recover our peace.' And in fact from that moment Peter Catanii did not perform any more miracles. AF III,31.

15. Jordan of Giano, who attended the Chapter of 1221, speaks of Brother Elias as already exercizing the functions of vicar general at that meeting; cf. Giano, n17; *II Celano*, 143.

16. [Sabatier would indeed be surprised to learn that his arch-villain Brother Elias is being "rehabilitated" in these decades. A judicious re-assessment, particularly of his role in the years 1221-1226, has been made not only by Conventual historians but also by such eminent scholars of the OFM as Fidentius van den Borne and the Quaracchi editors of Wadding's *Annales*. The latter (A240:I,-377) state that during the Saint's lifetime Elias *"minime defecisse"* and was always praised by Francis, and that his *"deflectere"* began during his Generalate. To this, van den Borne (E167) adds that the early sources show no trace of any dissension between the two and that the accusations against Elias in later texts must be heavily discounted. Alfonso Pompei, Conv, came to the same conclusions in a systematic and thorough study of contemporary and later literature (E165). Finally, Mrs. Brooke (E3), an independent (British and non-Catholic) observer, reached similar conclusions without hav-

24. Giano, n12. It is through John of Komerow that we know the name of the messenger from the Portiuncula. For the personality and authority of this chronicler, see A133:XIX-XXV & 11.

ing used the studies of either van den Borne or Pompei. Fortini's only significant contribution (E160) is rather startling and suggestive: he identifies Elias as the Dominus Bonus Baro who was Assisi's first Consul in 1198, and thinks he may even have been married and the father of a son before becoming a friar. Fortini has said that only a non-Italian could write a definitive biography of Elias — may one do so. For important recent studies, see E154-E165; for a brief biographical sketch, see Appendix VII.]

17. Giano, n19. [Esser (E75) and Brooke (E74a) have shown that despite his resignation, Francis remained in effect the superior general of the Order until he died. Brooke (E3:76-83) lists some cogent reasons for concluding that he resigned his office a year or two before going to Egypt; her reasons need further analysis. Ignatius Brady, OFM, in his critical review of the first English edition of Englebert's work, pointed out that there is almost no evidence for the hypothesis of Sabatier — and Englebert — that the Rule of 1221 was actually composed in 1220-1221; rather the anachronisms which it retained (e.g. in ch. VII) indicate that it was a revision of the *Regula primitiva* with the legislation and admonitions of the annual chapters; in this sentence, therefore, we have changed Englebert's *"rédigea"* to "revised". Numerous substantial studies of the Rules are listed in E78-E91; the only one in English in E91(b).]

18. [English texts of the Rules appear in A31-A33.]

19. "The true imitator of Christ, Francis, abhorred money above everything else. He urged his friars to flee from it as from the devil, and he taught them to look on it as so much dung. A layman who had come to pray in the chapel of the Portiuncula had placed a piece of money at the foot of its crucifix. A friar unthinkingly took the money in his hand and threw it on a window sill. When St. Francis heard about it, he severely reprimanded the friar for having touched the money; and he told him to go and pick it up with his mouth from the sill and carrying it thus in his mouth, to go and lay it on a heap of ass's dung." *Speculum*, 14. [For St. Francis' concept of poverty, see D76-D95, especially D81-D82, D84 & D87, as well as D114-D119.]

20. Brother Giles declared: "To say of anyone that he is a Friar Minor is to say that he should place himself beneath the feet of the whole world. And this is the reason why St. Francis gave this name to his religious, after a revelation which he stated he had received from God Himself." *Dicta beati Aegidii* (E119:94); [cf E77.]

21. "The blessed Francis trained those who were ministers or preachers in the performance of good works. He would tell them that their charge or office of preacher must never cause them to forsake holy and devout prayer; that they ought to beg and work with their hands like the other friars for the sake of a good example, for the good of their own souls and those of others." *Legenda antiqua*, 71. [On manual labor see D81 & B57.]

22. "Do not these naive repetitions have a mysterious charm that winds its way into your very heart? Is there not in it a sort of 'sacrament' for which the words serve but as the vehicle? Francis takes refuge in God like a child in its mother's bosom, and in the incoherence of his weakness and his joy, lisps to Him all the words that he knows, and by means of which he desires only to repeat the eternal 'I am Thine' of love and faith." Sabatier, *Vie* (A305:351).

23. Jordan of Giano, n16, and Psalm 143:1.

15   THE THIRD ORDER

1. *II Celano*, 70.

2. *Fioretti*, XVI. [The origins of the Third Order Secular remain obscure. In opposition to the generally accepted date of 1221, Sarasola (A316:(a)425-440; (b)361-38), followed by Habig (E31: 401-403; & E229:17-18) interpret *I Celano*, 36-37, as indicating that the Saint organized groups of lay persons soon after returning from Rome to Assisi in 1209. This theory has not yet had the definitive analysis which it merits. Fortini establishes that Cannara, the traditional site of the first Umbrian group, was a flourishing small town then (FNV II,458).]

3. *III Celano*, 181.

4. [On Brother Jacopa, the fundamental work is still Edouard d'Alençon's booklet in its 2d edition (E243); cf E113, E244, E246, F122. One major problem had been the year of her death: about 1239 (Wadding) or much later? Was she the *domine Iacobe de Roma* mentioned in an Assisi will of 1258 and in another of 1273? If so, the young widow (in her twenties when Francis met her) lived to

be over eighty. But a papal letter of 1288 (omitted by Fortini) also names a *Jacoba de Roma dicta Christiana*, leading the Capuchin historian to conclude that she was not Brother Jacopa for these reasons: she would then be about 100 years old; the last two words suggest a virgin consecrated to God; and the wills of 1258 and 1273 list her as recipient of clothing (E243:62-63; FNV II,456). Terzi (F-122:63) claims that the painting by Simone Martini in the Lower Church of San Francesco Basilica, hitherto identified as St. Clare, is Brother Jacopa; cf E190.]

5. *Bonaventure*, VIII,7.

6. [English tr. in A31-A33.]

7. The author of a contemporary life of Gregory IX attributes the foundation of the Third Order to Cardinal Hugolin (RIS III,575).

8. On this subject, see the works of Callaey (E228), Van den Wyngaert (E-236), [Van den Borne (E235), and Habig (E31:399-410 & 427.)]

9. These documents are: (1) the text of Capistrano published by Sabatier in OCH (P 1903) I; (2) the text of Koenigsberg published by Lemmens in AFH 6(1913)249ff; (3) the text of the library of H. de Landau at Florence, published by Bughetti in AFH 14(1921)109ff. The first of these texts is of 1228; the second somewhat later; and the third appears to be prior to 1228; [cf E31:405 & 427.]

10. Scarcely was the third Order founded than the citizens of Faenza entered it en masse, so as not to have to answer the call to arms of their suzerain. The latter, who was a Ghibelline (and therefore of the party opposed to the Pope), wished to compel them to take up arms by reason of their oath. They had recourse to their bishop, who appealed to the Supreme Pontiff. In a Bull of December 16, 1221, Honorius III replied that the tertiaries of Faenza were released from their vassals' oath, and that it was the duty of the bishop to protect them against their lord. See the Bull in BF I,8.

11. For the political and social influence of the Third Order, see: Leo L. Dubois, *St. Francis Social Reformer* (NY, 1905); Cuthbert, (A288:339-345); Felder, *Ideals* (D161(b):295; [Van den Borne's (A320:280-286) and Clasen's ar-

ticles (D79), as well as the works listed in Note 8 above.].

12. In *The Ideals of St. Francis* (D161 (b):295), Felder writes: "That St. Francis was a social reformer, whose equal the world has not seen since the time of Christ, is generally admitted by the authorities of various camps and convictions." "It is in the Rule of St. Francis," declares Gino Capponi, "that the consecration, and in a manner, the beginning, of Italian democracy is to be found." *Storia della Republica di Firenze* (F 1875) I,180. For H. Thode, *Franz von Assisi und die Anfaenge der Kunst* (Berlin 1885) 52, "the Beggar of Assisi is the representative of the great mass of 'little people,' of the Third Estate, which, on the whole, aspires to independence and self-government. He is likewise the representative of every man possessed of an awareness of his rights . . . in the world."

There is, doubtless, much of truth in these generalizations. Yet it must be said that neither in his writings nor sermons does Francis ever appear to be prepossessed by political or social matters. Like Christ, he seems unconcerned by the temporal fate of the group as such. His primary concern is the individual and his eternal salvation. To be sure, he preaches the love of neighbor, peace, interior joy, the right of every man to fulfill his spiritual destiny. But all this is the Gospel, whose practice, we well know, effectively conduces to the temporal happiness of the individual and of society. Perhaps it is therefore better, in defining with precision the political and social role of the Poverello, to limit ourselves to saying that, more than anyone else in the world, Francis brought the Gospel home to men's souls.

13. Mariano of Florence fixes the date of this event as March 20, 1221; cf. A. Van den Wyngaert, E236:42-44.

14. [For outstanding Tertiaries, see. *These Made Peace* by Cecily Hallack and Peter F. Anson, rev. and ed. by Marion A. Habig, O.F.M. (E230); and *The Franciscan Book of Saints* by Marion A. Habig, O.F.M. (E106)]

15. [On Blessed Luchesio, see *These Made Peace* (E230:2-9, 243), and E246-E247.]

16 THE FOUNDING OF THE FIRST FRANCISCAN SCHOOL

1. It is especially in relation to the subjects dealt with in this and the following chapter (XVI and XVII) that Franciscan sources give rise to varied inter-

pretations and that historians disagree. The divergence comes from the inclination of some toward the views of St. Bonaventure and of others toward those of

Brother Leo. As for Thomas of Celano, although he assuredly is closer to the views of the latter than of the former, everyone succeeds in ranging him on his side.

Since it is necessary, if we are to make any progress, to make a definite choice between these two divergent viewpoints, we prefer to refer to the testimony of Brother Leo for our account. Should the reader, however, desire to embrace the opposite opinion, we call his attention, among other works, to those of Felder and Beaufreton, where he will find it briefly and learnedly defended: "Franciscan Science," in the former's *Ideals of St. Francis* (D 161 (b):351-379) and the latter's chapter on "La crise et la réorganisation de l'ordre des frères mineurs," in his *Saint François d'Assise* (A80:20-226).

To be fair to St. Bonaventure, we must note that he did much to save the spirit of St. Francis, not only by his wise direction of the Order, but also by his writings, in which he was able to cast the deeds and examples of the Founder into an image accessible to all the friars.

2. For Felder, in his history of studies in the Order (E18) and in his *Ideals* (see Note 1 above), the Poverello positively encouraged the scientific movement in his Order. This thesis has been challenged by E. Gilson in *The Philosophy of St. Bonaventure* (D164(a):46-50); Carvalho y Castro, *Saint Bonaventure* (P 1923) 35ff; Cuthbert (A288: 346ff); Gratien, *Histoire* (E23:81-96); and Jordan (E29).

3. On the culture of St. Francis and his understanding of the needs of his times, see Vito da Clusone's *Cultura e pensiero di S. Francesco d'Assisi* (D184). [Despite its erudition and Bihl's courteous preface, reviews describe this vast compendium as uncritical and inclined to exaggeration.]

4. *I Celano,* 82.

5. *Testament.*

6. *II Celano,* 163; [cf Notes 27 & 29 below].

7. Giano, n12.

8. *Legenda antiqua,* 73; *Speculum,* 4. Mark 4:11; Luke 8:10.

9. *II Celano,* 195; *Speculum,* 69.

10. *Legenda antiqua,* 7; [*Speculum* 4; cf Admonition 6].

11. *II Celano,* 194.

12. *Legenda antiqua,* 77 [condensed paraphrase]: "The Blessed Francis caused it to be written in his Testament that all the houses of the friars were to be of wood and mud, as a sign of holy poverty and humility, and that the churches for their use were to be small. Many observed that in certain countries wood cost more than stone. But he did not argue the point with them, since he was then very ill, even at death's door. We who were with him when he composed the Rule and nearly all his writings, testify that he introduced in it many prescriptions which were opposed by the friars, especially by the superiors. It was from fear of scandal, but against his will that he gave in to them. He would often say, however: 'Woe to those friars who oppose what I know to be God's will! ... The thing that afflicts me is their opposition to that which I obtain from God's mercy through prayer and meditation.' "

13. "Without condemning, of course, theological science (any more than he condemned property), and even honoring it in others, he wished none of it for his Order. This follows from the silence on this point and the spirit pervading all his Rules." Jordan (E29:90).

14. *Legenda antiqua,* 73.

15. *Ibid.,* 72-74; *Speculum,* 4; *II Celano,* 195.

16. Rule of 1223, X.

17. *II Celano,* 194.

18. *Ibid.,* 189. Thomas of Celano wrote that for Francis, "True simplicity is that which glories in the fear of God and knows not how to do or say evil. It examines its own self and does not judge others. It respects the power entrusted to its betters and does not desire it for itself. Judging that 'the Grecian glories' are not man's highest title to fame, it prefers action to study and teaching.... It seeks not the bark but the pith, not the shell but the kernel, not many things but that good that is highest and unchanging."

19. *II Celano,* 191-192.

20. The state of studies and preaching in the Church at this period is fully described by P. Mandonnet, M. H. Vicaire, and R. Ladner in *Saint Dominique* (P 1937. 2v.); condensed Eng. tr.: *St. Dominic & His Work* (St. Louis, 1944. 487 p).

21. *Legenda antiqua,* 71; [*Speculum,* 72.]

22. *Legenda antiqua,* 43-44; [*Speculum,* 100.]

23. Rule of 1223, IX; [*I Celano,* 72; *II Celano,* 107.]

24. *I Celano,* 73. Etienne de Bourbon (d. 1261) likewise mentions this improvised sermon, but he certainly is mistaken when he claims that Francis went so far as to inveigh against the dissolute lives of

prelates; cf. Lecoy de la Marche, *Anecdotes . . . d'Et. de Bourbon* (P 1876) 215 & 407, & *La chaire française au moyen âge* 2e éd. (P 1886) 323; [and Lemmens, *Testimonia minora* (A80:93-94).

25. A80:9-10.

26. "While refusing to become the promoter of science in his Order, Francis had no desire to forbid it . . . He even consented to its cultivation, but under certain specified conditions designed to render it immune to the all too real dangers that he dreaded. Forbidden to the laics, study was rightly permitted to those whose profession it was . . . (However) the true Friar Minor should not, according to Francis, devote himself to study chiefly with preaching in mind . . . but for his own sanctification, i.e. that he might learn to do better, to love better, and to live better." Gratien, *Histoire* (E23:93,95).

This is that author's summary of his chapter (pp. 81-96) consecrated to this question: "We may conclude that St. Francis, deeming learning unnecessary to the fulfillment of his ideal, and struck by its possible dangers, neither desired to promote it in his Order nor to make of it one of its essential means of action. He nevertheless consented to permit, to scholars only, the study of sacred science, to the exclusion of the profane sciences, and on the condition that this study should be first of all a means of sanctification."

[On St. Anthony of Padua, see A55-A56, E133-E153, E167.]

28. *Fioretti*, XXXIX & XL. [Candido Mesini, OFM, has recently set forth a strong but not definitive claim (E144) that the hermitage of San Paolo, in which

Anthony spent his first year in Italy, is on a hill just south of Bologna and not near Forlì.]

29. At this time Francis wrote to Anthony of Padua: "To Brother Anthony, my 'bishop,' Brother Francis sends greetings. It pleases me that you teach Sacred Theology to the brethren, but on condition that by this study they do not destroy the spirit of holy prayer and devotedness, as it is written in the Rule." *Opuscula* (Q 1904) 179. [The authenticity of this letter seems to have been established, despite the objections of Bonman (A55), by Esser (A56) and Clasen (E136(c):112ff; cf E16:213n114. Cambell (A44:244-249), writing after Bonman but before Clasen, considered it probably authentic. See also Ch. 14, Note 9.]

30. *Poesie spirituali*, B. Brugnoli, ed. (F 1914) 57; [*Le laude*, I,10 (F 1923) 84: "*Mal vedemmo Parisi — ch'ane destrutto Ascisi.*"]

31. *Dicta* (E119) App. 1,6. [For the background and Giles' opinions of "egghead" friars, see Brown, *Franciscan Mystic*, ch. 17, "The Franciscan" (E121:154-179).]

32. *Vita B. Aegidii*, AF III,101. [On Brother Giles and St. Bonaventure, *Franciscan Mystic*, pp. 174-179. In connection with the anecdote of the old woman, the Seraphic Doctor has the following related passage in his *Collationes in Hexaemeron* (*Opera Omnia*, V,418): "*Sic ecce, quod una vetula, quae habet modicum hortum, quia solam caritatem habet, meliorem fructum habet quam unus magnus magister, qui habet maximum hortum et scit mysteria et naturas rerum.*"

17 THE FINAL RULE AND THE TEMPTATION OF ST. FRANCIS

1. *Speculum* I; *Bonaventure*, IV, 11; *Verba S. Francisci*, 4; AF III,29.

2. He dictated the Rule to Brother Leo, as the latter told Brother Conrad of Offida, who so advised Ubertino de Casale; see the latter's *Arbor Vitae*, V, Ch.5.

3. *Legenda antiqua*, 113.

4. *II Celano*, 209; *Bonaventure*, IV, 11.

5. *Legenda antiqua*, 113; [*Speculum* I; *Verba*, 4.

6. *Epistola III*, in *Opuscula* (A28: 109).

7. Hugolin, later, as Pope, declared in the Bull *Quo elongati* (Sept. 8, 1230)

that he had collaborated on the Rule of 1223. The Bull *Quo elongati* is reproduced in BF I,68-70; [critical text in E24.] The Bull *Solet annuere* is contained in BF I, 15ff.

[Nine lines above, the editors changed Englebert's "*on sait*" to "[I surmise]".]

There were intransigents who were displeased by the Pope's approval of the Rule of 1223 and who disregarded it. The number of these rebels must have been considerable since, less than three weeks later, a new Bull enjoined the prelates to treat them as excommunicated (Bull *Fratrum minorum* of December 18, 1223, in BF I,19). For different reasons, Elias and his friends were likewise not satisfied. Elias declared later that having made his vows under the Rule of 1209, he was not obliged to observe the Rule of 1223; Eccleston, ed. Little (A135:68).

8. "The second Rule does not reproduce the intentions of the founder in their entirety and with all the vital force that he would have liked to put into it; and this by reason of the suppression of certain words of the Holy Gospel which were especially expressive of his ideal." Gratien, *Histoire* (E23:105).

9. *Legenda antiqua*, 80: "Although this article does not figure in the Rule, because the ministers did not judge it opportune to oblige the Brethren on this point, the holy Father nevertheless desired in his Testament . . . to bequeath to his friars the expression of his will on this subject. He likewise desired that friars should be sent into all the provinces carrying good and fair irons for making hosts." (cf *Speculum*, 65).

10. *Legenda antiqua*, 69; "The ministers knew well that, according to the Rule, the friars were obliged to observe the holy Gospel. Nevertheless, they caused to be suppressed that passage of the Rule wherein it is said: 'Take nothing for your journey.' . . . That is why the blessed Francis, warned by the Holy Spirit of what his ministers had done, exclaimed in the presence of several friars: 'The ministers think to deceive God and to deceive me. But that all the friars may know that they are bound to observe evangelical perfection, I wish to have written these words at the beginning and end of the Rule: 'The friars are obliged to observe the holy Gospel of our Lord Jesus Christ.' And that the friars may be without excuse before God, I desire, with God's help, to perform and observe forever the ordinances God has put in my mouth for the salvation and utility of my soul and of the souls of my friars." [cf A320:273-277.]

11. "Whereas the first Rule stipulated that the friars could have only those books necessary for the Office, the second Rule (III) makes no such restriction." Gratien, *Histoire* (E23:105).

12. *Speculum*, 6; *II Celano*, 58.

13. Bulls *Cum dilecti filii* of June 11, 1219, and *Pro dilectis* of May 29, 1220.

14. Bull *Devotionis vestrae* of March 29, 1222.

15. Bulls *Quia populares* of December 3, 1224; *In hiis quae* of August 28, 1225; & *Non deberent* of September 18, 1225.

16. Bull *Ex parte vestra* of March 17, 1226.

17. Bull *Nimis iniqua* of August 21, 1231.

18. Bull *Quo elongati* of September 28, 1230.

19. Among these writers may be mentioned Renan, Hase, Thode, Kybal, and Sabatier. The latter constitutes himself their spokesman when he writes, for example: "The Gospel of the Beatitudes was rediscovered . . . Alas! The Church, personified by Cardinal Hugolin, if it did not render abortive the Franciscan movement, was at least so to block it that a few years later it had lost all its original characteristics." *Vie* (A305:199). And elsewhere: "One of two things is true. Either [Hugolin] did not understand the profoundness of the Franciscan effort; or, understanding it, spent the rest of his life flourishing the Franciscan banner while betraying it. There could be another solution. Hugolin was one of those men who see no difference between the religious interests of the world and the political interests of the Holy See. For this old man of indomitable energy, whose whole intellectual and moral strength was thus oriented, the success of Franciscan preaching had awakened only one quite practical idea: 'How can I use this force?' " (*Ibid.*, 278-279). It is just to observe that some non-Catholics, such as W. Goetz and H. Tilemann, do not share their views.

20. Two critics among those in France who have best studied the first century of Franciscan history, Gratien and Jordan, consider that, in view of the situation of the Church in the 13th century, the ideal of St. Francis needed clarification before being put into practice.

According to the first, "Between the views of the prudent cardinal and those of the fervent initiator, there was . . . an important difference. Hugolin strove to harmonize the enthusiastic views of the Saint and the practical considerations of the ministers. He knew . . . that St. Francis' plan was the answer to the needs of the Church and of the people. But to him this plan appeared incomplete. . . . It did not seem fitting to him to keep the Friars Minor in the obscure role which the Poverello had assigned to himself and his first disciples. . . . What regeneration of the Church might one not expect from these men who, once raised to ecclesiastical dignities, should preserve . . . the evangelical spirit of poverty, of simplicity, of humility! An admirable dream, a grandiose conception, from which the holy cardinal was unable to detach his gaze; and which, it would seem, ought to have captivated the idealistic Francis. . . . Perhaps (the latter) was wrong not to fall in more freely with the views of Cardinal Hugolin and the clerics by widening his own scope of action." Gratien, *Histoire* (E23: 67-68) and *St. François*. . .(D127(a)67; not in (b).

Edouard Jordan writes: "In his Rules, in his Testament . . . St. Francis had forbidden to his friars the ownership of all property, either as a group or as individuals. . . . Now a great effort in legal dialectics was displayed to assure to the Order, as an essential condition of its activity, a semi-ownership based on the quasi-intervention of others. . . .St. Francis had especially forbidden luxury in construction, even of churches. Yet some of the most beautiful religious edifices of the Middle Ages are Franciscan churches. . . . Without condemning the science of theology, he desired none of it for his Order. And the Franciscan Order was speedily transformed into an Order of students. If I were to have, says the Testament, 'as great a wisdom as Solomon possessed, and were to meet poor priests of this world, I do not wish to preach without their consent in their parishes.' And yet the Order exhausted itself in quarrels and arguments with the secular clergy, a good share of them on this very subject of preaching.. . . . The Testament forbade the friars to 'ask for any letter of privilege at the Roman Curia' But the apostolic privileges solicited by the Order would fill volumes.. . . Foreseeing possible relaxation, Francis had thought to forestall it by proscribing casuistry. But the glosses and explanations of the Rule — official, pontifical, and private — fill a whole library. . . In a word, nothing could have been farther from the thought of St. Francis than the idea of the inevitable growth of all living organisms. Yet the Order has lived. In this perpetual opposition between what the Saint wanted and what happened lies the drama of the first century of Franciscan history." — E. Jordan, "Le premier siècle franciscain," (E29:90-91).

21. Salimbene, *Chronica* (A136:161).

22. One of the oldest is that of the Observants, who were in a certain sense heirs of the Spirituals of Angelo Clareno. The latter, after having been approved by St. Celestine V (1294), were condemned and suppressed by John XXII (1317). Some fifty years later the Observants began, following many of the same ideals but acting with greater prudence and ability. Their name came from their resolve to observe the Rule strictly and simply, whereas "Conventual" was the name given to the friars who continued to live in large "convents" in the towns; [cf E27:133ff]. These designations remained when the Observants, after their first zeal, abandoned their hermitages to take up residence again in cities. At the Council of Constance (1415), they obtained a sort of autonomy, although their head, called the Vicar General, remained theoretically under the obedience of the Minister General, elected by the Conventuals only. [On the Observants see Iris Origo's masterpiece, *The World of San Bernardino* (NY, 1962. ix,303p. illus.).]

Three divisions took place in the Observants of the fifteenth century: the Coletans, inspired by St. Colette of Corbie; the Amadeans, inaugurated by Blessed Amadeus of Portugal; and the Discalced Friars, influenced by Blessed John of Puebla. In 1517, however, deeming that these reform groups no longer had any justification, Leo X joined their members to the Observants, who received on this occasion the privilege of electing the Minister General of the Order. The Conventuals thus found themselves dispossessed, and had to be content with a Master General who depended theoretically on the head of the Observants.

To these two Franciscan families, the Capuchin reform added a third in 1528, which became autonomous in 1619.

There were never any divisions among the Conventuals and Capuchins. With the united Observants it was a different story. "Once more," writes Fr. Gemelli, "the Franciscan trunk renewed its youth as a result of sacrificing rigid unity to the liberty of evolution, in keeping with the law of life." (A. Gemelli, *Le Message de St. François d'Assise au monde moderne* (P 1935)130.

Leo X had hardly re-established the unity of the Observance when it gave birth to three important reforms: the Alcantarines in Spain, the Reformed in Italy, and the Recollects in France and the Low Countries. Although theoretically under the head of the Observants, Alcantarines, Reformed, and Recollects nevertheless had their own constitutions and hierarchy until the day when "perhaps without great advantage," writes Fr. Gemelli (*ibid.*, p. 220), Leo XIII reunited them with the Observants (1897).

Since that time, the First Order is divided into Friars Minor, Conventuals, and

Capuchins. These groups are autonomous, having their own minister general; and in 1959 comprised about 26,300, 4,100, and 15,500 religious, respectively [(E34:89; statistics & chart)].

Since we are on the subject of figures, we note that the Second Order, the Poor Clares, consists of more than 16,000 nuns. The Third Order is divided into the Third Order Regular and the Third Order Secular. The first is composed of congregations leading the authentic religious life in which vows of obedience, chastity, and poverty are taken. It numbers about 180,000 members. The third is composed of both single and married people who do not leave the world or take religious vows. It numbers about 2,200,000 members [(E34:477, 518, 419). On the early history of the Order, see E1-E73.]

23. He did not consent to treat his body gently until too late, and even then he profited by the opportunity to mock it: "When the hour came when against his will he had to use appropriate remedies for the sufferings that were exhausting his strength, . . . Francis said jokingly to his body: 'Rejoice, brother body, and forgive me. I am ready now to satisfy your desires, and I shall make haste to supply all your needs.' But what could now have afforded pleasure to a body already wasted away? How is one to support anything

when it is falling in ruins?" *II Celano,* 210-211.

24. *Ibid.,* 211.

25. *Legenda antiqua,* 21; *II Celano,* 115.

26. *Fioretti,* XV; *II Celano,* 205.

27. *II Celano,* 152; *Bonaventure,* VI,4.

28. *II Celano,* 156; *Legenda antiqua,* 17.

29. AF IV,428.

30. *Legenda vetus,* in OCH I,97.

31. *Speculum,* 64; *Legenda antiqua,* 83; *Bonaventure,* VI,5.

32. *Admonition III,* in *Opuscula.*

33. *II Celano,* 157; *I Celano,* 103.

34. *II Celano,* 188: "A little later, in the midst of his great sufferings, he sat up in bed and in exaltation of soul cried out: 'Who are these men who have snatched from my hands my Order and that of my friars? If I am able to go to the General Chapter, I will show them what my will is.' " See also *Speculum,* 41.

35. *Speculum,* 71; *Legenda antiqua,* 76.

36. *Legenda antiqua,* 114; *II Celano,* 188; *Speculum,* 68.

37. *II Celano,* 158; *Legenda antiqua,* 86.

38. *II Celano,* 188; *"Vivant pro libitu!"; Speculum,* 81.

39. *II Celano,* 115; *Legenda antiqua,* 21; *Speculum,* 99.

18 CHRISTMAS AT GRECCIO

1. *Legenda antiqua,* 61; *Speculum,* 23.

2. *II Celano,* 120; [for Brother Giles' stay with a Cardinal, see E121:110-111; on the Cardinal, F106].

3. Eccleston, AF I,231; ed. Little (E135:30-31).

4. *II Celano,* 119-120; *Legenda antiqua,* 92; *Speculum,* 67; *Bonaventure,* VI,10.

5. It was this double sentiment of joy and compassion that was his inspiration for the following psalm. It forms part of the short *Office of the Lord's Passion* that Francis was accustomed to recite, in addition to the usual canonical hours:

"Sing joyfully to God our helper: acclaim the Lord, the living and true God, with a loud cry of joy!

"For the Lord is terrible and great, the Great King over all the earth. Because the most high Father in heaven, our King before the ages, has sent His beloved Son from on high; and He has been born of the Blessed Virgin, Holy Mary.

"He shall cry out to me: Thou art my

Father; and I will make Him the First-born high above the kings of the earth.

"In that day the Lord God sent us His mercy: and in that night His song. This is the day the Lord has made: let us be glad and rejoice therein.

"For the most holy and beloved Child is given us and born for us on the way and laid in the manger: because He found no place in the inn.

"Glory in the highest to the Lord God: and peace on earth to men of good will.

"Let the heavens be glad and the earth rejoice: let the sea be moved, and the fulness thereof; the fields and all things that are in them shall be joyful . . .

"Give to the Lord, O countries of the nations, give to the Lord glory and honor: give to the Lord the glory due His Name.

"Offer your bodies in sacrifice and carry His holy Cross: and follow unto the end His most holy commandments."

Officium Passionis Domini, in *Opuscula* (A28:126-148). [For recent studies of this *Office,* see A57-A60.]

6. *II Celano*, 199-22; *Legenda antiqua*, 110; *Speculum*, 114; "The blessed Francis said of the lark: 'Our sister lark wears a hood like the friars. She is a humble bird, glad to go along the roads to find a few grains. Even if she finds them in the droppings of animals, she picks them out and eats them. Even as she flies, she praises the Lord, like a good religious who despises earthly things and whose life is in Heaven. And her clothing, that is, her plumage, is the color of earth. Thus she gives a good example to the friars, who ought not to wear showy or sumptuous garments, but those of a dull hue like that of the earth.' And for all these reasons, the blessed man Francis was very fond of our sister larks and liked to watch them." *Legenda antiqua*, 110.

7. Bonaventure, X,7: "*Miles virtuosus qui propter Christi amorem saeculari relicta militia. . .*" [cf C137:8].

8. [The Christmas Crib at Greccio has been the subject of considerable discussion; for outstanding studies, see C124-C142; and on Greccio, F354-F356. Three principal topics can be discerned: the event at Greccio, the history of the Christmas crib before St. Francis, and the influence of the Saint on the later development of the crib. (1) Why did he obtain the Pope's permission? Because in 1207 Innocent III had forbidden the *ludi theatrales* enacted in churches (cf Ch. 1, Note 33), because live animals were to be present, because the Mass was to be outdoors in a grotto and not in a chapel, and perhaps to avoid any friction with the local pastor or ordinary. Msgr. Terzi has recently engaged in a minor controversy

with Prof. Maria Sticco, opposing her denial that a statuette *bambino* was used (C138); Thomas of Celano's basic text (*I Celano*, 86) is ambiguous on this point. Important archaeological discoveries, particularly of the long-hidden private cell of the Poverello, have been made at Greccio by Msgr. Terzi and amply described in his *Memorie* (F356). A new church for pilgrims has replaced the one built fifty years ago. (2) Greccio is not the first example of a Christmas crib. Well-known cribs existed for centuries in Santa Maria Maggiore and Santa Maria in Trastevere in Rome; instances of live animals being used in the mystery plays of the shepherds (*officium pastorum*) are found in France in the 12th century. Francis had probably visited Bethlehem, and had certainly seen the Nativity realistically represented in Byzantine and Italian Romanesque mosaics and paintings. (3) Contrary to generally accepted notions, it would appear that the Christmas of Greccio had relatively little direct influence on Italian art and especially on the development of the craft of the creche, which begins to flourish only in the 16th century. However, it had a profound influence on Franciscan spirituality, which was reflected in and stimulated by Jacopone da Todi's popular Christmas hymn, *Stabat Mater speciosa*. The specific originality of the Greccio Mass lay in its typically Franciscan fusion of stark simplicity and realistic dramatizaton. Its ever growing influence on the recent "Put Christ back into Christmas" movement has yet to be traced.]

9. *I Celano*, 84-87; *Bonaventure*, X,7.

19 THE STIGMATA

1. *II Celano*, 61; *Legenda antiqua*, 32; *Speculum*, 20; *Bonaventure*, VII, 9. [The first friars' refectory and dormitory are well preserved at Greccio; see illus. in C138 & F356.]

2. *I Celano*, 115.

3. *II Celano*, 61.

4. The principal sources for this chapter are: (1) the letter which Brother Elias addressed to Gregory of Naples on the morrow of the Saint's death (A72 & C196); (2) *I Celano*, 91-96 & 112-114; *II Celano*, 135-139 & 203; *III Celano*, 2-13; (3) *Bonaventure*, VIII,10, & XIII, 1-10; *The Five Considerations on the Holy Stigmata* in most eds. of the *Fioretti* [See E166:29, 171-216, 343-347, for background, English text, & commentary)]; (5) *Legenda antiqua*, 93. For

Oktavian von Rieden's masterly treatise on the subject, see C143; for materials on La Verna, F373-F383, with works on Franciscan Italy F26-F49.

5. [Of the companions with the Saint on La Verna, only Illuminato is named by Bonaventure; Leo, Masseo, and Angelo are mentioned in the *Third Consideration*. The late apocryphal "Farewell" adds Sylvester, but must be disregarded; see Note 25 below.]

6. *First Consideration*.

7. [Today three excellent roads (from Bibbiena or Rassina on the west or Pieve S. Stefano in the Tiber Valley on the east) lead numerous pilgrims to the famous Shrine of La Verna, with its large friary (novitiate of the Tuscan Province) and basilica, chapels, and beautiful oak

and beech forest, with relics and memories of the Poverello and Blessed John of La Verna, one of the heroes of the last chapters of the *Fioretti*. Unknown to most visitors and even to many Franciscans, just above and connecting with the Chapel of the Stigmata is one of the few hermitages left in the Order, inhabited by two elderly Fathers and a Brother who, however, take their meals with the other friars. On a clear day one can see the round hump of Mount Subasio from La Verna, on the southern horizon. A pilgrimage to this holy site of the stigmatization should if at all possible be arranged by all who visit Franciscan Italy; the most practical way is for several persons to share the reasonable fare of an all-day automobile excursion from either Florence or Assisi. Every mile of the way the pilgrim will be traveling — in comfort — in the very footsteps of St. Francis. A restaurant and overnight accommodations are also available. Read Gemelli's vivid account of a retreat there (D162).]

8. *First Consideration.* [Even in an automobile on a sunny spring day, one notices how dry one's throat becomes in the Apennines above an altitude of 3000 feet.]

9. *Second Consideration.* [The welcome by Count Orlando of course occurred on the first of the Saint's several visits to La Verna. A little-known document of about 1300 states that the *"locus* of the Holy Mount La Verna was accepted" on September 8, 1218 (A136:657).]

10. Sabatier, *Vie* (A305:397).

11. *Second Consideration.* [For an interesting analysis of the remarkable series of chasms and ravines, resulting from a severe earthquake, see F372.]

12. *Ibid.*

13. *Legenda antiqua*, 93; *Speculum*, 99.

14. *Second Consideration; II Celano*, 168; *III Celano*, 25; *Bonaventure*, VIII, 10. [La Verna is today a wildlife sanctuary.]

15. *Third Consideration; I Celano*, 91.

16. *Third Consideration; I Celano*, 92; *Bonaventure*, xiii,2. The custom of drawing lots to learn God's will is still in use among the Orthodox. It was very ancient in the Church; cf the selection of the Apostle Matthias in Acts, 1:23-26. [For other instances in early and medieval church history, see Karrer (A86:741).]

17. *Third Consideration. Bonaventure*, XIII,3: *circa Festum*.

18. *Third Consideration.*

19. *Bonaventure*, XIII,3; cf *Third Con-* *sideration; Actus*, IX,69; *I Celano*, 94-95; *III Celano*, 4; Eccleston, quoted in AF X, 247n2., (cf A135:75); *Encyclical Letter of Brother Elias* (AF X,526): "I announce to you a great joy and a new miracle. It is a sign that has been unheard of from the very beginning of time, except in the Son of God, Christ the Lord. Not long before his death, our Brother and Father was seen to resemble the Crucified Lord, bearing in his body the five wounds which are the marks of Christ. His hands and feet had the wounds of the nails and were pierced on each side, bearing the marks and showing the color of nails. His side seemed opened with a lance, and often bled."

20. *II Celano*, 138 & 214; *Bonaventure*, XIII,4 & 8; *Third Consideration.*

21. *I Celano*, 95 & 112-113; *III Celano*, 39; Elias' *Letter; Fourth Consideration; Bonaventure*, XIII,8: "At his death, more than fifty brethren were able to see them, as well as Clare, her sisters, and a great many seculars." [For data on the latter, cf FNV II,448-451.]

22. [For Englebert, the best refutation of rationalist explanations are those by Bihl (AFH 3,1910,393-432) and Gemelli (SF 1,1924,368-404). Much has been written on the subject since then; the reader must turn to Oktavian von Rieden's definitive work (C143) for the bibliography and the best analysis. A brief Appendix on the phenomenon of stigmatization appears in E166:32-324.]

23. *Opuscula*, p. 124.

24. *II Celano*, 49; *Bonaventure*, XI,9; *Second Consideration.* [There has been much discussion over the drawing of the cross or Tau over a mountain (Calvary or La Verna) or a head (Adam's or Francis'); see refs. in A53-A54, & Von Matt's illus. in F43:150.]

25. [The short Farewell in the last paragraph first appeared in 1818. On the equally apocryphal farewell attributed to Brother Masseo, see F375. Its earliest source is a 17th century manuscript in the friary of La Verna, where it is read to the community each year on September 30. For a paleographical analysis, see A380:6-7. Perhaps the writer of genius hiding under Brother Masseo's name was the Fra Salvatore Vitale (1576-1647) who, as we have seen (cf Ch. 4, Note 3), "contaminated" the early history of the Portiuncula. He spent three years at La Verna and wrote four books totaling over 1400 pages about it (F383:436). It should not be hard to ascertain whether the handwriting of the Farewell manuscript

is his. If so, this clever pseudephigraphon might be said to redeem somewhat the harm he did to the truth about the Portiuncula.]

[Mencherini (A380:27-29; cf D70:57] has shown that an alleged Bull of Alexander IV dated May 3, 1256, which asserts that the Blessed Virgin frequently appeared to St. Francis on La Verna — as indeed may well have happened — is spurious "and must have been fabricated by some fanatic of the 17th century." Perhaps a handwriting expert could help here too.]

[Late in the 15th century a tradition existed at La Verna (A380:140; cf D70:

58) that Mary had in fact appeared to Francis there and had "pointed out to him the site and the foundations and the shape" of "the devout church" which he caused to be built there. The historical origins of the 13th century chapel or first church need clarification. The local tradition that the Saint himself named it "Santa Maria degli Angeli," like the Portiuncula, is first documented only in 1568 (A380:169). This problem was first disclosed in 1954 (D70:57), but the latest history of the shrine (F376) ignores it. A critical study of the early history of such an important Franciscan "holy place" is overdue.]

20   THE CANTICLE OF BROTHER SUN
[On this Chapter, see Appendix VIII.]

1. A pair is still in existence at [Santa Chiara in Assisi; cf illus. n133 in F43.]

2. *II Celano,* 98.

3. *Fourth Consideration; I Celano,* 68, 70; *Bonaventure,* XII,11.

4. *I Celano,* 98; *Legenda antiqua,* 54.

5. *I Celano,* 109; *Legenda antiqua,* 64; [cf Appendix II].

6. *I Celano,* 98, 99; *Legenda antiqua,* 26,42,46.

7. *II Celano,* 213; *Legenda antiqua,* 43; *Speculum,* 100; *Fioretti,* XIX.

8. [See Appendix VIII on the important recent controversy over the place of composition of the Canticle of Brother Sun.]

9. "Because he thought that the sun is the most beautiful of creatures, being that most closely resembling our Lord, who is called in the Scriptures the Sun of Justice, he gave its name to the Lauds that he wrote on God's creatures when God assured him of His Kingdom, calling them the *Song of Brother Sun.*" *Speculum perfectionis,* 119.

10. *II Celano,* 213; *Speculum,* 119 & 120; *Legenda antiqua,* 43. For the abundant literature to which the *Canticle of the Sun* has given rise, see [C144-C185.]

11. *Legenda antiqua,* 25; *Speculum,* 104; *Fioretti,* XIX. [See also Note 8.]

12. *Legenda antiqua,* 44; *Speculum,* 101.

13. Some will be tempted to smile at these marks of veneration. Yet six and a half centuries later, French rationalists were still more exuberant in expressing their enthusiasm. We read in the historians of the French Revolution that on Federation Day La Fayette mounted the raised platform on the Champ-de-Mars and deposited his sword on the altar of

the fatherland. "Hardly had he descended when the Federals flung themselves upon him, some of them kissing his face, others his hands, and those less fortunate, his garments. No sooner was he on horseback, than they started kissing his legs, his boots, the horse's harness, and finally the horse itself." L. Madelin, *Les Hommes de la Révolution* (P 1928) 21-22.

14. *II Celano,* 41; *Bonaventure,* XI,5; *Legenda antiqua,* 58.

15. *Bonaventure,* V,11; *II Celano,* 126; *Legenda antiqua,* 24. According to the *Legenda antiqua,* Francis was at that time "in the house of Teobaldo Saraceni," where he remained a few days." [Terzi, *Memorie* (F59:13-60). supplies local background data on the homes of Teobaldo, the well-known doctor Maestro Nicola, and Br. Angelo's family.]

16. *II Celano,* 166; *III Celano,* 14; *Legenda antiqua,* 46, 48; *Speculum,* 115.

17. *Legenda antiqua,* 45; *Speculum,* 90.

18. *I Celano,* 103; *Bonaventure,* XIV, 1.

19. *Opuscula, Epistolae* III & IV.

20. *I Celano,* 105.

21. *II Celano,* 93; *Bonaventure* VII,6. [On the site, cf F161; on the Rieti-Siena itinerary, A90:323n196; A105:312n228.]

22. *II Celano,* 103, 137, 170.

23. *Legenda antiqua,* 17; *Speculum,* 87.

24. *Legenda antiqua,* 64.

25. *I Celano,* 105; *II Celano,* 87-88; *Speculum,* 30, 131, 35. "One day when St. Francis was returning from Siena, upon meeting a poor man, he said to his companion: We must give my cloak to this poor man. It belongs to him; we received it only as a loan until we should find someone poorer than we are. His com-

panion, considering the need the generous Father had of the cloak, objected strenuously to this generosity which would have deprived him to supply the other. But St. Francis said to him: I do not want to be a thief. And we would be thieves not to give this cloak to a man who needs it worse than we do. So the good Father gave his cloak to the poor man." *Speculum*, 30.

26. *II Celano*, 77; *Bonaventure*, VII, 10; *Speculum*, 22; [*Legenda antiqua*, 59. Over 40 years ago Delorme published the *Legenda antiqua* of Perugia containing an apparently authentic text dealing with

this part of the Saint's life which did not appear in any other source. It stated clearly that from Cortona he returned to the Portiuncula, and then, due to the summer heat, was taken to the hermitage of Bagnara near Nocera; on the latter, see F396. But Fortini did not use this text in 1926 (FNV 347), nor did Englebert in 1956 (A290(a):366). However, in his new biography, Fortini devotes many pages (FNV I/2,310-317; II,462-470) to this episode, concentrating especially on the history of the village of Satriano in the hills between Nocera and Assisi.]

27. *I Celano*, 105; *Speculum*, 109.

21 THE TESTAMENT AND DEATH

1. *II Celano*, 184-186; *Speculum*, 80.

2. *Epistola II*, in *Opuscula*. Ubertino da Casale, in the *Arbor vitae*, V, Ch. 7, declares that this letter was written toward the end of St. Francis' life. This is one of the chief reasons for thinking that it was addressed to the Chapter of 1226.

3. "The cult of St. Francis for the Blessed Sacrament is as strong as that which he felt for the Scriptures. Like devout Christians of all time, (he) found in the Bible passages meant especially for him. He mined it with the enthusiasm of a farmer delving into soil whose richness he has experienced and to which he looks for food." Sabatier, *Etudes inédites* (A-307:19). [For studies of Francis and the Bible, see D1-D5.]

4. "*Moneo . . . ut una tantum missa celebretur in die. Si vero plures fuerint in loco sacerdotes, sit . . . alter contentus audita celebratione alterius sacerdotis.*" *Opuscula*, p. 104. Francis thus desired that in friaries where there were several priests, only one of them should celebrate Mass. This practice, still in use in the Orient, was likewise the custom for several centuries in the West. It was not until quite late that the custom of Latin priests of celebrating the Holy Sacrifice daily became general. Felder, *Ideals* (D-161:445) thinks that the Saint acted out of respect for the Eucharist — *assueta vilescunt*. Cuthbert (A288:441) judges, however, that he was legislating *in concreto*, against an actual evil: the simoniacal habits of some priests whose zeal was in proportion to the gifts they received. [See D45, D65, D66, & my Guide, p. 9.]

5. See the critical monograph of Esser (A62). [The English text in this book is by Ignatius Brady, OFM, who retains all rights to it.]

6. The Bull *Quo elongati* (Sept. 28, 1230) said: *. . . ad mandatum illud (Testamentum) vos dicimus non teneri; quod sine consensu fratrum maxime ministrorum, quos universos tangebat, obligare nequivit, nec successorem suum quomodolibet obligavit, quum non habet imperium par in parem.* The Testament had not been assented to by the friars, still less by the ministers; and from a canonical point of view, Francis, supposing that he still was Minister General, could in no wise bind his successors, who enjoyed the same powers as himself. *Non habet par in parem imperium.*

7. We may be surprised at Francis' attempt to take back in this Testament of 1226 what he had granted to the Pope's representative in the Rule of 1223. But that obedience entailed sacrifice of one's "judgment" was not so wide-spread an idea in his time as it has become since. It was St. Ignatius of Loyola who best formulated the theory: "Let it be clearly understood," he writes, "that the obedience which consists in the *execution* of that which is commanded is the first and lowest degree of obedience. It does not deserve the name of obedience because it is worthless if it does not go on to the second degree, which is to make the superior's *will* one's own; so that not only is the order received carried out, but the soul itself conforms in the same willing or not willing . . . If anyone intends to make a complete and perfect oblation of himself, he must surrender not only his will but his understanding. The third and supreme degree of obedience is not only to be of the same will as one's superior, but of the same thought, submitting one's own *judgment* to his." — *Ignatii episolae*, IV,669-681, in *Monumenta historica S.J.*

8. St. Luke 18:19.

9. *Legenda antiqua,* 65; *Speculum,* 122. [Fortini (FNV II,536-542) identifies the doctor as a judge of Assisi, though none of the documents he cites describes him as *medicus.* Arezzo archives have a tenuous reference to a *"mag. Buongiannis (medici)"* at this time (A194:228).]

10. Eternal death.

11. *Legenda antiqua,* 64; *Speculum,* 121, 123.

12. *I Celano,* 107.

13. *Ibid,* 108. [See Note 18 below.]

14. *Legenda antiqua,* 99; *I Celano,* 108. [The gate was the Porta Moiano (FNV I/2,328).]

15. *Legenda antiqua,* 99; *Speculum,* 124; For the various texts of this blessing of Assisi, cf Sabatier, *Speculum* (A151: 245nl), [& FNV I/2,329n2].

16. *I Celano,* 106; *Legenda antiqua,* 9-10; *Speculum,* 55 & 83. "We who have lived with him, bear witness that we heard the blessed man Francis solemnly declare that of all the churches dedicated to the Blessed Virgin, this was the one she loved best. Thus, shortly before his death, he said before the Minister General and the other brethren: 'I want the clerics who live here to be chosen from among the better, the more holy, and those who know best how to recite the office. And let the lay brothers who serve them be also chosen from among the most humble and sincere, who do not gossip with them or tell them news of the world. And when one of them passes away to God, the Minister General is to take care to replace him by another friar of like holiness. For I want this place to stay blessed and always be the mirror and model of my Order." —*Speculum,* 55.

17. *II Celano,* 214-215.

18. *I Celano,* 109; *Legenda antiqua,* 107; *Speculum,* 107; *Fioretti,* VI; AF III,42. [Brooke (E3:17-19) analyses the differences between the accounts of the blessings in *I Celano* and *II Celano,* but does not treat the special blessing of Brother Bernard reported only in the later sources, which the *Actus-Fioretti* distorted. The *Legenda Neapolitana* or *Umbra* (A203:245), probably written about 1254 (E3:19) has Francis say to Elias: *"fratrum necessitates viriliter supportasti."*

19. *Legenda antiqua,* 109; *Speculum,* 108; *Opuscula,* p. 76; Rule of St. Clare, VI,3 (E10:74).

20. *III Celano,* 37-39; *Legenda antiqua,* 101; *Speculum,* 112; Bernard of Bessa, AF III,687; *Fourth Consideration; Liber exemplorum,* 67.

21. *II Celano,* 217; *Legenda antiqua,* 117; *Speculum,* 88; *Bonaventure,* XIV,4. [Some confusion in the precise order of the events in the last days of the Saint prevails in both early and modern accounts. In *II Celano,* 217, Friar Thomas corrects a slip he made in *I Celano,* 110: the Gospel of the Passion read to the dying Francis at his request (omitted by Englebert) began with John 13 and not John 12. Also *Bonaventure,* XIV,5, seems to correct *I Celano,* 110, by having the Saint die singing the Psalm, which Thomas reported was sung before the Gospel reading.

22. *I Celano,* 110-113; *II Celano,* 217; *Legenda antiqua,* 109-110; *Speculum,* 112; *Bonaventure,* XIV,6, & XV,1-8. [For studies of the Poverello's last days and death, see C195-C200; on his relics, C-201-C216; and on his canonization and cult, C217-C232.]

A

FRANCIS OF ASSISI
RESEARCH BIBLIOGRAPHY

Comprehensive for 1939-1963
Selective for Older Materials

compiled by

RAPHAEL BROWN

EXPLANATORY NOTE

A few brief notes on the sources and technical style of this Bibliography may be helpful to its users.

In accordance with that law of research which states that one reference leads to another, it is based primarly, of course, on the data in its own 1575 items. Secondarily, naturally, on the excellent bibliographies listed under A1-A26, especially the invaluable wealth of materials in the *Collectanea Franciscan's Bibliographia Franciscana* (A2). Other useful sources have been the major religious encyclopedias: *Enciclopedia cattolica; Lexikon für Theologie und Kirche*, 2d ed.; *Dictionnaire d'histoire et de géographie ecclésiastiques* and *Dictionaire de spiritualité ascétique et mystique* (unfortunately neither has yet treated François d'Assise); and *Dictionnaire de théologie catholique*, especially its recent *Tables générales*. Still too new to be of much help, yet richly promising for the fuure are the *Bibliotheca Sanctorum* (E103), also to appear in English; *Dictionnaire de biographie française;* and *Neue deutsche Biographie*. No doubt the *New Catholic Encyclopedia*, with articles on Francis and Clare by Lothar Hardick, OFM, will become a standard reference work.

In addition, mention should be made of the major current national bibliographies: *Bibliografia nazionale italiana, Bibliographie de la France, Deutsche Nationalbibliographie* and *Deutsche Bibliographie, Das Schweizer Buch, Nieuwsblad voor de Boekhandel, Bibliographie de Belgique,* and *Libros del mes;* as well as the various national cumulations similar to our *Cumulative Book Index*. Not least in usefulness have been two union catalogs: the National Union Catalog in the Library of Congress, on cards and in recent years in published author and subject catalogs; and the Franciscan Union Catalog at St. Bonaventure University, St. Bonaventure, N.Y.

A careful perusal of the cumulative indexes of the following periodicals (see Abbreviations) has also been rewarding: AFH, EF, MF, & DSPU; but that of IF has not been available. Still more enriching has been a systematic coverage of their pages, as well as those of the other principal Franciscan historical journals (FF, FS, IF, & SF), especially for important reviews and abstracts, from 1963 back to beyond 1939.

As to *bibliographical style*, perhaps to the annoyance of some users, the principles governing the editing of this Bibliography have been deliberately Franciscan: simplicity and economy. Hence the liberal use of *contractions*, e. g. Cap for O.F.M. Cap.; 13th for thirteenth century; & for and; and of *abbreviations*, not only for periodicals and monographic series, but also for place names in imprints and even for S(aint) F(rancis) (of) A(ssisi) — see lists below.

It is hoped that the user will be helped by the equally generous number of *cross-references*, usually indicated by cf (even after a period, to avoid any possible confusion with the frequent CF); as they will lead him to other important data on the subject. For the same reason, references to outstanding *reviews* (Rev:) and *abstracts* (Abs:) have been included, often with the name or initials of the reviewer. It must be stressed that these items will frequently include significant corrections of fact and additional references.

Lastly, a single *asterisk before* an entry number (e.g. *A266) indicates that the book or article contains a useful bibliography of older materials, while two asterisks before the entry number (e.g. **A7) are used only for major bibliographies or for works having a comprehensive bibliography. For a list of the latter, see the index under Bibliographies. (Asterisks after page numbers denote a separate pagination in certain CF volumes; see list in A2.)

In the Bibliography, Notes, Appendices, and new Introduction, the system adopted for *page references*, though somewhat unorthodox, could hardly be more simple and economical: C185:37-42, for instance, means pages 37-42 in item C185 in the Bibliography.

In the still chaotic realm of *capitalization*, the rule adopted (with almost exceptionless consistency) has been to follow the more or less standard practice of each language.

The *Bibliography Subject Index* will prove helpful in finding various subjects, but it does not cover authors. The Bibliography is not included in the Index at the end of the book.

The reader will also do well to study carefully the table of Contents of the Bibliography, as it is much more inclusive than the brief outline of the Bibliography in the general Table of Contents in the front of the book.

BIBLIOGRAPHY

CONTENTS

A. DOCUMENTATION

C. LIFE

D. SPIRITUALITY

E. ORDERS

A   DOCUMENTATION

I ABBREVIATIONS

1 NAMES & PLACES IN TITLES & IMPRINTS

A   Assisi, Assise
Ba   Barcelona
Brux   Bruxelles
Chi   Chicago
Dü   Düsseldorf
F   Francesco, Francis,
    François, Franciscus,
    Franziskus (not Franz)
FA   Francesco di Assisi,
    Francis of Assisi,
    François d'Assise
Fi   Firenze
Fr/Br   Freiburg im Breisgau
L   London
Man   Manchester, England
Mi   Milano
Milw   Milwaukee
NY   New York

P   Paris
Phil   Philadelphia
Q   Quaracchi
R   Roma
S   San, Sanctus, Saint, Sankt
SF   San Francesco, Saint Francis,
    Saint François, Sankt
    Franziskus, Sanctus
    Franciscus
SFA   SF with Assisi, Assise
SMA   Santa Maria degli Angeli
    (Assisi)
To   Torino
Tü   Tübingen
Ven   Venezia
Wa   Washington
We   Werl/Westfalen
Z   Zürich

AB   *Analecta Bollandiana*
Actus   *Actus Beati Francisci et Sociorum Ejus.* See A158
AF   *Analecta Franciscana.* Q, 1885-1941. 10v. See A133,
    A134a, A191, A193, A64.

AFH	*Archivum Franciscanum Historicum.* Q, 1908-. (OFM) With *AFH Indices tomorum 1-50* (1908-1957). Q, 1960. 435p.
AFP	*Archivum Fratrum Praedicatorum*
Anonymus Perusinus	see A126.
AHR	*American Historical Review*
AIA	*Archivo ibero-americano.* Madrid, 1914—. (OFM)
AKG	*Archiv für Kulturgeschichte*
ALKG	*Archiv für Litteratur und Kirchengeschichte des Mittelalters.* Fr/Br, 1885-1900, 7v.
Ant	*Antonianum.* R, 1926—. (OFM)
AOFM	*Acta Ordinis Fratrum Minorum.* Q, R, 1882—. (OFM)
ASF	*Les amis de saint François.* P.
ASS	*Acta Sanctorum.* See A281.
Bartholi, *Tractatus*	see F247.
BF	*Bullarium Franciscanum.* See F109.
BISI	Instituto Storico italiano per il Medio Evo *Bollettino*
Bonaventure	*Legenda Maior.* See A74.
BSFS & BSFS-ES	British Society of Franciscan Studies Publications & Extra Series
BSS	*Bibliotheca Sanctorum.* See E103.
CC	*Civiltà cattolica*
CCM	*Cahiers de civilisation médiévale*
CED	*Collection d'études et de documents sur l'histoire religieuse et littéraire du moyen âge.* Paul Sabatier, ed. P, 1893-1909. 8v. See A151, F247, A158, A133.
I *Celano*	*Thomas of Celano, Vita Prima.* See A65
II *Celano*	*Thomas of Celano, Vita Secunda.* See A67.
III *Celano*	*Thomas of Celano, Tractatus de Miraculis.* See A68.
CF	*Collectanea Franciscana.* A, R, 1931—. (Cap) cf A2.
CHR	*Catholic Historical Review*
CISSA	Congresso internazionale di scienze storiche *Atti.* R, 1904.
CISSR	X Congresso internazionale di scienze storiche *Relazioni.* Fi, 1955.
COCR	*Collectanea Ordinis Cisterciensium Reformatorum*
Conv	*Convivium*
CVF	*Cahiers de vie franciscaine*
DA	*Dissertation Abstracts*
DASP	Deputazione Abbruzese di storia patria *Bullettino*
DBI	*Dizionario biografico degli italiani*
DDC	*Dictionnaire de droit canonique*
DHGE	*Dictionnaire d'histoire et de géographie ecclésiastiques*
DSAM	*Dictionnaire de spiritualité ascétique et mystique*
DSPM	Deputazione di storia patria per le Marche *Atti e memorie*
DSPU	Deputazione di storia patria per l'Umbria *Bollettino*; for its 1895-1954 index, see F185.

DTC & DTC-TG   *Dictionnaire de théologie catholique;* & *DTC Tables générales*

EC   *Enciclopedia cattolica*

EF   *Etudes franciscaines.* P, 1899-1938; ns 1950—. (Cap) With *Table générale des EF 1909-1928.* P, 1932. 172p.

EHR   *English Historical Review*

EstF   *Estudios franciscanos.* Ba, 1907-1911 as *Revista de EstF;* 1923-1936 as *Estudis franciscans.* (Cap)

FEC   Franciscan Educational Conference, *Report of the Annual Meeting.* Wa, 1919—.

FF   *Frate Francesco.* A, R, 1924—; ns 1954—. (OFM)

Fioretti   see A161-A165 for Italian eds; A166 English; Englebert used his own ed: A168.

FL   *Franciscaans Leven.*

FnSs   *Franciscan Studies.* St. Bonaventure, NY, 1924—; ns 1941—. (OFM)

FNV   Fortini, *Nova vita di SFA.* Mi, 1926. See A295.

FNV I-IV   Fortini, *Nova vita di SF.* A, 1959. See A296.

FQ   *Franziskanische Quellenschriften.* We, 1956—. 7v. (OFM) See A41, E191, E120, E140, A90, A132, A105.

FrFr   *La France franciscaine.* P, 1912-1939. 22v. (OFM)

FS   *Franzikanische Studien.* Münster, We, 1914—. (OFM)

GBB   Golubovich, *Biblioteca* . . . See C94.

Giano   *Chronica Fratris Jordani.* See A133.

Gratien, *Histoire*   see E23.

GWU   *Geschichte in Wissenschaft und Unterricht*

HJ   *Historiches Jahrbuch der Görresgesellschaft*

IF   *Italia francescana.* R, 1926—. (Cap) With *Indice generale (1926-1945).* R, 1945. 103p.

Laur   *Laurentianum.* R, 1960—. (Cap)

Legenda antiqua   Delorme's *Legenda antiqua de Pérouse.* See A148. Englebert cites Paris ed.

Lex Cap   *Lexicon Capuccinum.* See A12a.

Liber exemplorum   see A221.

Little Flowers   see *Fioretti;* English tr. A166.

LTK   *Lexikon für Theologie und Kirche.* 2 Aufl. Fr/Br, 1957—

LS   *Luce serafica.* Ravello (Salerno).

MA   *Moyen âge*

MAH   *Mélanges d'archeologie et d'historie de l'Ecole française de Rome*

MF   *Miscellanea Francescana.* Foligno, R, 1886—. (Conv) With *Indice dei primi XXXIII volumi (1886-1930).* R, 1935. lxxivp.

MFE   *Miscellanea Francesco Ehrle.* R, 1924. 3v.

MGH-SS   *Monumenta Germaniae Historica, Scriptores*

MS   *Medieval Studies*

NRT   *Nouvelle revue théologique*

NYT	*New York Times*
OCH	*Opuscules de critique historique.* Paul Sabatier, ed. P, 1901-1919. 3v.
Opuscula	see A28.
OR	*Osservatore romano*
OS	*Oriente serafico.* SMA. (OFM)
QF	*Quellen und Forschungen aus Italienischen Archiven und Bibliotheken*
QSF	*Quaderni di spiritualità francescana.* SMA, 1961—. (OFM)
RB	*Revue bénédictine*
RF	*Revue franciscaine.* Montréal. (OFM)
RH	*Revue historique*
RHE	*Revue d'histoire ecclésiastique*
RHF	*Revue d'historie franciscaine.* P, 1924-1931. 8v.
RIS	*Rerum Italicarum Scriptores;* ed. Muratori.
RQ	*Römische Quartalschrift*
RSB	*Rivista storica benedettina*
RSCI	*Rivista di storia della Chiesa in Italia*
RSI	*Rivista storica italiana*
RSR	*Revue des sciences religieuses*
Sabatier, *Vie*	Englebert cites 1931 ed. See A305.
SC	*Scuola cattolica*
SF	*Studi francescani.* Fi, 1914—; 1903-1911 *La Verna.* (OFM)
SFA	*San Francesco d'Assisi.* A, 1920-1930. 10v. (Conv)
SintF	*Sint Franciscus.* Brummen, Holland, 1955—(ns.). (OFM)
SISF	Società internazionale di studi francescani in Assisi *Bollettino.* A, 1904—.
SM	*Studi medievali*
SMon	*Studia Monastica*
SP	*Studia Picena*
Spec	*Speculum*
Speculum	*Speculum Perfectionis.* See A151 & A152.
SRSP	Società romana di storia patria *Archivio*
TO	*Tertius Ordo.* R, 1939—. (Cap)
Trad	*Traditio*
Tres Socii	see A143.
Verba	see A123.
VM	*Vita Minorum.* Ven, 1929—. (OFM)
VP	*Vita e pensiero*
VS	*Vie spirituelle*
VV	*Verdad y vida.* Madrid, 1943—. (OFM)
WW	*Wissenschaft und Weisheit.* M.-Gladbach, 1934— (OFM)
ZKT	*Zeitschrift für Aszese und Mystik*
ZAM	*Zeitschrift für katholische Theologie*

II BIBLIOGRAPHIES

Bibliografia storica nazionale. R, 1939—. Indispensable. **A1

Bibliographia Franciscana, "Relationes de SF." In CF (1931)— & as supplements:

      1 (1931) 98-106, 239-240, 383-407 (for 1929-30);
      3 (1933) 436-459 (1931);
      5 (1935) 125-176 (1932-33);
      9 (1939) 120-152 (1934-35);
     10 (1940) 128-160 (1936-37);
  VI 12 (1942) 9*-30* (1938-39) with separate pagination;
 VII 18 (1948) 23*-50* (1940-46);
VIII 20 (1950) 48*-92* (1947-48);
  IX 22 (1952) 65*-84* (1949-50);
   X -[195?] 62*-92* (1951-53) published separately;
  XI -[1963] 56-132 (1954-57)   **A2

BRLEK, Michael, OFM, "De historia fontium et institutorum OFM," Ant 31 (1956) 83-91. *A3

DI FONZO, L. Conv, "Bibliographia Franciscana, VII," MF 50 (1950) 652-656. *A4

ENGLEBERT, Omer, *Vie de SFA* (P 1956) App. III, "Ouvrages français sur SF," p. 408-415. *A5

——, *SFA* (NY 1950) App. III, "English Works & Translations on SF & His Order before Sabatier's Life of SF (1894)," p.333-335. *A6

FACCHINETTI, V., OFM, *Guide bibliografiche. SFA.* R, 1928, xlviii, 352p. Rev. AFH 24 (1931) 274. **A7

FNV IV, 7-30. Regrettably not comprehensive. *A8

HERSCHER, Irenaeus, OFM. *Franciscan Literature, A Checklist*. St. Bonaventure, NY, 1958. viii, 148p. 9000 items in one author list. **A9

ILARINO DA MILANO, Cap, "La bibliografia francescana." In *Il libro e le biblioteche. Atti del primo Congresso bibliologico francescano internazionale* (R 1950) II, 183-220; & CF 19 (1949) 224-246. Rev: AFH 45 (1952) 193-210; FS 33 (1951) 319-322; CF IX, 35*. *A10

International Guide to Medieval Studies, A Quarterly Index to Periodical Literature. Darien, Conn., 1961—. **A11

Lexicon Capuccinum. R, 1951. xlvii, 1868 col. illus. Rev: FnSs 14 (1954) 114. *A12

LITTLE, A. G., "Guide pour les études franciscaines," EF 40 (1928) 517-533; 41 (1929) 64-78 (mis à jour par le P. Gratien). *A12a

MASSERON, Alexandre, & Marion A. Habig, OFM, *The Franciscans* (Chi 1959) App. II, "Bibliography of English Franciscana. I. SF," p.480-490. *A13

OOMS, H. J., *Bibliographia de bibliographia franciscana*. Brux, 1961. xxv, 81p. *A14

——, & Ermenegildo Frascadore, OFM, "Bibliografia delle bibliografie francescane," AFH 57 (1964) [150p.] Basic. **A15

PALANDRI, E., OFM, "Rassegna bibliografica sanfrancescana dell'ultimo trentennio," SF 37 (1940) 161-231. Rev: CF 11 (1941) 493. *A16

PIANA, Celestino, OFM, "Le fonti medioevali della storia e del pensiero francescano nell'ultimo settantennio." In Istituto Storico Italiano per il Medio Evo, *La Pubblicazione delle fonti del medioevo europeo negli ultimi 70 anni (1883-1953)* (R 1954) 283-312; on SF: 286, 310. CF XI, 10.   **A17

PITTOLET, C., "Bibliographie franciscaine de 1920 à 1926," RHF 3 (1926) 579-591.   *A18

PIZZI, F., "Per l'unificazione della bibliografia francescana," SF 45 (1949) 163-166.   A19

PREZZOLINI, G., *Repertorio bibliografico della storia e della critica della letteratura italiana dal 1932 al 1942*. NY, 1946. 2v.   **A20

Progress of Medieval & Renaissance Studies in the United States & Canada. Boulder, Colo., 1-25 (1923-1960).   **A21

Repertoire générale de sciences religieuses. R, P, 1950-53, 4v.   **A22

Repertorium fontium historiae medii aevi, primum ab Augusto Potthast digestum, nunc cura collegii historicum e pluribus nationibus emendatum et auctum. R, 1962—. Basic.   **A23

SARRI, F., OFM, "Saggio bibliografico di studi francescani," SF 12 (1926) 518-546.   *A24

SMOLINSKI, Arcadius, OFM, *Franciscan Literature. A Selected, Evaluated, Annotated Bibliography*. Wa, 1957. 105p. CF XI, 9. (Cath. Univ. MA thesis)   *A25

VICINELLI, A., See A38a: 399-407.

VITO DA CLUSONE, Cap., *Cultura e pensiero di SFA* (Modena 1952) xv-lxiv. cf D184.   *A26

III THE WRITINGS OF ST. FRANCIS

1 EDITIONS

a. LATIN

BOEHMER, H., ed., *Analekten zur Geschichte des F von A*. 3. Aufl. durchgesehen von F. Wiegand. Tü, 1961. xvi, 75p. Rev: CF 33 (1963) 327.
A27

Opuscula Sancti Patris F Assisiensis. Ed. 3a. Q, 1949. xvi, 209p.   A28

b. ENGLISH

Memorable Words of SF, A. Masseron, ed.; M. Sullivan, tr. Chi, 1963, viii 123p. Tr. of A40.   A29

SFA, His Life & Writings as Recorded by His Contemporaries . . . Tr. by Leo Sherley-Price. L & NY, 1960. 234p. Rev: CF 31 (1961) 101.   A30

The Words of SF, An Anthology. Comp. by James Meyer, OFM. Chi, 1952. viii, 345p. Rev: CF X, 63; FnSs 13 (1953) 209-213.   A31

The Writings of SFA. Tr. by Paschal Robinson, OFM. Phil, 1906. xxxii, 208p.   A32

The Writings of SFA. Tr. by Benen Fahy, OFM. Intr. & notes by Placid Hermann, OFM, L & Chi, 1964. 181p.   A33

510 *Saint Francis of Assisi:* A *Biography*

c. FRENCH

Ainsi parlait SF. P, 1955, 255p. Rev: CF 26 (1954) 84. A34

Les écrits de SFA, remis en langage populaire par le P. Willibrord de Paris. P, 1959. 197p. Rev: AFH 52 (1959) 472; Ant 37 (1962) 311; CF 30 (1960) 103; FS 44 (1962) 112. A35

Le message spirituel de SFA dans ses écrits. Willibrord de Paris, Cap, ed. Blois, 1960. xvi, 367p. Rev: Ant 38 (1963) 241; AFH 53 (1960) 472; CF 31 (1961) 101. A36

Oeuvres latines et Cantique de frère soleil. Tr., intr. & notes de Alexandre Masseron. P, 1959. 264p. Rev: AFH 52 (1959) 472; CF 30 (1960) 102. A37

Les opuscules de SF. Texte latin & tr. fr. de l'Abbé Paul Bayart. P, 1945. viii, 263p. Rev: MF 46 (1946) 343. A38

Les opuscules de SFA. Texte latin de Quaracchi. Intr., tr. fr. & tables du R. P. Damien Vorreux, OFM, de l'Abbé Paul Bayart & des FF. MM. de la Clarté-Dieu. P, 1956. 353p. Rev: CF 26 (1956) 308; MF 57 (1957) 305; (1945 ed. 262p.): CF 15 (1945) 227; MF 46 (1946) 343. *A39

Paroles mémorables de SFA. Tr. & notes de Alexandre Masseron. P, 1960. 182p. Rev: CF 31 (1961) 230. cf A29. A40

d. GERMAN

Die Schriften des hl. F von A. Einführung, Übersetzung, Auswertung Kajetan Esser & Lothar Hardick, OFM. 3. verb. Aufl. We, 1963. 258p. (2. verb. Aufl. 1956. 258p.; 1st ed.: 1951. xii, 204p.) Rev: AFH 47 (1954) 171; CF 22 (1952) 387-390; CF XI, 56; FS 34 (1952) 327-329. Basic. *A41

e. ITALIAN

Gli scritti di SFA. Intr. e note di Mons. Vittorino Facchinetti, OFM. Testo riveduto e aggiornato da Fr. Giacomo Cambell, OFM. 5a ed. Mi, 1957. 211p. Rev: CF 27 (1957) 327; CF 15 (1945) 227; MF 45 (1945) 193. A42

VICINELLI, A., *Gli scritti di S F e i Fioretti.* See A165. *A43

2 STUDIES

CAMBELL, Jacques, OFM. "Les écrits de SFA devant la critique," FS 36 (1954) 82-109, 205-264; & We, 1954. 91p. Rev: CF XI, 58-59. Fundamental study of textual problems. **A44

——, "SF a-t-il composé une paraphrase du Pater?" SF 45 (1963) 338-342. No. *A44a

CHINI, Mario, *SF poeta.* R, 1937. 46p. Rev: CF 12 (1942) 23*. A45

DANIELE DALLARI DA BARI, Cap, "SFA 'scrittore'," IF 33 (1958) 94-102, 163-179, 188, 233-243, 328-336; 34 (1959) 11-20, 84-95, 175-183; & R, 1959. 86p. Rev: MF 62 (1962) 500-502. A46

ESSER, K., OFM, "Die älteste Handschrift der Opuscole des hl. F (cod. 338 von A)," FS 26 (1939) 120-142. cf C183: 159-174. *A47

——, "Le langage de SF," CVF 4 (1957) 116-123. A48

FALOCI-PULIGNANI, M., "Gli autografi di SF," MF 6 (1895) 33-39. With large facsimiles. A49

LAMPEN, Willibrord, OFM, "De quibusdam sententiis et verbis in opusculis S.P.N.F." AFH 24 (1931) 552-557. A50

MORETTI, G. M, (a) *I santi dalla scrittura; [esami grafologici].* Padova, 1952. 408p. facsims. Ch. on SF in RF nov. 1953. (b) *Saints through Their Handwriting.* NY, 1964. 269p. See p. 47-49. A51

OTTAVIO DA ANGERS, Cap., "SF e il canto," IF 3 (1928) 257-268, 417-424. A52

3 INDIVIDUAL WRITINGS

(on THE CANTICLE see C144-C159; on
THE LETTER TO ALL THE FAITHFUL, D48)

a. THE BLESSING OF BROTHER LEO

ATTAL, Salvatore, "La benedizione di Frate Leone," MF 32 (1932) 245-248; cf CF 30 (1960) 24 n63-64; FS 36 (1954) 218-222 (Cambell); C70: 364. A53

VAN DIJK, S.J.P., OFM, "SF's Blessing of Brother Leo," AFH 47 (1954) 199-201. Abs: CF XI, 62. A54

b. THE LETTER TO ST. ANTHONY

BONMAN, Ottokar, OFM, "De authenticitate epistolae SF ad S. Antonianum Patavium," AFH 45 (1952) 474-492. Abs: CF X, 64. Reply to A56.
*A55

ESSER, K., OFM, "Der Brief des hl. F. an den hl. Antonius von Padua," FS 31 (1949) 135-141. Abs: CF IX, n125; cf FS 36 (1954) 244-249 (Cambell). *A56

c. THE OFFICE OF THE PASSION

BRACALONI, Leone, OFM, "L'ufficio composto da SFA," SF 37 (1940) 251-265. A57

DE SCHLAMPHELEER, Jacques, OFM, *L'Office de la Pâque. Commentaire de l'Officium passionis de SFA.* P, 1953 & 1963, 156p. Rev: CF 34 (1964) 185. A58

FRANCESCHINI, Ezio, "Note sull'Ufficio della passione del Signore." In QSF (SMA 1962) IV, 42-62. A59

OKTAVIAN VON RIEDEN, Cap., "Das Leiden Christi im 'Officium passionis' des hl. F," in his "Leiden Christi . . ." (see D139), CF 30 (1960) 129-145; cf CF 33(1963) 328; WW 25 (1962) 135-142. **A60

d. THE RULE FOR HERMITAGES

ESSER, K., OFM, "Die 'Regula pro eremitoriis data' des heiligen F. von A," FS 44 (1962) 382-417. Fundamental analysis, with critical text. *A61

e. THE TESTAMENT

——, *Das Testament des heiligen F. von A.* Münster/Westf., 1949. 212p. Abs; FnSs 10 (1950) 77-81. Rev: AFH 42 (1949) 312-315 (Oliger); FS 31 (1949) 214-217 (Hardick); MF 49 (1949) 633-635. Definitive. **A62

TITO DA OTTONE, Cap., *Il Testamento di SF*. Genova, 1957. 61p.
Rev: IF 33 (1958) 231. A63

IV SOURCES
(see also E27:533-567, & Appendix I)

1 COLLECTIONS & ANTHOLOGIES

a. LATIN

Legendae S. F. Assisiensis saeculis XIII et XIV conscriptae. AF X, Q.
1926-1941. lxxxvii, 755p. Critical edition. Rev: AFH 30 (1937) 235; 34 (1941)
420. Contains (also pub'd separately): *A64
THOMAS DE CELANO, O. Min. *Vita Prima S. F*: 1-117. A65
——, *Legenda ad usum chori*: 118-126. A66
——, *Vita Secunda S. F*: 127-168. A67
——, *Tractatus de Miraculis S. F.*: 269-330. cf A249: 20-54, 161-205. A68
IULIANUS DE SPIRA, O. Min, *Vita S. F*: 333-371. A69
——, *Officium rhythmicum S. F*: 372-388. A70
HENRICUS ABRINCENSIS, canonicus, *Legenda Versificata S. F*: 405-
521. A71
(cf BIHL, M., OFM, "De 'Legenda Versificata' S. Fauctore Henrico Ab-
rincensi," AFH 22 (1929) 3-53; cf 193-195. A71a
HELIAS, Fr., O. Min, *Epistola encyclica de transitu S. F.*: 523-528. cf
C196. A72
ANON., *Legenda choralis Umbra*: 543-554. cf A202. A73
S. BONAVENTURA, O. Min. *Vita seu Legenda Maior S. F.*: 555-652.
A74
——, *Vita seu Legenda Minor S. F.*: 653-678. A75
IACOBUS DE VORAGINE, OP, *Vita S. F. in eius Legenda Aurea*:
681-693. A76
BERNARDUS DE BESSA, O. Min, "Liber de laudibus b. F." In AF
III (Q 1897) 666-692. A77
(cf DELORME, F.M., OFM, "A propos de Bernard de Besse," SF 13,
1927, 217-228). A78
Florilegium Franciscanum. In usum scholarum excerpsit Sam. Cavallin. Lund,
1957. 116p. Rev: CF 28 (1958) 426. A79
LEMMENS, Leonardus, OFM, (a) "Testimonia minora saeculi XIII de
S.P.F." AFH 1 (1908) 68-84, cf E16:98-106, & F108:248-266. (b) 2d ed.
Q, 1926. 127p. Rev: AFH 20 (1927) 154-157 (Bihl). **A80
Via Seraphica; Selected Readings from the Early Documents & Writings Per-
taining to SF & the Franciscan Order; ed. by Placid Hermann, OFM. Chi,
1959. 221p. A81

b. ENGLISH

Early Franciscan Classics. Tr. by the Friars Minor of the Franciscan Province
of Saint Barbara, Oakland, California. Paterson, N.J., 1962. vii, 257p. Contains tr. of A65, A72, A112, & A133. A82.

The Little Flowers of SF, tr. by T. Okey. *The Mirror of Perfection* by Leo of A, tr. by Robert Steele. *The Life of SF* by St. Bonaventure, tr. by Miss E. Gurney Salter. Intr. by Hugh McKay, OFM. L & NY, 1963. xi, 397p. [4th ed.] (Everyman's Library, 485)   A83

SFA, His Holy Life & Love of Poverty. The Legend of the Three Companions, tr. by Nesta de Robeck. And *The Sacrum Commercium or F & His Lady Poverty,* tr. by Placid Hermann, OFM. Chi, 1964. ix, 204p.   A83a

A New Fioretti, A Collection of Early Stories about SFA Hitherto Untranslated. Tr. & ed. by John R. H. Moorman. L, 1946. 90p. Invaluable.   *A84

SFA, The Legends & Lauds. Ed. by Otto Karrer; tr. by N. Wydenbruck. L & NY, 1948. xiv, 302p. Lacks some of notes in A86.   *A85

c. GERMAN

Franz v A: Legenden und Laude. Otto Karrer, ed. Z, 1945. 811p. illus. Rev: AFH 41 (1948) 296 (Bihl).   *A86

d. SPANISH

San F de Asis. Sus escritos. Las Florecillas. Biografías del Santo por Celano, San Buenaventura y los Tres Compañeros. Espejo de Perfección. Ed. prep. por los P. Fray Juan R. De Legísima, OFM, y Fray Lino Gómez Cañedo, OFM. 3a ed. Madrid, 1956. xxxix, 857p. illus. Rev: CF VII, n247, & XI, n168; VV 4 (1946) 349. Has useful index.   *A87

2 MAJOR 13TH-CENTURY SOURCES
(see also A64-A80, A82)

a. THOMAS OF CELANO
(see also A65-A68, E210, E211, F210)

(1) TRANSLATIONS

SFA: First & Second Life of SF, with Selections from Treatise on the Miracles of Blessed F. Tr. from the Latin with Intr. & notes by Placid Hermann, OFM. (a) Chi, 1963. xxx, 245p. illus., map. Richly illustrated; notes based on AF X. Excellent tr. Useful index. (b) Also paperbound ed. Chi, 1964. liv, 405p. (without illus.).   *A88

Vie de SFA, tr. intr. & notes du R. P. Damien Vorreux, OFM. P, 1952. 462p. Crit. rev: EF ns6 (1955) 102; MF 52 (1952) 635-639.   *A89

Thomas von Celano. Leben und Wunder des Heiligen F von A. Einführung, Uebersetzung, Anmerkungen von Engelbert Grau, OFM. We, 1955. 621p. (FQ, 5) Rev: FS 38 (1956) 437. Fundamental work; notes based on AF X.   *A90

Fra Tommaso da Celano. Vita di SFA (Prima e Seconda) e Trattato dei miracoli. Fausta Casolini, tr. & ed. SMA, 1952 & 1960. liv, 481p. Rev: AFH 48 (1955) 147; CF 24 (1954) 402. Important intr.   *A91

Tommaso da Celano. Le due Vite e il Trattato dei miracoli di SFA. Nuova versione integrale, intr. e note di Luigi Macali, Conv. R., 1954. xxix, 563p. Rev: AFH 48 (1955) 147; MF 56 (1956) 599-601.   *A92

(2) STUDIES

CASOLINI, Fausta, "Il primo biografo francescano a sette secoli dalla morte (1260?)," FF 26 (1959) 154-161. cf her art. in EC XII, 243.   A93

——, *Profilo di fra Tommaso da Celano*. R, 1960. 75p. illus.   *A94

CHIAPPINI, Aniceto, OFM, "La sequenza 'Dies Irae, Dies Illa' di Fra Tommaso da Celano," CF 32 (1962) 116-121. Impt. refs.   *A95

COMITATO PER LE ONORANZE AL BEATO TOMMASO DA CEL-ANO. *Numero commemorativo per il VII centenario della morte di fra Tommaso da Celano. Celano, 1960*. R, 1960. 29p. cf FF 27 (1960) 172.   A96

DE BEER, Francis, OFM, *La conversion de SF selon Thomas de Celano. Etude comparative des textes relatifs à la conversion en Vita I et Vita II*. P, 1963. 367p. Abs: MF 63 (1963) 380-383. Crit. rev: CF 34 (1964) 183 (OvR). Important   *A97

HOONHOUT, P., *Het Latijn van Thomas van Celano Biograaf van sint F*. Amsterdam, 1947. 262p. Rev: AFH 40 (1947) 276-279; EF nsl (1950) 105.   *A98

HULL, Mona C., *The Usefulness of the Original Legend of SFA in Religious Education*. Boston, 1962. vi, 281p. (Boston Univ. diss.) Abs: DA 23 (1962) 1433.   *A99

MANCINI, Norberto, OFM, "Tommaso da Celano nel VII centenario della morte," IF 35 (1960) 252-257.   A100

SPIRITO, Silvana, *Il francescanesimo di Fra Tommaso da Celano*. SMA, 1963. 154p. cf E166.   *A101

VAN DEN BORNE, Fidentius, OFM, "Thomas van Celano als eerste biograaf van F," SintF 2 (1956) 183-213. Abs: CF XI, 75-76; RHE 52 (1957) 787.   *A102

WDZIECZNY, Gilbert, Conv, "The Life & Works of Thomas of Celano," FnSs 26 (1945) 55-68.   *A103

b. ST. BONAVENTURE

(1) TRANSLATIONS
(see also A74, A75, E174)

The Greater Life of SF, & The Shorter Life of SF. Tr. by Benen Fahy, OFM with intr. & notes by Placid Hermann, OFM. Chi, 1965. 200p.   A104

Saint Bonaventure. Vie de SFA. Tr. fr., intro. & notes du R. P. Damien Vorreux, OFM. P, 1951. 254p. Rev: MF 51 (1951) 635; EF ns2 (1951) 363-365.   A104a

F. Engel des Sechsten Siegels. Sein Leben nach den Schriften des Heiligen Bonaventura. Intr., tr., & notes by Sophronius Clasen, OFM. We, 1962. 631p. (FQ, 7) Rev: CF 33 (1963) 442; AFH 56 (1963) 214-217 (Esser); MF 63 (1963) 129-131. Contains impt. intr., tr. of A74 & A75 & 7 sermons. Basic.   **A105

SFA, di san Bonaventura. Agostino da Melilli, Cap, tr. Bari, 1957. 213p.   A100

S. Bonaventura. Vita di SF. Tr., intr. e note del P. F. Russo, Conv. R, 1951. xii, 208p. Rev: AFH 46 (1953) 99-104; CF 23 (1953) 352; MF 51 (1951) 634.   A107

(2) STUDIES

CLASEN, S., OFM, "S. Bonaventura S. F. Legendae maioris compilator," AFH 54 (1961) 241-272; 55 (1962) 3-58, 289-319. Fundamental study. *A108

——, "Die Sendung des hl. F. Ihre heilsgeschichtliche Deutung durch Bonaventura," WW 14 (1951) 212-225. CF X, 83. *A109

CRESI, Domenico, OFM, "San Bonaventura biografo perfetto di SF," SF 54 (1957) 355-364. (In A258.) A110

LAURAND, L., SJ, "Le 'Cursus' dans la Légende de SF par Saint Bonaventure," RHE 11 (1910) 257-262. *A111

c. *SACRUM COMMERCIUM*
(see also A82, A83a, E207)

Sacrum Commercium S.F. cum domina Paupertate. Q, 1929. 77p. Rev: EF 43 (1931) 118; CF 1 (1931) 102; cf FF ns4 (1931) 218-222. A112

The Lady Poverty, A Thirteenth Century Allegory. Tr. & ed. by Montgomery Carmichael. L, 1901. 209p. A113

SF e Madonna Povertà. Raoul Manselli, ed. Fi, 1953. 97p. Rev: IF 30 (1955) 196. A114

Le sacre nozze del Beato F con Madonna Povertà. Tr. with useful intr. & notes by Nello Vian. Mi, 1963. xxii, 70p. *A115

COSMO, Umberto, "Il primo libro francescano." In D157:33-58. A116

ENGELS, J., "De Convivio Paupertatis cum Fratribus." In *Mélanges offerts à Mademoiselle Christine Mohrmann* (Utrecht 1963) 141-151. A117

SABATIER, P., "Kurze Bemerkungen zur historischen Bedeutung des Sacrum Commercium Beati F cum Domina Paupertate," FS 13 (1926) 277-282. Also in Fr. in A30:335-362. A118

SANTONI, Enrico, OFM, "SF e Madonna Povertà," FF 16 (1939) 285-292. Abs: CF VII, 11*. A119

d. LEMMENS' *DOCUMENTA ANTIQUA FRANCISCANA*

Documenta Antiqua Franciscana, edidit Fr. Leonardus Lemmens, OFM. Q, 1901-1902. 3v. Contains, with important intrs. & comments: *A120

Pars I. *Scripta Fratris Leonis.* (1901. 107p.). Includes: A121

    A. *Vita B. Aegidii Assisiastis:* 37-62; *Verba:* 63-65; App.: 66-72. A122

    B. *S.P.F. Intentio regulae:* 83-99; *Verba S.P.F.:* 100-106. A123

Pars II, *Speculum Perfectionis, Redactio I,* (1901. 107p.) 23-84. A124

Pars III. *Extractiones de Legenda Antiqua.* (1902. 75p.) A125

e. ANONYMUS PERUSINUS

VAN ORTROY, F., SJ, "La leggenda latina di SF secondo l'Anonimo Perugino," MF 9 (1902) 33-48. Latin text & comment. A126

ABATE, Giuseppe, Conv, "L'Anonimo Perugino e le sue fonti." In A147: 230-237. *A127

Note: Ghinato is preparing a critical ed. (C112:166n 12).

f. *JACQUES DE VITRY*
(see also F85:545-557)

Lettres de Jacques de Vitry (1160/1170-1240, évêque de Saint-Jean-d'Acre.
Ed. crit. par R.B.C. Huygens. Leiden, 1960. viii, 166p. Rev: AFH 54 (1961)
227-229; SM 3s2 (1961) 240-244; Spec 36 (1961) 658-660. Definitive ed.
                                                                    *A128
McDONNELL, Ernest W., *The Beguines & Beghards in Medieval Culture, With Special Emphasis on the Belgian Scene*. New Brunswick, NJ, 1954.
xvii, 643p. Rev: AFH 48 (1955) 153. Important. Author working on his *Sermones*.   **A129

g. *FRANCISCAN CHRONICLES*
(see also A230, A236, A240, E3, E16)

LAUREILHE, Marie Thérèse, *Sur les routes d'Europe au XIIIe siècle;
chroniques de Jourdain de Giano, Thomas d'Eccleston, et Salimbene d'Adam*,
traduites et commentées. P, 1959. 229p. maps. Rev: AB 79 (1961) 205-208;
CF 30 (1960) 466.   *A130
———, *XIIIth Century Chronicles*. Tr. by Placid Hermann, OFM. Chi, 1961.
xvii, 302p. maps. Rev: CHR 49 (1963) 226.   *A131
HARDICK, Lothar, OFM, ed. & tr.   *Nach Deutschland und England. Die
Chroniken der Minderbrüder Jordan von Giano und Thomas von Eccleston*.
We, 1957. 293p. (FQ, 6) Rev: AFH 50 (1957) 445; CF 28 (1958) 233-235.
                                                                    *A132
Chronica Fratris Jordani. Edidit, notis et commentario illustravit H. Boeh-
mer, P, 1908. lxxxii, 95p. Rev: AFH 2 (1909) 647-650 (Bihl). (CED, 6)
cf AF I, 1-19; C10.   *A133
AUWEILER, Edwin J., OFM, *The "Chronica Fratris Jordani a Giano."*
Wa, 1917. 63p. (Cath. Univ. diss.)   *A134
Chronica Fratris Nicolai Glassberger. In AF II.   *A134a
*Fratris Thomae vulgo dicti de Eccleston Tractatus de Adventu Fratrum Min-
orum in Angliam*. A. G. Little, & J. Moorman, ed. Man, 1951. 115p.   *A135
Cronica fratris Salimbene de Adam Ordinis Minorum. Edidit Oswaldus Hol-
der-Egger. Hannover, 1905-13. xxxii, 755p. (MGH SS32) Rev: AFH 1 (1908)
443-446; 6 (1913) 759-765; cf 3 (1910) 348.   *A136
Salimbene. Cronica. F. Bernini, ed. Bari, 1942. 2v. Latin.   A137
BIHL, Michael, OFM, "Salimbene," EF 16 (1907) 520-532.   A138
CLEDAT, Léon, *De fratre Salimbene et de ejus Chronicae auctoritatae*. P,
1876. 116p.   A139
LAUREILHE, M. T., "Les idées religieuses des Frères Mineurs au XIIIe
siècle, d'après la chronique de Salimbene," EF nsl (1950) 5-22.   A140
———, "Les Frères Mineurs et les puissances de l'Europe occidental au XIIIe
siècle, d'après la chronique de Salimbene," EF nsl (1950) 313-328.   A141
SCIVOLETTO, N., *Fra Salimbene da Parma e la storia politica e religiosa
del secolo decimoterzo*. Bari, 1950. 182p. Rev: AFH 48 (1955) 436-440; CF
X, 275*.   A142

3 14TH-CENTURY *LEGENDAE* & COMPILATIONS

a. THE SO-CALLED LEGEND OF THE THREE COMPANIONS
(see also A83a, A85-A87, A219)

"Legenda S. F. Assisiensis tribus ipsius sociis hucusque adscripta. Redactio antiquior iuxta Cod. Sarnanensem," Giuseppe Abate, Conv, ed., MF 39 (1939) 375-432. Best text available, though incomplete. See A147. *A143

La légende des trois compagnons. Tr. du latin par l'Abbé Louis Pichard. P, 1926. 232p. A144

La Leggenda dei Tre Compagni. Testo senese inedito del XV secolo. Appendice e discussione critica. Zefferino Lazzeri, OFM, ed. Fi, 1923. ix, 171p. *A145

La Leggenda dei Tre Compagni. Ezio Franceschini, tr. & ed. Mi, 1957 (3a ed.) xvii, 87p. Rev: CF XI, 72; MF 47 (1947) 615-617; Ant 32 (1957) 475 (Cambell). *A146

ABATE, Giuseppe, Conv., "Nuovi studi sulla leggenda di SF detta dei 'Tre Compagni'," MF 39 (1939) 1-55, 225-262, 359-373, 635-655 (for text see A143); also R, 1939. 186p. Rev: CF 12 (1942) 9*; cf CF 29 (1959) 515. Fundamental study. **A147

Note: Clasen has announced a new study (WW27, 122); cf C45a.

b. THE LEGENDA ANTIQUA OF PERUGIA
(see also FNV II, 479-485; A249:461-496 & C160:348-353)

"La 'Legenda Antiqua S. F.' Texte du Ms. 1046 (M. 69) de Pérouse," Ferdinand M. Delorme, OFM, ed. (a) AFH 15 (1922) 23-70, 278-382. (b) P, 1926. 70p. Rev: AB 45 (1927) 198; AFH 20 (1927) 596-598 (Bihl); EF 38 (1926) 555; RHF 1 (1924) 236-238; Note: (a) have different numbering; Englebert follows b. See Table II in A265:23-26. *A148

SFA raconté par ses premiers compagnons. Tr. fr. de la Legenda Antiqua par l'Abbé M.-J. Fagot, P, 1927 & 1946. 205p. A148a

BURKITT, P. C., "La Légende de Pérouse et le ms. 1/73 de Saint Isidore," RHF 2 (1925) 457-466. A149

GRATIEN DE PARIS, Cap, "La 'Legenda Antiqua' de Pérouse," FF 1 (1924) 142-147. A150

c. THE SPECULUM PERFECTIONIS OF SABATIER
(see also C160:344-348)

Speculum Perfectionis seu S. F. Assisiensis Legenda Antiquissima, auctore fratre Leone. Nunc primum edidit Paul Sabatier. P, 1898. ccxiv, 376p. (CED, 1). *A151

Le Speculum Perfectionis, préparé par Paul Sabatier. Man, 1928-31. 2v. (BSFS 13 & 17) Rev: AFH 26 (1933) 497-518 (Bihl); RHE 25 (1929) 309-311 (Masseron). *A152

SFA, His Life & Writings as Recorded by His Contemporaries. A New Version of The Mirror of Perfection ... (see A30 & another tr. in A83). A152a

Frate Leone. Lo Specchio di Perfezione. F. Pennacchi, tr.; E. Franceschini, ed. 3a ed. Mi, 1945. xxiii, 175p. Rev: SF 39 (1942) 189-192 (Pennacchi); MF 43 (1943) 338; 49 (1949) 196; CF VII,27*. A153

Lo Specchio di Perfezione. F. Pennacchi, tr.; F. Russo, Conv, ed. R, 1950. xxvii, 248p. Rev: AFH 46 (1953) 99-103; CF 22 (1952) 79-81; MF 51 (1951) 632. A154

BIHL, Michael, OFM, "Zur Kritik des Speculum Perfectionis gelegentlich der Neuausgabe desselben von P. Sabatier," FS 22 (1935) 113-148. Abs: CF 9 (1939) 123. *A155

d. THE A. G. LITTLE MANUSCRIPT
(see also A249:3-19 & 182-194)

LITTLE, A.G. "Description of a Franciscan Manuscript Formerly in the Phillipps Library." In BSFS (Aberdeen 1914) V, 9-113. *A156

——, *Un nouveau manuscrit franciscain, ancien Phillipps 12290, aujourd'-hui dans la bibliothèque* A. G. Little, P, 1919. 110p. (OCH, 18) Rev: AFH 12 (1919) 567-569 (Oliger). *A157

e. THE ACTUS-FIORETTI
(see also bibl. in A166)

(1) EDITIONS & MANUSCRIPTS

Actus Beati F et Sociorum Ejus. Paul Sabatier, ed. P, 1902. lxiii, 271p. (CED, 4) *A158

BUGHETTI, Benvenuto, OFM, "Descriptio Novi Codicis 'Actus Beati F' Exhibentis (Florentiae, Bibliotheca Nationalis Centralis II, XI, 20)," AFH 32 (1939) 412-438. *A159

KRUITWAGEN, Bonaventura, OFM, "Descriptio nonnullorum codicum MSS. quibus insunt libelli 'Speculum Perfectionis' et 'Actus B. F.'," AFH 1 (1908) 300-412. *A160

I Fioretti di SF. Le Considerazioni sulle Stimate. La Vita di Frate Ginepro. La Vita e i Detti del Beato Egidio. Capitoli aggiunti. Il Cantico di Frate Sole. Con note del P. Benvenuto Bughetti, OFM, nuova edizione riveduta dal P. Riccardo Pratesi, OFM. Fi, 1959. 465p. Rev: AFH 53 (1960) 460-462. Useful notes. *A161

I Fioretti di SF. Le Considerazioni sulle Stimmate. Il Cantico de Frate Sole. R. Pratesi & G. Sabatelli, OFM, eds. Fi, 1961. 212p. *A161a

I Fioretti di SF, con una introduzione storico-critica (& notes & bibl.) del P. Giacinto Pagnani, OFM. R, 1960. 253p. illus., map. Rev: AFH 53 (1960) 325-327 (Pratesi). Important intr. & notes. *A162

I Fioretti di SF. G. M. Bastianini, Conv, ed. R, 1950. xxii, 267p. Rev: AFH 46 (1953) 99-101; CF 21 (1951) 431-433; MF 50 (1950) 657; SF 47 (1951) 131. A163

——. Agostino Gemelli, OFM, ed. Mi, 1957. 304p. 4a ed. Rev: CF XI, 74; MF 47 (1947) 617. A164

Gli scritti di SF e "I Fioretti," a cura di Augusto Vicinelli. Mi, 1955. 427p. illus. Rev: AFH 50 (1957) 120-123. Important. *A165

The Little Flowers of SF. First Complete Ed., with 20 Additional Chapters. Also The Considerations of the Holy Stigmata, The Life & Sayings of

Brother Giles, The Life of Brother Juniper. A Modern English Tr. from the Latin & the Italian with Intr., Notes, & Biographical Sketches by Raphael Brown. Garden City, NY, 1958. 359p. map. Rev: AFH 52 (1959) 352. 105-item bibl. includes 36 refs. to studies. **A166

The Little Flowers of SF. With 5 Considerations on the Sacred Stigmata. Tr. with an intro. by Leo Sherley-Price. L. & Baltimore, 1959. 202p. map. (Penguin Classics, L91) A167

The Little Flowers of SF & Other Franciscan Writings. Tr. with Intr. by Serge Hughes. NY, 1964. 222p. A167a

Les Fioretti de SF. Ed. complète. Omer Englebert, tr. & ed. P, 1945. 420p. A168

Les Fioretti. Tr. nouvelle d'après l'Incunable de Milan par le R.P. Godefroy, Cap. P, 1947. 314p. Rev: CF 20 (1950) 130. A169

Les Fioretti de SF, suivis des Considérations sur les Stigmates et autres textes traditionnels. Tr., intr. et notes de Alexandre Masseron. (a) P, 1953. xxxviii, 510p. Most useful French ed. (b) P, 1963. xii, 195p. illus.; abridged juvenile ed. *A170

(2) STUDIES
(see bibl. in A166)

BROWN, Sr. M. Anthony, "Historical Value of Certain Chapters of the Fioretti," *Cord* 8 (1958) 214-220. A171

CLASEN, Sophronius, OFM, "Zur Problematik der Fioretti," WW 25 (1962) 214-218. Important. *A172

CRESI, Domenico, OFM, "I Fioretti di SF," SF 55 (1958) 35-50. A173

DABOVICH, Elena, "Syntaktische Eigentümlichkeiten der Fioretti." In *Syntactica und Stilistica. Festschrift fur Ernst Gamillscheg* (Tü 1957) 83-109. A174

DAMIANI, Quinto, OFM, "Raffronto tra alcuni codici a stampa dei *Fioretti* e il codice di Amaretto Manelli," CF 28 (1958) 397-400. *A175

DEFRENZA, Giuseppe, "La poesia dei Fioretti," IF 34 (1957) 1-8, 73-82, 163-168, 217-224, 289-295, 380-384. A176

PAGNANI, Giacinto, OFM, "Il codice di Fabriano dei Fioretti di SF," SP 25 (1957) 1-23. CF XI, 79. *A177

——, "Contributi alla questione dei 'Fioretti di SF'," AFH 49 (1956) 3-16. Rev: CF XI, 78. Fundamental study, with new data on author. *A178

——, "Ricerche intorno al B. Liberato da Loro Piceno, O. Min.," MF 58 (1958) 76-98. Important new research; cf F132, F139, F142. *A179

PELLEGRINI, Leo, "I Fioretti del glorioso Messere Santo F e de' suoi frati," *Annali della Scuola Normale Superiore di Pisa* ser. II, 21 (1952) 131-157. CF X, 67-68. *A180

PETROCCHI, Giorgio, "Dagli 'Actus Beati F' al Volgarizzamento dei Fioretti," Conv 22 (1954) 534-555, 666-677; also in his *Ascesi e mistica trecentesca* (Fi 1957) 85-146. CF XI, 78. *A181

——, "Inchiesta sulla tradizione manoscritta dei 'Fioretti di SF'," *Filologia romanza* 4 (1957) 311-325. *A182

QUAGLIA, Armando, OFM, "Il 'Floretum' e i 'Fioretti' del Wadding," SF 50 (1953) 107-112. CF X, 68. See also A228. *A183

———, "Il mondo ideale dei Fioretti." SF 56 (1959) 3-9. A184
———, "Perchè manca un'edizione critica dei Fioretti di SF," SF 52 (1955)
216-223. CF XI, 77. A185
TOSI, G., "Coordinazione e subordinazione nei 'Fioretti' di SF," *Archivio
glottologico italiano* 27 (1935) 40-63. *A186

f. THE AVIGNON COMPILATION

SABATIER, Paul, "Compilation franciscaine d'Avignon," RHF 1 (1924)
425-431. cf A44:88-96 (Cambell). *A187
VALENTI, Tommaso, "Gl'inventari di Fr. Federico de Pernstein, O.M.,
Arcivescovo di Riga (1304-1341)," MF 33 (1933) 46-66; cf MF 43 (1943)
177; AFH 42 (1949) 34; AFH 41 (1948) 12. *A188

g. MINOCCHI'S LEGGENDA ANTICA
& RELATED DOCUMENTS

La Leggenda Antica. Nuova fonte biografica di SFA tratta da un codice
vaticano e pubblicata da Salvatore Minocchi. Fi, 1905. xxviii, 184p. cf AFH
11 (1918) 47-65; MF 49 (1949) 359n25. A189
"Vita di SF e dei suoi compagni. Testo inedito di volgare umbro del XIV
secolo," M. Faloci-Pulignani, ed., MF 8 (1901) 81-119. A190
(For related writings of Angelo Clareno & Ubertino da Casale, see E57-E66
& E68-E73.)

h. THE CHRONICLE OF THE 24 GENERALS

Chronica XXIV Generalium Ordinis Minorum (1209-1374) [by Arnaud de
[Sarrant or Samatan]. In AF 111 (Q. 1897) 1-575. cf A213. *A191
Cronica da Ordem dos Frades Menores (1209-1285). Jose Joaquin Nunes,
ed. Coimbra, 1918. 2v. Rev: AFH 11 (1918) 543-546 (Oliger). A192

i. THE BOOK OF THE CONFORMITIES

De conformitate vitae Beati F ad vitam Domini Iesu, auctore Fr. Bartholo-
maeo de Pisa. In AF IV-V (Q 1906-12). Rev: AFH 6 (1913) 170. *A193
FALOCI PULIGNANI, M., "Il 'Liber Conformitatum' del P. Bartolomeo
da Pisa," MF 8 (1901) 137-148. A194
GOYAU, G., "Les étranges destinées du Livre des Conformités." In D178:
90-147. A195
LINDEBOOM, J., "De Satyren naar aanleiding van het 'Liber Conformitatum'," Akademie van Wetenschappen (Amsterdam) *Mededelingen Afdeling
Letterkunde* nrd7 (1944) n6 (14p.) A196

4 MINOR CODICES & COMPILATIONS
(13TH TO 15TH CENTURIES)
(alphabetically by editor)

ALBAN STOECKLI VON HERMETSWIL, Cap, "Die Franziskuslegende
des 'Passionals'," CF 7 (1937) 529-566; 8 (1938) 5-37, 165-193. cf F107.
A197

——, "Notae die Franziskuslegende des 'Passionals' praeliminaria crisis censurae 'De Legenda quadam S. F. anonyma,'" CF 7 (1937) 209-214. A198

BIHL, M., OFM, "De Legenda quadam S. F. anonyma et incognita nuperrime in 'Legenda Aurea' et in 'Passionali' arbitrarie detecta," AFH 28 (1935) 305-323. *A199

HILARIN [FELDER] VON LUZERN, Cap, "Die Mitteldeutsche Legendendichtung Passional (um 1240) und ihr Leben von Sante F und Sante Elisabeth," CF 3 (1933) 481-517. Rev: CF 5 (1935) 127-129; cf CF 9 (1939) 121. A200

BIHL, M., OFM, "De Legenda S. F. Neapolitana integra et nunc 'Legenda Umbra' aptius nuncupanda," AFH 28 (1935) 3-36. Abs: CF 9 (1939) 121. cf E3:19. *A201

——, "Legenda S. F. Neapolitana supplentur ex eadem aliqua in *Vita II* deficientia," AFH 21 (1928) 240-268. *A203

ABATE, G., Conv, "La Leggenda Napoletana di SF e l'ufficio rimato di fra Giuliano da Spira secondo un codice umbro," MF 30 (1930) 129-155; & A, 1930. 91p. Abs: CF 1 (1931) 384. *A204

BIHL, M., OFM, "Narrationes VII de S. F. (In cod. Florentino Laurent. Ashburnh. 326)," AFH 17 (1924) 560-568. *A205

——, "Novus flosculus legenda S. F.," AFH 15 (1922) 202-203. A206

BUGHETTI, B., OFM, "Analecta de S. F. Assisiensi saeculo XIV ante medium collecta (e cod. Florentiae Nation. C. 9.2878)," AFH 20 (1927) 79-108. *A207

——, "Una nuova compilazione di testi intorno all vita di SF (dal cod. Universitario di Bologna, n.2697)," AFH 20 (1927) 525-562. *A208

CAMBELL, J., OFM, "Glanes franciscaines: la compilation d'Angers (Angers, bibliothèque Municipale, ms. 821)," FS 45 (1963) 41-82. *A209

——, "Glanes franciscaines. La première compilation de Barcelone. (Barcelona, Biblioteca Central, cod. 645.)," AIA 23 (1963) 65-91 & 391-453. *A210

DELORME, F. M., OFM, "Descriptio codicis 23.J.60 bibliothecae Fr. Min. Convent. Friburgi Helvetiorum," AFH 10 (1917) 47-102. A211

——, "Les Flores S. F.," MF 43 (1943) 171-178. *A212

——, "Pages inédites sur SF écrites vers 1365 par Arnaud de Sarrant Min. Prov. d'Aquitaine," MF 42 (1942) 103-131. cf A191. *A213

ELIZONDO, Jose Maria de, Cap, "Le Leyenda de SF segun la versión catalana del 'Flos Sanctorum'," REF abril-mayo 1910, 43p. A214

FIERENS, A., "La Question Franciscaine, Vita S. F. Anonyma Bruxellensis, d'après le Manuscrit II.2326 de la Bibliothèque Royale de Belgique," RHE 9-10 (1908-09); & Louvain, 1909. 123p. Rev: AFH 3 (1910) 343; cf MF 40 (1940) 490. *A215

GRATIEN DE PARIS, Cap, "Sermons franciscains du Cardinal Eudes de Châteauroux (†1273)," EF 29 (1913) 171-195, 647-655; 30 (1913) 291-317, 415-437; & P, 1915. *A215a

LAMPEN, W., OFM, "Auctoris anonymi saeculi XIII Collatio de S.P.N. F.," AFH 26 (1933) 549-550. A216

LAZZERI, Z., OFM, "Una piccola vita inedita di SF," *Rivista di Liv-*

orno 1 (1926) 404-409; English tr. in NYT Feb. 13, 1927, VIII: 7.　A217
LITTLE, A. G., "Flos novus Legendae S. F.," AFH 8 (1915) 675-676.
　　　　　　　　　　　　　　　　　　　　　　　　　　　　　A218
MARCELLINO DA CIVEZZA & Teofilo Domenichelli, OFM,　*La Leggenda di SF scritta da tre suoi compagni.* R, 1894. cxxxvi, 267p. Rev: AB 19 (1900) 457.　A219
MATTHAEI AB AQUASPARTA, O. Min. (d. 1302),　*Sermones de S. F., de S. Antonio et de S. Clara.* Q, 1962. 222p.　*A219a
OLIGER, Livarius, OFM, "Descriptio codicus S. Antonii de Urbe unacum appendice textuum de S. F," AFH 12 (1919) 321-401.　*A220
———, "Liber exemplorum Fratrum Minorum saeculi XIII. (Excerpta e Cod. Ottob. Lat. 522)," Ant 2 (1927) 202-276; cf FNV II, 59, 61; MF 49 (1949) 131.　*A221
PENNACCHI, F., "Actus S. F in Valle Reatina. Leggenda tratta dal Codice 679 della Biblioteca Comunale di A," MF 13 (1911) 3-21; & Foligno, 1911. 63p.　A222

5 LATE COMPENDIA & CHRONICLES

a. THE SPECULUM VITAE

Speculum vitae Beati F et sociorum eius. Ven, 1504. xi, 397p. (Metz, 1509; P, 15[??]; Antwerp, 1620; Köln, 1623; Györ (Raab), 1752, vi, 589p.)　*A223
BIHL, M., OFM, "L'édition du 'Speculum Vitae B. F' parue à Györ en 1752 et l'origine hongroise du 'Speculum Vitae'," AFH 20 (1927) 132-153. Basic.　*A224
GOYENS, F., "Les éditions du 'Speculum Vitae B. F' parues en 1620 et 1623," AFH 20 (1927) 116-131.　*A225
SABATIER, P., "Description du Speculum Vitae b. F et sociorum eius (éd. de 1504)." In OCH (P 1903) VI, 298-397.　*A226

b. THE SPANISH FLORETO

El Floreto de Sant Francisco. Sevilla, 1492. (R. Brown has microfilm of rare Madrid Biblioteca Nacional copy.)　A227
QUAGLIA, A., OFM, " 'El Floreto': fonte storica sconosciuta di Marco da Lisbona e del Wadding," SF 54 (1957) 40-49. CF XI, 80. cf A183.　*A228

c. LA FRANCESCHINA

La Franceschina. Testo volgare Umbro del secolo XV scritto dal P. Giacomo Oddi di Perugia, edito per la prima volta nella sua integrità dal P. Nicola Cavanna, OFM. Fi., 1931. 2v. cf AFH 44 (1951) 111; 51 (1958) 120.
　　　　　　　　　　　　　　　　　　　　　　　　　　　　　*A229

d. THE CHRONICLES OF FRA MARIANO DA FIRENZE
(see also A178, C209, E236, F374)

MARIANUS DE FLORENTIA, O. Min., "Compendium chronicarum Fratrum Minorum," AFH 1 (1908) 98-107; 2 (1909) 92-107, 305-318, 626-641; 3 (1910) 294-309, 700-715; 4 (1911) 122-137, 318-339, 559-587; & Q, 911. 171p.　*A230

ABATE, G., Conv, "Le fonti storiche della cronaca di fra Mariano da Firenze." MF 34 (1934) 46-52. *A231

CANNAROZZI, Ciro, OFM, "Una fonte primaria degli 'Annales' del Wadding (II 'Fasciculus Chronicarum' di Mariano da Firenze)," SF 27 (1930) 251-285. Rev: AFH 25 (1932) 136; cf A178. *A232

——, 'Pensiero di fra Mariano da Firenze," SF 26 (1929) 4-28, 121-179, 295-326. A233

——, "Ricerche sulla vita di fra Mariano da Firenze," SF 27 (1930) 31-71 A234

CRESI, D., OFM, "Le origini dell'Ordine Minoritico nella narrazione di Mariano da Firenze," SF 56 (1959) 139-147. *A235

e. THE CHRONICLES OF MARK OF LISBON

MARCOS DE LISBOA, OFM, *Cronicas da Ordem dos Frades Menores.* Lisboa, 1557-62. 2pts. (Span. tr. Alcala, 1568; Salamanca, 1570). A236

——, *Croniche degli Ordini instituiti dal Padre SF.* Tr. by Horatio Diola. Ven, 1585. 2v. Also other eds.; for list, see Streit's *Bibliotheca Missionum* (Münster 1916) I, index. A237

——, *The Chronicle & Institution of the Order of the Seraphical Father SF.* Wm. Cape & Christopher Davenport, tr. S. Omers, 1618. 759p. A238

——, *Chronique . . . P,* 1622. 2v. in 1. A239

f. WADDING
(see also A183, A232)

WADDINGUS, Lucas, OFM, *Annales Minorum* (Q, 1931) I-II & XXVI (1934): Index Generalis. Rev: AFH 28 (1935) 273-279. *A240

——, *Annales des Frères Mineurs.* P. Silvestre Castet, tr. Toulouse, 1680. 2v. in 1 (1208-1300). Abridged. A241

ABATE, G., Conv, "Un profilo storico di Fra Luca Wadding. Gli 'Annales Minorum' e la loro recente edizione," MF 40 (1940) 269-285. *A242

CASOLINI, F., *Luca Wadding, OFM, l'Annalista dei Francescani.* Mi, 1936. 282p. Rev: CF 9 (1939) 229-233; & A242. *A243

Father Luke Wadding. Commemorative Volume, Edited by the Franciscan Fathers, Dun Mhuire, Killiney. Dublin & L, 1957. 652p. illus. Rev: AFH 51 (1958) 211-215; CF 28 (1958) 116; MF 59 (1959) 260-262. *A244

PANDZIC, Basilio, OFM, "Gli 'Annales Minorum' del P. Luca Wadding," SF 54 (1957) 275-287. Useful list of editions, vols., years, & editors: 287; cf AFH 28 (1935) 579-582. *A245

V STUDIES OF SOURCES

See A90, C219a, D156, D157, & E27; also important studies in the biographies by Beaufreton (A280), Cuthbert (A288), Fortini (A296), Joergensen (A298), Sabatier (A 303), & Sarasola (A316); likewise the articles by Abate (A147 & C33) and Cambell (A44, A209, A210).

BIGARONI, M., OFM, "La questione delle fonti." In C164:23-68 *A246

BIHL, M., OFM, "Contra duas novas hypotheses prolatas a Ioh. R. H. Moorman," AFH 39 (1946) 3-37, 279-287. cf A268. *A247

——, "De vero sensu Definitionis Capituli generalis an. 1266 Legendas antiquiores S. F. proscribentis," AFH 30 (1937) 274-281. *A248

——, "Disquisitiones Celanenses," AFH 20 (1927) 433-496; 21 (1928) 3-54, 161-205. Indispensable; analyzes A148, A156, A68. *A249

——, "La questione francescana riveduta dal signor prof. M. Barbi alla luce dell'opera dei Tre Compagni," SF 32 (1935) 6-47, 121-141. Abs: CF 9 (1939) 120. *A250

BURKITT, F. C., "SFA & Some of His Biographers." In *Franciscan Essays* (Man 1932) II, 19-40 (BSFS-ES III). CF 4 (1934) 328. A251

——, "Scripta Leonis and Speculum Perfectionis." In MFE (R 1924) III, 1-24. Rev: RHF 2 (1925) 423. *A252

——, "The Study of the Sources of the Life of SF." In D178:13-61. A253

CAVALLIN, S., "La question franciscaine comme problème philologique," *Eranos* 52 (1954) 239-270. Rev: CF XI, 75; FS 37 (1955) 325. *A254

CHIAPPINI, Aniceto, OFM, "Fr. Ioannes de Celano, OFM, S. F. Assisiensis biographus coaevus," Ant 35 (1960) 339-342. Important *A255

——, "Fr. Joannis de Celano Sermones duo saec. XIII," CF 28 (1958) 401-403. A256

CLASEN, S., OFM, & Julius van Gurp, Cap, "Nachbonaventurianische Franziskus Quellen in niederlandischen und deutschen Handschriften des Mittelalters," AFH 49 (1956) 434-482. Rev: CF XI, 77. *A257

CRESI, D., OFM, "Discussione e documenti di storia francescana," SF 54 (1957) 351-380. Abs: CF XI, 76. cf A110. *A258

——, *Discussioni e documenti di storia francescana.* Fi, 1959. 183p. Rev: CF 29 (1959) 537. *A259

FALOCI PULIGNANI, M., "I veri biografi di SF," MF 7 (1899) 145-174. A260

FIERENS, A., "La question franciscaine. Les écrits des zélateurs de la Règle aux premiers temps de l'histoire franciscaine d'après les récentes controverses," RHE 7 (1906) 410-433; 8 (1907) 57-80. CF X, 467. *A261

FREDEGAND [CALLAEY] D'ANVERS, Cap, "De fontibus litterariis ad vitam S. F. Assisiensis speciatim pertinentibus brevis disquisitio," CF 1 (1931) 433-456. *A262

GOETZ, W., *Die Quellen zur Geschichte des hl. F. von* A. Gotha, 1904. x, 259p. *A263

LEMMENS, L., OFM, "Die Schriften des Br. Leo von A (Gest. 1271)." In MFE (R 1924) III, 25-48. *A264

LITTLE, A. G., "Some Recently Discovered Franciscan Documents & Their Relations to the Second Life by Celano & the *Speculum Perfectionis*," British Academy (L) *Proceedings* 12 (1926) 147-178. Rev: AFH 21 (1928) 127-129. Includes indispensable Tables of Parallel Passages. *A265

MARTIN DE BARCELONA, Cap, *Estudio critico de la fuentes historicas de SF y Santa Clara.* Ba, 1921. xii, 254p. Rev: AFH 15 (1922) 173-181. *A266

MASSERON, Alexandre, "Les sources de la vie de SFA." In D179:9-67. *A267

MOORMAN, John R. H., *The Sources for the Life of SFA.* Man, 1940. 176p. Despite Bihl rev. (A247) very useful; cf A84, A300. *A268

OKTAVIAN VON RIEDEN, Cap, *Zum kritischen Wert der bedeutenderen Quellen für die Erforschung der Geistigkeit des hl F von A. R*, 1956. Unpub'd typescript. CF 30 (1960) 7n9. *A269

OLIGER, Livarius, OFM, *De Fontibus Vitae S. F. R*, 1949. 62p. Typescript. A270

——, *Le Leggende di SF*. R, 1950. 43p. Typescript. *A271

POU Y MARTI, Jose, OFM, "Studia recentiora circa vitam S F," Ant 2 (1927)3-20. *A272

SALTER, E. G., "Sources for the Biography of SFA," Spec 5 (1930) 388-410. CF 3(1933) 453*. A273

SALVATORELLI, Luigi, "La storiografia francescana contemporanea." In CISSR III, 403-448. Abs: RHE 50 (1955) 1103. cf E55a. *A274

VAN DEN BORNE, Fidentius, OFM, *Die Franziskusforschung in ihrer Entwicklung dargestellt*. München, 1917. x, 106p. Rev: AFH 15 (1922) 175. *A275

——, "Zur Franziskusfrage," FS 6 (1919) 185-200. *A276

——, "Het probleem van de Franciscus-biografie in het licht van de moderne historische kritiek," SintF 57 (1955) 241-320. Abs: CF XI, 89; RHE 52 (1957) 369. See also A318-A321. *A277

VI MAJOR BIOGRAPHIES

ATTAL, Francesco Salvatore (Soter), *SFA*. 2a ed. Padova, 1947. 515p. illus. Rev: (1st ed. Livorno, 1930. 517p.) CF 1 (1931) 393-395; IF 6 (1931) 347-355; 7 (1932) 101-104. CF 20 (1950) 53*; MF 49 (1949) 176-178. *A278

BARGELLINI, Piero, *SF*. To, 1941. 233p. illus. Rev: CF 11 (1941) 265; SF 39 (1942) 87-89. 2a ed. Brescia, 1951. 215p. CF X, 69; MF 53 (1953) 129. *A279

BEAUFRETON, Maurice, *SFA*. P, 1925. 340p. Rev: AB 44 (1926) 202; RHF 2 (1925) 418-420 (Gilson); EF 38 (1926) 549; cf A322, C45. *A280

BOLLANDISTS, *Acta Sanctorum* (P 1868) L, Oct. II, 545-1004; & Dec. *Propylaeum* (Brux, 1940) 433-434. cf MF 34 (1934) 70-93. A281

BATTISTINI, Mario, "I Padri Bollandisti Henschenio e Papebrochio nelle Marche nel 1660," DSPM s4v10 (1933) 93-105. A282

——, "I Padri Bollandisti Henschenio e Papebrochio nell'Umbria nel 1660," MF 34 (1934) 53-59. Abs: CF 9 (1939) 132. A283

FALOCI PULIGNANI, M., "SF ed i Bollandisti," MF 16 (1915) 65-69. A284

——, "Corrispondenza tra il P. Suyskens ed il P. Tebaldi," MF 16 (1915) 93-123. A285

CHALIPPE, Candide, OFM, *Vie de SFA*. P, 1727; 1874, 3v. (Torino, 1787. Madrid, 1796). Based on Wadding. A286

——, (a) *The Life of SFA*. Tr. by the Congregation of the Oratory. NY, 1899. 483p. (b) *The Life & Legends of SFA*, rev'd & re-ed. by Fr. Hilarion

Duerk, OFM. NY, 1918. xxxiii, 405p. Lacks notes in (a). A287

CUTHBERT OF BRIGHTON, Cap, *Life of SFA.* L & NY, 1912; 2d ed. 1913; 3d ed. 1921. xv, 536p. illus. Rev: AFH 6 (1913) 338-343 (Oliger); 18 (1925) 593; CF 3 (1933) 436-439; EF 38 (1926) 191-194; cf A328. *A288

DAL GAL, Girolamo, Conv, *SFA.* Padova, 1947. xix, 412p. Rev: MF 48 (1948) 409-412; SF 44 (1947) 122-124 (Cresi). *A289

ENGLEBERT, Omer, *Vie de SFA* (a) P, 1947, 461p. illus. Rev: MF 48 (1948) 412-414; RF (1948) 92-95 (Bonin); CF 20 (1950) 127-129. (b) Ed. rev. & corr. P, 1957. 452p. Rev: AFH 54 (1961) 431-432 (VdBorne); cf *Praeco Regis* 4 (1952) 186-190, & *Franciscana* 5 (1950) 47-62. *A290

———, *SFA*, tr. & ed. by Edward Hutton. L & NY, 1950. x, 352p. illus. Rev: FnSs 13 (1953) 198-206 (Brady); CF 21 (1951) 94. *A291

Also Speyer, 1952. Rev: FS 35 (1953) 443-444 (Hardick).

FACCHINETTI, Mons. Vittorino, OFM, *SFA nella storia, nella leggenda, nell'arte.* (a) Mi, 1921. xlviii, 542p. illus. Rev: CC 73/3 (1922) 244-254. (b) 2da ed. arrich. e migliorata. Mi, 1926. xlviii, 542p. Sumptuously illus. Rev: AFH 20 (1927) 416-422. Important. cf A331. *A292

———, *SFA dans l'histoire, dans la legende, dans l'art.* Tr. par la Comtesse de Loppinot & F. Feugère. Vanves, 1926. lxiv, 744p. illus. Rev: RHF 4 (1927) 378-383. (Also Span. ed. Ba, 1925). *A293

FORTINI, Arnaldo, "I documenti degli archivi assisiani e alcuni punti controversi della vita di SF," AFH 43 (1950) 3-44. Abs: MF 51 (1951) 651.
*A294

———, *Nova vita di SFA*, Mi, 1926. 483p. Rev: AFH 20 (1927) 157-161 (Bihl). A295

———, *Nova vita di SF.* A, 1959. 4v in 5. Rev: AFH 53 (1960) 324-327; MF 62 (1962) 498-500. Indispensable. *A296

GRATIEN DE PARIS, Cap, "SFA. Essai sur sa vie et son oeuvre d'après les derniers travaux critiques," EF 18 (1907) 359-482. cf A335, D127, E23.
*A297

JOERGENSEN, Johannes, *SFA, A Biography.* (a) L & NY, 1912. Tr. by T. O'Conor Sloane. ix, 428p. (Editions & tr. in all major languages). (b) Garden City, NY, 1955, 354p.; lacks impt. app. on sources. Rev (various eds.): EF 20 (1908) 377-387 (Felder); AFH 6 (1913) 338-343 (Oliger); CW 95 (1912) 385-391 (Robinson); cf SintF 58 (1956) 25-30; abs: RHE 521 (1957) 369. cf A337. *A298

LOPES. Fernando Felix, OFM, *O Poverello S. F. de Asis.* Braga, 1951. 458p. A299

MOORMAN, JOHN R. H., *SFA.* L, 1950. 127p.; & 1963. viii, 118p. cf D177. A300

OSCAR DE PAMEL, Cap, "La psychologie de SFA," EF 33 (1921) 489-505; 34 (1922) 327-345, 500-519; 36 (1923) 267-274. AFH 18 (1925) 421. Well documented, almost a biography. *A301

PAPINI, Niccola, Conv, *La Storia di SFA. Opera critica.* Foligno, 1825-27. 2v. cf MF 20 (1919) 56-64. Still useful. cf A341. *A302

SABATIER, Paul, *Vie de SFA.* P, 1894. cxxvi, 418p. (On Index.) *A303

———, *Life of SFA.* Tr. by Louis Seymour. L, 1894 (& 1942). 448p. A304

——, Vie de SFA. Edition définitive. P, 1931. li, 580p. Rev: AFH 25 (1933) 525-533 (Bihl); CF 2(1932) 249. *A305
——, "L'enfance et la jeunesse de SF. Etude comparative des sources." [1900-06] SM 6 (1933) 1-28; "Première partie de la vie de SFA," 7 (1934) 24-51, 165-184; 8 (1935) 72-97; 9 (1936) 150-161. *A306
——, Etudes inédites sur SFA. P, 1932 (& 1953). ix, 386p. Rev: AFH 25 (1932) 525-533 (cf 533-536); CF 5 (1935) 130-132. Important. A307
COSMO, U., "L'ultimo Sabatier." In D157:114-145. A308
FALOCI PULIGNANI, M., "SFA secondo Paolo Sabatier," MF 9 (1902) 65-74. A309
GOFFIN, Arnold, "Les Etudes Inédites de Paul Sabatier sur SFA," RHF 7 (1930) 129-132 (cf 134-138). A310
JOERGENSEN, J., "Paul Sabatier storico francescano," IF 3 (1928) 344-347. A311
MAUGAIN, G,. "Paul Sabatier. Notes biographiques," RHF 5 (1928) 1-22 (bibl. of Sab.'s works, 14-22); P, 1928. 22p. 2e éd. P, 1931. 28p. Rev: AFH 25 (1932) 533 *A312
ROBINSON, Paschal, OFM, "The Saint of A and M. Sabatier," *The Dolphin* (Phil) 8 (1905) 33-43, 148-165; cf A342. A313
——, *The Real SFA.* 2nd ed. rev, L, 1904. 112p. Valuable. A314
VEUTHEY, L., Conv, "Il pensiero definitivo di Sabatier sulla vita di SF e sulle sue fonti storiche," MF 33 (1933) 3-14. Abs: CF 5 (1935) 130. cf. A343. *A315

SARASOLA, Luis de, OFM, *SF de Asis.* (a) Madrid, 1929. 603p. Rev: EF 41 (1929) 440; CF 1 (1931) 388; FF ns 3 (1930) 149. (b) 2da ed. Madrid, 1960. xv, 616p. Rev: CF 31 (1961) 658. *A316
SPARACIO, Domenico, Conv, *Storia de SFA.* A, 1928. xxiv, 508p. 271 illus. Rev: AFH 22 (1929) 226-229; EF 41 (1929) 322; SFA 8 (1928) 117-119. Important. *A317
VAN DEN BORNE, Fidentius, OFM, "Het 'Drama' in de moderne Franciscus biografie," SintF 58 (1956) 248-287. Abs: RHE 51 (1956) 788; CF XI; 92. *A318
——, "De Franciscus-biografie als litterair werk. Een vraagstuk van methodiek," SintF 58 (1956) 31-80. Abs: RHE 52 (1957) 370; CF XI, 90. *A319
——, "Voornamste feiten uit het leven van F in het licht van de historische kritiek," SintF 59 (1957) 163-239, 243-316. Abs: RHE 53 (1958) 1110; CF XI, 92. *A320
CLASEN, S., OFM, "Das Schriftum von P. Fidentius van den Borne," FS 40 (1958) 251-255. cf A275-A277. *A321

VII BIO-BIBLIOGRAPHICAL NOTES ON 24 DECEASED FRANCISCANISTS

1. MAURICE BEAUFRETON (d. 1927); RHF 5 (1928) 62-68. *A322
2. MICHAEL BIHL, OFM (1878-1950): AFH 37 (1944) 355-402; CF

VII, 16*; SF 7 (1951) 138; DTC-TG II, 442; RSCI 4 (1950) 296; LTK II, 457.   *A323

3. BENVENUTO BUGHETTI, OFM   (1875-1944): CF 13 (1943) 112; MF 47 (1947) 316; AFH 35 (1942) 133-152.   *A325

4. ANDRE CALLEBAUT, OFM (1876-1958): AFH 51 (1958) 366; MF 59 (1959) 280; *Franciscana* 14 (1959) 50-64.   *A325

5. MONTGOMERY CARMICHAEL   (1857-1922):   CW   103   (1916) 360-364; 144 (1936) 328-333.   *A326

6. NICOLA CAVANNA, OFM   (1876-1942): DSPU 39 (1942) 217-220.   *A327

7. CUTHBERT OF BRIGHTON, Cap   (1866-1939): CF 9 (1939) 316-320; CF XI, 43; EC IV, 1098; Lex Cap 485; HPR 39 (1939) 1179-84.
   *A328

8. FERDINAND M. DELORME, OFM   (1873-1952): AFH 46 (1953) 357-368; CF X, 457*; SF 50 (1953) 137-139; Ant 28 (1953) 215.
   *A329

9. EDOUARD D'ALENCON, Cap   (1859-1928): EF 40 (1928) 575-594; RHF 5 (1928) 412-418; CF X, 444; DTC-TG VII, 1109, 1735; Lex Cap 525; EC V, 84.   *A330

10. VITTORINO FACCHINETTI, OFM   (1883-1950): SF 47 (1951) 133; CF X, 451*; FF ns9 (1936) 189-192; 27 (1960) 116-121; 28 (1961) 62-70.   *A331

11. MICHELE FALOCI PULIGNANI   (1856-1940): MF 41 (1941) 1-19, 227-247, 464-501; MF 52 (1952) 401-424; EC V, 968.   *A332

12. HILARIN FELDER, Cap   (1867-1951): CF X, 454*-456*; LTK IV, 63; Lex Cap 571.   *A333

13. GIROLAMO GOLUBOVICH, OFM   (1865-1941): AFH 35 (1942) 338-345; MF 41 (1941) 393; 57 (1957) 453; 47 (1947) 314; CF XI, 150, 659; EC VI, 911.   *A334

14. GRATIEN DE PARIS, Cap   (1873-1943); CF 14 (1944) 402; 20 (1950) 69*; EF nsl (1950) 93-96, cf 146; Lex Cap 697.   *A335

15. RAPHAEL HUBER, Conv   (1897-1962): NYT Sept. 24, 1962: 39; CF 30 (1964) 232; CHR 49 (1964) 620.   *A336

16. JOHANNES JOERGENSEN   (1866-1956): CF 20 (1950) 51*; CF IX, 76*; *Cord* 3 (1953) 119-121 (tr. from D177); MF 57 (1957) 631; FF 22 (1955) 113-121, 165-170; FF 24 (1957) 67-70; IF 31 (1956) 300; J. A. NUYENS, OP, *Johannes Joergensen*. Antwerp, 1959. 62p. cf D177.
   *A337

17. LEONARD LEMMENS, OFM   (1864-1929); CF X, 444*; EC VII, 1097; Ant 4 (1929) 337-350; LTK VI, 942; CF 1 (1931) 138; SF 26 (1929) 290-293.   *A338

18. ANDREW G. LITTLE   (1862-1945): CF 15 (1945) 270; FnSs 6 (1946) 112; MF 47 (1947) 313; cf AFH 31 (1938) 475.   *A339

19. LIVARIUS OLIGER, OFM   (1875-1951): Ant 20 (1945) 1-32; 26 (1951) 210-214; FS 32 (1950) 362-381; AFH 44 (1951) 252-255; CF X, 451*; EC IX, 95; SF 47 (1951) 139-140.   *A340

20. NICCOLO PAPINI, Conv   (1751-1834): MF 20 (1919) 56-64; EC IX, 782.   *A341

21. PASCHAL ROBINSON, OFM (1870-1948): FnSs 8 (1948) 317-320.
*A342
22. PAUL SABATIER (1858-1928): RHF 5 (1928) 1-22; FF 5 (1928) 35-40, 104, 477; SFA 8 (1928) 194; *Cont. Rev.* (L) 74 (1898) 505-518; *J. des Débats* Ed. Hebd. (P) 35 (1928) 473-474; *History* (L) ns13 (1928) 31-32 (Little); *Rev. of Revs.* (L) 76 (1928) 337-340; EC X, 1510; A. G. LITTLE, *Paul Sabatier, Historian of SF.* Man, 1929. 14p., rev: AFH 25 (1932) 533; SISF 25 (1928) 1-60. cf A303-A315. *A343
23. EDOUARD SCHNEIDER (1880-1960): CF 31 (1961) 132; 11 (1941) 694; 29 (1959) 550. *A344
24. WALTER W. SETON (1882-1927): CF 1 (1931) 138-139. *A345

B BACKGROUND

(see also C29-C32, C68, D197-D204, F63-F106, F182-F197, F230-F245)

I TEMPORALITIES

BOYD, Catherine E., *Tithes & Parishes in Medieval Italy.* Ithaca, NY, 1952. xi, 280p. Rev: AHR 60 (1955) 345. *B1
BREZZI, P., *Roma e l'impero medioevale (774-1252).* Bologna, 1947. 663p. (Storia di Roma, 10) *B2
HEER, Friedrich, (a) *Mittelalter.* Z, 1961. 747p. illus. (b) *The Medieval World: Europe 1100-1350.* Tr. by J. Sondheimer. Cleveland, 1962. 365p. illus. (c) NY, 1963. 432p. illus. *B3
HURTER, Friederich E. von, *Geschichte Papst Innocenz der dritten und seiner Zeitgenossen.* Hamburg, 1892. 4v. Still useful for documented survey of institutions in last vol. (Also P, 1855, 3v.; Mi, 1857. 4v.) *B4
MORGHEN, R., *Medioevo cristiano.* 3a ed. Bari, 1962. 364p. *B5
NANNI, L., "L'evoluzione storica della parocchia," SC 81 (1953) 475-544. *B6
PLESNER, J., *L'émigration de la campagne à la ville libre de Florence au XIIIe siècle.* Copenhagen, 1934. xvi, 240p. *B7
Regesta imperii, V. Böhmer, Ficker, Winkelmann, eds. Innsbruck, 1881-1901. 3v. *B8
RENOUARD, Y., *Les villes d'Italie de la fin du Xe siècle au début du XIVe siècle.* P, 1961—. *B9
ROTA, E., et al., *Questioni di storia medioevale.* Mi, 1957. lxviii, 837p. *B10
SALVATORELLI, Luigi, *L'Italia comunale dal secolo XI alla metà del secolo XIV.* Mi, 1940. 948p. 424 illus. Basic. *B11
VERGOTTINI, G. de, *La rinascita politica medievale.* Mi, 1961. xxv, 619p. *B12
WALEY, Daniel, *The Papal State in the Thirteenth Century.* L & NY, 1961. xv, 337p. Fundamental work. cf his "Lo stato papale nel XIII secolo," RSI 73 (1961) 429-472. *B13

II ITALIAN ROMANESQUE ART & ARCHITECTURE
(see also C69, C70, C233-C253, F195, F197)

AINAUD, Juan & André Held, *Romanesque Painting*. NY, 1963. 36p. 176pl.   B14

BARGELLINI, Piero, *L'arte romanica*. Fi, 1960. 314p., 173 illus.   B14a

BOLOGNA, F., *Early Italian Painting*. NY, 1964. 227p. illus.   *B15

CERONI, I., *Periplo dell'arte romanica nell'Umbria*. R, 1950 illus.   B15a

CRICHTON, G. H., *Romanesque Sculpture in Italy*. L, 1954. 172p., 92pl.   B16

DECKER, Heinrich, *Romanesque Art in Italy*. NY, 1959. 82p., 263pl.   *B17

Encyclopedia of World Art (NY & L 1959) VIII, 404-407, 646-680. Best bibls.   **B17a

GAETA, Wanda, "La pittura a Spoleto nell'età romanica," *Spoletium* 1-2 (1954-55).   B18

GARRISON, Edward B., *Studies in the History of Medieval Italian Painting*. Fi, 1953-56. 2v.   B19

GILARDONI, V., *Il romanico*. Mi, 1963. 188p. 122 illus.   *B19a

LAVAGNINO, Emilio, *L'arte medioevale*. 2da ed. To, 1960. 942p., 732 illus. Has useful index of places & monuments in Italy.   *B20

MAIURI, A., et al., *Painting in Italy, from the Origins to the 13th Century*. NY, 1959. 199p. Many col. pl.   B21

MALERBA, Luigi, *Forme e spazio*. Vol. II: *La chiesa, dalle catacombe all'arte gòtica*. Bologna, 1958. 106p., 356 fig.   B22

MARINELLI, Manlio, *L'architettura romanica in Ancona*. 2da ed. agg. Ancona, 1961. 342p., 68pl.   *B23

MORETTI, M., *L'architettura romanica religiosa nel territorio dell'antica repubblica senese*. Parma, 1962. 350p. illus.   *B24

SALMI, Mario, *Chiese romaniche della Toscana*. Mi, 1961. 38p., 80pl. cf F197.   B25

SERRA, Joselita, *La diocesi di Spoleto*. Spoleto, 1961. 126p. 63 pl. (Corpus della scultura altomedievale, 2) Basic. Rich bibl.   *B26

SERRA, Luigi, *L'arte nelle Marche*. Pesaro, 1929. I. 366p. 575 illus.   *B27

TARCHI, Ugo, *L'arte cristiano-romanica nell'Umbria e nella Sabina*. Mi, 1937. 8p., 232 illus.   B27a

La Vita medioevale italiana nella miniatura. R, 1959. 127p., 80 illus.   B28

III HERESIES
(see also D198 & D199a)

BORST, A., *Die Katharer*. Stuttgart, 1953. xi, 372p. (Schriften der MGH, 12) Rev: RSI 55 (1953) 574-581. Fundamental.   **B29

CLASEN, S., OFM, "Armutsbewegungen." In LTK I, 883-886.   *B30

DONDAINE, H., OP, "La hiérarchie cathare en Italie," AFP 20 (1950) 234-324.   *B31

ESSER, Kajetan, OFM, "FvA und die Katharer seiner Zeit," AFH 51 (1958) 225-264.   *B32

FRUGONI, A., *Arnaldo da Brescia nelle fonti del secolo XII*. R, 1954, x, 198p. cf EC I,2001; LTK I,893. *B33

GUNDMANN, H., "Neue Beiträge zur Geschichte der religiösen Bewegungen im Mittelalter," AKG 37 (1955) 129-182. cf D199a. Basic. **B34

ILARINO DA MILANO, Cap, "Le eresie medioevali (sec. XI-XV)." In *Grande antologia filosofica* (Mi 1954) IV, 1599-1689. *B35

KOCH, Gottfried, *Frauenfrage und Ketzertum im Mittelalter*. Berlin, 1962. 210p. (Forsch. zur mittelalt. Ges., 9) *B36

MANSELLI, R., *Studi sulle eresie del secolo XII*. R, 1953. vii, 124p. Rev: AFH 47 (1954) 431. *B37

MARIANO D'ALATRI, Cap, "L'inquisizione francescana nell'Italia centrale nel secolo XIII," CF 22 (1952) 225-250; 23 (1953) 51-165; & R, 1954. 151p. Rev: EF ns6 (1955) 230; FS 39 (1957) 93; MF 56 (1956) 610-612; SF 55 (1955) 184. *B38

"Movimenti religiosi popolari ed eresie del medioevo." In CISSR III, 344-365; cf 383-402. *B39

SAVINI, Savino, *Il catarismo italiano ed i suoi vescovi nei secoli XIII e XIV*. Fi, 1958. 181p. *B40

SHANNON, Albert C., *The Popes & Heresy in the Thirteenth Century*. Villanova, Pa., 1949. 148p. *B41

SOEDERBERG, Hans, *La religion des cathares. Etude sur le gnosticisme de la basse antiquité et du moyen âge*. Uppsala, 1949. 301p. *B42

WERNER, Ernst, *Pauperes Christi; Studien zu sozial-religiösen Bewegungen im Zeitalter des Reformpapsttums*. Leipzig, 1956. 225p. *B43

WALDENSES
(see also D94 & D208)

GONNET, G., ed., *Enchiridion fontium Valdensium (Recueil critique des sources concernant les Vaudois au moyen âge.) Du IIIe Concile de Latran au Synode de Chanforan* (1179-1532). Torre Pelice, 1958—. I (1179-1218) 188p. *B44

HUGON, A. A., *Bibliografia valdese*. Torre Pelice, 1953. 275p. **B45

IV THE HUMILIATI
(see also D197)

DE STEFANO, Antonio, "Delle origini e della natura del primitivo movimento degli Umiliati," *Archivum romanicum* (Genève) 11 (1927) 31-75; cf his *Riformatori ed eretici del medioevo* (Palermo 1938) 125-208. B46

ILARINO DA MILANO, Cap, "Umilati." In EC XII, 754-756, with rich bibl. *B47

MEERSEMAN, G. G., OP, & E. Adda, "Pénitents ruraux communautaires en Italie au XIIe siècle," RHE 49 (1954) 343-390. B48

V LITERATURE & DRAMA
(see also B61; C144-C159; F195; Umbrian Folklore, F200-F204; & Troubadours, C54-C62)

BERTONI, Giulio, *Il Duecento*. 3a ed. riv. & aum. Mi, 1960. xv, 423p. B49

CELLUCCI, Luigi, *Le Leggende francescane del secolo XIII nel loro aspetto artistico*. 2da ed. corr. & accresc. Modena, 1957. 249p. Rev: AFH 52 (1959) 123-125. Important. *B50

FORTINI, Arnaldo, *La Delfo italica. Discorso*. SMA, 1961. 17p. B51

——, *La Lauda in Assisi e le origini del teatro italiano*. A, 1961. 560p. illus. Rev: CF 32 (1962) 339. Indispensable for history of Assisi. *B52

GHILARDI, Fernando, "Le origini del teatro italiano e SF," IF 30 (1955) 341-351; 31 (1956) 81-87. B53

LIUZZI, Fernando, *La Lauda e i primordi della melodia italiana*. R, 1935. 2v. *B54

TERRUGGIA, Maria, *Contributo allo studio del teatro sacro umbro*. R, 1947. (Univ. di Roma tesi). *B55

VITTORINO, Domenico, *The Age of Dante. A Concise History of Italian Culture in the Years of the Early Renaissance*. Syracuse, NY, 1957. xv, 188p. Text & bibl. also cover pre-Dante period. *B56

VI MONASTICISM

1 CENOBITICAL

COUSIN, Patrice, OSB, *Précis d'histoire monastique*. P, 1959. 594p., maps. Invaluable for bibl. **B57

DE WARREN, H. B., "Le travail manuel chez les moines à travers les âges," VS Suppl. 52 (1937) [80-123]. cf D81. *B58

GROSSI, Paolo, *Le abbazie benedittine nell'alto medioevo italiano*. Fi, 1957. xxix, 168p. B59

KAPSNER, Oliver, OSB, *A Benedictine Bibliography*. 2d ed. Collegeville, Minn., 1962. 2v. **B60

LECLERCQ, Jean, OSB. (a) *L'amour des lettres et le désir de Dieu*. P. 1957. 269p. (b) *The Love of Learning & the Desire for God*. NY, 1962. 336p.; see its bibl. of his writings. Rev: Spec 37 (1962) 138-140. *B61

——, et al., *La spiritualité au moyen âge*. P, 1961. 718p. (Histoire de la spiritualité chrétienne, 2) Rev: SMon 5 (1963) 237. To appear in English. *B62

MATT, Leonard von, *Saint Benedict*. Tr. by Ernest Graf. Chi, 1961. 226p. Useful for illus. of Central Italy. cf F43. B63

PENCO, Gregorio, OSB, *Storia del monachesimo in Italia dalle origini alla fine del Medio Evo*. R, 1961. 608p. Rev: RSCI 15 (1961) 356-360. Basic. **B64

VICAIRE, Marie-Humbert, OP, *L'Imitation des apôtres, moines, chanoines, mendiants (IV-XIIIe s.)*. P, 1963. 93p. Important. *B65

2 EREMITICAL

ANSON, Peter A., *The Call of the Desert*. L, 1964. xix, 278p. (New version of his 1932 *The Quest of Solitude*.) Valuable history & bibl. of Western eremiticism. **B66

BLUM, Owen J., OFM, *St. Peter Damian. His Teaching on the Spiritual Life*. Wa, 1947. 224p. (Cath. Univ. diss.) *B67

CACCIAMANI, Giuseppe, Er. Cam., *La reclusione presso l'Ordine camaldolese.* Camaldoli, 1960. 48p. *B68

DRESSLER, F., *Petrus Damiani, Leben und Werk.* R, 1954. xviii, 247p. (Studia Anselmia, 34). Basic. *B69

L'Eremitismo in Occidente nei secoli XI e XII. Atti della Settimana internazionale di studio, sett. 1962. Mi, 1964. *B70

GIABBANI, Anselmo, Er. Cam., *L'Eremo; vita e spiritualità eremitica nel monachismo camaldolese primitivo.* Brescia, 1945. xx, 238p. Basic. *B71

LECLERCQ, Jean, OSB, *Saint Pierre Damien ermite et homme d'Eglise.* R, 1960. 284p. Rev: RSCI 15 (1961) 340-344; SM 3 ser. 1 (1960) 571-574. Basic. *B72

Lettres des premiers chartreux. S. Bruno. Guigues. S. Anthelme. P, 1962. 270p. (Sources chrétiennes, 88). B73

MANSUETO DELLA SANTA, O. Cam, *Ricerche sull'idea monastica di San Pier Damiano.* Camaldoli (Arezzo), 1961. xx, 220p. With B72, fundamental. Rev: SM 3 ser. 3 (1962) 626-632. *B74

MASON, Mary E., *Active Life & Contemplative Life, A Study of the Concepts from Plato to the Present.* Milw, Wis., 1961. 137p. *B75

PAGNANI, A., OSB, *Storia dei Benedettini Camaldolesi, cenobi, eremita, monache ed oblati.* Sassoferrato, 1949. 327p. *B76

Petri Damiani Vita Beati Romualdi, a cura di Giovanni Tabacco. R, 1957. lxiv, 125p. (Fonti per la Storia d'Italia, 94). Rev: AB 78 (1960) 486. *B77

PIERDAMIANO, S., *Scritti monastici.* A cura di B. Ignesti. Siena, 1959. 2v. (Also *Lettere e discorsi.* 1956. 350p.) B78

Saint Pierre Damien et Saint Bruno Querfurt. Textes primitifs camaldules. ("*La vie du bienheureux Romuald*" et "*La vie des Cinq Frères*") Tr. par le P. L.A. Lassus. Namur, 1962. 225p. (Les Ecrits des Saints) B79

WANG, John, *St. Peter Damian as Monk.* NY, 1958. iii, 244, 12p. (Fordham Univ. diss.) *B80

3 ST. FRANCIS & MONASTICISM

(see also D13, D99, D151, E88, E205, F50, F123-F128, F258-F261, F292)

BINDANGOLI-BINI, B., "SF, la Porziuncula e i benedettini," OS 29 (1916/17) 222-250. cf F254. B81

BULLETTI, Enrico, OFM, "SF nell'Eremo di Camaldoli," *Unità Cattolica* 26 ag, 1928. Abs: FF 6 (1929) 112. B82

HUIJBEN, J., OSB, "Sint F en Sint Benedictus," FL 10 (1927) 125-143. Abs: EF 40 (1928) 312. B83

LAMPEN, W., OFM, "Utrum S.P.N.F. cognoverit regulam S. Benedicti," AFH 17 (1924) 445-448. B84

LAURI, A., "S. Benedetto e SFA nella loro regione," IF 21 (1946) 305-311; cf 3-6. CF VII, 33*. B85

LIBERATO DA STOLFI, OFM, "SF e l'Ordine di S. Benedetto," FF 26 (1959) 19-25. B86

MATURA, M. C., OFM, "SF et l'Ordre bénédictin," *Studium* 2 (1947) 171-175. CF VIII, 62*. B87

C LIFE

I CHRONOLOGY
(see also Appendix II; & E196)

CRESI, D., OFM, "Cronologia della vita di SF," SF 55 (1958) 50-64. Rev: MF 56 (1956) 608. Not sufficiently critical. C1

FISCHER, HERMANN, *Der hl. F. von A. während der Jahre 1219-1221. Chronologische-historische Untersuchungen.* Fribourg, 1907. 144p. Rev: AB 13 (1912) 451-462; AFH 1 (1908) 630-633. Still useful. *C2

FORTINI, A., *Nel 750o anniversario della fondazione dell'Ordine dei Frati Minori (1209-1959). Storia, cronaca, discussioni.* SMA, 1959. 33p. illus. Abs: AFH 53 (1960) 342. C3

GNOCCHI, Ludovico U., OFM, "In quale anno, mese e giorno il Crocifisso di S Damiano parlò a SF," SF 23 (1926) 274-279. C4

HERMANN, Placid, OFM, "The Chronology of SFs' Life." In A81:1-10. C5

MANDIC, Dominik, OFM, *De legislatione antiquia OFM.* Mostar, 1924. xvi, 140p. Rev: AFH 18 (1925) 272-278 (Bihl). *C6

——, "Kronolski pregled zivota sv. Franje Asiskoga," *Bogoslovska Smotra* (Zagreb) 15 (1927) 36-43, 170-176, 349-357. Summary of a ms burned in World War II. cf EF 40 (1928) 290 & 535. *C6a

PATREM, Léon, OFM, "Appunti critici sulla cronologia della vita di SF," MF 9 (1902) 76-101. cf AFH 1 (1908) 30. Fundamental. *C7

ROBINSON, P., OFM, "Quo anno Ordo Fratrum Minorum inceperit," AFH 2 (1909) 181-196. Important. *C8

TERZI, Arduino, OFM, *Cronologia della vita di SFA.* R, 1963. xvi, 182p. Indispensable though not sufficiently critical. *C9

VAN DER VAT, Odulf, OFM, "Das chronologische Rätsel in der Chronik des Jordanus von Giano," AFH 24 (1931) 395-398. cf A133. *C10

II HOME
(see Appendix V)

ABATE, Guiseppe, Conv, *La casa dove nacque SFA, nella sua documentazione storica.* R, 1939. 56p. C11

——, *La casa dove nacque SFA nella sua nuova documentazione.* Gubbio, 1941. xxiv, 424p. illus. Also in MF 40 (1940) 321-744. Basic. **C12

——, "Storia e leggenda intorno alla nascita di SFA," MF 48 (1948) 515-549; 49 (1949) 123-153, 350-379. Valuable discussion. cf C33. *C13

ATTAL, Francesco Salvatore, *La casa dove nacque SF. Studio critico.* R, 1942. 48p. Summarizes C12. C14

——, "La casa paterna e il parentado di Santa Chiara. Falsi e falsari dei secoli XVI e XVII," MF 46 (1946) 157-197; on the casa of SF: only 170-172, 175-177. cf E216. C15

BARRADO, Arcangel, OFM, "La casa donde nació SF de Asis, patronado del Estado Español," VV 2 (1944) 471-512. *C16

BRACALONI, Leone, OFM, "Casa, casato e stemma di SF." CF 2 (1932) 520-534; 3 (1933) 81-102. Abs: CF 5 (1935) 146*. *C17

——, *La Chiesa Nuova di SF Converso, casa paterna del Santo in A.* Todi, 1943. xix, 304p. illus. *C18

——, *La Chiesa Nuova, casa paterna di SF. Capo aggiunto.* SMA, 1955. 15p. Rev: AFH 49 (1956) 227. C19

——, *La Chiesa Nuova, casa paterna di SF. Secondo capo aggiunto.* SMA, 1960. 28p. Rev: AFH 53 (1960) 341. C20

BUGHETTI, B., OFM, "Per la casa paterna di SF in A," AFH 34 (1941) 243-260, 449-455; 35 (1942) 328-337. *C21

CANALETTI GAUDENTI, Alberto, "Un parere giuridico sugli atti del Comune di A relativi alla Casa Natale di SF," MF 42 (1942) 313-317. C22

FORTINI, A., "La casa paterna di SF." FNV II, 21-90. *C23

GOLUBOVICH, G., OFM, *La storicità e autenticità della casa paterna di SFA oggi "Chiesa Nuova" e la popolare leggenda della "Stalletta." Studio critico.* Fi, 1940. xv, 112p. illus. Rev: SF 12 (1940) 151-154; 13 (1941) 237-240. *C24

JACOVELLI, A., Conv, *La casa natale di SFA intorno al 1615.* A, 1959. 20p. C25

PERALI, Pericle, "Lettera intorno alla Casa Paterna e Natale di SF, intorno ad un documento 'perentorio' ma superfluo, e intorno ad una casa dei nipoti del Santo prospiciente sulla 'Platea Nova Communis'," MF 41 (1941) 297-325J. map, facsim. Has 1395 taxlist. *C26

——, "Ottavio Ringhiere, Vescovo di A, e la casa dove nacque SF," MF 42 (1942) 277-312. C27

TERZI, A, OFM, '*La Chiesa Nuova' in A casa natale di SF.* R, 1960. 33p. map. Rev: EF ns12 (1962) 94. Quotes principal docs. *C28

III FAMILY, BIRTH, CHILDHOOD
(see also Appendices III & IV; cf D156)

1 BACKGROUND

ARIES, Philippe, *Centuries of Childhood, A Social History of Family Life.* Tr. by R. Baldick, NY, 1962. 447p. illus. C29

FACE, Richard D., *The Caravan Merchants & the Fairs of Champagne; a Study in the Techniques of Medieval Commerce.* Ann Arbor, Mich., 1957. lii, 175p. Abs: DA 17 (1957) 1318. Fundamental study. *C30

RENOUARD, Yves, *Les hommes d'affaires italiens du moyen âge.* P, 1949. ix, 262p. map. Rev: MA 57 (1951) 403-415. C31

SAPORI, Armando, *Le marchand italien au moyen âge.* P, 1952. lxx, 126p. Bibl: 1-115; cf B11:691-722. **C32

2 ST. FRANCIS

ABATE, G., Conv, "Storia e leggenda intorno alla nascita di SFA," MF 48 (1948) 515-549; 49 (1949) 123-153, 350-379; & R, 1949. 102p. Abs: CF VIII, 58* & CF IX, 65*. Fundamental new research on Stalletta, Pica, family, name, & birth legends. See Appendix III & IV. *C33

ATTAL, S., "Pietro Bernardone." In A278: 59-96. Rehabilitation.   C34
BIHL, M., OFM, "De nomine S. F.," AFH 19 (1926) 469-529. Basic.
*C35
FORTINI, A., FNV I/1, 102-116; II, 93-112 (chart, 100).   *C36
MARINANGELI, Bonaventura, Conv, "Sulle orme di SF. Il fonte battesimale," SFA 1 (1920-1) 159-162.   C37
ORTOLANI, Ciro da Pesaro, OFM, *La madre del Santo d'A.* Tolentino, 1926. 301p. Rev: FF 4 (1927) 210-213; EF 41 (1929) 322.   C38
UBALD D'ALENCON, Cap, "De l'origine française de SFA," EF 10 (1903) 449-454.   C39

IV YOUTH

1 GENERAL

DUGGAN, Alfred, *Growing up in 13th Century England.* NY, 1962. 213p.   C40
MANACORDA, Giuseppe, *Storia della scuola in Italia. I. Il medioevo.* Mi, 1913.   C40a
MEYER, Paul, "De l'expansion de la langue française en Italie pendant le moyen âge." In CISSA IV, 61-104; on SF: 68-69.   C41
OZANAM, Antoine Frédéric, *Documents inédits pour servir à l'historie littéraire de l'Italie depuis le VIIIe siècle jusqu'au XIIIe.* P 1897. 418p. cf "Des écoles et de l'instruction publique en Italie aux temps barbares," 3-79.
C42
SALVIOLI, G., *L'istruzione in Italia prima del mille.* Fi, 1912. 192p.   C43
THOMPSON, J. W., *The Literacy of the Laity in the Middle Ages.* NY, 1939 (& 1960). 198p. cf ch. III: "Italy."   *C44

2 ST. FRANCIS
(see also A306, A307:89-114; D156)

BROCART, Yves, OFM, "Une singulière nouveauté sur SFA," FF 2 (1925) 318-326. Opposes Beaufreton (A280).   C45
CLASEN, Sophronius, OFM, "F, der Gottes Absicht noch nicht erkannte," WW 27 (1964) 117-128. Important.   *C45a
DOMENICHELLI, Teofilo, "Il Celanese e i primi venticinque anni di SFA," *Luce e Amore* 4 (1907) 21-30.   C46
FALOCI PULIGNANI, M., "Il maestro di SF," MF 22 (1921) 57-64.
C47
FORTINI, A., "La giovinezza del Santo." FNV I/1, 105-149; II, 93-129.
*C48
——, "SF e i Tripudianti di S. Vittorino," FF ns3 (1956) 84-88. Abs: CF XI, 93. cf FNV I/1, 164-178.   C49
FREDEGAND [CALLAEY] D'ANVERS, Cap, "Come visse SFA in veste e costume secolareschi," RISS 106 (1926) 181-201. Basic, with C51.   *C50
——, "L'allegra giovinezza di SFA. Esame critico," IF 1 (1926) 273-292. cf EF 40 (1928) 535-537; EstF 38 (1926) 356-374. cf C50.   *C51
MASSERON, A., "L'enfance et la jeunesse de SF," ASF (1946-47) n.41, 4-8; n.45, 1-5. CF 20 (1950) 59*.   C52

OLIGER, O., OFM, "De ultima mutatione officii S.F.," AFH 1 (1908) 45-49. *C53

3 CHIVALRY & TROUBADOURS
(see also D69, D151, F35)

BEDIER, J., "Les chansons de geste et les routes d'Italie." In his *Les légendes épiques* 2e éd (P 1917) II, 145-293. *C54

CHAYTOR, Henry J., *The Troubadours*. NY, 1912. vii, 151p. cf ch. III. *C55

D'ANCONA, A., "Le tradizioni carolingie in Italia." In his *Saggi di letteratura popolare* (Livorno 1913) 3-44. *C56

DUPIN, Henri, *La courtoisie au moyen âge (d'après les textes du XIIe et du XIIIe siècle)*. P, 1931. 167p. C57

FELDER, Hilarin, Cap. *Der Christusritter aus A. Z*, 1941. 165p. *C58

———, *Le chevalier du Christ au pays d'A*. Genève, 1943. 146p. *C59

———, *The Knight-errant of A*. Tr. by B. Bittle, Cap. Milw, 1948. 152p. Rev: (various eds.) CF 12 (1942) 557-559; Ant 17 (1942) 313; FnSs 7 (1947) 100-102; WW 12 (1949) 59-61 (Clasen). *C60

FREDEGAND [CALLAEY] D'ANVERS, Cap, *L'animo cavalleresco del Giullare di Dio*. Reggio Emilia, 1927. C61

OLIGER, L., OFM, "S F cognovitne pseudo-Turpinum?" Ant 2 (1927) 277-280. *C61a

VINCENTI, E., *Bibliografia antica dei trovatori*. Mi, 1963. lxiii, 179p. **C62

V MILITARY SERVICE
(see Appendix VI)

1 ASSISI-PERUGIA WAR

FORTINI, A., "La guerra di Perugia," FNV I/1, 151-210; "Le fazioni e la guerra di Perugia," FNV II, 131-219. *C63

GIARDINA, Camillo, "I 'boni homines' in Italia, contributo alla storia delle persone e della procedura civile e al problema dell' origine del consolato," *Riv. di storia del diritto italiano* 5 (1932) 28-98, 313-394. *C64

2 WAR IN APULIA

CALAMITA, F. P., "Chi era il conte Gentile?" MF 27 (1927) 151-152. C65

FALOCI PULIGNANI, M., "Perche SF voleva andare nelle Puglie," MF 27 (1927) 33-36; & IF 2 (1927) 325-329. Rev: C67. C66

ORZA, Mariano, *Gualteri III conte di Brienne*. Napoli, 1940. 348p. C66a

OTTAVIO DA ALATRI, Cap, "Perche F voleva andare nelle Puglie?" IF 2 (1927) 321-334. Important. *C67

VAN CLEVE, Thomas C., *Markward of Anweiler & the Sicilian Regency*. Princeton, NJ, 1937. x, 231p. Basic. **C68

VI CONVERSION

BRACALONI, Leone, OFM,   (a) "Il prodigioso Crocifisso che parlò a FS," SF 36 (1939) 185-212;   (b) SMA, 1958. 18p. illus. Based on   (c) Evelyn Sandberg Vavalà's masterpiece, *La Croce dipinta italiana e l'iconografia della Passione.* Verona, 1929. xiii, 943p. 585 illus.   *C69

——, "SF architetto secondo Paolo Sabatier," CF 5 (1935) 353-369.   *C70

DE BEER, Francis, OFM,   *La conversion de SF* . . . See A97.

EDOUARD D'ALENCON, Cap,   "La fenêtre de l'argent," *Annales franciscaines* 16 (1889) 370-372. cf EF 40 (1928) 580.   C71

ESSER, Kajetan, OFM,   "Das Gebet des hl F vor dem Kreuzbild in San Damiano," FS 34 (1952) 1-11. CF X, 77*; CF 30 (1960) 16n34. Important. *C72

FALOCI PULIGNANI, M.,   "Il messale consultato da SF quando si convertì," MF 15 (1914) 32-43. cf AFH 7 (1914) 784; CF 30 (1960) 361n102. C73

FORTINI, A., FNV I/1, 213-317; II, 221-272.   C73a

VII MISSIONS

1 DALMATIA

MANDIC, Dominik, OFM,   "Boravak sv. Franje Asiskoga u hrvatskim krajevima. Sur le séjour de SF dans les contrées croates," *Nova Revija (Makarska)* 5 (1926) 223-229. With French summary. cf EF 40 (1928) 537; FF ns6 (1933) 52.   *C74

2 SPAIN (& CORSICA)

CHIAPPINI, Aniceto, OFM,   "La Corsica francescana," *Archivio storico di Corsica* 17 (1941) 507-515.   C75

ERNEST-MARIE DE BEAULIEU, Cap,   "Le voyage de SF en Espagne," EF 15 (1906) 384-399; 16 (1906) 60-75; cf CF 30 (1960) 369n129.   *C76

FORTI COGUL, E.,   "Sant Francesc d'Assis a Santes Creus," SMon 2 (1960) 223-231.   C77

LOPES, Atanasio, OFM,   "El viaje de SF a Espana," AIA 1 (1914) 13-45, 257-289, 433-469. Rev: AFH 4 (1911) 769; 7 (1914) 395, 798. cf CF 30 (1960) 369. Basic.   *C78

ROSSETTI, Felice M., Conv,   "SF ospite dei Codina," OR 7 feb, 1952: 4. CF X, 74*.   C79

3 EGYPT & THE HOLY LAND

a. GENERAL

BOEHM, Ludwig,   *Johann von Brienne, König von Jerusalem, Kaiser von Konstantinopel um 1170-1237.* Heidelberg, 1938. 106p. cf C68, C 82.   *C80

DONOVAN, Joseph P.,   *Pelagius & the Fifth Crusade.* Phil, 1950. 124p. cf C84.   *C81

GEROLA, Giuseppe,   "Giovanni e Gualtieri di Brienne in SF di A," AFH

24 (1931) 330-340. cf MF 56 (1956) 22. On John's tomb in the Basilica.
*C82

GOTTSCHALK, Hans L., *Al-Malik al-Kamil von Egypten und seine Zeit.* Wiesbaden, 1958. x, 256p. (On his personality: 23-26; on Damietta: 58-88; on SF: nothing.) Rev: AFH 52 (1959) 331-333. *C83

MANSILLA, D., "El Cardenal hispano Pelayo Gaitan (1206-1230)," *Anthologica Annua* 1 (1953) 11-66. cf C81. *C84

MAYER, Hans E., *Bibliographie zur Geschichte der Kreuzzüge.* Hannover, 1960. xxxii, 272p. **C85

OLIVER OF PADERBORN, *The Capture of Damietta.* Tr. by John J. Gavigan, Phil, 1948. ix, 112p. Rev: CHR 34 (1949) 475. *C86

THETMARI, Magistri, *Iter ad Terram Sanctam.* T. Tobler, ed. St. Gall, 1851. 16p. C87

———, "Voyages faits en Terre Sainte par Thetmar, en 1217 . . ." In Académie royale des sciences, des lettres et des beaux-arts de Belgique *Mémoires* 26 (1851) no. 6; 61p. C88

VAN CLEVE, Thomas C., "The Fifth Crusade." In *A History of the Crusades* (Phil 1962) II, 377-428. Basic. **C89

ZACOUR, Norman F., "The Children's Crusade." *Ibid.*, 325-342.
**C90

b. EARLY FRANCISCAN MISSIONS

BIHL, M., OFM, "Die Franziskaner-Missionen im Morgenlande während des 13. Jahrhunderts," *Der Katholik* 35 (1907) 365-376; cf CF 30 (1960) 373n138. *C91

DE ROECK, Hildebrand, OFM, *De normis Regulae OFM circa missiones inter infideles ex vita primaeva franciscana profluentibus.* R, 1961. 125p. Rev: AFH 55(1962) 524-526. *C92

DURIGON, Natale, OFM, *L'istituzione dei missionari nell'Ordine dei Frati Minori (studio storico-giuridico).* Cairo, 1959. 134p. *C93

GOLUBOVICH, Girolamo, OFM, *Biblioteca Bio-bibliografica della Terra Santa e dell'Oriente francescano.* Q, 1906-19. Ser I, I-III. cf C97, C113. Rev: AFH 7 (1914) 132-138. Cited GBB. cf A334. **C94

GOVERNANTI, Gaudenzio, OFM, *I Francescani in Acri.* Gerusalemme, 1958. 96p. C95

KRUEGER, Hilmar C., OFM, "Reactions to the First Missionaries in Northwest Africa," CHR 32 (1946) 275-301. CF VII, 44*. *C95a

ODOARDI, Giovanni, Conv, "La Custodia francescana di Terra Santa nel VI centenario della sua costituzione (1342-1942)," MF 43 (1943) 217-256.
*C96

RONCAGLIA, Martiniano, *Storia della Provincia di Terra Santa. 1. I Francescani in Oriente durante le Crociate (sec. XIII).* Cairo, 1954. xxvi, 107p. (GBB, ser. IV, Studi 1) Rev: AFH 47 (1954) 232. Useful. *C97

———, *SFA & the Middle East.* 2d ed. Tr. by Stephen A. Janto, OFM. Cairo, 1957. v, 93p. *C98

RUSSO, Francesco, Conv, *I protomartiri francescani.* Padova, 1948. 31p.
C99

La scimitarra del Miramolino: Relazione della passione dei primi martiri

francescani del Marrocco (1220). Tr. e pres. del P. Alberto Ghinato, OFM. R, 1962. 64p. cf AFH 23 (1930) 390.   C100

SIMONUT, Noe, *Il metodo d'evangelizzazione dei Francescani tra i Mussulmani e Mongoli nei secoli XIII-XIV*. Mi, 1947. 164p. Rev: CF 21 (1951) 393.   *C101

VAN DER VAT, Odulphus, OFM, *Die Anfänge der Franziskanermissionen und ihre Weiterentwicklung im nahem Orient und in den mohammedanischen Landern während des 13. Jahrhunderts*. We, 1934. xi, 267p. Rev: AFH 31 (1938) 477-486; CF 5 (1935) 277.   *C102

c. ST. FRANCIS IN EGYPT & THE HOLY LAND

ANASAGASTI, Pedro de, OFM, *El alma misionera de SF de Asis*. R, 1955. 106p. Rev: CF 27 (1957) 328; EF ns7 (1956) 224.   C103

BASETTI-SANI, Giulio, *Mohammed et SF*. Ottawa, 1959. 284p. Rev: CF 30 (1960) 220.   *C104

DELORME, F., OFM, "Les Espagnols à la bataille de Damiette," AFH 16 (1923) 245-246. cf C84.   *C105

DIOTALLEVI, Ferdinando, OFM, "SF nei suoi viaggi e nel possesso dei Luoghi Santi." In F38: 274-293.   C106

FISCHER, H., "Der Aufenthalt des hl F im Orient . . ." In C2:20-42.   *C107

FORTINI, A., "Damiata." FNV I/2, 43-109.   *C108

——, *SF in Egitto*. SMA, 1959. 71p.   C109

——, *Gli ultimi Crociati, cronaca del VI centenario della Custodia di Terra Santa, celebrato in A nell'anno giubilare 1933*. Mi, 1935. 268p.   C110

GABRIELI, Gabriele, *Del viaggio di SF in Egitto e del frate reatino che ve l'accompagnò. Ricerca storica*. Rieti, 1927. 21p.   C111

——, "SF e il Soldano d'Egitto," *Oriente Moderno* 6 (1926) 633-643.   *C111a

GHINATO, Alberto, OFM, "S. F in Oriente Missionarius ac Peregrinus," AOFM 83 (1964) 164-181. Basic.   *C112

GOLUBOVICH, Girolamo, OFM, "SF e i Francescani in Damiata," SF 12 (1926) 307-330. cf AFH 19 (1926) 559; 25 (1932) 129. See also C105.   *C113

"L'incontro d'El-Mansurah," OR 4mag, 1947: 3. CF VIII, 61*.   C114

JACOPOZZI, Nazzareno, OFM, "Dove sia avvenuta la visita di SFA al Sultano Melek-el-Kamel." In 11e Congrès international de Géographie *Comptes rendus* (Cairo 1926) V, 141-156; & FF 2 (1925) 379-393. maps. Useful.   *C115

LEMMENS, Leonard, OFM, "De SF Christum praedicante coram Sultano Aegypti," AFH 19 (1926) 559-578.   C116

——, " 'F vir catholicus et totus apostolicus.' De primordiis missionum Ordinis Minorum," Ant 2 (1927) 21-58.   *C117

NATALI, Augusto, "Gli Arabi e SF alle Crociate," IF 33 (1958) 154-162.   C118

NILO, M., "SFA e l'Oriente," IF 2 (1927) 3-8. On possible Orthodox links. cf D211.   C119

OKTAVIAN VON RIEDEN, Cap, "Die Sehnsucht des hl F nach dem Martyrium." In D139:365-372. Fundamental. **C120
RONCAGLIA, Martiniano, "Fonte Arabo-musulmana su SF in Oriente?" SF 50 (1953) 258-259. CF X, 74*. *C121
——, "SFA in Oriente," SF 50 (1953) 97-106. CF X, 74. Basic. *C122
ZWEMER, S. M., "F of A & Islam," *Moslem World* 39 (1949) 247-251.
C123

VIII THE CHRISTMAS CRIB
(for Greccio, see F311, F354-356)

BERLINER, Rudolf, "The Origins of the Creche," *Gazette des Beaux Arts* (NY) 30 (1946) 249-278. *C124
——, *Die Weihnachtskrippe*. München, 1955. 244p. illus. Rev: CF 27 (1957) 445-447; CF XI, 97. Abs: C133. *C125
BERNAREGGI, A., "Le fonti del presepio francescano di Greccio," SC ser. 6 3 (1924) 7-29, 99-108. Rich bibl. *C126
CANTINI, Gustavo, OFM, "L'infanzia divina nella pietà francescana," SF ns9 (1923) 283-313; cf 437-463. On post-SF evolution. C127
DAUSEND, H., OFM, "Die Weihnachtsfeier des hl F von A in Deutschland und Greccio," FS 13 (1926) 294-304. C128
DE ROBECK, Nesta, *The Christmas Crib*. L, 1938. 153p. Basic.
*C129
GOUGAUD, L., OSB, "La crèche de Noël avant SFA," RSR 2 (1922) 26-34. Abs: AFH 19 (1926) 135. Important. *C130
GRISAR, H., SJ, "Archeologia del presepio in Roma (V-XVI secolo)," CC 59 (1908/4) 702-719; cf s16 (1895/4) 467-475. *C131
GROUSSET, René, "Le boeuf et l'âne à la Nativité du Christ," MAH 4 (1884) 334-344. *C132
MOLS, Roger, SJ, "Historie de la crèche de Noël d'après un ouvrage récent," NRT 81 (1959) 1049-1072. Abs-rev of C125. C133

OKTAVIAN VON RIEDEN, Cap, "De Kerstviering van Greccio in het licht van haar tijd," FL 40 (1957) 163-177; 41 (1958) 21-27. Rev: CF XI, 96. *C134
——, "Die Krippenfeier von Greccio in zeitgenössischer Beleuchtung," St. Fidelis 44 (1957) 8-20. Abs: CF XI, 96. Important. *C135
ROSENTHAL, Erwin, "The Crib of Greccio & Franciscan Realism," Art Bulletin (NY) 36 (1954) 57a-60a. Abs: CF XI, 125. C136
STEFANUCCI, Angelo, *Storia del presepio*. R, 1944. 570p. 292 illus. Rev: CF 14 (1944) 349-351. Useful but not sufficiently critical. *C137
TERZI, A., OFM, *Nella selva di Greccio nacque il presepio plastico*. R, 1961. 45p. 16pl. C138
TIME, Inc., "The Rich Poverty," *Time* (NY) Dec. 28, 1959; 34-37.
C139
VAN HULST, Cesario, OFM, "Crèche," DS II, 2520-2526. *C140
——, *De historia Praesepii Nativitatis Domini a Bethlehem usque ad Graecium*. R, 1941. 200p. (diss.) *C141

YOUNG, Karl, "Officium Pastorum. A Study of the Dramatic Developments with the Liturgy of Christmas," *Wisconsin Academy of Science, Arts & Letters Transactions* 17 (1914) 299-396. *C142

IX THE STIGMATA

OKTAVIAN VON RIEDEN, Cap, "De Sancti F Assisiensis Stigmatum susceptione. Disquisitio historico-critica luce testimonium saeculi XIII," CF 33 (1963) 210-266, 392-422; 34 (1964) 5-62, 241-338. Masterpiece, Fundamental study with comprehensive bibl. **C143

X THE CANTICLE OF BROTHER SUN
(see Appendix VIII)

1 MEANING

BENEDETTO, Luigi Foscolo, "Laudato si', mi' Signore, per . . ." *Pegaso* 2 (1930) 170-185. Rev: CF 1 (1931) 397. C144 .

——, *Il Cantico di frate Sole.* Fi, 1941. 263p. Rev: AFH 34 (1941) 236-242 (Bihl); CF 12 (1942) 71-73; MF 43 (1943) 305-314; SF 40 (1943) 185-189 (Bughetti); SM 14 (1941) 150-163. First basic study favoring per-by & S. Fabiano. *C145

BRANCA, Vittore, "Il Cantico di frate Sole. Studio delle fonti e testo critico," AFH 41 (1948) 3-87; & Fi, 1950. 130p. Rev: CF 20 (1950) 62*; CF IX, n127; MF 52 (1952) 640. Critical ed. *C146

CAMBELL, Jacques, OFM, see A44:225-230. Favors per-for. *C147

CASELLA, Mario, "Il Cantico delle Creature," SM 16 (1943/50) 102-134. Favors per-propter. *C148

CHIMENZ, Siro A., "La poesia religiosa umbra del duecento." In F195: 167-192. Abs: CF XI, 65. Favors per-through or as in Mass-Preface. C149

GETTO, Giovanni, *FA e il Cantico di Frate Sole.* To, 1956. 70p. *C150

GUERRIERI CROCETTI, Camillo, "Ancora sul Cantico di frate Sole," *Rassegna della lett. ital.* 59 (1955) 440-445. Abs: CF XI, 66. Favors per-propter. C151

MONTANO, Rocco, "Il Cantico delle Creature," *Delta* ns7/8 (1955) 107-109. Abs: CF XI, 66. Against per-by-through-for; favors an obscure mystical sense. C152

MONTEVERDI, Angelo, "Prime testimonianze di lingua e di poesia volgare in Umbria." In F195:149-163. Abs: CF XI, 64. Agrees with Pagliaro. C153

PAGLIARO, Antonio, "Il Cantico di frate Sole," *Quaderni di Roma* 1 (1947) 218-235. Abs: CF XI, 65 (with 2 later art.) Favors Preface instrumental per. C154

PAX, Elpidius, OFM, " 'Bruder Feuer.' Religionsgeschichtliche und volkskundliche Hintergründe," FS 33 (1951) 238-249. Has per-durch. C155

PLATZECK, E. W., *Das Sonnenlied des Hl F von A. Eine Untersuchung seiner Gestalt und seines inneren Gehaltes nebst neuer deutscher Übersetzung.* München, 1956. 84p. Rev: CF 29 (1959) 105; FS 40 (1958) 431. C156

Research Bibliography 543

SABATELLI, Giacomo, OFM, "Studi recenti sul Cantico di Frate Sole," AFH 51 (1958) 3-24. Basic survey of recent studies. *C157

SPITZER, Leo, "Nuove considerazioni sul 'Cantico di Frate Sole'," Conv 23 (1955) 257-270; "Postilla all'articolo 'Nuove .... Sole'," 24 (1956) 234-235; "Altre considerazioni sul 'Cantico di Frate Sole'," 25 (1957) 84-87. Abs: CF XI, 66-67. *C158

VICINELLI, A. See A165:219-252. Outstanding literary analysis. Favors per-for. *C159

2 WHERE COMPOSED
(arranged chronologically under authors)

ABATE, G., Conv, "La nascita del Cantico di Frate Sole nel Palazzo Vescovile di A," MF 56 (1956) 333-415. Rev: RSCI 11 (1957) 262-265. Basic. *C160

ATTAL, F. S., "San Damiano e il Cantico di Frate Sole," FF 25 (1958) 139-141. Summarizes controversy; favors San Damiano. C161

BENEDETTO, L. F., Il Cantico . . . See C145:128-156. C162

BIGARONI, Marino, OFM, "A proposito di una rischiosa tesi sul Cantico di Frate Sole," Accademia Properziana del Subasio Atti 5 (1955) 46-52. Abs: CF XI, 70; RSCI 11 (1957) 262. C163

——, Il Cantico di Frate Sole. Genesi del Cantico. SMA, 1956. 158p. illus. Rev: AFH 50 (1957) 248; FF 23 (1956) 142; RSCI 11 (1957) 262-265. *C164

CASOLINI, F., "San Damiano o S. Fabiano?" FF 23 (1956) 25-33. C165

CAVANNA, N., OFM, "Il Santuario della Foresta presso Rieti rivendicata alla storia," SF 37 (1940) 265-273; & Fi, 1941, 11p. *C166

FORTINI, A., "Di alcune questioni riguardanti la composizione del Cantico del Sole." In E206:275-298. [1954] Rev: CF XI, 69. *C167

——, Infondatezza di una recente critica che vorrebbe contestare al luogo di San Damiano la gloria del Cantico del Sole. A, 1955. 24p. *C168

——, Altra ipotesi sul luogo dove fu composto il Cantico del Sole. A, 1956. 38p. *C169

——, "Questioni sulla composizione del Cantico del Sole." [1959] FNV II, 471-543. Fundamental. *C170

L.V.R. [Benigno Luciano Miglorini], Il santuario francescano di San Fabiano Papa alla Foresta. Rieti, 1949. 11p. C171

SABATELLI, Giacomo, OFM, Fatti e ipotesi sul luogo di nascita del Cantico di Frate Sole. SMA, 1959. 16p. *C172

SACCHETTI SASSETTI, Angelo, Anecdota . . . [1926] In F58:5-32. C173

——, "Franciscana Reatina," SF 38 (1941) 103-108. *C174

——, Per la storia del Convento della Foresta. Rieti, 1948. 19p. C175

——, Ancora due parole sul Convento della Foresta. Rieti, 1949. 10p. C176

——, S. Fabiano della Foresta o S. Maria della Foresta? Rieti, 1955. 15p. C177

——, Nuovi documenti sul Convento della Foresta. Rieti, 1955. 23p. C178

——, *Replica a Mons. Terzi sul Convento della Foresta.* Rieti, 1956, 20p.
C179
——, *Questioncelle francescane.* Rieti, 1959. 22p. Abs: AFH 53 (1960) 342. C180
TERZI, A., OFM, *Memorie*. [1955] See F59:255-402. Fundamental, *C181
——, *Risposta al VI opuscolo del Prof. Sacchetti contro "La Foresta."* R, 1956. 16p. re C177. C182
——, *S. Fabiano de "La Foresta" ascoltò per primo il Cantico di Frate Sole (Supplemento al Volume "Memorie francescana nella Valle Reatina").* R, 1957. 223p. Rev: AFH 51 (1959) 219; CF XI, 68; MF 59 (1959) 253-255. Important. *C183
——, *Il Poverello* . . . [1959] See F 60:81-104, 123-142. Summarizes his case. *C184
——, *Ultime battute sul luogo di nascita del Cantico di Frate Sole.* R, 1960. 53p. Also important, with app. on Companions. *C185
——, *Cronologia* . . . [1963] See C9:126-151 & 158-171. Latest summary. *C186

XI ILLNESSES & DOCTORS
(see also C143)

ANDRESEN, Carl, "Asketische Forderung und Krankheit bei Franz von A.," *Theologische Literaturzeitung* 79 (1954) 129-140. Abs: CF XI, 97; CF 30 (1960) 27-29. *C186a
——, "Franz von A. und seine Krankheiten," *Wege zum Menschen* 6 (1954) 33-43. Abs: CF XI, 97; CF 30 (1960) 27. *C187
BONADIES, Antonio, *SF medico.* R, 1960. 51p. Rev: EF ns13 (1963) 225. C188
BOURNET, Albert S., *SFA, Etude sociale et médicale.* Lyon, 1893. 198p. Rev: AB 13 (1894) 301. C189
GILBERT, Judson B., *Disease & Destiny, A Bibliography of Medical References to the Famous.* L, 1962. 535p. On SF:173-174. *C190
GUALINO, L., "La morte del Santo," *Illustrazione medica italiana* 8 (1926) 201-204. Abs: EF 40 (1929) 538. C191
HARTUNG, Edward F., "SF & Medieval Medicine," *Annals of Medical History* ns7 (1935) 85-91. Well documented study of sources. *C192
LODATO, Gaetano, *La malattia d'occhi di SFA.* Mi, 1927. 8p. Rev: MF 30 (1930) 64. C192a
PARISOTTI, Orestes, *Quo morbo oculi sensum amisit F ab Assisio.* R, 1918. 26p. C193
STREBEL, J., "Kulturhistorisches aus der Geschichte der Ophthalmologie und Medizindiagnose des Augenleidens des hl. F von A," *Klinische Monatsblätter für Augenheilkunde* 99 (1937) 252-260. Abs: CF 22 (1952) 81.
C193a
VIVIANI, Ugo, "Sulla identificazione dei vari medici di SFA," Accademia Petrarca (Arezzo) *Atti e Memorie* ns 28-29 (1940) 221-234. cf DSPU 55 (1958) 258; FF 6 (1929) 71. C194

XII DEATH
EDOUARD D'ALENCON, Cap, "La bénédiction de SF mourant à Frère Elie," EF 9 (1903) 204-207. cf MF 9 (1902) 107. C195

BIHL, M., OFM, "De epistola encyclica Fr. Heliae circa transitum S.F.," AFH 23 (1930) 410-418. Abs: CF 1 (1931) 398. cf A72. *C196

CARMICHAEL, Montgomery, "The Gospel Read to SF in transitu," *Dublin Review* 132 (1903) 321-335; & with P.S.: "Il Vangelo letto a SF in transitu," MF 9 (1904) 149-156. C197

CERMINARA, T., OFM, "Il B. Agostino d'A," SF 29 (1932) 208-219. C198

HABIG, Marion A., OFM, *As the Morning Star, The Passing of SF.* NY, 1947. 218p. Rev: CF 21 (1951) 280; FnSs 8 (1948) 88. *C199

RENE DE NANTES, Cap, "La mort de SF," EF 18 (1907) 483-506. C200

XIII RELICS
BRACALONI, Leone, OFM, "Le sacre reliquie della Basilica di S. Chiara in A," AFH 12 (1919) 402-417. *C201

CANNAROZZI, Ciro, OFM, "Storia dell'abito col quale SFA ricevette le Sacre Stimmate," SF ns10 (1924) 262-282. cf C209. *C202

FALOCI PULIGNANI, M., "L'ultima tonaca di SF," MF 14 (1913) 73-95; illus. Abs: AFH 6 (1913) 403. *C203

FOSCO, A., "La sindone di SF," SFA 5 (1925) 158. C204

GOFFAERTS, Camille, "L'écuelle de SFA," *Revue de l'art chrétien* 4 (1893) 48-49. cf "The Soup Bowl of SF," *Dublin Review* 23 (1890) 191-192. C205

GRATIEN DE PARIS, Cap, "SFA au Musée du Trocadero," EF 38 (1926) 493-507. C206

JEAN DE COGNIN, Cap, "Une prétieuse relique de SFA: une manche de son habit," MF 32 (1932) 138-140. Abs: CF 5 (1935) 174*. C207

LAURI, Achille, "A proposito del calice di SF," *Luce serafica* 16 (1940) 216-129, CF VII, 33*. cf FNV III, 31; CF 5 (1935) 361. cf C210. C208

LAZZERI, Zeffirino, OFM, "Fra Mariano da Firenze, La storia della translazione dell'abito di SF da Montauto a Firenze," AFH 17 (1924) 545-549. cf C202. Habit on display at Ognissanti OFM church in Florence. *C209

LY, A., "Il calice di SF," OR 5ott, 1940:3. CF VII, 44*. cf C208. C210

MARINANGELI, Bonaventura, Conv, "Le reliquie di SF nella Basilica di A," SFA 3 (1922/3) 51-52, 67-69, 111-112; 4 (1924) 228-231. Basic. cf earlier series in MF 14-18 (1912-17). *C211

PARSI, Ettore, "Storia di una insigne reliquia del sangue di SF," OR 30dic, 1943:2. Abs: CF VII, 42*. cf SFA 9 (1929) 223-226; MF 34 (1954) 357. C212

Il saio delle stimmate nel suo pellegrinaggio tra le genti di Daunia, Lucania, Molise, Lupinia e Campania nell'anno 1957. Foggia. 1959. 66p. C213

STICCO, Maria, "I vestiti di SF," VP 32 (1949) 415-420. Abs: CF IX, 67*. *C214

TAMBURINI, Elisa, "Bigello," FF 16 (1939) 361-364. Abs: CF VI, 19*. C215

VALAGRA, Giuseppe, "Il sacco di SF a Montella," IF 2 (1927) 232-239. C216

XIV CANONIZATION & CULT

1 GENERAL

BIHEL, E., OFM, "S. F. fuitne angelus sexti sigilli? (Apox. 7,2)" Ant 2 (1927) 59-90. C217

BIHL, M., OFM, "De canonizatione S. F.," AFH 21 (1928) 480-514. Basic. *C218

DELORME, F. M., OFM, "Elevations théologiques sur SF 'l'autre ange'," SF 10 (1924) 233-253. *C218a

FORTINI, A., *Il ritorno di SF. Cronaca del settimo centenario francescano.* Mi, 1937. 467p. 78 illus. Rev: CF 8 (1938) 80-83. C219

LAZZERI, Z., OFM, "La Questione francescana e il processo di canonizzazione di SF," FF ns10 (1963) 171-175. C219a

ROSSETTI, Felice M., *Alla tomba di SFA.* To, 1957. 267p. illus. Rev: CF XI, 115. *C220

SISTO DA PISA, Cap, "La invenzione del corpo di SF ad Assisi 1818-1820," IF 13 (1938) 81-92. Rev: CF VI, 18*. Not critical. C221

2 IN LITURGY
(see also C53)

Liturgia di SFA. Testi latini liturgici. Intr. di Giacomo Cambell, OFM. Versione di Fausta Casolini, TOF. Santuario della Verna (Arezzo), 1963. xxxi, 159p. Rev: CF 34 (1964) 185 (OvR). *C222

ABATE, C., Conv "Da chi e quando fu composto il Prefazio della Mesa di SF," MF 36 (1936) 511-514. CF 10 (1940) 142. *C223

CORNET, Bertrand, OFM, "Le 'Proles de coelo prodiit' de Grégoire IX en l'honneur de SF," EF ns2 (1950) 427-461. C224

CRESI, D., OFM, "Il Prefazio di SF in un Messale sconosciuto," Ant 35 (1960) 95-102. *C225

OLIGER, L., OFM, "De Praefatione S. F. Assisiensis," Ant 11 (1936) 351-370. *C226

PAVOLINI, Francesco M., OFM, "Il Prefazio del P. SFA," VM 11 (1939) 67-71, 93-96. Abs: CF VI, 25*. C227

3 PAPAL VISITS TO SAN FRANCESCO

ABATE, G., Conv, *La maestà del romano pontefice sulla tomba di SF.* A, 1931. 112p. *C228

FORTINI, A., *Il significato storico e spirituale della visita di Giovanni XXIII alla tomba di SF.* A, 1962. 31p. C229

ROSSETTI, F. M., Conv, "Papa Giovanni XXIII sulla tomba di SF trovò il suo santo prediletto," IF 33 (1958) 388-393. (As Cardinal, Oct. 2, 1953.) Author's C220 includes visit of Pius IX. C230

STANO, Gaetano, Conv, "I papi e la basilica di SF in A (Da Gregorio IX a Sisto IV)," OR 25mag, 1953:2. CF X, 89*. C231

S. S. Giovanni XXIII pellegrino alla tomba di SF. A, 1963. 95p. illus.
C232

XV ICONOGRAPHY
(see also A292, D36, E245, F123, F214)

ANDRISANI, Gaetano, "L'iconographie franciscaine dans l'oeuvre du Titien," EF ns12 (1962) 84-92. C233

ANHEUSER, Clemens, & P. Plaseller, *F. und seine Gefolgschaft. Philatelistische Studie über den Fr. Orden.* Saarbrücken, 1959. 96p. illus. Rev: CF 32 (1962) 195. C234

BARGELLINI, P., "Il ritratto di SF," *Città di Vita* 5 (1950) 401-404. Abs: CF IX, 81* (Bonav. Berlinghieri's.) C235

BASCAPE, Giacomo C., "Note sui sigilli dei Francescani (secoli XIII-XVI)," CF 32 (1962) 148-164; illus. cf AFH 4 (1911) 425-435. cf C248, *C236

BOVING, Remigius, "Das aktive Verhältnis des hl. Franz zur bildenden Kunst," AFH 19 (1926) 610-635. C237

BUGHETTI, B., OFM, "Vita e miracoli di SF nelle tavole istoriate dei secoli XIII e XIV," AFH 19 (1926) 636-732; 32pl. *C238

FACCHINETTI, V., OFM. See A292. Richest coll. of illus. & refs.

GUDIOL, J., "Iconography & Chronology in El Greco's Paintings of SF," *Art Bulletin* 44 (1962) 195-203. cf Paul GUINARD, "SF dans l'oeuvre de Greco," RHF 2 (1925) 1-20. C239

JULIAN, René, "Le franciscanisme et l'art italien," *Phoebus* (Basel) 1 (1946) 105-115. Important. *C240

KAFTAL, George, *SF in Italian Painting.* L, 1950. 121p. illus. Rev: CF 22 (1952) 193. *C240a

LAMY, M., "La vie de SF racontée par les artistes de la Renaissance au XIXe siècle," ASF 3 (1937) 97-100; 4 (1938) 11-14. CF VI, 29*. C241

LAZZERI, Z., OFM, "Un ritratto di SF eseguito nel 1225?" OR 20 dic, 1959:3. por. Detail of mosaic by Iacopo da Torrita in Florence Baptistery.
C242

MARINO MAZZARA, S., "Il sentimento francescano di Benozzo Gozzoli," SF 7 (1921) 236-245. cf. C247. C243

MASSERON, A., "Note d'iconographie franciscaine. A propos de la fresque du baptistère de Parme," EF ns2 (1950) 463-466. C244

MARINANGELI, B., Conv, "La serie di affreschi giotteschi nella Chiesa Superiore di A," MF 13 (1911) 97-112. cf MF 49 (1949) 151n9. C245

NERI, Damiano, "Iconografia del transito di SF," SF 12 (1926) 495-517. C246

NESSI, Silvestro, "La vita di SF dipinta da Benozzo Gozzoli a Montefalco," MF 61 (1961) 467-492. Basic. *C247

RAOUL DE SCEAUX, Cap, "SF d'après les sceaux," ASF n61 (1950) 7-13. C248

REAU, Louis, *Iconographie de l'art chrétien.* P., 1955-59. 3v. in 6. On SF:t. III, pt. 1, 516-535. Useful.   *C249

REMY D'ALOST, Cap, "L'oeuvre franciscaine de Rubens," EF 50 (1938) 637-659; 51 (1939) 23-54.   *C250

SCHNEIDER, Reinhold, *Franziskus.* Freiburg, 1953. 17p.; 25pl.; also in English: SF. CF X, 87*. Coll. of early portraits.   C251

SCHRADE, H., *Franz von A und Giotto.* Köln, 1964, 184p.   *C251a

TINTORI, Leonetto, & M. Meiss, *The Painting of The Life of SF in A, with Notes on the Arena Chapel.* NY, 1962. xv, 205p.   *C252

VILLAIN, Maurice, "SF et les peintres d'A," EF 49 (1937) 509-531; 50 (1938) 35-62, 172-193, 415-441; & P, nouv. éd. 1950. 232p. illus. Rev: CF VI, 29*; CF IX, 82*.   *C253

FIVE OUTSTANDING MODERN ILLUSTRATORS OF THE LIFE OF ST. FRANCIS

BENLIURRE Y GIL, Jose, *SF de Asis,* comentarios del P. Antonio Torro, OFM. Valencia, 1926. xxxvii, 265p. 66 illus. (49 of SF). Rev: AFH 25 (1932) 537; EF 41 (1929) 438.   C254

BOUTET DE MONVEL, Louis Maurice (1850-1913), *SFA.* P, 1921. 126p. 21 illus.   C255

BURNAND, Eugene, *The Little Flowers of SF.* NY, 1919. 178p. 30 illus.   C256

SEGRELLES, Jose, (a) *Florecillas de SF de Asis.* Ba, 1926. 344p. Rev: AFH 20 (1927) 408, 422; EF 41 (1929) 438.   (b) *La leggenda francescana.* Mi, 1927. 49 illus.   C257

SUBERCASEAUX ERRAZURIZ, Pedro, OSB. *SF d'Assise.* Intr. by J. Joergensen. Boston, 1925. xviii, 198p. 50 col. illus. Rev: Ant 2 (1927) 280 (Oliger); EF 41 (1929) 439; cf AFH 24 (1931) 271. cf his autobiography: Pedro SUBERCASEAUX, *Memorias.* Santiago de Chile, 1962. 272p.   C258

D   SPIRITUALITY

I BIBLE
(see also D77, D93)

BIHEL, E., OFM, "Deux citations bibliques de SF," FrFr 12 (1929) 529-539. Abs: CF 1 (1931) 101.   D1

CHIMINELLI, PIERO, "SF e la Bibbia," FF 15 (1942) 132-136, 177-182.   D2

EUGENE D'OISY, Cap, "SFA la Bible et le Saint Evangile," EF 39 (1927) 498-529, 646-656; 40 (1928) 69-80. List of scriptural passages in SFs' works, but not based on critical ed.   D3

FRANCESCHINI, Ezio, "Il Vangelo nella vita a negli scritti di SF." In QSP (SMA 1963) VI, 71-77.   D3a

LAMPEN, W., OFM, "De textibus S. Scripturae allegatis in opusculis S.P.N. F," AFH 17 (1924) 443-445.   D4

MIKL, J. M., *Die Bedeutung des Evangeliums im Leben des hl. F von A.* Neunkirchen, 1963. xiii, 168, 13p. (Typescript Wien Kath.-Theol. diss. *D4a
VITUS A BUSSUM, Cap, "De veneratione SFA erga Sacram Scripturam," TO 2 (1941) 114-120; 3 (1942) 14-19; & *Verbum Domini* 21 (1941) 161-168, 202-208. *D5

II CONTEMPLATION, MYSTICISM, & PRAYER
(see also A61, B66, B82, C72, F344-F403)

BLUMA, Dacian, OFM, *De vita recessuali in historia et legislatione OFM.* R, 1959. 145p. Rev: AFH 53 (1960) 343; CF 30 (1960) 468. Fundamental. *D6
BORGESE, Maria Pia, *L'esperienza mistica di SF.* Palermo, 1930. 395p. Rev: CF 1 (1931) 395; AFH 24 (1931) 412; EF 44 (1932) 606, cf 733-743; EF 46 (1934) 225; SF 28 (1931) 94-96. Reviews quite critical. D7
BRACALONI, L, OFM, "SF nella sua vita mistica," SF 26 (1929) 423-476. Abs: CF 1 (1931) 98. D8
BRADY, Ignatius, OFM, "The History of Mental Prayer in the Order of Friars Minor," FnSs ns11 (1951) 317-345. *D9
CLASEN, S., OFM, "Das beschäuliche Leben des Eremitentums." In D152: 176-179. *D10
CRESI, Angelo, OFM, "Il valore ascetico-mistico della perfetta letizia francescana," SF 45 (1948) 1-17. Abs: CF VIII, 71-72*. D11
CUTHBERT OF BRIGHTON, Cap, "The Mysticism of SFA. His Sacramental View of the Visible World," *Ecclesiastical Review* 87 (1932) 225-237. Abs: EF 46 (1934) 223-225. cf his *The Romanticism of SF & Other Studies . . . L*, 1924. ix, 311p. D12
DE BOER, Bertilo, OFM, "La soi-disant opposition de SFA à Saint Benoît," EF ns8 (1957) 181-194; 9 (1958) 57-65. Abs: CF XI, 62. D13
ESSER, K., OFM, "Die 'Regula pro eremitoriis data' . . ," see A61. *D14
GILSON, Etienne, "La conclusion de la Divine Comédie et la mystique franciscaine," RHF 1 (1924) 55-63. D15
GOAD, Harold E., "The Dilemma of SF: A Study of the Two Traditions." In D178:129-162. Abs: EF 40 (1928) 314. D16
MANACORDA, Guido, *Poesia e contemplazione.* Fi, 1947. On SF: 59-105 & 187-191. D17
MELCHIOR A POBLADURA, Cap, "Déserts franciscains." In DSAM IV, 539-550. Rev: CF XI, 284. Important though mostly on post-SF evolution. *D18
MEYER, Rudolf, *F. von A, Stufen des mystischen Lebens.* Stuttgart, 1951. 147p. CF XI, 101. Anthroposophical. cf D218. D19
NICHOLSON, D.H. S., *The Mysticism of SFA.* L, 1923. 393p. D20

OKTAVIAN VON RIEDEN, Cap, "Die Stellung Christi im Beten des hl. F von A," WW 25 (1962) 128-145, 188-212. cf his "Leiden . . ." (D139) *D21

POURRAT, P., "La mystique de SF." In D179:178-203. D22
SCHWENDINGER, Fidelis, "Franziskanische Frömmigkeit. Das Beten des hl. Franz von A," WW 8 (1941) 85-93. D23
Note: a basic art. will appear in 1964 (?) in DSAM under "Frères mineurs."

III CREATURES
(see also Canticle C144-C159; D12, D129, D146, F294, F316)

AMEDEE DE RENNES, Cap, *Pour la route, le jardin, l'oratoire. Thèmes de réflexions sur SF et les animaux.* Le Mons, 1945. 248p. CF VII, 41*. D24
BERNARDY, Amy A., *SF & the Animals.* Fi, 1928. D25
BIHL, M., OFM, "De praedicatione a S. F. avibus facta," AFH 20 (1927) 53-58. D91
——, "De S. F. aliisque Sanctis lepusculos foventibus," AFH 20 (1927) 206-209. D27
BROWN, Raphael, *Fifty Animal Stories of SF, As Told by His Companions. Transcribed from the Early Franciscan Chronicles.* Chi, 1958. 96p. illus. Complete but not documented. D28
——, *SF et nos frères les animaux. Cinquante histoires tirées des anciennes chroniques franciscaines.* Tr. par Serge-M. Lefébure, OFM. Montréal, 1963. 80p. illus. D29
CELLUCCI, Luigi, "Varie redazione della predica di SF agli uccelli," *Archivum romanicum* 24 (1940) 301-308. Abs: CF VII, 42*. *D30
DETTLOFF, W., OFM, "Franciscus en de dieren," SintF 2 (1956) 243-247. D31
EMIDIO DA ASCOLI, Cap, "Il sentimento della natura" & "La fraternità con le creature." In D158:211-226 & 227-256. D32
FA, protettore degli animali. Tr. dal tedesco dalla Marchesa E. del Bufalo della Valle. R, 1901. D33
JUNGE, Liselotte, *Die Tierlegende des hl. Franz von A.* Leipzig, 1932. ix, 129p. Rev: AB 53 (1935) 429-432; AFH 26 (1932) 203-206; CF 4 (1934) 411-414. Abs: FS 13 (1926) 33-53. *D34
KLINGENDER, F. D., "SF & the Birds of the Apocalypse, "Warburg & Courtauld Institutes *Journal* (L) 16 (1953) 12-23. *D35
"Sconosciuto affresco di SF che predica agli uccelli," OR 12dic, 1959:3. cf F132:53. D35
SILVESTRI, Domenico, *SF e gli animali.* R, 1927. 194p. Rev: FF 5 (1928) 395; IF 4 (1929) 189. Also R, 1928. 133p. (EF 43, 1931, 117.) D37
VITUS A BUSSUM, Cap, "L'atteggiamento spirituale di SF verso il creato," IF 21 (1946) 4-12. D38
WHITE, Lynn, Jr., "Natural Science & Naturalistic Art in the Middle Ages," AHR 52 (1947) 421-435. Important. *D39
ZIMEI, Artemisia, *La concezione della natura in SFA.* R, 1929. 257p. Rev: AFH 25 (1932) 536, CC 81/4 (1930) 246-250; CF 1 (1931) 391. *D40

IV EUCHARIST
1 GENERAL

BARBERO, Giuseppe, *La dottrina eucaristica negli scritti di papa Innocenzo III.* R, 1953. xix, 226p. *D41

BROWE, Peter, SJ, *Die Verehrung der Eucharistie im Mittelalter.* München, 1933. xi, 195p. Rev: AB 54 (1936) 217. *D42

DUMOUTET, Edouard, *Corpus Domini. Aux sources de la piété eucharistique médiévale.* P, 1942. 194p. D43

——, *Le désir de voir l'hostie et les origines de la dévotion au Saint Sacrement.* P, 1926. 112p. Rev: *Irenikon* 9 (1932) 469. D44

FREDEGAND [CALLAEY] D'ANVERS, Cap, *L'origine della Festa del "Corpus Domini."* Rovigo, 1958. 100p. *D45

——, *Origine e sviluppo della festa del 'Corpus Domini.'* In *Eucaristia* (R 1957) 907-933; & *Euntes Docete* 10 (1957) 3-33. Abs: CF XI, 106. *D46

KENNEDY, V. L., OSB, "The Date of the Parisian Decree on the Elevation of the Host," MS 8 (1946) 87-96. Basic. · *D47

2 ST. FRANCIS
(see also D114-D116)

CORNET, Bertrand, OFM, "Le 'De reverentia Corporis Domini', exhortation et lettre de SF," EF 6 (1955) 65-91, 167-180; 7 (1956) 20-35, 155-171; 8 (1957) 33-58. Rev: CF XI, 61. Important. *D48

ESSER, K., OFM, "Missarum sacramenta. Die Eucharistielehre des hl. F von A," WW 23 (1962) 81-108. Basic. *D49

FRANCESCHINI, Ezio, "L'Eucarestia negli scritti di SF." In QSF (SMA 1962) III, 38-49. D50

QUIRINUS VAN ALPHEN, Cap, "Het H. Sacrament des altaars en Sint F van A.," FL 22 (1939) 364-374. Abs: CF VI, 24*. D51

V LITURGY
1 GENERAL

ABATE, G., Conv, "Il primitivo breviario francescano (1224-1227)," MF 60 (1960) 47-227. Fundamental; but see D59. *D52

HANSSENS, Ioannes M., SJ, *Aux origines de la prière liturgique. Nature et genèse de l'office de Matines.* R, 1952. 130p. *D53

KENNEDY, V. L., OSB, "The Calendar of the Early Thirteenth Century Curial Missal," MS 20 (1959) 119-126. *D54

KING, Archdale A., *The Liturgies of the Religious Orders.* L, 1955. xii, 431p. Rev: COCR 18 (1956) 170-172. *D55

NUSSBAUM, Otto, *Kloster, Priestermönch und Privatmesse; ihr Verhältnis in Westen von den Anfangen bis zum hohen Mittelalter.* Bonn, 1961. 286p. Rev: CHR 49 (1963) 224; COCR 25 (1963) 71; RHE 57 (1962) 925-929; SMon 4 (1962) 428. On SF:15. cf D65, D66. *D56

PENCO, G., OSB, "Per la storia liturgica del monachesimo italico nei

secoli VII-IX. Correnti ed influssi," *Rivista liturgica* 44 (1957) 168-181.
*D57

SALMON, Pierre, *L'office divin, histoire de la formation du bréviaire.* P, 1959. 252p. *D58

VAN DIJK, Stephen J. P., OFM, "An Authentic Copy of the Franciscan 'Regula Breviarii'," *Scriptorium* 16 (1962) 68-76. Critical of D52. *D59

——, & J. H. Walker, *The Origins of the Modern Roman Liturgy: The Liturgy of the Papal Court & the Franciscan Order in the Thirteenth Century.* Westminster, Md., 1960. xxxi, 586p. illus. Rev: CHR 47 (1961) 215; CF 31 (1961) 235-237; History 46 (1961) 126 (Brooke). Fundamental.
**D60

——, "The Urban & Papal Rites in Seventh & Eighth-Century Rome," *Sacris Erudiri* 12 (1961) 411-487. Summarizes D60 on p. 416-422. D61

——, *Sources of the Modern Roman Liturgy. The Ordinals of Haymo of Faversham & Related Documents (1243-1307).* Leiden, 1963. 2v. **D62

WALKER, J. H., "Early Franciscan Influence on Thirteenth Century Roman Liturgy," *Sobornost* s3,n19 (1956) 344-361. Useful. D63

2 ST. FRANCIS
(see also A52, D12, D21, D23, D48, D152)

BERTWIN, OFM, "Die Liturgie im Frömmigskeitsleben des hl. F," *S. Fidelis* 33 (1946) 139-143, 322-324. Abs: CF VII, 41*. D64

DAUSEND, Hugo, OFM, "Die Brüder dürfen in ihren Niederlassungen täglich nur eine hl. Messe lesen," FS 12 (1925) 207-212. cf RHF 4 (1927) 437. See also D56, D66. D65

OCTAVE D'ANGERS, Cap, "La messe publique et privée dans la piété de SF," EF 49 (1937) 475-486. cf CF VII, 149; CF 5 (1935) 164. cf D56, D65. *D66

VAN DIJK, S., OFM, "The Breviary of Saint Clare," FnSs 8 (1948) 25-46, 351-387. Abs: CF 21 (1951) 486*. *D67

——, "The Breviary of Saint Francis," FnSs 9 (1949) 13-40. *D68

VI MARIOLOGY
(see also F246-F255, Portiuncula)

BENOIT, Ignace-M., OFM, *Le chevalier courtois de Notre-Dame-des-Anges.* Montréal, 1952. 103p. Rev: CF X, 69*. *D69

BRLEK, M., OFM, "Legislatio OFM de Immaculata Conceptione B.V.M.," Ant 29 (1954) 3-44. *D69a

BROWN, Raphael, *Our Lady & SF; All the Earliest Texts.* Chi, 1954. x, 80p. Rev. CF XI, 106. *D70

——, *Notre Dame et SF. Compilation et trad. des plus anciens textes.* Adapté de l'anglais par Romain Légaré, OFM. Montréal, 1960. 96p. Rev: EF ns10 (1960) 96. *D71

——, "SFA & Our Lady." In *The Marian Era* (Chi 1960) I, 53-55, 109-116. D72

ESSER, K., OFM, "Die Marienfrömmigkeit des hl. F von A," WW 17

(1954) 176-190. Rev: CF XI, 107. Also in D118, D119. Fundamental, with D74, D75. *D73

FELICIANO DE VENTOSA, Cap, "La devoción a Maria en la espiritualidad de SF," EstF 62 (1961) 249-274; 63 (1962) 5-21. *D74

GHINATO, Alberto, OFM, "La Madonna nella pietà e nella vita di SF." QSF (SMA 1963) V,41-56, cf 221. *D74a

OKTAVIAN VON RIEDEN, Cap, "De Seraphici Patris F habitudine erga Beatissimam Virginem Mariam," TO 15 (1954) 132-152; & in *Regina Immaculata*, Melchior a Pobladura, Cap, ed. (R 1955) 15-47. Rev: CF XI, 107; AFH 49 (1956) 228, cf 238. Definitive study. *D75

VII POVERTY
(see also A112-A119, D114-D119)

ANASTASIO DA MONTECASTELLI, Cap, "Il diritto di questua negli Ordini Mendicanti dal suo sorgere fino al Codice di Diritto Canonico," CF 21 (1951) 241-345. On SF:255-265. Basic. *D76

"De armoede van Sint F en het heilig Evangelie," SintF 57 (1955) 65-119. Abs: RHE 52 (1957) 367; cf 53 (1958) 1112. D77

AUGUSTINUS A TILS, Cap, *Der hl. F von A und die Armut.* R, 1957. Univ. Gregoriana typescript diss. D78

CLASEN, S., OFM, "F und die soziale Frage," WW 15 (1952) 109-121. Abs: CF X, 76*. *D79

CUTHBERT OF BRIGHTON, Cap, *SF & Poverty.* NY, 1910. vii, 84p. D80

ESSER, K., OFM, "Die Handarbeit in der Frühgeschichte der Minderbrüderordens," FS 40 (1958) 145-166. Important. See also B57. *D81

——, "Leben in höchster Armut." In his *Ordo ...*, E16:334-345. *D81a

——, "Mysterium paupertatis. Die Armutsauffassung des hl. F von A," WW 14 (1951) 177-189. Abs: CF X, 77*. *D82

FRIEND, Julius W., *Holiness & Poverty: A Study of the Influence of the Franciscan Poverty Movement on the Early Secularist Philosophers.* Chi, 1960. 244p. Univ. of Chi diss. *D83

GHINATO, A, OFM, *La Regola e la povertà francescana nella evoluzione dell'Ordine.* R, 1953. I, 322p. *D83a

HARDICK, L, OFM, "Pecunia et denarii. Untersuchungen zum Geldverbot in den Regeln der Minderbrüder," FS 40 (1958) 192-217, 313-328; 41 (1959) 268-290; 43 (1961) 216-243. Fundamental. *D84

HUGUET, Paul, OFM, *Dame sainte pauvreté.* P, 1963. 95p. Rev: CF 34 (1964) 188. D85

——, *Richesses de la pauvreté.* P, 1962. 123p. D86

LAMBERT, Malcolm David, *Franciscan Poverty. The Doctrine of the Absolute Poverty of Christ & the Apostles in the Franciscan Order, 1210-1323.* L, 1961. 269p. Rev: AFH 55 (1962) 383-386; FS 44 (1962) 124-128 (Hardick); *Month* ns27 (1962) 148-155 (Knowles). Fundamental. *D87

LECLERC, Eloi, OFM, "La pauvreté de SF." In *La pauvreté* (P 1952) 71-84. D88

——, "The Poverty of SF," In *Poverty* (Westminster, Md. 1954) 55-68.
D89

LUCA M. DA CARRE, Cap, "SF e i poveri," IF 31 (1956) 310-326
D90

MOLINA, Bruce, OFM, "SFA's Attitude toward Money," *Cord* 12 (1962) 53-58. D91

PETRY, Ray C., *F of A, Apostle of Poverty*. Durham, N.C., 1941. viii, 199p. Rev: CHR 27 (1942) 109; FnSs 23 (1942) 84. Basic. *D92

SOIRON, Thaddeus, OFM, "Die Armutsideal des hl. F und die Lehre Jesu über die Armut," FS 4 (1917) 1-17. cf RHE 52 (1957) 368 (Clasen).
*D93

VITO DA BUSSUM, Cap, "Il movimento di povertà di SF e quello di Pietro Valdo," IF ns34 (1959) 225-233, 299-307. cf B44, B45. D94

——, "SFA e i poverelli," IF 9 (1934) 561-575. Anecdotes in sources. D95

VIII PRIESTHOOD & DIACONATE
(see also E92-E99)

ALBAN VON HERMETSCHWIL, Cap, "Zur Diakonatsweihe des hl F," S. *Fidelis* 28 (1941) 7-11. D96

CALLEBAUT, André, OFM, "SF lévite," AFH 20 (1927) 193-196.
*D97

CLASEN, S., OFM, "Priesterliche Würde und Würdigkeit, Das Verhältnis des hl. F zum Priestertum der Kirche," WW 20 (1957) 43-58. Abs: CF XI, 108. Basic. *D98

LAURI, Achille, "SFA e S. Benedetto da Norcia non furono sacerdoti," *Latina Gens* 18 (1940) 234-236. D99

LECLERCQ, Jean, OSB, "On Monastic Priesthood According to the Ancient Medieval Tradition," SMon 3 (1961) 137-155. cf *Irenikon* 1963
*D100

QUIRINUS VAN ALPHEN, Cap, "De Priester en Sint F," *Priesterblad* 30 (1950) 130-135, 171-173, 204-206, 231-234, 307-310. Abs: CF IX, 74*.
D101

VITA DA CLUSONE, Cap, "Quando ebbe la tonsura SFA," IF 9 (1934) 15-28. Crit. rev: CF 9 (1939) 133-134. Important, with rev. *D102
(*Note*: QSF VIII will include a ch. on SF & the priesthood.)

IX THEOLOGY

AUSPICIUS VAN CORSTANJE, Cap, "F de Christusspeler," SintF 58 (1956) 7-24. Abs: RHE 52 (1957) 368. F as joculator Dei. D103

BACH, Kurt, "Christus am Kreuz und der hl. F." In *Ein Gabe der Freunde für Carl Georg Heise* (Berlin 1950) 103-112. D104

BENJAMIN [VAN NEERBOSCH], Cap, "De Kristus-beschouwing van Sint F," FL 19 (1936) 205-209, 272-274, 323-326. Crit. rev: CF 10 (1940) 147. D105

BERNARDS, Mattäus. "Nudus nudum Christum sequi," WW 14 (1951) 148-151. Abs: CF 28 (1958) 336. D106

BEYSCHLAG, K., *Die Bergpredigt und F von A.* Gütersloh, 1955. 243p. Rev: CF 27 (1957) 207-209 (OvR). (Erlangen Univ. thesis) D106

BUSENBENDER, Wilfrid, OFM, "Der Heilige der Inkarnation. Zur Frömmigkeit des hl. F von A," WW 15 (1952) 1-14. Abs: CF X, 76*. D107

CHAUVET, Fedele J., OFM, "La sapienza cristiana secondo SF," VM 30 (1959) 198-224 D108

DETTLOFF, Werner, OFM, "Die Geistigkeit des hl. F in der Christologie des Johannes Duns Scotus," WW 22 (1959) 17-28. D109

——, "Die Geistigkeit des hl. F in der Theologie der Franziskaner," WW 19 (1956) 197-211. Abs: CF XI, 117. D110

DUKKER, Chrysostomus, OFM, *Umkehr des Herzens. Der Bussgedanke des hl. F von A.* We, 1956. 172p. Rev: CF 27 (1957) 426; FS 40 (1958) 106. *D111

——, *The Changing Heart; The Penance-concept of SFA.* Tr. by Bruce Molina, OFM. Chi, 1959. 156p. cf D114-D119. *D112

ENGEMANN, Antonellus, OFM, *Entflammt vom Heiligen Geist. Die Sieben Gaben des Hl. Geistes im Leben des hl. F.* We, 1961. 126p. Rev: FS 45 (1963) 192. *D113

ESSER, K., OFM, & Engelbert Grau, OFM, *Antwort der Liebe. Der Weg des franziskanischen Menschen zu Gott.* We, 1958. 351p. (Also 2. Aufl, 196[?]) Rev: CF 29 (1959) 512; FS 40 (1958) 433. *D114

——, *Love's Reply.* Tr. by Ignatius Brady, OFM. Chi, 1963. 258p. Tr. of D114. *D115

——, *Pour le royaume.* P, 1960. 191p. Tr. of D114. *D116

——, *La conversion du coeur.* (Both) tr. par l'Abbé Virrion. P, 1960. 127p. Tr. of D114. *D117

—— (alone), *Repair My House.* Tr. by Michael D. Meilach, OFM. Chi, 1963. 222p. Tr. from D119. Collection of WW articles. *D118

——, *Thèmes spirituels.* Tr. par Luc Mely, OFM. P, 1958. 197p. *D119

——, "Bindung zur Freiheit. Die Gehorsamsauffassung des hl. F von A," WW 15 (1952) 161-173. Abs: CF X, 78*. *D120

——, "Freiheit zur Liebe. Keuschheit und Jungfräulichkeit in der Auffassung des hl. F von A," WW 19 (1956) 100-108. CF XI, 114. Also in D118-D119. *D121

——, "Gehorsam und Freiheit," WW 13 (1950) 142-150. Also in D118-D119. *D122

——, "Homo alterius saeculi. Endzeitliche Heilswirklichkeit im Leben des hl. F von A," WW 20 (1957) 180-197. Abs: CF XI, 109. Also in D118-D119. *D123

——, "Die Lehre des hl. F von der Selbstleugnung," WW 18 (1955) 161-174. Abs: CF XI, 112. Also in D114-D116. *D124

——, "Sancta Mater Ecclesia Romana. Die Kirchenfrömmigkeit des hl. F von A," WW 24 (1961) 1-26; & in *Sentire Ecclesiam: das Bewusstsein von der Kirche als gestaltende Kraft der Frömmigkeit* [K. Rahner Festschrift]. Jean Danielou & H. Vorgrimler, eds. (Freiburg 1961) 218-250. Basic. *D125

——, "Wer bist Du, Herr, und wer bin ich? Das Gottesbild des hl. F von A," *Bruder Franz* 2 (1949) 146-149, 195-197. "F's visie op God," SintF

2 (1956) 288-302. Abs: CF XI, 101. Also in D159:27-42. cf B32:241-258. **D126**

GHINATO, Alberto, OFM, "SF nella Chiesa e per la Chiesa." In QSF (SMA 1964) VII, 22-42 cf D125. **D126a**

GOOSSENS, Hilarion, "De Gods- en Christus visie van Sint F," SintF 1 (1955) 7-42. **D127**

GRATIEN DE PARIS, Cap, (a) *SFA, sa personnalité, sa spiritualité.* Nouv. éd. rev. et augm. P, 1928. 157p. 3e éd. P, 1943. 96p. (lacks notes). Rev: AFH 25 (1932) 289; CF 3 (1933) 439-441; CF 5 (1935) 159. Also 4e éd. Blois, 1963. 87p. (b) *I Know Christ. The Personality & Spirituality of SFA.* Tr. by Paul J. Oligny, OFM. St. Bonaventure, NY, 1957. 80p. (From 1943 ed.) Excellent. ***D127a**

KOPER, Rigobert, OFM, "F der Gottsucher," FS 40 (1958) 115-132. ***D128**

———, *Das Weltverständnis des hl. F von A; eine Untersuchung über das "Exivi de saeculo."* We, 1959. 156p. Rev: CF 30 (1960) 219; FS 43 (1961) 110. Important. ***D129**

LAMPEN, W., "De S.P. F cultu angelorum et sanctorum," AFH 20 (1927) 3-23. ***D130**

———, "S. F, cultor Trinitatis," AFH 21 (1928) 449-467. Basic. ***D131**

LORSCHEIDER, Luigi, "Gesù nella vita di SF." In QSF (SMA 1961) II, 40-50. **D132**

MATTESINI, Francesco, "La passione di Cristo nella vita di SF da S. Damiano alla Verna." In QSF (SMA 1962) IV, 32-41. **D133**

MAZZOTTI, Arcangelo, "La teologia dello Stimatizzato," VP 10 (1924) 604-610. **D134**

MEDERLET, Eugen, *Der Hohepriester des Alls. Ein Weltbild, gewonnen aus dem Christus-Erleben des Bruders Franz von A.* Marburg, 1961. 91p. **D135**

MERZAGORA, A., "L'apostolo Paolo e l'Araldo del gran Re," SF 34 (1937) 321-334. **D136**

NEYER, Paschalis, OFM, "Der hl. F und die armen Seelen seiner drei Orden." In *Kirchengeschichtliche Studien P. Michael Bihl als Ehrengabe dargeboten* (Kolmar 1941) 29-49. ***D137**

OKTAVIAN VON RIEDEN, Cap, preparing a study of "Franziszi Gedanken zur Nachfolge Christi." cf CF 30 (1960) 363n110. ***D138**

———, "Das Leiden Christi im Leben des hl. F von A. Eine quellenvergleichende Untersuchung im Lichte der zeitgenössischen Passionsfrömmigkeit," CF 30 (1960) 5-30, 129-145, 241-263, 353-397; & R, 1960. xx, 114p. Rev: AFH 54 (1961) 233; EF ns12 (1962) 94; & D141. Masterpiece. ****D139**

PETRY, Ray C., "Medieval Eschatology & SFA," *Church History* 9 (1940) 54-69. ***D140**

POMPEI, Alfonso, Conv, "SF e la Passione di G. Cristo in una recente indagine critica delle fonti," MF 61 (1961) 92-108. On D139. **D141**

SCHLUND, Erhard, OFM, "Die religiöse Gedankenwelt des hl. F," ZAM 1 (1926) 301-311; & "Das religiöse Wollen des hl F," ZAM 2 (1927) 17-33. Abs: AFH 24 (1930) 139. **D142**

SENFTLE, Alexander, Cap, *Menschenbildung in franziskanischer Geistigkeit; die Bedeutung der franziskanischen Poenitentialehre.* Fr/Br, 1959. 126p. D143

TERSCHLUESEN, Josef, OFM, "Die Pflicht der Liebe und das Recht der Strafe. Die Strafauffassung des hl. F von A," WW 16 (1953) 90-100. Abs: CF X, 79*. D144

VERHEY, Sigismund, "Das Leben in der Busse nach F von A," WW 22 (1959) 161-174. D145

———, *Der Mensch unter der Herrschaft Gottes; Versuch einer Theologie des Menschen nach dem hl. F von A.* Dü, 1960, 212p. Rev: CF 32 (1962) 168-170 (OvR); FS 45 (1963) 199; MF 61 (1961) 129-132. *D146

VITUS A BUSSUM, Cap, "De habitudine animae S.P. F ad tres divinas personas," TO 1 (1940) 21-25, 55-59, 90-92. *D147

———, "De Spiritus Sancti donorum efficacitate in anima B.P.N. F," TO 5 (1944) 48-56. *D148

———, "F strenuus Paternitatis divinae praeco," TO 4 (1943) 19, 49, 96. *D149

X MISCELLANEOUS STUDIES

1 GENERAL

ANSCHARI A PAMEL, Cap, "La psychologie de SF," EF 33 (1921) 489-505; 34 (1922) 327-345, 500-519; & FL 6-7 (1923-24). D150

CASUTT, Laurentius, Cap, (a) *Das Erbe eines grossen Herzens; Studien zum franziskanischen Ideal.* Graz, 1949. 222p. (b) "L'héritage d'un grand coeur," EF ns 5 (1954) 11-43, 205-218; 6 (1955) 5-42, 133-165; 7 (1956) 5-19. (c) *L'eredità di SF.* R, 1952. 254p. Rev: AFH 56 (1963) 225; CF IX, n177; CF X, n283; EF ns5 (1954) 227; MF 53 (1953) 130-132; MF 56 (1956) 499; WW 16 (1953) 57-61 (Clasen). Very important, with reviews; cf D156. Has chs. on SF's knightly spirit & on Francis & Benedict & Ignatius of Loyola. *D151

CLASEN, S., OFM, "Apostolisches oder liturgisches Franziskanertum? Die Antwort des hl F von A und seines ersten Biographen," FS 40 (1958) 167-192. Fundamental. cf D9. *D152

———, "Franz von A im Lichte der neueren historischen Forschung," GWU 3 (1952) 137-154. Abs: CF X, 72*. On sources, times, SF & Church. *D153

———, "Franz von A und Joachim von Fiore. Zur neuen F-biographie von Dimitri Merejkowski," WW 6 (1939) 68-83. cf E48. D154

———, "F der neue Moses," WW 24 (1961) 200-208. D155

———, "Kritisches zur neueren F-literatur," WW 13 (1950) 151-166. Abs: CF IX, 54. On sources, family, gay youth, influence of times (re Helder, Casutt, Grundmann). *D156

COSMO, Umberto, *Con Madonna Povertà. Studi francescani.* Bari, 1940. 303p. Rev: CF 12 (1942) 70. Collected older essays on *Sacrum Commercium* (A116), Brother Pacifico (E131), Elias (E156), Sabatier (A308), Lo Speco (F398), & Greccio (F354); also reprints of old, well-documented studies of sources. *D157

EMIDIO D'ASCOLI, Cap, *L'anima di SF.* Ascoli Piceno, 1949. 286p. Rev:

CF 21 (1951) 436-438; EF ns2 (1951) 109-111; SF 47 (1951) 130. D158
ESSER, K., OFM, *F und die Seinen. Gesammelte Aufsätze.* We, 1963.
223p. Misc. essays, incl. only D126 in this Bibl. D159
FALOCI PULIGNANI, M., *Conferenze francescane.* Città di Castello, 1924. 203p. Collected essays; list in MF 41 (1941) 499. Important.
*D160
FELDER, Hilarin, Cap, (a) *Die Ideale des hl. F von A.* Paderborn,
1923. xvi, 540p. (b) *The Ideals of SFA.* Tr. by Berchmans Bittle, Cap.
NY, 1925. xvi„ 518p. Other early eds. listed CF 1 (1931) 402. Rev: AFH
17 (1924) 433-437; FS 35 (1953) 451. Very useful. *D161
GEMELLI, A., OFM, (a) *SFA e la sua "Gente Poverella."* Mi, 1945.
vii, 288p. Rev: CF 15 (1945) 288; MF 45 (1945) 191; SF 40 (1943)
111. (b) *The Message of SF.* Tr. by Paul J. Oligny, OFM. Chi, 1964.
ix, 197p. Excellent essays. cf E20. D162
GHINATO, Alberto, OFM, *Profilo spirituale di SF tratto dai suoi scritti e dalle primitive biografie.* R, 1961. 206p. Also excellent. D163
GILSON, Etienne, (a) *La philosophie de saint Bonaventure.* 2e éd.
rev. P, 1943. 419p. On SF: 37-75. (b) *The Philosophy of St. Bonaventure.*
L & NY, 1938. xiii, 551p. On SF:40-86. *D164
GUALINO, Lorenzo, *L'uomo di A.* To, 1932. 112p. Rev: CF 5 (1935)
132. D165
LECLERC, Eloi, OFM, *Exil et tendresse.* P, 1962. 224p. Abs: MF 63
(1963) 390. D166
———, (a) *Sagesse d'un Pauvre.* P, 1959. 143p. (b) *Wisdom of the
Poverello.* Tr. by Marie Louise Johnson. Chi, 1961. 126p. Rev: CF XI,
511; CF 29 (1959) 511. D167
LEKEUX, Martial, OFM, *F, qui est-u? L'homme, son message, sa permanence.* P, 1962. 144p. Rev: CF 34 (1964) 182. D168
LORTZ, Joseph. (a) *Der unvergleichliche Heilige. Gedanken um F
von A.* Dü, 1952. 80p. (b) *F l'incomparable.* P, 1956. 96p. (c) *Un Santo unico.* Alba, 1958. 163p. Rev: CF X, 75*; EF ns8 (1957) 97; FS 35
(1953) 444 (Hardick: "one of the most valuable studies in modern Franciscan literature"). D169
LORTZING, J., "Franz von A als Reformator," WW 9 (1942) 61-70,
126-139. D170
LUCA M. CARRE, Cap, "Sulle vette del Francescanesimo," IF 30
(1955) 267-272. D171
MIGUEL DE ESPLUGUES de Llobregat, Cap, (a) *La vera efigie del
Poverello. Assaig psicologic.* Ba, 1927. (b) *Le véritable visage du Poverello.* Tr. par A. de Falgairolle. P, 1929. 235p. Rev: CF 1 (1931) 239; cf
CF 8 (1938) 491. D172
MOTTE, Ignace, & Gérald Hego, OFM, *La Pâque de SF.* P, 1958. 135p.
Rev: EF ns 9 (1959) 118. D173
PAPINI, Giovanni, "Il segreto di SF," FF 21 (1943) 18-21. cf ARSENIO DA CASORATE, Cap, "Giovanni Papini e il suo incontro con SF,"
IF 22 (1948) 241-258. CF VIII, 88*; & P. BARGELLINI, "Giovanni
Papini terziario francescano," IF 32 (1957) 361-370. cf D183. D174
Il Patrono d'Italia. 2a ed. R, 1956. 3v. richly illus. (v.1: *Il santo della*

patria; G. FORTINI. v.2: *La patria al suo santo*; A. FORTINI. v.3: SF *oggi*; I. GIORDANI.) Rev: CF XI, 122. *D175

ROSSETTI, Felice M., Conv, *SF e i carcerati*. Mi, 1956. 208p. Rev: CF 27 (1957) 329. D176

―――, ed., *SF vivo. Testimonianze di uomini d'oggi*. A, 1952. 285p. illus. Rev: MF 53 (1953) 276. Valuable autobiographical tributes by Harold Goad, Joergensen, Arnold Lunn, Moorman, Daniel-Rops, Clare Sheridan, Eugenio Zolli, et al. D177

SFA: 1226-1926. Essays in Commemoration. W. Seton, ed. L, 1926. 332p. Several important studies on sources (see A253), spirituality (D16), Rome (F121); see also D215. *D178

SFA; son oeuvre, son influence, 1226-1926. P, 1927. 320p. illus. Includes excellent studies on sources (see A267), Book of Conformities (A195), mysticism of SF (D22), his Basilica (F273). Rev: AFH 21 (1928) 371-375. *D179

SALVADORI, Giulio, *Il vessillo sul monte*. La Verna (Arezzo), 1963. 145p. Rev: FF ns10 (1963) 142. Collected writings on SF of the saintly Tertiary professor (1862-1928). cf LIBERATO DI STOLFI, OFM, "Il francescanesimo di Giulio Salvadori," FF ns9 (1962) 63-68; & *Lettere Italiane* 15 (1963) 253. cf F120. D180

SCARAMUZZI, Diomede, OFM, *Nella luce di Cristo e di Santo F*. R, 1953. xviii, 262p. Rev: CF 24 (1954) 428. 49 articles (some from OR). D181

SCHNEIDER, Reinhold, (a) *Die Stunde des hl. Franz von A*. Heidelberg, 1950. 100p. (b) *The Hour of SFA*. Chi, 1953. xiv, 113p. CF X, 53* & 72*. D182

Universitalità del francescanesimo. A, 1950. 247p. illus. Essays by Bargellini, Fortini, Papini, et al. D183

VITO DA CLUSONE, Cap, *Cultura e pensiero di SFA; opera critico-storica*. Modena, xcii, 534p. illus. Rev: CF X, n274; CF XI, 98; MF 55 (1953) 422-427. Uncritical erudite portrait of SF as a universal genius. cf A26. *D184

―――, "SFA e il lavoro," IF 8 (1933) 225-235. Survey of sources. D185

―――, "La 'Forma mentis' di SFA nel giudizio degli scrittori," IF 22 (1947) 286-298. Abs: CF 20 (1950) 58*. D186

2 PEDAGOGY

BERNARELLO, Franco, *La formazione religiosa secondo la primitiva scuola francescana*. R, 1961. 94p. Rev: CF 33 (1963) 109 (OvR). *D187

FERNANDO DE MALDONADO, Cap, "La pedagogia de SFA," Laur 3 (1962) 3-40, 289-348. Fundamental. *D188

HAMMER, Robert, OFM, "SFA as an Educator & His Pedagogical Method," FEC 11 (1929) 9-40. Abs: CF 1 (1931) 404. D189

HARDICK, L., OFM, "Geistige Menschenformung durch F von A," WW 23 (1960) 147-160. *D190

HUG, Pacific, OFM, "How SF Guided His Brethren," FEC 29 (1949) 43-81. Abs: CF IX, 75*. D191

LINDEN, Raymund [von Duisburg], Cap, *Vater und Vorbild. F: Forma Minorum.* We, 1960. 311p. Rev: CF 32 (1962) 167 (OvR). *D192
PAOLO ANTONIO DA BASSANO, Cap, "SF educatore," IF 4 (1929) 3-15, 193-206, 385-397. Abs: CF 1 (1931) 99. D193

3 PREACHING
(see also F108)

BELLUCCO, B., *De sacra praedicatione in OFM.* R, 1956. xix, 134p. Rev: AFH 50 (1957) 123. *D194
BIHL, M., OFM, "De S. F. praedicante ita ut de toto corpore faceret linguam," AFH 20 (1927) 196-199. D195
HOBRECHT, Hilary P., *SFA, the Model of Franciscan Preachers.* Wa, 1951. 48p. (typewritten Cath. Univ. MA thesis) *D196

4 RELATION TO MEDIEVAL SPIRITUALITY

DELARUELLE, Etienne, "L'influence de SFA sur la piété populaire." In CISSR III, 449-466. Rev: EF ns8 (1957) 98; RHE 50 (1955) 1103; CF XI, 117. *D197
ESSER, K., OFM, "Die religiösen Bewegungen des Hochmittelalters und F von A." In *Festgabe Joseph Lortz* (Baden-Baden 1958) II, 287-315. *D198
GILSON, Etienne, "SF et la pensée médiévale," *Etudes italiennes* 8 (1926) 12-27. *D199
GRUNDMANN, Herbert, *Religiöse Bewegungen im Mittelalter.* Berlin, 1935. 520p. Rev: AFH 29 (1936) 550-559 (Bihl); CF IX, 55*. cf B34. Basic. *D199a
HARDICK, L., OFM, "F, die Wende der mittelalterlichen Frömmigkeit," WW 13 (1950) 129-141. Abs: CF IX, 69*-70*. *D200
OPTATUS VAN VEGHEL, Cap, "F gezien tegen de achterground van zijn tijd," FL 39 (1956) 14-27, 36-52, 99-110. Abs: CF XI, 95. D201
SCHNEIDER, E., "SF et le rétablissement de l'unité spirituelle au XIIIe siècle," *Nouvelle revue historique de droit français et étranger* 60 (1939) 515-523. D202
VAN BEERS, B., "F en de Scholastiek," FL 16 (1933) 145-156. D203
WILLIBRORD DE PARIS, Cap, "Rapports de SFA avec le mouvement spirituel du XIIe siècle," EF ns12 (1962) 129-142. Important: in several ways SF was a man of the 12th century. *D204

5 ST. FRANCIS & NON-CATHOLICS

BROPHY, LIAM, "Non-Catholic Tributes to SF," *Catholic Digest* Dec. 1943, p. 31-32. (Ruskin & Oscar Wilde). D205
CHIMINELLI, P., "Einstein nel 'bel San Francesco' di Fiesole," FF 22 (1955) 126-128. His friendship with a friar there. D206
CONSTANTINUS [VAN SCHIEDAM], Cap, "Chassidisme, niewchassidisme en SF van Assisie," FL 14 (1931) 274-280. Abs: CF 3 (1933) 449. D207

EYNARD, Max, *Pietro e F.* Torre Pellice, 1951. 219p. By a Waldensian. D208

FORTINI, A., *D'Annunzio e il francescanesimo.* A, 1963. 275p. illus. Rev: FFns10 (1963) 138-141; MF 63 (1963) 388. Includes letters & interviews. D209

HESS, J., "Franz von A i n protestantischer Darstellung," *Schweizer Rundschau* 22 (1922) 1-18. D210

HEYLIGERS, A. R., "Franz von A oder die orientalische Mystik im Westen," *Internationale Kirchliche Zeitschrift* (Bern) 39 (1949) 104-114 Old-Catholic writer compares SF with Eastern Orthodox spirituality. cf. C119, D217. D211

JUILLARD, Pierre, *Le "Poverello" d'A, chantre de l'amour divin.* Genève, 1944. 163p. illus. Protestant biography; includes Rule of Les Veilleurs (Third Order) founded by Pasteur Alfred Monod in 1923. D212

LAVALLE, Guillaume, OFM, "Les littérateurs à la trace de SF," *Nos Cahiers* (later *Culture*, Montréal) 4 (1939) 344-368. D213

LUCA DA CARRE, Cap, "Il SF mutilato di Van Loon," IF 32 (1957) 254-258. Re latter's *The Arts.* D214

SETON, Walter, "The Rediscovery of SFA." In D178:245-266. D215

STEERE, Douglas Van, *On Beginning from Within.* NY, 1943. 149p. By a Quaker admirer of SF. D216

STEJN, Sergije, "Sv. Franjo Asiski i Rusija," *Nova Revija* 15 (1936) 30-48. Abs: CF 10 (1940) 150. cf *Cord* 4 (1954) 310-314; CF XI, 117. D217

STEINER, Rudolf, *Anthroposophical Ethics, with an Account of FA.* L, 1955(&1928). cf D19. D218

STYRA, Ambros, OFM, *F von A in der neueren deutschen Literatur.* Breslau, 1928. 182p. D219

WHITFIELD, Derek W. J., "SF & Reunion. Reflections on the Relevance of FA's Ideals to Current Oecumenical Thought," *Unitas* 11 (1959) 252-262. D220

E ORDERS

I FRANCISCAN HISTORY

1 GENERAL & EARLY

(see also A235)

ABATE, G., Conv, "Per la storia francescana. Osservazioni e proposte," MF 37 (1937) 575-585. E1

BRLEK, Michael, OFM, *De evolutione iuridica studiorum in Ordine Minorum (Ab initio usque ad annum 1517).* Dubrovnik, 1942. 111p. Rev: CF 16/17 (1946/47) 350-352. E2

BROOKE, Rosalind, *Early Franciscan Government; Elias to Bonaventure.* Cambridge, Eng., 1959. xv, 313p. illus. Rev: AB 79 (1961) 205-208; AFH 53 (1960) 210-212; CF 30 (1960) 112-114; FS 41 (1959) 439-

442 (Hardick); RHE 55 (1960) 572-574; 56 (1961) 676; Spec 35 (1960) 432. Fundamental. *E3

CALLEBAUT, A., OFM, "Les Provinciaux de la Province de France au XIIIe siècle," AFH 10 (1917) 289-356. *E4

CENCI, Caesar, OFM, "Constitutiones Provinciales Provinciae Umbria anni 1316," AFH 56 (1963) 12-39; with list of published early Italian provincial constitutions, p. 12. cf F198, F199. *E5

CRESI, Domenico, OFM, *Discussioni e documenti di storia francescana.* Fi, 1959. 183p. Rev: EF ns10 (1960) 98. *E6

———, *SF e i suoi Ordini.* Fi. 1955. 335p. Rev: AFH 49 (1956) 228; Ant 31 (1956) 435-437; CF 26 (1956) 92-95; MF 56 (1956) 606-609; SF 54 (1957) 250-259. Important, with corrections in revs. *E7

———, "Statistica dell'Ordine Minoritico all'anno 1282," AFH 56 (1963) 157-162. E8

DI FONZO, Lorenzo, Conv, "I Francescani." In *Ordini e congregazioni religiose,* a cura di Mario Escobar (To 1952) I, 157-344. Abs: MF 54 (1954) 323. Rev: MF 53 (1953) 135. *E9

———, " 'Lezioni storiche' sull'Ordine dei Frati Minori del P. Paolo Sevesi, OFM (1942)," MF 44 (1944) 143-166. See E46. *E10

———, *Series quaedam historicio-statistica OFM Conv. 1209-1960.* R, 1961. 88p. *E11

———, "Studi, studenti e maestri nell'Ordine dei Francescani dal 1223 al 1517," MF 44 (1944) 167-195. Abs: CF 16/17 (1946/47) 352. *E12

DOUIE, D., *The Conflict between the Seculars & the Mendicants at the University of Paris in the 13th Century.* L, 1954. 30p. *E13

DUPEYRAT, Elisabeth, *De Gengis-khan à la Chine populaire, sept cents ans d'histoire franciscaine.* P, 1962. 127p. E14

EMERY, Richard W., *The Friars in Medieval France; A Catalogue of French Mendicant Convents, 1200-1550.* NY, 1962. xix, 130p. maps. *E15

ESSER, K., OFM, "Ordo Fratrum Minorum. Ueber seine Anfange und ursprünglichen Zielsetzungen," FS 42 (1960) 97-129, 297-355; 43 (1961) 171-215, 309-347. Rev: AFH 56 (1963) 224. Masterpiece. Supersedes his previous shorter surveys in FS 31 (1949) 225-246 & 39 (1957) 1-22. To be rev'd & pub'd as book. **E16

———, (a) *Der Orden des hl. F.* 2. Aufl. We, 1952. 56p. (b) *The Order of SF. Its Spirit & Its Mission in the Kingdom of God.* Tr. by I. Brady, OFM. Chi, 1959. 60p. Essay, not history. E17

FELDER, Hilarin, Cap, (a) *Geschichte der wissenschaftlichen Studien im Franziskanerorden bis um die Mitte des 13. Jahrhunderts.* Fr/Br, 1904. xi, 557p. (b) *Histoire des études dans l'Ordre de SF . . .*P, 1908. vii, 574p. Rev: AFH 2 (1909) 131-136. *E18

FIDELIS ELIZONDO, Cap, "Bullae Quo Elongati Gregorii IX et Ordinem Vestrum Innocentii IV," Laur 3 (1962) 349-394. Basic. cf E24. *E19

GEMELLI, Agostino, OFM, (a) *Il francescanesimo.* 7a ed. riv. e agg. Mi, 1956. xvi, 563p. Revs of earlier eds: AFH 28 (1935) 517-527; 31 (1938) 485-487; CF 3 (1933) 105-108; CF 11 (1941) 496-499. (b) *Le message de SFA au monde moderne.* P, 1948. xviii, 483p. (c) *The Franciscan Message to the World.* L, 1934. 244p. (condensed). A classic. cf D162. *E20

GHINATO, A., OFM, *La letteratura storica francescana del primo secolo.* R, 1952. 264p. *E21

GOAD, Harold, *Greyfriars. The Story of SF & His Followers.* L, 1947. 238p. illus. Rev: AFH 41 (1948) 297-299; CF 21 (1951) 277*. E22

GRATIEN DE PARIS, Cap, (a) *Historie de la fondation et de l'évolution de l'Ordre des Frères Mineurs au XIIIe siècle.* P, 1928, xxiv, 699p. Rev: AFH 22 (1929) 187-192 (Bihl); EF 41 (1929) 345 (Cuthbert); MF 29 (1929) 93; RHE 25 (1929) 312-314. (b) *Historia de la fundación y evolución de la Orden de Frailes Menores en el siglo XIII.* Tr. del P. Victoriano M. de Larrainzar, Cap. Buenos Aires, 1947. 624p. CF 20 (1950) 401. Masterpiece. *E23

GRUNDMANN, H., "Die Bulle 'Quo elongati' Papst Gregors IX," AFH 54 (1961) 3-25. Important: critical text. cf E 19. *E24

HANLEY, Boniface, & Salvator Fink, OFM, *The Franciscans: Love at Work.* Paterson, NJ, 1962. 247p. illus. Readable current survey, not history. E25

HOLZAPFEL, Heribert, OFM, (a) *Handbuch der Geschichte des Franziskanerordens.* Fr./Br, 1909, xxi, 732p. (b) *Manuale historiae OFM.* Fr/Br, 1909. xxi, 662p. (c) *The History of the Franciscan Order.* Tr. by Antonine Tibesar & Gervase Brinkmann, OFM. Teutopolis, Ill, 1948, xiv, 608p. Rev: AFH 2 (1909) 485-489; *Thought* 24 (1949) 748. *E26

HUBER, Raphael M., Conv, *A Documented History of the Franciscan Order from the Birth of SF to the Division of the Order under Leo X, 1182-1517.* Milw. 1944. xxxiv, 1028p. illus. Rev: CF 18 (1948) 303-306; FnSs 26 (1945) 88; 27 (1946) 93-99; MF 47 (1947) 263-266; Spec 21 (1946) 261-263. **E27

ILARINO DA MILANO, Cap, "L'incentivo escatologico nel riformismo dell'Ordine francescano." In Accademia Tudertina, 30 Convegno Storico *Atti* (Todi 1961) 55p. Abs: MF 63 (1963) 133. E28

JORDAN, Edouard "Le premier siècle franciscain. In D179:68-89. E29

——. "Les premiers franciscains et la France," *Etudes italiennes* 8 (1926) 65-84, 129-139. E30

KNOWLES, David, *The Religious Orders in England.* Cambridge, Eng, 1948. 2v. On SF: I, 114-126. Splendid. *E31

LAZARO DE ASPURZ, Cap, *Manual de historia franciscana.* Madrid, 1954. 536p. Rev: AFH 47 (1954) 461; Ant 30 (1955) 200-202; CF 25 (1955) 192-195; MF 56 (1956) 603-609. *E32

LEON, Achille, OFM, *Histoíre de l'Ordre des Frères Mineurs. SFA et son oeuvre.* P, 1954. xviii, 395p. Rev: (1st ed.) AFH 22 (1929) 186. *E33

MASSERON, Alexandre, & Marion A. Habig, OFM, *The Franciscans: SFA & His Three Orders.* Chi, 1959, xxi, 518p. illus. Rev: CF 30 (1960) 465. Includes useful statistics, lists, tables, etc. *E34

MATANIC, Atanasio, OFM, *Compendio di storia dell'Ordine dei Frati Minori. I,1: Il medioevo francescano, 1182-1517.* R, 1956. 174p. *E35

MOORMAN, J. R. H., "The Foreign Element among the English Franciscans," EHR 62 (1947) 289-303. E36

ODOARDI, Giovanni, Conv, "'Inizi e sviluppi del Primo Ordine francescano nel mondo," *Città di Vita* 14 (1959) 726-739. E37

——, "Il nuovo 'Conspectus missionum' dei Frati Minori. Presentazione e rilievi critici," MF 58 (1958) 306-315. *E38

——, *SF e i Francescani. Sintesi storica del francescanesimo nei suoi tre ordini e loro varie famiglie.* 2a ed. riv. e agg. A, 1961. 95p. Rev. of 1st ed: MF 52 (1952) 307. E39

OZANAM, Antoine Frédéric, (a) *Les poètes franciscains en Italie au XIIIe siècle.* P, 1852. 440p. (b) *The Franciscan Poets in Italy of the Thirteenth Century.* NY, 1914. xvi, 333p. Still useful. E40

SCHMITT, Clement, OFM, "Frères mineurs." In DTC-TG VII, 1696-1733. **E41

——, *Un pape réformateur et un défendeur de l'unité de l'Eglise: Benôit XII et l'ordre des Frères Mineurs (1334-1342).* Q, 1959. xxxvii, 419p. Rev: CF 30 (1960) 115; RSCI 15 (1961) 498-500. Bibl. useful also for 13th century. *E42

SCUDDER, Vida D., *The Franciscan Adventure. A Study in the First Hundred Years of the Order of SFA.* L & NY, 1931. 409p. Rev: CF 5 (1935) 171. *E43

SESSEVALLE, François de, *Histoire générale de l'Ordre de SF.* Le Puy, 1935-37. 2v Rev: AFH 28 (1935) 279, 30 (1937) 239-243; Ant II (1936) 580-582 (Oliger); CF 6 (1936) 262-268; EF 47 (1935) 736-739; 50 (1938 120. cf author's letter, "A propos de l'Histoire . . .," EF 50 1938 88-91. *E45

SEVESI, Paolo M., OFM, *L'Ordine dei Frati Minori. Lezioni storiche (an. 1209-1517).* Parte prima. Mi, 1942. xvi, 314p. Rev: CF 14 (1944) 328-330. Parte 2da, Tomo I. Mi, 1958. xix, 352p. Rev: AFH 52 (1959) 333-335; CF (1959) 535-537. Parte 2da, Tomo II. Mi, 1960 xxiii, 322p. Rev: IF 35 (1960) 146; CF 32 (1962) 188. See also E10; cf his obit., CF 34 (1964) 230. *E46

2 THE SPIRITUALS & JOACHIMISM

a. GENERAL
(see also A166:21-26 & AFH 29 (1936) 242-254)

of the Franciscan Spirituals. R, 1963. 84p. *E56a

FREDEGAND [CALLAEY] D'ANVERS, Cap, "L'infiltration des idées franciscaines spirituels chez les Capucins." In MFE I, 388-403. *E51

FRUGONI, A., "Dai 'Pauperes eremite domini Celestini' ai 'Fraticelli de paupere vita'." In *Celestiniana* (R 1954) 125-167. Rev: AFH 47 (1954) 431-434. *E52

his Canon, Teachings, Sources, Biography & Influence," Trad 13 (1957) 249-311. Masterpiece, with comprehensive bibl. **E48

CHIAPPINI, Aniceto, OFM, "I processi di Frate Andrea da Gagliano Aterno," DASP ser6 (1953-55) 45p. cf AFH 55 (1962) 286. cf E56. *E49

DOUIE, Decima L., *The Nature & Effect of the Heresy of the Fraticelli.* Man, 1932. 292p. Rev: RHE 29 (1933) 722-725; AFH 26 (1933) 531-535. Fundamental. *E50

MANSELLI, R., "Dagli spirituali all'osservanza. Momenti di storia francescana," *Humanitas* (Brescia) 6 (1951) 1217-1228. *E53

OLIGER, L., OFM, *De secta spiritus libertatis in Umbria saec. XIV.* R, 1943. 166p. *E54

——, "Spirituels." In DTC (P 1941) XIV, 2522-2549. Basic. *E55

PASZTOR. Edith. "Il processo di Andrea da Gagliano (1337-1338)," AFH 48 (1955) 252-297. With text. cf E50. *E55a

SALVATORELLI, L., "Movimento francescano e Gioachimismo." In CISSR III, 403-448. cf A274. *E56

THADDEUS [MacVICAR] OF NEW DURHAM, Cap, *The Doctrine*

BARTOLOMASI, Bonaventura, Conv, "Storia genuine e sincera della fondazione de' Frati Zelanti Spirituali," MF 28 (1925) 127-141, 163-175; 29 (1926) 49-61, 75-92. Written in 1823. E47

BLOOMFIELD, Morton W., "Joachim of Flora. A Critical Survey of

b. ANGELO CLARENO

ANGELUS A CLARINO, *Chronicon seu Historia septem tribulationum Ordinis Minorum.* Prima ed. integrale, a cura di P. Alberto Ghinato, OFM. Vol. I, Testo. R, 1959. 231p. Corrected ed. of Tocco & Ehrle texts. Notes & commentary not yet published. E57

——, "Cronaca delle tribulazioni," L. Malagoli, ed., *Didaskaleion* (To) 10 (1931) 75-236. 14th century Italian translation. E58

BATTELLI, Guido, "Il Breviloquio di fra Angelo Clareno," IF 26 (1951) 213-235. Abs: CF X, 337*. E59

DOUCET, Victorin, OFM, "Angelus Clarinus ad Alvarum Pelagium Apologia pro vita sua," AFH 39 (1946) 63-200. Basic. *E60

OLIGER, L, OFM, ed., *Expositio Regulae Fratrum Minorum auctore Fr. Angelo Clareno.* Q, 1912. lxxx, 251p. Rev: AFH 6 (1913) 168-170 (Bihl). Basic. *E61

——, "Fra Angelo da Chiarino nel VI centenario della sua morte," FF 14 (1937) 169-176. Important. E62

[ORTOLANI], Ciro da Pesaro, OFM, *Il Clareno (studio polemico).* Macerata, 1920. cxi, 444p. Also in part in MF 15-18 (1914-1917). *E63

VON AUW, Lydia, *Angelo Clareno et les Spirituels franciscains.* Lausanne, 1952. 59p. Rev: AFH 47 (1954) 223; FS 37 (1955) 326. Important. Author is editing his Letters. *E64

——, "Clemente V ed Angelo Clareno." *Religio* 15 (1939) 119-133. *E65

——, "Quelques notes sur Angelo Clareno," BISI 66 (1954) 115-128. *E66

c. PIERRE JEAN OLIVI (OLIEU)

STADTER, E., "Das Glaubensproblem in seiner Bedeutung für die Ethik bei Petrus Johannis Olivi, OFM," FS 42 (1960) 225-296. See its comprehensive Olivi bibl: 290-296. **E67

d. UBERTINO DA CASALE

UBERTINO DA CASALE, *Arbor vitae crucifixae Jesu.* Tr. e intr. di Fausta Casolini. Lanciano, 1937. xxiv, 205p. Rev: SF 39 (1942) 89-91. Contains only Lib. I Lib. IV, cap. 9, & Lib. V, cap. 3-9; but includes all material on SF. Important. *E68

COLASANTI, Giovanni, Conv, "I Ss Cuori di Gesu e di Maria nell' 'Arbor Vitae' (1305) di Ubertino da Casale, O. Min.," MF 59 (1959) 30-69. *E69

FREDEGAND [CALLAEY] D'ANVERS, Cap, *L'idéalisme franciscain Spirituel au XIVe siècle. Etude sur Ubertin de Casale.* Louvain, 1911. xxviii, 280p. Rev: AFH 4 (1911) 594-599; AB 31 (1912) 371-374. Basic. E70

——, "L'influence et la diffusion de l'*Arbor Vitae* d'Ubertin de Casale," RHE 17 (1921) 533-546. Important. *E71

GODEFROY, Cap, "Ubertin de Casale." In DTC (P 1950) XV/2, 2031-2034. *E72

SARRI, Francesco, OFM, "Pier di Giovanni Olivi e Ubertino da Casale Maestri di Teologia a Firenze (sec. XIII)," SF 22 (1925) 88-125. Basic. *E73

II THE FIRST ORDER

1 MISCELLANEOUS, (CHAPTER, ETC.)

(see also E16)

BROOKE, R. B., "The Chapter of Mats." In E3:286-291. *E74

——, "The Constitutional Position, 1217-27." In E3:106-118. cf E75. *E74a

ESSER, K., OFM, "Das 'Ministerium generale' des hl. F von A," FS 33 (1951) 329-348. Abs: CF X, 77*. Important. cf E74a. *E75

——, "Die regelmässigen Kapitel." In his *Ordo . . .*, E16:316-326. Basic. *E75a

MARINUS VON NEUKIRCHEN, Cap, *De capitulo generali in primo Ordine Seraphico.* R, 1952. 543p. Rev: AFH 45 (1952) 462-465; MF 53 (1953) 282-284; SF 52 (1955) 321. Fundamental. *E76

VITO DA CLUSONE, Cap, "Quando ebbe nome l'Ordine dei FF. Minori?" IF 8 (1933) 561-567. Important: cf Esser, "Die Name des neuen-Ordens." In his *Ordo . . .* E16:116-118. E77

2 RULES

(see also C6, D83a, E19)

CASUTT, Laurentius, Cap, *Die älteste franziskanische Lebensform; Untersuchungen zur Regula prima sine bulla.* Graz, 1955. 172p. Rev: AFH 49 (1956) 227; CF 26 (1956) 202; FS 38 (1956) 123-125 (Hardick). Basic. *E78

——, "Die Regeln des franziskanischen Ersten Order, übertragen und eingeleitet." In *Die grossen Ordensregeln,* 2. Aufl., Hans Urs von Balthasar, ed. (Einsiedeln 1961) 261-321. Rev: (1948 ed.) CF VIII, 64*. E79

CUTHBERT OF BRIGHTON, Cap, "La Règle primitive des Frères Mineurs de SF (1209)," EF 29 (1913) 140-153; & App. I in A288:465-476. E80

ESSER, K., OFM, "Zur Textgeschichte der Regula non bullata des hl. F," FS 33 (1951) 219-237. Abs: CF X, 64*. Basic. *E81

GHINATO, A., OFM, "De ordinis agendi ratione ad regulam S. F.,"

Ant 35 (1960) 3-48. Important. cf D83a. *E82

HARDICK, L., OFM, "Vom F-leben zur Franziskanerregel," WW 17 (1954) 27-39. Also in E91(a):55-73. Abs: CF XI, 60. *E83

OLIGER, L., OFM, ed., *Expositio Quatuor Magistrorum super Regulam Fratrum Minorum (1241-1242).* R, 1950. xv, 203p. Rev: AFH 43 (1950) 181; CF 21 (1951) 434; EF ns 1 (1950) 361; MF 51 (1951) 630-632. Important. *E84

——, *S. F. regula anni 1223 fontibus locisque parallelis illustrata.* R, 1950. 31p. Also a reply to E86 & E87. E85

QUAGLIA, Armando, OFM, *L'originalità della Regola francescana.* Sassoferrato, 1943. x, 172p. Rev: AFH 39 (1946) 287-293; CF 16/17 (1946/47) 343-347; MF 45 (1945) 193; Ant 21 (1946) 168; SF 43 (1947) 119-131. E86

——, *Origine e sviluppo della Regola francescana.* Napoli, 1948. viii, 155p. Rev: AFH 39 (1946) 287-305; MF 52 (1952) 308-311; SF 44 (1948) 180-182. E87

——, *Originalità della Regola francescana.* 2a ed. Sassoferrato, 1959. xix, 187p. Rev: AFH 54 (1961) 220; EF 10 (1960) 85-88 (Cambell); MF 62 (1962) 502; WW 25 (1962) 230 (Clasen). Important, with critical reviews. *E88

Seraphicae legislationis textus originales. Q, 1897. 310p. *E89

VAN DER LUUR, Vittoricus, OFM, *Regola e vita dei Frati Minori.* SMA, 1960. xv, 403p. Rev: CF 31 (1961) 600. *E90

(a) *Werkbuch zur Regel des heiligen F von A.* Herausgegeben von den deutschen Franziskanern. We, 1955. xvi, 434p. (b) *The Marrow of the Gospel; A Study of the Rule of SFA,* by the Franciscans of Germany. Tr. & ed. by Ignatius Brady, OFM. Chi, 1958. xiv, 346p. Rev: CF 29 (1959) 514 (OvR); FS 40 (1958) 94-96. (c) *La règle des Frères Mineurs, étude historique et spirituelle.* Tr. de J.-M. Genvo. P, 1961. 239p. Fundamental. *E91

3 CLERICUS & LAICUS
(see Appendix VII & D96-D102)

ALESSANDRO DA RIPBOTTONI, Cap, "l fratelli laici nel primo Ordine francescano," *Ius Seraphicum* 1-2 (1955-1956); & R, 1956. xx, 294p. Rev: AFH 50 (1957) 447; CF 28 (1958) 113. Basic. *E92

BOCK, Colomban, OCR, "Tonsure monastique et cléricale," *Revue de droit canonique* (Strasbourg) 2 (1952) 375-406. Basic. *E93

BONDUELLE, J., "Convers." In DDC IV, 562-582. *E94

BROCKHAUS, T. A., *Religious Who Are Known as Conversi.* Wa, 1946. 127p. (Cath. Univ. diss.) *E95

HALLINGER, K., OSB, "Sui primordi dell'istituto dei fratelli conversi," *Camaldoli* (now *Vita Monastica*) n38 (1954) 115-119. E96

——, "Woher kommen die Laienbrüder?" *Analecta S. O. Cist.* 12 (1956) 1-104. Basic. *E97

HARDICK, L., OFM, "Gedanken zu Sinn und Tragweite des Begriffes 'Clerici'," AFH 50 (1957) 7-26. Rev: CF XI, 60. Important for SF. *E98

LANDGRAF, A. M., "Zum Gebrauch des Wortes "Clericus' im 12. Jahrhundert," CF 22 (1952) 74-78. E99

4 FRANCISCAN BIOGRAPHY

a. COLLECTED WORKS
(see also A229)

ARTHUR DU MOUSTIER, OFM Rec. (d. 1662), *Martyrologium franciscanum*, recognitum et auctum a PP. Ignatio Beschin et Juliano Palazzolo, OFM R, 1938. xxviii, 551p. Rev: AB 59 (1941) 355-357; CF 11 (1941) 91; MF 44 (1944) 111-142 (Di Fonzo) with many corrections.   *E100
——, *Martirologio francescano*, riv., corr, ed aum. dai PP. I. Beschin e G. Palazzolo, OFM. Prima versione italiana del P. G. Palazzolo con corr. e agg. R, 1946. xi, 459p. Rev: MF 47 (1947) 267. Indispensable.   *E101
——, *Ménologe franciscaine*. Première tr. fr. d'après la réédition latine de 1939 et la version italienne de 1946. Par le P. Jacques Cambell, OFM. Rennes, 1952. 286p. (mimeogr.)   *E102
Bibliotheca Sanctorum. R, 1961—. Standard new ref. work with rich illus. & bibls. By end of 1963, v.1-3, A-B, pub'd. To be pub'd in English.   *E103
Fragmenta minora. Catalogus sanctorum fratrum minorum. L. Lemmens, OFM. ed. R, 1903, xii. 54p. cf ME 34 (1934) 50.   *E102
GONZALO DE CORDOBA, Fray, *Del solar franciscano. Santoral de las tres Ordenes.* Madrid, 1958. 869p.   E105
HABIG, Marion A., OFM, *The Franciscan Book of Saints.* Chi, 1959. 1006p. illus. Useful tables & bibl. (English only).   *E106
JACOBILLI, Lodovico, OFM, *Vite de' Santi e Beati dell'Umbria e di quelli i corpi dei quali riposano in detta Provincia.* Foligno, 1647-1656. 3v.   E107
LEON DE CLARY, OFM, *Aureola serafica. Vite dei Santi e Beati dei tre Ordini di SF.* 2a ed. corr, migl., agg. dal R.P Gian-Crisostamo Guzzo,. OFM Ven, 1951-54. 6v. Rev: CF 23 (1953) 395; MF 53 (1953) 278: MF 55 (1955) 292. Useful.   E108
PIETR'ANTONIO DI VENEZIA, OFM, *Leggendario francescano.* Ven, 1721-22. 12v. Old, but longer biographies than later compendia.   E109
THOMA DE PAPIA, *Dialogus de gestis sanctorum Fratrum Minorum.* Ex integro edidit P. Ferdinandus M. Delorme, OFM. Q, 1923. 312p.   E110

b. COMPANIONS OF ST. FRANCIS (COLLECTED WORKS)
(see Appendix VII)

FORTINI, A., "Gli uomini di A compagni del Santo," FNV II, 273-314. cf FNV I/1, 319-378; I/2, 178-211.   *E111
GRAU, Engelbert, OFM, "Die ersten Brüder des hl F," FS 40 (1958) 132-144. Basic.   *E112
MacDONNELL, Anne, *Sons of F.* L & NY, 1902. viii, 436p.   *E113
MECCOLI, Antonio, "I compagni di SF verso la gloria degli altari?" VP 23 (1932) 640-650. Important for tombs in Basilica.   E114
TERZI, A., OFM, "I compagni del Santo: Filippo, Angelo, Illuminato sono Reatini . . ." App. A in his *Ultime battute . . .* C185:27-32.   *E115

c. INDIVIDUAL FRIARS

(1) BLESSED AGNELLUS OF PISA

GILBERT OF LONDON, Cap, B. *Agnellus & the English Grey Friars.*
L, 1937. xiv, 134p. por. Rev: CF 9 (1939) 210. *E116

(2) BROTHER ANGELO

PRATESI, R., OFM, "Angelo da Rieti." In DBI III, 233. cf E115. *E117

(3) BLESSED BENEDICT OF AREZZO

CRESI, D., OFM, *Il beato Benedetto Sinigardi d'Arezzo e l'origine dell'*
Angelus Domini. Fi, 1958. 63p. Rev: EF ns23 (1960) 222; MF 59 (1959)
543. E118

(4) BLESSED GILES OF ASSISI
(see bibl. in E121; cf F299, F303-F306)

Dicta Beati Aegidii Assisiensis. Q, 1905. 123p. E119
BEATO EGIDIO DI A., *I Detti.* Intr., versione e note di Nello Vian.
Brescia, 1933. lxix, 179p. Rev: AFH 28 (1935) 530; CF 5 (1935) 492-
494; Ant 9 (1934) 409; Conv 5 (1933) 947. Excellent intro. & notes.
2d ed Mi, 1964. vii, 205p. *E119a
Leben und "Goldene Worte" des Bruders Agidius. Einführung und Erläuterungen von Lothar Hardick, OFM. Uebertragen von Paul Alfred Schlüter. We,
1953, xii, 176p (FQ, 3) Rev: AFH 47 (1954) 172; CF X, 241*; FS 37 (1955)
119-122. Useful intr., notes, index. *E120
BROWN, Raphael, *Franciscan Mystic. The Life of Blessed Brother Giles*
of A, Companion of SF. Garden City, NY, 1962. 221p. Rev: AFH 56 (1963)
217-220: MF 62 (1962) 511-514. Complete but not documented, though
with 52-item bibl. of sources & studies. *E121
GAMBOSO, Vergilio M., Conv, *Il Beato Egidio d'A, compagno di SF.*
Padova, 1962. 144p. illus. Rev: AFH 56 (1963) 220. Excellent. E122
MATTESINI, Francesco, OFM, "Ricordano un cavaliere della Tavola
rotonda," SF 59 (1962) 207-212. E123

(5) BLESSED GUIDO OF CORTONA

BRUNI, N., *Le reliquie del beato Guido da Cortona, compagno di SF,*
al lume della leggenda e della scienza. Cortona, 1947, xii, 115p. Rev: CF
21 (1951) 282*; MF 47 (1947) 621. *E124
PRATESI, R., OFM, "Guido da Cortona." In EC VI, 1291. *E125
SERNINI CUCCIATTI, Ugo, *La leggenda del Beato Guido.* Cortona,
1900. 31p. Rev: AB 23 (1904) 121. E126

(6) BROTHER JUNIPER

CASOLINI, F, "Aroma di Fra Ginepro nel settimo centenario della
morte (1258-1958)," FF 25 (1958) 120-123. E127
FORTINI, A., *Nel settimo centenario della morte di Frate Ginepro da*
(1258-1958). Cronaca delle celebrazioni di R e di A (21-22 giugno 1958).
Ven, 1959. 34p. illus. E128

PETROCCHI, Giorgio, ed., *La vita di frate Ginepro.* Testo latino e volgarizzamento. Fi, 1960. xxxvi, 100p. Rev: AFH 53 (1960) 329. Fails to cover all extant texts. E129

(7) BROTHER LEO

GIUSEPPE DE SIMONE (Pinuzzo da Bonea), "Frate Pecorella del buon Dio." IF 1 (1926) 12-15, 96-101, 230-232, 293-300; 2 (1927) 204-217; 3 (1928) 182-194; & Ven, 1934. 92p. Rev: IF 9 (1934) 665. E130

(8) BROTHER PACIFICO

COSMO, Umberto, "Il re dei versi." In D157:59-81 & 128n25. *E131
OCTAVE D'ANGERS, Cap, "Du frère cithariste qui, à Rieti, se récusa," EF 44 (1932) 549-556. *E131a

(9) BROTHER RIZERIO OF MUCCIA

Ristampa di notizie sulla vita del Beato Rizerio e sul culto a lui dedicato. R, 1958. 82p. Reprint of G. A. ANTONUCCI's 1711 life. E132

(10) ST. ANTHONY OF PADUA
(see also A55, A56, E167)

ARNALDICH, Luis, OFM, *San Antonio, doctor evangelico.* Ba, 1958. 229p. E133
BENVENUTI, D. G., "Cronologia della vita di Sant Antonio di Padova (1195-1231). Esame e discussione dei documenti dei sec. XIII e XIV," MF 30 (1930) 155-157; 31 (1931) 35-37; & A, 1931. 55p. E134
CALLEBAUT, André, OFM, "Saint Antoine de Padoue. Recherches sur ses trente premières années. Notes, discussions et documents," AFH 24 (1931) 449-494. Fundamental. *E135
CLASEN, Sophronius, OFM, (a) *Antonius, Diener des Evangeliums und der Kirche.* M.-Gladbach, 1959. 136p. Many fine illus. Rev: CF 30 (1960) 226. (b) *St. Anthony, Doctor of the Gospel.* Tr. by Ignatius Brady, OFM Chi, 1961. 136p. illus. (c) Documentation under German title in WW 23 (1960) 53-67, 108-130. Basic. *E136
——, "Die geistige Gestalt des hl. Antonius von Padua," WW 12 (1949) 45-58. *E137
——, "Die Schriften des hl. Antonius von Padua," WW 13 (1950) 104-118. *E138
——, "Lehrer des Evangeliums; über die Predigtweise des hl. Antonius von Padua," WW 16 (1953) 101-121. *E139
——, *Lehrer des Evangeliums. Ausgewählte Texte aus den Predigten des hl. Antonius von Padua.* Einführung, Uebersetzung, Erläuterungen. We, 1954. xii, 390p. (FQ, 4) Rev: CF 28 (1959) 106. Important. *E140
Doctor Evangelicus. Vier studies over de H. Antonius van Padua. Hertogenbosch, 1949. 132p. See E167. *E141
FACCHINETTI, V., OFM, *Antonio di Padova. Il santo, l'apostolo, il taumaturgo.* Mi, 1925. xliv, 579p. 414 illus. Rev: AFH 22 (1929) 218-220. Still the most complete work. *E142
HUBER, Raphael M., Conv, *St. Anthony of Padua, Doctor of the Church*

Universal; A Critical Study of the Historical Sources of the Life, Sanctity, Learning & Miracles of the Saint of Padua & Lisbon. Milw, 1948. xiv, 209p. Comprehensive bibl:164-199. **E143

MESINI, Candido, OFM, "L'eremo di S. Paolo in Ponte o Monte Paolo nel quale avrebbe, soggiornato S. Antonio di Padova," AFH 55 (1862) 417-467 & 558. Claims it was near Bologna, not Forlì; important also for early Franciscan history of Bologna. *E144

PURCELL, Mary, *Saint Anthony & His Times.* Garden City, NY, 1960. 282p. Rev: RHE 56 (1961) 333. E145

RIGAULD, Jean, O. Min., *La vie de Saint Antoine de Padoue.* Tr., intr. et notes d'Alexandre Masseron. P, 1956. 153p. Rev: CF 27 (1957) 89-91. E146

SABATELLI, Giacomo U., OFM, "Antonio da Padova, santo." In DBI (R 1961) III, 561-566. illus. 2-col. bibl. *E147

S. Antonio di Padova secondo un contemporaneo. La "Vita Prima" o "Assidua," tr., ann. e corr. di riferimenti ad altre fonti dei secoli XIII e XIV, a cura di A. F. Pavanello. Padova, 1946. 153p. Rev: SF 44 (1948) 183. *E148

S. Antonio da Padova, Prediche scelte, a cura di P. Beniamino Rossi, OFM. To, 1961. 198p. E149

S. Antonio dottore della Chiesa. Atti delle settimane antoniane tenute a Roma e a Padova nel 1946. Città del Vaticano, 1947. xix, 520p. *E150

STANO, Gaetano, OFM, "Antonio di Padova." In BSS (R 1962) II, 156-179. 7-col. bibl. Basic reference study. See E103. **E151

VIAN, Nello, "Frate Antonio, il mio Vescovo." R, 1956. 310p. (2d ed.) E152

WILLIBRORD DE PARIS, Cap, *Saint Antoine de Padoue, Docteur de l'Eglise. Sa vie, son oeuvre.* P, 1947. 245p. Excellent with 3 important apps. on sources, miracles, & biogs. *E153

(11) BROTHER ELIAS
(see also A72, C195, C196, D62)

ATTAL, F. S., *Frate Elia compagno di SF.* R, 1936. 186p. Rev: EF 48 (1936) 395-397; impt. crit. rev. by Fr. Cuthbert CF 6 (1936) 600-605; author's reply MF 36 (1936) 515-524. Superseded by E155. E154

——, *Frate Elia, compagno di SF*; nuova ed. riv. e ampl. Genova, 1953. 325p. illus. Rev: CF 24 (1954) 405; MF 54 (1954) 671-673. Important. *E155

COSMO, U., "Il dramma di frate Elia." In D157:82-113. *E156

CRIVELLUCCI, A., "La penitenza di frate Elia," *Studi storici di Pisa* 4 (1895) 41-54. cf AB 16 (1897) 351. Includes text of 1253 doc. E157

DI FONZO, L., Conv, "Elie d'A." In DHGE (P 1961) XV/1, 167-183. Basic. *E158

FORTINI, A., "Frate Elia da A architetto della Basilica di SF," MF 37 (1937) 529-545. Eulogy. E159

——, "Frate Elia." In F233:79-155. Useful for 1226-1253. E159a

——, FNV II, 299-303; & index IV, 90. Not critical; stresses A origin. E160

GIROLAMO DA CIVITELLA, Cap, "I meriti e demeriti di Frate Elia,"
IF 4 (1929) 16-20, 232-246, 398-406. Abs: CF 1 (1931) 103. Objective.
*E161

GOAD, H. E., "Brother Elias as the Leader of the Assisan Party in the
Order." In *Franciscan Essays* (Man 1932) II, 67-84 (BSFS-ES III).   E162

MARINANGELI, B,. Conv, "Frate Elia fondatore della Provincia di
Terra Santa," MF 34 (1934) 3-14.   E163

ODOARDI, Giovanni, Conv, "Un geniale figlio di SF, Frate Elia di A
nel settimo centenario della sua morte," MF 54 (1954) 90-139. Fundamental.   *E164

POMPEI, Alfonso, "Frate Elia d'A nel giudizio dei contemporanei e dei
posteri," MF 54 (1954) 539-635. Comprehensive bibl.; fundamental.
**E165

SPIRITO, S., "Etude sur deux protagonistes du mouvement franciscain
au XIIIe siècle: Grégoire IX et Frère Elie," EF ns13 (1963) 181-199. Tr.
from A101.   E166

VAN DEN BORNE, Fidentius, OFM, "Antonius en Elias. Hun betek-
nis." In E141:80-132. Abs: CF 19 (1949) 270-273; MF 54 (1954) 135 &
622n294. Reaches conclusions similar to E165. Important, esp. for post-SF
period.   *E167

III THE SECOND ORDER

1 ST. CLARE
(see also D67, D118, D119, & F262-F265)

BEREL, Anne-Marie, *Au creux du rocher . . . Claire d'A*. Préface de
Georges Goyau. P, 1960. 128p. Rev: CF 30 (1960) 475.   E168

BRACALONI, L., OFM, "S. Chiara nell'arte." In E206:207-212.   E169

BRADY, Ignatius, & Sr. M. Frances, SMIC, *The Legend & Writings
of Saint Clare of A*. Intr., Tr., Studies. St. Bonaventure, NY, 1953. xiv,
177p. Based on E191. Fundamental.   *E170

BRETON, Valentin-M., OFM, (a) "La spiritualità di S. Chiara." In
E206:69-78. (b) "La spiritualité de Sainte Claire," EF ns6 (1955) 43-
64.   *E171

CALLEBAUT, André, OFM, "SF et les privilèges, surtout celui de la
pauvreté concéde à Sainte Claire par Innocent III," AFH 20 (1927) 182-
193. cf E193, E198, E204.   *E172

CASOLINI, Fausta, *Chiara d'A rilucente specchio*. 3a ed. riv. e aum.
A, 1954. xv, 294p. illus. Rev: AFH 47 (1954) 214. Excellent.   *E173

CLASEN, S., OFM, "Franziskanische Christusbrautschaft. Die Stellung
des hl. Bonaventura zum Orden der hl. Klara," FS 35 (1953) 313-317.
*E174

CRESI, Domenico, OFM, "Cronologia di S. Chiara," SF 50 (1953)
260-267. Rev: AFH 47 (1954) 213. Important. cf E196.   *E175

DANIEL-ROPS, Henri, (a) *Claire dans la clarté*. P, 1953 & 1962.
148p. (b) *The Call of St. Clare*. Tr. by A. Attanasio. NY, 1963, 144p.
illus. Excellent. cf D177.   E176

De ROBECK, Nesta, *St. Clare of A*. Milw, 1951. 242p. illus. Best biog.

in English. Includes Rule, Testament, Process. *E177

ESSER, K., OFM, "Die Briefe Gregors IX an die hl. Klara von A," FS 35 (1953) 274-295. Abs: AFH 47 (1954) 220. *E178

FARNUM, M.A., *Saint Clare, Patroness of Television.* Pulaski, Wis., 1961. 96p. cf E185. E179

FASSBINDER, Maria, "Untersuchungen über die Quellen zum Leben der hl. Klara von A," FS 23 (1936) 296-335. *E180

FORTINI, A., *Cronache dell'Anno di santa Chiara.* Perugia, 1953. 33p. E181

———, *Nel settimo centenario della translazione del corpo di S. Chiara (A, 3 ottobre 1260-3 ottobre 1960).* SMA, 1960. 16p. Abs: MF 63 (1963) 390. E182

———, "Santa Chiara," FNV I/1, 409-453; "La famiglia di Santa Chiara," FNV II, 315-349 (chart 349); "Luoghi e persone che si ritrovano nella vita di Santa Chiara," FNV II, 384-426. Fundamental. *E183

———, "Nuove notizie intorno a S. Chiara di A," AFH 46 (1953) 3-43. Abs: AFH 47 (1954) 211. cf E183. *E184

———, *Santa Chiara patrona della televisione.* SMA, 1960. 61p. Abs: AFH 53 (1960) 480. cf E179. E185

FRANCESCHINI, Ezio, "Biografie di S. Chiara," Aevum 27 (1953) 455-464; & in E206:263-274. Basic critical survey. *E186

———, "I due assalti dei saraceni a S. Damiano e ad A," Aevum 27 (1953) 289-306. Rev: VP 37 (1954) 116. Basic; includes impt. text of A Mss. *E187

———, "La notte di Natale del 1252," Chiara d'A 2 (1954) 69-74. E188

———, "Storia e leggenda nella vita di S. Chiara," VP 36 (1953) 394-404. Valuable critical examination of historicity of 20 incidents. Rev, with E186 & E187: AFH 47 (1954) 211-213. *E189

GALLINO, T., "La cosi detta "S. Chiara" di Simone Martini," Chiara d'A 1 (1953) 89-92. Abs: CF 27 (1957) 426. E190

GRAU, Engelbert, OFM, *Leben und Schriften der heiligen Klara von A.* Einf., Uebersetz, Erläut. We, 1952. xii, 173p. (FQ. 2) Rev: AFH 47 (1954) 218; FS 35 (1953) 137-142. 3. verb. Aufl. We, 1960. 204p. Important. cf E170. *E191

———, "Die päpstliche Bestätigung der Regel der hl. Klara," FS 35 (1953) 317-323. *E192

———, "Das Privilegium Paupertatis Innozenz' III," FS 31 (1949) 337-349. cf E172. *E193

———, "Die Regel der hl. Klara in ihrer Abhängigkeit von der Regel der Minderbrüder," FS 35 (1953) 211-274. Basic. Abs: AFH 47 (1954) 219. *E194

HARDICK, Lothar, OFM, *Spiritualité de sainte Claire.* Tr. par Damien Vorreux, OFM. P, 1961. 126p. Rev: AFH 55 (1962) 410. E195

———, "Zur Chronologie im Leben der hl. Klara," FS 35 (1953) 174-210. Rev: AFH 47 (1954) 219. Basic; more critical than E175. *E196

J'ai connu Madame Sainte Claire. Le procès de canonisation de Sainte Claire d'A. Toulouse & P, 1961. 176p. Rev: Ant 38 (1963) 242; CF 32 (1962) 480; EF ns12 (1962) 219. Useful notes, bibl., apps., & tables. *E197

LAZZERI, Z., OFM, "La 'Forma Vitae' di S. Chiara e la Regole sue e del suo Ordine." In E206: 79-122. Crit. rev. by Hardick: FS 37 (1955) 122-124. Basic, with rev. For impt. earlier arts. & eds. of texts by Lazzeri, see AFH *Indices*, p26. *E198

LONGPRE, Ephrem, OFM, "Sainte Claire d'A (1194-1253)," EF ns4 (1953) 5-21. Fundamental; uses all impt. sources. *E199

MARIE DE SAINT-DAMIEN, *Sainte Claire d'A, lumière dans le Christ*. P, 1962. 190p. E200

OLIGER, L., OFM, "De origine regularum ordinis sanctae Clarae," AFH 5 (1912) 181-209, 413-447. Still indispensable. *E201

Il processo di S. Chiara d'A. Con una notizia di Nello Vian. Mi, 1962. xxxiv, 110p. Excellent intr. & tr. E202

"Il ricamo di S. Chiara." In E206: 145-149, illus. Two studies of an alb she made. E203

SABATIER, Paul, "Le privilège de la très haute pauvreté accordé à Saint Claire d'A par Innocent III. Son authenticité, son histoire de 1215-1253," RHF 1 (1924) 1-54. cf E172, E193, E198. *E204

SALVI, G., "La Regola di s. Benedetto nei primordi dell'ordine di S. Chiara," *Benedictina* 8 (1954) 71-121. Important. *E205

Santa Chiara d'A. Studi e cronaca del VII centenario (1253-1953). A, 1954. 722p. illus. Rev: AFH 48 (1955) 149-152; FS 37 (1955) 122-125. Besides C167, E169, E171(a), E186, E198, includes 1253 Rule, Letters, & surveys of Order throughout the world. Fundamental. *E206

SCHNEIDER, Edouard, *Sainte Claire d'A*. Préface du R.P. Leone Bracaloni, OFM. P, 1959. 237 p. Includes tr. of *Sacrum Commercium*. Crit. rev: CF 29 (1959) 550. E207

SETON, W., "The Letters from Saint Clare to Blessed Agnes of Bohemia," AFH 17 (1924) 509-519. cf E213 & E222a. E208

SPAETLING, Luchesius, OFM, "Die geistige Gestalt der hl. Klara von A," FS 35 (1953) 145-173; cf 36 (1954) 132. Well documented. *E209

TOMASO DA CELANO, *La leggenda di Santa Chiara*... per cura di Guido Battelli. Mi, 1952. vi, 147p. Rev: AFH 47 (1954) 209. E210

——, *La leggenda di Santa Chiara d'A*. Con intr. di Arnaldo Fortini. R, 1953. xxx, 133p. illus. Rev: AFH 47 (1954) 210; MF 56 (1956) 602. cf E210. E211

——, *La leggenda di S. Chiara Vergine*. Testo latino dal cod. 338 di A. Tr di Fausta Casolini. A, 1953. xii, 94p. Rev: AFH 47 (1954) 208. E211a

VAN DIJK, S., OFM, "Il culto di S. Chiara nel Medioevo." In E206: 155-206. *E212

VYSKOCIL, J.K. & Barabas, L., OFM, "Le lettere di S. Chiara alla Beata Agnese di Praga." In E206: 123-144. With crit. text & Ital. tr. cf E222a. *E213

2 THE HOME OF ST. CLARE

ABATE, G., Conv, "La casa paterna di S. Chiara, e falsificazioni storiche dei secoli XVI e XVII intorno alla medesima Santa e a SFA," DSPU 41 (1944) 34-160, 8pl.; & A, 1946. 128p., 8pl. Rev: CF 16/17 (1946/47) 348-350. Condensed in E216. Fundamental. *E214

——, *Nuovi studi sull'ubicazione della casa paterna di S. Chiara d'A.* A, 1954. 37p. illus. plans. Rev: EF ns9 (1959) 229; CF X, n3939. Basic *E215

ATTAL, Francesco Salvatore, "La casa paterna e il parentado di Santa Chiara. Falsi e falsari dei secoli XVI e XVII," MF 46 (1946) 157-197. Condenses E214. Important. For data on SF, see C15. *E216

FORTINI, A., "Della casa paterna di S. Chiara," AFH 48 (1955) 160-194; reprinted in FNV II, 351-382: "La casa paterna di Santa Chiara." Fundamental, with E215, both for the home of St. Clare & the history of San Rufino. *E217

ZOCCO, Emma, "L'identificazione della casa paterna di S. Chiara in A," MF 54 (1954) 651-656. Agrees with Abate. E218

3 EARLY POOR CLARE HISTORY & BIOGRAPHY
(see also E174, E205)

AGATHANGE DE PARIS, Cap, "L'origine et la fondation des monastères de Clarisses en Aquitaine au XIIIe siècle," CF 25 (1955) 5-52. *E219

CASOLINI, F, *Il protomonastero di S. Chiara in A. Storia e cronaca (1253-1950).* Mi, 1950. xxiv, 390p. Rev: AFH 48 (1955) 149-152; CF 21 (1951) 237-240; IF 26 (1951) 201-210; MF 51 (1951) 648-651. Basic. cf F282, F283. *E220

FASSBINDER, Maria, (a) *Die selige Agnes von Prag.* We, 1957. 180p. (b) *Princess et moniale, Agnès de Bohéme.* Tr. par G. Daubie. P, 1962. 144p. cf E213, E222a. *E221

GRATIEN DE PARIS, Cap, "L'Ordre de sainte Claire." App. in his *Histoire...* E23: 593-617. Still indispensable. *E222

VYSKOCIL, Jan Kapistran, OFM, *The Legend of Blessed Agnes of Bohemia & The Four Letters of St. Clare.* Tr. by V. Buresh. Cleveland, 1963. ix, 287p. cf E213. *E222a

IV THE THIRD ORDER
1 THE THIRD ORDER REGULAR

PAZZELI, Raffaele, TOR, *Il Terz' Ordine regolare di SF attraverso i secoli.* R, 1958. 383p. illus. Crit rev: AFH 52 (1959) 127-130. *E223

2 THE THIRD ORDER SECULAR
(See also E34)

BETTEZ, Norbert M., OFM, *L'influence sociale de SFA et du Tiers Ordre franciscain.* Montréal, 1960 383p. Not critical. E224

FANTOZZI, A., & B. Bughetti, OFM, "Il Terz' Ordine francescano in Perugia dal secolo XIII al XIX," AFH 33 (1940) 56-113, 319-365. *E225

FORTINI, A., FNV II, 456-462. E226

FREDEGAND [CALLAEY] D'ANVERS, Cap, "La diffusione e l'influenza politica del Terz' Ordine di SF nel secolo XIII. Esame critico di una frase attribuita a Pier della Vigna," IF 1 (1926) 56-67, 161-171. From E228 (a). *E227

——, (a) "Le Tiers Ordre de SFA," EF 33 (1921) 360-382, 468-488;

34 (1922) 66-85, 195-210, 367-391, 538-560; & P, 1923. 135p. (b) English tr.: *The Third Order of SFA.* Pittsburg, 1926. 109p. Still unsurpassed.   *E228

HABIG, Marion A., & Mark Hegener, OFM, *A Short History of the Third Order.* Chi, 1963. 104p. illus. cf E34:401-403.   E229

HALLACK, Cecily, & Peter F. Anson, *These Made Peace. Studies in the Lives of the Beatified & Canonized Members of the Third Order of SFA.* Rev. & ed. by Marion A. Habig, OFM. L & Paterson, NJ, 1957. xix, 268p. illus. Reprinted: L, 1963. Rev: CF 28 (1958) 351. Useful bibl. Basic   *E230

MATTONE-VEZZI, E., "SFA a Poggio Bonizzo. La fondazione del Terz' Ordine," *Miscellanea storica valdelsa* 45 (1937) 16-28.   E231

MEERSSEMAN, Gillis, OP, *Le dossier de l'Ordre de la Pénitence du XIIIe siècle.* Fribourg, 1961. xvi, 346p. Rev: CHR 48 (1962) 384; FS 45 (1963) 193-196 (Hardick); SM s3/3 (1962) 638-645.   *E232

PEANO, Pierre, OFM, *Histoire du Tiers Ordre.* P, 1943. 128p.   E233

SARASOLA, Luis de, OFM, "Fraternidad de Penitencia." In A316:425-440 (1929 ed.); 361-378 (1960 ed.). Important for early origin.   *E234

VAN DEN BORNE, Fidentius, OFM, *Die Anfänge des Franziskanischen Dritten Ordens.* Münster, 1925. viii, 184p. Rev: AFH 20 (1927) 164-168 (Bihl).   *E235

——, "Ursprung und erste Entwicklung des Franziskanischen Dritten Ordens," FS 16 (1929) 177-192. Still useful.   *E235a

VAN DEN WYNGAERT, Anastasius, OFM, "De Tertio Ordine iuxta Marianum Florentinum," AFH 13 (1920) 3-77.   *E236

3 13TH CENTURY TERTIARIES
(contemporaries of St. Francis)

a. ST. ELIZABETH OF HUNGARY

ANCELET-HUSTACHE, Jeanne, *L'or dans la fournaise; vie de Sainte Elisabeth de Hongrie.* P, 1962. 142p. illus.   E237

——, (a) *Sainte Elisabeth de Hongrie.* P, 1947. 444p. illus. (b) *Gold Tried by Fire: St. Elizabeth of Hungary.* Tr. by Paul J. Oligny, OFM, & Sr. Venard O'Donnell, OSF. Chi, 1963. xxx, 313p. Thoroughly documented; basic. Rev: CF 18 (1948) 361.   *E238

DE ROBECK, Nesta, *Saint Elizabeth of Hungary, A Story of Twenty-four Years.* Milw, 1954. ix, 211p. illus. Rev: CF 26 (1926) 100. Excellent. *E239

KRANZ, Gisbert, *Elizabeth von Thüringen, wie sie wirklich war,* 3. Aufl. Augsburg, 1961. 64p. illus.   E240

LAVATER-SLOMAN, Mary, *Triumph der Demut. Das Leben der hl. Elisabeth.* Z, 1961. 444p.   E241

MARIL, Lee, ed., *Elizabeth von Thüringen; die Zeugnisse ihrer Zeitgenossen.* Einsiedeln, 1961. 174p,   *E242

b. BROTHER JACOPA
(see also E113)

EDOUARD D'ALENCON, Cap, *Frère Jacqueline,* Nouv. éd P, 1927. 65p. Rev: AFH 21 (1928) 375. Basic.   *E243

FORTINI, A., FNV II, 453-456, & index. E243a

HUMANI, Maria Castiglione, "Frate Jacopa," FF 5 (1928) 10-24, 137-142, 205-210. & re-ed. with bibl.: R, 1933. 80p. illus. Rev: FF 7 (1934) 308; CF 5 (1935) 149. *E244

MASSERON, Alexandre, "Jacqueline de Settesoli aux funérailles de SFA d'après un tableau de Sassetta," EF nsl (1950) 329-336. *E245

c. BLESSED LUCHESIO

DUHAMELET, Geneviève, *Lucchese, premier tertiaire franciscain (1181-1260)*. P, 1959. 134p. illus. Rev: AFH 53 (1960) 481; CF 30 (1960) 345. Useful. *E246

NATALI, Augusto, "Luchesio (La vita nello sfondo dei suoi tempi, di Poggibonsi e nell'arte," IF 35 (1960) 237-247, 297-309; 36 (1961) 125-130. Basic. *E246a

Numero dedicato al settimo centenario di S. Lucchese 1260-1960. Poggibonsi (Siena), 1960. 82p. illus. E247

V ST. FRANCIS & ST. DOMINIC
(see also A80:97-99 & F116)

ALTANER, Berthold, "Die Beziehungen des hl. Dominikus zum hl. F von A," FS 9 (1922) 1-28. Rev: AFH 17 (1924) 300-302. Basic *E248

FALOCI PULIGNANI, M., "SF e San Domenico," MF 9 (1902) 13-15. *E249

FISCHER, H., "Begegnung zwischen F und Dominikus." In C2:83-108. Basic. *E250

HINNEBUSCH, William A., OP, "Poverty in the Order of Preachers," CHR 45 (1960) 436-453. On SF: 450-452. Fundamental. *E251

MATT, Leonard von, & M. H. Vicaire, OP, *St. Dominic, A Pictorial Biography*. Chi, 1957. vii, 88p. 159 illus. Splendid illus. & excellent short life. Eds. in many languages. cf E255. E252

OLIGER, L., OFM, "Ein pseudoprophetischer Text aus Spanien über die heiligen F und Dominikus (13. Jahrhundert)." In *Kirchengeschichtliche Studien P. Michael Bihl als Ehrengaben dargeboten* (Kolmar 1941) 13-28. *E253

SARASOLA, Luis de, OFM, "San F y Santo Domingo." In A316: cv-cvii (1929 ed.); 580-582 (1960 ed.). *E254

VICAIRE, M. H., OP, (a) *Histoire de Saint Dominique*. P, 1958. 2v. Rev: Spec 34 (1959) 337-341 (Hinnebusch). (b) *Geschichte des heiligen Dominikus*, Freiburg, 1962. 2v. Rev: FS 44 (1962) 330-333 (v.1). (c) *St. Dominic & His Times*. Tr. by K. Pond. NY, 1964. XI, 548p. Fundamental. On SF, see index. cf E252. **E255

F   PLACES

I CENTRAL ITALY

1 MAPS

Carte topografiche delle diocesi italiane nei secoli XIII e XIV. Città del Vaticano, 1932-52. (Made for *Rationes decimarum Italiae* series; available for Latium, Marchia, Tuscia, Umbria.) Indispensable.   F1

Marche-Umbria. Plastico fisico-politico. 1:550,000. 27x19"; covers Imola-Grosseto-Pescara area in plastic relief. Fi [196?] Excellent.   F2

Touring Club Italiano, Carta automobilistica, 1:200,000. Mi. Foglio 13-17. Very useful.   F3

United States Army Map Service, Washington, D.C. Ser. 1302, *Plastic, The World,* 1:1,000,000. No. 321 "Vesuvio." 27x30"; covers Florence-Naples-Brindisi area in plastic relief. Excellent.   F4

2 MEDIEVAL ROADS & TOPOGRAPHY
(see also F1)

HOFMANN, Albert von, *Das Land Italien und seine Geschichte in einer historischen-topographischen Darstellung.* Stuttgart-Berlin, 1921. 458p. maps. Fundamental.   *F5

LUDWIG, Friedrich, *Untersuchungen uber die Reise- und Marschgeschwindigkeit im XII. und XIII. Jahrhundert.* Berlin, 1897. 193p. Basic.   *F6

MARTINORI, E., *Via Cassia.* R, 1930. 241p. illus., maps. Historical.   *F7

——, *Via Flaminia.* R, 1929. 233p. illus., maps. Important.   *F8

MILLER, Konrad, *Itineraria Romana. Römische Reisewege an der Hand der Tabula Peutingeriana.* Stuttgart, 1916. lxxv, 992p. illus., maps. Basic.   *F9

PARKS, George B., *The English Traveler to Italy.* R, 1954. I. The Middle Ages (to 1525). xx, 669p. illus.   *F10

PIVEC, Karl, "Italienwege der mittelalterlichen Kaiser." In *Die Brennerstrasse* (Bozen 1961) 84-110.   F11

SCHROD, Konrad, *Reichsstrassen und Reichsverwaltung im Königreich Italien (754-1197).* Stuttgart, 1931. xii, 220p.   *F12

SPRINGER, Otto, "Medieval Pilgrim Routes from Scandinavia to Rome," MS 12 (1950) 92-122.   *F13

3 TRAVEL & GUIDEBOOKS

BRAUNFELS, Wolfgang, (a)*Toskana, Umbrien.* Dü, 1956. 128p., plans, maps (b) *Central Italy: Tuscany & Umbria.* Tr. by Salvator Attanasio. Baltimore, 1959. 139p. plans, maps, illus. Excellent.   F14

COATES, Robert M., *Beyond the Alps; A Summer in the Italian Hill Towns.* NY, 1961. 159p. illus. Includes Orvieto, Assisi, Alviano, Gubbio, Cortona, Arezzo.   F15

DELETTREZ, Jean-Marie, *Toscane, Ombrie*. P, 1958. 368p illus. Good
F16
E.N.I.T., *Italy (7): Latium, Umbria, The Marches*. R, [195?] 56p. illus.,
maps. Excellent. F17
LAEUBLI, Walter, *Sonnenland Toskana and Umbrien* Z, 1961. 95p. illus.
F18
NOTESTEIN, Lucy L., *Hill Towns of Italy*. L, 1963. 256p. illus., map.
Includes Siena, Arezzo, Cortona, Chiusi, Montepulciano, Gubbio, Ascoli, Spoleto, Todi, Orvieto; but not Assisi & Perugia. Excellent. F19
PATMORE, Derek, *Italian Pageant. A Tour through the Cities of Tuscany
& Umbria*. L, 1949. 132p. illus. F20
RHODES, Anthony, *A Sabine Journey to Rome in Holy Year*. L, 1952.
196p. illus. Includes Rieti, Aquila, Tagliacozzo. F21
TOURING CLUB ITALIANO, *L'Italia in automobile. Toscana e Umbria*. Mi, 1957. 196p. maps, plans, illus. Includes 13 useful altimetric profiles
of passes. F22
TROLLOPE, Thomas A., *A Lenten Journey in Umbria & the Marches*.
L, 1862. 308p. F23
Umbrien, Latium und Abruzzen. München, 1964. 205p. maps. (Grieben
Reiseführer, 250). F23a
UTZINGER, Ernst, *Wanderungen zu den historischen Hügelstädten und
in der Landschaft der Toscana und Umbriens*. Z, 1961. 87p. F24
WIESEL, J.M., *Toskana, Umbrien. Ein Reiseführer*. Stuttgart, 1956.
258p. F25

II FRANCISCAN CENTRAL ITALY
1 AS A WHOLE

ANSON, Peter F., *The Pilgrim's Guide to Franciscan Italy*. L, 1927.
xx, 243p. illus. with fine drawings by the artist-author; bibl. Excellent. Rev:
AFH 21 (1928) 376. *F26
BRACALONI, Leone, OFM, *Terres franciscaines*. Tr. par Barthélemy
Héroux, OFM. Montréal, 1933. 294p. Articles from FF, revised; bibl. Useful.
*F27
BROWN, Raphael, "In Franciscan Italy," *Padre* (NY) 10 (1959) 22-25,
66-70, 110-113, 154-158, 198-201, 242-245, 286-288; illus. F28
CANONICI, Luciano, OFM, "Itinerari francescani Umbri," VM 30
(1959)-32(1961). Reprinted, revised, in *La Porziuncula*, 1962-64. Excellent.
F29
CAVANNA, Nicola, OFM, *L'Umbria francescana illustrata*. Perugia, 1910.
xv, 415p. illus., maps. Rev: AFH 3 (1910) 755-757 (Oliger). Fundamental,
with rich bibl. notes. *F30
——, *L'Ombrie franciscaine*. Tr. de T. de Wyzewa. P, 1926. xiv, 293p.
illus., maps. *F31
DE SELINCOURT, Beryl, *Homes of the First Franciscans in Umbria,
the Borders of Tucsany & the Northern Marches*. L & NY, 1905. 325p. illus.
Useful. F32
FACCHINETTI, V., OFM, *I santuari francescani*. Mi, 1925. 3v. (v.l: *La*

Verna nel Casentino; v.2: *Assisi nell'Umbria;* v.3: *Nella Valle Reatina.*)
Illus. with 79 fine color paintings by Luigi Zago. Rev: AFH 20 (1927) 413-
415. Also Span. ed.: Ba, 196?. 3v.   F33

FELLER, Jean, *François d'Assise.* P, 1958. 128p. 121p. illus., map.   F34

GILLET, Louis, "Sur les pas de SFA," *Revue des Deux Mondes* 34 (1926)
578-603 (Assise), 746-777 (D'Assise à Vezelay); 35 (1926) 128-157 (Rieti
Valley), 315-337 (Greccio & Poggio Bustone), 563-594 (La Verna); also P,
1926. 252p. Excellent.   F35

GIOVAGNOLI, Enrico, *Sulle Orme di SFA.* A, 1928. 164p. illus. From
SFA 8 (1928) & 9 (1929). Rev: AFH 24 (1930) 437; MF 30 (1930) 64.
F36

GOAD, Harold. E., *Franciscan Italy.* L, 1926. xii, 284p. illus. Useful.
F37

L'Italia Francescana nel settimo centenario della morte di SF. SMA, 1927.
392p. 121 illus. Still important for regional history. *F38

JOERGENSEN, Johannes, *Pèlerinages franciscains.* Tr. par Teodor de
Wyzewz. P, 1919. x, 324p. illus. A classic.   F39

——, *Das Pilgerbuch aus franziskanischen Italien.* München, 1922. xv,
349p.   F40

——, *Pilgrim Walks in Franciscan Italy.* L, 1908. 176p.   F41

KIRSCH, B., & H.S. Roman, *Pèlerinages aux sanctuaires franciscains.*
Lille, P, 1920. viii, 420p. illus., maps, good bibl. One of the best. *F42

MATT, Leonard von, (a) *Franz von A.* Z, 1952. 310p. 200 illus., maps.
(b) *SFA, A Pictorial Biography.* Chi, 1956. vi, 106p. maps. Rev: CF 24
(1954) 404; CF X, n345-50. Important for fine views of Franciscan Italy;
text by Walter Hauser. Eds. in numerous languages. cf **B63**.   **F43**

——, (a) *Franz von A.* Z, Würzburg, 1962. 48p. text, 78p. illus. (b)
SFA. NY, 1963. 48p. text, 72p. illus. Condensed ed. of F43.   F44

RAYMOND, Ernest, *In the Steps of SF.* L & NY, 1939. 372p. illus. Good.
F45

SCHREURS, Jacques, *Pelgrimstocht door Franciscaans Italië.* Utrecht,
1954. 163p. illus.   F46

SECRET, Jean, & Fidèle Durieux, *A et les chemins de SF.* P, 1960. 151p.
illus. maps. Rev: AFH 53 (1960) 477. Excellent.   F47

Terres franciscaines. Actualité de SFA. Préface de François Mauriac, 64
photographies de Jean M. Marcel. P, 1950. 16, 64, 11p. Rev: CF IX, 76*;
EF nsl (1950) 237. Good views.   F48

THANS, Hilarion Antonius, OFM, *Terra d'amore; door oud en nieuw
Italië.* Tielt, 1949. 216p. illus.   F49

2 LAZIO

a. THE PROVINCE AS A WHOLE
(see also F346-F359a)

IGINO DA ALATRI, Cap, "SF e i Francescani in Cioceria," IF 34 (1959)
336-343, 391-403. Includes Subiaco, Alatri, Sora, M. Cassino, Ceprano, Arpino,
Ceccano, Piglio, etc. Documented; important. *F50

——, "Il viaggio di SF da Subiaco a Gaeta," IF 2 (1927) 406-415.   F51

SPILA, Benedetto, OFM, *Memorie storiche della provincia riformata romana.* Mi, 1896. 3v. illus. *F52

TOURING CLUB ITALIANO, *Attraverso l'Italia, v. 11: Lazio.* Mi, 1943. 240p. 435 illus. map. Fine illus. of art & scenery. F53

——. *L'Italia in automobile. Lazio.* Mi, 1953. 164p. maps, plans, illus. Useful. F54

——, *Lazio (non compresa Roma).* Mi, 1935 & 1954. 486p. maps, plans; rich bibl. (Guida d'Italia) Indispensable. **F55

b. ALATRI

IGINO DA ALATRI, Cap, "Fu SF in Alatri?" IF 4 (1929) 207-231. Abs: CF 1 (1931) 101. cf F50. F56

c. THE VALLEY OF RIETI
(see also A222, C160-C185, F350-F356, F359, F359a)

PALMEGIANI, Francesco, *Rieti e la Regione Sabina.* R, 1932. 775p. illus. *F57

SACCHETTI SASSETTI, Angelo, *Anecdota franciscana reatina.* Potenza, 1926. 91p. illus. Rev: AFH 20 (1927) 424-426, cf 200; EF 41 (1929) 324. Important. *F58

TERZI, Arduino, OFM, *Memorie francescane nella valle reatina.* R, 1955. x, 507p. maps, plans, & many illus.; rich bibl. Rev: AFH 50 (1957) 245-248; CF 26 (1956) 80-83; MF 56 (1956) 500-504. Fundamental. **F59

——, *Il Poverello di A nella valle reatina.* R, 1959. viii, 146p. illus. *F60

VARANO, Venanzio, *Itinerari francescani. La Valle Santa.* 2da ed. R, 1950. 239p. illus. Rev: CF IX, 79*. Not critical. F61

VERANI, Cesare, *La provincia di Rieti.* Terni, 1960. 185p. F62

d. ROME & THE PAPACY
(1) ROME & THE CHURCH IN THE 13TH CENTURY
(see also B1-B6, B13, B31-B48)

ARMELLINI, Mariano, *Le chiese di Roma dal sec. IV al XIX.* Nuova ed. a cura di Carlo Cecchelli. R, 1942. 2v. illus. Basic. *F63

FLICHE, A., et al., *Histoire de l'Eglise* (P 1950) X, 11-424. *F64

HERDE, Peter, *Beiträge zum päpstlichen Kanslei-und Urkundenwesen im dreizehnten Jahrhundert.* Kallmünz, 1961. xiii, 259p. *F65

HOMO, Léon, *Rome médiévale (476-1420). Histoire, civilisation, vestiges.* P, 1934. 327p. *F66

MATT, Leonard von, *Rom im Mittelalter.* Würzburg, 1960. xvi, 48pl. *Roma medioevale.* Genova, 1961. xvi, 48pl. *Medieval Rome.* Genova, 1961. xii, 48pl. F67

POTTHAST, A., *Regesta Pontificum.* Berlin, 1874. 2v. *F68

SCHULLER, Sepp, *Schwann Travel Guide: Rome.* Baltimore, 1958. 128 p. illus., maps, plans. Excellent. Data arranged by eras, see "Rome of the Monks": 61-71. F69

SEPPELT, F. X., *Geschichte der Päpste,* 2 Aufl. (München 1956) III, 319-411, & 614. *F70

(2) POPE INNOCENT III
(see also F107, F112, F113, F116, F119-F122)

BULTOT, Robert, "Mépris du monde, misère et dignité de l'homme dans la pensée d'Innocent III," CCM 4 (1961) 441-456. Basic. cf DA 14 (1954) 2069. *F71

FLICHE, Augustin, "Innocent III et la réforme de l'Eglise," RHE 44 (1949) 87-152. Fundamental. cf F74; F64:139-213. *F72

MACCARRONE, Michele, "Innocenzo III prima del Pontificato," DRSP 65 (1942) 59-134. Important. *F73

——, "Riforma e sviluppo della vita religiosa con Innocenzo III," RSCI 16 (1962) 29-72. Basic. cf F72. *F74

POWELL, James M., ed., *Innocent III, Vicar of Christ or Lord of the World?* Boston, 1963. 74p. Anthology of excerpts from leading modern historians showing evolving interpretations of Innocent's motives. *F75

SMITH, Charles E., *Innocent III, Church Defender.* Baton Rouge, La., 1951. vi, 203p. *F76

TILLMANN, Helene, *Papst Innocenz III.* Bonn, 1954. xv, 315p. Basic. *F77

(3) POPE HONORIUS III

CLAUSEN, J., *Papst Honorius III. (1216-1227); eine Monographie.* Bonn, 1895. viii, 414p. *F78

DELORME, F.M., OFM, "La bonne date de la bulle 'cum dilecti' d'Honorius III," AFH 12 (1919) 591-593. cf AFH 19 (1926) 539. *F79

FALOCI PULIGNANI, M., "Una bolla sconosciuta di Onorio III a SF," MF 27 (1927) 177-181; cf AFH 25 (1932) 146. F80

PRESSUTI, Pietro, ed., *Regesta Honorii papae III.* R, 1888-1895. 2v. *F81

VERNET, Felix, *Etude sur les sermons d'Honorius III.* Lyon, 1888. xi, 118p. F82

(4) CARDINAL HUGOLIN — POPE GREGORY IX
(see also E19, E24, E166, E178, F96, F120-F122)

AUVRAY, Lucien, ed., *Les registres de Grégoire IX.* P, 1896-1907. 2v. *F83

BREM, Ernst, *Papst Gregor IX. bis zum Beginn seines Pontifikats.* Heidelberg, 1911. 118p. Rev: AFH 5 (1912) 752. F84

CALLEBAUT, André, OFM, "Autour de la rencontre à Florence de SF et du Cardinal Hugolin (en été 1217)," AFH 19 (1926) 530-558. Fundamental. *F85

CRISPOLTI, Virgilio, "Il VII centenario della morte di Papa Gregorio IX, commemorato nella Basilica di A (1241-21 agosto-1941)," MF 41 (1941) 411-423. F86

FELTEN, J., *Papst Gregor IX.* Fr/Br, 1886. xii, 409p. F87

LEVI, Guido, ed., "Documenti ad illustrazione del Registro del Card. Ugolino d'Ostia, legato apostolico in Toscano e Lombardia," SRSP 12 (1889) 241-326. *F88

——, *Registri dei cardinali Ugolino d'Ostia e Ottaviano degli Ubaldini.* R, 1890. xxviii, 247p. (Fonti per la storia d'Italia, 8). *F89

LIBERATO DI STOLFI, OFM, "Gregorio IX 'Padre e signore' di SF," FF 14 (1941) 249-256. F90

SIBILIA, Salvatore, *Gregorio IX (1227-1241).* Mi, 1961. 406p. illus. *F91

THOUZELLIER, C., "La légation en Lombardie du cardinal Hugolin (1221)," RHE 45 (1950) 508-542. Basic. *F92

ZARNCKE, Lilly, *Der Anteil des Kardinals Ugolino an der Ausbildung der drei Orden des hl. Franz.* Leipzig, 1930. 144p. Rev: AFH 25 (1932) 81-85 (Bihl). Important. *F93

ZOELLIG, Benedikt, Cap, "Die Beziehungen des Kardinals Hugolino zum hl. F und zu seinem ersten Orden," FS 20 (1933) 1-33; 21 (1934) 34-79; & Münster, 1934. 79p. Rev: CF 9 (1939) 141-143. Important. *F94

(5) THE COLLEGE OF CARDINALS

"Essai de liste générale des cardinaux." In *Annuaire pontifical catholique* (P) 1928-29. Useful biographical sketches of 13th-century cardinals. F95

BERNARDINO DA SIENA, Cap, *Il cardinale protettore negli Istituti religiosi, specialmente negli Ordini francescani.* Fi, 1940. 185p. Rev: CF 10 (1940) 588. cf E3:59-76 (Brooke). *F96

CRISTOFORI, Francesco, *Storia dei cardinali.* R, 1888. lxii, 507p. F97

GANZER, Klaus, *Die Entwicklung des auswärtigen Kardinalats im hohen Mittelalter. Ein Beitrag zur Geschichte des Kardinalcollegiums vom 11. bis 13. Jahrhundert.* Tü, 1963. xxxiv, 217p. *F98

JANSSEN, Wilhelm, *Die päpstlichen Legaten in Frankreich vom Schisma Anaklets II. zum Tode Coelestins III. (1130-1198).* Köln, 1961. vii, 206p. *F99

KARTUSCH, Elfriede, *Des Kardinalskollegium in der Zeit von 1187 bis 1227.* Wien, 1948. 454p. (Wien Univ. diss.) *F100

ZIMMERMANN, Heinrich, *Die päpstliche Legationen in der ersten Hälfte des 13. Jahrhundert...(1198-1241).* Paderborn, 1913. xv, 348p. *F101

(6) CARDINAL JOHN OF ST. PAUL

ALTANER, B., "Zur Biographie des Kardinals Johannes von St. Paul," HJ 49 (1929) 304-306. *F102

BIHL, M., OFM, "De Iohanne de S. Paulo, cardinali episcopo Sabinensi, primo S. F in Curia Romana an. 1209 fautore," AFH 19 (1926) 282-285. Basic. *F103

PASCHINI, Pio, "Il cardinale Giovanni di San Paolo." In *Studi di storia e diritto in onore di Carlo Calisse* (Mi 1940) III, 109-118. Indispensable. *F104

WENCK, K., "Der Designationsversuch Weihnachten 1197. Kardinal Johann von St. Paul..." In *Papstum und Kaisertum* (München 1926) 456-474. *F105

(7) CARDINAL NICHOLAS DE ROMANIS

BIHL, M., "Nicolaus de Romanis (1219) fueritne primus cardinalis O.

F.M.?" AFH 19 (1926) 287-289. cf AFH 54 (1961) 229. cf F105:471.
*F106

(8) ST. FRANCIS & ROME
(see also D125, D126a, D153, D199a, E3, E16)

ALBANUS AB HERMETSCHWIL, Cap, "Visio papae Innocentii III de Basilica Lateranensi collabenti secundum Legendam S. Dominici in carmine 'Passional' contentam cum fontibus franciscanis comparata," TO 22 (1961) 29-33, 146-151. cf A197. *F107

BIHL, M., OFM, "S. F. parabola in sermonibus Odonis de Ceritonia an. 1219 conscriptis," AFH 22 (1929) 584-586. Abs: CF 1 (1931) 102. Add to A80. F108

Bullarium Franciscanum, Joannes Hyacinthus Sbaralea et al., ed. R, 1759-68. v.1-4; *Bullarii Franciscani Epitome*, Conrad Eubel, Conv, ed. Q, 1908. 349p. Rev: AFH 2 (1909) 646. *F109

BULLETTI, E., OFM, "Ospedale e chiesa di S. Antonio presso il Laterano," SF 26 (1929) 267-268. Important. *F110

CECCHELLI, Carlo, "Memorie romane del Serafico," *Capitolium* 2 (1926) 329-347. illus. Basic. *F111

CERAFOGLI, G., "Il Concilio Lateranense IV e SF," OR 22dic, 1963: 7. F112

FRANCISCUS, Fr., "F en het IVe Lateraans Concilie," FL 45 (1962) 47-59, 78-94, & cont. *F113

LIBERATO DI STOLFI, OFM, "SF e Roma," FF 15 (1938) 24-34.
F114

——, *SFA e Roma*. R, 1947. 27p. Rev: CF 20 (1950) 61*. Useful.
*F115

MATANIC, Atanasio, OFM, "Papa Innocenzo III di fronte a San Domenico e SF," Ant 35 (1960) 508-527. Abs: AFH 54 (1961) 445; RSCI 15 (1961) 366. *F116

MIGUEL DE PAMPLONA, Cap, "Viajes de SF a Roma," *Verdad y Caridad* 10 (1933) 236-239, 267-269, 305-308, 338-339. Rev: CF 5 (1935) 147. F117

OLIGER, L., OFM, "SF a Roma e nella Provincia Romana." In F38: 65-112. Important. *F118

ORTH, Clement R., Conv, *The Approbation of Religious Institutes*. Wa, 1931. 171p. (Cath. Univ. diss.) Useful. *F119

SALVADORI, Giulio, "SFA nei suoi rapporti con i pontefici dell'età sua a Roma," Univ. del Sacro Cuore (Mi), *Pubblicazioni Scienze filologiche* Ser. 4 16 (1933) 321-340. Abs: CF 5 (1935) 173. cf D181. F120

STRONG, Mrs. Arthur, "SF in Rome." In D178:267-306. F121

TERZI, Arduino, OFM, *SFA a Roma*. R, 1956. xviii, 100p. illus., plans. Rev: AFH 51 (1958) 203; CF 27 (1957) 424; MF 58 (1958) 340-342. Indispensable. *F122

e. SUBIACO
(see also B81, B83-B87, F50)

BUGHETTI, B., OFM, "Di un presunto nuovo ritratto di SF," AFH 19 (1926) 937-939. F123

FEDERICI, Domenico, "SF si preparò alle stimmate nel Sacro Speco," Società tiburtina di storia e d'arte *Atti e memorie* 26 (1953) 175-204; & Tivoli, 1954. 62p. Abs: CF IX, 94; rev: EF ns7 (1956) 228; MF 55 (1955) 627. *F124

FRUGONI, Arsenio, "Subiaco francescano," BISI 65 (1953) 107-119. CF X, 89*; AFH 47 (1954) 462. *F125

SALVI, Guglielmo, OSB, "La cappella di S. Gregorio al Sacro Speco di Subiaco," RSB 22 (1953) 1-28. *F126

——, "La data della venuta di SF a Subiaco," IF 31 (1956) 28-44; "Ancora su SF a Subiaco," 344-347. Abs: CF XI, 95. F127

—— ,"SF si preparò alle stimmate nel Sacro Speco?" IF 30 (1955) 109-118. Abs: CF X, 90*. Important. F128

f. VICALVI

FACCHINETTI, V., OFM, "Vicalvi in quel di Sor," FF 9 (1936) 16-21. cf AFH 21 (1927) 138. F129

3 THE MARCHES OF ANCONA & FERMO
(see also B23, B27)

a. AS A WHOLE

FOGLIETTI, Raffaele. *Le Marche dal 586 al 1230.* Macerata, 1907. F130

HUTTON, Edward, *The Cities of Romagna & the Marches.* L, 1913 (& 1925). xix, 309p. illus. Excellent. F131

PAGNANI, Giacinto, OFM, *I viaggi di SFA nell Marche.* Mi, 1962. 114p. illus., map. Rev: AFH 56 (1963) 357-359; CF 33 (1933) 329. Fundamental. *F132

STRAPPATI, Tarcisio, Conv, "Il Piceno 'Provincia stellata'," IF 34 (1959) 121-127, 131, 203-209, 265-269, 273, 344-348; 35 (1960) 51-54, 56, 128-133, 266-272, 347-352. *F133

TALAMONTI, Antonio, OFM, *Cronistoria dei Frati Minori della Provincia Lauretana delle Marche.* Sassoferrato, 1939-62. 7v. Rev: CF 9 (1939) 569; 10 (1940) 415; 13 (1943) 324-326; 20 (1950) 148; 33 (1963) 453; MF 38 (1938) 579-587 (Abate); 63 (1963) 373-385. Histories of friaries. Important. *F134

TOURING CLUB ITALIANO, *Attraverso l'Italia, v. 19: Marche.* Mi, 1953. 240p. 438 illus. of art & scenery. F135

——, *Marche.* 3a ed. Mi, 1962. 507p. maps, plans, rich bibl. Guida d'Italia, 13. Indispensable. *F136

b. PARTICULAR LOCALITIES

ALLEVI, Febo, *Poesia delle rovine. Contributi storico-artistico-letterari d'una valle picena.* R, 1956. 298p. Abs: CF XI, 78. Not critical. F137

BUGHETTI, B., OFM, "San Leo nel Montefeltro." In *La Verna* (Arezzo 1913) 1-6. Basic. *F138

DAMIANI, Quinto, OFM, "San Liberato da Loro Piceno," CF 32 (1962) 325-335. cf A179, F132, F142. F139

DONATI, Luigi, *SF a S. Leo.* S. Leo, 1959. 31p. illus. cf F132. F140

FACCHINETTI, V., OFM, "Il convento di Villa Verucchio," FF 6 (1929) 344-348. cf 3 (1926) 287.   F141

PAGNANI, Giacinto, OFM, *San Liberato e il suo convento.* Falconara M. (Ancona), 1962. 149p. illus. Rev: CF 33 (1963) 329. Important. cf A179, F139.   *F142

PECCI, Giuseppe, *Cenni storici artistici sul convento di Villa Verucchio.* Bologna, 1926. 23p. illus. Rev: FF 6 (1929) 346.   F143

TANI, Antonio, *SF nel Montefeltro.* Città di Castello, 1926. 272p. Rev: FF 4(1927) 378-379.   *F144

4 TUSCANY

a. AS A WHOLE
(see also B24, B25, F360-F383)

HUTTON, Edward, *In Unknown Tuscany.* L, 1909. xi, 244p. illus. 3d ed.: *A Wayfarer in Unknown Tuscany.* L, 1925. xii, 212p. illus. Excellent. F145

——, *Siena & Southern Tuscany.* L & NY, 1955. xiii, 274p. illus. Excellent. F146

SISTO DA PISA, CAP, "SF in Toscana," IF 7 (1932) 449-461; 8 (1933) 3-15, 337-349; 9 (1934) 113-120, 337-351. Abs: CF 5 (1935) 132 & 9 (1939) 136. Useful but not critical.   F147

TOURING CLUB ITALIANO, *Attraverso l'Italia, v.6: Toscana.* Mi, 1941. 240p. Over 200 illus. of art & scenery.   F148

——, *Toscana (non compresa Firenze).* 3a ed. Mi, 1959. 880p. maps, plans, rich bibl. (Guida d'Italia, 11). Indispensable.   *F149

b. AREZZO

RENZONI, Marco, OFM, "SF ed Arezzo," SF 46 (1950) 129-155. Basic.   *F150

RUSSO, Francesco, "Figure francescane di Arezzo," MF 41 (1941) 107-111.   F151

WIERUSZOWSKI, Helene, "Arezzo as a Center of Learning & Letters in the Thirteenth Century," Trad 9 (1953) 321-391.   *F152

c. CORTONA
(see also F360-F362)

BERNARDINI, A., & A. Castri, *Cortona, guida turistica.* 2da ed. Arezzo, 1955. 64p. illus.   F153

LIBERATO DI STOLFI, OFM, "Ricordi francescani di Cortona," FF 24 (1957) 14-18.   F154

d. FLORENCE
(see also B7, E6, F85)

MONTANO, Giovanni, OFM, *Motivo francescano in Piazza S. Gallo.* Fi, 1955. 108p. illus. Rev: CF 26 (1956) 321; EF ns7 (1956) 228; FS 40 (1958) 438; MF 58 (1958) 143-147; SF 54 (1957) 123. Revs. important, with F156.   *F155,

TEUCCI, Raffaele, "Dove era il primo convento dei Minori a Firenze?" SF 54 (1957) 103-106. Important, with F155 revs. *F156

e. SIENA
(see also B24, F368-F371)

SF e Siena, a cura di Piero Misciatelli e Aldo Lusini. Siena, 1927. 311p. illus. Fundamental. *F157

f. MISCELLANEOUS LOCALITIES
(cf E231)

GIACINTO DA PISTOIA, Cap, "Montauto, SF, i Cappucini," IF 17 (1942) 113-135. cf C202 & C209. F158

MARRI MARTINI, Lilia, "SF a Piancastagno sull'Amiata," FF 12 (1939) 88-92. F159

RICCI, Ivano, *Storia di Borgo Sansepolcro*. Sansepolcro, 1956. 123p. F160

ROSATI, Nazario, OFM, "Sposalizio di SF con Madonna Povertà alle Briccole tra Campiglia e S. Quirico d'Orcia," FF 13 (1940) 271-277. Basic. cf AF X, 185n10. *F161

5 UMBRIA
(see also B27a, F 384-F400)

a. AS A WHOLE

(1) DESCRIPTION
(see also F26-F49, F182)

BERIOLI, Orlando, *Alla conoscenza dell'Umbria*. Terni, 1960. 103p. illus. F162

BRION, Marcel, *L'Ombrie*. P, 1956. 116p. 162 illus., map. Rev: CF 27 (1957) 330. One of the best, esp. on art. F163

CAMERON, Mary Lovett, *Umbria, Past & Present*. L, 1913. 324p. illus. Excellent chs. on feasts, fairs, confraternities, customs. F164

CRUIKSHANK, J.W. & A.M., *The Umbrian Cities of Italy*. Boston, 1901. 2v. in 1. illus. 2d ed. rev. NY, 1912. 391p. illus. F165

EGERAAT, L van, *Umbrië, het mysterieuze Italië*. Den Haag, 1958. 104p. 50 illus. F166

ETNA, Giacomo, *Il sole dell'Umbria. Figure, paesi francescani*. To, 1960. 217p. 24 illus. Excellent. F167

FAINA, Carlo, *Umbria verde*. To, 1925. 266p. illus. F168

FEDERER, Heinrich, (A) *Umbrische Reisegeschichtlein*. Luzern, 1948. 304p. (b) *A travers l'Ombrie. Contes et récits de voyage*. Mulhouse, 1951. 2v. (c) *Storie e leggende nel cuore d'Italia*. Ven, 1930. xii, 263p. Rev: CF 5 (1935) 175; 25 (1955) 179. cf his *Der heilige Habenichts*. München, 1926. 30p. Rev: EF 40 (1928) 542. Also Sigisbert FRICK, OSB, *Heinrich Federer und Italien*. Sarnen, 1949. 155p. And *Federer-Briefe*. Luzern, 1963. 229p. F169

HUTTON, Edward, *The Cities of Umbria*. L, 1905. xvi, 303p. illus. F170

——, *Assisi & Umbria Revisited*. L & NY, 1954. xi, 247p. illus. Excellent.
F171
JACQUET, Pierre,   *Ombre, terre de S F*. Photos de Fulvio Roiter. Lausanne, 1955. x, 110p. illus. Disappointing.   F172
KELLER, Harald,   (a) *Umbrien; Landschaft und Kunst*. Wien, 1959. 185p. 145 photographs by Konrad Helbig.   (b) *Umbria, The Heart of Italy*. NY, 1961. 215p. 145 illus. Splendid.   F173
LUCONI, Geremia,   *Umbria ignorata*. R, 1939. 104p. Rev: MF 43 (1943) 205. Useful for region around Gubbio, Nocera, & Scheggia.   F174
MAUREL, André,   (a) *Petites villes d'Italie*. P, 1920. 4v.   (b) *Little Cities of Italy*. NY, 1911-13. 2v. On Umbria: v.2. Excellent.   F175
MEYER, Willy,   *Das Herz Italiens. Umbrische Miniaturen*. Bern, 1955. 188p. illus. Good.   F176
PRETE PEDRINI, Maria Rosa,   *Umbria*. To, 1963. x, 442p. maps, plans, many illus. (Le Regioni d'Italia, 9). Excellent economic & geographical survey. Series includes similar works by other authors on other provinces.   F177
RIZZATI, Ferruccio,   *Umbria verde*. Bologna, 1926. 380p. 143 illus. 2d ed. of 1911 work. Useful.   F178
SODINI, A.,   *L'Anima umbra*. Mi, 1928. 66p. illus. Excellent. List of famous foreign writer-tourists, p. 35.   F179
TOURING CLUB ITALIANO,   *Attraverso l'Italia, v.12: Umbria*. Mi, 1944. 240p. 429 illus. of art & scenery. Indispensable.   F180
——, *Umbria*, 3a ed. Mi, 1950. 392p. maps, plans, rich bibl. (Guida d'Italia, 11). Indispensable   *F181

(2) HISTORY OF UMBRIA

ADAMS, Michael,   *Umbria*. L, 1964. 240p. illus., maps. Excellent   F182
Archivio per la storia ecclesiastica dell'Umbria, Mons. Michele Faloci Pulignani, ed. Foligno, v.1-5, 1913-21.   *F182a
BRIGANTI, Francesco,   *Città dominanti e comuni minori nel medio evo, con speciale riguardo alla Repubblica perugina*. Perugia, 1906. 300p.   *F183
——, *L'Umbria nella storia del notariato italiano. Archivi notarili nelle provincie di Perugia e Terni*. Perugia, 1958. 250p. illus. cf F236   *F184
Deputazione di storia patria per l'Umbria *Bolletino*. (DSPU) *Indici dei volumi 1 (1895)-51 (1954)*, Olga Marinelli, comp., in v.52/53 (1957); 389p.
**F185
FAINA, Maria Caterina, *I palazzi comunali umbri*. Mi, 1957. 159p. 79 illus. Useful. For A: 77-88; depends on FNV (1926).   *F186
FISHER, Craig B., *The Beginnings of Communal Historiography in Central Italy*. Ithaca, NY, 1961. v, 265p. (Cornell Univ. diss.) Abs: DA 22 (1961) 2369.   *F187
ITALY MINISTERO DELL'INTERNO. SOPRINTENDENZA ARCHIVISTICA PER IL LAZIO, L'UMBRIA E LE MARCHE, *Gli archivi dell' Umbria*. R, 1957. 202p. (Pubblicazioni degli Archivi di Stato). Abs: CF XI, 27.   *F188
KEHR, P. F.,   *Italia Pontificia, sive Regesta pontificum romanorum*. Berlin, 1909. IV: Umbria, Picenum, Marsia. xxxiv, 336p. Useful bibls.   *F189

LANZONI, Francesco, *Le origini delle diocesi d'Italia. Studio critico.* R, 1927. 2v. (Studi e testi, 35). Basic. *F190

MOCHI ONORY, Sergio, *Ricerche sui poteri civili dei vescovi nelle città umbre durante l'alto medioevo.* R, 1930. 257p. Important. *F191
——, "L'Umbria bizantina." In F195:57-77. *F192

PALAZZOLI, Maria Rosa, "Trasformazione delle classi rurali nell' Umbria medioevale," *Nova Historia* 12 (1960) n4 45-82, 13 (1961) n2 46-79, n3 53-61. *F193

PALUMBO, Pier F., *Le terre arnolfine.* Perugia, 1945. F194

PERUGIA. UNIVERSITA DEGLI STUDI. ACCADEMIA DI LETTERE, *L'Umbria nella storia, nella letteratura, nell'arte.* Bologna, 1954. 347p. illus. Fundamental. Includes C149, C153, F192, F204. *F195

REGGIANI, Angelo, *Ricerche sulle origini del cristianesimo nell'alta valle del Tevere.* Città di Castello, 1960. 58p. F196

SALMI, Mario, "La cosidetta 'Porta del Morto'," *Lares* 21 (1955) n3-4, 1-8; illus. Basic refutation of modern legendary explanation of raised medieval Umbrian housedoors. F197

(3) FRANCISCAN PROVINCIAL HISTORY
(see also E51, E107)

ANTONIO D'ORVIETO, OFM Rif., *Cronologia della Provincia serafica riformata dell'Umbria, o d'A.* Perugia, 1717. 811p. Fundamental. F198

BAZZOCHINI, Benvenuto, OFM, *Cronaca della Provincia serafica di S. Chiara d'A.* Fi, 1921. 437p. map. Indispensable. *F199

(4) UMBRIAN FOLKLORE
(cf EC XII, 749-753)

CHINI, Mario, *Canti popolari umbri.* Todi, 1917. 286p. F200

GRIFONI, Oreste, *Poesie e canti religiosi dell'Umbria.* 4a ed. SMA, 1927. 165p. On SF: only p. 105. F201

MAZZATINTI, G., *Canti popolari umbri raccolti a Gubbio.* Bologna, 1883. 321p. F202

MAZZIER, Alessio, "Il Ciclo della vita umana nelle tradizioni popolari umbre," *DSPU* 49 (1952) 11-108. Important. F203

TOSCHI, Paolo, "Le tradizioni popolari umbre." In F195:333-346.
F204

b. ASSISI
(1) DESCRIPTION

BARGELLINI, Piero, (a) *Visitare e sentire A. Guida itinerario.* Fi, 1951. 101p. illus. (b) *How To See & Appreciate A.* Fi, 1956. 95p. illus.
F205

BIZZARRI, Mario, *Guida di A e dintorni.* 2a ed. Perugia, 1954. 86p. illus. F206

BOELL, Heinrich, *A.* München, 1962. 23p. maps, 36 illus. Includes brief excerpts from tribute to A by 15 writers. F207

BONNET, Pierre, *Le colloque d'A.* P, 1955. 165p. illus. Moods. F208

BOVINI, Giuseppe, (a) A, *la città del Santo.* Mi, 1957. 36p. 64 illus. (b) A. *Die Stadt des Heiligen.* Z, 1959. 38p. 64 illus. F209

CAMERON, Mary L., *The Inquiring Pilgrim's Guide to* A. L, 1926. ix, 275p. illus. Includes Thomas of Celano's First Life. Good for fairs, small churches, customs. F210

CHIERICHETTI, Sandro, A, *An Illustrated Guidebook.* Mi, 1957. 110p. illus., map. Best recent guidebook; available in several languages. F211

FORTINI, Arnaldo, *Settimana santa di* A. A, 1957. 72p. illus. F212

FORTINI, Gemma, *Calendimaggio di* A. Perugia, 1955. 21p. F213

GOFF, Mrs. Robert (Clarissa), *A of SF.* L, 1908. 290p. maps; illus. by Col. R. Goff. Includes "The Influence of the Franciscan Legend on Italian Art," by J. Kerr-Lawson, p. 237-282. Excellent. F214

JACOVELLI, Anacleto, Conv, (A) V*isitiamo* A. 9a ed. A, 1954. 95p. illus. (b) V*isiting* A. 2d ed. A, 1954. 83p. illus. Also French & German eds. F215

JUD, Karl, & Hans Krömler, (a) A. *Bilder einer Stadt.* Z, & Stuttgart, 1954. 12p. text by H.K.; 48p. fine photos by KJ. (b) A. *Images d'une ville.* Fribourg & P, 1954. 12p.; 48p. F216

LEKEUX, Martial, OFM, *Dans la lumière d'*A. Bruxelles, 1950. 65p. illus. Rev: EF ns2 (1951) 113. F217

MAJARELLI, Stanislao, OFM, (a) A, *itinerario francescano.* SMA, 1956. 64p. illus. plan. (b) A, A *Franciscan Pilgrimage.* SMA, 1957. 64p. illus. F218

MASSERON, Alexandre, A. P, 1950. 191p. map, plans, illus. Excellent. F219

MAUCLAIR, Camille, A. P, 1923. 172p. 30 col. pl. by J.F. Bouchor. F220

NEWTON, Francis, Conv, *S. F. & His Basilica,* A. A, 1926. 296p. illus. F221

POMPEI, Alfonso, & Costantino Troiano, Conv (a) *Guida dei santuari di* A. A, 1958. 119p. 126 illus. (b) *The Sanctuaries of* A. A, 1961. 142p. illus. F222

RICHMOND, Sir William, A, *Impressions of Half a Century.* L, 1919. viii, 210p. illus. Excellent. F223

SCHNEIDER, Edouard, A. P, 1933. 214p. illus. F224

——, A. P, 1953. 222p. illus. F225

——, *Le petit pauvre au pays d'*A. P, 1926. x, 260p. Excellent. F226

ZOCCA, Emma, *Catalogo delle cose d'arte e di antichità d'Italia,* (9): A. R, 1936. 383p. illus. Lists & describes all works of art & relics. *F227

——, *A e dintorni.* 3a ed. R, 1960. 92p. illus. F228

(2) HISTORY OF ASSISI

ATTAL, F. S., "A città santa. Come fu salvata dagli orrori della guerra," MF 48 (1948) 3-32. Rev: CF 21 (1951) 370*. Important for 1939-45. F229

BRACALONI, Leone, OFM, "A medioevale. Studio storico-topografico," AFH 7 (1914) 3-19; illus. Still useful. *F230

BRUNACCI, Aldo, "Leggende e culto di S. Rufino in A," DSPU 45

(1948) 5-91. Basic for that Saint. cf F284-F286. *F231

CRISTOFANI, Antonio, (1828-83), *Delle storie d'Asisi libri sei.* A, 1886. xvi, 568p. *Le storie di A.* 4a ed., curata dal Prof. Giustino Cristofani. Ven, 1959. xxiv, 645p. illus. Still fundamental. F232

FORTINI, Arnaldo, *A nel medio evo, Leggende, avventure, battaglie.* R, 1940, viii, 629p. Rev: AFH 33 (1940) 210-214 (Bihl); CF 11 (1941) 491; FF 13 (1940 238-240. Indispensable. cf B52. *F233

——, *Le corporazioni artigiani medioevali nella città di SF.* R, 1962. 52p. illus. Abs: AFH 56 (1963) 228. F234

——, *I fioretti delle Carcerelle.* Ven, 1956. 188p. illus. Valuable history of Capuchin friary on Monte Subasio. cf CF 5 (1935) 241-260. F235

[——], *Il millenario dell'Archivio Capitolare di A.* (963-1963). SMA, 1963. 25p. F235a

——, *I notai nella città di SF.* SMA, 1962. 59p. 21 illus. Rev: CF 33 (1963) 443. cf FNV III, 525-530: list 1372-1750. cf F184. *F236

——, FNV: "Signori e servi," I/1, 5-52; "La città dei guerrieri e dei mercanti," I/1, 55-102; "A al tempo del Santo," III, 7-227. Basic. *F237

——, *Il piu ardente poeta d'amore.* Foligno, 1931. cf FNV III, 7 nl. On Propertius & the Roman period. F238

——, *Nella luce di A.* Mi, 1934. Rev: FF 7 (1934) 159. Speeches & articles 1921-33. F239

FORTINI, Gemma, *Città di poeti. Storia dell'Accademia* [properziana] *assisana del Subasio.* A, 1954. 398p. Rev: AFH 48 (1955) 164; CF XI, 130; FF nsl (1954) 179; IF 30 (1955) 129-132. (1949 Univ. di Roma tesi.) cf FNV II, 117. *F240

GORDON, Lina Duff, *The Story of A.* L, 1901. 372p. illus., map. F241

PAGLIACCI, A., "Fonti archivistiche per una storia economica di A," Univ. degli Studi di Perugia, Facoltà di scienze economiche e commerciali *Annali* ns4 (1955/56) 581-608. *F242

PENNACCHI, Francesco, *Diario storico Assisiano francescano.* A, 1927. 104p. Rev: FF 5 (1928) 396. *F243

THEOBALD, Père, Cap, "A au temps de SF," EF 50 (1938) 385-414, 497-532. Based on FNV (1926) & on local archives. *F244

ZACCARIA, G., Conv, *Catalogo degli incunabili della Biblioteca comunale di A.* Fi, 1961. 114p. (Biblioteca di bibliografia italiana, 38) *F245

(3) CHURCHES & MONASTERIES OF ASSISI

(a) THE PORTIUNCULA

ABATE, G., Conv, "Della data della consacrazione della Porziuncula e dei racconti sulla celebre Indulgenza," MF 37 (1937) 183-197. Rev: AFH 33 (1940) 208-210 (Bihl). Important, with rev. *F246

Fratis Francisci BARTHOLI de Assisio, *Tractatus de Indulgentia S. Mariae de Portiuncula,* ed. Paul Sabatier. P, 1900. clxxxiv, 204p. (CED,2)Fundamental coll. of docs. *F247

CANONICI, Luciano, OFM, *La Porziuncula e gli inizi dell'Ordine francescano. Ricerche storiche.* SMA, 1963. 157p. illus. Rev: CF 34 (1964) 186. Basic. *F248

——, *La Porziuncula nei piu antichi documenti francescani*. SMA, 1959 144p. Popular anthology of early texts. F249

CICIONI, G. C., "Le rose di SF in Santa Maria degli Angeli," MF 18 (1917) 3-7. Rev: AFH 14 (1921) 314. Botanical analysis. F250

EDOUARD D'ALENCON, Cap, "Des origines de l'Eglise de la Portioncule et de ses diverses dénominations," EF 11 (1904) 585-606; & Couvin, 1909. Still useful. *F251

FIERENS, Alfons, *De Geschiedkundige Oorsprong van den Aflaat van Portiunkula*. Gent, 1910. 301p. Includes text of Frater Andreas Bajuli's important early *Historia Indulgentiae*, p. 77-103. Rev: AFH 4 (1911) 601-603. Fundamental. cf A210. *F252

FORTINI, A., FNV III, 92-99; cf II, 427-445. *F253

GIUSEPPE DE SIMONE, "SF, la Porziuncula e i Benedettini," IF 9 (1934) 121-125. Abs: CF 9 (1939) 134*. Data on history of annual fish-gift. cf B81, F248:116. F254

HUBER, Raphael M., Conv, *The Portiuncula Indulgence from Honorius III to Pius XI*. NY, 1938. 207p. Comprehensive bibl. Rev: AFH 33 (1940) 199-210 (Bihl), with other works on subject; CF 11 (1941) 499-501. **F255

(b) RIVO TORTO
(see also FNV II, 306-314)

CARMICHAEL, Montgomery, (a) "The First Franciscan Convent," *Downside Review* 21 (1902) 1-17. (b) "Il primo convento francescano," MF 9 (1902) 22-29. F256

GIOVAGNOLI, E., "Rivotorto, la culla dell'Ordine," SFA 8 (1928) 222-230. F257

(c) SAN BENEDETTO
(see also B81-B87)

BACHECA, Michelangelo, "La cripta triastila di San Benedetto al Subasio," Accademia properziana del Subasio (A) Atti Ser. 5 (1956)n4. *F258

EDOUARD D'ALENCON, Cap, "L'Abbaye de Saint-Benoît au Mont Soubase," EF 22 (1909) 376-424. Fundamental. *F259

FORTINI, Arnaldo, FNV I/1, 22-26; III, 163-169. Basic. *F260

PANTONI, Angelo, "San Benedetto al Subasio," *Benedictina* 2 (1948) 47-74. Fundamental. *F261

(d) SAN DAMIANO
(see also E168-E213)

BRACALONI, Leone, OFM, *Storia di San Damiano in A*. 2da ed. Todi, 1926. xii, 199p. illus. Rev: AFH 23 (1930) 568. Fundamental. *F262

FORTINI, Arnaldo, FNV III, 86-91; IV, 190 (index). *F263

GIORGI, Antonio, OFM, *San Damiano il santuario della fedeltà*. A, 1950. ix, 174p. 66 illus. Valuable coll. of historical data & descr. *F264

TINI, Andrea Pier, "La culla delle Damianite e Guido Vescovo," MF 14 (1912) 33-37. With texts of 1030 & 1253 docs. F265

(e) THE BASILICA OF SAN FRANCESCO & THE SACRO CONVENTO
(cf C82, C228-C232, C251a, E114, E159)

ABATE, G., Conv, "Per la storia e l'arte della Basilica di SF in A," MF 57 (1957) 3-36. Misc. 15th-century items. *F266

BRACALONI, Leone, OFM, "Apoteosi francescana nella Basilica Inferiore d'A," FF 23 (1956) 116-123. *F267

BRUNI, Bruno, "Le pitture giottesche nella parete sinistra della Basilica Superiore di SF in A," MF 48 (1948) 329-344. F268

CARATTOLI, L., M. Guardabassi, & G.B. Rossi Scotti, "Descrizione del santuario di SF D'A," DSPU 28 (1928) 89-237; text of 1863 report. cf 1-87, Fra LUDOVICO DA PIETRALUNGA (d. 1580), "Descrizione della Basilica di SF in A." *F269

COLETTI, L., *Gli affreschi della Basilica di Assisi*. Bergamo, 1949. 133p., 200 pl. *F269a

CRISPOLTI, V., *Guida della Basilica Papale e del Sacro Convento di SF di A*. A, 1947. 144, 54p. CF VIII, 92*; MF 47 (1947) 634. F270

CRISTOFANI, Giustino, "Le vicende di un grande monumento nell' ultimo sessantennio: la Basilica francescana di A." In V Convegno nazionale di storia dell'archittetura, Perugia 1948, *Atti* (Fi 1957) 639-642. *F271

FRUTAZ, Mons. Pietro Amato, "La Chiesa di SF in A 'Basilica Patriarchale e Cappella Papale'," MF 54 (1954) 399-432. *F272

GILLET, Louis, "Nouvelles études sur la basilique d'A." In D179:268-287. *F273

GNOLI, Umberto, "Il tesoro di SF d'A," *Dedalo* 2 (1921/22) 421-441, 555-579. Important. *F274

KLEINSCHMIDT, Beda, OFM, *Die Basilika SF in A*. Berlin, 1915. 3v. Rev: AFH 21 (1928) 130-133 (Bihl). Basic. *F275

MARINANGELI, B., Conv, "Cenni storici della Basilica e del S. Convento di SF," SFA 9 (1929) 6-11, 53-55, 104-106, 162-169, 218-222. Abs: CF 1 (1931) 105. *F276

SCHOENE, Wolfgang, "Studien zur Oberkirche von A." In *Festchrift Kurt Bauch* (München 1957) 50-116; 27 illus. Basic. *F277

SCIAMANNINI, Raniero, Conv, *La Basilica di SF e gli altri santuari di A*. Fi, 1952. 107p. Rev: MF 53 (1953) 284. *F278

ZACCARIA, Giuseppe, Conv, "Diario storico della Basilica e Sacro Convento di SF in A (1220-1927)," MF 63 (1963) 75-120, 290-361, 495-536; & cont. Basic. *F279

(f) SAN GIACOMO DE MURORUPTO

FORTINI, Arnaldo, FNV I/1, 183-184; III, 60-64; IV, 192 (index). F280

PARIS, Ugolino, OFM, *L'antica chiesa e monastero di San Giacomo de murorupto in A*. A, 1937. 87p. *F281

(g) SAN GIORGIO, later SANTA CHIARA
(see also C218, E220)

BRACALONI, Leone, OFM, "La chiesa di S. Giorgio in A," CF 8

(1938) 493-511. Supersedes his art. in FF 2 (1925) 332-342. *F282
FORTINI, A., FNV III, 54-60. *F283

(h) SAN RUFINO
(see also E214, E215, E217, E218, F231)

BERTINI CALOSSO, A., "Giovanni da Gubbio e la sua attività in A." Unpub'd; cf V Convegno nazionale di storia dell'archittetura, Perugia 1948, *Atti* (Fi 1957) 600, & EC II, 176. *F284
FORTINI, A., FNV III, 34-42; IV, 199 (index). *F285
———, "Sull'epoca in cui fu costruita la primitiva chiesa di S. Rufino in A," IF 30 (1955) 352-358. *F286

c. CITERNA

ASCANI, A., *Citerna. Memorie storiche e religiose.* Sansepolcro, 1944. 224p. F287

d. CITTA DI CASTELLO

BRENTANO, Robert, "The Bishops' Books of Città di Castello," Trad 16 (1960) 241-254. *F288
TORRIOLI, Ascanio, *Panorama storico dell'alta valle del Tevere, con particolare riguardo alle vicende di Città di Castello.* Città di Castello, 1960. 85p. F289

e. FOLIGNO

FALOCI PULIGNANI, M., "SF e la città di Foligno," MF 6 (1895) 3-15. F290

f. GUALDO TADINO

FALOCI PULIGNANI, M., "SF a Gualdo Tadino," MF 9 (1905) 185-193. *F291

g. GUBBIO

FALOCI PULIGNANI, M., "SF e il monastero di S. Verecondo presso Gubbio," MF 10 (1906) 1-8. *F292
GOLUBOVICH, G., OFM, "I conti Spadalunga di Gubbio e SF," AFH 1 (1908) 144-147. *F293
MacCRACKEN, Laura, *Gubbio, Past & Present.* L, 1905. xvii, 319p. illus. F293a
PARIS, Ugolino, OFM, *SF e i Francescani nella città di Gubbio.* 2a ed. accr. ed illus. A, 1941. 221p. Rev: CF VII, 38*; MF 43 (1943) 196. Basic.
*F294

h. NOTTIANO

[FORTINI, A.], A, AZIENDA AUTONOMA DEL TURISMO, *24 Giugno 1957: Inaugurazione della restaurata chiesa di Nottiano.* Ven, 1957. 7p. F295

i. ORVIETO

CARPENTIER, Elisabeth, *Une ville devant la peste. Orvieto et la peste noire de 1348.* P, 1962. 295p. illus. *F296

RICCIONI, Giuseppe, *Guida di Orvieto.* Orvieto, 1960. 80p. illus. *F297

WALEY, Daniel, *Medieval Orvieto.* Cambridge, Eng., 1952. xxv, 170p. illus., map. Basic *F298

j. PERUGIA
(see also C63, E119 E123, E225)

FANTOZZI, Antonio, OFM, "Alcune memorie intorno al culto di SFA, di S. Antonio di Padova e del B. Egidio d'A nella città di Perugia," AFH 33 (1940) 227-233. Mostly 15th-century docs. *F299

HEYWOOD, William, *A History of Perugia.* L & NY, 1910. xvi, 411p. *F300

JOHNSTONE, Mary A., *Perugia & Her People.* Perugia, 1958. 261p. F301

MARINELLI, O., *Momenti di storia perugina.* Perugia, 1960. 84p. F302

MAZZARA, Marino, OFM, *Il santuario francescano di Monteripido in Perugia.* Perugia, 1920. 29p. illus. F303

Il movimento dei Disciplinati nel settimo centenario dal suo inizio (Perugia, 1260). Atti del Convegno internazionale, Perugia 25-28 sett. 1960. Perugia, 1962. 652p. *F304

RICCI, Ettore, "Luoghi francescani," OS 27 (1915) 100-106. Abs: AFH 14 (1921) 320. F305

SORBI, Salmareggi, *I primordi della chiesa di SF al Prato in Perugia (VII centenario della morte di Frate Egidio, 1262-1962).* SMA, 1963. 96p. illus. Rev: AFH 57 (1964) 246. F306

k. SPELLO

FRANTINI, Luigi, Conv, "Antichi ricordi di SF a Spello," MF 17 (1916) 156-159. Rev: AFH 14 (1921) 314. Important. *F307

LAZZERI, Z., OFM, *L'antico monastero di Vallegloria vicino a Spello (con appendice di documenti).* Arezzo, 1913. 87p. From *La Verna* 9-10 (1911-13). Rev: AFH 6 (1913) 775. Basic. *F308

l. SPOLETO
(see also B18, B26, F390-F394)

FAUSTI, Luigi, "SF a Spoleto," SFA 3 (1922/3) 137-139. F309

MONELLI, Paolo, *High Spoleto.* R & NY, 1960. 22p., 76 illus. F310

m. TERNI (DISTRICT)

LANZI, Luigi, *Escurzioni francescane nei dintorni di Terni.* Perugia, 1907. 92p. illus. On Stroncone, Greccio, Eremita di Cesi, Sant'Urbano. *F311

n. TODI

MANCINI, Franco, *Todi e i suoi castelli. Pagine di storia e d'arte.* Città di Castello, 1960. viii, 428p. illus.   F312

o. TREVI

BONACA, Aurello, "Le memorie francescane di Trevi," SF ns13 (1927) 12-35, 113-148. Basic.   *F313

III NORTHERN ITALY
1 EMILIA

BUGHETTI, B., OFM, "In che anno predicò in Imola SFA," *Il Diario* (Imola) 22 mag, 1926.   F314

STRAPPATI, Tarcisio, Conv, "Il convento, lo studio e la chiesa della SS. Annunziata e SF di Bologna," MF 34 (1934) 25-41. cf E144.   F315

2 PIEMONTE

ABATE, G., Conv, "SF in Alessandria e il miracolo della lupa," MF 38 (1938) 259-261. Abs: CF 9 (1939) 136; cf CF VI, 19*. Important.   *F316

DE FERRARI DI BRIGNANO, Umberto, "SF in Alessandria," *Alexandria* 3 (1935) 307-311. Source of F316.   *F317

FACCHINETTI, V., OFM, "Il santuario di Belmonte," FF 5 (1928) 429-434.   F318

SALSOTTO, Carlo, "SFA nel Novarese (storia e leggenda)," *Bolletino storico per la provincia di Novara* 54 (1955) 103-112; 55 (1956) 160-173. Basic.   *F319

3 VENETO
(see also F401-F403)

BERNARDINO DA CITTADELLA, Cap, "E stato SF nel Veneto?" IF 1 (1926) 224-229.   F320

FAINELLI, V., "Lebbrosi e francescani a Verona ai tempi di SF," Istituto Veneto di scienze, lettere ed arti, Classe di scienze morali e lettere, *Atti* 112 (1953/54) 97-106.   *F321

SARTORI, Antonio, Conv, *La provincia del Santo dei Frati Minori Conventuali. Notizie storiche.* Padova, 1958. 351p. Rev: CF 28 (1958) 115.   *F322

SPIMPOLO, Timotee, OFM, *La provincia veneta dei Frati Minori di S. Antonio da Padova. Profilo storico.* Ven, 1951. 136p. Rev: SF 51 (1954) 122.   *F323

IV SOUTHERN ITALY
1 ABRUZZI & MOLISE

CHIAPPINI, Aniceto, OFM, *L'Abruzzo francescano nel secolo XIII.* R,

1926. 54p. illus. From *Rassegna di storia e d'arte d'Abruzzo e Molise* 2 (1926) n3-4. Rev: AFH 21 (1928) 138. *F324

———, "Codici liturgici di Sulmona e Tagliacozzo," CF 30 (1960) 208-216. Important. cf F329. *F325

———, "La fondazione dell'Aquila e le sue origini francescane," SF 45 (1949) 37-51. *F326

———, "Le falsificazioni del P. Nicolo Colagreco da Guardiagrele e la storiografia francescana abruzzese," SF 11 (1925) 187-206. cf F329. *F327

DE CAESARIS, G., *Memorie francescane Pennesi.* Lanciano, 1927. 45p. illus. F328

ODOARDI, Giovanni, Conv, "Equivoci sui codici liturgici di Tagliacozzo e pretese falsificazioni del P. Nicolo Colagreco. OFM, Conv. (†1770), MF 63 (1963) 15-64. Attacks F325 & F327. Important. On SF: 52-58. *F329

SEBASTIANO, Isidoro, OFM, "Appunti e ricerche storiche sull'Abruzzo francescano (Circa l'origine della Minoritica Provincia Pennense)," SF 30 (1933) 70-83. *F330

———, "SFA a Chieti," FF 18 (1941) 214-217. F331

———, "SF e i primi francescani a Chieti e nei dintorni," SF 28 (1931) 446-463. Important. *F332

2 CALABRIA

COCO, Primaldo, OFM *Saggio di storia francescana di Calabria dalle origini al secolo XVII.* Taranto, 1931. xxxv, 251p. On author: Adiuto PUTIGNANI, *P.A. Primaldo Coco, storico del Salento.* Taranto, 1962. 34p. cf his obit. CF 34 (1964) 230. *F333

RUSSO, Francesco, Conv, "Su alcuni apocrifi del primitivo francescanesimo calabrese," MF 43 (1943) 315-320. *F334

3 CAMPANIA

OTTAVIO DA ALATRI, Cap, "SF e i suoi figli in Avellino," IF 7 (1932) 3-19, 181-200. F335

4 APULIA
(see also C65-C68)

ACOCELLA, Vito, "SFA e il conte Raone di Balvano," LS 9 (1933) 222-231. Abs: CF 5 (1935) 153. Important. F336

ANGELILLIS, Ciro, "Un punto inesplorato nella vita del Poverello: il pellegrinaggio al Gargano," IF 3 (1928) 3-41, 97-122. Well-documented though not critical. cf his *Il santuario del Gargano e il culto di S. Michele nel mondo.* Foggia, 1956. 2v. *F337

BACCI, Domenico, OFM, *SFA attraverso le leggende pugliesi.* Brindisi, 1925. 296p. Rev: AFH 21 (1928) 427. Important. *F338

COCO, Primaldo, OFM, *I francescani nel Salento. Vol. I: Dalle origini al 1517.* 2da ed. riv. e ampl. Pref. del P. L. Oliger. Taranto, 1930. xxxiv, 321p. Rev: (1st ed. AFH 16, 1923, 237-241); CF 3 (1934) 419-421; CF 5 (1935) 152; IF 7 (1932) 142-151; SF 28 (1931) 227. cf F333. *F339

GUASTAMACCHIA, Gabriele M., Conv, *Francescani di Puglia. I Frati Minori Conventuali (1209-1962)*. Bari-R, 1963. xii, 167p. Rev: CF 34 (1964) 207.   *F340

LA SORSA, Saverio, "Il culto di SF in Puglia," *Lares* 10 (1939) 102-126. Based mostly on F338.   F341

LIBERATO DI STOLFI, OFM, "SF sullo sperone d'Italia," FF 13 (1940) 152-160.   F342

5 SICILY

LEANTI, Giuseppe, "L'ordine francescano in Sicilia nei secoli XIII e XIV," MF 37 (1937) 547-574.   *F343

V THE HERMITAGES
(see also A61, D6, D10, D18, F26-F49, F57-F62, F132, F198-F199)

1 AS A WHOLE

[BROWN, Raphael, *The Hermitages of SF*. In preparation.]   *F344

SCHNEIDER, Edouard, *Le petit pauvre dans ses ermitages*. P, 1927. xvi, 303p. illus. Excellent.   *F345

2 LAZIO

a. BELLEGRA

GUERINI, Rocco, "Visite di Papi al S. Ritiro di Bellegra," FF 26 (1959) 184-189.   F346

MARIOTTI, Candido, OFM, *Il ritiro di SF presso Civitella (Bellegra)*. R, 1899. 303p. illus. Rev: AB 19 (1900) 471; AFH 5 (1912) 595-597.
*F347

Sua Santità Giovanni XXIII visita il S. Ritiro di Bellegra: 25. VIII. 1959. R, 1959. 63p. illus.   *F348

TULLI, Alberto, "La finestra della cella del Poverello tornata alla luce a Bellegra," IF 1 (1926) 28-30.   F349

b. FONTE COLOMBO

BURKITT, F. C., "Fonte Colombo & Its Traditions." In *Franciscan Essays* (Man 1932) II, 41-56. (BSFS-ES III)   F350

CERMINARA, Teofilo, OFM, "Dove SF ha composto la Regola del 1223," SF 30 (1933) 60-70. Rev: CF 5 (1935) 154.   F351

LIPPENS, Hugolinus, OFM, "De vero titulari ecclesiae minoriticae Fontis Columbae," AFH 25 (1932) 286-288.   F352

TERZI, A., OFM, "Fontecolombo." In his *Memorie*. . .See F59:61-135 & tav. XXIV-XL. Basic   *F353

c. GRECCIO
(see also C124-C142 on Crib; & F311)

COSMO, U., "Greccio." In his *Con Madonna Povertà*. See D157:152-177. Local traditions.   *F354

SOLINAS, Mario, *Greccio*. Pref. di A. Sepinski, OFM. Perugia, 1956. 41p. illus.   F355

TERZI, A., OFM, "Greccio." In his *Memorie*. . . See F59:139-203 & tav. XLI-LX. Basic. See also C138. *F356

d. ORTE

CAMILLI, Alessandro, *Memorie francescane in Orte*. Subiaco, 1927. *F357

MARINI, Piero, "Il soggiorno di SF e dei suoi undici compagni in Orte," FF 25 (1941) 260-268. Illus. Based on F357. cf FNV I/1, 382nl. F358

e. POGGIO BUSTONE

TERZI, A., OFM, "Poggio Bustone." In his *Memorie*. . . See F59:207-253 & tav. LXI-LXXVI. Basic. *F359

f. SAN FABIANO — S. MARIA DELLA FORESTA
(see C160-C185; esp. C181 & C183)

BIHL, M., OFM, "De raris racenis Reatinis vinum abundans, iuxta S F promissum, fundentibus," AFH 20 (1927) 200-202. F359a

3 TUSCANY

a. LE CELLE DI CORTONA
(see also F153-F154)
GIULIANO DA LECORE, Cap, *Ricordo del santuario delle Celle*. 2da ed. Cortona, 1950. 32p. illus. F360
LEOPOLDO DA CORTONA, Cap, *Il primo convento francescano*. Fi, 1915. 192p. 20 illus. *F361
ODOARDI, Giovanni, Conv, "Il convento delle Celle," *Ecclesia* (R) 6 (1947) 532-537. illus. Rev: CF 20 (1950) 61*. F362

b. MONTE CASALE

ANDREOZZI, Gabriele, TOR, "Monte Casale nei Fioretti e nella nostra storia," *Analecta T.O.R.* 5 (1952) 812-819, 914-925. F363
GIOVAGNOLI, E., "Monte Casale," SFA 8 (1928) 411-418. illus. F364
GIUSTINO DAL BORGO S. SEPOLCRO, Cap, *Relazione dell'antico santuario di Montecasale*. Nuova ed. (1st ed. Ven, 1755) Fi, 1901. 62p. F365
NEDIANI, Tommaso, *Romitaggi francescani. Montecasale*. Fi. 1915. 119p. illus. F366
RENE DE NANTES, Cap, "L'ermitage de Monte Casale," EF 24 (1910) 353-365. *F367

c. SIENA: L'ALBERINO
(see also F157)

DE ANGELIS, Luigi, *Del albero di SF vicino alle mura di Siena*. Siena, 1827. 88p. illus. Basic. *F368
FACCHINETTI, V., OFM, "L'Alberino di Siena," FF 7 (1934) 205-210. F369
MAURICI, Mario, "Oasi francescane. La parrochia di SF all'Alberino

di Siena." *La Vetta* (L'Aquila) 2n11-12 (1960) 1-3. Important.   F370
MISCIATELLI, Pier, *Eremi senesi*. Siena, 1936. 131p. Basic.   *F371

d. LA VERNA
(see also C143, C202, C209)

ASTRE, Gaston, "Fissures et dislocations des rochers de l'Alverne," FrFr 16 (1933) 337-344. Geological analysis: result of a severe earthquake.   F372
BARGELLINI, Piero, & Vittorio Vettori, *Amoroso viaggio in terra francescana. Itinerario casentinese illustrato*. Fi. 1949. 94p. illus.   F373
CANNAROZZI, Ciro, OFM, *Dialogo del Sacro Monte della Verna di Fra Mariano da Firenze*. Pistoia, 1930. xxiii, 143p. Indispensable for history.
*F374
CARMICHAEL, Montgomery, "The Addio of SF to Mount La Verna," *Capuchin Annual* (Dublin) 5 (1934) 126-130. Abs: CF 9 (1939) 137.
F375
CRESI, Domenico, OFM, "Per la storia del Santuario della Verna," SF 59 (1962) 391-403. Basic.   *F376
DE TREMAUDAN, H., "L'etymologie du mot 'Alverne'," EF 47 (1935) 86-87.   F377
JOERGENSEN, Johannes, *La montée de l'Alverne*. Tr. & illus. par A. Carof. P, 1923. 265p. Excellent.   F378
MASSERON, Alexandre, "Comment Napoleon faillit détruire le célèbre couvent franciscain de l'Alverne," *Ecclesia* (P) n. 90 (Sept. 1956) 93-98. illus.   F379
MENCHERINI, Saturnino, OFM, ed., *Codice diplomatico della Verna e delle SS. Stimate di SFA nel VIIo centenario del gran prodigio*. Fi, 1924. 759p. illus. Rev: AFH 18 (1925) 594 (Bihl). Fundamental coll. of docs.
*F380
———, *Guida illustrata della Verna*. 3a ed. Q, 1921. 384p. illus.   *F381
SOLINAS, Mario, *La Verna*. Perugia, 1959. 190p.   F382
La Verna, Contributi alla storia del Santuario (studi e documenti). Arezzo, 1913. 397p. illus. Rev: AFH 7 (1914) 374-380. Indispensable.   *F383

4 UMBRIA

a. LE CARCERI ON MONTE SUBASIO
(see also F223)

BRACALONI, Leone, OFM, "Il Monte Subasio e le Carceri," FF 1 (1924) 171-181. French tr. in F27:87-102.   F384
FORTINI, Arnaldo, FNV III, 153-162, & IV, 67 (index). Basic.   F385
GAETANO DA NORCIA, OFM, *Memorie storiche di S. Maria delle Carceri*. A, 1844. 81p. Important.   F386
LOCCATTELLI PAOLUCCI, Tommaso, "Il Santuario di Santa Maria delle Carceri presso A," *L'Apologetico* (Perugia) 3 (1865) 261-275; & MF 13 (1911) 65-70. Important.   F387
NICCOLA DA VITORCHIANO, OFM, *Memorie antiche e breve descrizione del Santuario di Santa Maria delle Carceri d'A*. 2da ed. Perugia, 1774. 58p. Important.   F388

SOLINAS, Mario, *Le vie del silenzio: le Carceri*. Perugia, 1950. 31p. F389

b. MONTE LUCO (SPOLETO)
(cf F309)

BANDINI, Carlo, *Monte Luco*. Spoleto, 1922. 235p. illus. Basic. *F390
CASTELLUCCI, A., "Monte Luco. Tebaide dell'Umbria." In *Le conferenze al Laterano* (Grottaferrata 1921) 75-181. Indispensable. *F391
FACCHINETTI, V., OFM, "Monte Luco sopra Spoleto," FF ns5 (1932) 382-386. F392
GUERINI, Rocco, "Una tebaide medioevale nella mistica Umbria," *Latina Gens* (R) 19 (1941) 227-231. illus. F393
LIBERATO DI STOLFI, OFM, "Il convento di Monteluco e il suo santo," FF 25 (1958) 174-178. F394

c. PANTANELLI (near ORVIETO)

OLIGER, Livarius OFM, *Pantanelli presso Orvieto, romitorio dei tempi di SF e i Signori di Baschi*. R, 1932. xxiv, 240p. illus. Rev: AFH 25 (1932) 396; CF 4 (1934) 83. Basic. *F395

d. LA ROMITA DI NOCERA (& BAGNARA)

SIGISMONDI, Gino, "Origine della Romita di Nocera Umbra," SF 36 (1939) 245-249. Basic. *F396

e. LO SPECO DI SANT' URBANO (near NARNI)

CERONI, D.G., *Lo Speco di Frate F. Storia, leggenda e canti*. R, 1929. Rev: CF 9 (1939) 136; FF ns3 (1930) 151. Important. F397
COSMO, Umberto, "Lo Speco." In his *Con Madonna Povertà*. See D157:146-152 & 173-174. Useful. *F398
MANCINI, Giulio, OFM, *Lo Speco di Narni, luogo inedito di SF*. SMA, 1960. 64p. 27 illus. Model brochure. *F399

f. TRASIMENE ISLAND

MARINI, Piero, "La quaresima di SF sul Trasimeno," FF 19 (1941) 73-78. F400

5 VENETO

a. SAN FRANCESCO DEL DESERTO (near VENICE)

BARBAN, Bernardino, OFM, *L'isoletta di "SF del Deserto" nelle lagune di Venezia*. Vicenza, 1927. vii, 239p. illus. Rev: AFH 24 (1931) 431. Basic. *F401
BOTTOME, Phyllis, "Brother Leo," *The Century* (NY) 86 (1913) 181-191. Reprinted in her *Innocence & Experience* (Boston 1934) 81-102; & in Sister Mariella Gable's *They Are People* (NY 1943) 151-170. Fictional sketch of a modern friar, with superlative descr. of the island-ritiro. F402
FACCHINETTI, V., OFM, "SF del Deserto," FF 6 (1929) 45-51. F403

Bibliography Subject Index

Index

MAP 3 ITALY

Grand St. Bernard
Mont Cenis
Novara
PIEMONTE
Allesandria
Pavia
Piacenza

LOMBARDY
Bergamo
Milan
Brescia

TRENTINO
Trent

VENETO
Verona
Vincenza
Padua
Venice
Islet near Burno
S. Francesco del Deserto

LIGURIA
Genoa
Pontremoli

Parma
Modena
Bologna
EMILIA
PO RIVER

Imola
Piacenza
Cesena
Forli
Rimini
San Marino
San Leo
Fano
Urbino
Cagli
Ancona

Lucca
Pisa
Livorno
ARNO RIVER
Florence
Fucecchio
La Verna
San Sepolcro
Bagno

TUSCANY
Siena
Arezzo
Chiana Swamps
LAKE TRASIMENE
Gubbio
Chiusi
Assisi
Perugia

MARCHE
Nocera
Fermo

UMBRIA
Orvicto
Todi
Spello
Duchy of Spoleto
Viterbo
Orte
Cerni
Narni
NERA
Rieti
Penne
Chieti

CORSICA

SARDINIA

CASSIA
Rome
Bellegra
Subiaco
Celano
Sulmona

LAZIO
Ceprano
Sora
ABRUZZI
Monte Cassino
Monte Gargano

Gaeta
CALORE RIVER
Foggia

CAMPANIA
Naples
Avellino
PUGLIA
Bari

BRADANO RIVER
BASILICATA
Brindisi
Lecce

TYRRHENIAN
SEA

CALABRIA

SICILY

Adriatic Sea

© 1965, Franciscan Herald Press